German Social Policy 3

Edited and introduced by
Lutz Leisering

German Social Policy

Edited and introduced by Lutz Leisering

The 5-volume series "German Social Policy" presents a unique multidisciplinary approach to the history of German social policy and is written by the doyens of their respective disciplines. The volumes expound the contribution of the German tradition to the rise of social policy in the Western world in the 19th and 20th centuries. Germany pioneered modern social policy in the 19th century when Bismarck introduced social insurance. After the Second World War, Germany's Social Market Economy became a model of social integration. The volumes cover the history of ideas (volume 1), the legal and political history before and after 1945 (volumes 2 and 3), the German Democratic Republic (1949-1990) and the impact of German reunification (1990) (volume 4). Volume 5 embeds the German case in a major comparative study of European welfare states, complemented by a study of the USA and the Soviet Union. The volumes also yield insights into general theoretical issues of social policy beyond the empirical case of Germany. Each volume has an introduction by the editor who summarizes the contribution made by the volumes and looks into the future of German social policy.

Volume 1:
F.-X. Kaufmann: Thinking About Social Policy – The German Tradition
2013. ISBN 978-3-642-19500-6

Volume 2:
M. Stolleis: Origins of the German Welfare State – Social Policy in Germany to 1945
2013. ISBN 978-3-642-22521-5

Volume 3:
H.F. Zacher: Social Policy in the Federal Republic of Germany – The Constitution of the Social
2013. ISBN 978-3-642-22524-6

Volume 4:
M.G. Schmidt and G.A. Ritter: The Rise and Fall of a Socialist Welfare State - The German Democratic Republic (1949 – 1990) and German Unification (1989 – 1994)
2013. ISBN 978-3-642-22527-7

Volume 5:
F.-X. Kaufmann: Variations of the Welfare State – Great Britain, Sweden, France and Germany Between Capitalism and Socialism
2013. ISBN 978-3-642-22548-2

Hans F. Zacher

Social Policy in the Federal Republic of Germany

The Constitution of the Social

Translated from the German by Thomas Dunlap

Springer

Prof. Dr. Dr. h.c. mult. Hans F. Zacher
Max-Planck-Institut für Sozialrecht und Sozialpolitik
Amalienstraße 33
80799 München
Germany
zacher@mpisoc.mpg.de

Operative editors: Günter H. Ast, Lutz Leisering

Published with the financial support of:

VolkswagenStiftung

Federal Ministry
of Labour and Social Affairs

Parts of this volume have been published previously in German in the following publication: Bundesministerium für Arbeit und Sozialordnung [Federal Ministry of Labour and Social Order] and Bundesarchiv [Federal Archive] (eds.): Geschichte der Sozialpolitik in Deutschland seit 1945, vol. 1 (of 11 volumes published 2001-2008): Grundlagen der Sozialpolitik, Baden-Baden, Nomos, 2001, ISBN 3-7890-7314-8

ISBN 978-3-642-22524-6 ISBN 978-3-642-22525-3 (eBook)
DOI 10.1007/978-3-642-22525-3
Springer Heidelberg New York Dordrecht London

Library of Congress Control Number: 2012945416

Printed on acid-free paper

Springer is part of Springer Science+Business Media (www.springer.com)

Preface to the Book Series "German Social Policy"

The welfare state originated as a project of nation states, with roots in the nineteenth century. This book is part of a book series about the German tradition of social policy, which is one of the three paradigmatical European traditions of social policy besides the British and the Swedish traditions. The book series covers modern social policy in Germany from its beginnings under the early modern state to its breakthrough in the nineteenth century to the present day, ranging from poor relief to Bismarckian social insurance to the post World War II "social market economy" and the current crisis. The series provides even more: it also locates Germany in the wider context of a comparative study of European welfare traditions, complemented by a study of the USA and the Soviet Union proposed to be non-welfare states (vol. 5). Furthermore, vol. 4 contrasts a democratic welfare state with a communist "welfare state", namely the Federal Republic of Germany with the German Democratic Republic which resided side by side 1949–1990, followed by an analysis of the transition to the new unified Germany in 1990.

Beyond the empirical case of Germany, the work yields insights into general issues of social policy which have been addressed in German discourses in-depth and at an early stage. This includes the distinction "state versus society" which is essential for a theoretical understanding of the welfare state; the meaning of "the social" and the "social question"; the identification of what a "welfare state" is compared to non-welfare states; and social policy issues arising during the transition from communism to democratic capitalism.

The unique quality of the book series derives from its authors. The grand old men of German scholarship on social policy, coming from diverse disciplines, have rendered their legacy to the scientific community and to politics: *Franz-Xaver Kaufmann* (sociology) writes on the history of the idea of "social policy" in German politics since the nineteenth century (vol. 1); *Michael Stolleis* (legal history) presents an overview of social policy in Germany from the middle ages to 1945, with an emphasis on the years after 1871 (vol. 2); *Hans F. Zacher* (constitutional law) investigates the history of the German post-war welfare state and its normative foundations (vol. 3); *Manfred G. Schmidt* (political science) analyses communist East Germany, the German Democratic Republic (GDR, 1949–1990), followed by *Gerhard A. Ritter's* study of German unification (1989–1994) (volume 4); and *Franz-Xaver Kaufmann* provides an international comparison of welfare states (and some non-welfare states) (vol. 5). All authors take a distinctly historical approach to their subject, elaborating the formative forces of social policy in Germany.

The book series is a translated, revised and up-dated version of the first of the 11 large volumes of the "History of Social Policy in Germany Since 1945".[1] While two contributions of the first volume have been left out, a study of German unification by Ritter (based on his award-winning study of the subject) has been added to the English version. The 11 volumes of the German work add up to the most ambitious and comprehensive study of the history of German social policy ever published. The work not just displays the state of the art but includes original studies which draw on historical sources that have not been accessible before. Especially for this work the government lifted confidentiality from many documents. Volume 1, which underlies this book series, provides a general framework for the more specific Vols. 2–11 that cover 17 fields of West and East German social policy chronologically. The work was initiated by Chancellor Kohl in 1994. The idea was to take stock of the German social policy tradition at a historical moment: the Iron Curtain over East Europe had fallen, the Treaty of Maastricht had created the "European Union" (1992/1993) and German politics had eventually realized that the "golden years" of the post war welfare state had come to a close. At the same time, the new challenges of globalization and demographic change had become apparent. In the early 1990s, German politics was only just beginning to face up to these challenges while the authors of Vol. 1 of the German work were already sensible of the inherent tensions and uncertainties of the advanced post war welfare state.

Translating, revising and extending the original German "History of Social Policy in Germany Since 1945" was not an easy task. It required a joint and protracted endeavour of a number of persons and a considerable sum of money. I am indebted to Richard Hauser for bringing up the idea of a translation (and joining, with Werner Abelshauser, my application for funding with the Volkswagen Foundation); to Franz-Xaver Kaufmann for continuously supporting the project in many ways and with verve; to Thomas Dunlap, David Antal and Ben Veghte who translated the demanding texts with admirable skill and care; to Günter H. Ast, formerly Federal Ministry of Labour and Social Affairs, who acted as operative editor of the texts with unceasing commitment and patience; to Werner A. Müller, Katharina Wetzel-Vandai, Irene Barrios-Kezic and Kay Stoll from Springer publishers who supported the project with diligence; and, last but not least, to the authors for their support and patience.

---

[1] Geschichte der Sozialpolitik in Deutschland seit 1945. Edited by the Federal Ministry of Labour and Social Affairs (*Bundesministerium für Arbeit und Soziales*) and the Federal Archive (*Bundesarchiv*). 11 volumes, Nomos publishers, Baden-Baden. 2001–2008. The book series is based on a translation of the first volume, *Grundlagen der Sozialpolitik* (See footnote on p. 391).

I thank the Volkswagen Foundation, Hannover/(Germany), for generously funding the translation under their scheme "'Deutsch plus' – A Program for Multilingualism in Teaching and Research" (Az. II/83 610). I equally am indebted to the Federal Ministry of Labour and Social Affairs, Berlin/Bonn which co-funded the project, approved by the minister, Ursula von der Leyen, and processed by Thomas Biewer. I also thank the Ministry and the Federal Archive, Nomos publishers, Suhrkamp, C.H. Beck and VS publishers for granting permission to translate the German work. Sage gave permission to adopt passages for the introduction from an earlier article I wrote.[2] Finally, I am most indebted to my wife Maria who gave me time to finish this undertaking.

Lutz Leisering

[2] Leisering L (2003) Nation state and welfare state. An intellectual and political history. Journal of European Social Policy 13, pp. 175–185.

Contents

List of Abbreviations

ABl	Amtsblatt (Official Gazette)
AEMR	Allgemeine Erklärung der Menschenrechte (Universal Declaration of Human Rights)
Art	Article
AuR	Arbeit and Recht (Work an Law, a journal)
AV	Amsterdamer Vertrag (Treaty of Amsterdam)
BAGE	Entscheidungen des Bundesarbeitsgerichts (Decisions of the German Federal Labour Court)
BAnz	Bundesanzeiger (Federal Gazette)
BErzGG	Bundeserziehungsgeldgesetz (Federal Child-Raising Allowance Act)
BGB	Bürgerliches Gesetzbuch (German Civil Code)
BGBl	Bundesgesetzblatt (Federal Law Gazette)
BGHZ	Bundesgerichtshof, Entscheidungen in Zivilsachen (Federal Supreme Court Judgments in Civil Cases)
BKGG	Bundeskindergeldgesetz (Federal Child Benefit Act)
BMAS	Bundesministerium für Arbeit und Soziales (Federal Ministry of Labour and Social Affairs). For changes in the name of the German Ministry of Labour see the note on page 391.
BRD	Bundesrepublik Deutschland (Federal Republic of Germany)
BRDrs.	Bundesratsdrucksachen (documents of the second chamber of the Federal German parliament)
BSGE	Entscheidungen des Bundessozialgerichts (Federal Social Court Judgments)
BSHG	Bundessozialhilfegesetz (Federal Social Assistance Act)

BTDrs.	Bundestagsdrucksachen (parliamentary papers and documents, including drafts of laws)
BVerfGE	Entscheidungen des Bundesverfassungsgerichts (Decisions of the Federal Constitutional Court)
BVerwG	Bundesverwaltungsgericht
BVG	Bundesversorgungsgesetz (Federal War Victims Relief Act)
CDU	Christlich-Demokratische Union (Christian Democratic Union)
CSU	Christlich-Soziale Union (Christian Social Union)
DDR	Deutsche Demokratische Republik (German Democratic Republic)
DGB	Deutscher Gewerkschaftsbund (German Federation of Trade Unions)
DM	Deutsche Mark (German Mark)
DP	Deutsche Partei (German Party)
e.g.	exempli gratia
EAGV	Vertrag über die Europäische Atomgemeinschaft (Treaty establishing the European Atomic Energy Community)
ed.	Editor/ Edition
EEA	Einheitliche Europäische Akte (Single European Act, SEA)
EEC	European Economic Community
EG	Europäische Gemeinschaft (European Community, EC)
EGKSV	Vertrag über die Gründung der Europäischen Gemeinschaft für Kohle und Stahl (Treaty on the Foundation of the European Coal and Steel Community)
EGV	Vertrag zur Gründung der Europäischen Gemeinschaft (Treaty on the Foundation of the European Community)
EMRK	Europäische Menschenrechtskonvention (European Convention on Human Rights)
esp.	Especially
et al.	et alii (and others)
etc.	et cetera
EU	Europäische Union (European Union)
EuSCh	Europäische Sozialcharta (European Social Charter)
EWG	Europäische Wirtschaftsgemeinschaft (European Economic Community, EEC)
EWGV	Vertrag zur Gründung der Europäischen Wirtschaftsgemeinschaft (Treaty on the Foundation of the European Community)
f.	Following
FAO	Food and Agriculture Organisation of the United Nations
FDP	Freie Demokratische Partei (Free Democratic Party)
ff.	Following

FRG	Federal Republic of Germany
GATT	General Agreement on Tariffs and Trade
GB/BHE	Gesamtdeutscher Block/Bund der Heimatvertriebenen und Entrechteten (All-German Bloc/League of Expellees and Deprived of Rights)
GDR	German Democratic Republic
GG	Grundgesetz (Basic Law)
GVBl.	Gesetz- und Verordnungsblatt (Law and Ordinance Gazette)
GWB	Gesetz gegen Wettbewerbsbeschränkungen – Kartellgesetz (Law against Restraints of Competition – Anti-Trust Law)
HGrG	Gesetz über die Grundsätze des Haushaltsrechts des Bundes und der Länder (Law on Budgetary Principles for Federation and Länder)
IDA	International Development Association
i. d. F.	in der Fassung (in the version)
ibid.	ibidem (in the same place)
ILO	International Labour Organization
IPBPR	Internationaler Pakt über bürgerliche und politische Rechte (International Covenant on Civil and Political Rights)
IPWSKR	Internationaler Pakt über wirtschaftliche, soziale und kulturelle Rechte (International Covenant on Economic, Social and Cultural Rights)
KPD	Kommunistische Partei Deutschlands (Communist Party of Germany)
LVerf.Baden	Constitution of Baden
LVerf.Bay	Constitution of Bavaria
LVerf.Bb	Constitution of Brandenburg
LVerf.Be	Constitution of Berlin
LVerf.Be 1950	Constitution of Berlin from 1 September 1950
LVerf.Be 1995	Constitution of Berlin from 23 November 1995
LVerf.Br	Constitution of Bremen
LVerf.BW	Constitution of Baden-Wuerttemberg
LVerf.He	Constitution of Hesse
LVerf.HH	Constitution of Hamburg
LVerf.MV	Constitution of Mecklenburg-Western Pomerania
LVerf.Nd	Constitution of Lower Saxony
LVerf.NRW	Constitution of North-Rhine –Westphalia
LVerf.RP	Constitution of Rhineland-Palatinate
LVerf.SH	Constitution of Schleswig-Holstein
LVerf.Sl	Constitution of the Saarland
LVerf.Sn	Constitution of Saxony
LVerf.SnA	Constitution of Saxony-Anhalt
LVerf.Th	Constitution of Thuringia

LVerf.WB	Constitution of Wuerttemberg-Baden
LVerf.WH	Constitution of Wuerttemberg-Hohenzollern
MV	Maastrichter Vertrag (Maastricht Treaty)
NDV	Nachrichtendienst des Deutschen Vereins für öffentliche und private Fürsorge (News service of the German Association for Public and Private Welfare)
Nos.	Numbers
NRW	North-Rhine-Westphalia
NSV	Nationalsozialistische Volkswohlfahrt (National Socialist People's Welfare)
o. J.	ohne Jahrgang (n.d. – no date given)
o. O.	ohne Ort (s.l. – sine loco, no publishing place given)
OECD	Organization for Economic Cooperation and Development
OEEC	Organization for European Economic Co-operation
Para.	paragraph
PDS	Partei des Demokratischen Sozialismus (Party of Democratic Socialism)
pp.	Pages
RAF	"Rote Armee Fraktion"
RGBl.	Reichsgesetzblatt (Reich Law Gazette)
RVO	Reichsversicherungsordnung (German National Insurance Code)
S.	Seite (page)
SDSRV	Schriftenreihe des Deutschen Sozialrechtsverbandes e. V.
Sent.	Sentence
SGB	Sozialgesetzbuch (Social Security Code)
SH	Schleswig-Holstein
SPD	Sozialdemokratische Partei Deutschlands (Social Democratic Party of Germany)
StWG	Gesetz zur Förderung der Stabilität und des Wachstums der Wirtschaft (Law to Promote Economic Stability and Growth)
UD	United Nations
UN Convention on Racial Discrimination	United Nations Convention on the Elimination of All Forms of Racial Discrimination
UN Convention on Women	United Nations Convention on the Elimination of All Forms of Discrimination against Women
UNICEF	United Nations International Childrens Emergency Fund
UNRRA	United Nations Relief and Rehabilitations Administration
VO	Verordnung
vol.	Volume
vols.	Volumes

VVDStRL	Veröffentlichungen der Vereinigung der Deutschen Staatsrechtslehrer (Publications of the Union of German Constitutional Law Teachers)
WAV	Wirtschaftliche Aufbau-Vereinigung (Union for Economic Reconstruction)
WHO	World Health Organisation
WIGBl.	Gesetzblatt der Verwaltung des Vereinigten Wirtschaftsgebietes (Military Government Gazette Germany)
WoBauG	Wohnungsbau- und Familienheimgesetz (Housing and Family Home Law)
ZeS	Zentrum für Sozialpolitik der Universität Bremen (Centre for Social Policy Research at the University of Bremen)

Nation State and Social Policy: An Ideational and Political History

Introduction to the Book Series "German Social Policy"

Lutz Leisering

Advances in social policy were often related to processes of nation-building, like the introduction of social insurance by Chancellor Bismarck during the years 1883–1889 which contributed to the social integration of the new German Empire. The Empire had been created through the unification of the numerous German states in 1871. Critical periods in a country's history that went along with a renewal of the national spirit also propelled social reform, like the New Deal during the Great Depression in the 1930s and the creation of the British "welfare state" in the immediate aftermath of World War II. Today, the golden age of the welfare state, the decades after WW II, has passed. Domestic problems combine with the impact of globalisation. Some authors assume that globalisation makes nation states increasingly irrelevant. What, then, is a history of a national welfare state as presented in this book series good for in the contemporary debate?

Western welfare states have proved to be resilient amidst domestic and global crises. While welfare states are undergoing far-reaching change there is no sign that welfare statism is disappearing. To the contrary, the "social" and social policy have been spreading to the global South since the 1990s to become a key issue of global politics – "socialization of global politics" (Deacon 1997). Looking into the intellectual and political history of one of the great traditions of social policy, indeed the pioneer of modern social policy, Germany, may then shed light on key issues of social policy that continue to underlie political debates and conflicts. Stolleis (in volume 2 of the work) argues that the past is still present in current policies and institutions, like layers that have piled up in the course of history, including pre-Bismarckian social policies.

The analysis of the last 130 years of German social policy (plus earlier periods) as presented in this work uncovers key issues of social policy which are relevant beyond the German case: the disjunction "state versus society" to which social policy is seen as a response in the German intellectual tradition; the meaning of "the social", the "social question" and "social policy"; the meaning of "welfare state" as compared to non-welfare states; and social policy in different societal settings like monarchy, national socialism, communism, democracy and affluent society – and during periods of transition.

H.F. Zacher, *Social Policy in the Federal Republic of Germany*,
German Social Policy 3, DOI 10.1007/978-3-642-22525-3_1,

1 The Distinction "State Versus Society"

The history of social policy has been riddled with debates about individualism versus collectivism, about state versus market and related dichotomies. In current controversies about "globalisation", free marketeers quarrel with advocates of social and ecological regulation of global markets. While these are world-wide issues, Germany, more than any other country, has developed an intense political discourse on "the state" and on the distinction between "state" and "society" that goes back to the early nineteenth century and is worth looking at.

Franz-Xaver Kaufmann's *Thinking About Social Policy* (volume 1 of the book series) traces the political history of the concept of social policy. "Social policy" as a political and scholarly concept originated in Germany in the second half of the nineteenth century, to become more prominent only after World War II. In Britain, France and other countries it gained ascendance only in the 1970s. Kaufmann argues that "social policy" has emerged as a response to problems of societal integration which, from the point of view of Hegelian philosophy, arose from a disjunction between "state" and "society".

Kaufmann's point – which sets the theme for the whole book series – is that the history of social policy is the history of the changing relationship between state and society and of the ensuing problems of social integration. The German Philosopher Hegel (1770–1831), after first allusions by Montesquieu, diagnosed the disintegration of the ancient and early modern idea of a unitary, politically integrated society – the Lockean "political society" – into two heterogeneous spheres, "state" versus "society" or "public" versus "private". "It was here [in Hegel's philosophy – L.L.] that the political and the social appeared for the first time as two separate spheres dominated by *different* legal principles, and the *relationships* between them subsequently became the fundamental issue of 'social policy'" (Kaufmann, volume 1, p. 29). The problem, as the Hegelians saw it, was that "society", mainly the economy, was a source of uncontrollable dynamics and social problems.

The diagnosis of separate spheres was further developed in the twentieth century by the sociologists Talcott Parsons and Niklas Luhmann under the name "structural" or "functional" "differentiation" of society (Luhmann 1982). In their view, too, functional differentiation generated a problem, namely the necessity of enabling persons to participate in functional systems. Drawing on T.H. Marshall they referred to this requirement as the problem of "inclusion".

While Marx (1818–1883), who was a Hegelian, proposed communism as a solution, that is, a fusion of the Societal and the Political, his contemporary Lorenz von Stein (1815–1890), also a Hegelian, proposed a compromise solution (which today could be termed "social-liberal") which he called "social-policy". Social-policy was to link the Societal and the Political (through "social administration") while preserving a basic autonomy of the Societal (in modern terms: to intervene in the economy, family etc. in a non-totalitarian way). Lorenz von Stein, a lawyer and economist, was the intellectual father of the welfare state, precisely 100 years before Beveridge (von Stein 1842) and two years before Marx published his first concept of communism (not yet termed as such; see Marx 1978, first published in 1844) based on the same diagnosis of class conflict in industrial society as von Stein's. The distinction between "state" and "society" and the analysis of their precarious relationship has shaped the German tradition of thinking about the state and social policy ever since (Luhmann 1987).

Germany was a latecomer to industrialization and to nation-building but the pioneer of state welfare. Bismarck's social insurance was a means of integrating the new nation state and securing support by the laboring classes. German liberalism was weak and the "Manchester theory" had eventually fallen in disrepute after the economic crisis of 1873, as Stolleis points out in his *Origins of the German Welfare State – Social Policy in Germany to 1945* (volume 2 of the book series, p. 52). During those years the term social policy started its career in politics. Social policy set out as a comprehensive "workers policy" (*Arbeiterpolitik*) in a society divided by class. During the nineteenth and twentieth centuries the concept of "social policy" changed its meaning several times, mirroring new challenges of societal integration and new ideas of "the social".

After World War II, social policy expanded in an unprecedented way, connected to two new formulas designed to denote the place of social policy in post-war society. The first formula, "Social Market Economy", aimed to integrate the economic and the social. The second formula, "social state", the German version of "welfare state", was contained in the post-war constitution of the new Federal Republic of Germany 1949, the *Grundgesetz* (1949). (The year before, 1948, had witnessed the creation of the British "welfare state".) The year 1949 marked a "double state building" (Christoph Klessmann) which reflected the link between social policy and nation building. While the German Constitution of 1919 had already included articles on social welfare regulations, the West German Constitution of 1949 was the first to establish the "social state" as constitutive principle of the German polity, not to be changed even by a majority in Parliament. In the same year, the German Democratic Republic (GDR) was founded in East Germany under the influence of the Soviet Union. The GDR opted for "socialism", presented as an alternative to the West German social state (see below). The meaning of "Social Market Economy" and "social state" was indeterminate and contested. Political controversies during the 1950s generated some clarification but the two formulas continued to indicate the openness of the idea of the "social" in the development of the Federal Republic of Germany.

2 "The Social"

Out of the three components of "democratic welfare capitalism" – "the hyphenated society" (Marshall 1981) – the component "welfare (state)" has remained more contested than the other two, democracy and market. This hints at problems of identifying "the social". "... the systemic character of social policy is not nearly as evident as that of the market economy. What 'the social' means in distinction to the economic and the political . . . – to this day no clarity has emerged on this question" (Kaufmann, volume 1, p. 97f.). Nullmeier, in his political theory of the welfare state (2000, Chapter VI, p. 2), points at the inferior legitimacy of social rights as compared to civil and political rights.

Like the distinction between state and society, the term "(the) social" is part of the German tradition. Hans F. Zacher, in his *Social Policy in the Federal Republic of Germany* (volume 3 of the book series): "The social is in a very special way part of Germany's national identity" (pp. 315). Germans call their welfare state a "social state". In France, the term "solidarity" has played a comparable role from the nineteenth century and still shapes present-day debates on social policy. The term "social" emanated in the 1830s in Germany, with influences from France, and soon fed into the term "social policy" and other nineteenth century semantics like the "social question". Unlike British and French usage, the word "social" assumed a strongly normative and critical connotation in the German language: the word was contrasted to "the individualistic" to denote something that was seen to be absent from civil society (*bürgerliche Gesellschaft*; Kaufmann, volume 1, p. 32). After World War II, the "social" became a common element of the political and scholarly language in Germany. In the British community of social policy researchers, the term "the social" figures less though increasingly. Remarkably, the term has recently even reached the global level, as indicated by novel semantics of global social policy like "social pensions", "social cash transfers", "corporate social responsibility" and "social sustainability".

". . . '*social*' has something to do with *equality* and *inequality*. '*Social*' *negates* a certain measure of *inequality* – or more precisely: certain constellations of inequality. . . . '*social*' is a mandate to distinguish unreasonable inequalities from reasonable or at least tolerable ones (or less important ones), and to eliminate, compensate for, or at least diminish the unreasonable ones" (Zacher, volume 3, p. 24). This implies that the meaning of the "social" may change, and that it varies across time and between social groups. In politics, the semantic field of the social encompasses ideas like social justice, individual social rights, protection and security. In the British debate, the social is often defined with reference to "need" but need is an equally fluid concept. Despite or rather just because of its vagueness, reference to the "social" may exert considerable political pressure on policy-makers. What appears to be a deficiency is in Zacher's view the very essence of the "social". He sees the openness and changeability of the "social" as an intrinsic feature of a welfare state in a free and democratic society, a feature that was lacking, e.g., in the German Democratic Republic.

The difficulty to pin down the meaning of social policy and the "social" indicates the compromise character and the historical changeability of social policy: "From the point of view of the great political doctrines of liberalism, socialism and conservatism, 'social policy' has evolved as a seemingly heterogeneous sequence of inconsistent compromises. By contrast, this analysis rests on the assumption that the history of social policy in Germany reflects an independent 'reformist' strand which developed against the backdrop of the three 'great ideologies' but has independent roots and points of view. The social-democratic, Christian-social, and social-liberal position appear not only as a more or less consistent compromise between liberal, socialist, and conservative ideas, but in many cases also as a productive synthesis with far-reaching positions of its own" (Kaufmann, volume 1, p. 26; for Christian Democracy and the welfare state see van Kersbergen 1995). Therefore, remarkably, unlike British textbooks on social policy, Kaufmann in his *Thinking About Social Policy* (volume 1) pays scant attention to liberal, socialist and conservative thought when tracing the history of the idea of social policy.

The great ideologies do not tell us a lot about questions of social development and institutional design in a complex and changing society. Esping-Andersen has used these ideologies to label two of his three welfare regime types, the liberal and the conservative regime. Kaufmann's alternative approach to comparative welfare state analysis (see below) shows that these labels are inadequate to distinguish between welfare states. In line with Kaufmann's interpretation of social policy as an ideological compromise, Schmidt's (2005) and Obinger and Wagschal's (1998) empirical analyses of the impact of political parties have shown that the German welfare state is more accurately characterised as "centrist" rather than "conservative" (see below).

In the post-war period, the social has been strongly associated with state welfare and the idea of the welfare state. In Germany, the term "social state" is preferred to "welfare state", the latter sounding egalitarian or even totalitarian to German ears, and makes some people think e.g. of Sweden.[1] Zacher (volume 3) challenges the social democratic orthodoxy of equating the social with "social" intervention by the government. Rather, Zacher defines "the social" by a "basic formula" which posits work and family as the primary sources of providing for human needs, with the law enabling, securing and compensating the operation of work and family. "Only the state and society together can adequately bring about the social" (Zacher, volume 3, p. 46). Zacher (volume 3, p. 43) also speaks of a "constant intermingling of private, societal-public, and state activities". In Zacher's view the actual ability of the welfare state to impact on the welfare of individuals is mostly overrated, by advocates and critics of the welfare state alike.

The *doyen* of German post-war social policy thinking, Hans Achinger (1979, first published 1958) also objected to equating the social with the welfare state. In his view, social policy cannot lay claim to representing unique "social" values. Achinger challenged the claim that the social constitutes an independent normative province: "the idea of an autonomous normative sphere of social policy is a delusion. Social policy relies on ideas of order stemming from other social spheres" (Achinger 1979, p. 7; transl. L.L.). In the British debate, Robert Pinker, in his critique of the Titmussian orthodoxy (Pinker 1971, 1979), similarly rejected the notion of a moral superiority

---

[1] In addition, "social state" is a term of German constitutional law denoting the "social" obligation of the state. Therefore, Kaufmann and Zacher (volumes 1, 3 and 5) use the term "social state" rather than "welfare state" when they refer to Germany. The other authors of the series mostly use the Anglo-Saxon term "welfare state", which is also used as a theoretical term by German scholars. See Ritter (volume 4, footnote 64) for further explications of the terms.

of the "social market" (Titmuss) over the economic market. Rather, "the social", "welfare" and social policy are pluralistic concepts. "Welfare state" always means "welfare state in a free society" ("liberal welfare state"; "*freiheitlicher Wohlfahrtsstaat*"; Zacher, volume 3, p. 45), that is, a state in a mixed society in which "the social" is not primarily promoted by the government. State provision is part of a wider welfare mix, and in Germany even "state" often means "intermediary" agencies like social insurance, which in Germany are non-state agencies with separate budgets, or voluntary welfare associations.

3 Variations of Modern Society: Distinguishing Welfare States and Non-Welfare States

Studies of the welfare state normally assume that every Western society is a welfare state. Franz-Xaver Kaufmann's *Variations of the Welfare State* (volume 5 of the series) questions that assumption. Cross-national comparisons which use the typological method, most prominently Esping-Andersen's work, often cannot distinguish between welfare states and non-welfare states. In Kaufmann's view, the instability of the classification of countries (noted by many commentators especially with regard to Esping-Andersen's original classification of 1990) indicates that the dimensions of comparison have been insufficiently worked out in theoretical terms. Esping-Andersen, from a political economy point of view, defines welfare statism by decommodification but his decommodification index has no cut off point that could distinguish between welfare states and non-welfare states. Other authors define "welfare state" in descriptive institutional terms, by a list of social services (common in the Anglo-Saxon literature), but then any country with a range of social services may appear as a welfare state.

By contrast, Kaufmann emphasizes the normative and cultural dimension of the welfare state by distinguishing two sides of the welfare state: the "*welfare sector*" as a range of social services and administrations and *welfare politics* as political action revolving around "social" issues. We can speak of a "welfare state" if and only if social services are linked to normative orientations: if political actors assume a collective responsibility for the well-being of the entire population (Kaufmann, volume 5, p. 35). Kaufmann subscribes to the definition by Harry Girvetz (1968, p. 512) which emphasizes law and normative orientations: "The welfare state is the institutional outcome of the assumption by a society of legal and therefore formal and explicit responsibility for the basic well-being of all of its members. Such a state emerges when a society or its decision-making groups become convinced that the welfare of the individual [...] is too important to be left to custom or to informal arrangements and private understandings and is therefore a concern of government." The core of a welfare state is the commitment to social rights (inclusion) embedded in a culture of social responsibility.

This ambitious definition of "welfare state" has methodological consequences. It implies a new approach to the comparative study of nation states that emphasizes norms, culture and history. Kaufmann elaborates such a socio-cultural approach (see the next section). It is a holistic and institutionalist approach which yields rich analyses of the *gestalt* of a welfare state and, if used comparatively, produces accounts of the "idiosyncrasy" (*Eigensinn;* Kaufmann, volume 5, p. 31) of each welfare state (Ginsburg 1992 and Castles 1993 are cited as kindred approaches). In this way, the variety of welfare states is exposed while avoiding a coarse typology.

Moreover, the socio-cultural approach enables Kaufmann to show, based on meticulous secondary studies of the USA and the former Soviet Union, that not all modern nation states are welfare states. Some are just "capitalism" – the USA –, some are "socialism" – the former Soviet Union –, and others, especially countries of the global South, may muster some social services for privileged groups mostly related to government or the military but lack a normative concern that defines a welfare state.

In this light, the (essentially West European) welfare state appears as a third way between capitalism and socialism. Anglo-Saxon researchers easily classify the USA as welfare state or welfare capitalism. The USA has not ratified the International Covenant on Economic, Social and Cultural Rights of 1966. During the war on poverty in the 1960s there "arose – perhaps the only time in US history – a political and public majority opinion that believed in the potential of social policy to shape society" (Kaufmann, volume 5, p. 84). The departure of the 1960s was triggered by a moral and civil crisis, not by an economic crisis as in the case of the New Deal of the 1930s.

In the burgeoning literature on welfare regimes and typologies Kaufmann's comparative approach that highlights the "idiosyncrasy" of welfare states offers a stimulating new perspective. By including and identifying non-welfare states Kaufmann also contributes to the more general debate on the "varieties of capitalism" opened up by David Soskice and others (for an overview see Hall and Soskice 2001). The "varieties of capitalism" debate concentrates on the economy, on industrial relations and the labor market while Kaufmann adds the fields of social security and personal social services and discusses them in conjunction with the economic fields.

Manfred G. Schmidt's *Social Policy in the German Democratic Republic* (GDR, communist East Germany; in volume 4 of the series) helps to put the distinction between welfare states and non-welfare states to the test. The welfare of the people was a major promise and source of legitimacy of the GDR. "All power serves the good of the people" (Constitution, article 4). "We are guaranteed social security and safety, full employment, equal educational opportunities for all children of the people" (Honecker in 1986, quoted by Schmidt, volume 4, p. 27). The right to work was seen as the showpiece of the GDR. The status of the GDR as an independent nation state beside the West German Federal Republic was always contested. Social rights and social security were meant to underpin the claim of the GDR to be a genuine socialist nation and the better alternative to West Germany. Again, social policy and nation building were closely linked. Schmidt's contribution aims to test the claim of the GDR to be superior in "social" terms.

Social policy was not seen as an original field of politics in the GDR till 1961. This was true to the original doctrine of communism, because "social policy" assumes a distinction between "state" and "society" while communism means a fusion of both spheres. The East German leaders opted for Marx, not for Lorenz von Stein. 1961–1971 under Ulbricht, the concept "socialist social policy" emerged though "the social" remained subordinated to the economic. The year 1961 when the Berlin Wall was erected was the true founding date of the GDR. Honecker (1971–1989) made the "unity of economic policy and social policy" a key formula of social development. The strategy was to increase consumption, to raise the motivation of the workers and to boost birth rates.

Social spending was low by international standards (around 15% of gross domestic product (GDP), measured by the International Labour Organization (ILO)) and social services offered not more than bare minimum standards or even less. However, if we take into account the cost of subsidies to basic consumption goods and the cost of securing full employment through unproductive work, social spending figures easily double. But the economy was too weak to sustain that degree of "security and safety". Schmidt's key thesis is that there was a grave, in fact excessive imbalance between the moderate economic performance and the high degree of social protection in the GDR. The sociologist M. Rainer Lepsius once remarked that the GDR in 1989 became "the first welfare state to collapse under the burden of its social services".

But was it really a welfare state? Did the GDR positively grant social rights? Schmidt's answer is negative. The GDR was "far removed" from all Western welfare regimes (Schmidt, volume 4, p. 131). The right to work, to education, to housing and to protection in case of illness, incapacity and old age was proclaimed but it was substantially qualified in its realisation (and subject to "societal requirements" even in the Constitution, article 24). The gap between the rights and the actual services was wide: the level of services was low (with an estimated 40% of pensioners living in poverty, measured by the 50% income threshold), benefits were increased irregularly by way of political discretion and the rights could not be claimed in court. The GDR was not a welfare state as defined by Kaufmann because the "social" was dominated by the political and the economic. Political considerations were paramount, with substantial legal privileges for state elites, e.g. with regard to old-age pensions, and discrimination of children from "bourgeois" or religious backgrounds in the educational system. In addition, social security was used for economic purpose. The GDR was more of a workfare state than the USA.

The GDR was neither a welfare state as defined by Zacher. A closed, static notion of social needs prevailed: the level of benefits met pre-war standards and provisions were not responsive to changing aspirations in an individualistic society that emerged in the 1980s even in the GDR. This was not an open and pluralistic concept of the social stipulated by Zacher as the core of a welfare state in a free society. The implicit formula of the GDR "social rights without civil and political rights" did not work out because social rights interlock with civil freedom and political participation. But central planning, not freedom, was the overriding concept of society. "It thus seemed possible even to plan individual and social consumption" (Schmidt, volume 4, p. 30). Work was not seen as a social but as a mere economic issue that had been resolved – the Ministry of Labour was dismantled in 1958, the labor exchanges even earlier (Kahlenberg and Hoffmann 2001, p. 181). Even family policy was reduced to boosting birth rates; the traditional gender arrangement was only half changed, with more women in employment but still doing the house work. This was not a welfare state. It was an "authoritarian, paternalistic work and welfare state" (Schmidt, volume 4, p. 131).

Gerhard A. Ritter's *The Politics of German Unification. Social, Economic, Financial, Constitutional and International Issues* (in volume 4 of the series) analyses the years from the eve of unification of West and East Germany in 1989 to the aftermath of unification (till 1994). The transition from communism to a new post-communist order in East European countries has been widely studied. East Germany was special since it had a Western counterpart. In this case transition meant merger with the Federal Republic of Germany. In some respects this made things easier compared to other Eastern countries that were left to fend for themselves even if international agencies offered some support. In other respects the transition was more difficult due to problems of making two worlds meet and of integrating a less modernized region into the Federal Republic of Germany.

German unification made the link between nation building and social policy explicit again. The "Social Union", that is, the integration of the two Germanys in social policy terms, turned out to be a critical strand of unification. The Social Union was initially contested. When planning for unification, three alternative strategies were considered: delaying the Social Union, that is, not (fully) transferring the generous West German social services and rights to the East in order to facilitate economic growth; transferring the West German system topped up by alleged or real "social achievements" of the GDR to be retained; and transferring the West German system without topping up. The latter solution prevailed as a compromise, turning the GDR into a modern welfare state in one day, at least legally. Failure to achieve a viable Social Union might have put the entire process at risk: "... in light of the economic problems and constellation of political forces, there was ultimately no alternative to extending the West German welfare state to the East. This is not to deny several grave errors in the social policy of unification" (Ritter, volume 4, p. 204).

4 Variations of the Welfare State: The Idiosyncrasy of National "State Traditions"

With his holistic cultural approach Kaufmann's *Variations of the Welfare State* (volume 5) analyses Britain, Sweden, France and Germany (besides the USA and the Soviet Union as non-welfare states). Each country is portrayed as a singular case with an "autonomous cosmology" (Kaufmann, volume 5, p. 33) rooted in history and culture. While this may sound rather vague and "soft", Kaufmann's analyses yield ample new and fascinating insights into the cultural and institutional diversity of a continent (Europe) which is moving towards political unity. Kaufmann also provides analytical categories that can be used by students of comparative politics to move beyond the standard ways of comparing welfare states. All country studies follow the same pattern (which is also applied in the analyses of the non-welfare states), with a focus on three themes:

1. The relationship between "*state*" *and* "*society*" in a country, that is, the historical "state tradition" (see also Dyson 1980) with regard to institutional patterns (government, public administration, courts; federal vs. unitary systems, central-local government relationships etc.) and ideas (about the proper scope of government, about ways and means of intervening or not intervening in the economy, family and "private" life). Germany, e.g., as explicated earlier, is imbued by the distinction between "state" and "society". Stolleis specifies the influence of the German state tradition in the historical situation of German unification after 1871. In the face of a weak liberal tradition, the legacy of the autocratic state and of the corporatist or "intermediary" structures of early modernity produced a "mixture of half-authoritarian and autonomous structures" (Stolleis, volume 2, p. 59) typical of German social policy ever since.
2. The *problem definition* prevalent in social politics: ". . . how the 'social question' is posed [in a country L.L.], that is, how the guiding problem of the respective social policy was articulated at the beginning of its development, will be postulated as a revealing key for understanding national developments of the welfare state" (Kaufmann, volume 5, p. 32f.). The guiding problem (*Bezugs-problem,* problem of reference) is assumed to influence both discourse and institutional practice even at much later stages in the development of social policy. The original "social question", the problem that has propelled social politics in Germany, was the "workers question", that is, the social risks and needs of the industrial worker to which Bismarck's social insurance was a response. The "workers question" was the key issue of social integration in the new German Empire founded in 1871: "National and social questions came together in a half-finished state structure and necessitated an intensive linkage of domestic and foreign policy" (Stolleis, volume 2, p. 57). By contrast, British social policy remained oriented towards the problem of poverty. The social question which permeates the Swedish system is the issue of inequality, which gave rise to universal services. In France the concern for family and population has been at the heart of social policy. These four different problem definitions (which do not follow a linear order) have left their traces in the institutional design of each welfare state. They define national welfare paths.
3. The *sectoral structure of social services* in a country. Kaufmann looks at three heterogeneous fields of social policy: production (labor law, industrial relations, labor market policy), (re-)distribution (income maintenance) and reproduction (personal social services, benefits in kind). The literature is mostly confined to

one or two of these fields or even parts thereof, so balances and imbalances, similarities and dissimilarities, between the three fields in one country cannot be identified (Esping-Andersen 1990, e.g., operationalizes "decommodification" only on the basis of cash benefits.) The relationship between the fields also reflects political problem definitions, indicating a national profile of a welfare state. Alber (1995) and Mayer (1997) also analyse the question of homogeneity and heterogeneity of social policy fields as a methodological challenge for welfare state analysis. Kaufmann (2012; Chapter first published in German in 1982) earlier developed a theory of socio-political intervention that yields a distinction of four heterogeneous types of intervention akin to four policy fields. Similarly, Kasza (2002) diagnoses "a disjointed set of welfare policies" in most countries. As a consequence he rejects the concept of welfare 'regimes' altogether and calls for restricting comparative analyses to specific policy areas. But this conclusion is not necessary. Kaufmann takes differences between policy fields as part of the profile of a welfare state.

The German welfare state, e.g., is biased towards income maintenance whereas the British welfare state is stronger on services. Old-age pensions are the "sacred cow" in German politics, a role which in Britain is played by the National Health Service. Labor law is more important in Germany than in Britain. Kaufmann is interested in tracing incongruent normative patterns in different fields of social policy in one country, indicating "package solutions" (Kaufmann, volume 5, p. 32) that have proved viable as a political compromise. The British welfare state, e.g., combines full egalitarian health services with a poverty approach to income security in old age. This is one reason for the difficulty of classifying the British welfare state.

With these three dimensions of welfare states in mind, the profiles of the British, the Swedish and the French welfare states emerge more clearly. For *Britain*, the most basic finding is that the distinction state versus society is not even applicable because it is rooted in the Roman legal distinction between public and private law which is not part of British common law. Since the Glorious Revolution and John Locke, "government" (not "the state"!) has been seen as the trustee of "civil society", a term that retained the old meaning of *res publica*, of a unitary, politically integrated "political society": "Thus, the notion of society was *not* depoliticized and was not infused with the derogatory aftertaste it acquired so often in continental political thought as the embodiment of particularist and mostly economic private interests" (Ritter 1964, p. 30, quoted by Kaufmann, volume 5, p. 93). In a paradoxical way, the weak notion of state enabled Britain to develop a system of government with powers that are constitutionally less restricted than in Germany. The British state tradition also includes a late professionalization and bureaucratization of the civil service and a liberal-utilitarian justification of state intervention that follows the logic of Benthamite rational collectivism. British utilitarianism and German Hegelianism have consistently ignored each other. The British labor movement was much more concerned with the idea of self-help than the German labor movement, and it produced a political (Labour) party much later (1900; Germany: 1863/1869/1875) even though Germany was industrialised much later than Britain.

The *Swedish* state-society tradition represents a third, peculiar type. "In Sweden, . . . similar to England, the tension between 'state' and 'society' hardly played any role, though for very different reasons" (Kaufmann, volume 5, p. 117): While Britain was a latecomer to modern state bureaucracy, Sweden (together with France) was a pioneer, even preceding Prussia, the dominant German state before German unification in 1871. But the evolving civil society in Sweden never really confronted the state as in Germany. On this basis, a modern interventionist state could develop which never became detached from "society" for a number of reasons, such as extensive participation of "societal" interests through associations and political parties, an efficient public administration with relative independence of government, strong local government, pragmatic rationalism, ethnic homogeneity and the tradition of a unitary state church.

France represents yet another singular type. The relationship between state and society is ambivalent. There is a tradition of a strong central state and public administration but the unity of the country is projected onto "society" as a whole, e.g. by the early sociologists Comte and Durkheim. The nation (not the state) as a cultural entity and the idea of "solidarity" constitute the social bond in society.

We can conclude that simple distinctions like strong vs. weak state or big vs. small government do not capture the complexity of the state and its role in a given society. This complexity needs to be taken into account in order to understand the diversity of national paths of welfare state development in Europe.

5 Post-War German Social Policy in Retrospect: The Genesis of a Welfare State

History is subject to continuity and discontinuity, to stability and change, and so is the history of social policy. National transitions of welfare are "path dependent", that is, departures from institutional structures established during the formative years require sustained efforts to materialize. Stolleis (volume 2, p. 23, 24f.) speaks of "layers of historical growth", including pre-Bismarckian sources, that linger in present-day systems of social welfare: "All forms of provisioning against risk and its consequences that we know and practice simultaneously can be assigned to specific chronological stages: from family and neighbourly help to co-operative self-help, the formation of foundations as the bearers of charitable institutions, the emergence of funds that are meant to ensure against conventional risks – all the way to the modern protection systems that encompass nearly the entire population. Some of these institutions go back to the early Middle Ages .... Others can be assigned to the period of the emerging cities, to the beginnings of trade, and the formation of the first large fortunes in the fifteenth and sixteenth centuries, such as urban hospitals, charitable foundations, or social housing projects like the 'Fuggerei' in Augsburg. Others are the products of the society-shaping powers of the churches in the early modern period and especially of the early-modern territorial state, which implemented a new notion of 'work," combated 'idleness', and created penitentiaries and workhouses." At the same time, the future of the historically grown institutional structure is uncertain. Twentieth century advanced Western societies with their extended systems of social protection remain "a historical experiment, in the same way that other cultures of world history have been experiments" (Stolleis, volume 2, p. 151).

Most authors agree that in the German welfare state change is difficult to achieve, due to the veto players in the political system, to the high degree of juridification and due to mentalities grounded in the strong state tradition. There have indeed been few path-breaking reforms in post-war Germany. Even under National Socialism (1933–1945), the institutional structure of public welfare had remained largely intact (Stolleis, volume 2, p. 155: "ruptures and continuity"). Still, there has been change after World War II, but largely in an evolutionary manner – "reformless change" (Czada 1999). The change was obscured by old semantics like "social insurance", "social state" and "social market economy" which were retained in public discourse despite substantial changes in institutional realities. These terms have become "semantics of continuity" (Leisering 2000a).

If we take stock of the changes in social policy during the post-war decades until the crisis of the welfare state was widely acknowledged in the 1990s, the change has been considerable. It was during that period that "social policy" fully turned into a "welfare state" (Kaufmann, volume 1), and German society became a mixed society, as indicated in T. H. Marshall's (1981) term "democratic welfare capitalism". Public welfare expanded dramatically in terms of spending, benefit schemes, levels of benefits, coverage of schemes and legal and bureaucratic apparatuses. New institutions were created which demarcated the sphere of social policy, like a consolidated Statute Book for social legislation (*Sozialgesetzbuch,* from 1976), specialized labor courts (established as independent branch of justice since 1953) and social courts (created in 1954) and mushrooming social reporting since the 1960s. Politically, social policy issues moved to centre stage, turning social policy into the main source of legitimacy of the state. Elections could be won and lost on social policy issues. The institutional structure also changed gradually but markedly. While the Bismarckian core, contribution-based financing of social security, remained, the segmentation of social provisioning typical for conservative welfare states was reduced. Separate institutions of social security were coordinated, integrated or even fused (such as the Statutory Pension Insurances for blue and white collar workers in 2005), and extensions to the core schemes rounded off the architecture of public welfare, resulting in a structured "quasi-universalism" of benefit systems (Leisering 2009).

The "welfare sector" grew, going along with the rise of social professions and semi-professions, of a new labor market sector for public welfare employees and of "welfare industries", that is, commercial providers which deliver services to public agencies or provide services themselves. The character of social policy changed. Social policy turned from "workers policy" into a growing, though less ambitious redistributive policy for the whole population. The focus of societal integration shifted (Kaufmann, volume 1, pp. 106–113): class politics gave way to politics geared to individual social rights and "social security", a term which came to define the welfare state (Kaufmann 2001). Old age insurance, for instance, turned into a question of relations between generations, not classes, and the delivery and implementation of social services became a prime focus of social policy beyond ideological controversies over the orientation of social policy. From the 1970s the emphasis of German social policy on cash transfers began to be gradually supplemented by expanding personal social services.

Regarding outcomes, welfare policies came to shape the every day life of most citizens, advancing the standard of living and promoting socio-cultural individualization but also juridifying and bureaucratizing life. Zacher (volume 3, p. 376) diagnoses a move to more equality, a "process by which inequalities have proliferated": ever new inequalities were discovered to be addressed by welfare policies. This refers to labor law, to inequalities of gender and between white collar and blue collar workers, to protective rights e.g. for tenants and consumers, and to allowances for various exigencies regarding family, housing, education and special needs. As a result, "welfare state generations" emerged whose lives have been shaped by the experience of extensive social services (Leisering 2000b). Much of the change just described could as well be observed in other Western countries. However, while numerous studies compare social spending or policies and policy outcomes cross-nationally, there is little comparative work on the institutional, social and cultural aspects of the post-war welfare state.

6 What Future for the Social?

Is the German welfare state facing up to the new challenges and crises since the 1990s? Is the welfare state changing? While Germany shares some of the challenges faced by other countries, some problems are specific to Germany. Globalization exerts particular pressures on the competitiveness of the German economy since Germany is one of the world's biggest export economies. Financing social benefits mostly by contributions rather than taxes makes the German benefit systems particularly vulnerable to crises in employment – and to competition by low-wage countries – because half of the contributions are paid by the employers as part of labor costs. Similarly, the design of social insurance as pay-as-you-go-systems rather than capital funding, in conjunction with high (if falling) replacement rates, exposes the system more directly to the effects of the ageing of the population, especially in the context of one of the world's lowest birth rates. Above all, German unification in 1990 "exacerbated decisively the latent crisis of the German welfare state" (Ritter, volume 4, p. 204): East Germany had a run-down economy with low productivity; unification generated a need for massive redistribution to the East; the cost of unification were largely passed on to the social insurance system (rather than to the tax system which would have spread the cost more widely; see Ritter, in volume 4); and the regional division East-west became a new social cleavage. In the early years after unification, social spending in the

East temporarily soared to two thirds of the Eastern gross domestic product, unprecedented in any country.

Regarding domestic problems, the 1990s confronted the Germans with a new – or newly perceived – world of social heterogeneity and social cleavage. This created new demands on social policy in view of integrating the nation state. First, there is the East/West divide since unification in 1990. Unemployment in the East is still higher than in the West, and economic growth is too slow. More than 20 years after unification, divisive resentments between East and West linger. Some Eastern regions are depopulated and racism has spread. Second, there is a problem of immigration and ethnic conflict. Germany has one of the highest proportions of immigrants in Europe but politicians have been slow in facing up to this fact. Between 1988 and 1996, 2.3 million "settlers" from Eastern Europe and the former Soviet Union (recognized as ethnic Germans) and c. two million asylum seekers came to Germany. The poverty rate among migrants is twice that of native citizens, just as the unemployment rate; some of the settlers are becoming marginalized. Some third generation immigrants are less integrated than their parents, and religious fundamentalism has grown, especially among persons of Turkish origin who are the biggest ethnic minority. For decades, Germany has facilitated the immigration of unskilled workers, without reaching out to highly qualified professionals as other countries have done. Third, a new low pay sector of the economy has produced a group of working poor, a problem hitherto unfamiliar to Germans. Fourth, both higher education and pre-school education are wanting, with a new problem referred to as "educational poverty" *(Bildungsarmut).*

To ascertain if the German welfare state has changed, we need to become clear what the German welfare state is. We discuss three conceptions of the welfare state in view of identifying the German welfare state and its recent changes: concepts from political economy (Esping-Andersen), from political science (M. G. Schmidt) and from sociology (as found in this book series, especially in Kaufmann, volumes 1 and 5, and in the related legal approach by Zacher, volume 3).

Following Esping-Andersen (1990), Germany is the epitomy of the *conservative welfare regime*: achieving a medium degree of decommodification (of enabling people to live independently of the market) by regulating labor markets and containing labor market participation; basing entitlements on occupational and social status, producing structured inequality; and upholding a conservative concept of society emphasizing family, traditional gender roles and intermediate social bodies such as churches, voluntary welfare associations and status groups. The conservative welfare regime contrasts with the Anglo-Saxon liberal regime and the Scandinavian social democratic regime. Studies agree that conservative or "*Bismarckian*" welfare regimes – Austria, France, the Netherlands, Luxembourg, Italy, Spain, Belgium, The Czech Republic, Poland, Slovakia and Hungary also come near this ideal-type (Palier 2010, p. 24) – are changing but they do not agree in which way (see Palier and Martin 2007; Palier 2010). Bismarckian regimes have adopted some of the new policies also found in other regimes, such as "activating" policies, deregulating labor markets and raising labor market participation (reducing "labor shedding"), cuts in benefits and social services, and marketization.

This brings Bismarckian welfare states closer to liberal regimes. In Germany, corporatism in industrial relations and closed arrangements of collective bargaining under the Statutory Health Insurance have opened up to a degree. By contrast, some authors diagnose a deepening of the divisions of Bismarckian regimes. Seeleib-Kaiser (2002) differentiates between policy areas, diagnosing a "dualization" of the German welfare state, that is, the traditional objective of status maintenance through insurance benefits weakens while family benefits and services are expanded. Models of gender and the family relations are being modernized. This brings Germany closer to a social democratic regime. Lessenich (2003) argued that the German welfare state has a hybrid, not just conservative character which allows flexible adaptation to new situations, even if in a gradual way. He depicted the opening of regional collective wage agreements and the creation of a statutory Long-Term Care Insurance in 1994/1995 – the fifth branch of social insurance, 111 years after Bismarck introduced the first branch – as cases in point.

Schmidt (e.g. 2005, 2010) also rejects the notion of a merely conservative German welfare state but in a different way and with more scepticism about the ability of the German welfare state to adapt than Lessenich. From a political science point of view, Schmidt argues that the German regime is "*centrist*" rather than conservative, shaped by a reformist centre/centre-right party (the Christian Democrats) in conjunction with a pragmatic, strong social democratic party (though mostly in opposition; the Social Democrats): "the policy of the middle way" (Schmidt 2010). Re-analysing Esping-Andersen's data, Obinger and Wagschal (1998) found that his conservative type actually falls into two types, a "centrist European social insurance state" (including Germany) and a type which really meets Esping-Andersen's criteria of conservatism (found in France, Italy and Austria). The policy of the middle way goes along with a pronounced consensus which underpinned the German welfare state well into the 1990s. Germany was and still is a country with two big welfare state parties.

However, the pressure to reach consensus has also acted as a check to major reforms. "Centrist" implied the aim of achieving high economic growth *and* generous social benefits (Schmidt 2010). Schmidt argues that the centrist model is still in operation but with increasing cost and side-effects. In fact, the performance of the German welfare state has diminished over the last 10 years, with more poverty and more inequality, even if this only means that among countries of the Organisation for Economic Co-operation and Development (OECD). Germany fell from a position better than average to an average position. At the same time, Germany is the biggest spender among Western welfare states, only topped by France and small countries like Sweden – medium performance at highest cost. At the beginning of the 2010s, Germany is caught between the old political middle ground (the carrier of the welfare state consensus) which acknowledges the need for change but shies away from distinct reforms, a new market liberalism which tends to break away from the welfare state consensus but is equally at a loss, and a new social populism.

Authors of this book series characterize the German welfare state in a more sociological way (than the authors just mentioned), conceiving of German social policy as the outcome of the idea of a precarious disjunction between "state" and "society". This idea has given rise to a strong concept of state and para-state institutions that "mediate" between state and society, tied to a strong notion of the "social" that permeates policies, law and mentalities. Has the German welfare state recently been changing with regard to these defining characteristics? The volumes in this series suggest a positive answer, though with qualifications.

The relationship between "*state*" *and* "*society*" has been changing since the 1990s. There are indications – in labor market policy and social assistance, in old-age security and (least) in education – that Germany is restructuring the state-society relationship, with more reliance on "society" and with new instruments of intervening in society. We maintain that Germany is moving from a provider state to an "*enabling state*" (Gilbert and Gilbert 1989; Gilbert 2002; Kaufmann 2012 [Chapter first published in German in 1994]),[2] or from direct to indirect social policy. The new policies include:

- enabling persons to participate in non-state welfare production – this facet of the enabling state figures in the literature since the 1990s as "*activating*" *social policy,* especially in labor market policy and social assistance
- enabling non-state welfare systems like markets, voluntary organizations and families to operate – this facet is addressed by the more recent literature on the "*regulatory state*" in social security (see Leisering 2011a).
- Furthermore, the concept "*social investment*" policies could also be grouped under "enabling state" since these policies, especially education and family policies, aim to enable individuals to provide for themselves in the long run.

Activating social policy in social assistance started in Germany well before the "Hartz IV" reforms of 2005, undertaken by the municipalities since the mid 1990s (Leisering 2001). *Regulatory* policies became more important with the new Long-Term Care Insurance (1994/1995) which opened care markets to private providers, and with the major pension reforms of 2001 (the *Riester* reform) and 2004 which boosted occupational and personal pension plans as part of a new multi pillar model. In a way, this reversed Adenauer's reform of 1957 which had turned the Bismarckian pension insurance into a quasi mono pillar model. The regulation of private providers by the state also extends to other fields, e.g. job centres rely on private temporary employment agencies. In this way, new links between state and society and new intermediate forms – public-private hybrids like the new *Riester* pension – have emerged. Moves towards *social investment* policies are weaker, contrary to the rhetorics from all political parties, with departures in family benefits and services but less in education.

However, the diagnosis of a move towards enabling policies needs qualification. First, enabling is not new. Historically, the German tradition already harboured

[2] In 1994, Kaufmann devised the concept of *"Steuerungsstaat"* independently of the concept "enabling state" which Gilbert and Gilbert had introduced 5 years earlier. The two concepts are akin.

a potential for change in the state-society relationship since "state" in "social state" primarily refers to the social responsibility of the state while the institutional realization of this responsibility, the "welfare sector", need not be "state" but is mostly in the hands of "intermediary" agencies like social insurance with separate budgets or voluntary welfare associations. Thus, there is a tradition of the state reaching out to "society" and regulating non-state welfare production rather than providing welfare by itself. But the intermediary agencies often had a symbiotic relationship with the state, operating in closed quasi-corporatist circles. This made the overall arrangement rigid and inert. Still, the tradition of "old" regulation may have eased the rise of the "new regulatory state" (Leisering 2011a). Second, in contrast to Gilbert, Kaufmann conceives of the move towards an enabling state *(Steuerungsstaat)* as a change in the *discourse* on the state, not as institutional or policy change, although the discursive change may reflect or spur "real" changes. In a state-oriented country like Germany, the new regulatory state indicates the (re-) "discovery of society" in social policy (using a phrase coined by Polanyi) by exposing the dependence of the provider state on societal forces (Leisering 2011b). Any complex policy intervention is of a regulatory nature. The notion of the provider state was a fiction cherished during the golden age of the welfare state. The advent of the new regulatory state helps to expose fictions underlying the provider state during its heyday like the notion of a neat separation of public and private and of the capability of the state to steer societal processes (Berner 2009) – the "heroic state" (Rüb 2003).

The changes in the relationship between state and society entail changes in the "*social*". In a study of recent changes in old-age security in Europe I suggested that the social is undergoing three kinds of transformation: 'rationalization', that is, an increasing emphasis on rational models and expert knowledge; 'civilization', that is, blending social rights and civil rights; and internationalization, that is, an increased influence of international law and global forces on national social law. In the process, the social takes on new sides – socio-technological, civil and international. This transformation pertains to both public and publicly regulated welfare production. While elements of the three transformations can be traced in several Bismarckian or even some other welfare states, all three are particularly momentous in the German context.

Rationalization: The 'social' in European welfare states has historically been framed by ideologies or social *Weltanschauungen* like social democracy, social liberalism, conservatism or Christian social thought. By contrast, in the Anglo-Saxon tradition, especially in the USA, the social is often related to rationalized models of producing welfare goods based on science and social technologies (Janowitz 1976), such as New Public Management in the administration of social services or Disease Management Programmes (DMP) and Diagnosis-Related Groups (DRG) in medical services. The rationalist approach implies a redefinition of the social. Efficiency, quality of services and "choice" hitherto associated with private provision become criteria of social policy-making. While social policy in Germany has been strongly framed in terms of ideologies, combined with a romantic distrust or even ignorance of scientific and technological approaches to the social, the pressure to restructure the welfare state has eventually led Germany to develop a more rationalist approach, often with imports from Anglo-Saxon countries. A "managerial state" has entered the social policy arena (Rüb 2003).

Civilization: Enabling policies – activation, regulation and social investment – aim to influence access, processes and procedures in social welfare rather than welfare outcomes. Rights of access to public and private social services, consumer rights and, e.g., "financial capability" in private pension markets become new objectives of policy. Organization-related norms include transparency of providers, procedural security, accountability and participation. In terms of rights, conventional social rights give way to civil rights set in a social context. Is this still a "social" state? The consequences of the civilization of the social are ambivalent: The substance of the social is attenuated as compared to the golden age of the welfare state, since the social refers only indirectly to welfare outcomes and redistribution. At the same time, the province of the social is extended beyond conventional domains of public welfare, to markets and civil society. Markets become socially regulated welfare markets. For Germany, with its history of distrust in "civil society", the new civil interpretation of the social is difficult to swallow.

Internationalization: While social policy originated as a project of nation states, social policy is increasingly embedded in international social policy contexts: regional associations like the European Union (EU), international organisations like the United Nations (UN), the World Bank and the ILO, global non-governmental organizations (NGOs) and international legal conventions and treaties have emerged as increasingly "social" regimes. Although ultimately based in nation states, these regimes have turned into a world *sui generis*, developing independent "social" ideas. In Zacher's view (volume 3), the internationalization of social policy generates new social ideas, in line with the openness of the concept of the "social". For example, in global discourses, the social and the ecological are often linked in semantics like "social and economic sustainability". This link has not been made in national welfare states. Being a large country with a distinct national tradition of social policy, Germany has been inward-looking and reserved about external influences. It was the European Court of Justice of the EU which had, e.g., to force gender equality on German labor law and social security law. But as a country situated in the centre of Europe, Germany is liable to migration and external influences. The "social state of the Federal Republic of Germany was never simply a nation state" (Zacher, volume 3, p. 315).

The message of the book series is that "the social" is a continuous subject of public deliberation and political struggle. It is constantly changing, it comes in many varieties, and its change is not linear. Some of the recent changes in German social policy in a way lead back to Bismarck, especially the increased emphasis on private provision by markets and families. Bismarck had conceived of social insurance benefits only as a supplement to other sources of income. In some ways, the current German welfare state even goes back to the time before Bismarck.

Bismarck's legislation established a distinction between policy for workers *(Arbeiterpolitik)*, above all social insurance, and policy for the poor (*Armenpolitik*), above all the poor law. The new German job seekers allowance created in 2005 ("*Hartz IV*") has blurred the distinction between the two policies by merging the former Unemployment Aid (the lower echelon of unemployment benefit) with social assistance. In this and other instances, Germany is making a step from an insurance state towards a social assistance state. In the wake of *Hartz IV*, more than 10% of the population are in receipt of social assistance, up from 1.2% in 1970.

Lockwood (1964) distinguished "social integration" and "system integration". From the onset, modern social policy was not only a response to problems of social integration in the process of nation building but also to problems of system integration, above all to problems of economic development. Without positive effects on the economy, the historical rise of social would have been inconceivable. But with the expansion of the welfare state, positive effects cannot be taken for granted. Imbalances between social concerns and economic development may even contribute to the breakdown of a society as experienced by Communist East Germany. The German distrust in "society" makes it difficult for Germans to acknowledge the societal functions of the entrepreneur. "... the political form of the state that guarantees rights of liberty and rights of participation acquires its social quality only on the basis of an efficient economic system. The greatest possible synergy of economic and social policy is therefore the prerequisite for the success of the policies of the welfare state" (Kaufmann, volume 1, p. 125). Against the backdrop of economic globalization, the need to adjust the social and the economic has assumed a new quality. Still, the volumes of this book series testify to the resilience of national welfare states, sustained by institutional and ideational traditions. Nation states continue to be "societal communities" (Talcott Parsons). The future of the welfare state depends on the future of the nation state, on new synergies between state, economy and civil society and on the availability of cultural ideas that mobilize people towards the "social". We are 130 years away from Bismarck's creation of social insurance. The next 130 years may bring less national and more trans-national social ideas and institutions but the "social" does not appear to be in retreat.

References

Achinger H (1979) Sozialpolitik als Gesellschaftspolitik. Von der Arbeiterfrage zum Wohlfahrtsstaat. 3rd edn (1st edn 1958). Eigenverlag des Deutschen Vereins für öffentliche und private Fürsorge. Frankfurt am Main New York

Alber J (1995) A framework for the comparative study of social services. Journal of European Social Policy 5:131–149

Berner F (2009) Der hybride Sozialstaat. Die Neuordnung von öffentlich und privat in der sozialen Sicherung. Frankfurt am Main New York

Castles FG (ed) (1993) Families of nations. Patterns of public policy in western democracies. Aldershot

Czada R (1999) Reformloser Wandel. Stabilität und Anpassung im politischen Akteursystem der Bundesrepublik. In: Ellwein T, Holtmann E (eds) 50 Jahre Bundesrepublik Deutschland. Politische Vierteljahresschrift, special issue 30/1999. Opladen Wiesbaden: 397–412

Deacon B, with Hulse M, Stubbs P (1997) Global social policy. International organizations and the future of welfare. London

Dyson K (1980) The state tradition in Western Europe. Oxford

Esping-Andersen G (1990) The three worlds of welfare capitalism. Princeton

Gilbert N (2002) Transformation of the welfare state. The silent surrender of public responsibility. Oxford New York

Gilbert N, Gilbert B (1989) The enabling state. Modern welfare capitalism in America. Oxford New York

Ginsburg N (1992) Divisions of welfare. A critical introduction to comparative social policy. London Thousand Oaks New Delhi

Girvetz HK (1968) Welfare state. In: Sills DL (ed) International encyclopedia of the social sciences, vol 16. New York, pp 512–521

Hall PA, Soskice D (eds) (2001) Varieties of capitalism. The institutional foundations of comparative advantage. Oxford

Janowitz M (1976) Social control of the welfare state. New York

Kahlenberg FP, Hoffmann D (2001) Sozialpolitik als Aufgabe zentraler Verwaltungen in Deutschland – Ein verwaltungsgeschichtlicher Überblick. In: Bundesministerium für Arbeit und Sozialordnung and Bundesarchiv (eds) Geschichte der Sozialpolitik in Deutschland seit 1945, vol 1. Baden Baden, pp 103–182

Kasza GJ (2002) The illusion of welfare 'regimes'. Journal of Social Policy 31:271–287

Kaufmann F-X (2001) Social security. In: Smelser NJ, Baltes PB (eds) International encyclopedia of the social and behavioral sciences, vol 21. Amsterdam, pp 14435–14439

Kaufmann F-X (2012) European foundations of the welfare state. New York Oxford

Leisering L (2000a) Kontinuitätssemantiken. Die evolutionäre Transformation des Sozialstaates im Nachkriegsdeutschland. In: Leibfried S, Wagschal U (eds) Der deutsche Sozialstaat: Bilanzen – Reformen – Perspektiven. Frankfurt am Main New York, pp 91–114

Leisering L (2000b) Wohlfahrtsstaatliche Generationen. In: Kohli M, Szydlik M (eds) Generationen in Familie und Gesellschaft. Opladen, pp 59–76

Leisering L (2001) Strategien des Umbaus im lokalen Sozialstaat. Chancen und Risiken der kommunalen Sozialhilfereformen (Hilfe zum Lebensunterhalt) unter besonderer Berücksichtigung neuer Informationssysteme. Final report of the research project 98-53-4 of the Hans-Böckler-Stiftung (with Bernhard Hilkert et al.). Manuscript. Bielefeld

Leisering L (2009) Germany: a centrist welfare state at the crossroads. In: Alcock P, Craig G (eds) International social policy: welfare regimes in the developed world, 2nd edn. Houndmills Basingstoke, pp 148–170

Leisering L (ed) (2011a) The new regulatory state. Regulating pensions in Germany and the UK. Houndmills Basingstoke

Leisering L (2011b) Afterword: rethinking the nation state. In: Leisering L (ed) The new regulatory state. Regulating pensions in Germany and the UK. Basingstoke, pp 289–312

Lessenich S (2003) Dynamischer Immobilismus. Kontinuität und Wandel im deutschen Sozialmodell. Frankfurt am Main New York

Lockwood D (1964) Social integration and system integration. In: Zollschan GK, Hirsch W (eds) Explorations in social change. London, pp 244–257

Luhmann N (1982) The differentiation of society. New York

Luhmann N (1987) Die Unterscheidung von Staat und Gesellschaft. In: Luhmann N (ed) Soziologische Aufklärung, vol 4. Opladen, pp 67–73

Marshall TH (1981) Value problems of welfare-capitalism. With afterthought – the 'hyphenated society'. In: Marshall TH, The right to welfare and other essays. London, pp 104–136 (article first published 1972)

Marx K (1978) On the Jewish question. In: Tucker RC (ed) The Marx-Engels reader, 2nd edn. New York, pp 26–52 (German 1844)
Mayer KU (1997) Notes on a comparative political economy of life courses. Comparative Social Research 16:203–226
Nullmeier F (2000) Politische Theorie des Sozialstaats. Frankfurt am Main New York
Obinger H, Wagschal U (1998) Drei Welten des Wohlfahrtsstaates? Das Stratifizierungskonzept in der clusteranalytischen Überprüfung. In: Lessenich S, Ostner I (eds) Welten des Wohlfahrtskapitalismus. Der Sozialstaat in vergleichender Perspektive. Frankfurt am Main New York, pp 109–135
Palier B (ed) (2010) A long goodbye to Bismarck. The politics of welfare reform in Continental Europe. Amsterdam
Palier B, Martin C (eds) (2007) Reforming the Bismarckian welfare systems. Social Policy and Administration 41(6) (special issue). Oxford
Pinker R (1971) Social theory and social policy. London
Pinker R (1979) The idea of welfare. London
Ritter GA (1964) Nation und Gesellschaft in England. Historische Zeitschrift 198:24–32
Rüb FW (2003) Vom Wohlfahrtsstaat zum "manageriellen" Staat? Zum Wandel des Verhältnisses von Markt und Staat in der deutschen Sozialpolitik. In: Czada R, Zintl R (eds) Politik und Markt. Politische Vierteljahresschrift, special issue 34. Wiesbaden: 256–299
Schmidt MG (2005) Sozialpolitik in Deutschland. Historische Entwicklung und internationaler Vergleich, 3rd edn. Wiesbaden
Schmidt MG (2010) The policy of the middle way: Germany since 1990. In: Bulmer S, Jeffery C, Padgett S (eds) Rethinking Germany and Europe. Democracy and diplomacy in a semi-sovereign state. Houndmills Basingstoke, pp 73–84
Seeleib-Kaiser M (2002) A dual transformation of the German welfare state. West European Politics 25:25–48
van Kersbergen K (1995) Social capitalism: a study of Christian democracy and the welfare state. London
von Stein L (1842) Der Socialismus und Communismus des heutigen Frankreich. Leipzig

Social Policy in the Federal Republic of Germany: The Constitution of the Social

Hans F. Zacher

The "Social" as the Guiding Concept of Politics and Law

1 The Normative Openness and the Concrete Historical Perceptibility of the "Social"

1.1 The Normative Power and Undeterminedness of the Social

The social policy of the Federal Republic of Germany is based on a social norm of great authority: this society seeks to be a *"social"* order. It wants its polity to be social, and through its policies and laws to bring about and guarantee a state of affairs that deserves to be called "social." This norm is so general that it cannot be adequately attested with a single piece of evidence. Rather, it is demonstrated by the totality of the political and legal development. It is grounded in a long and impressive history (Hockerts 1996, pp. 27–48; Stolleis 2013, German Social Policy, vol. 2), which after 1945 was initially picked up and vigorously carried forward by the *Länder*, and then in 1949 by the Federal Republic. By virtue of that continuity, this history constitutes an essential – and today presumably the most important – component of German identity (Ritter 1998b). At the same time, it is reinforced by the international embeddedness in a community of states whose economically developed and liberal-democratic members feel committed to the ideal of the welfare state (Ritter 1991; Schmid 1996, 1998), and who have also carried this ideal into the international community of states itself through shared institutions and norms (Köhler 1988; Schuler 1988). The law picks up this norm of the social above all in the social goal of the state and in the elevated ranking that it accords this goal (Zacher 1987a, pp. 1045–1111).

While this social commitment of the society and polity into which this human community has constituted itself is quite firm, it is unclear what it means concretely. The term *"social" is extremely indeterminate*. The individual who uses it, or the

H.F. Zacher, *Social Policy in the Federal Republic of Germany*,
German Social Policy 3, DOI 10.1007/978-3-642-22525-3_2,

group or organization that expresses itself "*socially*" by means of it, often has something very specific in mind. But the multitude of these specific meanings does not produce an intersubjective definitude, or a definitive clarity that holds for society as a whole. We can say only the following: *"social" means social conditions*. "*Social*" also means the individual state of being, though not in a solipsistically isolated sense, but with reference to the individual state of being of others and of society. "*Social*" is aimed at "correct" societal conditions (that is, those deemed correct), and thus also at "correct" individual states of being (that is, those deemed correct). "*Social*" refers to the criteria by means of which appropriate societal conditions and individual states of being are distinguished from inappropriate ones. "*Social*" gives rise to – indeed, compels – judgments about the existing societal conditions and individual states of being and their development.

But what, precisely, is meant by all of this? First this: "*social*" has something to do with *equality* and *inequality*. "*Social*" *negates* a certain measure of *inequality* – or more precisely: certain constellations of inequality (Mau 1997). The "social question" arose first in the guise of the "question of the poor": vis-à-vis the inequality between those who had a minimum livelihood or more, and those who lacked the bare necessities. It then manifested itself as the "workers' question": vis-à-vis the inequality of those who had to sell their labor like a commodity, and those who sold commodities as goods. Thus, the "social question" was ignited time and again by the constant perception of new inequalities. In that sense, "*social*" is a mandate to distinguish unreasonable inequalities from reasonable or at least tolerable ones (or less important ones), and to eliminate, compensate for, or at least diminish the unreasonable ones. In this regard, "*social*" *aims at more equality. Not equality as such.* This is the *difference between "social" and "socialist."* And at no time has there been a general consensus about the "socialist" approach. The basic norm that is generally endorsed aims at something more open. This version of the "social" means a selective, responsible approximation to equality. Thus, the expansion of the social across the nineteenth and twentieth century took place as a process of negating an ever growing number of inequalities and discovering more and more new equalities: and the latter were used to define the inequalities and to guide the efforts that would prevent, eliminate, compensate, or at least moderate them.[1] Thus, "more equality" can also be understood as "more equalities": not "equality" as such, but "many equalities."

Here we must insert a constriction, though. At its core, "social" is aimed at something economic (Zacher 1987a, p. 1087). "Social" refers to economically conditioned or economically relevant inequalities and equalities. But that, too, is a result of the history of the "social question." And it results from a basic liberal attitude. The goal is not to change the human being: a person should have autonomy over his or her own self. The goal is to change the conditions that surround people. What is given from the outside is to be altered. And those things are first and foremost the economic givens and the economic effects of non-economic givens.

[1] For a diagnosis of the reality of social inequality in Germany at the end of the twentieth century see Braun and Mohler (1998); Hradil and Schiener (1999), which also has a further discussion, including older material.

But what degree of proximity to the economic core is demanded? What must the relationship between economic and non-economic conditions be for social conditions and individual states of being to be measured by the yardstick of the "social"? There are no definitive answers to any of these questions. The latitude is wide and variable over the course of social and political developments. Exceptions, too, are conceivable.[2] The concept of the "social" is an open one.

This openness is by no means merely a default position. On the contrary: it alone can reconcile the lofty claim of the norm to validity and the multiplicity of conditions and the diversity of societal and political constellations that form the basis from which humans respond to the challenges of the social. Most of all, however, it manifests *another basic norm of this society: the willingness to accept inequality*. Inequality between people is not only perceived as the result of fate. It is *also* understood and accepted as something *truly human*, as a conditio humana. But it is also seen *as an opportunity*, as a sphere of freedom. And that applies especially in relationship to the economically conditioned or economically relevant circumstances – in other words: in relationship to the "*social*." Neither individuals nor the groups with which individuals associate themselves want to be equal above all else. Rather, the entire development is shaped by an ideal of social happiness, which fundamentally rejects disadvantages vis-à-vis respective others, accepts the disadvantages of the respective others, but also limits them, and, finally, regards advantages vis-à-vis respective others as legitimate, in fact, regards the possibility of advantages vis-à-vis respective others as essential. The *relativity of the maxims of equality*, which characterizes the *meaning of the "social*," has *two roots*, therefore: on the one hand, the *multiplicity of what equality can mean*, and on the other hand, the *proviso of inequality*, which has always been essential for the relationship of this society to the social.

1.2 The Concrete Historical Perception of the Social

1.2.1 Approaches

The *historical experiences* connected to the concept of the social can be perceived and depicted through two approaches. Both approaches can be derived from the self-evident societal and political nature of historically evolved socio-political institutions. They convey the concrete substance of what is meant by the word "social." They furnish images that form the basis for all further thinking and talking about the social.

One approach leads to the basic formula that every adult who is not old and bound by family work should have the opportunity, but also the responsibility, to earn a

[2] For example, a common phenomenon is the application of the principle of the social state to the protection of the individual in criminal law and in the penal system: BVerfGE 35, 202 (235f.); 41, 329 (331); 45, 187 (223, 228f., 238f.); Stern (1984, p. 901f.).

living through work and thus provide for his needs and the needs of those who live with him in a community of maintenance and depend on his support. This basic formula provides a rule from which socially appropriate conditions can – but do not have to – emerge. The first responsibility of society and the polity is to make the realization of this basic formula possible, legally speaking: through the organization of gainful work through private law and possibly also administrative law (especially labor law), through free-market and administrative and subsistence-providing legal conditions regarding the coverage of needs, and through family law. But the specifically social responsibility goes further than that. It is directed against unreasonable inequalities that emerge during the implementation of the basic formula: either as the inappropriate conditions of the implementation, or as the inappropriate circumstances and processes of the implementation. The implementation of the basic formula entails dangers (e.g. threats to health in the area of work, exploitation in the area of income, unusual needs or excessive costs of necessary goods in the area of basic needs, failure of members within a community of maintenance to perform their roles) and shortfalls (e.g. loss of the capacity to work in the area of labor, insolvency of the employer in the area of income, unbridgeable contradictions between needs and the costs of meeting them, death of a breadwinner). These dangers and shortcomings are the exceptions to the rule – or more precisely: the difference between the real implementation of the rule and a hoped-for realization of the basic formula. Overcoming this difference – counteracting the dangers and compensating for the shortcomings – is thus the specific social task. This is preceded by the more general task of making the basic formula operational and maintaining it that way by developing gainful employment, the meeting of basic needs, and the community of maintenance. It is also – but not only – a social task. Since the beginning of labor law and social insurance, social policy has gradually developed in this sense of an equally specific and comprehensive task. This was joined by the realization of the need for an economic policy that offers the best possible chance for realizing the social by implementing the basic formula. Moreover, since the establishment of public assistance, it has been clear that social policy must guarantee a minimum of subsistence coverage and maintenance also when the individual is blocked from access to work and an income.

The other approach to the historical perception of the social is constituted by the spheres of politics in which the social responsibility of the state is concentrated in a special way: first, the guarantee of a subsistence minimum for everyone; second, social protection against the rupture of an individual's life circumstances through social provisioning and social compensation; third, the multitude of measures of social protection and compensation to achieve greater equality; and, finally, the responsibility of the state for the economy. These four areas stand side by side in considerable autonomy. The substance of what they are concerned with is already very different. The guarantee of a subsistence minimum, social protection through provisioning and compensation, and a reduction in differences in levels of prosperity are aimed essentially at the microcosm of individual welfare. The responsibility of politics for the economy is related primarily to the economic system, the macrocosm. These areas also differ with respect to the criteria they employ. Guaranteeing a subsistence minimum, security, and equality can be juxtaposed as alien, indeed, contradictory goals, and the responsibility for the economy can be substantially untethered from a direct link to them. Still, all four areas of politics manifest essential experiences of social responsibility and decision-making. The landmarks of the concrete expression of these experiences is what citizens, politicians, experts, journalists, and so on think of when they hear the world "social" – together with the experiences that people have with the basic formula, with the warding off of dangers that accompany its implementation, and with compensation for the shortcomings it leaves unresolved.

The normative openness of the "*social*" is thus juxtaposed to its concrete manifestation in the historically given institutions. The nature of the basic social norm, which is characterized by abstract certainty with concrete uncertainty, thus seems to be inverted: abstract uncertainty with concrete certainty. In reality, what we see here is a relationship of tension. The price for the full authority of the basic social norm is its openness. The institutions provide a picture of a possible realization and in the process charge the basic norm with social and legal energy. But this poses the danger that what is understood as *social* is only what has been historically realized or can be measured by what is historically given.

1.2.2 The Functional Approach to the Concrete Historical Perception: the Basic Formula

The basic formula of work, income, meeting of essential needs, and maintenance draws a line along which the law makes possible the realization of the formula by the individual, counteracts threats that arise during its implementation, and compensates for shortcomings that make it impossible to make the formula a reality (Zacher 1982, pp. 329–337; Zacher 1983, pp. 943–978). The line follows the density of institutional concretization. That gives it weight and import, but also constitutes its weakness. The realization of the social through work, income, the meeting of essential needs, and maintenance requires more than the prescriptions of freedom, social protection, and social benefits that accompany the individual through the implementation of the basic formula. To put it differently: the realization of the social through work, income, the meeting of essential needs, and maintenance depends – also – on many other factors and more general regulations and policies apart from the norms and institutions that accompany and supplement the implementation of the basic formula by the individual. It is therefore necessary to see the relativity of the basic formula alongside its power of providing orientation.

Dependent Gainful Work, Independent Gainful Work, Unpaid Employment – Light and Shadow of the Basic Formula

Work in the sense of the basic formula is *gainful employment*. Gainful employment can be dependent, independent, or corporative (marginal in Germany). When it comes to an understanding of the basic formula, *dependent gainful employment is in the foreground*. This applies to the responsibility of society and the polity to make possible the realization of the basic formula. It is directed at dependent gainful employment in a different and more intensive way than at independent or corporative gainful employment. This holds for the responsibility of the individual to earn an income through work and thus meet the basic needs and provide maintenance. Satisfying that responsibility through independent or corporative gainful employment is a liberty. If that liberty is not exercised, the responsibility of satisfying the formula through dependent work becomes what is known in legal parlance as a "burden": a duty whose fulfillment cannot be compelled, but which cannot remain unfulfilled without disadvantages. The special status of dependent gainful employment is evident particularly in the responsibility of society and the polity for the socially appropriate realization of the basic formula. The individual who meets his responsibility to work through dependent employment enjoys extensive protection against the dangers that arise during the implementation of the formula, and extensive safeguards against the shortcomings left open by its implementation. Independent and corporative gainful employment do not enjoy a comparable protection, or at least not on the same scale.

The reason for this lies in the fact that dependent gainful employment is the norm within industrial society. But it also has to do with the very dependency that defines this kind of work and triggers the critique of inequality in several respects: in relation to the employer, in relation to non-dependent workers, in relation to the person whose income is not conditioned by work, and so on. During the misery of the workers in the early capitalist phase, it was precisely this complex inequality that turned the "workers' question" into the "social question." The concentration of the social on dependent gainful work also has to do with the very diverse category of the self-employed, many of whom are themselves employers. The need to bind the self-employed socially to "their" employees may have helped to repress the question about the social protection of the independent workers – in the extreme case as "just punishment" for the "class enemy." Finally, the reason why social intervention is so heavily focused on dependent gainful employment has to do with the specific power of workers' interests to assert themselves (as expressed especially in the unions). At any rate, the various ways in which the basic formula was manifested for *different areas of gainful employment* have shaped their structures. Social intervention has substantially reinforced the distinctions between independent or corporative and dependent work.

The basic formula has *no place* for *unpaid work. Familial work* is subsumed by the community of maintenance. *Unpaid work outside of the family* – "charitable" social, community-related or individually altruistic work – remains in limbo. *Gainful employment* incorporates *three levels of meaning*: first, *real effective action*, the doing itself; second, a *social position outside the private sphere* (in the workplace, in the company, etc.); third, *paid compensation*. The social responses to the challenges of the basic formula that are perceived as threats and shortcomings have considerably *expanded* these meanings, especially in regard to dependent gainful employment: the essence of the *social position* through a guarantee of freedom, of equality, and of security of labor relations, and especially through the institutions of workplace-based, enterprise-based, and public participation;

the element of *gainful compensation* through a guarantee of the ability to meet essential needs, also in situations of an unusual imbalance between income and the costs of covering basic needs (as in the case of illness or accident), through a continuation of income beyond the opportunity to work (as in the case of unemployment), beyond the ability to work (as in the case of illness or disability) or the end of a person's working life (as in the case of old age), indeed, even through a continuation of the ability (as in the case of the death of a breadwinner) to provide maintenance to dependants beyond death. Non-gainful work in principle means forgoing all of these "extensions."

While the social thus clearly sketches the line of dependent gainful employment, work income, the meeting of essential needs, and maintenance, the picture becomes very murky when the sequence begins with independent or corporative work. Non-gainful work finds no place within it. As a result, work that – embedded in the family, in organizations, and sometimes performed individually or in informal collectives – is carried out to prevent the inequality of others or to moderate and compensate it falls by the wayside. In other words, what falls by the wayside is work that is indispensable and exceedingly important for the production of human welfare.

In the Shadow of the Basic Formula: Wealth

The connection of work, income, need, and maintenance attained its relevance as the elementary basic formula of social responsibility from the challenges of the classic "social question": from the "question of the poor" already, for in its perspectives only the person who was unable to earn the bare necessities through work was "poor;" and then especially from the "workers' question," for it demanded the social protection and development of work and income. Grounded in these beginnings, the basic formula was conceived without concern for *wealth*, and it has stayed that way. But if wealth is present, that can substantially alter the realization of the formula. Wealth can replace income: either by earning "income" as capital, or by simply being used up. In this way, wealth can serve to meet basic needs and provide maintenance. And with respect to the individual who has wealth, it can relativize – if not completely abolish – the responsibility of earning income through work. Finally, as the "factor capital," wealth can be juxtaposed to the "factor work." The social unfolding of the formula then demands the integration of the "capitalist." At any rate: wealth can exist, but not invariably so. And it has no reliable connection to the arch of work, income, meeting needs, and maintenance. Social policy does not quite know what to do with wealth. On the one side, the pendulum swings into the negative judgment against "unearned income." On the other side, wealth is repeatedly taken into account as an additional path to social protection. For the most part, though, wealth is ignored – it remains in the slipstream of the social dynamic of work, income, meeting needs, and maintenance.

Wealth exists not only in the form of assets, but also in the form of liabilities: *debts*. Debts, in turn, at least as long as they are not balanced by assets, alter the reality of the connection between work, income, meeting needs, and maintenance.

Debts make income doubly necessary – to live and to repay debts. Work becomes essential to earn this income. But the purpose of work, to meet basic needs and provide maintenance, is reduced – if not entirely abolished – by the debt burden. The social maintains its own distance – and helplessness – also to this circumstance.

Meeting Basic Needs: The Alternative Responsibility of "Income Policy" and "Policies to Meet Basic Needs"

The basic formula aims at meeting needs: food, clothing, shelter, housing, education and training; medical care, nursing care, care and substitution for defects in the ability to provide for oneself, mobility and communication, information and counseling. Meeting needs has a general and an individual side.

The *general side* consists in the provisioning of relevant goods and services through public administration, the free market, and individuals, groups, or organizations that differ from the market in their renunciation of the profit motive, and from the bureaucracy through their private or social character (non-profit carriers). The responsibility of the polity for meeting needs extends further than the meeting of needs through the public bureaucracy. Depending on the significance of the goods and services in question, the polity has the responsibility of providing them – or more precisely: of deciding whether and, if so, how they are to be provided. Whether the polity will and can meet that responsibility directly through the public bureaucracy, or by creating the relevant leeways for the market and non-profit carriers and guaranteeing and regulating their efforts, is another question.

This *provision* of the *goods and services necessary* to meet needs is *not something social in and of itself.* It does not a priori have to be borne by the goal of equality and the negation of inequality. Providing goods and services is first of all a question of a society's *level of civilization* and of the living conditions of every member of that society – with no regard to his or her economically conditioned or economically relevant circumstance. When, as a result of the changed living conditions of a largely urban society dominated by science and technology, the role of the polity with regard to these challenges became increasingly apparent, the name *Daseinsvorsorge* (provision of basic services) was coined to describe it (Forsthoff 1938, 1959).

The *individual side* of the problem lies in the individual ability to make use of the goods and services offered in this way. It is only here that the problem of meeting needs connects to the question of the social. The most important reason why people have different access to goods and services lies in the economic realm: in their ability to pay the prices for them, and in their ability to bear the costs connected with making use of them. According to the basic formula, work and income should provide the ability to meet a person's basis needs. But every time the basic formula fails to work in this regard, every time people run the risk of being excluded from meeting their needs because they cannot afford to do so, the specific social responsibility that is meant by the basic formula becomes relevant.

There are *two possible ways* of responding to a misalignment between needs and the ability to meet them. The *first* addresses the *demand*: by increasing a person's earning capacity, either generally or limited to a certain need. The housing subsidy is one example. The *other* addresses the *supply*: by providing goods or services on favorable terms to those whose economic capacity is absent or inadequate. The corresponding example is "affordable" housing. *Social insurance* has combined the two approaches into the *synthesis of social provisioning*: the danger that the less economically productive will be excluded from medical care is countered by pooling all those who face a similar threat into health insurance. But the *social problem* can also be *neutralized*: by providing goods and services – administratively or through altruistic social carriers – at no or only a minimal cost, the economic differences among recipients become irrelevant. A *historically widespread variant* of this approach is to offer an important good through *price controls* or through *administrative provisioning* in such a way that it is "affordable" also to the socially weaker strata.

All told, the problem of meeting needs displays both a high degree of autonomy and a high degree of complexity. The agglomeration of social problems follows two lines: the line of a responsibility via income policy for a gainful or social assistance income that completely covers the needs of individuals and their communities of maintenance; and the line of the specific responsibility in terms of needs-policy, which arises from the unequal distribution of needs and the goods-specific conditions of meeting them.

The Linearity of the Basic Formula in the Earner-Consumer Household and the Non-linearity with the Inclusion of a Community of Maintenance

Once the basic formula arrives at its endpoint, the "community of maintenance," the contradiction between the *individual-unidimensional* and the *collective-multidimensional* implementation of the basic formula comes into play. In a one-person household, the number of (potential) earners is always equal to the number of consumers. In the marriage or family household, by contrast, the number of earners can lag behind the number of consumers. Accordingly, in a single-person household, the normality of income that can be earned by the labor power of *one* earner approaches the normality of the needs of *one* consumer. As a result, shortcomings in labor power and income in a one-person household always affects *one* earner and *one* consumer. But in the marriage and family household, a great multiplicity of constellations is conceivable. The number of earners and of consumers can match, as is typical of a household in a childless marriage (or of an unmarried couple of singles). For the family household, however, it is typical that the normality of income achievable by *one* earner confronts the needs of *two or more* consumers, or that the normality of the income achievable by *two* earners confronts the needs of *three or more* consumers.

The complication rises if the aspect of *services* is taken into account. In a one-person household, services are provided to the extent that this single person is willing and able to provide for him or herself. Beyond that limit, needs must be met administratively or by the market. By contrast, in the marriage and family household (with once again considerable variations in the specific circumstances), the needs that the members cannot meet by themselves are largely taken care of by the services from other members of the community of maintenance. The *community of maintenance* is not only an income community or only a consumption community, but also a *service-providing community*. The service-providing community of the family is indispensable to the regeneration of society, as well as to the care of people who need to be looked after. This service-providing community is thus a value-creating community. But this value-creation is not calculated in the same way as income that can be achieved by gainful employment, or in the way needs are calculated that are met by the market, by charitable carriers, or by the public sector.

A picture of social organization that is based primarily on work and income thus has difficulty with the *familial work performed in the complementarity of various roles*. The one-person household is an individual system linked entirely to this single person. This one person creates the connection between "work/income" and "meeting needs." He or she is the meaning *and* endpoint of the system. This holds in a functional sense: with the meeting of the needs of this one person, the system ends – in principle; the opening of the system towards others on a case-by-case basis is possible in a variety of ways. But the final piece of the formula, the community of maintenance, is missing. And it holds in a temporal-historical sense: with the death of the one person, the system ends. By contrast, a marriage, and even more so a family, is a supraindividual system in which interrelational roles are assigned to the members. If the person in an active role drops out of the picture or ceases to play that role, the system does not end. Instead, it suffers a deficit. If an earner who contributed his or her income to the family as maintenance dies, the systems of social protection face the challenge of replacing this maintenance through social benefits and services. If the roles within a family are divided among one earner and one service "provider," and if that "provider" dies, the familial system likewise suffers a deficit. But this deficit has nothing to do with gainful work and income. That is why the death of a "provider" is met with a social shrug. It is rarely seen as a social challenge. Rarer still are explicit responses. By contrast, the death of an earner has long since become self-evident as a social challenge, as have the positive responses to it.

There is a multitude of options for counteracting the inequalities that are connected to all of this: through the structure of family law itself, through social support for that law, through help in conflicts, and so on; through the substitution of role-bearers if they fail; through an expansion of social protection, especially by extending it to cover maintenance; by taking into account the familial structures and concerns when devising the structures to meet needs; by supplementing earned income through social services that reflect the burden of maintenance; by calculating familial burdens when it comes to taxing earners, and so on. The multiplicity of constellations and the even greater multiplicity of how to assess them opens up an extreme diversity in the way the problem is defined and resolved. The result is a considerable imbalance: in principle, the social gradient between a single-earner/single-consumer or a two-earner/two-consumer constellation, on the one hand, and the variety of more-consumers-than-earners constellations, on the other hand, is understood; but there are broad disagreements over which inequalities specifically should trigger a social intervention, what techniques should be used to counter social threats, and to what extent deficits should be compensated for. The *community of maintenance* is the *"open end" of the basic formula.*

Also in the Shadow of the Basic Formula: The Negative Income and Property Law – Taxes

The reality of the basic formula depends crucially on taxes. The *income* that can be earned through *gainful employment* depends on the burden of taxes imposed on wages and salaries. And that burden consists largely of taxes *and* social insurance contributions. The real relationship between income from dependent work and income from independent work, as well as the real relationship between earned income and other types of income (e.g. capital wealth), are also determined substantially by the burden of taxes and dues and by the way in which they are levied. Looking at the *meeting of needs*, we can see once again that the reality of meeting needs likewise depends on taxes and dues: on the fees for the services of public administration; on the sales tax, the transportation tax, and the consumption tax that enter into the prices of goods-commodities and services and services. All of this becomes differentiated yet again within the problem sphere of the *community of maintenance*. How do the taxes and dues take the structures and functions of the community of maintenance into account? And finally: how often are the taxes and dues relevant not only for the reality of the basic formula, but also for the case in which income is replaced or supplemented by social services? Should social services be taxed or not?

The reality of ways of life is thus shaped by two sides: first, by income and wealth and by the social services that replace or supplement income and wealth; second, by taxes and dues, which reduce the available funds and can increase the cost of living. If the law governing revenues and transfer payments can be aggregated into a "*positive income law*," the sum of taxes and dues constitutes a "*negative income law*." As obvious as this is, it remains *in the background of the basic formula*. The perception of the social is directed at the positive enactment of work, income, the meeting of needs, and maintenance. The perception of the negative elements of this enactment – defraying the specific costs of the social along with the general costs of the polity that make possible and guarantee this positive enactment – does not have the same kind of clarity. Moreover, the aspect of drawing up a balance sheet of what is left after the taking and giving, and the aspect of evaluation whether the result is social, recede into the background.

This does not rule out that individual levies – especially the income tax – are subject to an intense discussion with respect to the demands of the social. However, taxes are first and foremost subject to the law of their real mandate: that of making funds available (Franke 1993). Social criteria of how taxes are construed cannot be divorced from this original mandate. Moreover, social goals of individual regulations – for example, when tax exemptions are substituted for social services – cannot undo this connection to the goal of raising the funds for the polity from those who are able to contribute. Even social insurance contributions, in spite of their distinct social charge, are subject to the dominant purpose of raising funds.

In the Shadow of the Basic Formula: Supraindividual Programs

The basic formula traces out a line along which individuals shape and take responsibility for their own lives, a line of liberties by means of which it is realized, and of obligations that go hand in hand with it, a line of social protection and social services that accompany and supplement the enactment of work, income, the meeting of needs, and the community of maintenance. However, social inequality cannot be prevented, eliminated, moderated, or compensated by directly shaping individual circumstances. Large-scale collective disadvantages can often be dealt with better through measures that are more general in nature: improvements in infrastructure, the development of information, counseling, advising, and education, financial programs in favor of certain institutions and activities, and so on. To be sure, these measures can also affect individual conditions – gainful employment, income, the meeting of needs, and the community of maintenance. In fact, as a rule they are intended to improve individual living conditions, though as part of a broader category: the living conditions of farmers, miners, coastal dwellers, the inhabitants of border regions, and so on. This distance of regional, sectoral, structural and other programs from the individual implementation of the basic formula removes them from the foreground of the picture drawn by the basic formula. They are a later accretion.

1.2.3 The Institutional Access to the Concrete Historical Perception: Social Protection and Social Services, Responsibility for the Economy

The other approach to what German society is concretely aware of as the "social" are the *institutional areas* through which the society and the polity exercise social responsibility: the guarantee of the subsistence minimum, social protection through provision and compensation, concern for more equality, and responsibility for the economy (Zacher 1987a, pp. 1059–1083; Zacher and Kessler 1990, pp. 97–157).

Guaranteeing the Subsistence Minimum

Guaranteeing the subsistence minimum is the traditional task of the institution that is today referred to as social assistance (*Sozialhilfe*). It is the *heir of poor relief*, the oldest stage of the modern German social state (Sachße and Tennstedt 1988, 1992, 1998). Even after the development of other, "better" institutions of the social state, it did not relinquish the function of a basic provision; but all the changes in details notwithstanding, it has also preserved its concrete character: namely, that the aid depends fundamentally on individual circumstances and should do justice to them.

The guarantee of the subsistence minimum is in principle subsidiary *with respect to the implementation of the basic formula.* To the extent that work allows for the earning of income by which needs – including those of the community of maintenance – can be met, the provision of the subsistence minimum does not come into play. To put it differently: the guarantee of the subsistence minimum precedes the basic formula. It takes effect precisely when the premise of labor power does not exist, or if the capacity and willingness to work do not lead to gainful employment. At the same time, it does accompany the implementation of the basic formula. If no specialized systems are responsible, it reacts to shortcomings in the implementation of the formula wherever they occur: be it a mismatch between income and needs, be it a mismatch between income and the burden of maintenance.

Social Protection Through Social Provision and Social Compensation

Another category of social institutions is devoted to protection (Weisser 1956, pp. 396–412; Kaufmann 1973; von Hippel 1979; Kaufmann and Külp 1988): to the social protection of individual life circumstances – the protection precisely also of "better" life circumstances. In this way, social protection sets itself apart from the guarantee of the subsistence minimum. Social protection as such is the most important piece of evidence that the social is not concerned with "equality" but with "equalities:" social protection also carries on unequal life conditions. That is even more evident in the multiplicity of institutions of social protection. Bundled in the manifestations of *provision* (*Vorsorge*) and *compensation* (*Entschädigung*), they pick up on various inequalities and equalities: inequalities and equalities in the threats from the "vicissitudes" of life and the ability to make provisions against them; inequalities and equalities of harm and the responsibility for it.

Social protection through *provision* has dual *historical roots*: the development of the modern professional civil service, which went hand in hand with the promise of *maintenance* – that is, of income in case of old age and disability, later also of support for surviving dependants (Ruland 1983, pp. 73–104); and *social insurance*, which was preceded by a long history of solidarist protection among tradesmen, miners, and so forth, and which developed at all times as complementary and parallel to private insurance (Tennstedt 1976, pp. 385–492; Peters 1978; D. Zöllner 1981, pp. 45–180). Social provision begins with a history of provision whose target horizon is a desired risk (old age) or undesired risks (illness, disability, death that leaves dependants behind, unemployment). If the risk scenario comes to pass, the story of provision turns into a story of benefits. In that provision is set up in such a way as to reflect the life circumstances at the time it is put in place, the story of benefits thus also reflects these live circumstances.

Social protection through *compensation* is very different. It goes back to a history of responsibility: the person responsible initiates a development that has the potential of harming someone else, and if that happens, he must make up for it – whereby a standardized form of compensation is generally regarded as adequate. Compensation has multifarious *historical roots* (Schulin 1981; 1997, pp. 463–483): in *risk liability*, in the collectivization of the liability of employers for the risks of accident and illness associated with work through *accident insurance*, and most recently in that the responsibility of the state for war and its victims compelled the state to *care for the victims of war*. While risk liability remained essentially tied to the development of private liability and insurance law, and while accident insurance – which in its basic thrust represents a workers' insurance and joint provision by employers for the case of their liability – was always regarded as a part of social insurance (in keeping with its evolutionary history), it was the care of the victims of war that led to the breakthrough of a specific type of social compensation law that has by now developed into a richly elaborated system.

Provision and compensation have a related though differentiated relationship to the *basic formula* of work, income, the meeting of needs, and the community of maintenance. *Provision* presupposes not only the need for provision, but also the capacity for provision. As a result, social provision takes effect fundamentally only when the first two parts of the basic formula – work and income – have been individually realized. In other words: provision posits that the person who depends on work to earn an income is to a special degree in need of provision; and it also posits that the person who earns an income through work is able to make contributions to provision. In turn, the degree of the capacity to make provisions – that is, income – affects the need for provision: for provision is all the more urgent, the smaller the income. The degree of the capacity for provision has a more differentiated impact on the degree of the need for provision. If we are talking about income protection, income also determines the degree of the need for provision. By contrast, if we are talking about the next part of the basic formula, the meeting of needs, the question of the need for provision arises only in principle, while the level is derived from the needs that must be guaranteed. Still, the level of income can be relevant: as the measure of the capacity for provision and also as a measure of the individual contribution to the solidarist meeting of needs. The scene changes once again as one moves to the fourth "leg" of the basic formula, the community of maintenance. The need for provision now extends also to the needs of those dependent on maintenance and on the maintenance that the earner(s) can provide from earned income. However, the capacity for provision does not grow with the size and needs of the community of maintenance. As a result, the development of provision was slow to enter the arena of providing co-insurance for dependants (especially for the case of illness) and the substitution of the earner's capacity for maintenance (through insurance for dependants) for the time after his or her death. And after that step had been taken, the difficulties within the internal sphere of provision became apparent. The simple linearity of the one-earner/one-consumer sequence of work, income, and the meeting of needs, and the complex non-linearity of the more-consumers-than-earners sequence of work, income, the meeting of needs, and maintenance could not be combined without problems. But no matter how grave the doubts and need for decision-making that this situation gives rise to, the contribution that the systems of provision make to solving the problems connected to the communities of maintenance is significant.

All this is underscored by the gradient that exists between citizens who are incorporated into systems of social provision, and citizens who have no access to them. The concentration of the social into a basic formula that reads "*dependent* work, income, needs, and maintenance" derives added weight from this circumstance. That the possibility exists of creating access – e.g. in the case of social insurance for the disabled or the inclusion of time spent raising children in calculating eligibility for pensions – in the name of equality also where (dependent) gainful employment is not possible or is given up in favor of something accorded equal or higher value (for example, familial child-raising), is the exception that proves the rule.

Compensation faces largely similar problems where it addresses the impairment of labor power and income. Incidentally, compensation cannot depend on the characteristic tenor of the basic formula. Wherever harm occurs – with regard to labor power, income, needs, or maintenance – it becomes necessary to assess it in connection with the responsibility recognized by law. In the typical case of social compensation, i.e. the responsibility of the community, this means that it must be assessed in connection with the responsibility of the community for the victims of Nazi persecution, for the victims of the war and the expulsions in its wake, for the victims of immunizations, for the victims of civil crimes, and so on.

The Specific Obviousness of Provision

These interconnections are of *great institutional obviousness. First*, the institutions reflect the complementary interplay between the *minimum protection* provided by welfare/social assistance, and an *"elevated" social protection* that is realized by provision and compensation. This also reveals the difference between a *narrower* and a *broader conception of social protection*. While the narrower conception is aimed at protecting individual life conditions, the broader conception includes the protection of general – at least minimal – life opportunities. Just as in German usage, "social protection" has for a long time incorporated also welfare (*Sozialhilfe*).

Second, what becomes apparent is the complementarity between a *universal* conception, as realized in the minimum protection, and a *selective* conception that is typical of provision. In this regard, compensation assumes a mediating role. While it is fundamentally conceived as *universal* with respect to persons, de facto – because of the specific nature of the circumstances that can trigger compensation – it is *selective*. Of course, during catastrophic times – such as the Second World War and the collapse of the German Reich – circumstances can assume such a level of generality that compensation appears to express a second mode of universality.

Third, a narrower, *organizational sense of institutions* mirrors a structure that accords an *eminent position to provision*. In keeping with its historical evolution, whose ripple effects are felt to this day, the most important types of provision are found, on the one hand, in social insurance, and, on the other hand, in provision for civil servants. As different as the two types are, both work with equal clarity toward the realization of the interests embodied within them (Rieger 1992; Nullmeier and Rüb 1993). In the case of *social insurance*, this is expressed, firstly, in the communality of interests of the insured and in the capacity of those affected to respond democratically. Clashes of interests, as can occur for example in pension insurance with respect to a generational conflict, can curtail the political effect of this communality. The institutional power of social insurance becomes even clearer in view of the fact that it is in principle an insurance of employees and therefore shares in the ability of the interests of employees to organize and assert themselves.

But the most effective institutional characteristic, finally, is the self-administration that is traditionally linked to social insurance. It ensures the intensive participation of the interested parties involved, which includes not only the insured, especially employees, but also their employers. In actuality, the organizations of these groups – especially the unions and the employers' associations – mediate this participation. That triggers an interaction: unions and employers' associations can use their status within social insurance to strengthen their influence also in other contexts; even more so, however, they can use their organizational power to assert the positions of social insurance. This participation refers not only to the internal decision-making process and the articulation and assertion of interests on the outside, but also to the formation of an autonomous bureaucracy and leadership management. Participating interest groups and an integrative administration together lend the concerns of social insurance special weight.

The principle of *provision for civil servants* is different in its approach. The organizational selection is absent. But civil servant provision is the shared interest of nearly all of those individuals whose service the state needs to fulfill its tasks: not only civil servants in the narrower sense, but – after a long development – also judges, soldiers, with modifications ministers and parliamentary state secretaries, with even greater modifications the delegates of parliament, and within the framework of special arrangements of supplementary insurance also the private law employees of the public sector. It is obvious that these two basic types – social insurance and civil servant provision – compete with each other, that they differ in substance, and that the powers standing behind them have an interest in setting them apart from each other. In the same way, there are differences in the ways the participating interests formulate themselves, the techniques by which they are pushed through, and the chances for their realization. On the other hand, the two types of systems are also mutually supportive, in that the successes of one trigger claims by the other, and the resistance of one reinforces the resistance of the other. *Provision* is thus an *area of high institutional weight*. That is very evident with respect to social insurance, and rather more concealed with respect to the provision of civil servants.

The *guarantee of the subsistence minimum* through social assistance is the other extreme. Its *amorphous generality and the principle of neediness* as the criterion of incidence make it more difficult for those affected to organize their interests. The administration cannot be in their hands. Traditionally, it is entrusted to the communities and to communal associations as one task among many. And the welfare associations have a dual status: they are the carriers of implementation *and* the advocates of their "clients."

The situation is different again when it comes to *compensation*; group-related commonalities in the histories of responsibilities (with war victims, for example) and the histories of benefits (with the disabled, for example) open up access to the organization of interests. The administrative implementation is entrusted to special bureaucratic bodies. Still, compensation, too, is far removed from the intrinsic institutional weight of provision.

The Multitude of Paths to "More Equality"

No matter how it is defined, welfare/social assistance guarantees *equality in the sense of a minimum level*. Provision guarantees *equality with respect to the possibility of protecting acquired living conditions* – but that means that it also secures unequal living conditions. Compensation seeks to establish a certain degree of equality *toward the inequality of victims*. But in the process, it, too, can continue the inequality of living conditions.

But if "social" means above all "more equality" or – put in different terms – the negation of inappropriate differences in wealth and dependencies, the described strategies alone are not sufficient to fulfill a comprehensive social mandate. Rather, the term "more equality" retains its elemental, a priori importance. It is, as it were, the *general clause of the social*. And accordingly, it trails off into the infinite.

Historically, a general principle of "social equality" emerges fairly late – and even then only as an overly general name for specific, concrete notions of equality. To be sure, the law has always known efforts aimed at equality. For example, the legal institution of guardianship to compensate for a person's inability to look after his or her concerns, and in family maintenance law the action of those capable of providing support for those who need it. But since social and legal history is much more a history of inequality than of equality, we find the concern over equality much more frequently integrated into regimes of inequality that could derive their meaning and justification from minimum guarantees of equality. For example, in children's law the obligation of parents to provide for their children. We find something similar in the law governing domestics, where the obligations of providing maintenance inject traces of the equality of human beings into a system of inequality. In the early stages of the modern social state, we find new concretizations of equality: the equality of the minimum in poor relief, or the minimum equality of educational opportunities through the free and obligatory attendance of the *Volksschule* (elementary school). Further steps toward more equality went hand in hand with the answers to the workers' question: the regulation of the imbalance of power wielded by employers toward employees through work protection law; initial approaches to a balance between employers and employees through the recognition of unions; efforts on the part of social insurance legislation to allow for a minimum level of equal access to social protection; very late then the approximation to even more equality through the development of the law governing labor struggles and especially the law on collective bargaining. The idea of "more social equality" achieved a further breakthrough only in the wake of the First World War, the Revolution of 1918, and the democratization of the polity through the Weimar Constitution.[3] It was not only the position of the worker and

---

[3] Time itself has not comprehensively recorded – let alone systematized – the diversity of value conceptions and political projects. It clung to principles or to the history of social law. On the latter see Frerich and Frey (1996, pp. 171–244). Nothing provides a better overview of the way the problem was perceived during the Weimar Period than the state constitutions of the first post-war

employee that was improved in many ways. Entirely new topics were articulated: children and youths, mothers, families with many children; promoting equal access to the educational institutions; access to property by those willing to settle; protection of tenants[4] and leaseholders[5]; protection of the *Mittelstand* (medium-size business community); protection of intellectual work and of copyrights; equality of taxation. In the Federal Republic of Germany, the basic and general charge of "more quality" was taken up even more openly and broadly. The inequalities of labor power, work, income, needs and the expense of meeting them, the size and structure of the community of maintenance and the individual positions within it, were joined by an increasing number of life situations (e.g. disability, old age), economic sectors (e.g. mining, agriculture), regions (e.g. border regions), and even topical areas (e.g. health care, education).[6]

Manifestations

But it was not only the *better-worse relationships,* which became the target of the charge of inequality, that could be *multiplied in many dimensions*. The same was and is no less true of the *patterns by which the polity can eliminate or moderate differences in prosperity* or *control the dependencies* arising from them: the social alteration of private-law relationships (e.g. through the development of labor law, tenant law, consumer protection law, etc.); the compensation of social disadvantages through the relevant obligations imposed on private individuals (e.g. in favor of the severely disabled); state intervention in social relations (e.g. occupational safety, institutional supervision, youth welfare, etc.); the guarantee of universal access to the essential goods and services (price maintenance, compulsive contracting); the reduction of economic inequalities through the socialization of economic goods and their conveyance into the *Gemeinwirtschaft* (common economy); the redistribution of economic goods (e.g. land reform); the provision of public institutions (e.g. in the area of the provision with universally necessary goods [water, electricity, gas] transportation and communication services, education and health care); the promotion of social offerings (especially through subsidies); the compensation of unequal economic and life conditions through supra-individual programs (regional, sectoral, and structural advancement programs) and through measures of financial equalization (federal financial equalization, local financial equalization; special economic levies and equalization funds); compensation for

---

years (see below section "Further Development and the Formulation of New Goals"). The drafters of these constitutions drew for the most part on the stock of ideas from the Weimar period.

[4] The beginnings go back to the time of the First World War (see Weiß 1993).

[5] A first leasehold protection decree was issued already during the First World War: "Verordnung über die Festsetzung von Pachtpreisen für Kleingärten vom 4. April 1916" RGBl., p. 234, and 12 October 1917, RGBl., p. 897; "Kleingarten- und Kleinpachtlandordnung vom 31. Juli 1918" RGBl., p. 1371.

[6] Zacher (1987a, p. 1066), with references. Probably the richest, though invariably incomplete, collection of examples regarding the preceding in Lampert (1998).

social disadvantages through the structure of public dues (taxes, contributions, fees, etc.); the equalization of social disadvantages in procedures (e.g. in access to the legal system, in the representation of interests), and so on. Added to this was the further development of the techniques linked to the guarantee of the subsistence minimum, social provision, and social compensation: the differentiation of the subsistence minimum according to special life situations (e.g. illness, disability); the facilitation of access to social insurance through the substitution of the ability to make provisions (through the payment of contributions from one branch of insurance to another – e.g. of unemployment insurance to sickness and pension insurance – or from the federal government; through the granting of benefits without contributions); the dismantling of regional, sectoral, or structural differences in capacity through the financial equalization between social insurance carriers; inclusion of particularly stressful periods (e.g. military service) as a contribution or work period in social security; compensation for inequalities resulting from harm within the framework of social compensation (e.g. through supplementary benefits of social protection for dependants or the meeting of individual needs when caring for war victims).

Thus, in contrast to the relative institutional cohesiveness of the guarantee of the subsistence minimum and of social protection through provision and compensation, the realization of "more equality" goes hand in hand with a broad *institutional openness*. Still, that principle has also led to the construction of a *separate branch of social services*. Together with public assistance, those services constitute the *aid and promotion systems* which – unlike the *provision systems* that are linked to a *history of provision*, and unlike the *compensation systems* that are based on a *history of responsibility* – are aimed directly at a *life situation*: maintenance advance, child-raising allowance, child subsidy, children and youth aid, promotion of vocational training, promotion of work, unemployment assistance, housing allowance (Zacher 1987b, pp. 572–592).

These interventions have the *most multifarious connections* to the *basic formula*. For the most part, they serve to equalize or moderate an imbalance between income and paying for one's needs (e.g. housing allowance), and an imbalance between income and the costs of maintenance (e.g. child allowance). They can also serve to provide access to work and income (work promotion). Finally, they can – in competition, one the one hand, with the benefits of social provision and social compensation, and, on the other hand, with benefits for a basic subsistence guarantee – represent an alternative to work and income (e.g. unemployment assistance).

But "more equality" means above all to *inject "more equality" into the implementation of the basic formula*: to broaden freedom and participation, security and prosperity in the implementation of the basic formula. To put it another way: to counter the dangers in the implementation that lead to an inappropriately unequal distribution of freedom, security, and prosperity. The most important example of this is *labor law* in the broadest sense: during the century-and-a-half of its modern history, it was developed ever more intensively in the direction of eliminating, compensating, or at least moderating the disadvantages that threatened employees from their inequality vis-à-vis employers, but also vis-à-vis the self-employed and those not dependent on work or income. These disadvantages are seen to lie in an unequal distribution of freedom and participation, security and prosperity, and lastly also in inequalities among employees themselves. Another example of the realization of "more equality" in the implementation of the basic formula is *social tenant law*. While labor law is situated within the fields of work and income, social tenant law belongs to the field of meeting basic needs. *Child and youth assistance* supplements family law accordingly. It addresses itself to the field of the community of maintenance.

The Responsibility of the State for the Economy

The responsibility of the state for the economy is the *most recent manifestation of the social state* (Stern 1984, pp. 903–906). To be sure, the state's concern for the economy has a long history: a concern for its internal structures and its processes and effects (R. Schmidt 1990, pp. 1–33; Piepenbrock 1964). But the social responsibility for the economy as a fundamental component of the social state is a product of the period immediately preceding the Weimar Constitution: on the one hand, the experience of the war economy, on the other hand, the basic challenge to the private sector by the revolutionary forces of 1918/1919. The Weimar Constitution responded to this new challenge primarily with Article 151, which began with the statement: "The economy has to be organized based on the principle of justice, with the goal of achieving a life of dignity for all" (Article 1, Para. 1). In fact, the Weimar period was marked by a multifarious struggle for socially useful, or at least socially justifiable, structures and effects in the economy (Apelt 1964, pp. 356–362; Ballerstedt 1958, pp. 1–90; Zacher 1965a, pp. 65–73). The *alternative between a state guarantee and freeing of a market economy whose product could create immediate social utility directly* (*in the process of distribution*) *or indirectly* (*through redistribution*), *and an arrangement of the structures of the economy aimed at social goals* (e.g. through the socialization of enterprises) *and a direct social guidance of its effects* (e.g. through guidance, compulsory contracting, or price regulations) was not aired out during the Weimar period. Thus, it was not clearly and generally known at the time. Only the forces that eventually paved the way for the path to a social market economy explained that the primacy of the free market economy was justified only if effective regulation of competition optimized the free market system and thereby enabled it to maximize the national output, which generated the appropriate social utility either directly (in the process of distribution) or indirectly (in the process of redistribution). This alternative was then brought to bear in the postwar period – already in the Unified Economic Area and then in the Federal Republic. The concept of the social market economy is based on the superiority of an internally optimized market economy over an economy of less-than-optimal performance with a direct social structure and guidance – a social *and* an economic superiority.

Of course, this did not answer the question of whether certain social concerns should not find expression in the structures of the economy. The development of works constitutions and co-determination is the most important example of this. But social questions persist also regarding the effects of the economy. Even if direct social guidance – in the sense of price maintenance, for example – receded into the background, the social duties of the state remained relevant in a variety of ways: in the focus of the overall guidance on direct or indirect social goals (such as especially full employment, price stability, and growth), in legal structures that were also intended (as in consumer protection) to counter the exploitation of social inferiority, in the particular care of politics and the law for socially appropriate conditions in various areas of life (as for example in housing), and well beyond that in the incentive practices of subsidies, tax breaks, and so on, which were intended to affect social conditions directly or indirectly. Responsibility for the economy thus articulates a social charge that requires development and has proven to be open to development.

The social responsibility of the state stands in a differentiated correspondence to the *basic formula*. The state's responsibility for the *organization of the economy precedes the basic formula*. The economic system is, in a sense, the landscape in which the basic formula realizes itself. But wherever this organization of the economy leaves room for concrete relationships – between the economy and work, the economy and income, the economy and the meeting of basic needs – a particular social *responsibility* of the state for the economic conditions in the respective sphere can arise. Examples are employment policy (for the area of work), monetary stability (for the area of income), price stability (for the area of the meeting of needs), as well as more specialized policies for meeting needs (e.g. consumer protection). But even then, the state's responsibility for the economy remains fundamentally macrocosmic in nature – committed to regulatory policy and overall guidance. The basic formula, by contrast, must realize itself in individual states of being – and in individual legal circumstances.

2 The Fundamental Interpretation of What Can Be Concretely Observed in History

2.1 *The Multi-layered, Dynamic Openness of the Social*

2.1.1 The Constant Intermingling of Private, Societal-Public, and State Activities – The Constant Interaction of Also-But-Not-Only Social Activities and Targeted Social Shaping – The Constant Difference Between Intent and Effect

Examinations and descriptions of the social, and especially of political projects and arguments, all too often create the impression that the social is restricted to activities: to intervention that is targeted at shaping and correcting the social realm. Likewise, talk of the social creates the appearance that the social is limited to *a single* carrier: the state. By contrast, the basic social norm refers to a private, societal and governmental overall process. It refers to a functional overall activity of actual life *and* legal shaping, ordering, and implementation. It refers to a diversity of purposeful endeavors: to the also-but-not-only social "normality" of private, societal, and governmental action, *and* to the socially purposeful shaping and correcting. This overall activity is a continuous interaction – an unceasing flow of pre- and after-effects, a constant side-by-side, coincidence, and clash of intentions and effects. No single element of this overall activity must be isolated and identified with the social as such. This overall activity is always merely an approximation to the social – to an individual or collective, societal or political "ought" of the social.

We can cast all of this into the following *image*: the *social* has a *three-fold locus* in a *dialectical structure*. The *thesis* is the infinity of prevailing and constantly developing private, societal, and political conditions in which social, asocial, ambivalent, and irrelevant elements are intermixed. How social the thesis is depends on the circumstances. Under favorable circumstances, it can accomplish much that is social. But it will always require the multiplication of the social through the antithesis. The *antithesis* is social by aiming in response to these conditions at the creation – a "more complete" creation – of the social. These are the effects of private, societal forces, but especially of the state, its policy, and its law. The antithesis represents the ideas that the forces engaged in shaping and corrective intervention have about the social. For that reason, alone, it cannot be identified with "the social." What is more important, however, is that the antithesis crucially presupposes the thesis, and that it becomes effective only by combining with it. The thesis, too, must not be identified with the social. The *synthesis* is formed of the private, societal, and state conditions that arise from the interaction of thesis and antithesis. It is social in that the social potential of the thesis and the social effects of the antithesis coincide and interact in a positive sense. This is what is meant by the term "*mixed welfare production*" (Kaufmann 1997a, pp. 99–113), which has broken open the equating of governmental social policy and the social, and which has revealed that the social can be reasonably conceived only as the *total achievement of the society and the state* (Zapf 1981, pp. 379–400; Evers and Olk 1996; Kaufmann 1999, pp. 800–830).

The "theoretical" extreme that underlies the conventional equation of socio-political intervention and the social is the following: the synthesis is social because the antithesis transforms the asocial conditions of the thesis into the social conditions of the synthesis. However, empirically this is an underestimation of the thesis as well as an exaggeration of the antithesis. The *social* in the thesis is something that emerges, something that can be incipient in the structures of the thesis but is not being realized. The social is not *the* norm of the thesis, it is not its purpose as such. Still, the overall social activity cannot forego the potential of the thesis. How social the synthesis can be and in fact is, depends crucially on how social the thesis is. By contrast, the social *is the norm* of the antithesis – of course, in an incomplete, polemical, critical, correcting sense. Still, in this specific meaning, the social is the purpose of the antithesis. The *social of the synthesis* is two-sided: it is an "ought" in the direction of which the antithesis alters the conditions of the thesis; and it is a reality that qualifies as social through its always incomplete approximation to this norm.

The *social* is therefore *not an a priori, self-contained* phenomenon of consistently social conditions and of a reliably social development. Nor is the social the correspondence of reality to an ideal. Rather, the social is a process that takes place in targeted and untargeted activities, in congruencies and differences, in tensions and contradictions. This dialectic of the social implies the risk of incompleteness. This is the price for allowing the activities of the thesis to remain creative and productive, to resolve social problems also on their own, or to provide resources for the solution to social problems.

This dialectical model of the social *does not describe a temporal process*, such that the multiplicity of the also-but-not-only social happens first, the "social intervention" then corrects, and the social finally emerges as a tolerable reality. Rather, all phases are constantly interacting. Every correction alters what is. Likewise, the dialectical model of the social does not describe sharp substantive distinctions, such that one sphere comprises the existing conditions, another sphere is where social intervention takes place, while the third sphere is where the social can be perceived as a tolerable reality. Again, everything is interconnected and interacts.

2.1.2 The Dialectical Structure of the Social and the Relationship Between the State and Society – The Liberal Social State

While the issue is thus not one of mapping the roles of the state and of society onto the elements of the dialectic, it is clear that the social, as a total interaction of society and state, can be conceptualized only within the structure of the dialectic I have described. Wherever one starts from, the result is always the same. Whoever wants the side-by-side existence and interaction of society and state can only want the social by having it take place within the structure of that dialectic. Or to put it differently: whoever wants the social without eliminating the side-by-side existence and interaction of society and state will find himself directed to the structure of this dialectic. A society that is to be committed to an a priori, self-contained social would not be a free society. And as the great historical experiment of Socialism has shown, every concept of the social confronts the alternative of renouncing either a priori self-containment or the values and forces of a free society. The *dialectic of the social* is the *medium of a liberal social state*, of a *liberal welfare state*.

The first issue is the fundamental *relationship of tension between freedom and equality*. Even if the social does not mean equality pure and simple, it does negate certain economically conditioned or economically relevant inequalities. Every correction of inequalities uses up freedom. But it also expands freedom. The redistribution of income expands for everyone the freedoms whose use presupposes financial resources. The social guarantee of medical treatment expands – in a very complex way, to be sure – the freedoms whose use presupposes "more health" and "less illness." Support for education and training expands the freedom to enter into and complete a certain course of training. But it is quite obvious that all of this also takes away freedom: from those who generate the resources. They suffer a curtailment of the liberties whose use presupposes the availability of the resources taken from them. It should be noted, though, that the taking away or withholding of money still leaves room for a personal decision about priorities or posteriorities. The situation is different when the creation of equality takes place directly – that is, when the increase of liberty and the decrease of liberty are directly connected not only with respect to the subjects involved, but also with regard to factual situations. That is largely the case when solutions to social problems alter legal circumstances that also serve purposes other than the social goal – which are, for the most part, carried by and determined by purposes other than the social one. The classic example is labor law. The social intervention in working conditions increases the freedoms of employees and reduces the freedoms of employers. But it is not only the freedoms that accrue to the employee that are constrained by the a priori purposes of the work relationship. The freedoms that are taken from the employer, as well as the freedoms that remain, are limited by the factual and legal context. The final verdict, then, is this: social intervention creates freedom, and it uses up freedom. But one cannot simply add and subtract the freedoms gained and lost, for freedom itself is politically altered by this process. On the one side, freedom, as soon as it is accorded, is also a political and legal construct. On the other side, freedom is also politically and legally defined when it is reduced or constrained. The further the reach of these changes and the more deeply they penetrate into the circumstances of life, the more they alter the character of freedom – the more the state grows into the sphere of freedom, and the more freedom becomes a creature of the state. For the sake of freedom, the political and legal formulation of the social must therefore impose a certain asceticism upon itself. Society needs room to develop and unfold. This means: to unleash forces that might also stand opposed to and endanger the social – forces that work toward inequalities and bring uncertainty with them.

Space for society means space for "asocial" developments. Space for society also means space for the social itself. The basic social formula of work, income, the meeting of needs, and maintenance is by its nature entrusted primarily to private and societal realization. And even the warding off of the dangers that lurk in its realization, and the compensation of shortcomings that might arise from its realization, are primarily matters for those affected. If those involved did not to use their freedom out of a sense of responsibility toward themselves and their environment, if they did not counteract the threats themselves, if they did not avoid, endure, and remedy the shortcomings on their own, the state would soon be exhausted in its responsibility to ward off dangers and make up for shortcomings. The state can only intervene beyond a certain threshold of what is important and typical.

While the importance of the individual, the private, and the societal for the realization of the social is thus evident, one must not overlook *the tasks and responsibility of the state*. Only the state and society together can adequately bring about the social. But they are not equals in this complementary relationship. Rather, they are sequentially arranged: *the individual, private, and societal takes the lead. The societal realization of the social takes precedence*. While the realization of the social through the state is indispensable and no less crucial, it presupposes the societal realization of the social. It is only under this premise that a *liberal social state*, a *liberal welfare state,* is possible.[7]

2.1.3 The Alternative of Internalizing and Externalizing Intervention

However, the state in its responsibility and effectiveness is not limited to the realm of its institutions. The state has responsibilities and functions also and particularly toward social life. It has a regulatory responsibility. It must combine freedoms and responsibilities, make cooperation possible, and ensure the resolution of conflicts. In essence, we are talking about the responsibility of the state for private law. In the sense of this regulatory task, the state also bears responsibility for allowing the basic social formula to be realized: through work, income, the meeting of needs, and the community of maintenance. To that extent it also has a very general concern to control dangers that arise during the implementation of the basic formula and to compensate for shortcomings. The criminal assault on labor power or income, harm inflicted on the consumer in the wake of meeting basic needs, or the impairment of a community of maintenance by harming its breadwinner are examples for the state's responsibility to provide protection and orderliness. The warding off of dangers and compensation for harm suffered are not inherently social tasks. They are such tasks when threats and shortcomings have a specific connection with economically conditioned or economically relevant inequalities.

When this purpose of ameliorating or eliminating economically conditioned or economically relevant inequalities comes to the fore, we leave the realm of the thesis and enter the realm of the antithesis. That begins the process of social critique and social correction. For this, too, there are societal possibilities: societal structures and forces that counteract social threats and seek to more or less compensate for social deficits. Along the way, the transitions from the open normality of the thesis and the critical correction of the antithesis are difficult. Where to place "mere" altruism, by which one person helps another? Where to place the generosity of a landlord who does not raise his rent for social reasons? Where to place the advantages that the employer offers his employees? These questions need not be pursued any further here. There are, at any rate, societal activities and institutions whose purpose of a critical correction assigns them to the antithesis. Charitable associations and foundations are the central examples. Thus, no matter how many societal elements of the antithesis exist, it is clear that the state has a necessary and central role in the area of the antithesis. Its social intervention determines whether a social synthesis occurs. In the long run, society is not capable, on its own, of adequately effectuating the necessary measure of social correction "against itself."

[7] On the primacy of the private and societal realization of the social as one implication of the social state goal of the Basic Law see Zacher (1987a, pp. 1060–1082).

An important question that now arises is whether this intervention integrates the socially purposeful guidance or supplementation into the existing structure – that is, internalizes it – or whether it takes paths that lead out of the context of the prevailing structure – that is, externalizes problems and problem solutions (Zacher 1982, 1983, 1984c, pp. 11–72; Zacher and Kessler 1990; Fuchs 1992, esp. pp. 8–12, 81–83, 229–233). The following are examples of this alternative: if an employee's labor power is impaired by illness, this creates the problem that income is in danger of failing because work is not being performed. The internalized solution: the continued payment of wage or salary at the expense of the employer. The externalized solution: compensation of the discontinued wage or salary by way of sick pay at the expense of sickness insurance. Or: income and rents are not infrequently imbalanced – especially if we are talking about family housing. The internalized solution: rent control. The externalized solution: housing allowance. A final example is the compensation for harm suffered, which affects employers in cases of occupational accidents. The internalized solution: the employer's liability. The externalized solution: accident insurance. Internalized solutions have in their favor a closeness to the life situation they regulate. As a result, dangers, especially, can be warded off only through internalization (as is expressed for example in the employer's duty of care (Fürsorgepflicht)). Internalized solutions have against them that they can enter into a relationship of tension with the primary regulatory purpose of a legal relationship. For example, the basic constellation of the work relationship, the exchange of labor for remuneration, has over time become ever more intensively overlaid with the concern to protect and develop the equality, freedom, security, and participation of employees. However, the correspondence between a service and a return service cannot be abolished at will. An employer can be asked to continue paying a wage or salary in cases of illness for a limited period of time. Beyond that, it becomes a public function – securing the income of individuals who are unable to work because of illness – which cannot be imposed upon an employer without risks to the survival of the business and its ability to provide work. But the risk of an excessive burden can exist also on the side of the worker and employee. A work-based retirement that is paid from a company's profits – without externalized, insurance-like provisions of savings and set-asides – is worth as much as the company's earning power. If the company "dies" before the (former) employee does, the security is gone. Or to use another example: rental prices regulate supply and demand in the housing market. Rent control alienates prices from this function. The result is either a shortage of supply or the compensation of earnings shortfalls through subsidies. In the extreme case, administrative supply takes the place of market supply. Externalized solutions avoid these conflicts. They isolate and integrate the social purpose. Their problem lies in the fact that the circumstances of life are rendered "public": they become generalized, typified, and their financing becomes anonymous. Their particular character in terms of distribution psychology lies in the fact that the benefit is essentially seen as an advantage, while the burden of financing is not perceptible in the same way. This peculiarity of externalized systems is an essential reason why the social state is measured against the benefits and performance of externalized systems, as expressed, for example, in the social expenditure rate.

All told, the *alternative of internalizing and externalizing solutions* is thus a crucial building block of the social. *Internalization* means making societal conditions more social in themselves. But its forms of regulation thereby also end up in a relationship of tension with their primary purpose. In the extreme case, they are alienated from their primary meaning: just as, for example, price controls can suspend essential preconditions of exchange transactions – especially the motivation of supply and the capacity to cover the costs of the supply. To what extent internalization, by bringing to effect the social purpose of a legal condition in addition to its primary purpose, serves to integrate the essential nature of a regulatory type or leads to the disintegration of its essential nature, is an exceedingly difficult question. For the most part, there is only one concrete answer. By contrast, *externalizing solutions* differentiate between the original nature of societal legal and living conditions and their social supplementation. They dispense with the direct social change of the existing legal and living conditions, but in so doing they also avoid the conflicts that this entails. They multiply the number of regulatory arrangements for the same life condition. The end of a working relationship, for example, is not only a matter of labor law. It is potentially also a matter of unemployment insurance and work promotion, of pension insurance, accident insurance, and so on. Internalizing solutions create self-contained orientations of individual, private, and societal behavior (e.g. for the termination of employment contracts). Externalizing solutions create additional orientations of individual, private and societal behavior. Accordingly, internalizing solutions create a self-contained political issue (an assessment of whether the original purpose of the legal condition has been brought into an appropriate or inappropriate relationship to the social purpose). Externalizing solutions create a complicated political issue (the critique of the shape of the existing legal condition is joined by a debate over the distribution of advantages and disadvantages through externalization).

Internalization has its locus in the material structures and the legal conditions of the existing systems: in the work relationship and in labor law, in the relationship to the meeting of needs (e.g. rent) and in the relevant benefits law (private or administrative), in the community of maintenance and in family law – to name only the most important fields. *Externalizing solutions* take us out of these contexts. Where to? They can remain within the realm of *the societal* as well as in the realm of *private law*. In that sense, the thrust of externalization can be in the direction of cooperatives, unions, tariff organizations, private law foundation, insurance companies, welfare organizations, and charitable carriers. What these manifestations of the social share is the activation of relevant private and societal energies. They also have in common that – subject to special legal arrangements – they rely on the voluntary nature of initiative and participation. If those additional energies are lacking and voluntariness is not adequate, the state becomes necessary: at least to legitimize compulsion, and usually also to take responsibility for implementation. In the German tradition, therefore, externalization in the direction of the *state*, *of its regional administrative subdivisions* (communities, associations of communities) or of *specifically established institutions, especially communities of solidarity* (social insurance carriers, other public-law corporate bodies, institutions, and public foundations) has been particularly important. What argues in favor of externalization in the direction of the state and public law is the broad shaping power of the state legislator (including his sovereign authority to tax) and the state executive's power of self-assertion. However, this externalization is subject to the jurisdictional arrangements of the polity and the specific legal principles of public administration. Above all, it is subject to the general conditions under which the politics of the polity unfolds.

Externalization serves the *specific integration of the social purpose*. This essential nature of externalization sets it apart from the internalizing realization of the social purpose. The *difference* lies in the *regulatory context*: in its unity with the internalizing solution, in its separation with the externalizing solution. The *other criterion* that *constitutes the specific concept of the externalizing solution* is the *social purpose* itself. And therein lies the essential difference to a *phenomenon that is similar to the externalizing solution of social problems through the tendency toward "state takeover" and the absorption into public law*. I am referring to cases in which the *state* (understood in the broadest sense, including also the carriers integrated into and established by it) *assumes a task without the intention of thereby creating a specific social solution*. The *central field* of these phenomena is the *meeting of needs*. The recognition and exercise of state responsibility for the meeting of certain needs is generally referred to as *Daseinsvorsorge* (generally translated as 'services of the general interest'). If one wants to avoid the historical, multivalent meaning of this concept, it might be better to speak of a *civilizational responsibility* of the state. In many instances the proximity to a social purpose is not apparent: for example, in the public water supply, the sewage system, transportation systems, and so on. Other "state takeovers," however, are set within contexts that suggest the presumption of a social purpose. But even then the way in which the process works is different. The social problem as such is not solved. Rather, it is neutralized, it becomes irrelevant. The prime historical example is the development of the elementary school system in the nineteenth century. As long as elementary schools were voluntary and fee-based, social differences had a lasting impact on whether or not children attended school, and thus also on life opportunities connected with education. With the establishment of public schools across the land, with the introduction of obligatory school attendance and the abolition of school fees, elementary schools became manifestations of the nation's standard of civilization. Of course, the social differences of the families from which the children came remained relevant. But the decision of whether or not a child attended school was now in principle independent of the economic inequality of families.[8] In Germany, this method of neutralizing social problems – with a voluntariness of offerings, needless to say – has expanded beyond secondary schools to the universities.

[8] An analogous example, which has not been implemented in Germany, is the introduction of a national health service, like the one created by Great Britain after the Second World War, and by now established – for the most part in a more developed form – by a number of other countries.

A more complex example that included societal and state factors was the provision of goods in the war economy – a system for guiding the production and distribution of goods that was reflected above all in regulations governing economic activity and price controls. It guaranteed this universality in the distribution of goods, that is, *Daseinsvorsorge*. And it prevented prices from reflecting scarcity and thereby turning into a social problem. This technique of neutralizing social problems – whereby a public provision of goods prevents a particular good from becoming so scarce and expensive that only the rich have access to it – determines in general the *relationships of 'Daseinsvorsorge' to the social.*

2.1.4 In Particular: The Social Market Economy

All these phenomena are manifested once again in the organization of the economy. *The economy is the central medium of the social.* The economy is the broadest sphere in which inequalities among people become social aggravations: either because economic inequalities have inappropriate consequences within the economic realm itself, or because non-economic inequalities have inappropriate effects in the economic realm. That is why the organization of the economy assumes crucial importance for the realization of the social. And that is also why the temptation is so strong to guide the economy – as in Socialism – toward a politically defined social goal in a centralized, planned, self-contained process. The critical concern about Socialism has always been that this paralyzes the efficiency of the economic processes, and that it exaggerates the claim of politics to rule the lives of people. Experience has provided ample proof that this concern is well founded. At the same time, it remains true that the economy is the sphere in which the inequality among people is perceived more clearly than elsewhere.

But it remains equally true that the economy is an essential sphere for allowing people to experience and productively develop their diversity and freedom. This experience of freedom, diversity, and productivity in the economic realm has a name: prosperity. And inherent in the living conditions that are built up in this way by virtue of freedom and diversity is the longing for security: they are not to change for the worse. But the economy is not only the realm in which people develop themselves through their own economic activity. On the contrary: the economy is also the realm from which people derive the goods they need to develop beyond the economic sphere – goods, at least, that they need to live. For that reason, an expectation of equality is always directed at the economy as well – at least equality in the sense that every person finds a subsistence minimum. The economy is thus a realm in which values overlap, values that can be discerned from the concrete, historical perception of the social: subsistence minimum, security, and equality. At the same time, the economy is a sphere in which these values stand in complex competition to the freedom and diversity of human beings. In the process, the energies that the economy requires to achieve the goals of the subsistence minimum, security, and equality, arise fundamentally from the investment of freedom on the path to prosperity. Finally, it is also evident that the goals of prosperity and security, wherever they have been achieved, "abrogate" the goal of the subsistence minimum and relativize the goal of equality – at least for the individual person who may believe that he has assured prosperity and security for himself. But how can this take shape within the fabric of diverse institutions and processes that constitute the economy? This shaping, in particular, is the specific quality of the "*social market economy.*"

The *concept of the social market economy* (Müller-Armack 1956, pp. 390–392; Blum 1980, pp. 153–166; 1988; Rupp 1997, pp. 129–148) must be understood first of all as the concept of a *free market economy*. Such an economy rests on a series of freedoms and creates space for them: professional freedom, especially freedom of economic activity, freedom of contract, freedom of consumption, and free choice of a job. The decision about consumption, savings, and investment freely rendered by economic subjects presuppose private property and realize it – including private ownership of the means of production. The most important mechanism by which a free market economy operates are competition, the mediation of supply and demand via prices, the allocation of profit and the risk of loss. The system of the free market does not constitute or maintain itself. It requires care and attention from the polity and its regulatory policy: the creation of legal rules and institutions that impart to the free market the order appropriate to it, from the guarantee of the necessary freedoms to the law governing competition and the maintenance of appropriate structures of competition. The free market system is not a priori autonomous. It takes place within a world of given conditions: external trade, public order, infrastructure, the state's policy of revenue collection and spending. These conditions are partly responsible for the ability of the free market to operate and the way in which it does. Still, even if one posits an optimal regulatory policy, the free market does not achieve everything that the economy is intended to bring about for the state, society, and individuals. Certain economic tasks must or should be undertaken directly by the state and its sub-units, or at least maintained under its control. This is the administrative dimension that also exists and must exist within the free market: the production and distribution of goods that the free market does not accomplish, or does not do so reliably. The dimension of *Daseinsvorsorge* enters the picture once again. The final upshot is this: on its own, the free market economy does not adequately serve the goals of prosperity, freedom, security, equality, and the subsistence minimum. As a result, there is need for a multitude of interventions to guide and supplement free market processes.

The Free Market Economy

Crucial to the *free market character of the structure as a whole* are the *rules by which the functions in question interact* (Zacher 1981, pp. 715–761). The structure of the economy, the complementary economic actions by the state, all guidance and intervention must proceed from *the primacy of the free market* and from *the primacy of its competition-driven optimization*. That means the following:

1. The production and distribution of goods takes place as much as possible *through private economic subjects* whose relationship is one of *competition*. The crucial task of regulatory policy is to ensure competition and to prevent or control market-dominating positions.
2. The *production and distribution of goods by the state* – including its incorporated administrative units (local communities, community associations, social insurance carriers, public banks, etc.) – comes into play (a) for goods which the free market might be able to provide, but whose provision seems to require direct democratic legitimation and oversight, constitutional structures, and possibly also a priori equality (as in the educational system); (b) for goods which the free market would not provide as reliably and universally as the common weal requires (as in *Daseinsvorsorge*); and (c) for goods which the free market does not allocate to those who need them, or at least insufficiently, because they are unable to contribute an adequate amount of land, capital, or labor. This is the area of social services.
   A vague *principle of subsidiarity* exists to *demarcate the realm of the free market from the realm of administration*: this principle states that the state economy should not do what the private economy can accomplish. Where private economic interests are to be curtailed through strict legal restrictions, this principle of subsidiarity is realized through the requirement of occupational freedom that "objective restrictions on activity" must be justified by "outstandingly important common goods."
   But the administrative economy must also take care not to improperly constrain the free market economy with which it interacts (postulate of market compatibility).
3. Even where production and distribution are organized according to the *free market*, the state bears a multi-layered *responsibility to ensure the effective operation of the free market through interventions*, especially (a) in the direction of securing provision with basic goods, (b) in the direction of efficiency (the growth of the economy), foreign trade balance, and the general participation by those who can contribute labor (full employment), (c) to control harmful temporal instabilities (price stability, economic policy) and to moderate frictions that accompany structural changes (e.g. technological developments and international shifts), and (d) to control tensions in terms of geography (regional policy) and between individual spheres and groups (sectoral economic policy). Finally, (e) the free market requires correction and supplementation where neither its inherent functioning nor the policies indicated above generate an adequate measure of social protection, equality, and defense against hardship (social policy).

The *guidance and correction of the free market through interventions* is subject to the well-known and vague principle of *market compatibility* (*Marktkonformität*). It means that interventions should leave the price mechanism and competition untouched, and that beyond that, for example in decisions about investments, the decision that the individual economic subject considers the right one must not be replaced by one that a bureaucracy regards as economically correct. And where decisions by individual economic actors are to be changed, this is to be achieved through information, persuasion, and incentive, not through coercion. The principle of market compatibility thus leads to the primacy of *global guidance* over individual guidance.

The Social Market Economy

In what way is this free market economy social? It is so, first of all, through its productivity and its openness to freedom and diversity, and in the final analysis through its creation of prosperity. That is its crucial advantage – also with regard to the social. Still, this alone does not give rise to a socially optimal or even tolerable state of affairs. In the absence of any social correctives, the competitive economy would give free rein to many of the dangers that emerge during the realization of the basic formula of work, income, the meeting of needs, and maintenance, and many of the shortcomings it left in place would remain unaddressed. Or, to return to the institutional approach to the concrete historical perception of the social: there would be no general guarantee of the subsistence minimum; social protection through provision would be unattainable precisely to the socially weaker members, while social compensation is already a largely political problem for which the economy is not responsible; a sheer endless multitude of inequalities that call for "more equality." It is therefore not enough to enshrine what is historically perceived as the concrete responsibility of the state for the economy in the constitution of a free market system. There is need for additional social guidance and supplementation. But the techniques of guidance and supplementation are subject to the dual *primacy of (first) the free market and (second) the competition-driven inherent optimization of the free market economy.* It is this complementarity that characterizes the social market economy: the optimization of the economy *and* the social engagement of the state where the free market would not effect the social. Thus, through the overarching dialectic of thesis, antithesis, and synthesis, the *economy is placed in service to goals of aid against need, equality, security, freedom, and prosperity* – a multitude of goals that complement and contradict one another, and the pursuit of which makes possible and ensures a complex, open realization of the social.

2.1.5 Social Pluralism

The social that is inherent in the basic norm of "more equality" and can be concretely perceived historically thus proves to be essentially *pluralistic*.[9] That applies to individuals, their priorities, their guiding pictures of the social, but also their guiding pictures of privacy, society and community, the economy and

[9] Zapf (1981, pp. 379–400); Evers and Olk (1996); Kaufmann (1999, pp. 800–830).

non-economic self-realization, civilization and culture, being, and the meaning of life. Plurality applies to all the methods by which the social is produced: to the shaping of life and the self-responsibility of the individual, to the important role of the private community of maintenance, to all social services between people, to small groups, and also to societal organizations that are altruistic in nature, to non-profit organizations, and, finally, to the production of the social through free-market enterprises (from commercial nursing care to private insurance). Plurality applies also to the political, legal, and administrative intervention of the state, the multitude of its approaches and its institutions. Finally, plurality also dominates the reality that emerges from the efforts on behalf of the social, for what is socially achieved will always be different from what is socially intended.

This plurality has a very crucial temporal dimension. It is not static. Changes may occur faster in one area, slower in another. On the whole, however, this plurality always moves across time. This permanent process may go hand in hand with fears and anxieties. But this process is no less a potential of expectation – a potential for all individuals and for all the forces into which they aggregate themselves. It is a potential of their hope that the future might lead social reality closer to their needs and guiding images. This openness in time is of crucial importance to the experience of the social and for the way the social is dealt with.

2.2 On the Specific Openness of the Social

2.2.1 The Appearance of Normative Closedness – The Reality of Openness

The assumption that the basic social norm lays down a closed circle of interpretations and concrete expressions thus proves false, from two sides: from the normative starting point, because the issue is not "equality" but "more equality," that is, an open multitude of "equalities" in opposition to an open multitude of "inequalities;" and from the conditions of its realization, because every social conception and intent encounters ever-changing circumstances. This stands in fatal opposition to attempts at imparting fixed content to the social. Those attempts arise for two reasons: from the authority of the basic social norm, and from the existing phenomenon of their historical concretization.

In reality, social conditions are the stuff of endless inequalities, from which, in a process of intersubjective, collective, and eventually political (and for the most part also constitutional – legislative or judicial – process) of concentration, new better-worse or worse-better relationships are constantly highlighted. Social problems are defined and problem solutions found through a constant back-and-forth between the stuff of inequalities and the possibilities of preventing, eliminating, moderating, controlling, or compensating for them. The result is the contrast between the "solid land" of the better-worse relationships that are perceived societally, politically, or legally as the object of correction, and the "sea" of inequalities that are not perceived, or at least not from the perspective of correction. Of course, this picture is not entirely accurate, since the shape of the solid land changes. The better-worse relationships change their shape. New problems are continually drawn from the "sea" of inequalities and stabilized through solutions. And occasionally, worse-better relationships that were modulated long ago dissolve, and their inequalities return to the "sea." Still, the picture points to something essential: the historical problem definitions and solutions make the social visible, whereas it remains shapeless in the "sea" of inequalities. Moreover: the concrete historical problem solutions of "solid land" provide an orientation: they can be appropriated, expanded, and also defended. The "sea" of inequalities is devoid of orientation, and it escapes appropriation – except in the process of shape-giving agglomeration, in the process of "land reclamation." But wherever problems and solutions are "molded" and "land is won," the social seems to have become once again visible. The claim of the concretely existing stock of social problem definitions and solutions to be equated with the social finds an explanation in this picture, but so does the need to question that claim.

2.2.2 The Verticality of the Openness of the Social: Agglomeration "Below," Openness at the "Top"

At the same time, the basic norm of the social does allow for a delimitation: the *lower limit of the subsistence minimum.* Equality in the participation in the necessities of life escapes the relativity of equalities.

That does not mean, however, that the social has some kind of focal point at this limit. On the contrary: the *social is open toward the "top."* The equality-focused energy of worse-better relationships does not seem to depend on how close it gets to the lower limit of the subsistence minimum. It does not seem to wane in the same degree to which the worse-better relationships rise into the zones of prosperity. There are many reasons for this.

First: historical experience. The history of the social – the social movement, the welfare state, the social state – is a history of success. It is a history of success in the interpretation of the specifically social and its realization. And it is a history of success with respect to the civilizational environment (economy, infrastructure, etc.) of the social. The standards of civilization have risen. Like boats in a harbor in which the water is rising, the claims of the social have risen along with this environment. The social and political motor function of the social privileges the specific – individual as well as collective – advantage. The competition of social demands takes place much more amenably by way of the improvement of each demand, rather than by way of the worsening of the others.

Second: this uptrend of social demands continues in the *background of their justification.* New justifications for one's demands are more effective than the invalidation of old justifications for the vested rights of others. Even where, under the aspects of equality, a "worse off" can be seen by some as an approximation to equality just as a "better off" can be seen that way by others, a "better off" has a much easier time being "socially" evaluated and accepted than a "worse off." One important piece of evidence for this is monetary social benefits. They are an advantage that can be calculated and which everyone involved can imagine. Where the money comes from – that is to say, the fact that someone is being burdened, that prosperity is reduced somewhere else, freedom is reduced, and new inequalities are perhaps created – is of far less interest.

Third: the process of the recognition and assertion of social problems and solutions takes place in accordance with the *social and political power of the groups, strata, etc.* that are disadvantaged by the problems and favored by the solutions. That power comes from quantitative and qualitative components and from the possibilities of aggregation (especially the formation of coalitions to push through shared interests). The weight of these factors does not increase as one moves "down." On the contrary: it grows toward the "middle," and then at best wanes again closer to the "top."

Fourth, and foremost: the consensus that carries the basic norm of the social is subject to the *caveat of inequality*. The opportunity of advantages is not to be excluded: neither the meritocratic advantage by virtue of freedom, nor the socio-political advantage by virtue of the political power to assert oneself. And so the proviso of inequality became reconciled with the goal of "more equality" in such a way that the rise in society's prosperity and the broadening of participation in it became an essential element of the social. Slogans such as "Prosperity for all" and "More quality of life" are the pithy expression of this understanding of the social.

With all this, *economic growth* became a central medium for realizing the social. And concern about that growth became an essential element of the social responsibility of politics. Growth expanded the maneuvering room of freedom and the maneuvering room of a politics aimed at "more equality." Growth allowed for improvements without the need to make the burdens explicit. "Equality through growth" (Hirsch 1977, pp. 166–174; 1980) added a special effect to the social: inequalities disappear in the process of growth, in the course of which many will have tomorrow what is today still reserved for the few. But if growth fails to materialize, the social becomes socially and politically more strenuous: the "overtaking effect" from the increase in prosperity, which relativizes and defuses social problems in various ways, does not occur. The problems of securing one's livelihood emerge anew. Guaranteeing social protection through provision becomes more difficult. The demand for equality discovers new worse-better relationships. The responsibility of the state for the economy finds itself acutely challenged. The fairly frictionless co-existence of an increase in freedom and equality through growth is replaced by the opposition of freedom to distribution through intervention and coercion and by the dangers of new inequalities this entails. Political pacification through the ongoing allocation of shares of growth to ever changing groups (Zacher 1978, pp. 15–36) gives way to political unrest from the distribution of disadvantages. Because the absence of growth reactivates the most original and urgent social goal, the struggle against need, the political realization of the social does not get easier, but more difficult.

2.3 *The Basic Norm, the Concrete Historical Situation, the Dialectical Locus, and the Openness of the Social Relative to the Supply of Normative Principles*

There is an ongoing presumption that the uncertainty about the concrete meaning of the basic social norm can be moderated or even replaced by certainty by drawing on other principles to clarify the social. Human dignity, equality, justice, solidarity, participation and inclusion, security, subsidiarity, and, finally, *Daseinsvorsorge* are invoked to take the place of or supplement the concept of the social. In fact, with the help of these concepts, the value conceptions of the social become more clearly visible, especially in a more differentiated manner. However, they are not able to abolish what is specific, historically evolved, and politically topical in the consensus – so unambiguous in principle, so vague in substance – that stands behind the basic social norm. And these principles do not constrain the inner diversity of the social, but explain and clarify it.[10]

2.3.1 Human Dignity: The Deepest Bedrock of the Social

The social stands in service to *human dignity*.[11] "The dignity of man, no more of that, I pray you. Give him food to eat, a place to live; if you have covered his nakedness, dignity will follow by itself" (Schiller). But as obvious as this core of the social is, it leaves one helpless when it comes to the concrete manifestation of the social. To be sure, in the implementation of the basic social norm there are dangers and shortcomings whose perception is imperative for the sake of human dignity. But which particulars of labor law and the practice of collective bargaining, which protections in the case of illness, disability, old age, or death are called for by human dignity? What needs must be met for the sake of human dignity? On what conditions? What intervention in the community of maintenance is necessary on behalf of human dignity? And what interventions should be refrained from for the sake of human dignity? The most important thing that can be learned from human dignity aims at the multiplicity of meanings and the openness of the social: the tension between the certainty that the deepest bedrock of the social is the concern for human dignity, and the irrelevance of so many decisions – including fundamental ones – about the shape of the social in relation to this bedrock. Many details lack any connection at all. And at times the argument of human dignity, if it is used to justify social demands, becomes an annoyance.

---

[10] On the socio-political literature for what follows see Kaufmann (2013, German Social Policy, vol. 1), on the historical setting see Stolleis (2013, German Social Policy, vol. 2).

[11] Soziale Sicherung in der Bundesrepublik Deutschland (1966, p. 53). On human dignity as the end of the goal of the state see Zacher (1981, p. 679f., notes 4–6).

2.3.2 The Comprehensive Explanations of the Social

Equality

The pathos of the "equality of all who bear the human face" is probably the most potent motive of the social. As I have said before, it is the foundation of the *basic norm of the social.*

The *constitutional recognition of equality* (Art. 3, GG) seems to impart positive form and effect to this spirit of equality. But equality per se is not representable. Any such attempt is thwarted by the diversity of human beings, conditions, value conceptions, and freely chosen options. Even of one focuses on what is economically conditioned and economically relevant, there is an infinite number of comparabilities to define inequalities, to guide, circumscribe, and question the equalization. Thus, what the constitution prescribes as "equality" *becomes concretized as an arbitrary prohibition*, as a *relative yardstick for objective justice (Sachgerechtigkeit) and consistency.*[12] Only where *society and the communal policy negate very specific inequalities or demand very specific equalities* must this also have consequences in the field of social equality (Zacher 1987a, p. 1068). And this applies especially to the equality of men and women, or to the prohibitions against discrimination (of the disabled, by race, origin, etc.). In terms of constitutional law, "equality" thus locates itself in three different contexts: the general maxim of equality (Art. 3, Para. 1, GG) serves to obviate arbitrariness – also, but by no means only, in the area of the social; the special maxims of equality (see esp. Art. 3, Para. 2 and 3, GG) have equality before their eyes also substantively and therefore point increasingly in the direction of the basic social norm of "more equality;" the principle of the social state – and the social constitutional program that embodies the social goal of the state – broadly incorporates the basic norm of "more equality."

One central formula for concretizing social equality in the sense of the basic social norm concerns the *protection of the weaker* (Hippel 1982) – the negation of the inequality between the socially stronger and the socially weaker. Perhaps it extends already to the protection of the socially weaker against the socially "normal." This approach invokes a better-worse relationship, but its locus is not fixed. The formula would be clearer if it spoke about the *socially weak.* That could keep the social stuck to what is socially "at the bottom." But that is not the generally intended meaning. Instead, what is meant is the openness that is so clearly expressed in what is concretely, historically manifest – also as "openness" toward "the top." Thus, one can speak only of the "socially weaker," even if the normality to which this "weaker than" refers is located in the realm of prosperity.

[12] "Der Gleichheitssatz," VVDStRL 47 (Berlin, 1988). On the specifically social see Zacher (1968a, pp. 341–383; 1990, pp. 67–90).

Freedom

Freedom takes its place alongside equality as the elementary explanation of the social (Lampert 1992, pp. 19–48). In the same way that human dignity demands the acknowledgement and realization of equality, it demands the recognition of individuality and of the individual person's status as a subject, and their development through freedom. The social has the meaning of expanding freedom – of allowing the freedom of the greatest number of people to become reality. That is why the social must, where necessary and possible, translate the status of formal freedom into a status of material freedom: through the allocation of real individual factors of freedom, and through restrictions on the freedom of others who are excessively powerful. To put it in constitutional terms: the principle of the social state articulates the responsibility for the reality of the rights of freedom. This is a difficult, risky mandate, since "created" freedom is not the same as "natural" freedom. And the allocation and denial of real factors of freedom can constrain the leeway of freedom in the same way as the interventionist limitation of freedom – only in a less palpable form, paralyzing instead of challenging the "immune responses" of freedom. Once again, our thinking encounters the very boundary that marks the transition from a liberal social state to a socialist state. The liberal social state must maintain the balance between "*more equality*" and "*more freedom.*" And the *proviso of inequality* finds its most important justification – in addition to the respect for the individuality of people, which is expressed also in fate, in good fortune and misfortune – in freedom. Freedom is also freedom for inequality – toward "the top" and toward "the bottom."

Freedom is not only the freedom of the person whose social state of being is the immediate concern. It is also the freedom of others: the freedom of those who create the conditions in which that person lives; the freedom of those who help, who can open up opportunities, who can allocate goods; and the freedom of those who can anticipate opportunities because they compete.

Justice

"Social justice" is among the most frequent and most important labels given to the social (Zacher 1981, p. 678f., note 3). Justice has many faces, however (Höffe et al. 1986), and that is true also of social justice. *Social justice* exists always in the diversity of *justice of needs, justice of effort,* and *justice of property ownership* – as well as justice of opportunity, whether one sees it as an extension of the justice of needs and justice of effort or as something separate (Kerber, Westermann and Spörlein 1981, pp. 5–75). These "justices" – each in itself fundamental and thus open and sufficiently vague – must be constantly weighed against one another if on the whole a socially just state is to be attained. Especially what can be historically and concretely perceived of the social consists of the implementation of the justice of needs, the justice of effort, and the justice of property ownership (Zacher 1988, pp. 669–691). And nothing would indicate that the consensus underlying the basic social norm would ever dispense with having *all* of these "justices" brought to bear at all times. As a result, the possible meaning of "social justice" remains all the more uncertain. Still, this is precisely the social mandate: to find the proper relationship between the justice of needs, the justice of effort, and the justice of property ownership.

Solidarity

Yet another example for the value backdrop but also for the openness of the social is the principle of *solidarity*.[13] Solidarity demands a polity and a society that seek a balance between the individual and the common and implements it. Solidarity negates both individualism and collectivism. And solidarity affirms the complementarity of individuals and their communities with the state and all the intermediary structures in which these two poles of solidarity encounter each other – whether within the framework of society, the framework of the state, or in the area of mutual interpenetration. Much like the principle of justice, the principle of solidarity circumscribes above all one task. The specific quality of that task lies in the relationship between the individual and the polity. The individual and the polity are recognized as autonomous and of their "own right," but they are simultaneously dependent on each other. The individual needs the community for his self-realization, and the polity can only do justice to itself if it acknowledges and respects the status of the individual as a subject. The individual must integrate himself into the community and contribute to the development of its nature; the community must guarantee and promote the life opportunities of the individual. To that end, the state's mandate of regulation and protection plays a central role. However, the relationship between the individual and society cannot be reduced to the polarity between state and society. Rather, the individual depends on the ability to self-realize himself within communities and societal structures; the state, meanwhile, depends on standing face to face not only with the individual person, but with the diversity of communal and societal entities. On the flipside, the state will be unable to fulfill its mandate of solidarity if it seeks to realize it through monopolizing exclusivity. The state must become differentiated – divide and subdivide itself – in order to do justice to the diversity of conditions and tasks.

This complex mandate of solidarity is comprehensive also in concrete terms. It concerns everything wherein individuals and communities develop themselves: the environment and the economy, civilization and culture, internal and external security, and so on. Solidarity is not a specifically "social" principle. At the same time, solidarity takes on special importance and special content in combination with the social. The central challenge of the social, the nuisance of economically conditioned and economically relevant inequalities, begins with the autonomy and the rights of the individual, with his freedom and responsibility, continues with the everyday life of private and societal entities, and can receive a satisfactory

[13] Grimm (1987, pp. 3144–3147); Rauscher (1988, pp. 1191–1194); Hondrich and Koch-Arzberger (1992); Gabriel, Herlth and Strohmeier (1997, pp. 13–27); Volkmann (1998); Isensee (1998).

answer only from the state, its differentiations, from societal affiliations and communities, and coexistence in private life. Thus, if solidarity cannot be reduced to the denominator of the social, the social *can* be reduced to the denominator of solidarity.

But this exemplifies once again the diversity of the social.[14] Solidarity realizes itself not only in the diversity of communities, of societal entities, the differentiation of the state, and the state itself. Moreover, solidarity realizes itself not only nationally, but also transnationally, supranationally, and internationally. Solidarity is also realized by virtue of very different principles: in *general entities* like the family and the state, and in *specific purpose entities* like a club or an insurance; as *vertical solidarity* between the "stronger" and the "weaker," of which families and the state are the most important examples, and as *horizontal solidarity* between those who share a common interest or a common fate, as is typical of the great mass of all purpose-driven organizations (clubs, societies, insurances). The social has articulated the "*small solidarity*" of the essentially equal with the essentially equal no less than the "*great solidarity*" also among the essentially unequal systems such as welfare/ social assistance, compensation for victims of the war and its aftereffects, and so on, represent the "great solidarity" – for the most part a "national" one. Systems like social insurance represent in principle the "small solidarity": the solidarity that is restricted to a particular community of solidarity, the solidarity of a select group of individuals who are in need of provision in the same way and capable of providing that provision. And in all too many aspects it remains unclear what exactly is meant. Finally, it has always been imperative to understand solidarity also in a *temporal dimension*. Those who need help *now* are not necessarily those who have *always* needed help. And they will not necessarily always remain those who need help. Conversely, those who can offer help *now* are not necessarily those who can *always* provide help. The opposite is much more likely. In the comprehensive structures of "great" vertical solidarity, these scenarios are usually intermixed in an irregular fashion. But the more specific solidarity is expressed, the more clearly the *diachronous* dimension of solidarity can be distinguished from the *synchronous* dimension. Social insurance offers examples of this: the short- or medium-term solidarity of the healthy with the sick in sickness insurance, or that of the "job holders" with the unemployed in unemployment insurance, or the long-term solidarity of the "active" with the elderly, disabled, and surviving family members in pension insurance. The picture of the "generational contract" shows the kind of difficult terrain into which this diachronous solidarity can take us.

Inclusion and Participation

The person who has access to the community of solidarity experiences this as participation – or more strongly: as inclusion (Luhmann 1981, pp. 25–32). The person

[14] Some aspects of the internal differentiation of solidarity in Schulin (1988, pp. 85–93).

who does not have this access experiences it as non-participation – or more strongly: as exclusion.[15] Participation and inclusion are therefore understood as important formulas for describing the social. Exclusion appears as one name for the unsocial as such. That perception is untenable. Every community, every societal structure, every state polity possesses its own boundary. The criterion of inclusion is therefore first a question, and only then an answer. And the critique of exclusion depends on this answer.

In the broadest sense, "inclusion" appears as a state-focused status that manifests itself in rights to social inclusion – more generally: in the consequence of social participation. Traditionally, this status is situated in citizenship and/or residency in the country, together with the right to that residency. But the social consequences unfold on very different levels. There is the *elementary inclusion* into the *national community of solidarity*, as is currently expressed in the guarantee of the subsistence minimum through social assistance. There is the *inclusion into the working world and the economy*, reflected by the basic social formula. The "state goal of full employment" develops that inclusion, which finds its most common expression in work and income, social protection of those who work, their social safety, but also in their participation in the workplace, as entrepreneurs, and in social policy. This, then, is *inclusion in a societal normality*, which is manifested above all in those social benefits which – like the child allowance, housing allowance, and so on – aim at a "more equal" participation in the prosperity.

But then there is also *private and societal inclusion*, as realized above all through the family. The state has a responsibility of imparting to this inclusion the appropriate regulatory structure and to compensate for shortcomings – for example, through the law of aid to children and youths, through the homestead law, and so on. If the familial inclusion of a child is endangered, the relevant authorities and courts must intervene in a supportive manner – and it is the state's responsibility to make the relevant normative and institutional provisions for doing so. If a child (to stay with the example) loses its familial inclusion, a surrogate must be created by activating the extended family, arranging an adoption, locating a foster family, placing the child in a home, or the like. Here, too, it is the state's duty, ahead of individual cases, to make adequate normative and institutional provisions. Beyond this fundamental familial inclusion of children, the state no doubt does not have the same duty to step in with respect to private inclusion. However, the openness of private and societal conditions to inclusion – and the corresponding negation of exclusions (including, for example, the legal regulation of conditions for admission and exclusion procedures in private organizations, unions, and so on) – is one of

[15] Luhmann (1995, pp. 237–264); Leisering (2004). "Exclusion" is a central term of the international, European, and foreign discussion. See, for example, Gaudier (1993); Rodgers, Gore and Figuerido (1995). On Europe see Social Exclusion Indicators (1995).

the responsibilities of the state. On the whole, we are dealing with phenomena of inclusion that are not consistently social in nature, but which can and do have a multitude of social meanings.

Participation – especially the alternative of inclusion and exclusion, which seems so simple when one talks about it – shares the *diversity of the social*: as inclusion by virtue of membership in a nation, participation in the working world and the economy, a share of the normality of prosperity, and as the opening up and guarantee of private and societal inclusion. The various dimensions of inclusion are the *legacy of diverse historical layers* of the social. *Elementary inclusion* in the sense of a participation in the subsistence minimum is an expression of the oldest layer: the solution to the poverty question. Inclusion originally concerned the local community and was tied to stringent preconditions of civic rights. Over decades, this participation expanded more and more into a national inclusion – a process that culminated for the time being in the Reich Law on Relief Residency (*Unterstützungswohnsitz*) of 1871. Soon after, *inclusion mediated by working life* achieved a decisive breakthrough in the form of labor protection legislation and social insurance. The fact of engaging in work in the country – and thus neither mere citizenship nor mere residency – became the decisive criterion of participation. The *inclusion in the participation in the normality of living conditions* mediated by social services is a later addition. That inclusion became a meaningful reality only in the Federal Republic of Germany. Once again, residency in the country took on crucial importance for one dimension of social participation, supplemented or replaced only secondarily by the criterion of citizenship. The situation is very different with the historical evolution of *private and societal inclusion*. It is the oldest manifestation of inclusion. The Middle Ages and the Early Modern Period are dominated by the principle of inclusion into concrete entities: the family, the house, the farm, the princely court, the monastery, a military unit, and so on. Whoever was not included in one of them was essentially excluded. Ecclesiastical institutions and secular foundations provided help that moderated this stark scenario. Still, entities of particular inclusion increasingly lost the strength to "incorporate" the growing and structurally changing population. The consequence of this increasingly intolerable shortcoming was the emergence of the "modern" system of poor relief. In the nineteenth century, then, the conditions of societal-private inclusion underwent a new development. The feudal structures increasingly dissolved, bourgeois society arose and determined the rules of private and societal inclusion. And the industrial proletariat embarked – slowly – on the path to becoming the working class, and thus assuming its place in an expanded, differentiated mosaic of civil society. In this phase, the order of societal-private inclusion was focused on the classic functions of private law. But it happened time and again that the state and social forces – above all the welfare organizations – took on additional functions. By far the most important example is the emergence of the institutions of youth welfare, and its development down to the present-day child and youth services.

The *importance of the national point of reference* as the base line of inclusion has undergone various changes over time.[16] The beginnings of the social state in poor law were marked by the communal form of citizenship, civil right the so-called *Heimatrecht* [local citizenship]. The oldest phenomenon of a relativization is social insurance. Its invention was a crucial, exceedingly significant step in the expansion of inclusion by virtue of participation in the working world. Social insurance meant disconnecting the guarantee of income from the direct connection with the work performed, and to ensure the coverage of certain needs (medical care in case of sickness or accident, rehabilitation to remedy the consequences of an accident) independent of the funds presently available. But access to this kind of provision came with the capacity to make provision, which was manifested in the wage or salary. Now that the support systems of welfare had been joined by the provisioning system of social insurance, the place of the criterion of membership in a state or communal polity had been taken by the personal-functional criterion of participation in the working world. Categories like state or communal territory or state or communal citizenship were pushed to the margin. The important thing was that a history of provision existed between the insured person and an insurance carrier. But this did not render the national boundaries of inclusion meaningless. Whether a German history of gainful employment and provision can develop depends fundamentally on the right to be in the country. Germans have the right to be in the country (Art. 11 GG) and the freedom to freely choose their vocation and job there (Art. 12 GG). For all others, the right of residency becomes the key to social participation.

The paths on which the national framework of inclusion was relativized have *multiplied* considerably over the course of time. It was increasingly in line with the guiding images of a modern society to dissolve the union of citizenship and residency as a premise for national inclusion: on the one hand, to grant citizens social inclusion also when they resided abroad, and on the other hand, to open up social inclusion without the prerequisite of citizenship to those living in the country. Many reasons were behind this trend: the distortions in the relationship between residency and citizenship that arose from processes of forcible removal, expulsion, and flight in connection with the war and the totalitarian political systems during the Second World War and after; the increase in migratory movements in the wake of economic, civilizational, and political developments; but also the need to integrate state-transcending regions as political, cultural, and social communities. The Europe of the Council of Europe proved a basic model for this kind of thinking. But the wider the doors of access opened up, the greater the need became to differentiate the consequence of participation: in social assistance between Germans and foreigners, even if they are legal residents; to control the access of foreigners to participation in the world of work (work permit), even if they are legal residents; to withhold benefits of participation in prosperity (especially child allowance) from foreigners, even if they are legal residents, and so on. The international opening up

[16] See below Chaps. 10 and 11; and Bundesministerium für Arbeit und Soziales and Bundesarchiv (2001b–2008a), Geschichte der Sozialpolitik in Deutschland, vols. 2–7, Chap. 3, no. 16.

of inclusion and exclusion developed in the direction of a new level through the development of the *supranational European Community.*

Finally, we must take a look at the *global reach and relativization of the mechanism of inclusion and exclusion,* which lies in the fact that the nations of this world – through common institutions, common policies, and merely by the sum of their actions – regard themselves as obligated to cooperate and join together for the welfare of all inhabitants of this planet. It is quite evident that this development does not leave the diversity of what inclusion and exclusion mean unaffected.

2.3.3 Structural Principles of the Social

While human dignity is the final bedrock of the social and gives rise to the basic norm of equality, and while justice, solidarity, and participation make visible specific dimensions of the social, other principles of the social also carry a significant, if narrower, meaning: these are the principles of security and subsidiarity.

Security

Security is a basic value in the history of states: time and again, external security, internal security, and legal security have been the – honest or mendacious – justifications of state power (Isensee 1983; Robbers 1987). It was only during the last two centuries – implicitly in the nineteenth century, explicitly in the twentieth – that a new dimension of security was added, that of *social security* (Weisser 1956, pp. 396–412; Kaufmann 1973; von Hippel 1979; Kaufmann and Külp 1988). It has grown out of the basic formula of work, income, the meeting of needs, and maintenance. It went hand in hand with the challenge that the expectations of employment, income, the meeting of needs, and the capacity for maintenance were in danger of being disappointed in many different ways. From the beginning of the nineteenth century, *civil service law* gradually created a model that ameliorated – if not eliminated – these dangers (Ruland 1983, pp. 73–104). As a result, they became all the more obvious for workers and employees in the private sector. After a variety of approaches, social insurance confronted this problem (Tennstedt 1976, pp. 385–492; Peters 1978; Zöllner 1981, pp. 45–180). With it there arose, different from the provision for civil servants, a concept of securing living conditions against the "vicissitudes of life" that was capable of being generalized. Over time, *this concept loosened the connection to its roots in insurance* (Köhler and Zacher 1983). In this process, international developments coincided with national ones (Schmid 1981). The international trends had two central causes: first, the acceptance of the social insurance model was running increasingly into limitations in the period between the two world wars. The US Social Security Act of 1935 overcame these limitations verbally by replacing social insurance with "social security;" second, the social insurance model focused on workers and employees, who were regarded as particularly in need of protection when the model was "invented." By contrast, the understanding had spread that the state bore a more general responsibility: for all gainfully employed citizens, for example, or for the entire population as such. The latter was especially true in countries in which the principle of a general, basic inclusion, which characterized the German provision system, had not yet been effectively instituted. At any rate, the predominant relationship between income, contribution, and benefits was supplemented – if not displaced – by greater consideration of more general aspects (more general contribution and benefit rates) and by drawing on more general sources (tax financing). "Social security" in this sense did not have to mean that the state-regulated system established the most precise possible ratio between income subject to contributions and income replacement benefits. It could also be that "social security" was aimed at providing a participation in prosperity that was appropriate according to general principles (demogrants) – whereby in the various sectors of gainful employment, at least additional guarantees in the sense of an approximation to an income relationship were established.[17]

In the *Federal Republic of Germany*, the names and guiding models were mixed together. The term "*soziale Sicherheit*" (social security) entered only gradually into German usage. In substance, the traditional concept of *social insurance* maintained itself. It was and remained the core also of "social security." However, gradually a more differentiated and more expansive vision of "social security" evolved: security not only against the "vicissitudes of life," against harm in public responsibility, but also (as in the case of child allowance or housing allowance) against life circumstances that could lead to disadvantages vis-à-vis the general standard of prosperity. Finally, public assistance was also understood as an element of "social security:" the basic inclusion. In the German understanding, "social security" is thus an *intrinsically diverse system*, an ensemble of institutions. A clear definition of this ensemble has not been able to assert itself.

Before all else, though, *security* is *a material concept*. It refers to freedom from threat and the guarantee of protection against potential dangers. More precisely: security negates negative changes, disadvantageous developments, and the uncontrollable negative flow of events over time. A peculiar orientation arises in the process: the dominance of the individual, indeed, of the biographical. Negative changes that affect society as a whole or essential areas – sectors, regions, and so on – are not amenable to institutional coping in the same way as individual changes are – for example, through unemployment, illness, old age, and so on. The latter are repeated in an endless succession of cases and can therefore be typecast and standardized. By contrast, general changes, like those of economic conditions, tend toward a certain uniqueness. Avoiding them may be formulated as a task of politics. However, whether that task is possible or impossible, a success or a failure, there is no sanction. And the reactions to a negative development are fundamentally entrusted to the realm of politics. By contrast, the consequences from changes in individual life circumstances can be regulated in principle legally, and with a high degree of effectiveness. This creates a certain pull: the intertemporal security of individual life conditions is equated "pars pro toto" with "social security."

[17] On the comparative typology see Zacher (1991a, esp., pp. 73–84).

As much as social security manifests itself in externalizing social benefits systems, security is by no means a concept *only* of these systems. *Security* as protection against disadvantageous changes is a *general principle* that holds not only for the field of *externalizing solutions*. It applies equally to *internalizing solutions*. The civil service law has already been mentioned. Security is likewise a value that has increasingly determined and pervaded also labor law. It is a field of abundant examples not only with its protection against dismissal, but with all the protections with which it opposes disadvantageous changes in working conditions. Tenant protection, too, is a legal good that is indebted to security.

In spite of this comprehensive and multifarious meaning, *security is only one aspect of the social*. Security stands in a *relationship of tension to equality* – much like legal security has always been in a relationship of tension with material justice. To be sure, social security serves to balance out the differences in the threats to which people are exposed, and differences in the ability to protect oneself against disadvantageous changes. In that sense, security and equality point in the same direction. But security also protects inequality. Security protects the better life conditions from adjusting downward to the lower life conditions of others. Social security is as much an expression of "more equality" as an expression of the caveat of inequality.

Subsidiarity

Subsidiarity (Herzog 1987, pp. 3563–3571; Rauscher and Hollerbach 1989, pp. 386–390) is the central formative principle of the liberal social state. Subsidiarity guarantees that the social happens: either on the level of primary responsibility *or* on the level of a "higher," "more comprehensive" secondary responsibility. Subsidiarity activates a multitude of possible forces. Subsidiarity creates room for autonomy and allows the entire system in which the social takes place to breathe. But subsidiarity is much more a principle of interpretation – the interplay of all the liberties, autonomies, or special jurisdictions with all the responsibilities of "higher," "more comprehensive," or "more powerful" carriers – than a norm that would indicate operationally what needs to be done, and who can regulate what. Subsidiarity is much more a result than a system.

Subsidiarity presupposes that an overall, overarching task is distributed onto a *multitude of carriers* that complement each other, and which contribute their part to the accomplishment of the overall task. At times this principle of subsidiarity seems to allow itself to be expressed in simple pictures. They all amount to the formula that the larger unit should not do what the smaller unit is able to. This formula seems useful when we are in fact dealing with obvious relations between larger and smaller units, as is the case especially in the relationship between the federal government and the *Länder*, or the state and local communities. And it still seems useful when the state confronts specific carriers with defined tasks (e.g. social insurance carriers). But in the latter case it already becomes evident that the formula creates difficulties. While the relationship of state/local community can itself be reduced to the formula bigger/smaller in the same way the relationship of state/social insurance carriers can, that is not true for social insurance carriers and communities amongst themselves. The dilemma becomes more pronounced still if, for example (as in the controversy over how to implement the social welfare and youth welfare laws), churches and charitable organizations claim that in relationship to the communities and the districts (*Landkreise*) and unincorporated (*kreisfreie*) cities, they are the "smaller entities."

As it is, subsidiarity is *not limited to the relationship between organizations*. Subsidiarity must also refer *to the relationship of the private to the public*: the relationship of individuals, families, and private groups to societal and state carriers. And subsidiarity must also mean the *relationship of society and state*: not only the relationship of the carriers of specific social tasks (such as businesses or associations) vis-à-vis the state, but also the *relationship of social activity to the state* (Isensee 1968; Rupp 1987, pp. 1219–1212). This subsidiarity of the state to society revolves around the overall system of subjects and effects that can be understood as constituting society. We are talking about "civil society" as such. Subsidiarity must respect and activate its powers. But at the same time, subsidiarity must also describe the task of the state. The *concept of subsidiarity must be understood from the perspective of the total complexity of a solidarity that is realized through individuals, communities, social entities, and the state and its substructures*.

All in all, *solidarity and subsidiarity* are mutually complementary and permeating principles of a liberal system (Engelhardt 1981, pp. 55–80; Brück 1984, pp. 197–200). In the process, the principle of solidarity expresses a positive and comprehensive concept: the reciprocal allocation of the common and general and the particular and individual; the essentialness each of the whole and the parts, but also the same essentialness of the orientation of the whole to the parts and of the parts to the whole. By contrast, subsidiarity accentuates a specific aspect: the differentiation of the tasks and subjects and that of the allocation of tasks to the subjects. This example, too, shows that the concepts that are used to label and describe the social are open-ended. Contrary to a widely held belief that the social can be precisely defined through alternative or supplementary concepts, and thereby circumscribed but also rendered more capable of being implemented, we see time and again that all concepts that truly do justice to the social also reveal once more the diversity and openness of the mandate of the social.

2.3.4 The Alternative Concept of *Daseinsvorsorge*

The term *Daseinsvorsorge* is also used repeatedly to describe the social (e.g. Stern 1984, p. 897f.). And it does in fact touch on the social.[18] The area of encounter is to be found in the basic formula: the satisfying of needs. The *social* is concerned about

[18] Rüfner (1988, pp. 1037–1085) distinguishes between "*Daseinsvorsorge* in the narrower sense" (the provisions and services of the public sector) and "*Daseinsvorsorge* in the wider sense" which includes social benefits.

the individual capacity to satisfy needs, principally through income earned by work. As a result, it is primarily interested in income. But an income may not be adequate to satisfy all appropriate needs. The social must therefore make provisions for bridging the distance between the individual capacity to satisfy needs and the costs of doing so. The basic types of provision are interventions in the process of distribution (e.g. price maintenance and control), or redistributive social benefits that supplement income accordingly (e.g. housing allowance, subsidy for educational expenses). Intervention in the mechanism of distribution might impair the quantity and quality of the supply. The redistributive intervention takes a different stance toward the problem: if the goods for satisfying needs are in short supply, their price rises, and that widens the gap between the individual capacity to satisfy needs and the cost of doing so. Social provisions must adjust to this fact. The *approach of Daseinsvorsorge* is very different (Zacher 1981, pp. 37–40; Zacher 1987a, p. 1082f.). Here the concern is that the goods necessary to meet needs are available in sufficient quantity and at the requisite quality, depending on their importance. The costs of this availability can be defrayed from general financial revenues. But they can also be payable as prices – as real, free-market prices or as administrative fees – by those who demand the goods. In the process, it is necessary to take into account the universal interest in the ability to satisfy basic needs.

The approach of the social is this: satisfying needs must not be unreasonably impeded by economic inequalities. The approach of *Daseinsvorsorge* is this: the universality of the provision with goods must be guaranteed. In their realization, the two approaches largely overlap. As a result, *Daseinsvorsorge* can be extraordinarily important for the reality of the social. However, in terms of their intentional direction, the social and *Daseinsvorsorge* are at odds.

2.3.5 The Integration of the Society Constituted in the State – The Goals of the Defense Against Hardship, of Equality, Security, Freedom, and Prosperity

Finally, the social is rightly credited with playing a crucial role in integrating and binding together the society that has constituted itself in Germany (Kaufmann 1997b, pp. 5–19). This becomes clear not least when a policy that does not advance the standards of social protection and social benefits, or even takes them back, is accused of causing the disintegration, fragmentation, subversion, and dissolution of society. In actuality, the social is not the only action of the community that creates meaning, cohesion, and identity. The guarantee of freedom already on this side of the social, internal security, law and public order, infrastructure and communication, culture and education, the protection of the environment, as well as participation in the European and international community of nations are among the most important achievements of the polity. Still, the social is one of the central dimensions of meaning and operation of this polity.

The social state accomplishes this achievement of integration only by showing itself as diverse and open. The normative foundation of the social and its mode of operation share this quality – and must share it. The basic norm of the social is borne by the general consensus only in its internal diversity and openness. And thus the social can bring about the unity of society only by doing justice to this diversity and openness. All concrete historical experience with the politics of the social, as well as all normative approaches to the meaning of the social, can be understood only in the sense that this society pursues *this kind of wide-ranging set of goals as the defense against hardship, equality, security, freedom, and prosperity*. This is what the basic norm means by "more quality," by the concentration on guaranteeing the subsistence minimum, by the caveat of inequality.

But the social consensus does not mean by this selectivity or arbitrariness. It means the *totality of this set of goals*. Each of these goals is an element of the social only in connection with all other basic values. A social policy that integrates society must therefore orient itself not only toward all of these goals individually. It must also *realize the inner connection between these goals*. Shortcomings in the integrative effect become visible not only when there are imbalances between these goals, or if individual goals are neglected outright, but also and already when the inner connection between the goals is lost: when it is no longer obvious that the defense against hardship and prosperity are mutually connected; when it is no longer obvious that freedom presupposes equality and requires the complement of equality, but that equality no less requires freedom and individualization through freedom; when it is no longer obvious that security cannot be an absolute vis-à-vis the other goals, but must complement them all.

3 The Institutional Shaping of the "Social"

3.1 The Primary (Historical) and the Secondary (Constitutional) Shaping

3.1.1 The Historical Shaping of the Social

From the outset of the period under discussion here, the social was characterized by a high degree of historical self-evidence. Anyone who had to deal with the social knew of essential examples in which the social manifested itself or was supposed to. Though a general *idea* of the social was for the most part vague, controversial, and unconscious, and though there was little consensus about a substantive *definition*, it was *obvious what it expressed itself in*. Even before principles such as the defense against adversity or the guarantee of the subsistence minimum were articulated and accepted, it was clear that public assistance existed. Even before German linguistic usage was familiar with "social protection" or "social security" as mere conceptual imports, social insurance existed. Long before anyone spoke of the social compensation law, there was public provision for victims of the war. Long before anyone raised the question of how much equality made sense socially, there was "more equality" through labor law, tenant protection law, leaseholder protection law, and so on. And well before the fog lifted from the future of an economic policy that was still entirely captive to the demands of *Daseinsvorsorge*, it was generally held that the economic sector would always give rise to and exacerbate inequalities if the state did not look after the economy. All social policy that happened after the collapse of the German Reich was grounded in history. The conceptual world of the social was rife with images. Those images had a long history behind them, in which a good deal of what they reflected achieved the claim of being a social necessity. It was a long history of controversies as well as serious conflicts. But it was also a long history of these ideas being put to the test and spreading (Frerich and Frey 1993, vol. 1; Stolleis 2013, German Social Policy, vol. 2). Above all, the thinking after 1945 picked up this thread, and all those who wanted something different and new also had to come to terms with this legacy. History had laid out the path that was taken after 1945. Everything that happened could be measured by this path: as a continuation or a departure. As a result, all of the ways in which the openness of the social was dealt with would present themselves as variation, development, new orientation.

The diversity and breadth of the idea of the social thus corresponds to the path dependency of the social in concrete terms. The path that is taken in the process is institutional in nature, not normative or principled.[19] Normatively the social always remains vague – it is always more of a challenge than an answer. By contrast, what exists institutionally provides the templates that are used to contemplate the answers. This approach has proved to be quite potent. It dominates the concretization of the social. All principled, normative contents of the social are arguments. Their selection, constellation, force, and direction in which they point always depend on the circumstances: from the objective circumstances – the occasions out of which they are articulated, and the purposes for which they are articulated; from the subjective circumstances – the social and political factors that take hold of the principled-normative content to define problems, design problem solutions, and implement them. To be sure, the interpretation and relevance of what is institutionally given is always dependent on circumstances. But it has a different degree of patency and complexity. And it always has an enormous power of persistence, thanks to all the interests invested in the existing institutions and their development.

3.1.2 The Constitutional Shaping

The real political unfolding of the social is subject to an institutional shaping from yet another side: that of the political-legal system in which decisions are made about the development of the social. This is the system of the *constitutional state*. In the summer of 1945, there was no German constitutional state. What did exist were local, regional, and functional administrations. Most of all, however, there was an

[19] On the example of social insurance see Rieger (1992).

occupation regime. That regime did not think of itself as a constitutional state. But the conditions that prevailed after the collapse of the Nazi regime – at least in the occupation zones from which the Federal Republic would emerge – were geared toward the development of the constitutional state: on the German side in the sense of turning the back on National Socialism and remembering the long development of the constitutional state that had preceded the Third Reich. For the occupation regime it emerged out of the tradition of the three western occupying powers, to which the Soviet occupying power initially also seemed to be paying a certain deference. As early as 1946/1947, the states of the American, French, Soviet, and in part also the British zone received constitutions. Zonal and bi-zonal structures were set up in the American and the British zone, which simultaneously initiated the further development of the constitutional state. Eventually, the constitutional development in the East and the West was completed with the founding of the two states in 1949, but it also sealed Germany's division for four decades. In spite of the – degressive – continuation of the occupation regime, the structure of the constitutional state now determined life in West Germany.

The social was given a *constitutionally normative title*: that of the *social state*. And it becomes clear right away that this embedding within the constitutional state asserts its own claim. Baden called itself a "democratic and social *Freistaat*" (Art. 50, Para. 1, LVerf.Baden), Wuerttemberg-Baden a "democratic and social *Volksstaat*" (Art. 43 LVerf.WB), and Rhineland Palatinate a "democratic and social member state of Germany" (Art. 74, LVerf.RP). Bavaria referred to itself as a "*Freistaat*" (Art. 1, Para. 1, LVerf.Bay), and "*Volksstaat*" (Art. 2, Para. 1, LVerf. Bay), and a "legal, cultural, and social state" (Art. 3, Para. 1, Sent.1 LVerf.Bay).[20] The Basic Law developed two different sequences: for the Federal Republic as a whole the formula of the "democratic and social federal state" (Art. 20, Para. 1, GG); for "the democratic system in the states" the formula of the "republican, democratic, and social state governed by the rule of law, within the meaning of the Basic Law" (Art. 28, Para. 1, Sent. 1, GG). In the process, the concepts of democracy, republic (and *Freistaat* [free state]), *Rechtsstaat* (state under the rule of law), and federal state have essentially *also* a state-organizing meaning. By contrast, the concept of the social state does not trigger any state-organizing association. This already manifests the problem we are dealing with. "Social state" refers to content. Democracy, republic, *Rechtsstaat*, and federal state label the structures of political power in which it is concretely spelled out how the "social state" is to realize itself.

A number of *state constitutions* had, of course, laid down different sets of social rights and programs (see section "Further Development and the Formulation of New Goals"), but that did not substantially alter the situation. Although these stipulations painted an impressive picture of the problems that the drafters of these state constitutions considered socially relevant and of the solutions they deemed appropriate, these programs, too, were entrusted to the general apparatus

[20] Bremen (Art. 65 LVerf.Br) invoked the formula of "social justice." Only Hesse refrained from a comparably general pronouncement.

of the constitutional state. Their realization was a matter for the democratic and constitutional institutions. The primary, historical-institutional shaping of the social was thus joined by a second, very different institutional shaping of the social: that of the constitutional state.

3.2 *The Social Federal State*

3.2.1 The Normative Meaning – The Unitary Orientation of Social Policy in the German Federal State

The formula of the social federal state certainly suggests a normative meaning.[21] The federal state is an entity in which autonomous members and the central government interact. This way the social state seems to correspond in a particular way to the principle of solidarity. The Basic Law elevates this situation by declaring the entire state of the Federal Republic of Germany – the central government *and* the member states – a social state (Art. 20, Para. 1, GG), while at the same time obligates every state to be a social state (Art. 28, Para. 1, Sent. 1, GG). This seems all the more significant, as the Basic Law obligates this federal state to subsidiarity: the jurisdiction of the states is constitutionally the rule, the jurisdiction of the federal government the exception (Art. 30, GG). Thus, diversity *and* totality complement each other in bringing about the social.

However, juxtaposed to this initial impression of a balance of diversity and totality is the *unitary a priori understanding* of this federal state (U. Münch 1997, esp. pp. 46–78): not so much – or at least not only – a general unitary a priori understanding, but a specific unitary a priori understanding of the social state. This has deep historical roots (Frerich and Frey, vol. 1, 1996; Stolleis 2013, German Social Policy, vol. 2). Already in the German Confederation and the Customs Union, in the North German League and the German Empire of 1871, and then once more in the Weimar Republic, the unity of the economic realm was the purpose and mandate of an overarching unity – first as a league of states, then as a federal state. And freedom of movement was the corresponding right of the citizens to take advantage of the opportunities of this common economic sphere. But social legislation, too, revealed itself as essentially unitary from the outset. Already the North German League had to stipulate:

[21] Thus, for example, Fechner (1955, pp. 161–168). The prevailing opinion, however, rejects a separate normative meaning of the compound term composed of social state and federal state. On the interpretation in the early years of the Federal Republic see Zacher (1981, pp. 45, 686–688, 737). On the more recent interpretation see Münch (1997, pp. 92–95).

> Every northern German must be treated as a national in every state of the League with respect to (a) the manner and degree of public assistance that is to be granted in case of need, and (b) the acquisition and loss of residential relief.[22]

After the founding of the German Empire, the concept was immediately applied to southern Germany.[23] The next great new approach, Bismarck's social insurance legislation, took place essentially on the level of imperial politics. The development of social legislation during the Weimar Period, too, was clearly in the hands of the Empire. The fact that whatever happened during the National Socialist period in terms of social policy was a matter for the Reich was a result of its transformation into a unitary state.

The Basic Law, by emphasizing the social mandate of the federal government *and* the states, was not able to break this fundamental political orientation, the push of the social toward unitary realization. On the contrary: while the old premises that the central state is responsible for the unity of the entire national economic sphere (e.g. Art. 73, nos. 3–7, 9, GG) and for the freedom of movement within the territory of the federal state (Art. 11, 73, no. 3, GG) persisted, there were new reasons for the concentration of the social within the political sphere of the federal state. The states that formed the Federal Republic in 1949 continued to be the result of occupation policy. Most lacked any kind of social identity. And a great many of the new social problems – and especially the most pressing among them – were the legacy of the politics of the Third Reich. For them, it was anyhow necessary to make central state solutions possible.[24] The Basic Law underscored this a priori unitary nature of the social by stipulating (Art. 72, Para. 2, no. 3, GG, old version) that "equal living conditions throughout the federal territory" constituted one of the criteria legitimizing federal jurisdiction in the area of concurrent legislative powers (Art. 74, GG). From the outset, one of the concerns of the Basic Law was to secure the "financial capacities also of the states with weak tax revenue" (Art. 106, Para. 4, Sent. 1, GG in the original version). Later, there was reference to a "reasonable equalization of the disparate financial capacities of the *Länder*" (Art. 107, Para. 2, Sent. 1, GG[25]). Taxes were to be distributed so as to "preserve uniform living conditions within the federal territory" (Art. 106, Para. 4, Sent. 4, no. 2, GG[26]).

[22] Section 1 Para. 1 of the "Gesetz über den Unterstützungswohnsitz vom 6. Juni 1870," BGBl, p. 360.

[23] Bavaria kept aloof from the common system until 1916.

[24] For example, matters concerning refugees and expellees (Art. 74, no. 6, Art. 119, 131, GG), war damages and reparations (Art. 74, no. 9, GG), benefits for persons disabled by the war and the survivors of deceased war victims, as well as assistance for prisoners of war (Art. 74, no. 10, GG), the costs of occupation and burdens resulting from the war (Art. 120, GG), soon supplemented with laws regarding the equalization of burdens (Art. 120a, GG, inserted through the law of 14 August 1952, BGBl. I, p. 445).

[25] Inserted by the "Gesetz zur Änderung und Ergänzung der Finanzverfassung (Finanzverfassungsgesetz) vom 23. Dezember 1955," BGBl. I, p. 817.

[26] Inserted as Art. 106, Para. 4, Sent. 2, no. 3 through the *Finanzverfassungsgesetz*, ibid. Amended by the "Finanzreformgesetz vom 12. Mai 1969" BGBl. I, p. 359.

And once again we hear of the mandate of the federal legislator to “ensure that the disparate financial capacities of the *Länder* are appropriately equalized” (Art. 107, Para. 2, Sent.1, GG). Finally, the federal government was authorized to intervene with financial assistance to “equalize differing economic capacities within the federal territory” (Art. 104a, Para. 4, Sent. 1, GG[27]). At the same time, the constitution-amending legislator indicated with the introduction of joint responsibilities (Art. 91a, 91b, GG[28]) that certain social, economic, civilizing and cultural gaps were to be overcome through joint action by the federal government and the states. After the reunification of Germany, the criterion of federal jurisdiction with respect to concurrent legislation was newly formulated: “to the extent that the establishment of equal living conditions throughout the federal territory.... renders federal regulation necessary in the national interest” (Art. 72, Para. 2, GG, new version[29]). However, it remains clear also in this version that the Basic Law includes significant regional differences in the inequalities whose equalization the social should bring about (Depenheuer 1997, p. 163f.).

On the whole, then, we see a relationship of tension. The basic normative approach affirms the diversity of the federal government and the states also with regard to the social. What matters is not that the social is shaped in a unitary manner, but that the total entity made up of the federation and the states is obligated to the social. This basic approach seems to affirm the openness of the social: clearly the federation and the states can pursue different concepts and arrive at different concrete expressions. At the same time, though, one can also observe a centripetal orientation of the social – a tendency that negates regional differences of the social and expects the optimal realization of the social from the largest possible unit: whether in the sense of relevant jurisdictions by the federal government and their use, or in the sense of joint action by the federal government and the states. This approach is in line with the historical and political self-conception. The unitary approach overlays the federal one. The normative meaning of the “social federal state” recedes into the background.

3.2.2 The Institutional Significance

The Institutional Effect of the Unitary Premise

Within this social unitarianism, the presumption of state jurisdiction (Art. 30, GG)[30] takes on surprising importance. The general regulatory setup of the constitution in the Federal Republic is this: as a rule, the states are in charge; the federal

[27] Inserted by the *Finanzreformgesetz,* ibid.

[28] Inserted by the *Finanzreformgesetz*, ibid.

[29] “42. Gesetz zur Änderung des Grundgesetzes vom 27. Oktober 1994” BGBl. I, p. 3146.

[30] See also specifically with respect to legislation (Art. 70, Para. 1, GG), administration (Art. 30, 83, GG), and the courts (Art. 92, GG).

government is responsible for the exceptions enumerated in the Basic Law. The historical-political orientation of the social points in the opposite direction: as a rule, the federal government should act, the states at best by way of exception. The practical effect of this is the following: the realization of the social is relegated to the sphere of "exceptions" that the Basic Law explicitly assigns to the federal government. With that, the formula of the "social federal state" takes on a peculiar one-sidedness. According to the literal text of the Basic Law, the federal government and the states together would have at their disposal the full scope that is meant by the openness of the social. Of course, the federal government could only act within the boundaries of the jurisdictions assigned to it. The open diversity of tasks would be a matter for the states. They would only be kept from what the federal government is explicitly responsible for. But the unitary proviso of the social turns this picture completely upside down: the *paths of federal responsibility* become the *paths of the social.*

In this scenario, then, the primary institutional shaping that emerges from the history of the German social state and the secondary institutional shaping that emerges out of the institutions of the constitution of the German social state enter into a highly effective union. When creating the Basic Law, the Parliamentary Council looked at what existed and what could be remembered: at "public welfare" (Art. 74, no. 7, GG), at "labor law, including the organization of enterprises, occupational safety and health, and employment agencies, as well as social security, including unemployment insurance" (Art. 74, no. 12, GG).[31] And it provided to the federal government corresponding regulatory possibilities – not as exclusive jurisdictions, but certainly with preeminence over the states (Art. 72, GG). It also saw the current problems that National Socialist rule and the war had left behind: "matters concerning refugees and expellees" (Art. 74, no. 6, GG), "war damages and reparations" (Art. 74, no. 9, GG), and "benefits for persons disabled by war and for dependants of deceased war victims as well as assistance to former prisoners of war and the care of war graves" (Art. 74, no. 10, GG). But scope for a comprehensive social reform is nowhere mentioned. What was meant? Should a far-reaching social reform – the introduction, for example, of tax-funded "citizen provision" or of a national health service – be reserved for an amendment to the Basic Law? Or for Germany as a whole? After all, the Federal Republic was to be only a provisional entity. Was a far-reaching social reform to turn into the hour of truth for the "social federal state"? For what the federal government is not authorized to regulate, the states should (Art. 30, GG), and they, too, are obligated to the social (Art. 28, Para. 1, Sent. 1, GG). Or was it simply that the legislators who created the Basic Law believed that they could manage quite well also politically with the system elements they incorporated into their catalog of responsibilities – and would be able to do so in the future, as well?

[31] On social insurance see also the regulation of administrative powers in Art. 87, Para. 2, GG, and the regulation of financing in Art. 120, Para. 1, GG.

The Basic Law's catalogs of responsibilities thus grew into an importance that would point the direction in two ways. On the one hand, they were suited to exemplifying the goal of the social state, which stands so alone within the constitutional text, unaccompanied and broad (Art. 20, Para. 1; Art. 28, Para. 1, Sent. 1, GG). On the other hand, they pointed the unitary road for the realization of the social. More still: the Basic Law largely anticipated this path. Old law essentially remained in force provided it did not conflict with the Basic Law (Art. 123, GG). Laws respecting matters under the legislative power of the federal government continued to exist, in principle, as federal law (Art. 124, 125 GG). When the federation came into being, it was already master over broad swathes of the traditional social law. The states would have had maneuvering room in this regard only if the federal government had created it by abolishing old law (Art. 72, GG). The constitution-altering legislation of the federation could certainly have altered this system of responsibilities (Art. 79, GG). But it, too, fit itself into the institutional reality. The elements it contributed are of limited importance: the equalization of burdens (Art. 106, Para. 1, no. 5, Art. 120a, GG), the regulation of educational and training grants (Art. 74, no. 13, GG), the economic viability of hospitals and the regulation of hospital charges (Art. 74, no. 19a, GG). An attitude critical toward the traditional cannot be inferred from this.

The Allocation of Responsibilities and the Picture of the Social

The Basic Law's system of responsibilities thus pointed the way for the social federal state. What image of the social and what image of the social federal state does this give rise to?

If one asks this question *from the vantage point of the basic social norm*, what becomes strikingly evident is the emphasis that the *original version of the Basic Law* places on concern for dependent work: for work in general (Art. 74, no. 12; Art. 120, GG) and for work within the public sector (Art. 73, no. 8; Art. 75, no. 1, GG). Provision against shortcomings in the developments of income, the satisfying of basic needs, or in maintenance was addressed as "social insurance" (Art. 74, no. 12; Art. 87, Para. 2; Art. 120, GG). When it came to service in the public sector, this provision was one of the traditional principles of the professional civil service (Art. 33, Para. 4 and 5, GG). The social problems of satisfying basic needs found scattered mention, beyond what provision could contribute to resolving them, for example with respect to housing (Art. 74, no. 18, GG).[32] The social problems of the community of maintenance are not explicitly addressed. But wherever the basic social formula does not take hold or runs into crucial limits of its realization, "public welfare" can help (Art. 74, no. 7, GG).

If we look at the question *from the perspective of the traditional institutions of the social*, the responsibility for public welfare (Art. 74, no. 7, GG) brings to bear

[32] A long catalog of responsibilities (Art. 74, nos. 17–23, GG) is not essentially aimed at social problems.

the tradition of poor relief. Social protection through provision is specified as social insurance (Art. 74, no. 12, GG) and no doubt also as a private insurance system (Art. 74, no. 11, GG), and is sufficiently clear in the traditional principles of the civil service (Art. 33, Para. 4 and 5; Art. 73, no. 8; Art. 75, no. 1, GG). Social protection through compensation emerges through examples related to history: matters concerning refugees and expellees (Art. 74, no. 6, GG), war damages and reparations (Art. 74, no. 9, GG), benefits for those disabled by war and the dependants of those killed in the war, as well as care for former prisoners of war (Art. 74, no. 10, GG). The concern for "more equality" is not explicitly addressed in the catalogs of responsibilities, nor can it be by its very nature. Otherwise the mandate of the social state would turn into a general clause of federal responsibility. However, some of its themes appear implicitly: for example, in the responsibilities regarding labor (Art. 74, no. 12, GG), land law and housing (Art. 74, no. 18; Art. 75, no. 4, GG). The responsibility for the economy is articulated in a great many differentiated ways (Art. 73, nos. 4, 5, and 9; Art. 74, nos. 11, 17, 18, 20; Art. 88, GG). A specific social meaning can be read especially from the responsibilities for "the transfer of land, natural resources, and means of production to public ownership or other forms of public enterprise" (Art. 74, no. 15, GG), and for the "prevention of the abuse of economic power" (Art. 74, no. 16, GG).

These *targets* clearly showed the "social federal state" the path: *first*, in that it should *focus* its concern on *dependent labor*, whereby the two basic patterns adumbrated in the system of competencies – the civil servant relationship and the work relationship – complemented each other; *second*, in that the externalizing *social benefits systems* gave emphatic expression to the *two categories of social inclusion* – the elementary national inclusion tied to the history of poor relief, and the industrial-economic inclusion tied to the history of social insurance; *third*, in that the *political and legal responsibility of the state for damages* well beyond the care for the victims of war found expression in a differentiated system of compensations and restitution benefits as well as other forms of aid.

Crucial to the continued course of social policy was a critical juncture about which the system of competencies was neutral, at least directly. The idea of the social market economy entailed a *priority in favor of externalizing solutions* to social problems; in other words: a presumption in favor of resolving social problems through special systems of social benefits, and a presumption against resolving them through a social change of existing legal conditions. Against this backdrop, policies that sought, for example, to equalize shortcomings in the capacity to meet basic needs in the direction of "more equality" through price controls or the stipulation of contractual conditions (social tenant law) lost importance, while relevant social benefits systems (housing allowance, child allowance) became central techniques of social policy. Social benefits by virtue of basic national inclusion (welfare/public assistance) and social benefits by virtue of inclusion in work and the economy (social insurance) were joined over time by *benefits by virtue of the general prosperity of society*. This also means: the traditional types of social benefits that the creators of the constitution had in mind were joined by new types. No federal responsibility was identified for them. Yet there was only one constitutional amendment for this purpose, namely for "educational and training grants" (Art. 74, no. 13, GG).[33] And there were very few serious attempts to invoke state responsibility in this regard. Rather, the given federal responsibilities were interpreted in a way that also provided a basis for social benefits systems of this "third kind." Here and there, an existing responsibility could be employed: for example, the responsibility for housing (Art. 74, no. 18, GG) for the housing allowance. As for the rest, the two central responsibilities for social benefits law were expanded accordingly: wherever the regulatory technique allowed a linkup, "social insurance" was invoked as the jurisdictional authority of federal legislation (Art. 74, no. 12, GG).[34] By contrast, for tax-funded benefits, the jurisdictional authority of "public welfare" was invoked (Art. 74, no. 7, GG).[35] Thus, the differentiation and expansion of the system of social benefits became the dominant trend. However, fundamental new departures could not have been justified with the help of these federal competencies.

Different once again was the development of the use of the federal government's competencies with respect to the *responsibility of the state for the economy.* Structural changes in the economy that went hand in hand with the *participation of labor* were – as labor or economic law – a priori open to the jurisdiction of the federal government (Art. 74, nos. 11, 12, GG). Other federal powers remained unused. The central example of that is the authority to carry out socializations (Art. 74, no. 15, GG). When it came to the organization of economic processes by the federal government, the Basic Law provided numerous competencies from the outset (Art. 73, 74, 75, 88, 105, GG). They were also employed in the sense of social guidance. However, as Germany rebuilt, the practice of direct intervention quickly receded, and the primacy of global guidance asserted itself. In the process, special importance was accorded over time to budget management and supra-individual financing programs (Art. 104a, 109, 115, GG).[36] However, what evolved into the foundation of the economic-political system were above all the jurisdictional norms that gave the federal government the possibility of guaranteeing the free market system as such (Art. 73, no. 4; Art. 74, nos. 11, 16; Art. 88, GG).

Of course, the allocation of responsibility between the federal government and the states cannot be seen *only* as the distribution of *legislative responsibilities*. The *competencies* are distributed differently for the *administration* and for the *legal system* (Art. 30, 83ff., 92, GG). The states seem to possess the greater leeway here.

---

[33] Inserted through the "22. Gesetz zur Änderung des Grundgesetzes vom 12. Mai 1969" BGBl. I, p. 363.

[34] For example, the early social-security like form of child allowance (BVerfGE 11, 105). See also the recognition of social insurance for artists (BVerfGE 75, 108), and the legitimation of contribution-free child-raising periods (BVerfGE 87, 1).

[35] As for child and youth services (BVerfGE 22, 180), the equalization of burdens on families (BVerfGE 87, 1), and aid to disabled children (BVerfGE 42, 263).

[36] The central law is the "15. Gesetz zur Änderung des Grundgesetzes vom 8. Juni 1967" BGBl. I, p. 581; and the "21. Gesetz zur Änderung des Grundgesetzes vom 12. Mai 1969" BGBl. I, p. 359.

However, the principles of the constitutional state and of democracy, as well as that of the federal state itself, accord the law a central and comprehensive guiding function (Art. 20, Para. 3; Art. 28, Para. 1, Sent. 1; Art. 84ff.; Art. 97, Para. 1, GG). What non-legislative administration can accomplish is not unimportant, but it cannot shape the social in a sweeping manner. The legislative power, finally, is not subject to politics, in any case, but to the law and is borne – within the framework of the laws – by the guiding function of the Federal Constitutional Court (Art. 93, 94, GG) and the higher courts, and these are courts of the federation (Art. 95, 96, GG of the original version).[37] With this, our analysis for the first time encounters a general observation with an importance that cannot be overestimated: the *connection between the federal, the constitutional, and the democratic function of the law* has contributed substantially to the concrete shaping of the social. In general, this has given rise to a *concentration of perception on the central and the formal*, and a *waning of the perception toward the decentral and the informal.* A number of differentials can be explained by this connection: the *emphasis on federal policy* as well as the *neglect* of the social structures and modes of operation of the *states*, *local communities*, and *societal forces*; the *emphasis* on all *legal* regulations and all *calculable* and thus legally directly regulatable *benefits* and the *neglect of services.*

The Federal Organization of Financial Resources and the Development of the Social

From the outset, a special kind of socio-political effect emanated from the fact that the financial arrangement of the Basic Law restricted itself to two aspects: in terms of revenue to taxes (Art. 105ff. GG), in terms of budget management to the budgets of the federal government and the states (Art. 109, GG). The flipside: the Basic Law said nothing about revenue other than taxes (fees, contributions, and special levies; fines etc.; revenue from the private sector) and – initially – only formal things about credit (Art. 115, GG). It said nothing explicit about the budget management of administrative units of legal capacity below and within the federal government and the states; and it said – again: initially – nothing explicit about spending. To be sure, over time there were reforms to the financial constitution (*Finanzverfassung*).[38] Their result was that the budget management of the federal government and the states, especially also borrowing, was regulated more intensively (Art. 109, 115, GG),

[37] Art. 95 in the version of the "16. Gesetz zur Änderung des Grundgesetzes vom 18. Juni 1968" BGBl. I, p. 657.

[38] "Finanzverfassungsgesetz vom 23. Dezember 1955," BGBl. I, p. 817; "Gesetz zur Änderung und Ergänzung des Art. 106 GG vom 24. Dezember 1956" BGBl. I, p. 1077; "Gesetz zur Änderung des Grundgesetzes vom 8. Juni 1967" BGBl. I, p. 581; "20. Gesetz zur Änderung des Grundgesetzes vom 12. Mai 1969" BGBl. I, p. 357; "Finanzreformgesetz vom 12. Mai 1969" BGBl. I, p. 359; "Gesetz zur Änderung des Grundgesetzes vom 3. November 1995" BGBl. I, p. 1492; "44. Gesetz zur Änderung des Grundgesetzes vom 20. Oktober 1997" BGBl. I, p. 2470.

that fundamental statements were made also about federal and state spending (Art. 104a, GG), and that the fiscal management of local communities and community associations (*Gebietskörperschaften*) were regulated within the federal fiscal system in an increasingly differentiated manner (Art. 28, Para. 2, Sent. 3; Art. 104a, Para. 4, Sent. 1; Art. 106, Para. 3, Sent. 1, and Para. 5–9, GG). Still, a *profound split of the fiscal system remained: an explicit federal system exists only for taxes*, while all other revenues are regulated implicitly in the separate material contexts in which they are embedded; explicit budget directives exist *only for the* budgets of *"territorial entities"* (that is, the federal government, the states, local communities, and community associations), while directives for the budget management of other administrative entities must be looked for once again in the particular substantive contexts in which they are embedded. And the constitutional system of expenditures (Art. 104a, GG), too, deals only with those of territorial entities.

This constellation holds profound importance for the development of the social. Most significant is that the *creative freedom* of the federal government *and* the states is substantially *greater when social benefits programs are financed by means other than taxes* and when they can be *administered other than by the federal government and the states*. To put it differently: the creative freedom is greater when social benefits programs are financed with the help of non-tax revenues, especially contributions or special levies (Kirchhof P 1990, pp. 87–233), and when they can be run by legal corporations, institutions, and public law foundations. In this setup the communities assume a special place. On the one hand, their position under fiscal constitutional law was increasingly strengthened; moreover, a financing of their social burdens by anything other than tax revenues is largely out of the question. However, the temptation of the federal government and the states to allocate tasks to communities across the board and to leave it to communal budgets to cushion the impact, remains in place. Far *greater*, however, is the *leeway with respect to the effective sphere of non-territorial entities*, institutions, and foundations. The *central example* is *social insurance*. Its real source of financing is contributions, and its real organizational form is that of a (non-territorial) corporation or institution (Art. 87, Para. 2, GG). But this sphere of creative leeway includes not only social insurance carriers in the narrower sense, but also other legal corporations, institutions, and foundations. The largest example is the Federal Labour Office (*Bundesanstalt für Arbeit*), which combines the task of a social insurance carrier (unemployment insurance) with a multitude of additional tasks: additional tasks of social protection (unemployment benefit, short-time work allowance, and so on; bankruptcy compensation payments/insolvency protection), and tasks of positive employment policy (job placement, job promotion). It likewise combines within itself various forms of financing: financing through contributions and levies with financing from federal funds (derived substantially from taxes). The fact that the Federal Labour Office performs its tasks in a three-tiered administrative structure (regions, states, the federal level) shows the extent to which the federal system can be circumvented by way of segregating out an area in terms of financing and organization. Finally, *special levies* (Kirchhof P 1990, pp. 184–202) – such as the "equalization of burdens levies" (Art. 106, Para. 1, no. 5; Art. 120a, GG), the levy to promote the employment of the severely disabled, or the levy on those inappropriately occupying subsidized housing – can serve social goals. However, unlike social insurance contributions, they are not tied to a particular organizational form.

The most important phenomenon to emerge out of this constellation, however, is the *fiscal autonomy of social insurance* (Kirchhof F 1990, pp. 395–423). By virtue of its responsibility for social insurance (Art. 74, no. 12, GG), the federal legislator can control this legal entity with its own budget without being subject to the constraints and consequences linked to the disposition over tax revenues and to changes in the fiscal relationship between the federal government and the states (Art. 104a, Para. 1–3, Art. 106, GG). The central place of social insurance in the development of the social is also grounded not least in this circumstance.

The fiscal system of the Basic Law, however, provides information also about another development of the social. The expansion of the federal fiscal constitution[39] articulated not only new values, but above all also new instruments. The budget management of the federal government *and* of the states was obligated to take account of the requirements of overall economic equilibrium, be responsive to economic trends, and engage in long-term financial planning (Art. 109, Para. 2 and 3, GG). Interventions in the borrowing and spending policy of the federal government and the states (Art. 109, Para. 4, GG), as well as additional borrowing by the federal government (Art. 115, Para. 1, GG), were authorized to "avert disturbances of the overall economic equilibrium." Finally, the federal government was empowered to "grant the states financial assistance for particularly important investments by the states or by municipalities (associations of municipalities), provided that such investments are necessary to avert a disturbance of the overall economic equilibrium, to equalize differing economic capacities within the federal territory, or to promote economic growth" (Art. 104a, Para. 4, Sent. 1, GG). A crucial supplement was the *Law to Promote Stability and Economic Growth* of 8 June 1967 (BGBl. I, p. 582), which provided for a differentiated set of instruments to coordinate the financial planning and the economic and borrowing policy of the federal government and the states. The practical importance of this set of tools has now receded to a modest level. However, the fundamental assertion that the financial management of the federal government and the states must be jointly obligated to take into account the requirements of the overall economic equilibrium, the stability of the price level, a high level of employment, the external economic equilibrium, as well as a steady and appropriate economic growth (Sect. 1, Sent. 2, StWG) carries even greater weight today.

[39] Especially the Fifteenth, Twentieth, and Twenty-First Law to Amend the Basic Law. See note 38.

The Collaboration of the Federal Government and the States – Integration of the State as a Whole

The basic unitary thrust of the social entered into a particularly lasting union with the possibilities of the states to influence politics – and especially legislation – at the federal level via the Bundesrat (upper house of parliament); (Das parlamentarische Regierungssystem und der Bundesrat 1999). As far as the relationship between the social policy of the federal government and the social policy of the states is concerned, the Bundesrat's rights of participation are inherently ambivalent. They could be employed equally to fight for the jurisdiction of the states, and to contribute to the development of federal competencies and influence their exercise. The states have largely opted for the latter. The unitary traditions of German politics and the mostly weak assertiveness of the states particularly during the first decades of the Federal Republic were reconciled in the direction of seeing the federal state not as the equal coexistence of autonomous spheres of statehood, but as a complex mechanism of integration (Lerche 1964, pp. 66–104). As time went by, it would also become increasingly difficult to distinguish whether the Bundesrat was exercising its competencies as an organ of the federal state or an organ of democracy, whether it brought to bear the concerns of the state and the expertise of the state governments (Art. 50, 51 GG), or whether, like the "upper house" of a bicameral parliament, it was realizing the opportunities for a constellation of parties that provided an alternative to the governing majority of the "lower house."

The Basic Law provided to the political *opposition* on the federal level another way *of articulating itself via the formation of governments in the states and the Bundesrat*. In keeping with a tradition that already went back to the Reich Constitution of 1871[40] and the Weimar Constitution,[41] Art. 43, Para. 2 of the Basic Law stipulated:

> The members of the *Bundesrat* and of the Federal Government as well as their representatives may attend all sessions of the *Bundestag* and of its committees. They shall have the right to be heard at any time.

This right of participation on the level of federal politics is also not restricted to the assertion of the interests of a state or the states. The importance of this constellation becomes clear from the fact that Kurt Georg Kiesinger, Willy Brandt, Helmut Kohl, and Gerhard Schröder were Minister-Presidents of a state before becoming Chancellor, and that Franz Josef Strauß, Johannes Rau, Hans-Jochen Vogel, Oskar Lafontaine, and Rudolf Scharping were Minister-Presidents of a state before they became candidates for the office of Chancellor.

---

[40] Art. 9, Sent. 1, GG: "Each member of the Federal Council shall have the right to appear in the Diet, and be heard there at any time when he shall so request, to represent the views of his Government, even when the same shall not have been adopted by the majority of the Council."

[41] Art. 33, Para. 2, Sent. 2, GG: "The states are entitled to send authorized representatives, who present the position of their state's government, into these sessions."

The *voters*, too, regard *state parliament elections*, the *formation of governments in the states*, and the *Bundesrat* as *instruments of opposition* (König 1999, esp., p. 32f.). Since 1972 it has been evident that after a change in the majority in the *Bundestag*, there is a tendency in the states, with some time lag, to prefer parties that stand in opposition to the policies of the federal government. This phenomenon was not nearly as clear before 1972, when the dominant perception was still that the *Bundesrat* was a chamber representing the states. Moreover, the coalitions in the states were even more colorful. Only the confrontation between a socially liberal federal policy with the CDU/CSU majority in a number of state parliaments gave rise to a sharp confrontation between the *Bundestag* and the *Bundesrat*, which would characterize the entire decade until the "*Wende*" of 1982. The year 1991, and even more so 1996, then saw the opposite constellation. The government policy of a CDU/CSU/FDP majority clashed with a SPD- dominated majority in the *Bundesrat*. This blockage of federal policy by the *Bundesrat* led in each case to a considerable paralysis.

The statehood of the *states* shifted from the individual autonomy of each state to the joint participation of all states in a complex overarching statehood. In the 1960s this trend began to manifest itself increasingly in new institutions – initially within the framework of the unwritten supplementation to the constitution. The year 1961 saw the so-called "*Fernsehurteil*" (Television Decision) by the Federal Constitutional Court (BVerfGE 12, 205). In it, the Court declared that if a federal jurisdiction (Art. 30, GG) did not exist but political action by the individual states was not sensible, the possibility of *interfederal cooperation* was preferable over the presumption of a natural jurisdiction by the federal government (BVerfGE 12, 251f.). This provided significant new impulses to interfederal cooperation, which previously had already found many forms (Rudolf 1990, pp. 1091–1132). The Federal Constitutional Court later reaffirmed once again the constitutional preference of interfederal cooperation over the establishment of unwritten federal competencies. In the Numerus Clausus Decision of 1972 (BVerfGE 33, 303), it pushed for a regulation of admission to university between the states via a state treaty (ibid, p. 357f.). With that, a social problem had also entered the purview of the courts: access to university was an equal educational opportunity.

However, the diversity of manifestations of interfederal cooperation did not assume any particular socio-political importance.[42] And yet: to the same degree in which the relationship between the federal government and the states was changed by interfederal cooperation, social policy and social administration also participated in this climate of the federal government's and the state's interaction and cooperation in agreements, conferences, and institutions. To be sure, much more specific for the reality of the social was a dimension of the cooperation that was rarely ever perceived as a component of interfederal cooperation, but which was in fact of the greatest importance for a *state-spanning cooperation in the realm*

[42] Münch (1997, pp. 92–142). An overview of the phenomena of interfederal cooperation in Zacher (1984d, pp. 521–530).

of the social: *associations*. They had *two central forms*, both of which had a prehistory that went back a long way. On the *one side* there was the *cooperation of the social insurance carriers* (Hein 1990). In individually very different ways, the various carriers of the statutory sickness insurance (*Ortskrankenkassen, Innungskrankenkassen, Betriebskrankenkassen, Ersatzkassen*) had been organizing themselves for a long time on their own but also on a higher level, the carriers of accident insurance (of commercial accident insurance and the accident insurance carriers of the public sector) and the carriers of the statutory pension insurance for the most part also on the state level, and in any case on the federal level. Through joint consultations, recommendations, joint organs, and so on, there emerged within the various branches of social insurance an overarching guidance of practice, and externally a formulation and realization of joint policies. *On the other side* was the *cooperation of the carriers of* welfare/public assistance and of child and youth services. Not only the concerns, but also the structures were substantially different here. The charitable and the communal carriers have a long history of responsibility for these social areas, which are largely realized in services, but also a long history of demarcation and competition. The joint task of such a large number and such a great diversity of carriers had also demanded early on an institution for clarification, consultation, information, exchange, cooperation, and finding and asserting a joint policy. This institution was the German Association for Public and Private Welfare (*Deutscher Verein für öffentliche und private Fürsorge*).[43] The Association was among the first actors that saw to the reestablishment of functioning social services and benefits in the occupation zones. With the founding of the Federal Republic, the Association established itself once again as the representative of the concerns of poor relief and youth welfare at the federal level. The realm in which the social was realized administratively and societally was thus filled in a very peculiar way by self-organization on the national level.

Eventually, the constitutional legislator itself in 1969 affirmed the development of integrative federalism by introducing the *joint tasks* into the Basic Law (Art. 91a, 91b, GG).[44]

The goal of these joint tasks is to moderate or abolish socially relevant differences between the regions of the federal territory. In substance they are an intensive affirmation of the unitary tendency of the social federal state. The political ramifications of this institution have by now proven to be problematic. To be sure, the joint effort by the federal government and the states – especially the use of federal finances in concert with the states – has produced considerable effects. However, the process of lifting entire political areas onto the national level has reduced the incentive for politics on the state level to solve problems on its own and creatively. The regime of joint tasks has paralyzed the responsibility of the relevant

---

[43] Founded in 1880 as "Deutscher Verein für Armenpflege und Wohltätigkeit" (German Association for Poor Relief and Charity), renamed in 1919 (Orthbandt 1980).

[44] "21. Gesetz zur Änderung des Grundgesetzes (Finanzreformgesetz) vom 12. Mai 1969" BGBl. I, p. 359.

level of politics, whether federal or state. State politics makes itself known largely through reproaches leveled against the federal government, and at times also against the other states. With the joint tasks, the development to integrative federalism has crossed a Rubicon. A reversal of the trend toward integrative federalism was indicated by a constitutional amendment in 1994:[45] the parameters within which the federal government can make use of concurrent legislative powers (Art. 72, GG) were drawn more tightly. It was further stipulated: "A federal law may provide that federal legislation that is no longer necessary.... may be superseded by state law" (Art. 72, Para. 3, GG). What use can be made of this, and whether this is in fact the beginning of a new development, only the future will tell.

3.3 *The Social* Rechtsstaat

3.3.1 The Normative Meaning

The relationship of the *Rechtsstaat* (rule of law; Schmidt-Aßmann 1987, pp. 987–1043; Benda 1994, pp. 719–797) to the social (Zacher 1987a, pp. 1101–1107; Bull 1988, pp. 13–39) may seem at first glance to be parallel – analogous to how the federal meaning of the federal state can be extended to solidarity and subsidiarity and thus to the basic principles of the social. The *Rechtsstaat* legitimizes itself by bringing forth justice.[46] Justice, however, is the target horizon of the social. Thus, by seeking justice, the *Rechtsstaat* must also seek the social. And justice is not justice if it is not (also) social justice. Therefore, the *Rechtsstaat can only legitimize itself by bringing forth social justice* (Bachof 1954, pp. 39f., 44).

This appears as a very simple truth. But it is an overly simple truth. Justice is not attainable in such a simple way, for it has many different forms. Just as the social takes on a diversity of forms, so too does social justice. Hence the *Rechtsstaat* cannot be recognized and legitimized by creating a particular kind of justice. Likewise, the social *Rechtsstaat* cannot be recognized by bringing forth a certain kind of social justice. The *Rechtsstaat* can legitimize itself as a just state only by accepting that it must approach justice anew time and again. It must have credibility for seeking to produce the greatest possible degree of justice. It must have credibility for seeking to avoid injustices – to keep them as small as possible, even if it cannot eliminate them altogether. That is the meaning of its institutions in terms of their history. And that meaning must be capable of being experienced in the present: their struggle for justice, their orientation toward justice. Perhaps one can say that the *Rechtsstaat* is a just state to the extent to which both are possible: that the *Rechtsstaat* can be recognized from the fact that it produces decisions that

[45] "42. Gesetz zur Änderung des Grundgesetzes vom 27. Oktober 1994" BGBl. I, p. 3146.

[46] Zacher (1981, pp. 663–672). For a rich discussion of the relationship between the *Rechtsstaat* and the social see Sobota (1997, pp. 90–104).

are seen as just, *and* that the decisions are accepted as just because the *Rechtsstaat* produced them. Alongside the democratic legitimation, this inseparable twofold achievement is the crucial political-legal legitimation of the social.

However, only the institutional is what is constitutionally doable (Zacher 1996, pp. 413–432). The normative meaning of the *Rechtsstaat* does not extend beyond that – leaving aside the extreme conflict of clearly unjust law. Thus, social justice, too, is doable only through institutions aimed at realizing it. Thus the social is once again entrusted to institutions.

3.3.2 The Institutional Meaning of the Social *Rechtsstaat*

Rechtsstaat – Social State

This institutional nature of the *Rechtsstaat* seems hard to bear by those for whom a certain conception of the social seems self-evident and valid as *the* social justice. That is *one* explanation for the protracted, vehement battle "here the *Rechtsstaat*, here the social state," which flared up time and again until the 1970s.[47] Champions of a seemingly *specific* social regarded the structure of the *Rechtsstaat* as a danger, in which the *true* social loses power and direction and can eventually be lost. The *Rechtsstaat*, meanwhile, was defended not only by those who saw in a "social *Rechtsstaat*" the best union of freedom and social justice. Rather, the *Rechtsstaat* was and is apparently *also* seen as a fortress wall behind which the values, concerns, and interests that must be weighed against the social can be securely protected. This is the *other* explanation for the protracted quarrel. In fact, this is the risk to which every social policy exposes itself by entrusting itself to the *Rechtsstaat*: that it will be truncated, that it will be "pruned back." But it is also the specific chance that the *Rechtsstaat* offers the social: that the projects of social policy are weighed against competing or conflicting values, goods, or interests in the never-ending process of disagreement, clarification, decision, and reassurance that constitutes the *Rechtsstaat*, so that in the end – "purified" as it were – it might be "more just" than a program that is formulated from only *one* perspective.

State and Society

The most important achievement of the *Rechtsstaat* is that it legally constitutes and guarantees the interplay of state and society (Böckenförde 1976; Rupp 1987). This is not to overlook that law cannot artificially create a vibrant society, a "civil society," where the preconditions are not in place. But the reverse is also true. In the long run, a civil society cannot be what it is supposed to be if it is not also legally guaranteed. Law and social reality have a reciprocal relationship here. The constitutional system of the Federal Republic of Germany does not explicitly mention

[47] Forsthoff (1968); Hartwich (1970); Kempen (1976); Degenhart (1983, pp. 537–553); Müller-Volbehr (1984, pp. 6–14).

that state and society are juxtaposed as autonomous entities and at the same time are to pervade each other. The Basic Law and the state constitutions presuppose this as given and intended. But they lay the foundation for the strength and the scope in which society can operate and guarantee their effectiveness.

The critical safeguarding of society lies in the *basic rights*. The constitution of society is chiefly a task of the civil rights and liberties. They create space for privacy and possibilities of communication and interaction. They open up room for private and societal cooperation and for the experience of coexistence and cooperation, of trust and disappointment, of altruism and selfishness. Inherent in them is also the mandate to the state to give these liberties a structure that develops them and brings them into some kind of balance. Of course, society and its relationship to the state are not established only by civil rights and liberties, but by the totality of basic rights. The rights of equality limit the emergence, continuation, and effect of social inequality. Procedural rights regulate the conflicts between the members of society, between them and societal forces, and also – and especially – between them and the state. Status rights create criteria of membership and eventually, as status activus, they reach across into the state; they channel the influence that citizens exert on the state. The society of the Federal Republic has filled this space. The large-scale suspension of societal normality under National Socialist rule was too short to alter the self-evident nature of societal life at its roots, let alone expunge it. And the collapse of 1945 quickly unleashed the societal forces, the control and restrictions of occupation law notwithstanding, with the result that even the earliest state constitutions with their systems of basic rights described and consolidated societal relationships whose rudiments already existed.

The constitution of a society in this sense means that the life of people takes place chiefly in the private sphere and in societal coexistence and interaction. It is evident that the state, through its legal system, through the infrastructure it provides or at least controls, through many of its functions, has a hand in shaping, carrying, and framing this private and societal life. Thus one can say that the processes of human life belong a priori to the interplay of society and state. But within this interplay the private and the societal takes precedence: the precedence of proximity, the precedence of everyday occurrence, and the precedence of autonomy – as well as the precedence of protection by the basic rights.

In that sense, the *juxtaposition of society and state is simply the most important institutional condition of the social*. Within this condition lies the crucial distinction between the "social" state and the "socialist" state. This condition rules out that the social – in the sense of a planned economy – is exclusively directed from a central point. On the contrary: no matter how centralized or decentralized the organization of the state may be, the social is entrusted first of all to the endless decentralization of the private and the societal. This basic condition *rules out* that the attempt is made to bring about the social through *a self-contained political process of distribution*. On the contrary: *distribution*, primarily a societal process, requires the *social correction of redistribution*. This fundamental condition also excludes the step of placing the economy exclusively or even primarily into the hands of the state. On the contrary: the primacy of the societal also entails a *primacy of the free market*. Without a free market economy, the primacy of the private and the societal cannot be realized. Finally, the basic condition of the juxtaposition of state and society demands a juxtaposition of private and public law as the framework conditions of the social. Everything taken together is a central reason for why the social cannot be directly and definitively politically conceived and realized at the same time – why we can never talk about anything more than the approximation of societal and political reality to the societal and political intention.

The freedom that underlies the juxtaposition of state and society can therefore not mean only "freedom *from* the social." It also means: "freedom *of* the social." In many respects the very fact is that the very thrust of freedom is toward the social. This is especially the case for the freedom of marriage and the family (Art. 6, GG). All freedoms of acquisition (Art. 2, Para. 1, Art. 12, GG) and all dealings with one's own property (Art. 14, GG) are, at any rate, set up in such a way that those who hold them are to care for themselves and their community of maintenance primarily on their own, while the state is relegated to a subsidiary role when it comes to the economic guarantee of their livelihood. Another dimension is the freedom to provide mutual support through the right of association (Art. 9, Para. 1, GG). Historically, this freedom has held great importance as the right to form cooperatives. Over the decades, this cooperative principle has lost much of its interest. But the same freedom also lays the foundation for more open, less binding unions, self-help groups that remedied specific shortcoming of contemporary society. Yet another direction opens up when we talk about the freedom to help others. It is included in the general freedom of self-development (Art. 2, Para. 1, GG). This altruistic help can take place privately or publicly; it can be done individually but also through the association of the helpers (Art. 9, Para. 1, GG). If economic resources come into play, this freedom can consist in motivating others to spend these resources (altruism, the charitable sector), or in organizing the meeting of basic needs in such a way that the costs are covered without making a profit (non-profit sector). Finally, the freedom can also consist in providing socially offered material benefits and services in return for free-market compensation. Another perspective lies in pursuing the societal and especially the political assertion of social concerns through associations (Art. 9, Para. 1, GG): it could be the personal concerns of those organized into an association, of which the unions are a particularly venerable and effective example (Art. 9, Para. 3, GG); or it could be a championing of the concerns of others, an advocacy function that especially charitable organizations associate with their task of organizing altruistic, non-profit aid.

Structures and Functions of the Rechtsstaat (Rule of Law) – The *Gesetzesstaat* (Statutory State) – The *Richterstaat* (Judiciary State)

The state is a *Rechtsstaat* because it seeks to subject itself to the rule of law. But since the state is at the same time the master of the law, this can be accomplished only in a complicated system, one that constrains state action through norms while providing ways of changing the binding norms themselves. The core pieces of this conception are the tri-partite division of power (Art. 20, Para. 2 and 3), the hierarchy of legal norms and especially the supraordination of the constitution over the law (Art. 1, Para. 3; Art. 20, Para. 3, GG), the subordination of the administration and the courts to the law (Art. 20, Para. 3, GG), the ability of the courts to review acts of the state as to their legality (Art. 19, Para. 4, GG), and especially the capacity of the constitutional courts to object to laws on the grounds that they violate the constitution (Art. 93 and 100, GG).

When it comes to the social, this system implies especially the following: politics focuses on the form of the laws. The formal law binds the administration and the courts (Art. 20, Para. 3; Art. 97, Para. 1, GG). If a law is correctly enacted, its effect extends across the trenches that protect the independence of the states against interference by the federal government (Art. 84, 85 GG) and remove the autonomy of municipalities (Art. 28, Para. 2, GG), social insurance carriers, and other independent administrative entities from the politics of the state. It is thus able to combine the need for uniform norms with the values of autonomy. The promulgation of its text (Art. 82, GG) assures the citizens of what the law is. It accords the individual rights that he or she can invoke vis-à-vis the administration and the courts. It is decided upon by parliament – or, to the extent to which this is provided for in the state constitution, by the people – as the central political organ of the polity and establishes political decisions first of all as binding. Finally, parliament's power to legislate moves the specific decision close to the financial responsibility of parliament, which is linked to its responsibility for budget legislation (Art. 110, 112, 115, GG). Wherever a regulation is intended to establish obligations, the tradition of the proviso of the law requires that it assume legal form. Over the decades, the decisions by the Federal Constitutional Court have expanded and changed this requirement by demanding that the legislature itself must enact all the regulations that substantially shape the content and use of a basic right (Der Grundrechtseingriff 1998). All in all, the formal law has become the most important regulatory instrument of the social. Moreover: the public perception of social policy is focused on legislation, and legislation is the dominant gesture of politics.

The proviso of the law applies with utmost clarity to all *externalizing social benefits systems*. As a rule, externalizing social benefits are state action. And because this state action shapes the sphere of the individual, it calls for legal regulation. But the legislator's transformative power extends also to *internalizing solutions*. The formal legislator can lay claim to regulating them – as for example the constant changes to a social rental law, the social occupational safety law, the works constitution law, or the co-determination law. However, internalizing solutions belong largely to private law. And private law is open to a special degree to the further development of the law by judicial decisions.[48] To that extent the distribution of roles between law and judge is a matter for the political powers that guide the legislative act, the judges who exercise their jurisdiction, and the societal forces involved, which urge one side or another to push forward or to hold back

[48] On the relationship between judge-made law and the reserved right of the law see Larenz and Canaris (1995, p. 246f.).

(Starck 1978, pp. 937–945). Especially labor law (Söllner 1994, pp. 325–335) has in this way preserved two core areas from which the formal legislator has kept his distance. The individual right to work was expanded – on the meager foundations of the Civil Code, supplemented by a series of individual laws – on the one hand by the practice of the parties to collective bargaining agreements, and on the other hand by the decisions of the labor courts.[49] All attempts at newly regulating individual labor law by statute have so far remained unsuccessful. The legislator has also omitted the right of the labor struggle and collective bargaining agreements, if one leaves aside the basic framework of the collective bargaining law. The Federal Constitutional Court and the Federal Labour Court established the relevant edifice of judge-made law on the basis of Article 9, Para. 3 of the Basic Law (Zacher 1980, pp. 509–536).

But even where the legislator has created systems, the *courts have attained maximum importance for the reality of the social*.[50] When the state was rebuilt after 1945, the power state and with it the state power of the government and the executive were disavowed. The legislative power offered the most attractive refuge of trust in the state and the law. Even before the Basic Law had been enacted, the administrative judges had been charged, through a so-called general clause, to protect the citizens against any violation of the law by the administration.[51] The Basic Law then secured the independence of judicial power with a protection that exceeded all tradition (Art. 92–101 GG). At the same time, it provided the courts with comprehensive jurisdiction to control public power, and the citizen with the corresponding possibility of appealing to that control (Art. 19, Para. 4, GG). But the authority of the courts was aimed not only at reviewing individual acts by the government or the administration, but also at examining the constitutionality of laws (Art. 93, Para. 1, no. 2; Art. 100, GG). Finally, the citizen was given the option of appealing to the Federal Constitutional Court to protect his basic rights (Art. 93, Para. 1, no. 4a, GG).[52] The final result, then, was a comprehensive jurisdiction of the courts to control the application of the law against the citizens, and to review whether all legal directives were in accord with higher-ranking law, and, in particular, to decide whether laws were constitutional.

---

[49] Of course, the field of labor law seeks to define the role of judicial decisions not as law-making but as the application of the law. See, for example, Richardi (1992, esp. pp. 62–66, 79–81).

[50] Sozialrecht in der Wechselwirkung der Gewalten (1975); Deutscher Sozialgerichtsverband (1979); Deutscher Sozialrechtsverband and G. Wannagat (1984); see also the documentation of court decisions in Maunz and Schraft (1963, 1968); Maunz and Schraft (1969, 1973); more substantial still Wannagat (1979–1988), and Wannagat and Gitter (1989–1998).

[51] Section 35 of the "Verwaltungsgerichtsgesetz für Bayern, Bremen, Hessen, und Wuerttemberg-Baden" of 1946/1947 = Sect. 24 of the "Verordnung Nr. 165 der Britischen Mililtärregierung" of 1948.

[52] Originally on the basis of the authority in Art. 93, Para. 2, GG, via Sect. 90ff. of the "Gesetz über das Bundesverfassungsgericht vom 12. März 1951" BGBl. I, p. 243, but now directly on the basis of the Basic Law (Art. 93, Para. 1, no. 4a, GG, in the version of the "19. Gesetz zur Änderung des Grundgesetzes vom 29. Januar 1969" BGBl. I, p. 97).

The effect of this mechanism was, *first*, to orient the application of legal prescriptions toward the *interest of the citizen*. The courts have no general mandate to supervise the other organs of the state on their own initiative. Leaving aside special exceptions, for example, when constitutional organs can appeal to them, they swing into action only when a plaintiff brings a case. Their essential business is to examine whether the rights of the citizens are protected. In performing that task, the courts are bound by the law (Art. 20, Para. 3; Art. 97, Para. 1, GG). In other words, their charge is to objectively determine the meaning and scope of the law. That also means: to realize the social meaning of the laws, which they are to posit on the basis of the principle of the social state (Köbl 1979, pp. 1040–1045). The interest of the citizen that is brought to bear in the court proceedings is often the interest of the citizen who can defend himself: because he is sufficiently skillful and assertive to bring his concerns before the court, or because the associations that organize his interests are competent and assertive. It is thus *not necessarily the weakest whose interests come to the fore*.

Second, the organization of the judicial jurisdictions reflects in a very peculiar way certain *structures of the social*. The Basic Law spoke from the outset about a regular, administrative, financial, labor, and social jurisdiction (Art. 96, GG, old version), thereby still leaving some question as to whether a joint labor and social jurisdiction should exist and what powers it would combine within itself. The legislator set up the indicated jurisdictions, namely, a *separate labor jurisdiction* and *social jurisdiction*. The initial effect was that *disputes related to labor law* rested with a *special branch of the courts*. This was all the more significant, as labor law, in particular, offered and offers great latitude for the continued development of the law by judicial decisions. The emergence of a special internal culture of labor law thus found an essential carrier in this jurisdiction. The *oversight of the administration*, to the extent that it was not still entrusted to the regular jurisdiction for historical or functional reasons,[53] was distributed among administrative, social, and financial jurisdictions.[54] The financial jurisdiction in all of this is a tax jurisdiction and has essentially nothing to do with specifically social levies – even if the social engineering of tax law time and again challenges also the financial jurisdiction from social perspectives. *Social jurisdiction*, at any rate, *is not* a jurisdiction to which is entrusted the realization of all socially relevant law, and that applies also to all social benefits law (Zacher 1965b, pp. 137–154). Compared to the broad scope of the mandate of the social state, the sphere of jurisdiction of social jurisdiction is narrow. It is the heir to the earlier institutions of legal protection of social insurance and provision for the victims of war (W. Bogs 1979, pp. 3–23). Constitutive for the

[53] That is especially true of restitution law and social compensation law that is not explicitly regulated by statute. In general, see the reports on social law within the decisions of the Federal Constitutional Court in Wannagat (1979–1988) and Wannagat and Gitter (1989–1998).

[54] On this see the reports about social law in the decisions of the Federal Administrative Court and the Federal Finance Court, and about social welfare law, child and youth law, and housing allowance law in Wannagat (1979–1988) and Wannagat and Gitter (1989–1998).

demarcation of its powers is the connection between the legal sphere and the relevant associations, which participate in the jurisdiction above all by virtue of the right to propose honorary judges who enjoy their trust: the unions and employers' associations can do so for the bodies that decide on disputes over social insurance, associations of war victims and similar organizations of the disabled can do so for the bodies that decide on social compensation law, and so on. The political representation of interests by the associations and their administrative participation in implementing the law thus carries over into participation in social jurisdiction (K. Müller 1979, pp. 879–910; Blättel and Fromen 1984, pp. 107–138). Therein lies the analogy to labor jurisdiction. By contrast, administrative jurisdiction is responsible for legal protection where social benefits systems are carried out without comparable associational representation of those affected by them: in the area of social welfare, child and youth services, housing allowance, education and training grants, the equalization of burdens, and so on. Thus, the institutional traditions of the social have a counterpart in the system of jurisdictions.

Third, with all the possibilities for the judicial application, interpretation, and supervision of the law, the *perspective of judges* – their milieu, experience, and interests – took on *outstanding importance* for the legal development of the social. Even if the judge does have the discretion that characterizes the shaping of the law by the legislator, but is bound by the law, one must not overlook the fact that the judicial process of discovery and decision-making does not – and cannot – take place in an atmosphere of objectivity that is independent of the subjects involved. But even more so than this circumstance, the judge's specific legal responsibility determines his contribution to the legal development of the social. Time and again, legal thinking has articulated values and perceived factual situations that are neglected by politics. The result has been the emergence of a far-reaching complementarity between the democratic and the constitutional shaping of the social.

Fourth, the guiding function of the highest federal courts (Art. 95, GG)[55] reinforces the *basic unitary thrust* of the social also from the perspective of judicial decision-making.

Fifth, and finally, the task of all courts, but most definitely of the *Federal Constitutional Court*, to review the constitutionality of laws is of utmost importance. By virtue of this function of the Federal Constitutional Court, *constitutional law* became *crucial* for the shaping of simple law, with a formerly unimagined intensity. In ever new ways, the court has in this way also driven forward, determined, and influenced the shaping of the law (Rüfner 1979–1998; Zacher 1987a, p. 1090).

---

[55] In the version of the "16. Gesetz zur Änderung des Grundgesetzes vom 18. Juni 1968" BGBl. I, p. 657; originally referred to as "Obere Bundesgerichte" (Art. 96, GG, old version).

Principles of the Rechtsstaat – The Legal Subject: The Center of the System – Security, Legal Security

The *Rechtsstaat* realizes itself not only in structures and functions. It realizes itself also in *principles*: in the principle that the citizen has a subjective right to the maintenance of the systems that constitute his personal sphere; in the principle of proportionality, that is to say, that the state's means in the pursuit of its goals are not disproportionate to its ends; in the principle of legal security, that is, in the protection of trust and the guarantee of legal peace; and, finally, in the principle that it makes up for damages it has caused in violation of the law (Art. 34, GG) and provide compensation for the imposition of unequal burdens (Art. 14, Para. 3; Art. 15, Para. 2, GG).

The *precept of subjective entitlement* creates between all law that shapes the sphere of the individual's life and that individual a relationship that gives him the power to call upon and assert the law. According to this precept, an exclusively objective enactment of benefits – a mere "treatment" of those affected – by which an administration would shape the life conditions of an individual, without entering into cooperation with him, and especially into an exchange about the material and legal correctness of the enactment of benefits, is not permissible (Simons 1985). The precept of a *subjective right* had its most spectacular impact on *provision*, which by its history was an objective enactment of benefits – in the final analysis a public regulation of the poor, which kept from the general community the dangers that might emanate from the poverty of the individual person. The transmutation of welfare into social assistance lies largely in the fact that social assistance was now recognized as a subjective right of the individual person to help (Zacher 1981, pp. 547, 679f., 767). In this way, the *Rechtsstaat orients the social* centrally *toward the individual*. This, along with the organization of legal protection, imparts a specific culture to the *Rechtsstaat*, and over time this culture pushes for continuous development. This raises the question, for example, of whether *subjective rights to social benefits* are not also subject to the constitutional conditions that the development of corresponding private rights must also follow. Private rights are an expression of individual disposition and shaping. Are the principles of their regulation not also the given pattern for designing the relationship of the individual to the social *Rechtsstaat*? The most important example of this is the *ownership of entitlements to social benefits*. At least claims to social insurance are acquired through contributions much in the same way as private rights to property values. And so the decisions of the courts – ultimately of the Federal Constitutional Court (Papier 1996, pp. 87–97) – have, over time, seen in social insurance claims, to the extent that they were acquired through personal contributions, property in the sense of Art. 14 of the Basic Law.

It is the principle of *legal security* that has attained the utmost importance – both fundamentally and in everyday life – for the social. If social protection is in any case one of the central building blocks of the social, the *Rechtsstaat*, with legal security, has placed a formal principle alongside this material principle of protection against a breakdown of living conditions: the reliability of the legal system.

We are talking about the limits that are set for the legislator when he alters regulations whose applicability the citizens have already adjusted to. We are talking about the validity of judicial decisions or administrative acts, if the court or the agency subsequently discovers that they were incorrect or at least not the best possible. We are talking about the scope of action that opens up when conditions change and old decisions no longer do them justice. Case law and legislation have developed a very extensive protection against all changes in legal regulations – laws, court decisions, administrative acts, and so on. These principles protect the confidence of those involved if they have already adjusted their lives to the regulations, and were allowed to do so, and when the change in the situation cannot be justified by them. But they also protect the legal peace, which is to be created above all by judicial decisions that were issued on the basis of extensive factual and legal clarification. All of this reduces the flexibility of the social, but it heightens its effect of making the lives of people more secure.

Essential to the shaping of social law, finally, was and is the constitutional principle of the restitution of harm caused in contravention of the law and the compensation for victims, for which the polity or the general public bears a heightened responsibility. The principle at stake here has a long prehistory (Stödter 1933; Schulin 1981): in entitlement to compensation if an individual makes sacrifices for the state or the common good; in compensation for expropriation; in the claim of official liability against the state whose officials have caused harm in contravention of the law; in compensation to victims of war, and so on. In the wake of National Socialism and the Second World War, there emerged problems on a broad front that went far beyond these examples. The result was the quick appearance of a variety of new law. In due course it became clear that the basic principles of compensation and restitution had taken on a new validity also for the society in peacetime – and required a new, differentiating development.

The Basic Rights State

The *Rechtsstaat* of the Federal Republic regards itself emphatically as a constitutional state, a state that subordinates politics to constitutional law. A central expression of this concept is found in the *basic rights and liberties*. They determine the sphere of the human being within the polity. A number of *state constitutions* sought to achieve a substantive binding of politics also through constitutional *programs*. However, given the unitary dynamic of the German federal state, they remained of minor importance. The *Basic Law*, by contrast, refrained from explicit, substantive political programs. It restricted itself to basic rights: to individual and, by way of exception, also collective rights of liberty, equality, process, and status. But precisely the *basic rights* that were adopted into the Basic Law to define and structure the individual sphere and secure societal interactions, were soon and increasingly regarded as the *basic order* not only of the polity, but also of society – as the expression of a system of values, the expression of basic values (Stern 1992, pp. 45–100). The issue was no longer to protect the basic rights from interference by the state and to assert them. Increasingly, these basic rights were understood as directives for the social, and the social was understood as a medium for the self-realization of the basic rights. The basic rights assumed the role of social programs. The principles of the social state (Art. 20, Para. 1; Art. 28, Para. 1, Sent. 1, GG) and the basic rights were drawing close (Neuner 1999). From the perspective of the basic rights, specific demands were made upon the principle of the social state. And the basic rights, conversely, encountered the challenge of the social state principle. Social law, which initially – much like tax law – seemed largely immune to the constitution's assertion of basic rights by virtue of its inherent technical nature, lost this autonomy and was gradually exposed more and more intensively to the claims of the system of basic rights (Papier 1996).

It was inevitable that problems would arise in the process. The law can alter realities only to a limited degree, while one of the expectations invested in the social is precisely that it transforms realities. This finds its most immediate expression in the system of public financing. The grant of social benefits presupposes the disposition over financial means, but those are always in limited supply. All of this means that the recognition as to which problem solution is impermissible in terms of the constitution says nothing definitive about which problem solution is commanded by the constitution. In doubtful cases there are several concepts of constitutionally possible solutions, and a multitude of possible ways to implement them. Making a choice among them cannot be the task of judges, but must be reserved for politics. The *Federal Constitutional Court devised the solution* that the court, under certain conditions, *determines not the invalidity of a contested norm, but only its unconstitutionality*, and that it *enjoins the legislator to remedy this unconstitutionality* within a specific period of time. This solution has accordingly shown itself to be important to the social on many occasions (Kleuker 1993, esp. pp. 182–184). Needless to say, this reconciliation between the mandate of the courts to demand what is constitutionally commanded, and the mandate of politics to choose among several constitutional solutions, has not always led to a positive result in real life. Over time there were more and more cases in which the legislator failed to do the "homework" imposed by the constitutional court. In spite of these caveats, there is no denying that the courts, especially the Federal Constitutional Court, have transported the basic structures that the Basic Law's system of basic rights imparts to private and societal life successfully and meaningfully into case law and into the law-supplementing and law-implementing judicial and administrative practice.

3.3.3 Imbalances in the Social *Rechtsstaat*: The *Rechtsstaat* and the Typology of State Interventions

The *Rechtsstaat* affirms the existing structures of the social. It pervades the social. The principles that determine the structures and functions of the state and the law in the *Rechtsstaat* share tendencies that also determined and determine the gestalt of the social. Their most important expressions are conformity to the law, subjective entitlement, and the judge's final jurisdiction. All of this together imparts to the political will that finds expression in the form of the law the utmost effectiveness, subjects everything that happens to the general norm, orients the application of the latter toward the subjectively entitled individual, and, finally, invests the judicial perspective with the greatest relevance.

This unfolds basic values of the social. But it also affirms the imbalances inherent in it. Social intervention can be understood as legal, economic, service-providing, pedagogical (competency-conveying), and ecological (environment-transforming) intervention (Kaufmann 1982, pp. 49–86). Legal intervention guides, secures, or changes the social conditions through law: through statutes, court decisions, and legal directives issued by the bureaucracy. Economic intervention guides, secures, or changes the allocation of money or monetary goods. Service-related intervention provides or organizes personal services (medical treatment, nursing care, counseling, etc.). Pedagogical intervention conveys individual and collective life skills. Environment-shaping intervention develops the external conditions of life (communication, mobility, housing, recreation, and so on). This is not a system of mutually exclusive manifestations. Rather, we are talking about the dimensions of social effectiveness that pervade and complement one another. All these types of intervention have their own relationship to the Rechtsstaat. And by virtue of this particular relationship to the Rechtsstaat, they also have a different relationship to each other. In the final analysis, this is how the Rechtsstaat substantially shapes the role that the various types of intervention assume in the edifice of the social.

As a result of the specific nature of the *Rechtsstaat*, the *legal intervention* largely dominates also the economic, service-related, pedagogical, and environment-shaping intervention. Furthermore, the relevance of the economic, service-related, pedagogical, and environment-shaping intervention depends largely on how the law can regulate them and bring them to effectiveness. From this vantage point a clear gradient becomes visible. In the form of the levying of taxes and especially the delivery of monetary benefits, *economic intervention* is most readily accessible to legal regulation. But that also means that is exposed to a special degree to the normative claims of the *Rechtsstaat*. *Service-related intervention*, by its very nature, asserts considerable spheres of freedom vis-à-vis legal regulation. That is true of the service providers, whose actions the law can program only to a limited extent. And it is also true of the recipients of services, whose basic rights largely demand consent and participation. Still, a number of professions – especially that of the physician and other medical professionals – have grown into a routine of dense regulation. And it is obvious that this distinguishes their position within the web of social action substantially from the position from those that offer "only" social services. When it comes to competency-conveying *pedagogical intervention*, legal regulation can refer at most to a framework of effectiveness. Finally, *environment-shaping intervention* means a broad array of different conditions – from private and public structures to ecology in the narrower sense. The law cannot lay its hands on this form of intervention in a comprehensive and self-contained way. And specific legal action enters into the most diverse contexts and in the process often loses its social clarity.

These contexts reveal how much the *Rechtsstaat* has contributed to the lopsided characteristics of the social, which have been recognized and described over time as the juridification, economization, monetarization, professionalization, and bureaucratization of the social (Henke 1980, pp. 369–378; Voigt 1980, 1983; Kübler 1984). It became very clear already in connection with the federal state how much these tendencies interact with those of the federal state and democracy: in the direction of the primacy of the formal over the informal, and of the central over the particular. The *Rechsstaat* heightens this disparity.

3.4 The Shaping of the Social by Democracy

3.4.1 The Normative Meaning

The social and democracy[56] have their deepest common roots in the legitimation of political power: as "government by the people" and as "government for the people." From the time of Enlightened Absolutism to the present, the names and substance of "social" and "democracy" have orbited around and substituted for each other. At the same time that the "government by the people" was gaining ground as vision and reality, the new necessity of justifying monarchy led to the beginnings of modern social policy – to a "government for the people." And when the democratic "government by the people" had long since become a diverse reality and it was evident that it was experienced to only a very qualified extent as a "government for the people," the "people's democracies" dispensed with the "formal" justification of a democracy to proclaim themselves fully a "government for the people." However, it is not possible to anticipate normatively what a "government for the people" is. It is not realistic to formulate a "democratic" norm from which the content of a "government for the people" will emerge. "Government for the people" is a product of "government by the people," even if "good" government for the people cannot emerge solely and directly from democratic institutions and processes, but requires the very complication of popular rule that is typical of the constitutional state. The *Rechtsstaat*, in particular, is an important precondition for the "government by the people" becoming a "government for the people."

Still, the notion that the word '*democracy*' is tantamount to a *statement about the content of the social* has become manifest repeatedly: in the concepts of "social democracy" and "economic democracy" (Zacher 1981, pp. 329–338; Zacher 1987a, p. 1098f.; Spieker 1986, pp. 157–221). Their thrust is in part toward extending democratic structures into society (Hartwich 1970, pp. 54–60, 344–351), in part toward implanting into the democratic system a "priority of power" for the socially disadvantaged (esp. unions: Ridder 1975), in part toward combining these two. To the extent that these concepts call for a "democratizing" change of society, their limits are set by the *Rechtsstaat*'s guarantee of a free society. To the extent that these concepts are aimed at shifts within the democratic system, they advance the

[56] Böckenförde (1987, pp. 887–952); Badura (1987, pp. 953–986); Maihofer (1994, pp. 427–536). On the relationship between democracy and the social see especially Zacher (1981, pp. 315–395) and (1987a, pp. 1096–1101).

value of group-based interests. And that ends up in contradiction not only to egalitarian democracy, but also to the openness of the social itself. *Democracy must prove itself as the state form of the smallest minority neglected over a sustained period of time* (Zacher 1968b, p. 30). This would not be made easier but more difficult by the special status of social groups – also and particularly with a view toward the social.

On the other side, the *legitimation of government through what it means 'for the people'* is basic. Human beings want both: to govern themselves, and to have government work to their benefit. If a democracy fails in a deep and sustained way to be the "government for the people," this circumstance may delegitimize it. But political success which the people experience as a benefit and as prosperity affirms the legitimation also of "formal" democracy. In this way, the *basic social norm enters into the legitimation of democracy.* The basic social norm is an essential yardstick for what the people regard as "for them." Thus, the fulfillment and failure of the basic social norm are criteria that contribute to determining the legitimacy of the constitutional order – not in the sense of positive, operational rules, but certainly as elements of the potential that can overcome crises of legitimacy or lead to catastrophe.

3.4.2 The Institutional Meaning of Democracy for the Social

The social requires the constant concretization through politics. Thanks to the openness of the social, politics has broad normative leeway. Its mandate is to convert the openness into the social here and now. In this regard, *politics* has something like a *power of definition.* In the extreme case, the definition of the social through politics can occur when concrete solutions are regarded *as the social per se*. This can be observed when certain solutions were and are determinative over a long period of time. And it is even more true, the more interests are tied to these solutions. The large branches of social insurance – sickness insurance and pension insurance – are disparate though good examples of this. In general, however, the power of definition is not exercised through the "canonization" of a particular solution, but through the *concrete narrowing of the scope of the discussion.* The major players in the competition over a political solution do not sound out what the openness of the social will yield. Instead, they tacitly circumscribe the scope of this openness. They articulate only what seems desirable or at least acceptable to their ideas and interests – and that means above all: to the ideas and interests of their clients. Depending on the assertiveness of the political and societal forces that are involved, broad swathes of what is socially possible are expunged from the framework of discussion. Taboos on ideas can form.

The Stuff of the Social and of Democracy

Within society, the search for the social takes place in the midst of an infinite number of competing demands – defined in personal or situational terms – *against* a socially "worse scenario" and *for* a socially "better scenario." The ensemble of these demands – in terms of both their selection and priority ranking – changes from group to group, in fact from subject to subject. It changes depending on the experience and articulation of the threat of something socially "worse" and the possibility of something socially "better." In the process, the comparison can refer to worse-better or better-worse relations that are individual or group-related, feared or hoped for. They can be articulated as past, present, or future better-worse or worse-better relations, or as a relationship between persons, groups, and situations (interpersonal/intercollective/intersituational comparison). They can also be formed non-contemporaneously over the course of a development (intertemporal comparison): as between "middle age" and old age, or between times of good health and times of illness.

Though this play of possibilities may seem infinite as a whole, each ensemble is in fact formed according to a common principle: *the basic assumption of a social normality*. This social normality has an orientational function: *against* subnormality, *for* access to normality, improvement *in the* normality, continuation *within the* normality, and *elevation of the* normality. But this social normality is relative. There is nothing absolute about it. The loci of where normality can be situated are inexhaustible. There is not *a normality*, only *normalities*. Normalities are not to be equated with a real level – say, a level of income, a basket of commodities, or the like. The level of a normality is open. Equally open is the diversity of ensembles of social valuation, expectation, and demands that individuals and groups arrange around a normality. In theory, every individual and every group could "invent" their normality that they would use to legitimate its claims to improvement or protection. Of course, an approach is practically meaningful only if it has a chance of being shared or at least accepted by others. But the decision of what is capable of attracting a consensus or a coalition also does not depend on an objective measure of need or prosperity – and that is the observation I am driving at here. That was not always so: not in the early stages of the "social question" and not in the early stages of democracy. Want and prosperity were still naturally evident. But over time, the quality of the social became generalized and available. More and more circles of society have learned to present *their* "social" ensemble, to assert *their* better-worse relation. In the competition of "social questions" they have learned to formulate *their* "social question." They have learned this because democracy derives the political chances of an interest largely from the quantitative givens of potential aggregation. Substantive, qualitative criteria are elementary conditions of quantitative aggregation. In the end, though, the effectiveness of the qualitative argument depends on how many votes invest it with what kind of significance. *In this way, the social and democracy have grown close to each other over time.*[57] More and more voters are using elections to make decisions not only about the social conditions of their society, but also about their own social interests.

[57] See the fitting title "Wohlfahrtsstaat und Massenloyalität" (Narr and Offe 1975).

The diversity of normalities, their level and the ensembles of valuation, expectation, and demands related to them, arises above all through *the course of history*. Social conditions change. Their experience changes. The ideas from which perceptions of problems and solutions are borne change. And the political constellations that bundle them into political programs change, as well. Social intervention itself continually alters the world of social normalities and of social valuations related to them. The social challenges lead to socio-political answers. Each socio-political answer, however, changes the world of social challenges. It is a fundamental experience of social policy that every solution to a social problem brings to light a multitude of new problems. Social injustices that were not perceived but endured as long as starker social injustices were in the foreground are no longer tolerated, or perceived in the first place, after those bigger problems have been solved. Moreover: social intervention replaces largely "natural" conditions and processes with "artificial" ones, and these require constant support and correction. The social therefore exists in a permanent process. The openness of the social is joined by the process-character of the social (Zacher 1978). Therein lies another essential communality between democracy and the social. *Democracy* is a *process*. The *social* is a *process*. And *both processes feed and drive each other forward.*

The Structures and Processes of Democracy – The Rule of the Middle Voter – The Temporal Pulse of Democracy

The mechanism by which the stuff of the social is continuously "shaken up" and newly solidified is generated by the institutions and processes of state democracy. It is dominated by universal and equal suffrage, by the central – especially legislative – decision-making function of parliament, and by the government's function of selection and integration. Historically, the victory of the universal and equal *right to vote* was an important step forward also for the assertion of social concerns. To this day, the universal and equal suffrage is an important instrument for asserting the interests that are given within society. Nevertheless, this suffrage as such is not a guarantee of the social. On the contrary: the social has become relativized in the degree to which the right to vote has become universal and its exercise permanent. Although there may be absolute ideas of the social, ideas about correct equality, correct justice, solidarity, participation, and so on, but what politics makes real as "social" is primarily a function of the democratic conditions.

In reality, what prevails under the rule of universal and equal suffrage are those opinions and interests that can be picked up and bundled by parties in a way that will allow them to become the programs of parliamentary and governing majorities. However, the degree to which an opinion or interest is capable of attracting a majority does not rise or fall with the degree of an "objective" social urgency of this particular opinion or that interest. Not infrequently the opposite is the case. By contrast, the "swing voter" in the middle of the electoral spectrum is most capable of attracting a coalition and thus represents the greatest potential for political consideration (Kort-Krieger 1994). The "marginal voter" on the verge of the electoral spectrum generally has the least assertive power. Now, the middle of the electoral spectrum and a dense field of concrete social "normalities" coincide with a certain probability, just as the "lower" band of the electoral spectrum coincides with social subnormality. Thus, behind the clearest and most urgent social tasks, the fight against want and help in cases of poverty, there usually stands less political force than behind the position battles around the "normalities" and behind the expectation of another life in normality. Of course, in the middle of the electoral spectrum there are also opinions and interests that cannot be brought to bear in political coalition-building processes. Likewise, at the margins of the electoral spectrum there are interests that are so obviously pressing or can be articulated in such an alarming way that the "middle voter," too, wants to see them addressed – and that they enter into his sense of responsibility, his interests, and possibly also into his fears. But the principled imbalance between social urgency and the democratic power of assertion remains.

Overall, then, egalitarian parliamentary democracy has the tendency *to shift the social toward the societal center*, to develop the social positions of the "middle voters," and to make their social issues the general criterion of social challenges. In the practice of the Federal Republic, this means above all that performance justice and ownership justice play a special role. It means that horizontal solidarity became more important than vertical solidarity. It means that the industrial-economic inclusion, as expressed in the systems of social provision, attracts the most acceptance and energy, while the political force of the elementary national inclusion, as reflected in the guarantee of the subsistence minimum, was always distinguished from it. The sensitivity to the subsidiarity of state intervention relative to the own productive energy of the person to be protected weakened. Instead, the aspect of the protection of the relative social status gained in importance. Increasing freedom was a central goal. But the risks of freedom were to be cushioned or at least moderated by systems of social protection.

Egalitarian *parliamentary democracy* influenced the social in a very different way through its *temporal pulse* (Zacher 1984a, p. 4f., pp. 10–12). Democracy is the rule of time. Democratic power must be periodically wrested from the voters. This is done by triggering positive expectations – in terms of effective campaigning: by promising advantages that can be perceived by groups. If we return to the picture of social normality and the better-worse relation connected to it, it means that from one election to the next new standards of normality are postulated, a different selection of better-worse relations is highlighted, and different expectations and demands are connected to them. The time horizon of election periods becomes the articulation and maneuvering room of social policy. Problems are picked up at the time of an election depending on the degree to which they are perceptible. Solutions are selected and designed in such a way that they provide the clientele on which the governing majority depends more advantages than disadvantages during the legislative period and/or that they promise more advantages than disadvantages at the time of the election. The consequences for the time after are given less consideration, the more they lie in the future. The temporal pulse of parliamentary democracy favors the short-term and momentary interests and harms the long-term and future concerns. The more urgently social problems are in need of long-term solutions, the more they suffer from the brevity of the temporal horizon. Pension insurance became the most striking example of this in the 1990s. At the time, the temporal pulse was gradually shortened because politics on the federal level became increasingly interested in state elections (*Landtagswahlen*), which meant that current voter reactions were able to overshadow ever more strongly the responsibility for long-term solutions.

3.4.3 Democracy and Societal Forces

What value concepts and interests prevail within democracy (von Winter 1995), especially which value concepts and interests enter into a governing majority's catalog of goals, depends on a complex web of interrelationships and contexts. They include the *voters* – their guiding ideas, their experiences, their expectations, and their fears. They include the *associations*, which in their own way bundle and articulate value concepts and interests. They include the *media*, which convey and shape public opinion. And they include not least the political *parties*, which – as intended by the constitution (Art. 21, GG) – spell out value concepts and interests in the transitional realm between society and political institutions, but which also pick them up and carry them into politics in what are for the most part ensembles capable of change. Lastly, they include *political leadership personalities*, who, even if they are tied into the parties, can in turn develop guiding images, respond to moods within society, and have a substantial part in determining which "normalities," which ensembles of problems and solutions, and which priority of value concepts and interests they wish to represent and realize together with their party. How this web reflects the problems of the social, addresses the social, articulates social problems, and assesses social solutions follows only a few sweeping laws.

The most important thing is that *politics pays attention to the perceptibility, effectiveness, and reliability of reactions* from the voters and to the forces that guide and reflect them. Value concepts and interests whose observance is rewarded by a discernible number of voters (presumably also after a longer period of time), or whose non-observance is punished by a discernible number of voters (presumably also after a longer period of time), have a good chance of being picked up by politics. Politics pays attention to which political moves and decisions trigger reactions that are discernible, estimable in numerical terms, and effective until the next election – by either attracting or repelling voters. This is the basis for the high priority that the improvement (or, alternatively, non-worsening) of statutory social cash benefit systems enjoys within politics. Affected individuals themselves can calculate their advantage (or disadvantage). Benefit recipients show predictably positive (or negative) reactions. Their numbers can be roughly estimated. This also explains, conversely, the democratic weakness of the care-providing sector. Politicians and the public presume, not without reason, that those who pursue a care-providing profession are shaped less by a concern for their own advantage and more by their compassionate engagement. Changes for the better – but also changes for the worse – in working conditions are less reliably transformed into political reactions by this group of individuals than is the case with other groups. The carriers who organize care carry no weight in electoral numbers. Individuals receiving care are themselves differentially "reactive" for a great many reasons. The more intensively and acutely they depend on care, the less their reaction needs to – in fact, can – be taken into consideration. And their family members, where they exist, hold opinions about the conditions and potential changes that are too diverse to be taken into account significantly as a politically effective clientele. The drastic result was the protracted *Pflegenotstand* (shortage of care providers) that was already diagnosed back in the 1960s. Eventually, however, too many interests were pushing for a change. Long-term care insurance was introduced. But the old contexts revealed themselves again in many ways. The *disparities of legal, economic, service-related, pedagogical, and environment-shaping intervention* find another explanation in these laws of democracy.

If voters, associations, parties, and politicians essentially fit into this explanatory model, that is not true for the *media*. The media have their own laws by which they articulate social problems and assess social solutions. And they have their respective laws for how they address the relationship between the parties and politicians, as well as the associations and the social problems and social solutions. Those laws include the market interests of the media and the journalists, which have a very vague influence on the selection and presentation of social problems and solutions, and on the evaluation of social policy. But they also include the self-perception: that of the institutions and of the individual journalists. Market interest and self-perception, in turn, can respond to socio-political challenges only in the way that one's own understanding and experience, value concepts and interests, allow or even command. The result is that the media process the social differently from associations, parties, and politicians. On the whole, the media probably represent a fairly aleatory corrective to the interplay between the public and politics that would otherwise take place.

Associations – Basic Pattern of Their Effectiveness

Associations are an equally central and multi-faceted phenomenon within the structure of social democracy (Grimm 1994, pp. 657–673). However, during the period under examination here, the role of associations within social democracy has undergone a *dual paradigm shift*. A *general paradigm shift* led from the *Verbändestaat* (association state) of the first decades (Kaiser 1987, pp. 149–170), by way of the differentiation, concentration, and intensification of the cooperation between state and associations, which is referred to as *"corporatism"* (Reutter 1991), to a regime of an increasingly differentiated, increasingly expansive opening of the state to societal entities (also businesses) and institutions carried by both the state and society (e.g. social insurance carriers). That regime is described only inadequately with labels such as *"negotiation democracy,"*, *"socialization of the state"*, *"privatization of the polity"*, and many others (Czada and Schmidt 1993; Mayntz and Scharpf 1995; Mayntz 1997). The *second paradigm shift* is *specific in nature*. It concerns the *"world of work"*: the interaction of dependent workers and employees with their "employers" in work-place, enterprise, and supra-enterprise contexts – in associational terms the interplay of unions with employers' associations, but also with entrepreneurs and business associations. This interplay began in a world in which the factors labor and capital saw themselves as self-evidently and inseparably dependent on each other, in the business as well as national context. Moreover, it began in a world in which the conditions for the effectiveness of the factors labor and capital seemed essentially firmly in place. This accorded with the notion of *"social partnership"*, which – with many transformations – dominated the world of work for decades. By now, technological and economic developments, as well as all the changes labeled "globalization" *have completely redefined the situation of labor and capital – each individually, in relationship to each, and in their relationship to the nation state*. It is too soon to tell what new order will emerge from this for the associations, their relationship to their "base", and for their relationship to the state. But it is quite clear that the old order is losing power.

The basic patterns that shaped the "association democracy" for the longest time were not abolished by these developments. Rather, they have been integrated into this change. Associations bundle the opinions and interests of the citizens, their groups, and possibly also their institutions. Associations can amplify the interests of the citizens and enhance their capacity for asserting themselves. But in doing so they must set priorities and form ensembles, and thereby always neglect or exclude some of the incorporated interests. Associations can mediatize politics. To the extent that politics places value on – or must place value on – acting in consort with the associations involved (or certain associations below them), there is inserted between the two poles of the "base" (voters, society, media, public opinion) and the "state" (parliament, government) an intermediate level on which politics and associations, but also the bureaucracy and associations, strike deals with each other. A level on which the state may no longer be able to act without having secured the consent or acquiescence of the relevant associations, but a level, also, on which associations are obligated to participate in legitimizing and implementing the solutions that were arrived at with their agreement or acquiescence. The element of the associations influences the functioning of democracy in a multitude of ways. *Organized interests* enter into politics largely *in keeping with the directives of this organization*: substantively, as formulated by the organization; tactically, as directed by the coalitions that are possible and are entered into between the organization and the political forces. This can substantially alter the allocation of the social "subject matter" to the spectrum of parliamentary party politics. But associational representation also creates *continuity*. It is not subject to the temporal pulse of parliamentary democracy; it can become its memory.

This encounter between democracy and associations becomes particularly dense where the influence of associations flows into *intermediary institutions* to which the state entrusts public tasks. The most important examples are the social insurance carriers (Nullmeier and Rüb 1993). Several "layers" of associational influence are here superimposed. First: the influence of unions, employers, and other voter groups of "social elections" on the insurance carrier, its work, its personnel, and especially its politics vis-à-vis the state. Second: the shared influence that the associations involved in self-governance can exert together with the management of the carrier on society, the state, and partner institutions. Third: the influence of the associations formed by the carriers. And the joint associations are generally able to exert considerable influence on the democracy.

Whom do the *associations organize* and represent? To begin with, there are associations formed by those who have and assert *shared interests*. Front and center in the social area are the associations which very specifically become the organizational home of *individuals who demand social protection*, expect and receive benefits, and so on. But there is also a wide variety of groups whose *interests are affected by the social in other ways*: as employers, as the providers of benefits, and so on. Of particular importance to the social area are also *associations that organize social activities or the carriers of social activities*: initiatives and their associations, charitable associations, churches, associations of social insurance carriers, and, finally, the Councils of Municipalities (*Gemeindetage*), German County Associations (*Landkreistage*), and the Association of German Cities and Towns (*Städtetag*) as the organizations of municipal and communal benefits carriers. They, especially, have a multiple role: to perform their tasks, to advocate on behalf of these tasks before the public and in the political arena and to work together with politicians, and, finally, to speak for the individuals who are their clients. This highlights a very essential mandate of the associations: to act as advocates, not only as the collective, self-interested advocates for all special interest associations, but also as *altruistic advocates* on behalf of those who are unable to organize their own interests or only with difficulty: the poor, the unemployed, children, those with severe care needs, and the mentally handicapped.

"Social Partnership" and "Social Self-government" of Dependent Work

The most far-reaching example that deeply marked the history of the German social state is the development of the working society into *the* home of the social. After the question of the poor, the nineteenth century recognized – and with even greater political intensity – the *workers' question as the social question*. With that, dependent work moved permanently into the center of social care. At the same time, dependent work proved itself an interest that was maximally open to being organized. Unions became a successful driving force for advancing social concern for dependent work. Parallel to this it became evident that the concerns of employers were also open to organization. This constellation initially created a system of conflict, but in due course also a system of cooperation, of joint regulation, and the cooperative administration of shared institutions.[58] Another feature of the development was that the interest of dependent work in politics was represented early on, but that it was at no time dependent on a single "workers' party", but found

[58] von Nell-Breuning (1964, pp. 216–223); Weddigen (1956, p. 557f.; 560f.); Sanmann (1977, pp. 52–59); Wulfhorst (1987); Külp (1989).

support also within other parties. Still, it remained characteristic that the special closeness of one party to the interests of dependent labor stimulated the competition among parties and the voters who backed them. The gradual result was that the concerns of dependent labor had to and were able to develop within a sphere whose reach was very deep: in factories and businesses, where employers encountered their employees and their union representatives; in the encounter between unions and employers' associations within the framework of the right to free collective bargaining; in the participation of the unions and employers' associations in institutions of social protection and the social security of the employed (from labor courts to social insurance); in the participation of unions and employers' associations in institutions devoted to administrative and political consultation and the search for solutions; and, finally, in the influence exerted by unions and employers' associations on politics – at times jointly, but for the most part in conflict and as rivals. These circumstances led to a substantial improvement in the conditions of dependent workers. The circumstances of real-life effectiveness benefited from technological and civilizational progress. The social integration into the working relationship was continuously improved through regulations pertaining to protection, equality, freedom, and security. Thanks to works constitutions and codetermination it was expanded through participation in the workplace and the company, and through the unions the participation in society and politics was differentiated and broadened. Within the framework of the right to free collective bargaining, the meaning element of earning was developed further. The capacities for satisfying basic needs and providing support that were connected to earning were extended further and further through the institutions of social protection, beyond the simultaneity of work and compensation.

The *unions* have always constituted the *core* of the institutional structure in which the concerns of dependent labor experienced this development (Briefs 1965, pp. 545–561; Wagenführ 1965, pp. 562–566; Beier 1981, pp. 641–659; Kleinhenz 1981, pp. 659–670; Mintzel and von Nell-Breuning 1986, pp. 1035–1050). They are the institutional representatives of the classic social claim that emerged with the workers' question and over time has repeatedly taken on new topicality. To that extent, the parity between the employers' associations (Herrmann 1956, pp. 285–291; Spiegelhalter 1985, pp. 235–238) and the unions is always an unbalanced one. The employers' associations do not represent an interest of comparable historical dignity and human immediacy. Moreover, they do not represent an interest that is enshrined in the fate of or shared by a comparably large number of individuals as the interest represented by the unions. Employers' associations do not represent an interest that equals the democratic electoral weight of workers. Finally, they do not represent an interest that can assert itself in a conflict with as much force as workers are able to do by virtue of the strike. As a result, the temptation of giving expression to this imbalance with the relevant legal recognition of union power was always strong. However, that would have called the cooperative system into question and, especially, delegitimized the shared autonomy of the social partners. The legal system of the Federal Republic thus maintained the concept of partnership: through the parity structure of free collective bargaining and the basically equal structure of the right to take collective action, through the essentially equal system of participation by the unions and employers' associations in the self-governance of social insurance, advice to the political realm, and so on, and above all also through the prohibition against the political strike (Scholz 1989, esp., pp. 1135–1146). Nevertheless, the disproportionate and system-transcending potential of the unions was, in some imponderable way, important for the development of dependent labor (Zacher 1977b). In this way, the organization of workers into unions, the corresponding organization of employers, and the interaction between the organized individuals and their organizations and the universal, egalitarian-parliamentary system have imparted a particular shape to both democracy and the social.

In the 1990s, the transformation of the world of work and the internationalization of capital called into question the labor and economic paradigm underlying these developments. It is still too early to tell what conditions will emerge from this. But the traditional edifice of unions, employers' associations, free collective bargaining, social partnership, and "social self-governance" is already showing a multitude of changes – and the same is accordingly true of the relationship between unions, employers' associations, and the state, especially also between unions, employers' associations, and democracy.

Areas of Weaker Organization

Other areas of the social are in distinct contrast to dependent labor, especially other systems of social benefits that lack, on the one hand, a corresponding organization of the interests concerned, and, on the other hand, specialized political and administrative structures. With that they also lack the interplay between the organization of interests and the political-administrative structures that is so characteristic of the concerns of the workers and their union representation. The most striking phenomenon is no doubt the area of *welfare/social assistance and youth welfare/child and youth services*. It provides an example of how the functions and structures of the concrete areas are interconnected with the institutional shaping of the social. Welfare/public assistance is rooted in the guarantee of a subsistence minimum, and from there it has increasingly developed over time into a system that also conveys an appropriate participation in the living conditions of society – that is, it has developed into the institutional space of "more equality". Youth welfare/child and youth services have undergone a similar evolution, though they are probably characterized by an even more complex connection between the concern for a subsistence minimum and the concern for "more equality" of life chances for children and young people. From this vantage point alone, it is understandable why the democratic conditions of these benefit areas are so substantially different from social insurance, which is oriented toward the interests of workers and their participation in the world of work and the economy. Poverty has always been an interest that is not very amenable to organization. In particular, the mere subsistence minimum is not an efficient common denominator around which the groups of interested individuals can constitute themselves effectively. Added to this is the inherent multiplicity of life situations into which social assistance is supposed to convey an elementary participation in society's living conditions. For the area of youth welfare/child and youth services, the weakness in its ability to be organized has analogous reasons. Added in this case is that the interests of children and youths, on the one hand, and the interests of parents and other legal guardians, on the other, can both coincide as well as conflict in exceedingly complex ways. The concrete substance of the benefits also determines the contrasting capacity for organization. Social insurance, for example, provides essentially legally regulated, calculable monetary benefits and correspondingly regulated, professional services. By contrast, for welfare/public assistance and youth welfare/child and youth services, the law is essentially only a framework that needs to be filled in by the organization and concretization of services and material benefits. Monetary benefits play a role only in welfare/public assistance, without attaining the calculability of social insurance benefits. The social services of these branches have a different professionalism than the professionalism of medical services, for example, which is characteristic of social insurance. "Social" professionalism is personal in nature and situationally open. "Socially non-specific" professionalism – such as medical professionalism – has a coherence that is borne by regulations, "guild-like" in terms of personnel, and institutionally supported. Moreover, to a degree very different from social insurance, welfare, public assistance, and youth welfare/child and youth services constitute also a pedagogical and environment-shaping intervention. Lastly, the realization of tasks of welfare/public assistance and youth welfare/child and youth services is divided up in a specific way: between the polity and societal forces. The polity acts fundamentally in the form of the communities (especially the *Landkreise* (counties) and independent cities, but also through "simple" municipalities and through higher-order territorial entities) (Schellhorn 1997, p. 679). Societal forces group themselves essentially into charitable associations (Diakonisches Werk, Caritas, Workers' Welfare, and so on) (Deufel 1986, pp. 687–694; Dörrie 1997, pp. 350–353). In the process there are once again considerable differences between the communities and the charitable associations. For the communities, social services are one task among many. On the other hand, communities, since they represent the polity, have a more general mandate than charitable organizations. For the latter, by contrast, the realization of social services is *their* particular purpose. Accordingly, their mandate is necessarily specific. Nevertheless, the charitable and communal carriers are the most effective representation of the interests associated with "their" areas of benefits and services: the interests of those who need and/or receive benefits; the interests of those who (as social workers and the like) provide the services; the interests of the carriers of these services – in other words, a very broad and in itself also contradictory spectrum of interests.

Associations display their effectiveness also in *many other areas* of the social: for example, *consumer associations* to optimize the meeting of needs; *renters' associations* to represent the concerns of tenants vis-à-vis the political realm as well as vis-à-vis the landlords; *family associations* as well as specific interest organizations in the area of families (parents' associations, associations of single parents, associations of those liable for maintenance, and so on) in order to influence family policies, and so on. But how effectively can these interests be organized? At any rate, what is lacking is the specific connection between the organization of interests, the organization of social regulation, and the organization of social benefits and services, such as exists in the area of dependent work, social insurance, indeed, even welfare/social assistance and youth welfare/child and youth services.

3.4.4 Spheres of Autonomy – Normatively Bound *Eigengesetzlichkeit* (Specific Intrinsic Laws) – Technocratic Structures

Autonomy

The phenomenon of autonomy overlaps with the phenomenon of associations. Autonomy services the *Eigengesetzlichkeit* of a matter – the unfolding of its specific rationality, the expertise of those especially competent in it. And it serves the collective self-realization of those specifically affected by this matter, those interested in it. In the process, the matter or the personal aspect may dominate. The autonomy I am talking about here constitutes a sphere of the public. Private freedom is another topic. To regulate autonomy, the legal system provides a broad array of forms: those of public law (corporations, institutes, foundations) and those of private law (associations and societies, but also foundations once again).

In the Federal Republic, *autonomy* became an important model for organizing the public sphere. That has positive reasons: precisely the self-realization of a matter or a plurality of people. And it has – and this is not intended as a value judgment – negative reasons. With autonomy, the matter and/or the formation of will on the part of those affected and interested become dissociated from the force fields and processes of the general state democracy. This can go hand in hand with an intensification of democracy among those affected and interested. But this compensation of the loss of "large democracy" through a gain in "small democracy" is not always the case and not always necessary. The self-realization of a matter at a remove from democracy can be more important. The other negative reason concerns the federal system. The division of all statehood between the federal level and the states leads, where a specific matter or a specific group of persons is concerned, at times to suboptimal processes and outcomes. Structures of autonomy can be helpful here if they overarch the boundaries between the federal government and the states.[59] An outstanding historical example is the introduction of social insurance during the Bismarck period. Its structures of self-governance avoided conflicts with the administrative jurisdictions of the states in the same way that the financing from contributions avoided a conflict with the financial system of the federal state.

[59] A very significant field of autonomous organization is scholarship and science. Autonomy combines the freedom of research and teaching with structures that span the states. Meusel (1999).

Social insurance rests on the principle of autonomy already as a result of this history (Selbstverwaltung in der Sozialversicherung 1991). *Externalizing provision* is fundamentally a matter that requires autonomous self-assertion. Private insurance, vocational insurance arrangements, the supplementary pension agency of the federal government and the states (*Zusatzversorgungsanstalt des Bundes und der Länder*), are examples of this. In the case of social insurance, however, there is the added necessity of giving expression to the community of solidarity. The autonomy of social insurance[60] is shaped by its mixed character: that social insurance is precisely that insurance, but also an institution of social policy. Thus the competencies of the state and the self-administration, the normative directives of the legislator and the financial obligations, burdens, and maneuvering room are distributed very differently from one branch of the insurance to the next – and not always in an unimpeachable way. Incidentally, over time the Associations of Social Insurance Carriers (Hein 1990) became increasingly important for the federal, democratic, *and* social relevance of the autonomy of social insurance.

A historically even older field of autonomy is *welfare/public assistance* and *youth welfare/child and youth services*. These emerged out of the statutory tasks of the communities and associations of communities, as well as the charitable civic engagement of citizens and societal carriers. It is precisely these two autonomous currents that characterize it to this day: the public-law autonomy of the communities and the societal-private law autonomy of the "charitable carriers" (leaving aside the special status of the churches). Incidentally, for these social areas, as well, the overarching structures – the governmental oversight of the states, the self-organization of the communities into Councils of Municipalities (*Gemeindetage*) and so on, associations of "charitable carriers," and the comprehensive cooperation of all those involved in the German Association for Public and Private Welfare (*Deutscher Verein für öffentliche und private Fürsorge*) – are of essential importance. If we add the various levels on which effects are felt, we arrive at a highly

[60] Only the *corporation* (*Körperschaft*] does unqualified justice to the denominator of a personal association (the insured, their employers, and so on). However, institutes and foundations are also suited to coordinating and representing particular collective interests. Significant for the reciprocal openness of the forms is the legislator's rather careless use of language especially in the social sphere: it has always assigned sickness insurances to the *Kassen* (funds] with an obvious corporate structure, accident insurance to the *Berufsgenossenschaften* (professional associations], and pension insurance to *Landesversicherungsanstalten* (state insurance agencies] and the *Reichs-/Bundesversicherungsanstalt* (Reich and Federal Insurance Agency]. Still today, the legislator speaks of all social insurance carriers as "legal corporations of public law with self-administration" (Sect. 29, Para. 1, SGB VI), which includes also the *Landesversicherungsanstalten*, the *Bahnversicherungsanstalt*, the *Seekasse*, the *Bundesversicherungsanstalt für Angestellte*, and the *Bundesknappschaft* (Sect. 125, SGB IV). Or see the terminologically bold text of Sect. 367, Sent. 1, SGB III: "Carrier of the promotion of labor is the *Bundesanstalt für Arbeit* as the legally responsible *Körperschaft* of public law directly under the federal government and with self-administration (*Bundesanstalt*)". See Bundesministerium für Arbeit und Soziales and Bundesarchiv (eds.), (2001b–2008a): Geschichte der Sozialpolitik in Deutschland, vols. 2–7, Chap. 3, no. 4.

differentiated, dense web that fills its own sphere of autonomy. However, the social tasks and possibilities of the *communities* go far beyond the working areas of welfare/public assistance and youth welfare/child and youth services (Schräder 1957, pp. 265–282; Pitschas 1996a, pp. 1257–1305). By virtue of their jurisdiction for "all matters relating to the local community" (Art. 28, Para. 2, Sent. 1, GG), they are in charge of a broad spectrum of social themes. That holds especially for the fields of activity where *Daseinsvorsorge* and the social interact.[61] Thanks to its broad and substantial competencies, the *autonomy of local communities* is a *basic pillar* of the social state. The fact that communal social policy *nevertheless attracts relatively little attention* is a symptom that is notable in various ways.

Expertise and Politics

A particular direction is assumed by the tendency to develop the intrinsic laws of a matter also within and against democracy where scientific and other professional expertise is introduced into politics (Brohm 1987, pp. 207–248). To that extent, organizational autonomy is more rare. For the most part, specific structures are created to reconcile the objective autonomy of expertise with the overarching and self-responsibility of politics. In this sense, the *social sphere* is characterized *rather by restraint*. Politics favors advice on a case-by-case basis, as evidenced by a multitude of ad-hoc expert commissions.[62] *Formalized procedures*, however, are the exception. One example in that direction is the *Bundesjugendbericht* (Federal Child and Youth Report), which the federal government has to submit to the German *Bundestag* and the *Bundesrat* once in each legislative session (Sect. 84, SGB VIII). The federal government must entrust its preparation to a commission composed of up to seven experts. The federal government must respond to the report. Other solutions are more complicated. In the *health care sector*, "those involved in providing health care to the population jointly develop, with the goal of adequate care for the insured and a balanced distribution of burdens,. . . medical and economic orientation data and. . . proposals for boosting performance, effectiveness, and efficiency in the health care sector and coordinate them (*concerted action in the health care sector*)" (Sect. 141, SGB V). To support this concerted action, the Federal Minister of Labour and Social Order in 1985 appointed an *Expert Commission*.[63] It usually issues annual reports, at the request of the Minister also special

[61] Bundesministerium für Arbeit und Soziales and Bundesarchiv (eds.), (2001b–2008a): Geschichte der Sozialpolitik in Deutschland seit 1945, vols. 2–7 and 11, Chap. 3, no. 14 in each.

[62] Examples of published reports of such commissions in Frerich and Frey (1996, p. 732f.).

[63] "Erlaß über die Errichtung eines Sachverständigenrates für die Konzertierte Aktion im Gesundheitswesen beim Bundesminister für Arbeit und Sozialordnung vom 12. Dezember 1985" printed in: Sachverständigenrat für die Konzertierte Aktion im Gesundheitswesen: Vorschläge für die Konzertierte Aktion im Gesundheitswesen. Jahresgutachten 1987: Medizinische und ökonomische Orientierung (Baden-Baden, 1987, p. 157f.). The jurisdiction over the Advisory Council has now passed to the Federal Minister of Health (Sect. 142, Para. 2, SGB V).

reports. These reports are made public. The setup allows for the results of the work of the experts to become publicly visible and effective. Within a different constellation is the expertise in the *Sozialbeirat der Rentenversicherung* (Social Advisory Committee of Pension Insurance).[64] The federal government's Pension Insurance Report and the Report of the Social Advisory Committee are to complement each other in providing factual information to the legislative bodies of the federal government and thus also to the public about the development of pension insurance. However, the Social Advisory Council includes not only experts, but also representatives of special interest groups: four representatives of the insured, four representatives of employers, one representative from the *Deutsche Bundesbank*, and three economists and sociologists.

Economic policy – and thus the manner in which the state's social responsibility for the economy is exercised – has incorporated *expertise* on a considerable scale. Already before the currency reform and the embrace of the free market in 1948, the Academic Advisory Board (*Wissenschaftlicher Beirat*) was set up with the Administration for Economics (Bundesministerium für Wirtschaft 1964, 1973, 1998). Since 1949, it has accompanied the economic *Ordnungspolitik* within the Federal Ministry of Economics. From the beginning, the monetary preconditions for a free market economy in the Combined Economic Area and then the Federal Republic were entrusted to an *independent central bank*: first to the *Bank deutscher Länder*, from 1957 to the *Deutsche Bundesbank*. The autonomy of the *Bundesbank*, bound to norms and carried by professional competence, was juxtaposed to the federal government in a carefully differentiated system of political responsibility.[65] In 1980 another independent element was built into the system of *promoting competition*: the *Monopolies Commission*.[66] A crucial additional step in the participation of independent expertise in economic policy was the establishment, already in 1963, of the *Council of Economic Experts* (*Sachverständigenrat zur Begutachtung der gesamtwirtschaftlichen Entwicklung*).[67] It is charged with "presenting in its reports the overall state of the economy and its projected development". The federal government is obligated to respond to the annual report; a response to special reports is optional. Only 4 years later, the Law for the Promotion of the Stability and Growth of the Economy expanded this approach in various ways.

---

[64] Originally Sect. 1273ff., RVO; now Sect. 154ff., SGB VI.

[65] On the independence of the *Bank deutscher Länder* see Buchheim (1998, pp. 106f., 114); on the independence of the Deutsche Bundesbank see Stern (1998, pp. 179–192); M. Neumann (1998, pp. 315–335).

[66] Section 24b of the "Gesetz gegen Wettbewerbsbeschränkungen i. d. F. des Vierten Gesetzes zur Änderung des Gesetzes gegen Wettbewerbsbeschränkungen vom 26. April 1980" BGBl. I, p. 458. Now Sects. 44–47, GWB.

[67] "Gesetz über die Bildung eines Sachverständigenrates zur Begutachtung der gesamtwirtschaftlichen Entwicklung vom 14. August 1983" BGBl. I, p. 685.

3.4.5 "Big Democracy" and the Structures in Which and with Which It Lives

Democratic reality thus presents itself as the interaction and cooperation of two "worlds." One "world" is the "*world of the 'big democracy'*": the "world" of the competition within the state as a whole for power within the state. This is the "world" that manifests itself in the interplay of government and opposition and expresses itself effectively through legislation, especially federal legislation. It encompasses also the interplay between government and bureaucracy: the reliance of the government (and its parliamentary majority) on bureaucracy, the latter's expertise, experience, and efficiency, the influence of the bureaucracy on the government, and the rule of the government over the bureaucracy. This is the "world" in which the social takes shape according to two central laws: first, depending on how the social principles, values, vested rights, and interests are picked up and implemented by the governing majorities; second, depending on how important the content of politics is for maintaining or winning power at the threshold between two election periods. In a broader sense this "world" of the "big democracy" includes also the judicature – especially the guiding judicial role of the higher courts and the review of legislation by the Federal Constitutional Court. Decisions by the courts can also counteract imbalances that arise from the formation of majorities and from the temporal pulse of democracy.

Then there is the "world" of *specific and intermediary structures*, which stand for individual groups, functions, or areas, provide societal forces with effectiveness vis-à-vis "big democracy" or differentiate the state, disencumber "big democracy," and, finally, open up the spheres of creativity and responsibility of "small democracies." What these particular structures mean for the social cannot be reduced to a common denominator. That is especially true in the thrust "away from the state" – in the direction toward democratization, becoming independent, and the autonomy of specific life contexts. After all, the autonomy of sickness, long-term care, accident, and pension insurance already means different things, as does the autonomy of the Federal Agency for Labour the implementation of public assistance and child and youth services by the communities, and the participation of "charitable carriers" therein. *One* purpose can be an opening to concrete proximity to the subject area (as traditionally in sickness insurance), another the freeing up of regulatory mechanisms (as especially in pension insurance), another the plurality of offerings (as in public assistance and in child and youth services), and yet another the extrication from the general political system and the transparency of the accounting system. There are also considerable differences in the degree to which the legislator exhausts or leaves open his regulatory spheres: whether in favor of formal, particular legislation (through statutes), or in favor of administrative practice or other implementing processes. To that extent, the connections between values and goals must be seen in very concrete terms in each case.

However, the *particular, intermediary structures* also represent the potential of exerting influence on the "*big democracy*" – though once again with substantial differences. One important example is pension insurance. Within its self-administration, the most important interest groups (unions, associations of the insured, associations of benefit recipients, employers' organizations) gain access to essential experiences and information, and especially to processes of clarification not only with the "opposing interests," but also with the management and the personnel of the carriers and their association. If this process of clarification produces congruent positions, the broad and diversely anchored power of this institution constitutes a highly influential force for the "normal" majority democracy. And there is almost always agreement about one thing: namely, the continuation of the system – in other words: the continuation of the institution. That the possibilities of effectively exerting influence differ from institution to institution needs no explanation. In most cases, however, the particular systems establish an important framework for the creation of the corporative will. Of the highest complexity in that regard is the example of sickness insurance: its system brings together not only the carriers and their associations and the organizations of the insured and their employers, but also the organizations of service providers. In the face of this complex variety of partners, the state, as the carrier of the overall responsibility for the functioning of the system, must live with the limited conflicts that go hand in hand with its corrective intervention. But for the most part *limited* conflicts is all the state can afford. When could the "big democracy" muster the strength for an all-out conflict that would come with the transition to a national health service? The institutions thus turn out to be an essential source but also the development-guiding framework of the social policy of "big democracy."

The situation is different again with respect to the *autonomy of expertise*. The expertise that is brought into the process can clarify the factual state of affairs, the possibilities of a meaningful assessment, and the consequences of certain legal or political decisions. If it is creative and courageous enough, it can free insights and assessments from the efforts to turn a blind eye suggested as much by the interests, opinions, and value concepts of those involved as by the political calculations of winning or preserving power. In addition, it can contribute to a clear grasp, understanding, and evaluation of the subject matter of the social. As such it can constitute an important counterweight to the temptations on the part of all parties involved and the politics of "big democracy" to engage in selective perception, understanding, and assessments – or simply to push through or leave in place only particular interests. Of course, this all depends on how suitable a particular matter is for evaluation and assessment. It depends on the professional and ethical qualities of the experts, for even the expert of the highest professional qualifications requires a moral impulse to fully exhaust the possibilities of a correct report. Assuming all these elements are in place, the independent expertise is a counterweight to the incompetence and biases of political structures, both "big" and "small."

3.4.6 Democracy and Constitutional State

Social democracy shares in the culture of the constitutional state – in the complex system which, as a democracy, seeks its central foundation in the mandate from the citizens, but which, as a state under the rule of law, embeds and protects the decisions of the people in *various spheres of the law*. All of these spheres have specific ways of contesting, clarifying, and deciding on the content and changes of the law. That holds by virtue of the *hierarchy or legal norms* – by virtue of the ranking of inviolable constitutional norms (Art. 79, Para. 3, GG), constitutional law that is changeable but requires a broad consensus (Art. 79, Para. 1–2, GG), simple laws that require parliamentary legitimation but in principle only a simple majority (Art. 76–77, GG), and the statutes and ordinances below the level of statutory law (e.g. Art. 28, Para. 2; Art. 80, GG). It applies analogously to the assignment of the courts to these layers of the law: the constitutional courts to deal with disputes over constitutional law (Art. 93 and 100, GG), the other courts to deal with disputes over statutory and sub-statutory law (Art. 92, GG). In all of these contexts, the "lower" and the "later" law is subject to the demand of overarching norms that it must respect their values and justify itself in relationship to them. In the final analysis, the issue is respect for the basic values of the polity that guide the development of the legal system, preserve older and broader consensuses, and can be altered only by decisions whose authority is equal to the very decisions by which the existing basic values were incorporated into the legal system.

This system of the constitutional state imparts to the politics and the law that develop within its framework a *legitimacy that goes beyond the legitimacy of mere majority rule of the moment*. It is a legitimacy that is fed by the agreement with older and broader consensuses, by a justification with respect to them, by the engagement with them, and possibly by the weighing and relevant will for innovation. It is the *legitimacy of an overall context*, of an ideational and temporal continuity.

This *legitimacy* takes hold also of *the social*. It is the *legitimacy of the democratic and social state under the rule of law*. The pacifying effect of the social is borne by this legitimacy. But the social pays a price for this: it is removed from the simple democratic majority rule; it must integrate itself into the overall context of legitimation; and it must integrate itself into the constitutional state's canon of values. For the most part this has a retarding, indeed, a conserving, effect. But time and again it also has a propelling effect, and it always provides guidance.

The *federal state* (*Bundesstaat*) deepens these regularities: through the "dual" hierarchy of norms of the federal government (*Bund*) and the states (*Länder*), through the constellations of disputes unique to the latter, through the contribution of the federal system to the formation (and failure) of broad consensuses, through the historical and societal substance that integrates itself in the individual states. In this way, the federal state makes a specific contribution to the retarding and conservative character of the constitutional state. But it also constitutes a special opportunity for the positive realization of its basic values, each of which can be of more value to one state than another.

3.5 The Institutional Deficit of the Social State

In view of all of this, what is the meaning of the *constitutional declaration that Germany is a social state* (Art. 20, Para. 1; Art. 28, Para. 1, Sent. 1, GG)? The goal of the social state is the normative constitutional *expression of the basic social norm* of the society as constituted by the Basic Law. The mandate of this basic norm is open-ended and constantly requires new concretization. This *concretization* is a process, and this process is *entrusted to the federal state, the Rechtsstaat, and democracy*. The constitution of the social state has *not given this social state its own institutions* for realizing itself.

To be sure, there are *particular institutions of the social*: the web of institutions in which the social has manifested itself historically. Yet these institutions – each by itself and all of them together – relate to the concretization of the social, to parts of the social, not to the open-end totality of the social. The federal state, the *Rechtsstaat*, and democracy relate as much to the totality of the polity and the society constituted within it as to the open totality of the social goals of the state. The concretization of the social thus takes on the specific legitimacy that is generated by the federal state, and above all the *Rechtsstaat* and democracy – and only by them. But the social is also exposed to all the biases and gradients with which these systems confront the social. And that, precisely, is the problem (Zacher 1987a, p. 1100f.).

What could *institutions that develop the social state as such look like?* Traditionally, the gaze has always been directed at "*social rights*" (Murswiek 1989, pp. 243–289), *social state goals* (Lücke 1982, pp. 15–60), *social programs*, and so on. But these entail significant problems. "Social rights," state goals, programs, and the like are always selective. In their selectivity, they reflect the assertiveness of those who stand behind the values and interests that have been articulated into a law or a program. The "critical law" that articulates otherwise neglected concerns is the exception. Moreover, social rights are very slow to develop – more slowly than social problems. They are comparatively late in bringing in new questions. Finally: how are social rights to be applied and implemented? Where the issue – as in labor law – concerns social rights in the relations among citizens, the judge may be able to realize them. But where the issue is the granting of social services and the provision of the necessary resources, the power of the judge is very limited. Giving the mandate to special commissions – especially expert commissions – instead of judges[68] may bring more expertise to the matter, but it simply expresses even more clearly the weakness of social rights. Apart from borderline cases – as for example disputes over the guarantee of a subsistence minimum – politics must have the final responsibility. As a result, the effectiveness of social rights is tightly circumscribed.

A normative remedy is therefore possible only to a limited extent. What can be done *institutionally and procedurally* in the narrower sense in order to *comprehensively assert the goal of the social state* and to protect it from being alienated and distorted by the specific operating conditions of the federal state, the *Rechtsstaat*, and democracy? Would it be conceivable to have specific "social parliaments"

[68] The solution, for example, of the European Social Charter.

compete against the regular parliaments? How would they be formed? What could be their competencies and powers? One cannot have a democracy alongside democracy, and a *Rechtsstaat* alongside the *Rechtsstaat*.

We are left with only this: the attempt to continuously explain to those who are in charge in the federal state, the *Rechtsstaat*, and the democracy the totality of the social, to show them what kind of imbalances and gaps the "is" of the social has, and the "ought" that is conceivable by contrast. What remains is to remove the individual worse-better relationships from their self-justifying isolation and place them within larger and eventually all-encompassing contexts. What remains is to rationally actualize the social so as to thereby strengthen the social responsibility of the federal state, the *Rechtsstaat*, and democracy, but without calling into question the federal, constitutional, and democratic legitimation of social policy and social law.

What is needed, therefore, is a *"technocratic" solution*. Conceivable would be an institution that comprehensively lays out the facts and develops criteria for assessing them, so as to expand the range of the discussion and improve the basis of political, administrative, and judicial decisions.[69] The decision itself could be made – depending on the circumstances – only in the democratic and constitutional process. The model could be the Council of Economic Advisors. In that sense one could think of the ongoing examination of social conditions and the effects of the political, legal, and administrative measures, as well as periodic reporting and assessment at the hands of the governments, the legislative organs, and thus also the public. The procedures of such an "Expert Commission for Examining the Social Development" could be further differentiated and intensified compared to its model. The crucial factor is this: the subject matter of the social and its rationality must be independently and comprehensively perceived, understood, and assessed, so as to increase the knowledge, insight, and responsibility of all those involved in the federal, constitutional, and democratic decisions regarding the social.

[69] See Item 17 of the "Beschlüsse der Sozialrechtlichen Abteilung des 55. Deutschen Juristentages" (Verhandlungen des 55. Deutschen Juristentages, vol. 2: Sitzungsberichte Teil N., München, 1984, p. 220): "An independent, expert office is to be established with the mandate of capturing the totality of social benefits systems in a comprehensive and continuous way, analyzing their effects, and preparing a forecast of their development. In this way, the public and politics are to be comprehensively and continuously informed about the reality and meaning of the social benefits systems, each by itself, compared to one another, and in their totality, and a reliable basis prepared for the application of the relevant constitutional principles." See also Zentrum für Sozialpolitik (1998, pp. 28–30, 44).

Social Policy and the Social in Post-war Germany: A Political and Legal History[70]

4 1945–1949: Adversity and New Beginning

4.1 The Political and Social Situation[71]

The end of the war and the collapse of the Nazi regime had left Germany in a disastrous state. Without a doubt, the end of the fighting was an eagerly awaited blessing. Without a doubt, the defeat of the criminal regime, which so many Germans had served, willingly or not, was a liberation not only for the victims of the Germans, but for the Germans themselves (von Weizsäcker 1985, p. 64). And yet it was a time of all-pervasive destruction: the destruction of human life and health, of families, housing, factories, and infrastructure. And it was a time of unimaginable deracination: through imprisonment, deportation, military service and captivity, flight and expulsion, evacuation and the destruction of cities and villages. For Germany and the Germans it was also a time of incapacity to act on their own. The structures of the Nazi party and of the state it had dominated had collapsed, or at the very least they were paralyzed, rendered useless, delegitimized. Societal forces had been either compromised through their connections to the Nazi systems, or they had to reconstitute themselves and connect again with their surroundings. Any normal contact with other countries was cut off. The political authority over Germany lay with the *occupying authorities*. But these authorities – the Control Council and the military government in the various zones, as well as the *Kommandantur* in Berlin – were anything but a well-organized government for the country with its competencies clearly delineated. And what was true for all those who assumed responsibility for Germany or any part of Germany at this time was also true for them: namely, that the situation they confronted was very different from the situation for which they had been prepared.

Still the occupation regime did not displace the *German polity* completely. Two phenomena, especially, make this clear: the continuity of the legal system, and the persistence of the lower and mid-level administrative structures. The Control Council did not by any means order the repeal of all German law. Rather, in its Law no. 1 of 20 September 1945 (von Münch 1968, vol. 1, pp. 52–54), it repealed Nazi laws. A number of Nazi-inspired laws and decrees were explicitly abrogated (Art. I). Other than that, the law worked with a general clause (Art. II).[72] In numerous additional individual regulations, the occupying powers repealed earlier German law (Etzel 1992). But all of this rested on the principle that German law as

[70] Hockerts (2001). In the discussion that follows, all figures – unless otherwise indicated – are taken from Bundesministerium für Arbeit und Sozialordnung (1999).

[71] Eschenburg (1983); Stern (2000, pp. 913–1197); Kahlenberg and Hoffmann (2001).

[72] Later clarifications were therefore invariably necessary. See Stolleis (1982, pp. 383–407).

such essentially continued to be in force. Far less transparent was the persistence of the actions of German state power – more precisely: of administrative, judicial, and finally also legislative institutions (Stolleis 1987, pp. 173–217). From the outset, the occupying powers regarded themselves as authorized to issue orders to local agencies and especially also to appoint new personnel (Dürig 1955, p. 31). This was established as a principle with the "Declaration in View of Germany's Defeat and the Assumption of Sovereign Governmental Authority with Respect to Germany" on 5 June 1945 (von Münch 1968, pp. 19–24). Functional remnants of state power were presupposed, activated, and pragmatically put to further use. And in fact, this was followed by a rapid revitalization of German administrative authorities and the *establishment of German states*, which reached its conclusion in 1946/1947 with the adoption of state constitutions.[73] The invigoration of German administrative and political structures went hand in hand with the development of a corresponding democratic life, especially through the authorization of political parties and elections at the local level. In the process, German state power always remained under the authority of the occupying forces. Over time, to be sure, that authority concentrated more and more on controlling the state governments. In addition, the American and the British zone also saw the emergence of zonal structures. In the *American Zone*, the *Länderrat* (Council of States), with its seat in Stuttgart, was created as early as the fall of 1945. It was a body made up of the Minister-Presidents of Bavaria, Wuerttemberg-Baden, and Hesse, and beginning in February 1947 also Bremen. Its most important function was the passing of laws for the entire zone. However, it was also supposed to become active in political, social, economic, and cultural questions. Alongside a merely advisory Parliamentary Council, it had a secretariat that became ever more differentiated. In the *British zone*, the establishment of the states was delayed. The British occupying power lacked the unquestioned federalism of its American counterpart. As a result, that area saw the *establishment of German central zonal offices* and of a *Zonal Advisory Council*.

An important further development of the interaction between the occupying powers and the central German authorities was the *Unified Economic Area* (Pünder 1966). At the end of 1946, the British and American occupying powers agreed to administer "their" zones in a coordinated manner and thereby improve the living conditions of the German population. Initial efforts in the first few months of 1947 did not prove very effective. Eventually, the occupying powers and German representatives agreed in the first months of 1948 on a state-like structure: a government (Executive Council: Directors as "Ministers" and one Chief Director as "Minister-President"), a bicameral parliament (*Wirtschaftsrat* and *Länderrat*), a High Court, a number of offices, and a Court of Auditors (Benz 1983b, pp. 406–418). Added to this was the *Bank deutscher Länder*, which was set up by the military

[73] The states in the American and French zones were given constitutions. In the British zone, only Hamburg was given one. Lower Saxony got a temporary state constitution in 1947. Schleswig-Holstein and North Rhine-Westphalia received constitutions only under the Basic Law (SH 1949; NRW 1950). Stolleis (1987, pp. 191–211). On the following see W. Vogel (1989).

government on 1 March 1948 (Buchheim 1998). Like no other institution of the Unified Economic Area, this bank, the precursor of the *Bundesbank*, would take on fundamental and lasting importance for the entire subsequent development.

The *French Zone* remained in an ambivalent relationship vis-à-vis the Bizone (Benz 1983a, p. 515f.). On the one hand, the French occupying power paid strict attention to separation. On the other hand, there were joint activities. Immediately after the currency reform, the central banks of the states in the French zone joined the *Bank deutscher Länder*, and the laws on the currency reform were issued jointly by the American, British, and French military governments. In the meantime, the occupying powers had set the course for a joint future of the "Trizone" with the Frankfurt Documents of 1 July 1948, with which they got the creation of a constitution for a "western state" off the ground (Mußgnug 1987, pp. 219–258).

If the organization and exercise of state power was already in constant flux and only gradually attained some kind of systematic structure, *society* was initially in a largely unstructured state (Broszat et al. 1988; Bucher 1990). In principle all institutions marked by the Nazi movement and regime had been outlawed and dissolved by the occupying powers. Many of the old institutions that had been destroyed or crippled during the Nazi period were very slow to reemerge – be it for factual reasons, be it because the occupying powers sought to control the new formation of social structures. That is especially true of the unions. The occupying powers were more open to charitable associations and their umbrella organization, the German Association for Public and Private Welfare. The highest degree of immediate presence belonged to the churches. At their core they had survived the Nazi period undamaged, without having been destroyed because of their opposition to the party and its ideology, but also without being compromised on account of their cooperation with the Nazi state. One exceedingly important circumstance was that the immediate concerns of all the groups affected by Nazi terror, the war, and the very divergent burdens of the postwar era found representation only slowly and with very different speed and effectiveness: the direct victims of Nazi rule (foreigners brought to Germany as prisoners or forced laborers, and Germans persecuted for racial, religious, or political reasons); the victims of the war (disabled veterans, surviving dependants of those killed in the war, those who had suffered property damage from the war – especially those who had lost their homes to bombing raids or other military actions; evacuees); the victims of the postwar period (prisoners of war and their families, the returnees from prisoner of war camps, all those who were legally, politically, or ethnically Germans who had fled or been expelled from territories outside of "Control Council Germany," as well as members of other states who found refuge in Germany from the expansion of communist rule in Central and Eastern Europe); those disproportionately affected by the currency reform; finally, those, as well, who in the wake of the denazification of Germany and the reparation of German guilt had ended up in difficult social situations (those harmed by reparations and persons removed from their old jobs, especially in the public sector). It is obvious that the conditions under which these groups would be able to assert themselves, in particular, be able to organize themselves, had to be extremely different because of actual circumstances and political reasons. By the end of the occupation period, nearly all had found a voice and representation. The social and political life of the Federal Republic was from the outset characterized by this fact. But this was the end of a development during the course of which the interests in question changed in many ways, in part emerged in the first place, and, at any rate, found a structure, a voice, and a hearing in very different ways.

This already points to how much the *old social problems were relativized* at that time. They had been absorbed into a chaos of new and old hardships. That applies also – and especially – to the classic "social question": the "workers' question" (Mooser 1984). To be sure, it had a claim of its own, the result of the traditions of social and political thought, but also of the fact that the "workers' question" had been immediately picked up and deliberated by the newly forming parties. Moreover, businesses and unions had fairly early created a new ground on which to assert themselves and bring the interests of workers to bear. But most of all it resulted from the fact that workers suffered especially from the circumstances of the times, the lack of food, clothing, housing, energy, transportation, and so on, while the entire population depended on the productive output of labor. Now, however, the entire population was exposed to the same lack of food, clothing, housing, energy, transportation, and so on. In other words: everyone was suffering the kind of hardship that had once been the concern of the poor and the lower strata of "wage workers." A deficient *social situation*, which had *once been the expression of inequality* within society, was in principle *universal at that time*. And the inequalities that existed with respect to a shortage of food, clothing, housing, energy, and so on no longer had a necessary connection with the old reasons of inequality – poverty and wage labor. And their social problematic essentially had little in common with the old categories of social inequality. The old *class differences* had *lost* their *precedence* as the embodiment of social inequality. In those initial postwar years, this expressed itself in a high degree of social pragmatism. And yet these beginnings would become a *legacy for the entire social history of the Federal Republic*. Even though there were surely many who – mostly because of their background, identity-shaping experiences, or guided by an ideology – regarded themselves as members of a specific class, and even though there were always political and journalistic forces that thought in terms of class conflict, indeed, class warfare, a traditional class mentality never again played a major role.

4.2 Principles and Concepts

The *world of social ideas at the time* was highly complex. One thing was certain: National Socialism was negated. Other than that, though, the most diverse approaches and currents were found. There were the guiding ideas of the Weimar period. But since Weimar itself had in fact been a time of searching and controversies, the echo it sent forth into the postwar period could not simply be one of unanimity. On the one hand, the ideas of the Weimar period were adopted;

on the other hand, the critique of these ideas continued. Particular weight was given to the experiences that had led to the failure of Weimar and the disaster of National Socialism. In addition, there were also ideas in the air that had emerged in other times and regions, and ideas, not least, that had arisen out of the opposition to National Socialism. These aspirations of principles, schools of thought, as well as ideologies were confronted by the miseries of the day: the challenge of hardship and millions of fractured life journeys, of millions of broken lives, or simply the general shortage of important necessities of life. All this consumed energies – equally among those who were simply affected by these circumstances, those who in some way bore responsibilities, and for the most part also those who held political and administrative power. All of this preoccupied the minds and paralyzed action. And it called for solutions, for immediate effectiveness, and not, or at least not in the same way, for large-scale concepts and ideas.[74] This deeply rattled society was not fertile ground for distant visions of something new. The saving proximity of the achievable drove people – and here once again: both those simply suffering from the conditions and those who were social, administrative, and political actors.

This gave the *traditional institutions*[75] a unique power. They were like machines which, shut down for weeks or months with the collapse of the Nazi regime and now restarted, were able to provide people with services they could not expect from anywhere else. To be sure, the grime of National Socialism had to be brushed off. Here and there, "machines" that National Socialism had set aside had to be or could be brought back into service. Here and there a "machine" had to be phased out. Where the "machines" had been tied into a system connected to the Reich, one now had to try and integrate them into a system focused on the states or the zones. But for the most part they proved robust enough to provide benefits even then. This lackluster triumph of the existing institutions went hand in hand with the power of traditional mindsets. Reforms of the traditional – that was the innovations that the time could bear. The outright new was reserved for ideologically committed individuals and groups, elite individuals and circles, and unrealistic eccentrics.

The social showed itself in those years distorted in a way that was not previously conceivable and was quickly consigned to the past again as the decade came to an end. If the core of the social is that the "nature" of societal conditions always brings forth *economically conditioned and economically relevant* inequalities among people, and that the social culture of social conditions lies in compensating, moderating, or at least controlling these inequalities, the peculiarity of those years was that the shortcomings that are the burden of the disadvantaged under "natural" societal conditions were now the fate of all. The degree of the impact may have varied – according to profession, region, and so on. And even the possibility of economically conditioned differences persisted, namely, in the black market. But in general, the misery *of the unequal had been joined by the misery of the equal*. Here

[74] See, however, Preller (1946; 2nd ed., 1947); Jostock (1946).

[75] For example, social insurance: see Rieger (1992).

we may recall the *basic formula* of the social: everyone has the possibility and bears the responsibility to earn an income through work and thus meet his needs and those of his family, while the task of the social state is to counter the dangers that arise in the implementation of the formula, and to compensate for the shortcomings left unaddressed by the realization of the formula. This formula assumes a notion of what is the rule and what is the exception. But that had been suspended at the time. An adequate meeting of needs was generally not possible even when there was work and income. And for many, the normality of access to work or familial support had been destroyed or at least suspended through physical or psychological injuries, through the loss of all social frames of reference, through traumatic changes to the family unit, and so on. Here, too, it was therefore the case that the *hardships that were the lot of the disadvantaged under the basic formula's model of the rule and the exception had become the hardships of everyone*. From this perspective, too, the question therefore arises: Should hardships that affect all be assessed, addressed, and compensated differently than hardships that fall on the "disadvantaged"? Or to put it differently: Should hardships that constitute a certain rule be assessed, addressed, and compensated differently from those that are the exception? And what does this difference mean for the responsibility of the state and society? In fact, a hardship that affects all is not conceptualized as "poverty" in the same way as a hardship that affects individuals, groups, or strata (von Wiese 1953/1954, pp. 43f., 47). Thus we should look not only to the later *Wirtschaftswunder*, but also to the experiences of the first postwar years, as an important reason why the German public and German politicians later refused for so long to even speak of poverty in the Federal Republic. Poverty is the hardship of the "unequal;" the universal hardship, the hardship of the "equal" is something else.

Accordingly, the responsibility of the polity presented itself differently. A suitable term had already been available for some time. *Ernst Forsthoff* had invented it in 1938: *Daseinsvorsorge* (see section "The Neighboring Concept of *Daseinsvorsorge*"). It was not coined for the kind of hardship that prevailed in the postwar period. Instead, it described more generally the task of the polity to provide individuals with the "life goods" they need to maintain their existence and, beyond that, to lead a decent life. In the midst of the Nazi regime, the term served to legitimize state and communal functions that were to be based no longer – or at least not comprehensively – on the law, but for which the invocation of the ubiquitous will of the Führer was not realistic and credible. The term survived the collapse of the framework conditions in which it had arisen. And precisely the first postwar years needed it to explain and understand the move to avail oneself of the state and local communities to provide the minimum conditions for the survival of the citizens. Of course, at the time it was a euphemism to speak of "Daseins*vorsorge*" (*Vorsorge* implies making provisions for the future); "Daseins*fürsorge*" or "Daseins*hilfe*" would have been more realistic (*Fürsorge* and *Hilfe* referring to relief and aid). At any rate: those years were a time of general hardship and a corresponding "*Daseinsvorsorge*" of the polity, while the mandate of the social to compensate, moderate, or at least control differences in prosperity was relativized by the extent of the general hardship, and only slowly assumed a new and valid gestalt in the exploding multitude of old and new differences in prosperity.

4.3 *An Interim Assessment: The Layers of Evolution*

The conditions I have sketched do not allow us to depict the shaping of the social on a single level. Even though it was only 4 years that separated the collapse of the Reich from the birth of the Federal Republic, three very different processes took place. Though they each have their temporal focal points, they are deeply interwoven. A *first phase* could be described as a *phase of political cleansing and of Daseinsvorsorge* (see below section "Political Cleansing and *Daseinsvorsorge*"). It concerns the basic restoration of the functions and institutions of society and, above all, of the polity – excluding the National Socialist legacy, but without asserting any new development. This phase dominated the years 1945 and 1946, after which time it receded increasingly behind the other two phases. The *second phase* is characterized by the *further development of conditions and new goals* (see below section "Further Development and the Formulation of New Goals"). It transcended the basic approach of the first phase and sought to establish and expand the new democracy, the new *Rechtsstaat*, and the new social state. This was done through the resumption of and new beginnings in political life. It was done through laws that went beyond the level of mere purging and mere restoration law. It was done above all – though of course only in the American and French occupation zones – through the creation of constitutions. Precisely the programmatic content of the state constitutions provides an insight into the world of ideas of the leading politicians and their advisors, the political parties, and the public that carried them. If laws must keep within the realm of the possible, constitutional texts can be formulated as signposts to an uncertain future. While the first phase was dominated substantially by the occupying powers, the second phase was primarily the responsibility of German politics – though of course under the control of the occupying force. This phase commences in 1946 and loses importance only in 1948, when the Unified Economic Area is created. The *third phase* is the phase of the Bizone, a platform on which the course of future developments is laid down in a fundamental way. The Bizone opens the gate to the *social market economy*, and in other ways, too, it provides lasting imprints to the *liberal social state* (see below section 4.6). This phase dominates the period from the spring of 1948 to the summer of 1949. In it, the American and British occupation power and the German organs of the Unified Economic Area cooperated in a fundamentally constructive way.

4.4 *Political Cleansing and* Daseinsvorsorge[76]

4.4.1 Responsibility for the Economy[77]

Capitulation and occupation meant little fundamentally for the structures and domestic functions of the economy. The comprehensive system of control of goods

[76] Bartholomäi et. al. (1977); Hudemann (1988); Frerich and Frey (vol. 3, 1996, pp. 1–15).

[77] Abelshauser (1993, pp. 13–40); Weimer (1998, pp. 11–30).

introduced as the war economy evolved was maintained. This system also determined the extent to which destroyed capacities could be rebuilt. The productivity of the economy had been substantially reduced through the events of the war. Foreign trade was completely under the control of the occupying powers. Some industrial plants were dismantled, with the scope varying from one zone to the next. In the wake of denazification, compromised managers were kept out of businesses. There were no changes, however, to the property system.

4.4.2 Labor[78]

The constitution of labor had been fundamentally altered by the *National Socialists* (Frerich and Frey 1996, vol. 1, pp. 270–288). Unions and employers' associations had been dissolved. The place of free collective bargaining had been taken by wage regulations issued by the Trustees of Labour. Organizing as well as disciplining the workers was the task of the German Labour Front. Labor conscription had been introduced. With the outbreak of the Second World War, the free choice of a job had been eliminated. A pay freeze in 1939 had abolished the freedom to negotiate pay; wages remained at the level of that year.

The *occupying powers* saw it as their first task to eliminate the specifically National Socialist elements. They began by prohibiting any further activity by the Reich Trustees of Labour. Control Council Law no. 1 (1945) dissolved the German Labour Front. Control Council Law no. 40 (1946) repealed the Law for the Regulation of National Labour. The restrictions on working life caused by the war were not eliminated in the same way. Youths and adults were initially required to register. The pay freeze was essentially maintained. In a next phase, the minimum preconditions for a liberal working life were restored. Unions and employers' association were permitted again[79] – even if the various occupying powers promoted this process in varying ways, with the Americans, in particular, limiting the establishment of unions to the level of the individual states. Dues could once again be agreed upon between unions and employers, though under the oversight of the relevant State Labour Offices. As a counterpart to free collective bargaining, the Control Council envisaged mediation bodies, with the precise form they would take left to the states to determine. In principle, they could only offer their services, not force them upon the parties.[80] Other important pieces were the restoration of labor courts – borne also by the social partners – and a framework regulation of the works constitution through Control Council Law no. 22 (1946). The actual introduction of

[78] See Bundesministerium für Arbeit und Sozialordnung and Bundesarchiv (eds.), 2001b: Geschichte der Sozialpolitik in Deutschland seit 1945, vol. 2, Chap. 3, nos. 1–3.

[79] See Bundesministerium für Arbeit und Sozialordnung and Bundesarchiv (eds.), 2001b: Geschichte der Sozialpolitik in Deutschland seit 1945, vol. 2, Chap. 2, 1.2.4., 3.3.1, and 3.3.2.

[80] On compulsory mediation, stipulated only in Rhineland Palatinate and South Baden, see Zacher (1981, p. 309f.).

works councils was the duty of the states, most of which fulfilled it – with the exception of Hamburg, Lower Saxony, and North Rhine-Westphalia (Fitting 1948).

4.4.3 The Family[81]

After 1945, the family was simultaneously the most burdened and most effective pillar of society. Nevertheless, those years were not a time of social family policy. The child allowance introduced under National Socialism (Frerich and Frey 1996, vol. 1, p. 318f.) was abolished again. In tax law, the burdens on and relief for families were changed in an unsystematic way (Frerich and Frey 1996, vol. 3, p. 11f.).

4.4.4 Social Provision[82]

Social insurance continued to operate after 1945 in spite of the collapse of its financing scheme and all centralized structures. The decentralized structure of social insurance evidently gave it enough flexibility to deal with the extraordinary situation. This ability to survive is one of the key reasons why social insurance largely retained its structure also in the subsequent decades and remained the core element of the social state of the Federal Republic. Only *unemployment insurance* faced greater problems. During the Nazi period, the labor administration had been moved onto the Reich level. The Reich Office for Job Placement and Unemployment Insurance, which had the task of collecting the income from dues and of spending it according to the directives of the budget, continued, though it was given the telling name "*Reichsstock für Arbeitseinsatz*" (Reich Employment Fund) (Peters 1978, p. 121f.). Nevertheless, the Labour Offices and State Labour Offices now sought to make payments to the unemployed (Frerich and Frey 1996, vol. 3, p. 8).

The other large branch of social provision was that of the *public sector* – divided into *provision for civil servants* (today: provision for civil servants, judges, and soldiers) and the supplementary retirement insurance for public sector employees. With respect to provision for civil servants there was essentially no break after 1945, provided the employer still existed. The supplementary retirement insurance for the public sector, by contrast, had been externalized by most employers, shifted especially onto the Supplementary Retirement Insurance Office of the Reich and the individual Länder. In this area there would invariably be problems of transition with the collapse of the Reich (Hautmann 1984, p. 17f.). A large-scale problem, however, arose from the fact that in countless cases, the employer disappeared or the

[81] Bundesministerium für Arbeit und Sozialordnung and Bundesarchiv (eds.), 2001b: Geschichte der Sozialpolitik in Deutschland seit 1945, vol. 2, Chap. 3, no. 10.

[82] Peters (1978, pp. 123–142); Bundesministerium für Arbeit und Sozialordnung and Bundesarchiv (eds.), 2001b: Geschichte der Sozialpolitik in Deutschland seit 1945, vol. 2, Chap. 3, nos. 3–7.

employment relationship could not be continued for a good reason, mostly having to do with denazification. That affected already existing provision relationships and the fate of individuals who were about to transition from active service to a provision relationship. In a great many cases, there was initially no solution. If, as for most refugees and expellees, the employer had disappeared, the states and other employers often helped out. Eventually, the federal legislator had to find general solutions on the basis of Art. 131 of the Basic Law (BVerfGE 3, 58, 162, 288; 28, 163).

4.4.5 Social Compensation[83]

An overarching, general concept of social compensation did not yet exist during the time under examination here (Zacher 1972a, pp. 461–471; Schulin 1981). It still had to develop, but it began to do so soon after 1945. The historically most potent dimension of social compensation was the *assistance for war victims*. However, it was initially negatively affected by the transfer of German state authority to the occupying powers (Trometer 1977, pp. 191–205). Only in the French occupation zone were supplementary pension payments continued, with limitations. In the British zone, pensions were paid in cases of need and within the framework of the statutory pension insurance. In the American zone, the Pension Offices were dissolved and the payment of pensions was stopped. Only from 1947 on was the assistance for war victims able to recover the character of a specific system of social benefits.

At that time, the analogy from "war damages to persons" to "war damages to property" and its expansion to those who lost wealth and property as a result of flight, expulsion, the currency reform, and so on was as unfamiliar as the analogy from "war damages to property" to "peace damages to property" subject to obligatory compensation (damages from riots and the like, of the "cases of sacrifice" first regulated in the General Prussian Code). Concrete help in the sense of accommodations for refugees and expellees dominated. By contrast, benefit systems to compensate damages did not exist at first.

As far as the occupying powers were concerned, their primary focus was on aid for the *victims of the Nazi system* (Goschler 1992; Pawlita 1992): for those persecuted on racial, religious, and political grounds, for displaced persons, and other individuals uprooted by the Nazi regime of terror and now living in Germany. Care had to be directed initially at actual help. This was above all care in the hands of the international community, on whose behalf the United Nations Relief and Rehabilitation Administration (UNRRA) was active. In addition, the occupying powers addressed the issue of the return of illegally confiscated assets (restitution). When it came to recompense for damages caused by Nazi persecution (compensation), on the other hand, they saw their responsibility in prevailing upon the German side to issue

[83] Bundesministerium für Arbeit und Sozialordnung and Bundesarchiv (eds.), 2001b: Geschichte der Sozialpolitik in Deutschland seit 1945, vol. 2, Chap. 3, no. 12.

relevant regulations. However, the necessity for a German state and German society to take responsibility for the damages from Nazi persecution was beyond question.

4.4.6 Public Care[84]

Countless people were living in the country without income, work, or possessions, and separated from their families. The systems of social provision – social insurance and civil service pension – that continued to function or began to operate again could address only a small portion of this need: because only some of those affected were protected by them in the first place, and because the benefits of these systems were not geared toward covering the kind of damages these people had suffered. Social compensation – whether conventionally prohibited, whether new and only emerging – could offer only inadequate help. As a result, the mass of these problems fell to public care, which was most suited to combating this flood of old and new hardships (Heisig 1995). But this public care was overextended not only by the magnitude of the misery and hardship. It also had its own internal problems. To be sure, financial assistance might find an adequate and largely workable basis in the traditional law of public care – the Reich Law on the Responsibility to Provide Public Assistance of 1924, and the Reich principles about the preconditions, nature, and extent of public assistance, and the multitude of supplementary regulations (Jehle 1950; 2nd ed., 1954). Moreover, the carriers of assistance – following the lead of the communal and general state administration – may well have been among the structures that felt the paralysis of the collapse the least and were the first to recover from it. Still, the benefits of public assistance were invariably out of all proportion to the need: first, because they were by their nature minimum benefits, while the need was vast; second, because there was an extensive shortage of funds to do justice to the abundance of need. Moreover, until that time, public care had been built on the distinction between group assistance (for disabled veterans, dependants of those killed in the war, pensioners, the severely disabled, needy minors, and mothers in childbed) and the general poor relief. This distinction no longer reflected the situation of people, many of whom were now dependent on assistance. But above all: assistance was not only cash benefits. Moreover, assistance could not be limited to what was regulated by law. Assistance always and essentially also meant services.[85] These services had always been only to a limited extent a matter of the welfare associations organized according to public law. They were always also a societal benefit, which was provided to a considerable degree by individuals, families, groups, and above all welfare associations. During the Third

[84] Bundesministerium für Arbeit und Sozialordnung and Bundesarchiv (eds.), 2001b: Geschichte der Sozialpolitik in Deutschland seit 1945, vol. 2, Chap. 3, no. 9.

[85] Bundesministerium für Arbeit und Sozialordnung and Bundesarchiv (eds.), 2001b: Geschichte der Sozialpolitik in Deutschland seit 1945, vol. 2, Chap. 3, no. 14.

Reich, the welfare associations had been displaced by the National Socialist People's Welfare (NSV). It no longer existed. And given the conditions at the time, the welfare associations could not simply be established at will – not even if it was a question, as was mostly the case, of reviving old associations. In this situation the welfare associations borne by the churches were somewhat ahead.[86] The churches had survived the Nazi era – in spite of persecution and compromising entanglements – and were able to act from the moment Germany collapsed *(Stunde Null)* in a way that probably no other non-state institution could. The non-church welfare associations[87] had a more difficult time, which was in part the result of their substrate and history, in part of the attitude of the occupying powers. In spite of all these difficulties, welfare – primarily the "public assistance" of the local communities, but increasingly again the complex blend of "public and private welfare" – was the broadest foundation for the new beginning of the social state. And so the German Association for Public and Private Welfare was the leading voice on social policy in the land.[88] Together with social provision, public assistance constituted, in the midst of the catastrophe, the core of the socio-political institutions that allowed the society and polity to pass through the grim days of those years.

4.4.7 Meeting Basic Needs

The basic formula of work, income, meeting basic needs, and the community of maintenance was profoundly challenged: by the inability of so many people to work, by the breakup of so many communities of maintenance, by the destruction of so many production processes, and quite generally by the extensive damage to the network of conditions under which the formula can be realized. The classic institutions of social protection and social aid might have been able to compensate the shortcomings in work, income, and maintenance within limits. The ability to meet basic needs, however, was subject to different, additional preconditions other than those of income or maintenance. Even individuals who had purchasing power – whether from income or wealth – were by no means able to meet their needs at will. For quite some time, the war economy had imposed tighter restrictions on an individual's access to basic goods than would have resulted from the distribution of money. The occupying powers retained this system of controls. In fact, it was

[86] Bundesministerium für Arbeit und Sozialordnung and Bundesarchiv (eds.), 2001b: Geschichte der Sozialpolitik in Deutschland seit 1945, vol. 2, Chap. 2, 3.3.3.

[87] Bundesministerium für Arbeit und Sozialordnung and Bundesarchiv (eds.), 2001b: Geschichte der Sozialpolitik in Deutschland seit 1945, vol. 2, Chap. 2, 3.3.4.

[88] The Association organized conferences in the early post-war years: 1946 in Frankfurt am Main on the topic "Stand und Entwicklung des deutschen Fürsorgewesens;" 1947 in Rothenburg ob der Tauber on the topic "Kriegsfolgehilfe;" 1949 in Bielefeld on the topic "Fürsorge im Dienst der wirtschaftlichen und sozialen Sicherung der Bevölkerung." See Deutscher Verein für öffentliche und private Fürsorge (1997, p. 12).

indispensable. On the one hand, the demand for goods had grown enormously from the fact that so many had lost all their possessions. On the other hand, the capacity to produce new goods was diminished by the destruction of manufacturing facilities and infrastructure, by the cutting off of the national economy from international exchange, and by the fragmentation of the land into zones. Added to this was the fact that a large segment of society had lost income and wealth as sources for meeting their needs, while others had not only been able to preserve their material wealth, but had also managed to accumulate more or less large monetary fortunes. An extreme shortage of goods thus confronted extreme divergences and distortions in the monetary demand capacity. This had to affect especially the basic goods – food, clothing, housing, and energy. The classic social problem, to control the inappropriate effects of economic inequality on the ability to meet basic needs, receded behind the danger of a struggle of all against all over the goods in short supply, and behind the danger that too many could emerge from this struggle with nothing. *Daseinsvorsorge* dominated the scene. The specific techniques varied. In the area of food, for example, the supply was placed under a compulsory regime of obligatory shipments, while distribution – subject to the directives of oversight and price controls – could be left to a rudimentary market. When it came to housing, however, new production was only a marginal prospect.[89] As a result, the existing units had to be distributed. The original mechanism of property and rent took a back seat to the public management of housing and rent control. Other areas of meeting basic needs had to get by with making full use of the existing possibilities. That was true of education and training. And it was also true of the area of medical treatment and nursing care.

4.5 Further Development and the Formulation of New Goals

However, the occupying powers and German politics in the states as well as in the zonal institutions of the British and American zone tried very soon to break the spell that the catastrophe of 1945 had cast over the land and to take steps in the direction of further development. This was done within the narrow parameters of concrete reality, as a number of laws implemented what was directly feasible. It was also done in the virtual world of broader visions.[90] These visionary concepts were created in the parties, the unions, economic associations, the churches, and by individuals and small groups. Broader consensuses were expressed in the state constitutions that were passed in 1946/1947 in the states of the French and American zones (Beutler 1973; Pfetsch 1990).

[89] Bundesministerium für Arbeit und Sozialordnung and Bundesarchiv (eds.), 2001b: Geschichte der Sozialpolitik in Deutschland seit 1945, vol. 2, Chap. 3, no. 15.

[90] Bundesministerium für Arbeit und Sozialordnung and Bundesarchiv (eds.), 2001b: Geschichte der Sozialpolitik in Deutschland seit 1945, vol. 2, esp. Chap. 1 and 2.

4.5.1 The Responsibility of the State for the Economy

Two Lasting Approaches

(a) Economic freedom (*Gewerbefreiheit*)
Two basic decisions had lasting importance for the development of the economy. The one approach would prove fundamental for the fact that the societal realization of the social later became self-evident. It concerned *economic freedom* (*Gewerbefreiheit*). Ever since the Commercial Code of the North German League of 1869, *Gewerbefreiheit* had been a pan-German principle – though very much in the legal sense of a principle: a rule that allowed for exceptions, indeed, needed them. And those exceptions multiplied over the course of time, not least during the Nazi period (Huber 1953, pp. 648–651). This growth and proliferation of exceptions needed pruning after 1945. A number of commercial licensing laws were passed (Huber 1953, pp. 651–655). However, the relative nature of the old *Gewerbefreiheit* was to be retained. And the constitutions of the time went even further in their restraint. Whenever they regulated the freedom of economic activity, they placed the economy's duty to the general welfare and the resulting constraints on freedom in the foreground.[91] The American military government created an alternative to this trend: its Order of 29 November 1948, proclaimed complete economic freedom. The only permissible restrictions would be those necessary to preserve public health, public safety, and the common welfare. And this was to apply not only to the conventional, narrow sphere of "commerce," but also to the free professions (Huber 1953, pp. 652–654). Although the French and British zones did not follow this example, it is clear that it shaped the subsequent development beyond the American zone. The regulation of professional freedom in Art. 12 of the Basic Law and its interpretation by the Federal Constitutional Court[92] picked up and carried on this approach.

(b) The codetermination of workers
The other approach that should be mentioned here concerns the structures of the economy – more specifically: the *influence of workers on the economy* and economic enterprises. A common feature was that the state constitutions spoke of a right of participation by workers and their union organizations on the level of both the individual enterprise and above.[93] But while the promise of codetermination above the enterprise level was nowhere realized, the path for influence by workers over their workplace was blazed at that time. On the

[91] Art. 43, LVerf.Baden; Art. 151, LVerf.Bay; Art. 38 I II, LVerf.He; Art. 52, 58, LVerf.RP; Art. 25 I, LVerf.WB; Art. 92 I, LVerf.WH. Only the LVerf.Br spoke of occupation freedom without restrictions (Art. 8 II).

[92] Beginning in 1958 with the "Apothecary Decision": BVerfGE 7, 377.

[93] Art. 38 and 39, LVerf.Baden; Art. 175 and 176, LVerf.Bay; Art. 46 and 47, LVerf.Br; Art. 37, LVerf.He; Art. 67, LVerf.RP; Art. 22, Para. 2, Art. 23, LVerf.WB; Art. 95, Para. 1.2, LVerf.WH.

most general level this was done through the economic right of codetermination by the works councils (Huber 1954, pp. 548–555). Control Council Law no. 22 had said nothing about this. Still, the works councils laws of the states envisaged a broader (Baden, Bavaria, Hesse, Wuerttemberg-Baden) or narrower (Rhineland-Palatinate, Schleswig-Holstein, Wuerttemberg-Hohenzollern) right of codetermination of the works councils also in economic matters (Huber 1954, p. 547). A step further was taken with the dispatch of workers' representatives onto the supervisory boards (Huber 1954, pp. 555–564). In this regard, Control Council Law no. 22 had stipulated only certain rights to information (Art. VI, Para. 1). However, a number of states (Baden, Bavaria, Hesse, and Rhineland-Palatinate) also called for the sending of works councils representatives onto the supervisory boards.[94] This development reached another level when, in the wake of the decartelization of the steel industry, supervisory boards with equal representation (five representatives each of the workers and the employers) were agreed upon for the enterprises that emerged from this process (Muszynski 1975, p. 76).

The Visions of the Time in the Mirror of the State Constitutions

(a) The general constraints on the economy
Germans at the time felt called upon not only to organize the economy at the moment, especially to develop it in the direction of covering the needs of the suffering population.[95] They also wrestled not less intensively with the future shape of the economy. The state constitutions were the most important place for these guiding visions to manifest themselves. In the process, the obligations imposed upon the economy emerged in a lasting way[96] – more lasting than economic freedom. Two examples:

[94] Hesse: only with an advisory voice. The states of Württemberg-Baden and Württemberg-Hohenzollern had relevant regulations in the law. However, since no implementing ordinances were passed, these were not realized.

[95] Impressive examples come from the earliest documents on the rebuilding of the political parties. One example is the appeal of the Social Democratic Party of Berlin on 15 June 1945 (Treue 1968, pp. 174–177): Subpara. 2 "Securing the food supply...," Subpara. 3 "Securing the essential needs of the broad masses of the population in housing, clothing, and heat...," Subpara. 4 "Rebuilding of the economy..." Or the appeal of the Christian-Democratic Union of Berlin on 26 June 1945 (Treue 1968, pp. 188–191): "The immeasurable misery amongst our people forces us to carry out the building of our economic life, the securing of work and food, clothing and housing, without any concern for personal interests and economic theories, with strict planning. The emergency program for bread, housing, and work takes precedence over everything."

[96] Art. 43 and 44, LVerf.Baden; Art. 151, LVerf.Bay; Art. 38 and 39, LVerf.Br; Art. 27 and 38, LVerf.He; Art. 51 and 52, LVerf.RP; Art. 25, LVerf.WB; Art. 92, LVerf.WH.

Art. 151 of the Constitution of Bavaria:
(1) The entirety of economic activity shall serve the common wellbeing, in particular a guarantee of dignified existence for all and a gradual enhancement of living standards for all sections of the community.
Art. 51 of the Constitution of Rhineland-Palatinate:
(1) The task of the economy... is to provide for all members of the people the material goods needed to satisfy the necessities of life. The organization of economic life must accord with the principles of social justice, with the goal of guaranteeing a dignified existence for all.

The state has a responsibility to oversee,[97] supervise,[98] protect,[99] promote,[100] and guarantee.[101] Occasionally we also hear of the state's mandate to guide the economy.[102]

The hardship of the time and probably also the familiarity with the planned war economy had initially given rise also to much more far-reaching ideas.[103] For example, the preliminary draft of a constitution for Bavaria gave the title "The Planned Economy" to the section that would later carry the heading "The Economic System." And instead of the later Art. 152, which obligated the state to supervise "the orderly production and distribution of economic goods to satisfy the population's necessities of life," it still contained an Art. 113, which stated:

(1) The economy is guided by the state government in accordance with a uniform plan.
(2) To that end, the state government shall use an advisory council, whose members are to be appointed based on suggestions by the economic organizations.[104]

The intervention by the American occupying authorities and the growing conviction of the delegates that this concept went too far in enshrining "the

[97] Art. 152, Sent. 1, LVerf.Bay.

[98] Art. 51, Para. 2, Sent. 1, LVerf.RP.

[99] Art. 153, Sent. 1, LVerf.Bay; Art. 51, Para. 2, Sent. 1, LVerf.RP.

[100] Art. 153, Sent. 3, LVerf.Bay.

[101] Art. 153, Sent. 2; Art. 164, Sent. 2, LVerf.Bay.

[102] Art. 39, Para. 1, LVerf.Br: "The state has the duty... to create through laws a meaningful guidance of production, manufacturing, and the exchange of good, and to guarantee everyone a just share in the economic productivity of labor." Art. 38, Para. 1, LVerf.He: "The economy of the state has the task to serve the people and satisfy their needs. To that end, the law must decree the measures that are necessary to guide production, manufacturing, and distribution in a meaningful way, and to secure everyone a just share of the economic result of his labor."

[103] On the need for a planned economy see also the "Politische Leitsätze der Sozialdemokratischen Partei Deutschlands vom 11. Mai 1946" (Treue 1968, pp. 182–188), Sect. I: "Social Democracy seeks a socialist economy through planned guidance and the shaping of the economy overall."

[104] Verfassungsauschuss der Bayerischen Verfassunggebenden Landesversammlung, 1946: Stenographische Berichte über die Verhandlungen, vol. 1, p. 10. See also the explanatory report, ibid, p. 14: "Under the current conditions, the committee came out unanimously in favor of a planned economy, the takeover of the ownership of mineral resources, power sources, important means of production, large banks, and insurance companies by bodies under public law, for the promotion of the cooperative system, and for a planned distribution of economic loans."

conditions today" (ibid.) eventually brought about that the project of a planned economy was replaced with more liberal, future-oriented formulations.[105]

The guarantee of economic freedom received another, very important accent through the prohibition on the formation of cartels and monopolies.[106] This was seconded, almost as a counterpart, by the emphasis on the freedom of economic activity in connection with the *Mittelstand.*[107]

(b) The binding of economic potentialities – nationalization (*Sozialisierung*) and land reform

In keeping with the mandate that was given to the economy, the economic potentialities were placed in service to the general public: "Capital formation is not an end in itself, but a means to develop the national economy."[108] This obligation was to be given structural expression by the transfer of important goods into *common property or property of the public sector, or by placing them under state supervision.*[109] The Constitution of Hesse went furthest in this regard:

> Art. 39
> (1) Every abuse of economic freedom – especially for the concentration of monopolistic power and political power – is prohibited.
> (2) Wealth that bears the danger of such an abuse of economic freedom is to be transferred into common property on the basis of legal provisions. To the extent that the transfer into common property is not economically expedient, this wealth must be placed under state oversight through legal provisions or administered by state-appointed bodies.
> Art. 40
> Common property is the property of the people. Control over this property and its administration shall, according to more specific legal provisions, belong to those legal entities that offer a guarantee that the property will serve exclusively the welfare of the entire nation and concentrations of power will be avoided.
> Art. 41
> (1) When this constitution takes effect
> 1. the following will be transferred into common property: mining (coal, potash, ores), the enterprises of iron and steel production, the enterprises of the energy sector and the transportation system tied to rails or overhead lines;

[105] Verfassungsauschusses der Bayerischen Verfassunggebenden Landesversammlung, Stenographische Berichte über die Verhandlungen, vol. 3, pp. 566, 567–572, 626, 647f.; Verfassungsausschuss der Bayerischen Verfassunggebenden Landesversammlung. Stenographische Berichte über die Verhandlungen, vol. 4, p. 168. On this and the corresponding events in Hesse see Fait (1985, pp. 420–455) and Fait (1998, esp. pp. 132f., 148f., 413–423, 438).

[106] Art. 46, LVerf.Baden; Art. 156, LVerf.Bay; Art. 41, LVerf.Br; Art. 39, Para. 1, LVerf.He; Art. 52, Para. 2, Sent. 2, LVerf.RP; Art. 99, LVerf.WH.

[107] Art. 43, Para. 1, Sent. 4, LVerf.Baden; Art. 153, LVerf.Bay; Art. 40, LVerf.Br; Art. 43, LVerf.He.

[108] Art. 157, Para. 1, LVerf.Bay.

[109] Art. 15, Para. 4, Art. 45, LVerf.Baden; Art. 160, LVerf.Bay; Art. 12, Para. 2, Art. 42 and 43, LVerf.Br; Art. 61 and 62, LVerf.RP; Art. 28, LVerf.WB; Art. 98, LVerf.WHz.

2. the following will be supervised or administered by the state: the big banks and insurance companies, and those enterprises listed under Item 1 whose headquarters are not in Hesse.

(2) Further details are determined by the law.

In keeping with this binding mandate of the constitution, Hesse subsequently became the only state in which the program of nationalization (*Sozialisierung*) was carried out on an appreciable scale.[110] A complex controversy ensued (Huber 1954, pp. 180–194; Krüger 1958, p. 322). Nationalization in Hesse came to an end (G. Winter 1976, pp. 119–153; Heiden 1995) with the final law on Art. 41 of the Constitution of Hesse of 6 July 1954 (GVBl., p. 126).

Apart from that, nationalization, which a large number of crucial political and societal forces after 1945 saw as an essential consequence from the lessons of the past and as an important precondition for a social path into the future,[111] remained from the outset a program of constitutional law (E. Schmidt 1981). The divergences between the intentions of the occupying powers and German ideas surely played a considerable role in all of this (Rudzio 1978, pp. 1–39; Steininger 1979, pp. 167–240). The thrust of the *German* idea was to place key objects of *Daseinsvorsorge* and economic life – be they qualitatively defined (mineral resources, energy sources, transportation systems, and so on) or quantitatively (such as large concentrations of wealth) or even combine both characteristics (big banks or insurance companies) – into the responsibility of carriers who would provide a special guarantee that their power would be exercised in loyal subordination to political democracy and in the interest of the polity and the society. Nationalization thus had primarily a positive goal, the "good" object of ownership. By contrast, the *occupying powers* had primarily a negative goal. This goal was to break up the concentration of economic rights of disposition into a small number of subjects and to destroy the power that was tied to this concentration. If one asks about a positive goal of the occupying powers, opinions diverged. The crucial consideration was not, as in German thinking about nationalization, the structurally "good" subject. What dominated was the goal of a multitude of independent subjects, by virtue of which the carriers of the economic power of disposition controlled one another. The thrust of the policy of the occupying powers was aimed at de-concentration, not nationalization (Huber 1953, pp. 335–337, 436–476; 1954, pp. 770–785).

[110] On 18 July 1947, Bavaria passed a "Erstes Gesetz zur Durchführung des Art. 160 der Bayerischen Verfassung" GVBl., p. 152, and later "Gesetz Nr. 110 zur Sicherung der Brennstoff-versorgung und zur Förderung der Braunkohlenwirtschaft (Zweites Gesetz zur Durchführung des Art. 160 Bayerische Verfassung) vom 31. März 1948" GVBl., p. 54. The two laws attained little practical significance. In Hesse itself, the legal situation was, of course, more complicated than the constitutional norm suggested. First, the published version of Art. 41 of the constitution deviated from its agreed-upon version; see Huber (1954, pp. 180–182). Second, the law envisaged in Art. 41, Para. 2 of the LVerf.He was never passed; instead, there was a "Treuhändergesetz vom 25. August 1947" GVBl., p. 72.

[111] See Mommsen (1982).

The situation was fundamentally different with respect to *land reform* (Trittel 1982). Land reform has never been a critique of the private ownership of land, but of the distribution of land, and of the system of laws about how the land can be used and disposed of (von Nell-Breuning 1985). The goal that the occupying powers and German forces unanimously pursued with a land reform was therefore not the creation of new, "good" carriers of landed property, but a better distribution among more owners and a better system to regulate the content of and constrain property. Thanks to the commitment of the occupying powers, the legal foundations for a land reform existed in all zones from 1946 on (Huber 1954, pp. 71–73). By contrast, the constitutions of the states lack the kind of pathos on this issue comparable to the articles dealing with nationalization. Only the Constitution of Hesse contained an explicit program of land reform (Art. 42). The Constitution of Bremen formulated a corresponding regulatory mandate.[112] Other constitutions touched the topic with even more restraint[113] or not at all.

4.5.2 Work – Income – Wealth – Taxes

The Central Place of Work

The constitutional programs of those years clearly reflected the basic assertion that every person should have the opportunity to earn a living through work, but that he also bears the responsibility to do so. All constitutions of those years, provided they were not only organizational statutes, imparted a pronounced structure to work.[114] Work is a basic value of the community.[115] Everyone has a right to work.[116] The corollary is an obligation to work.[117] This obligation to work is regularly subject to the proviso of personal freedom. Its fulfillment is not directly compelled, but its non-fulfillment can have negative consequences. In view of the importance that is

[112] Art. 45, Para. 1 LVerf.Br: "The state exercises oversight over how landed property is distributed and how it is used. It must prevent the continuation and new formation of excessively large landed property."

[113] Art. 163–165 LVerf.Bay.

[114] Art. 37, LVerf.Baden; Art. 166–177, LVerf.Bay; Art. 8, 37, and 46–58, LVerf.Br; Art. 27–37, LVerf.He; Art. 53–59, LVerf.RP; Art. 20, LVerf.WB; Art. 90, LVerf.WH.

[115] Art. 166, Para. 1, Art. 168, Para. 1, LVerf.Bay; Art. 37, LVerf.Br; Art. 53, Para. 1, LVerf.RP.

[116] Art. 37, Para. 1, LVerf.Baden; Art. 166, Para. 2, LVerf.Bay; Art. 8, Para. 1, LVerf.Br; Art. 28, Para. 2, LVerf.He; Art. 53, Para. 2, LVerf.RP; Art. 20, Para. 1, Sent. 3, LVerf.WB; Art. 90, Para. 1, Sent. 2, LVerf.WH.

[117] Art. 37, Para. 2, LVerf.Baden; Art. 166, LVerf.Bay; Art. 8, Para. 1, LVerf.Br; Art. 28, Para. 2, LVerf.He; Art. 53, Para. 2, LVerf.RP; Art. 20, Para. 1, Sent. 1, LVerf.WB; Art. 90, Para. 1, Sent. 1, LVerf.WH.

accorded to work, the capacity for work must be protected[118] – protection of the capacity of work first and foremost against the dangers of work, but also against other hazards. Particular attention was paid to mothers, children, and youths.[119]

Generally left open was the question of whether "work" meant specifically dependent gainful employment, or also self-employment and unpaid work. At any rate, the elaboration was focused on *dependent* gainful work: as with the regulations governing working hours,[120] vacation,[121] codetermination in the workplace and enterprise,[122] freedom of association and free collective bargaining,[123] labor struggle and mediation,[124] the shape of labor law,[125] and, finally, separate labor courts.[126] However, thought was also given to *independent gainful work*, especially in small and mid-size businesses and in agriculture.[127] The problem of *unpaid family* work was seen and honored: "The domestic work of the wife is seen as equal to the professional work of the husband."[128] The problem of a conflict between domestic work and participation in gainful and public life was also addressed: "The law. . .. establishes the guarantee that the woman can reconcile her tasks as a citizen and a productive person with her duties as wife and mother."[129] A few constitutions already saw to it that the domestic distribution of roles had to find a balance in the fact that the partner who assumed the domestic work attained a corresponding share

[118] Art. 37, Para. 4, Art. 41, Para. 2, LVerf.Baden; Art. 167, LVerf.Bay; Art. 49, Para. 1 and 2, Art. 52, Para. 1, Sent. 1, LVerf.Br; Art. 28, Para. 1, LVerf.He; Art. 53, Para. 1, LVerf.RP; Art. 20, Para. 1, Sent. 2, LVerf.WB; Art. 4, 91, Para. 1, LVerf.WH.

[119] Art. 41, Para. 2, 4, LVerf.Baden; Art. 52, Para. 1, Sent. 2, and Para. 2, Art. 54, LVerf.Br; Art. 30, LVerf.He; Art. 55, LVerf.RP; Art. 20, Para. 3, LVerf.WB; Art. 90, Para. 3, LVerf.WH.

[120] Art. 173, LVerf.Bay; Art. 55, Para. 2, LVerf.Br; Art. 31, LVerf.He; Art. 57, Para. 1, Sent. 1, LVerf.RP.

[121] Art. 41, Para. 1, LVerf.Baden; Art. 174, Para. 1, LVerf.Bay; Art. 56, LVerf.BR; Art. 34, LVerf. He; Art. 57, Para. 4, LVerf.RP; Art. 22, Para. 1, LVerf.WB.

[122] Art. 39, LVerf.Baden; Art. 175, LVerf.Bay; Art. 47, LVerf.Br; Art. 37, LVerf.He; Art. 67, LVerf.RP; Art. 22, Para. 2, LVerf.WB; Art. 96, Para. 1, LVerf.WH.

[123] Art. 38, LVerf.Baden; Art. 169 Para. 2, Art.170 LVerf.Bay; Art. 48, 50, Para. 2, LVerf.Br; Art. 29, Para. 2, Art. 36 LVerf.He; Art. 54, 66, 68, LVerf.RP; Art. 23, LVerf.WB; Art. 95, LVerf.WH.

[124] Art. 38, Para. 2, LVerf.Baden; Art. 177, LVerf.Bay; Art. 51, LVerf.Br; Art. 29, Para. 3, 4, and 5, LVerf.He; Art. 54, 66, Para. 2, LVerf.RP; Art. 23, Para. 3, LVerf.WB; Art. 97, LVerf.WH.

[125] Art. 41, Para. 1, LVerf.Baden; Art. 172, LVerf.Bay; Art. 50, Para. 1, LVerf.Br; Art. 29, Para. 1, LVerf.He; Art. 54, Para. 1, Sent. 1, LVerf.RP; Art. 22, Para. 1, LVerf.WB; Art. 96, Para. 4, LVerf. WH.

[126] Art. 177, LVerf.Bay.

[127] Art. 47, Para. 1, Art. 48, LVerf.Baden; Art. 153, 164, LVerf.Bay; Art. 40, Para. 1, LVerf.Br; Art. 43, Para. 1, LVerf.He; Art. 65, Para. 1, LVerf.RP; Art. 26 and 27, LVerf.WB; Art. 93 and 94, LVerf.WH.

[128] Art. 22, Sent. 2, LVerf.Br (amended 1997) – likewise Art. 21, Para. 2, Sent. 1, LVerf.Baden; Art. 16, Para. 2, Sent. 1, LVerf.WB; Art. 102, Para. 1, LVerf.WH.

[129] Art. 30, Para. 2, LVerf.He – likewise Art. 41, Para. 4, LVerf.Baden; Art. 54, LVerf.Br.

of the family income and family wealth.[130] Even *charitable and non-profit work* was addressed – though of course not directly in connection with the specific social goals of the constitutions. However, we find provisions about relevant obligations for the general public,[131] about emergency assistance,[132] and especially about access to "honorary posts" and the duty to assume them.[133] Of course, the constitutions provide no answers to the question of *how* the differences between dependent and independent work, between paid work and unpaid work, or also between familiar and trans-familial unpaid work are to be adequately assessed and dealt with. The statement in the Bavarian Constitution, "Every honest form of work has an equal moral value and a claim to appropriate remuneration,"[134] identifies the problem without solving it.

At this early stage, the constitutions thus already painted a *basic pattern that has remained determinative to this day*. The *first proposition* of that pattern states that the social structure is based on open *access to remunerative work* and on the fact that there is, in both societal and legal terms, an indirect *obligation* ("burden") *to make use of the access provided*. A *second proposition* states that there is *free choice between independent and dependent employment*. A *third proposition* asserts that *the state* is obligated to ensure *above all* the possibility of *dependent gainful employment* and to provide social protection for *dependent workers*, but that, on the other hand, the "*burden*" of taking on paid work *becomes concentrated on dependent paid work*. Finally, a *fourth proposition* maintains that the *polity, society, and individuals depend* on the circumstances that *individuals take on work without remuneration* – in the family, the realm of charitable interpersonal relations, in society's public sphere, and in clubs and organizations; that this unpaid work consequently deserves recognition; however, that a general norm of how the economic disadvantages entailed by this work should be compensated does not exist.

Income

Work is supposed to generate an *appropriate income*.[135] What *income from dependent work* is appropriate must be determined by the instruments by which wages are set, especially free collective bargaining and the mediation processes that complement it (see above notes 123 and 124). The setting of minimum wages was the

[130] Art. 21, Para. 2, Sent. 2, LVerf.Baden; Art. 16, Para. 2, Sent. 2, LVerf.WB; Art. 102, Para. 2, LVerf.WH.

[131] Art. 9, Sent. 2, LVerf.Br.

[132] Art. 122, LVerf.Bay; Art. 10, LVerf.Br; Art. 22, LVerf.RP.

[133] Art. 121, LVerf.Bay; Art. 9, Sent. 3, LVerf.Br; Art. 21, LVerf.RP.

[134] Art. 168, Para. 1, Sent. 1, LVerf.Bay; see also Art. 37, Sent. 2, LVerf.Br.

[135] Art. 41, Para. 3, LVerf.Baden; Art. 168, Para. 1, Sent. 1, LVerf.Bay; Art. 33, LVerf.He; Art. 56, Para. 1, Sent. 1, LVerf.RP.

exception.[136] Incidentally, equal pay was promised to women and young people.[137] In one instance there was reference to the possibility of securing for workers "in a suitable manner a fair share of the net profits by agreement, depending on the nature and productivity of the enterprises."[138]

In principle, the constitutions addressed *income from independent work* only indirectly – in connection with the need to promote the *Mittelstand* and agriculture.[139] One exception is the Constitution of Bavaria, which devised a program for securing agricultural income that was visionary, given the policies of the subsequent decades:

Art. 164, Para. 2, Sent. 1:

> An adequate agricultural income shall be ensured by means of price and wage regulations informed by general economic conditions as well as by market regulations.

Wealth

The constitutions at that time had a very differentiated relationship to wealth. On the one hand, they guaranteed all the basic rights of property.[140] At the same time, however, all of them emphasized that property was bound to the common welfare. That was especially true for the economic use of wealth (see above notes 108–113). The Constitution of Bavaria went especially far in this regard. It expanded the obligations imposed on economic activity (Art. 151 and 152) and especially on capital formation and the finance and credit systems (Art. 157) into the following requirement: "Unemployment benefits for persons fit for work shall be subject to special taxes as determined by the law" (Art. 168, Para. 2, Sent.1). Likewise, it expanded the statement "The distribution and use of land shall be supervised by the state" (Art. 161, Para. 1) into the demand: "Increases in the value of land that arise without particular effort or capital investment on the part of the owner shall be utilized for the general public" (Art. 161, Para. 2). In addition, it assigned to the inheritance tax the task of "preventing the amassing of huge individual fortunes" (Art. 123, Para. 3). On the other hand, it was certainly understood that property is an important foundation of free economic activity. This was emphasized especially for agriculture.[141] Likewise, it was recognized that property is an important principle for protecting the result of individual productivity. The example here is intellectual property.[142] Wealth, after all, is not only "assets," it could also be a "liability":

[136] Art. 169, Para. 1, LVerf.Bay.

[137] Art. 37, Para. 5, LVerf.Baden; Art. 168, Para. 1, Sent. 2, LVerf.Bay; Art. 33, Sent. 2, LVerf.He; Art. 56, Para. 2, LVerf.RP; Art. 20, Para. 2, LVerf.WB; Art. 90, Para. 2, LVerf.WH.

[138] Art. 56, Para. 1, Sent. 2, LVerf.RP.

[139] See above on notes 107 and 127.

[140] Art. 15, LVerf.Baden; Art. 103, LVerf.Bay; Art. 13, LVerf.Br; Art. 45, LVerf.He; Art. 60, LVerf.RP; Art. 8, LVerf.WB; Art. 4, LVerf.WH.

[141] Art. 47, Para. 2, LVerf.Baden; Art. 163, LVerf.Bay; Art. 42, Para. 2, LVerf.He.

[142] Art. 16, LVerf.Baden; Art. 162, LVerf.Bay; Art. 46, LVerf.He; Art. 40, Para. 2, LVerf.RP.

debts. That the latter could pose a social problem was seen in connection with agriculture (Art. 165, LVerf.Bay).

The question which role wealth can play in the individual implementation of the basic formula was posed only in fragmentary form. As was said before: wealth can form the basis for earning an income through independent work (see above notes 107 and 127). But wealth from which a person could live without working seemed problematic at the time (see above). Moreover, wealth was seen and assessed above all in terms of its political importance. Private ownership of certain key objects or "giant fortunes" seemed a threat to the general public (see notes 108–113 and above). The notion that wealth and the income from wealth could be a substitute for income based on work also in a positive sense appeared only in the Constitution of Bremen:

> Art. 58, Para. 1:
> A person who is not able to earn the necessary subsistence for himself and his family members entitled to support will receive it from public funds, provided he cannot derive it from existing wealth or has a statutory or other claim to subsistence.

In general, the inability to work or joblessness appeared as prerequisites for public assistance.[143] The tendency for social redistribution to be focused on work income and replacement for work income, while wealth and the income thereof are disregarded, was becoming apparent.

Taxes

The income and wealth that are available are determined not only by what a person has and acquires, but equally by the taxes that must be paid. The context of work, income, and wealth must therefore also include taxes and levies. The constitutions did not think of either the totality of taxes, or specifically of non-tax levies. With that, it initiated a perspective that would remain largely characteristic for the Federal Republic. Only two constitutions articulated programs of tax law:

> Art. 123, LVerf.Bay:
> (1) Everyone shall be required to bear the burden of public charges in proportion to this income, property, and financial obligations to dependants.
> (2) Consumer taxes and property taxes must be in an appropriate relationship to each other.
> (3) The inheritance tax also serves the purpose of preventing the accumulation of huge individual fortunes. It shall be tiered according to the degree of kinship.
>
> Art. 47, LVerf.He:
> (1) Wealth and income are taxed progressively according to social criteria, with special consideration given to familial burdens.
> (2) When imposing a tax, special consideration must be given to wealth and income earned through work.

[143] Art. 168, Para. 3, LVerf.Bay; Art. 49, Para. 3, LVerf.Br; Art. 28, Para. 3, LVerf.He.

4.5.3 Family – Community of Maintenance

Marriage and the family were recognized and protected as the foundation of social and political life.[144] There were two ways in which a family had different problems than an individual. On the one side was the demand that wages should do justice also to the needs of the family.[145] On the other side, the family was promised social promotion by the state and local communities[146] and social protection.[147] Since the social burden on families increases with the number of children, special social attention was paid to large families.[148] A particular need for social protection was recognized for mothers[149] and for children and young people.[150] Specific consideration was given in this regard to children born out of wedlock.[151] The responsibility of the parents[152] and the responsibility of the state for children and young people[153] were placed side by side. Special emphasis was placed on the responsibility of the states and local communities for orphans.[154]

4.5.4 Meeting Basic Needs

The general hardship and misery continued unabated during this phase. The constitutions declared the meeting of needs as a *task of the economy*, and they accorded the state essential responsibility for the scope of the economy's effectiveness (see above notes 95–102) With many variations, they expected from nationalization a guarantee of a socially appropriate meeting of basic needs (see above

[144] Art. 21, LVerf.Baden; Art. 124 and 125, LVerf.Bay; Art. 21, LVerf.Br; Art. 4, LVerf.He; Art. 23, Para. 1, LVerf.RP; also: Art. 16, LVerf.WB; Art. 101, LVerf.WH.

[145] Art. 41, Para. 3, LVerf.Baden; Art. 169, Para. 1, LVerf.Bay; Art. 33, Sent. 1, LVerf.He; Art. 56, Para. 1, Sent. 1, LVerf.RP.

[146] Art. 125, Para. 2, LVerf.Bay.

[147] Art. 24, Sent. 3, LVerf.RP.

[148] Art. 21, Para. 3, LVerf.Baden; Art. 125, Para. 3, LVerf.Bay; Art. 16, Para. 3, LVerf.WB; Art. 103, LVerf.WH.

[149] Art. 22, LVerf.Baden; Art. 125, Para. 1, Sent. 2, LVerf.Bay; Art. 54, LVerf.Br; Art. 30, Para. 2, LVerf.He; Art. 24, Sent. 2, LVerf.RP.

[150] Art. 24, Para. 1, Sent. 1, LVerf.Baden; Art. 125, Para. 1, Sent. 1, and Art. 126, Para. 3, Sent. 1, LVerf.Bay; Art. 25, Para. 1, LVerf.Br; Art. 30, LVerf.He; Art. 24 and 25, Para. 1, Sent. 1, LVerf. RP; Art. 19, Para. 1, Sent. 1, LVerf.WB; Art. 105, Para. 1, LVerf.WH.

[151] Art. 23, Sent. 2, LVerf.Baden; Art. 126, Para. 2, LVerf.Bay; Art. 24, LVerf.Br; Art. 25, Para. 2, Sent. 2, LVerf.RP; Art. 18, LVerf.WB; Art. 104, Para. 1, LVerf.WH.

[152] Art. 25, LVerf.Baden; Art. 126, Para. 1, LVerf.Bay; Art. 23, LVerf.Br; Art. 55, Sent. 1, He; Art. 25, Para. 1, Art. 27, Para. 1, LVerf.RP; Art. 17, Para. 1, LVerf.WB; Art. 106, LVerf.WH.

[153] Art. 24, LVerf.Baden; Art. 126, Para. 1, Sent. 2, LVerf.Bay; Art. 23, Para. 1, Sent. 2, LVerf.Br; Art. 25, Para. 1, Sent. 2, Para. 2, Sent. 1, LVerf.RP; Art. 17, Para. 2, Art. 19, LVerf.WB; Art. 104, Para. 2, 105, Para. 1, 3, Art. 106, LVerf.WH.

[154] Art. 23, Sent. 1, LVerf.Baden; Art. 17, Para. 2, LVerf.WB; Art. 104, Para. 2, LVerf.WH.

note 108f.). Other than that, they addressed the various themes in very different ways. The Constitution of Bavaria proposed a solution that was as original as it would be ineffective:

> Art. 155:
> For the purpose of an optimally balanced satisfying of the economic needs of all residents, particular areas of need may be established by law, taking into consideration the interests of independent productive enterprises; and to this end public bodies may be established on a cooperative basis. Such bodies shall have the right of self-administration within the provisions of the law.

Particular attention was given to the right to *housing*.[155] The *health care system* was seen primarily within the context of social insurance.[156] The Constitution of Hesse makes the strongest statements about the universality of the interest in *medical care*. It demands "a social insurance that binds together the entire people" (Art. 35, Para. 1, Sent. 1). And this social insurance it gives the mandate "to raise the people's state of health, also through preventive measures, to afford all necessary aid to the sick, the pregnant, and mothers-in-childbed, and to ensure adequate care for those with limited ability to work, those unable to work, survivors, and in old age" (Art. 35, Para. 2). But the universality of the task of medical care appears also in the statement: "The arrangement of the health care system is a matter of the state" (Art. 35, Para. 3, Sent. 1). The constitutions paid the greatest attention to meeting the need for *primary, secondary, and university education*,[157] to *access to education*,[158] and to *art and culture*.[159] A few constitutions articulated specifically the right of workers to participate in culture.[160]

4.5.5 Social Benefits

That the realization of the basic formula does not guarantee either the individual or families in every instance an adequate income remained self-evident, all these statements about work, income, the meeting of needs, and the community of maintenance notwithstanding. Likewise, the conventional view remained self-evident, namely that the need for social benefits had to be manifested in two fundamentally

---

[155] Art. 49, Para. 1, LVerf.Baden; Art. 106, Para. 1, Art. 125, Para. 3, LVerf.Bay; Art. 14, Para. 1, LVerf.Br.

[156] Art. 42, LVerf.Baden; Art. 35, LVerf.He.

[157] Art. 27 and 30, LVerf.Baden; Art. 129ff., LVerf.Bay; Art. 28ff., LVerf.Br; Art. 56ff., LVerf. He; Art. 27ff., LVerf.RP; Art. 37ff., LVerf.WB; Art. 108ff.; Art. 116 LVerf.WH.

[158] Art. 13, LVerf.Baden; Art. 128, LVerf.Bay; Art. 27, LVerf.Br; Art. 55, LVerf.He; Art. 35, LVerf.WB; Art. 107, LVerf.WH.

[159] Art. 41, Para. 2, LVerf.Baden; Art. 52, Para. 1, Sent. 1, LVerf.Br; Art. 30, Para. 1, LVerf.He; Art. 40, Para. 3, Sent. 2, Art. 56, Para. 1, Sent. 1, LVerf.RP.

[160] Art. 41, Para. 2, LVerf.Baden; Art. 52, Para. 1, Sent. 1, LVerf.Br; Art. 30, Para. 1, LVerf.He; Art. 56, Para. 1, Sent. 1, LVerf.RP.

different ways: in the form of the guarantee of a subsistence minimum through *public assistance* (*Fürsorge*)[161] and in the form of social provision against the vicissitudes of life through social *insurance*.[162] But should these institutions remain the way they were? Or should new approaches take effect? The Constitution of Hesse demanded a "social insurance that binds the entire people together" (Art. 35, Para. 1, Sent. 1). Any greater will to reform was not evident.

Social compensation did not get equal attention. A few constitutions spoke about restitution for "[t]hose who suffered harm at the hands of the National Socialist regime by virtue of their religious or political convictions or their race,"[163] especially also about the restitution of wealth.[164] Even less was said about the victims of the war[165] and about refugees and expellees.[166]

4.5.6 The Common Denominator: The Social State

To comprehensively describe the social task of the state, the constitutions for the most part used the term "*social state*" (*Sozialstaat*).[167] Among the other terms that were used to express the meaning of the social was *human dignity* as a basic right[168] in connection with educational goals,[169] as well as in connection with the economic system[170] and working conditions.[171] "*Social justice*" appeared among the goals of the state,[172] the educational goals,[173] in connection with the economic system,[174] and as a mandate of the administration of justice.[175] By contrast, "*solidarity*," "*participation*," or "*exclusion*" (*Ausschluss*) were not words used at the time. "*Subsidiarity*" remained a background concept. "*Social protection*" (*soziale Sicherheit*) was not

[161] Art. 14, LVerf.Baden; Art. 168, Para. 3, LVerf.Bay; Art. 58, LVerf.Br; Art. 28, Para. 3, Sent. 1, LVerf.He; Art. 89, Para. 1, LVerf.WH.

[162] Art. 42, LVerf.Baden; Art. 171, LVerf.Bay; Art. 57, LVerf.Br; Art. 35, Para. 1 and 2, LVerf.He; Art. 53, Para. 3 and 4, LVerf.RP; Art. 24, LVerf.WB; Art. 100, LVerf.WH.

[163] Art. 183, LVerf.Bay; Art. 139, Para. 2, LVerf.RP.

[164] Art. 139, Para. 1, LVerf.RP.

[165] Art. 139, Sect. 2 and 3, LVerf.RP; Art. 89, Sect. 2 and 3, LVerf.WH.

[166] Art. 139, Para. 3, LVerf.RP demands a "social equalization of burdens" for the "monetary and material losses as a consequence of National Socialist war and economic policy."

[167] Art. 50, Para. 1, LVerf.Baden; Art. 3, Sent. 1, LVerf.Bay; Art. 74, Sent. 1, LVerf.RP; Art. 43, Sent. 1, LVerf.WB.

[168] Art. 100, LVerf.Bay; Art. 5, Para. 1, LVerf.Br; Art. 3, LVerf.He.

[169] Art. 131, Para. 2, LVerf.Bay; Art. 26, Para. 1, LVerf.Br.

[170] Art. 151, Para. 1, LVerf.Bay; Art. 27, LVerf.He; Art. 51, Para. 1, Sent. 2, LVerf.RP.

[171] Art. 52, Para. 1, Sent. 1, LVerf.Br.

[172] Art. 65, Para. 1, LVerf.Br – see also Art. 3, Sent. 3, LVerf.WH: "just equalization."

[173] Art. 26, no. 1, LVerf.Br.

[174] Art. 51, Para. 1, Sent. 2, LVerf.RP.

[175] Art. 134, LVerf.Br.

yet familiar to the usage at the time. Finally, "*Daseinsvorsorge*" was used by everyone. The constitutions, however, did not employ the term: while they occasionally describe the matter,[176] the word itself was not incorporated. When it comes to "*equality*," the situation was ambiguous. All constitutions contained the general principle of equality.[177] They also laid down a number of prohibitions against discrimination: on the grounds of gender, ancestry, origin, social status, race, religion, political beliefs, and so on.[178] The constitutions also spoke of the equality of men and women – rarely in general terms,[179] and for the most part included in the prohibitions against discrimination[180] or limited to various spheres of life.[181] However, the economic dimension of equality that is specific to the social state was – with the exception of the requirement of equal pay (see note 189) – articulated only in the Constitution of Bremen: "All people are equal before the law and have the right to equal possibilities of economic and cultural development" (Art. 2, Para. 1).

4.6 Laying the Foundations of the Social Market Economy 1948/1949[182]

4.6.1 The Change to a Competitive Economy

The Starting Point: The Dominance of Inertia and Doubt

The economic reality of those years continued to be determined by economic guidance (Huber 1954, pp. 197–354). Opinion within society and politics was not pushing for a change. On the contrary: a part of public opinion believed that a planned economy was unavoidable, indeed, necessary and desirable; another part was at least unsure about whether the current problems could be solved without a planned economy. And planning and guidance seemed indispensable also for a

[176] For example, when the Constitution of Bavaria (Art. 152) speaks of the "ordered production and distribution of economic resources to meet the necessary needs of the population." See also Art. 38, Para. 1, LVerf.Br; Art. 38, Para. 1, Sent. 1, LVerf.He.

[177] Art. 2, Sent. 1, LVerf.Baden; Art. 118, Para. 1, LVerf.Bay; Art. 2, Para. 1, LVerf.Br; Art. 1, LVerf.He; Art. 17, Para. 1 and 2, LVerf.RP; Art. 2, Para. 1, LVerf.WB.

[178] Art. 2, Sent. 2, 3, and 7, Para. 2, Art. 37, Para. 6, LVerf.Baden; Art. 2, Para. 2, LVerf.Br.; Art. 1, LVerf.He; Art. 10, Para. 1, LVerf.WB; Art. 6, Para. 1, LVerf.WH.

[179] Art. 17, Para. 3, LVerf.RP.

[180] See note 178.

[181] Thus in regard to the equality of spouses (Art. 124, Para. 2, LVerf.Bay; Art. 22, Para. 1, LVerf. Br) and civic rights (Art. 118, Para. 2, LVerf.Bay; amended 1998), but especially with respect to the equality in the workplace (Art. 53, Para. 2, LVerf.Br; Art. 20, Para. 2, Sent. 1, LVerf.WB; Art. 90, Para. 2, Sent. 1, LVerf.WH) and equal pay (Art. 168, Para. 1, Sent. 2, LVerf.Bay; Art. 53, Para. 1, LVerf.Br; Art. 33, Sent. 2, LVerf.He; Art. 56, Para. 2, LVerf.RP; Art. 20, Para. 2, Sent. 2, LVerf. WB; Art. 90, Para. 2, Sent. 2, LVerf.WH).

[182] Weimer (1998, pp. 31–70).

more distant future which might not be characterized by the present problems of extreme shortages. That the economy should be placed in service to the common good, especially the social, was a widely held opinion, in any case. How would the mechanism of the free market and competition relate to this? Added to this was another aspect: the relationship between a free market economy and democracy (Zacher 1981, pp. 315–340). Is a democracy real or even conceivable, if it does not also govern the economic potentialities? Will a democracy not be undermined if the economic forces, and thus also powers, remain autonomous? How does the democratic equality and sovereignty of citizens square with their economic inequality as employers and workers, as market-dominating suppliers and dependent demanders, or simply as the rich and the poor? Must democratic structures and norms not be extended also into economic life? In other words: Is a democracy not a priori overextended if it is also responsible for the economy – not only its structure, but also the processes of production and distribution? Does a democracy not presuppose the dialectic of the state and economic self-fulfillment? The economic policy debate at the time came up with various answers to these questions. Overarching was the "yes" to nationalization: to the transfer of ownership in essential resources to subjects that were constrained politically or by the public sector.[183] Other than that, to control positions of economic power, the chosen path was workers' rights, especially also codetermination within the workplace and beyond, as well as restrictions on monopolies and cartels.[184] The question, however, of how much rule of political democracy over the economy is necessary (Arndt 1946), or how much "private law society" a democracy – especially a democracy – needs (Böhm 1946), was left in abeyance. The only thing that was beyond doubt is that the state should have a responsibility for the way in which the economy operated.

The crucial point was this: nothing seemed to overcome the forces of persistence that pointed toward the path of a guided economy. Perhaps – it might appear – there was still quite a bit left to be done to realize the programs of socialization, the control of monopolies and cartels, the obligations imposed on capital, and so on. Perhaps there was still quite a bit left to do to sound out anew the scope for the freedom of economic activity, and perhaps expand it. But that could very well be reconciled with economic guidance, and possibly even with central economic planning.

The Forces that Brought About the Change

The energy to overcome this inertia[185] came from a small group of actors – scholars who had begun to spell out the clear concept of a competitive economy in the midst of the deep and varied challenges of economic policy in the Weimar Period

[183] See above notes 108–120.

[184] See above notes 93f., 122.

[185] On what follows see Ambrosius (1977).

(Blumenberg-Lampe 1973). The core of this circle was formed by the economist *Walter Eucken* and the jurists *Franz Böhm* and *Hans Großmann-Doerth*. Their work was connected to the leading figures of the Neoliberal School: *Erwin von Beckerath, Friedrich A. von Hayek, Leonhard Miksch, Erich Preiser, Wilhelm Röpke, Alexander Rüstow*, and others. But *Walter Eucken* and *Franz Böhm* probably deserve the greatest credit for studying and powerfully explaining the free market and competition as both a self-carrying system of extraordinary efficiency – as an "*Ordo*"[186] – and a regulatory task of the state. With the picture of a "set of data" (*Datenkranz*) that surrounds the market economy, Eucken created a productive model for distinguishing between the market economy and the political fields that surround it (Eucken 1989, p. 262f., notes 51, 143–146, 156–162). It became clear that the market economy provides the greatest service to the social by realizing its productivity and generating prosperity, while it must remain the task of a complementary social policy to distribute this prosperity in a socially just way (Eucken 1948, pp. 113–131; Hohmann 1988, pp. 91–101). The system of the free market and of competition, including the state's responsibility for this system, could – indeed, had to – be thought of as separate from social policy without negating its concerns. *Alfred Müller-Armack* gave this system the name "social market economy" (*soziale Marktwirtschaft*).[187]

The person, whoever, who transformed these ideas into policy was *Ludwig Erhard* (Hentschel 1996). After finishing his studies and obtaining his doctorate in Economics, he had joined the *Institut für Wirtschaftsbeobachtung* of the Handelshochschule Nuremberg in 1929 as a scientific associate. Beginning in 1933, he became a deputy director there. His refusal to join a National Socialist Organization caused difficulties for him. In 1942 he saw himself compelled to leave the Institute. In 1945, the Americans appointed him head of the Office of Economics in his hometown of Fürth. At their urging he was put in charge of the Bavarian Ministry of Economics. However, with no talent and experience in managing a bureaucracy, he felt compelled to step down in January of 1947. In October of that year, though, he was appointed head of the newly established *Sonderstelle Geld und Kredit* in Bad Homburg, an expert commission that had been set up to prepare the currency reform for the three western occupation zones. In March 1948, immediately after the structure of government for the United Economic Area had been redesigned, Ludwig Erhard was elected Director of Economic Administration. It was the Free Democrats that had put him forth as a candidate for the post, and the CDU/CSU had supported them.[188] Ludwig Erhard was now in the post where he

[186] This is expressed by the central publications intended to provide a forum for these ideas: 1936–1937, the series "Ordnung der Wirtschaft," ed. by Böhm, Eucken and Großmann-Doerth; after 1948, then, the annual *ORDO*, ed. by Böhm, Eucken, Lutz and Meyer.

[187] Müller-Armack (1974). On this see also his own testimony in his "Soziale Marktwirtschaft" (1956, p. 392).

[188] The Economic Council, the parliamentary body f the United Economic Area, had the following party composition: CDU/CSU 40; SPD 40; FDP 8; KPD 6; DP 4; Zentrum 4; WAV 2.

could blaze the trail for the free market economy. And in the impending currency reform, which was being carried out under the responsibility of the occupying powers, he saw the decisive chance to free the economy of the Bizone from the fetters of a guided economy. The currency laws opened up the prospect of a healthy currency suitable to a productive economy. And the *Bank deutscher Länder* offered the institutional prospect that the development of the currency could not be put at risk by political interventions.

The extent to which Ludwig Erhard was sustained by the theoretical arguments of the Neoliberals, and the extent – on the other hand – to which his efforts on behalf of a free market and competition expressed above all his personality and experiences must remain an open question. The crucial element was that the Neoliberal school had created a framework of ideas and discussion that allowed Ludwig Erhard's policies to be understood and accepted beyond his own explanation. An important bridge in that process was the *Wissenschaftlicher Beirat beim Direktor der Verwaltung für Wirtschaft des Vereinigten Wirtschaftsgebietes* (Advisory Council to the Director of Economic Administration of the United Economic Area), which had been set up in January of 1948 at the initiative of *Walter Strauß*, at the time the Deputy Director of Economic Administration and head of the Legal Office of the United Economic Area. The Council included numerous representatives of the Neoliberal school. On the whole, though, its composition was pluralistic. In particular, it also included individuals who were close to the social democratic movement. In this way, their reservations about a liberalization of the economy carried weight in the Council.[189] In its first report dated 1 April 1948, titled "Measures for the regulation of consumption, rationing, and price policy after the currency reform" (ibid., 1–6), the Advisory Council formulated the decisions that would be at stake in the months to follow:

2. The currency reform makes sense only if a fundamental change of the previous guidance of the economy is tied to it. As an isolated, technical procedure it would be pointless, if not actually dangerous...
3. The Council is of the opinion that the function of prices, to guide the economic process, should come into play to the broadest possible extent. This opinion rules out allocation measures, unless there are compelling, especially social, reasons in their favor...
4. Guidance through prices serves to boost the national product. That is the most important socio-political task of the moment. This leaves open the further question which economic and social system should be pursued over the long run...
10. The majority of the Council is in favor of lifting the control measures also of basic commodities, in the interest of creating a relevant cost structure and gaining stringent possibilities of calculation for comparison within an enterprise and between enterprises. A minority regards at least a partial control of essential commodities as indispensable...

[189] On the founding composition of the Advisory Council see Bundesministerium für Wirtschaft (1973, p. 623f.).

13. In addition to the measures indicated above, the Council also believes it is absolutely necessary to overcome the currently disordered wage policy through an orderly wage formation, a process that proceeds from the fundamental assumption that obligations from collective bargaining agreements are recognized...
14. Neither the majority nor the minority proposals mean that an influence over the processes of the national economy via a credit and economic policy is abandoned.

The Events of June 1948

From that time on, the development proceeded rapidly and decisively in the direction of creating a free market economy. The Transitional Law on Price Formation and Price Controls (Price Law) went into effect on 10 April 1948 (WIGBl., p. 27). It replaced the Law on the Appointment of a Reich Commissioner for Price Formation of 29 October 1936 (RGBl. I, p. 927) and the Statute regarding the Commissioner for Price Formation and Price Controls of 29 August 1946 (Sect. 15 of the Price Law), and it accorded pricing law a foundation that was in keeping with a democratic state under the rule of law, though without anticipating the liberalization of the price maintenance laws. On 21 April 1948, Ludwig Erhard delivered his inaugural address to the Economic Council.[190] Only the currency reform and the Marshall Plan together, he argued, could secure the economic upswing. Currency reform was the point at which the economy must be once again accorded more freedom. He contended that only a system oriented toward competition and the strongest will to produce would be able to overcome the economic misery and make possible an economic policy with a social orientation. Prices would have to adjust to the supply of goods, which would in turn flow from new, honest work. In the market, money was to once again find complete backing from the goods economy. Currency reform, Ludwig maintained, initiated a dynamic process at the end of which stood a liberal, free market system.

Immediately before the currency reform, in June 1948, Erhard submitted to the Economic Council the draft of a law on "Principles for Control and Price Policy after the Monetary Reform."[191] The law gave both the Director of Economics and the Director for Food, Agriculture, and Forests extensive powers to suspend price and control regulations temporarily or permanently, or reinstitute them. Freedom from controls must be given preference over controls, price freedom over price setting.[192] "Loosening the state systems for distributing goods and setting prices has its limits where the issue is... to guarantee the protection of the economically weaker

[190] Wörtlicher Bericht über die 14. Vollversammlung des Wirtschaftsrates des Vereinigten Wirtschaftsgebietes, pp. 436–445.

[191] "Wirtschaftsrat Drucksache 331/1948 vom 1. Juni 1948" (issued on 10 June 1948). First reading on 17 June 1948: Wörtlicher Bericht über die 18. Vollversammlung des Wirtschaftsrates des Vereinigten Wirtschaftsgebietes, pp. 623–638; Second/third reading on 18 June 1948: Wörtlicher Bericht über die 18. Vollversammlung des Wirtschaftsrates des Vereinigten Wirtschaftsgebietes, pp. 652–666.

[192] Art. I, no. 1, Art. II, no. 1 of the Appendix to the law.

individuals" and "to prevent the exploitation of a situation of shortage through monopolistic influences."[193] The law was considered in a memorable debate in the Economic Council on 17 and 18 June. It was adopted with 50 votes to 37, with the CDU/CSU and FDP largely arrayed on one side, and the SPD and KPD on the other. On 19 June 1948, the three western occupying powers proclaimed the three laws on the restructuring of the monetary system: the Currency Law, the Emission Law, and the Conversion Law.[194] Effective 21 June 1948, the *Deutsche Mark* was the currency of the three Western occupation zones. The very day of the currency reform – and even before the occupying powers had approved the law on the guiding principles – Ludwig Erhard went on the radio to announce the sweeping lifting of rationing and price control, effective the following Monday, 21 June 1948 (Benz 1983b, p. 434). The occupying powers were angry about this move, but there was nothing they could do against this fait accompli. The Law on the Principles for Control and Price Policy after the Monetary Reform was passed on 24 June 1948.[195] There immediately followed Directive no. 71/48 on Price Formation and Price Oversight after the Currency Reform (Directive on the Freeing of Prices) of 25 June 1948 (WIGBl., p. 61). The free market economy had been put in place.

In the period that followed, economic conditions developed in contradictory ways: while the production of goods rose, real wages declined and unemployment grew (Benz 1983b, pp. 434–439). Doubts about the chosen path grew stronger. Opposition grew. But before the trends toward repealing the decisions of June 1948 could have their way, success arrived. Beginning in 1949 the rates of price increases declined, prices stabilized or dropped, the unemployment rate fell. The Marshall Plan had created a crucial precondition for the prosperity of the German economy.[196] George Marshall, the American Secretary of State, had announced the plan in a speech on 5 June 1947, and the US Congress laid the foundation for it on 3 April 1948, through the Foreign Assistance Act. It was an offer of partnership to 18 European countries, which on 16 April 1948, joined to form the Organization for European Economic Co-Operation (OEEC). The three Western zones were represented by their military governors.

With the far-reaching – though not complete – creation of a free market in goods and the concentration of responsibility for the young currency into the hand of the *Bank deutscher Länder*, the essential steps of what the United Economic Area could accomplish in laying the foundation of a free market economy had been taken. Additional steps were rather marginal.[197] In particular, there were no longer any

[193] Para. 2 of the Preamble.

[194] Military Government Laws nos. 61, 62, and 63, WIGBl., Appendix 5, pp. 1, 11, 13.

[195] However, the relevant "Gesetz- und Verordnungsblatt des Wirtschaftsrats des Vereinigten Wirtschaftsgebietes" was dated 7 July 1948: WIGBl., p. 59.

[196] On the extensive discussion over the interpretation of the economic development see Schröder (1990); Lindlar (1997).

[197] Examples: "Gesetz gegen Preistreiberei vom 7. Oktober 1948," WIGBl., p. 99; "Gesetz gegen Kompensationen vom 3. November 1948," WIGBl., p. 116; "Gesetz über die Errichtung von Fachstellen im Bereich der gewerblichen Wirtschaft vom 6. Mai 1949," WIGBl., p. 73;

regulations about the control of monopolies and cartels. Part of the reason was that the breakup of cartels and multi-corporate enterprises was an essential undertaking of occupation policy (Huber 1953, pp. 335–386, 436–478; 1954, pp. 770–794). Moreover, the subsequent development would show how difficult it was to find solutions for the control of cartels and monopolies that could garner majority support (Huber 1953, pp. 387–396; 1954, pp. 767–770).

4.6.2 The Further Development of the Social System

However, in the brief span between the currency reform and the establishment of the Federal Republic of Germany, some essential things could still happen to give expression also to the social character of this "social market economy."

The Development of the Labor Constitution[198]

An important step forward was the Law to Lift the *Wage Freeze* of 3 November 1948. That same day, the Economic Council passed a *Collective Bargaining Agreement Law.*[199] As a result of opposition from the military governments and proposed amendments from the legislative organs, it could not be passed until 9 April 1949.[200] The unions developed in tandem (Mielke 1987). In the process, they moved from the principle of (person-oriented) professional associations to that of (enterprise-oriented) industrial unions, and from the principle of (politically and ideologically oriented) *Richtungsgewerkschaften* to that of unified trade unions (oriented toward the overarching interests of the workers). The policy of the occupying powers toward the unions was, needless to say, neither uniform nor linear. While the unions initially seemed to the occupying powers as an important ally in democratizing the economy, over time they became concerned that the unions could become too powerful. It was not until 12 October 1949, that the German Federation of Trade Unions (*Deutscher Gewerkschaftsbund*) was founded, and with it the new beginning of the German trade union movement came to a conclusion for the time being. The development was complicated in a different way

"Wirtschaftsstrafgesetz vom 26. Juli 1949," WIGBl., p. 193; "Gesetz über den Kapitalverkehr vom 2. September 1949," WIBl., p. 305. – On the extension of these regulations beyond the Bizone into the French zone see Huber (1954, p. 212f.).

[198] Bundesministerium für Arbeit und Sozialordnung and Bundesarchiv (eds.), 2001b: Geschichte der Sozialpolitik in Deutschland seit 1945, vol. 2, Chap. 3, no. 1.

[199] "Wirtschaftsrat des Vereinigten Wirtschaftsgebietes Drucksache 672/1948. 2. und 3. Lesung vom 9./10. November 1948." Wörtlicher Bericht über die 24. Vollversammlung des Wirtschaftsrates des Vereinigten Wirtschaftsgebietes, pp. 1094–1100.

[200] WIGBl., p. 55. On the further development see "Drucksachen 706/1948, 752/1948, 961/1949, 1017/1949, 1023/1949, 1080/1949." Wörtlicher Bericht des Wirtschaftsrates des Vereinigten Wirtschaftsgebietes, pp. 1243f., 1447f., 1504f., 1560f.; on this see Nipperdey (1949, pp. 81–89).

on the side of the *employers*. While the organization of the economic enterprises seemed a necessity to the occupying powers (Plumpe 1987), the specific organization of the interests of employers remained tied to the reservations that they had toward free collective bargaining, let alone a conception of social self-governance that went beyond this. In the end, though, the amalgamation of the employers' associations for the Bizone took place already in 1949 – even before the German Federation of Trade Unions had been founded.

Social Insurance[201]

The policy of the United Economic Area emphatically confirmed also the social importance of social insurance. This is centrally exemplified by the Social Insurance Adjustment Act of 17 June 1949. This law raised the benefits of pension insurance in line with the wage and price developments. In addition, it introduced a number of structural improvements – not least also in the sense of an aligning of the regulations for workers and white-collar employees (Hockerts 1980, pp. 91–95). Other than that, though, it refrained from any criticism of the segmented system of German social insurance. On the contrary: the two accompanying laws – the *Knappschaft* Insurance Adjustment Act of 30 July 1949, and the Law on the Improvement of Statutory Accident Insurance of 10 August 1949 – affirmed essential elements of the traditional structure.

Social Compensation[202]

The politics of the Unified Economic Area provided essential impulses also to the development of the social compensation law. National Socialist rule had left behind two large groups of those who had suffered harm: those the regime had made into targeted victims, and those who had become victims of the war and the defeat as a result of the developments and events triggered by German politics. Against the backdrop of the problems that had thus arisen, compensation for the *harm the persecuted had suffered* had a special legitimacy and urgency. But the occupying powers had already taken on this problem and had either passed the first regulations themselves, or had the states or German authorities pass them at the zonal level. The Law about the Treatment of the Victims of National Socialist Persecution in Social Insurance of 22 August 1949, supplemented these regulations with the requirement that the secondary damage caused by the National Socialist persecution, especially through the interruption of professional careers, had to be compensated.

[201] Peters (1978, pp. 128–135); see Bundesministerium für Arbeit und Sozialordnung and Bundesarchiv (eds.), 2001b: Geschichte der Sozialpolitik in Deutschland seit 1945, vol. 2, Chap. 3, no. 3–7.

[202] Bundesministerium für Arbeit und Sozialordnung and Bundesarchiv (eds.), 2001b: Geschichte der Sozialpolitik in Deutschland seit 1945, vol. 2, Chap. 3, no. 12.

By contrast, opinions diverged widely when it came to the sacrifices that the Germans had made by virtue of their participation in the fate of the nation. Compensation for *war damage to individuals* (disabled veterans, surviving dependants of those killed in the war) had likewise drawn the special interest of the various occupying powers – even if that interest flowed in cross-currents. After all, the legal situation was different from one zone to the next. And in spite of the warlike past of the nation, compensation for *material war damages* had no regime or model within German legal history.

In this area the United Economic Area faced a specific task – and this all the more so as currency reform had created a new group of harmed individuals: those with "old" savings who had been disproportionately affected. A lot of questions were raised.[203] Should individuals be compensated relative to the harm they had suffered, so that the rich would end up as rich as before, and the poor once again as poor as before? Or should the damages be compensated relative to social urgency? Should the equalization of burdens be "quota-based" or "social"? But if one opted for a social equalization of burdens, why should the property situation of those not harmed be left unchanged? But if there is no social equalization: How could a general redistribution across the entire nation be accomplished? Of course it seemed obvious that the "wealthy" who had suffered no damages should bear the burden for compensating the "poor" who had been harmed. But even under this premise, there were exceedingly difficult questions relating both to gauging what was reasonable and sensible, and to the technique for liquidating "wealth" and transferring it to the "poor." The occupying powers, in the Preamble to the Conversion Law of 20 June 1948, placed the regulation of the equalization of burdens into the jurisdiction of the German legislative bodies. The Economic Council also took on this task.[204] However, coming to an agreement with the occupying powers, who advocated limiting it to social assistance, was not easy. The Immediate Aid Law could not be passed until 8 August 1949, on the eve of the establishment of the Federal Republic. It was limited to immediate aid to expellees and refugees to relieve urgent social hardships. The law was devised as a preliminary step to a comprehensive law on the equalization of burdens – according to the need-based principle and without a previous determination of harm. The costs were to be covered by the Mortgage Guarantee Act of 2 September 1948. This law laid claim to the difference between the claims of mortgagees, devalued at a ratio of 10:1, and the full mortgage debt on land for the benefit of the general public. An entry into the legislation on the equalization of burdens had been found. At the same time, though, its decisive principles had remained open.

---

[203] Schillinger (1985). On the development of the equalization of burdens see also Soziale Sicherung in der Bundesrepublik Deutschland (1966, pp. 11–48).

[204] Drucksachen 1192/1949 des Wirtschaftsrates des Vereinigten Wirtschaftsgebietes. Wörtlicher Bericht des Wirtschaftsrates des Vereinigten Wirtschaftsgebietes v. 5. November 1948, pp. 1079–1094; 19. November 1948, pp. 1135–1149, 1160–1186; 1. Dezember 1948, pp. 1194–1197.

4.6.3 The Basic Lines Are Drawn

Four years after the collapse of the German Reich, the basic lines of the future development had been laid down. *Tradition* had proved its worth. *Public assistance* had probably borne the greatest social burden. To be sure, it had not been able to guarantee everyone at all times a subsistence minimum. And not every time the existential necessities were put in place was it an achievement of public assistance. This was the great period also of spontaneous or compelled help among relatives and friends, or simply among human beings. Still, public assistance was the basis of survival for a large segment of the population. *Social provision* had also proven itself: both in its externalizing form as social insurance, and in its internalizing form as the civil service pension scheme. The latter had been affected severely and in multifarious ways by the political developments. Public sector employers had disappeared and employment relationships had ended. On the other hand: the system as such had endured. The development of *social compensation* proved much more difficult. It had gone into the catastrophe with the self-evident understanding that damages to life and limb (as specified by the provision for war victims) would be compensated, and the first thing that was called into question was this self-evident understanding. By contrast, the restitution for National Socialist injustice was pushing for regulation and implementation. But the mass of material and property damages that the war, expulsion, and other postwar conditions had caused also called for equalization. In the end, the social compensation law, in particular, had become – highly differentiated – a central medium for coming to terms with the past socially.

The "workers' question" – in the sense of both individual and collective employment relationships – was revived quickly and effectively. Incidentally, "more equality" was not an issue to which much constructive attention was devoted, for the hardships of the time were too universal. And their ubiquity covered up and concealed for now the old patterns of typical social inequality. This situation was much more in line with *general "Daseinsvorsorge"* than with efforts aimed at "more equality." But this had simply rendered the problems less important. Most of the solutions endured. And problems and solutions attracted new interest as the distance to the catastrophe grew and the tight grip of hardship and misery loosened.

Most surprising was the development regarding *the responsibility of the state for the economy*. While the power of the circumstances initially kept the idea of a free market economy at bay, they were soon joined by the concern that a free, entrepreneurial market economy could evade the social tasks asked of it. An economy that was structurally and functionally oriented toward the social seemed like the ideal or a necessary evil. Still, liberalization took place in connection with the currency reform – the dual strategy of the "social market economy", which combined an internally optimized free market and competitive economy and its inherent chance of prosperity with institutions of social protection and equalization. Success ensured that this model would endure. And with that, the *basic formula* also took on new strength. To be sure, the social values of the time were a priori built upon it, but the shortage of goods had suspended it. For a long time, work and income did not also bestow the guarantee of being able to meet basic needs – not even as a rule with all the exceptions that had always challenged social policy. Only the free market economy invested new probability in the presumption that work and income were fundamentally tantamount to the ability to meet basic needs. The willingness to embrace the basic formula was strong – the future was built upon it.

5 1949–1957: Laying the Constitutional and Social Foundations of the German Federal Republic[205]

5.1 The Construction of the New Constitutional Order

In January 1948, the United Economic Area had been given new and efficient structures. Shortly thereafter, the three western occupying powers embarked on the path that would eventually lead to the Federal Republic of Germany (Mußgnug 1987). February 1948 saw the start of the Six-Power Conference in London, where the three western occupying powers came together with the Benelux states. In a lengthy session, which lasted until June 1948, they laid down the basic outlines for a "western state." In the meantime, on 20 March 1948, the Soviet representative had left the Allied Control Council. The division of Germany was taking shape. On 16 June 1948, the Allied Command for Berlin also broke apart. This was followed by the currency reform in the West and the East and the Berlin blockade. On 1 July 1948, in Frankfurt, the military governors of the three western occupying powers presented the three *Frankfurt Documents* to the minister-presidents of the states that had been formed in the western zones. Document no. I authorized the minister-presidents to call a National Assembly to write a constitution. In addition, it laid out the parameters within which the constitution of the "western state" would have to lie. Crucial were the goals of a "democratic constitution" and a "federal type of government." The constitution would take effect once it was approved by two-thirds of the states through a simple majority in the state parliaments. In addition, it had to be approved by the military governors.

It was not easy for the *minister-presidents* to assume responsibility for underscoring the division of Germany by enacting a constitution for a "western state." They got around this by giving the new polity a provisional character, which they emphasized by using the term "Basic Law" instead of "Constitution." The constitutional assembly was given the name "*Parliamentary Council.*" Elections for this Parliamentary Council were carried out by the state parliaments, not the people. The CDU/CSU and the SPD came out of these elections with equal strength,

---

[205] Schwarz (1981); Stern (2000, pp. 1209–1472); Kahlenberg and Hoffmann (2001); Bundesministerium für Arbeit und Soziales and Bundesarchiv (eds.), 2005: Geschichte der Sozialpolitik in Deutschland seit 1945, vol. 3, Chap. 1 and 2.

each with 27 seats. The FDP received five seats, the DP, Zentrum, and KPD two each. Five Berlin delegates joined the Council without a vote. The Parliamentary Council was constituted in Bonn on 1 September 1948. Prior to that, the minister-presidents had already appointed an "Expert Committee on Constitutional Questions," which met on the island of *Herrenchiemsee* from 10–23 August. The Committee was a small circle of ministers and experts who prepared the "Herrenchiemsee Proposal." Although it could not anticipate the Parliamentary Council in any way, the proposal became a much-noted foundation for the work of the Council. The Parliamentary Council had to deal not only with the issue and the differences of opinion within its own ranks. The occupying powers also intervened – especially with respect to the federal structure. On 8 May 1949, the Parliamentary Council adopted the draft of the Basic Law with a vote of 53–12. The "No" votes came from the DP (2), the Zentrum (2), the KPD (2), and the CSU (6). With a letter dated 12 May 1949, the military governors put their stamp of approval on the Basic Law. The state parliaments voted on the Basic Law on 18, 20, and 21 May. With the exception of Bavaria, all voted in favor. Although Bavaria rejected the Basic Law, the Bavarian parliament noted emphatically that it recognized the rule stating the Basic Law would take effect once two-thirds of the state parliaments ratified it. The Basic Law for the Federal Republic of Germany was proclaimed on 23 May 1949. In the period from 14 August 1949 (the day of the *Bundestag* elections) to 20 September 1949 (when the first federal government took office), the Federal Republic constituted its constitutional organs. The state had been born. The tasks of the United Economic Area were done (Art. 122 and 133 GG).

5.2 *The Social Determinants of the Basic Law*

5.2.1 The Normative Statements

The Social Goal of the State

The Basic Law that had been created in this way refrained from a differentiated social program. The Herrenchiemsee Proposal had not contained anything about the social tasks of the state.[206] A broad majority of the Parliamentary Council also agreed that the Basic Law could not and should not attempt to prescribe the living conditions of the people (von Doemming and Füßlein 1951, p. 43f.). This is a clear departure from the practice of the state constitutions. One explicit reason behind this restraint was the provisional nature of the Basic Law. Another reason was probably the memory of the weakness of the social program in the Weimar Constitution. The fact that the Parliamentary Council was made up of exceptionally qualified members (Mußgnug 1987, p. 235f.) may have invested this comparison with Weimar with special importance. In addition, no contingent within the Parliamentary

[206] The text of the Herrenchiemsee Proposal can be found in Huber (1951, pp. 219–246).

Council was strong enough to unilaterally put its stamp on the Basic Law: "That, above all, is the reason behind the legal soberness that sets the Basic Law apart from the Weimar Constitution and from the West German state constitutions enacted earlier" (Mußgnug 1987, p. 236). What was clear is that the embrace of the social market economy, which had passed a first test while the Parliamentary Council was at work, counseled caution: What could be said beforehand about optimal solutions to the economic and social problems?

By contrast, a general orientation of the state to the social seemed harmless (Niclauß 1974). On 14 October 1948, the Policy Committee (*Grundsatzausschuss*) of the Parliamentary Council introduced into the draft a stipulation intended to express the essential characteristics of the state. It became *Art. 20 of the Basic Law* (*Entstehungsgeschichte*, pp. 244–262). In the process, the combination that included the word "social" changed. Compared to the initial proposals, which spoke of a "social *Rechtsstaat*," the Policy Committee, at its meeting on 14 October 1948, agreed on Carlo Schmid's suggestions of a "social Republic." That formulation survived a number of modifications of the paragraph and was confirmed once more by the Policy Committee at a meeting on 10 November 1948. However, on 16 November 1948, the general Editorial Committee recommended the compound phrase "social Federal Republic." Finally, in the second reading of the Main Committee on 15 December 1948, Theodor Heuss proposed the version that became part of the Basic Law as Art. 20, Para. 1: "*The Federal Republic of Germany is a democratic and social federal state.*" The Main Committee accepted the proposal. And that decision stood. During no phase of the debate was the meaning of the word "social" discussed.

The second place where the Federal Republic is committed to the goal of a social state is in *Art. 28 of the Basic Law*: the guarantee of an essential congruence of the constitutional order of the Federal Republic and the individual *Länder* Entstehungsgeschichte, pp. 244–262. The Herrenchiemsee Proposal had already included a corresponding stipulation (Art. 29), although it focused on democracy and the state under the rule of law. On 14 October 1948, at the same meeting where it agreed on the precursor to Art. 20, Para. 1, the Policy Committee decided to insert into the precursor of Art. 28 the following Para. 2, Sent. 1: "The constitutions of the *Länder* must conform to the principles of a democratic and social state under the rule of law in keeping with the Basic Law." The general Editorial Committee, at its meeting on 16 November 1948, simplified the entire provision, and this gave rise to the text of Art. 28, Para. 1, Sent. 1 of the Basic Law: "*The constitutional order in the Länder must conform to the principles of a republican, democratic, and social state governed by the rule of law, within the meaning of the Basic Law.*" This version survived all later efforts to formulate it differently. The deliberations regarding Art. 28 GG also yielded nothing about the meaning of the word "social."

The Indirect Program of the Basic Law

Of course, the Basic Law revealed in outline how the members of the Parliamentary Council had envisaged the implementation of the social. One important source for it was the structure of the federal system (see above section "The Institutional Significance"). By distributing the powers and resources of the state onto the federal state and the constituent *Länder*, it reflects a broad spectrum of state tasks. Since the federal state has only those jurisdictions that are explicitly granted to it by the Basic Law, a social policy above the *Länder* level is only possible within the framework of explicit federal jurisdictions. Given the unitary premise of social policy that is specific to the German tradition, this means that the circle of federal jurisdictions largely circumscribes also the effective sphere of social policy. It was all the more significant that the Basic Law gave expression even to the unitary premise of social policy: especially by making federal regulations of areas of so-called "concurrent legislation" contingent on the precondition that "the maintenance of the unity of living conditions beyond the territory of *Land*" rendered that regulation "necessary" (Art. 72, Para. 2, no. 3, GG, old version); and also by reserving to the federation the exclusive legislative authority for a number of matters that were essential especially for the unity of the economic area (Art. 73, nos. 3, 4, 5, 9, GG).

In detail, the Basic Law laid out the following picture (Zacher 1981). The *responsibility of the state for the economy* rested on three essential freedoms: occupational freedom (Art. 12 GG), freedom of property (Art. 14 GG), and the freedom "to form corporations and other associations" (Art. 9, Para.1, GG). The mandate of the state was addressed in an essentially open way through a circumscription of the legislative powers.[207] What the constitution said about the *Bundesbank*[208] hardly reveals the importance that this institution would attain for the constitution of the economy. It was only in the concurrent legislative authority for the "prevention of the abuse of economic power" (Art. 74, no. 16, GG) that the Basic Law addressed a core concern of the social market economy. But the new constitution also fell back on a central constitutional idea of the previous years: "Land, natural resources and means of production may, for the purpose of socialization, be transferred to public ownership or other forms of public enterprise by a law that determines the nature and extent of compensation."[209] When it came to the participation of social forces in economic policy, a very broad common denominator was found: the general freedom of association (Art. 9, Para. 1, GG), along with the "right to form associations to safeguard and improve working and economic conditions" which was "guaranteed to every individual and to every occupation or profession" (Art. 9, Para. 3, GG). Of course, the text gave no clue that the

[207] In the sense of an exclusive legislative authority of the federal state: Art. 73, nos. 3, 4, 5, 6, 7, 9, GG; in the sense of the concurrent legislative authority of the federal state and the states: Art. 74, nos. 11, 17, 18, 20, 21, 22, 23, GG.

[208] Art. 88, GG, old version: "The federation shall establish a note-issuing and currency bank as the Bundesbank."

[209] Art. 15, Sent. 1, GG. See also the explicit repetition of this option in the corresponding concurrent legislative authority (Art. 74, no. 15, GG).

interpretation of this norm, in particular, would develop in the judicial practice of the Federal Republic in a richly substantive, differentiated, and structurally potent way.

The foundation for the *structure of working life* was laid by a law of freedom: "All Germans shall have the right to freely choose their occupation or profession, their place of work, and their place of training."[210] The special importance of dependent work was very generally identified with the concurrent legislative authority for "labor law, including the organization of enterprises, occupational health and safety, and employment agencies" (Art. 74, no. 12, GG). Labor law appeared one more time in the constitution: alongside other "higher federal courts"[211] there was to be a supreme federal court for "labor and social jurisdiction." The Basic Law paid more intensive attention to *public sector law* than to general labor law: through guarantees of equality in the access to public offices (Art. 33, Para. 2, GG) and freedom of religious belief also in the public service (Art. 33, Para. 3, GG), through differentiated legislative jurisdictions (Art. 73, no. 8, Art. 75, no. 1, GG, old version), and through a series of remarkable transition regulations (Art. 130, Para. 2, Art. 131, 132, 137, GG, old version), and especially through guarantees for the tasks and the status of the professional civil service (Art. 33, Para. 4 and 5, GG). The freedom of *independent employment* was guaranteed in the freedom of occupational choice (Art. 12, Para. 1, Sent. 1, GG). Accordingly, its exercise could be "regulated by or pursuant to a law" (Art. 12, Para. 1, Sent. 2; GG). The stipulations of legislative powers saw this mandate above all in the guarantee of an orderly exercise of a profession (Art. 74, nos. 1, 11, 16–23, GG). *Uncompensated work* was not explicitly mentioned in the Basic Law. It was included in the autonomy of the family (Art. 6, Para. 1, GG) and in the right to the free development of one's personality (Art. 2, Para. 1; GG).

Income, the acquisition of which through work is an essential element of the basic social formula, is mentioned by the Basic Law merely as one of the bases of taxation (Art. 105, Para. 2, no. 2, GG, old version). *Wealth* was guaranteed as property (Art. 14 GG). Explicitly it was a theme for the Basic Law only as an issue of tax law (Art. 105, Para. 2, no. 2, GG, old version).

The law pertaining to the *community of maintenance* found an imprecise foundation in the order of the Basic Law: "Marriage and the family shall enjoy the special protection of the state" (Art. 6, Para. 1, GG). That statement was supplemented by the guarantee of the rights of parents (Art. 6, Para. 2 and 3, GG) and by the entitlement of "every mother.... to the protection and care of the community" (Art. 6, Para. 4, GG). Children born out of wedlock were the subject

[210] Art. 12, Para. 1, Sent. 1, GG, flanked by the prohibition against compelling a person to work (ibid., Para. 2) and against forced labor (ibid., Para. 3).

[211] The original version of the Basic Law posited that – notwithstanding the Federal Constitutional Court (Art. 93 and 94 GG) – "a supreme federal court shall be established to preserve the unity of federal law" (Art. 95, Para. 1, GG, old version). On the level below there were to be "higher federal courts for the area of regular, administrative, finance, labor, and social jurisdiction" (Art. 96, Para. 1, GG, old version).

of a special mandate of equality: they "shall be provided by legislation with the same opportunities for physical and mental development and for their position in society as are enjoyed by those born within marriage" (Art. 6, Para. 5). Important to an understanding of the guarantees of marriage and the family was the equality of men and women (Art. 3, Para. 2 and 3, GG). As impressive as the pronouncements of the Basic Law were regarding marriage and the family, it did not reveal what exactly was meant by the "protection of the state order."[212]

The *systems of social services* were reflected in the catalog of responsibilities. Two powers would prove central, even though their placement in the text would not lead one to suspect it: the concurrent legislative power for "public welfare" (Art. 74, no. 7, GG) and for "social security, including unemployment insurance" (Art. 74, no. 12; GG). It was evident that "public welfare" had the responsibility for the subsistence minimum. The formula left open to what extent the federal legislation of other services and benefits was covered by this norm. Social security was mentioned on two other occasions: with respect to the placement of the social insurance carriers into the structure of the federal state (Art. 87, Para. 2, GG, old version) and with respect to the obligation of the federation to bear "the subsidies to the burden of social insurance, including unemployment insurance" and unemployment benefits (Art. 120, Para. 1, GG, old version). *The civil service pension* was not explicitly addressed (an exception is Art. 131, Sent. 2, GG), though it was obviously included in the regulations concerning public service (Art. 33, Para. 4 and 5; Art. 73, no. 8, Art. 75, no. 1, GG). Far more expansive was the catalog of concurrent legislative powers to regulate the *consequences of politics*, especially in areas that would give rise more and more to a *social restitution law*: "matters concerning refugees and expellees" (Art. 74, Para. 6; on this, see also the power to issue statutory instruments in Art. 119 GG), "war damage and reparations" (Art. 74, no. 9, GG), and "benefits for persons disabled by war and for dependants of deceased war victims as well as assistance to former prisoners of war" (Art. 74, no. 10, GG).

The *meeting of needs* did not appear as a social theme. In the foreground were the organization of society and the orderly exercise of certain professions and other economic activities. Even though during the time when the Basic Law was being deliberated in the Parliamentary Council, the path of the United Economic Area in terms of its economic policy could still trigger doubts, the Basic Law already seemed to have returned to the normality of the provision with goods. One indirect exception – though a striking one, to be sure – was Art. 117, Para. 2, GG: "Laws that restrict the freedom of movement in view of the present housing shortage shall remain in force until repealed by a federal law." Social problems of meeting needs

[212] In particular, the was a lack of specific jurisdictional prescriptions, which are otherwise the most important indicators of what kind of social order the Basic Law has in mind. For the implementation of Art. 6 of the Basic Law, the concurrent legislative powers for civil law (Art. 74, No. 1, GG), public welfare (Art. 74, No. 7; GG), and for social security (Art. 74, No. 12, GG) come chiefly into consideration.

may well have been implicit in the legislative powers for the social benefits systems, problems of *Daseinsvorsorge* in a number of legislative powers for communications and transportation (Art. 73, nos. 6 and 7, Art. 74, nos. 21, 22, 23, Art. 87, Para. 1, GG), and probably also in the regulatory powers concerning economic and occupational law. Essential tasks fall to the local communities (Art. 28, Para. 2, GG) and to the *Länder* (Art. 30 GG). The Basic Law said nothing about this.

Among the peculiarities of the Basic Law with the greatest repercussions for social policy was that it addressed the *public tasks* only very selectively. It spoke only of *customs duties, dues on monopolies*, and *taxes* (Art. 105–108, GG, old version). The Basic Law did not mention or regulate other levies. Their legitimacy must be derived – and even that is not clear, it can only be inferred – from the relevant powers governing specific matters. Thus, the legitimacy of social security contributions followed from the powers regarding social insurance. Likewise, the authority for all other levies (fees, contributions, apportionments, special levies) follows from the authority for the specific matter with which they are connected (Kirchhof P 1990). That applies not only to legislation, but also to the inflow and the administration.[213] With that, the Basic Law created a fundamental schizophrenia: the "taxing state" does not know the "impost state"; and the overall effect of all levies on the living conditions of individuals is answered for even less than the effect of taxes. But the organization of taxes by the Basic Law was without social orientation.

The Early Interpretation of the Principle of the Social State

As multifarious as the mandates, suggestions, and restrictions were that the Basic Law laid out for the development of a social order, the interpretation of the principle of the social state was for a long time restrained (Art. 20, Para. 1, Art. 28, Para. 1, Sent. 1, GG).[214] *One current of interpretation* understood the word "social" in the most general, *value-neutral sense*, which can be more or less translated as "*societal*" and "*society-related.*" "Social State" in this sense means: the state has a responsibility for the condition of society. The autonomy of the latter is not absolute. Following the totalitarian grip on society, the pendulum was not to swing back to the liberal "night watchman state." A *different current* fell back on an understanding of the word "social" that aimed at the person's *reference and bond to community*, and in general parlance is better known in the negative version of the "asocial." In this sense, the "social state" means the obligation of the individual toward the community and toward others. Behind this understanding stood the concern that the pendulum, in the wake of the totalitarian subjection of the individual, could swing to the other extreme, complete detachment and lack of

[213] On taxes see Art. 105–108 GG.

[214] On the meaning of the word "social" see, for example, Geck (1963, pp. 676–684).

bonds – a mere liberation and entitlement. However, *the main current of opinion* flowed toward a *third understanding of the word*: toward a "*social state*" *that helps the weaker, that seeks to bring about the participation in the economic goods according to the principles of justice and with the goal of guaranteeing a decent human life for all*. This interpretation picked up the most quotidian meaning of "social" and placed the social state in connection with the concrete-historical, political social movement.[215] The need of the hour promoted this meaning as much as did the demand for a minimum of an objective statement about the direction in which society should develop. The questions of how the responsibility of that state for society (in the sense of the first, most general interpretation of the "social state") should be exercised, and in what way and for what goal the individual (in the sense of the second interpretation of the "social state" aimed at social obligations) should be bound by obligations, found a substantive answer in this current. The "third" understanding of the social state absorbed the "first" and the "second" into itself. With many differences in details, a consensus in the direction of this interpretation soon emerged. It was clear from the outset that this interpretation – contrary to the many temptations to regard a specific, concrete consequence as self-evident, compelling, and invariable – leaves broad leeway.

The *Federal Constitutional Court* (Zacher 1969, pp. 113–118) initially spoke only of "social justice,"[216] and only much later of "protection of the weaker"[217] and of a "just social order."[218] The first case in which it dealt with the social goal of the state was a complaint brought by a war widow who had been driven from her home. She demanded for herself and her children better support than what the war-victim law and the equalization of burdens were providing. The Federal Constitutional Court ruled as follows in 1951, in one of its earliest decisions:[219]

> Even if the phrase of the 'social federal state' does not appear in the basic rights, but in Art. 20 of the Basic Law (federation and states), it does contain an affirmation of the social state which can be of decisive importance in interpreting both the Basic Law as well as other laws. However, only the legislator can accomplish what is essential for the realization of the social state; he is surely obligated by constitutional law to engage in social activity, especially to strive for a tolerable conciliation of contending interests and the creation of tolerable living conditions for all who have fallen into hardship from the consequences of the Hitler regime. However, only if the legislator neglects this duty arbitrarily, that is, without objective reason, could this possibly give rise for the individual to a claim that

[215] Dürig (1953, p. 196): "It goes without saying that social does not equal socialist or should be read in the sense of a particular social theory. The decision by the Basic Law is a decision for what is common to the entire social movement. And the only thing that was and is common to the social movement, which entered the modern period as a countermovement, is its oppositional stance. The latter, however, is so unequivocal that it is also possible to positively define from the negative the minimum content of what the term 'social' means."

[216] BVerfGE 1, 97 (100); 5, 85 (198).

[217] BVerfGE 26, 16 (37); 35, 202 (236).

[218] E.g. BVerfGE 22, 180 (204); 59, 231 (263); 69, 272 (314).

[219] BVerfGE 1, 97 (105).

> could be pursued with a constitutional complaint. Given the extent of the general hardship, on the one hand, and the pension entitlement awarded after careful review, on the other hand, this is evidently not the case here.

Immediately thereafter, the Federal Constitutional Court applied the principle of the social state to access to legal protection by the courts. It found that the institution of poor law (today: legal aid) was necessary to prevent an unconstitutional disadvantage in legal protection.[220]

Another area that the Federal Constitutional Court addressed early on was public service law. The court elaborated, with a string of idiosyncratic assessments:[221]

> This clash of interests is, by its very nature, generally more intense in private employment relationships than in governmental employment relationships. That is why the Disabled Persons Act could posit that a government agency as the employer would not pursue its interests with the same kind of intensity that occurs in a private employment relationship. That is all the more the case after the Basic Law has declared the social state to be among the constitutive principles of our state.
>
> However, an agency is obligated to the principle of the social state to a heightened degree as part of the 'legality of administration' if it exercises sovereign power as an appeals body.

A short time later, the Federal Constitutional Court[222] based the individual right of civil servants to an appropriate livelihood on the necessity that they should be able "to preserve their constitutional position also legally, in conformity with the basic principles of the state under the rule of law and the social state." Finally, the Court derived the need for family equalization from the maxim of the social state.[223]

5.2.2 The Institutional Requirements of the Social: The Democratic Constitutional and Federal State

The Basic Law describes the new polity emphatically as a democracy (Art. 20, Para. 1, Art. 28, Para. 1, GG). What that is supposed to mean institutionally is spelled out in the basic outline for the central state, the federation. The *Länder* – constitutionally autonomous – are to organize themselves accordingly (Art. 28, Para. 1 and 3, GG). Democracy means *legitimation of the power of the state by the people* (Art. 20, Para. 2, Sent. 1, GG). However, the *exercise* of that power is *differentiated in three ways*. The *first of these differentiations* concerns the *exercise of state power by the representative organs*, whose structure must follow the classic tripartite separation of powers: legislative, executive, and judicial (Art. 20, Para. 2,

[220] BVerfGE 1, 109 (110f.).

[221] BVerfGE 3, 377 (381).

[222] BVerfGE 8, 1 (16f.).

[223] BVerfGE 6, 55 (80); not based in the same way on the principle of the social state: BVerfGE 11, 105 (113).

Sent. 2, GG). The *second differentiation* is *functional* in nature. The will *of the people expresses itself in layers*: in the *inalienable principles of the constitution*;[224] in the constitution, which can be changed only in a special process and with a broad majority (Art. 79, Para. 1 and 2, GG); in the *laws* that bind the administration and the judiciary (Art. 20, Para. 3, GG), and to which it is left to shape the subject-sphere of the citizen in accordance with the basic rights (Art. 1, Para. 3,GG). The *third differentiation* of democracy pertains to the *distribution of state power among various subjects*: the federation and the *Länder* as autonomous bearers of state power,[225] districts and municipalities (Art. 28, Para. 1 and 2, GG), as well as other corporations, institutions, and foundations.[226] This *multiple fragmentation of democracy* accords with the tradition within which the German constitutional state developed until Weimar times. The Basic Law deepened that tradition – especially in reaction to the National Socialist era and all its consequences. What this means for the social was explained by the Federal Constitutional Court in its decision outlawing the German Communist Party in 1956:[227]

> Thus, if progress toward '*social justice*' is established as a guiding principle of all state measures, a demand that was given a special accent in the Basic Law with its strong emphasis on the '*social state*,' it is a principle that is to a high degree capable of and in need of concrete expression. What must be practically done is thus determined in the continuous debate among all the individuals and groups involved in shaping social life. This struggle intensifies in the battle over political power in the state, but it does not exhaust itself in that battle. What takes place in the struggle for power is a simultaneous process of clarifying and altering these ideas. To be sure, the decisions eventually arrived at will surely accord more with the desires and interests of one group or social strata or another; however, the tendency of the system, and the possibility of the free contention between all real and intellectual powers inherent in it, works – as will be shown – in the direction of accommodating and sparing the interests of all. The common welfare is not equated a priori with the interests or desires of a certain class; a more or less equal promotion of the welfare of all citizens and a more or less equal distribution of the burdens is fundamentally aspired to. What exists is the *ideal of 'social democracy within the forms of the state under the rule of law.'*
>
> The system of government of liberal democracy must accordingly be set up systematically toward the task of adjustment, improvement, and social compromise; in particular, it must impede abuses of power. Its task is essentially to keep open the path for all conceivable solutions, namely, to enforce the will of the actual majority of the people for individual decisions, but at the same time to force this majority to justify its decision before the people as a whole, and also before the minority.

[224] More precisely: in the Basic Law (Art. 20, Para. 3), provided it has not been declared unchangeable through Art. 79, Para. 3 GG.

[225] Art. 20, Para. 1, Art. 28, 30–32, 35, 37, 70–100, 105–108 GG.

[226] For the federation see Art. 87, Para. 3, Art. 88, GG; for the federation *and* the *Länder*, the Basic Law gives only the example of the social insurance carriers (Art. 87, Para. 2, GG).

[227] BVerfGE 5, 85 (198); emphases added.

5.3 *The Political New Beginning – Establishing the Liberal Social State*

5.3.1 The Political Conditions[228]

First/Second Bundestag – First/Second Cabinet of Adenauer

The *Landtag* elections that took place between 1946 and 1949 (Ritter and Niehuss 1991, pp. 127–180) produced a dominant position of the CDU and the SPD, and flanking positions for the FDP and the KPD. Parties that reflected the special situation of the times hardly appeared at first – with the exception of the "Economic Reconstruction League" (*Wirtschaftliche Aufbauvereinigung*) in Bavaria.

The elections for the *First German Bundestag* did not alter the party-political picture fundamentally. However, the relative weight of the two large parties shrank. The smaller parties – led by the Liberals and the German Party (*Deutsche Partei*, DP) – gained weight. The Bavarian Party (*Bayernpartei*) broadened the political spectrum (Ritter and Niehuss 1991, p. 100). *Adenauer's first cabinet* was based on a coalition of CDU/CSU, FDP, and DP. The majority in the *Bundestag* was clear but narrow: 208 of 402 seats.

The elections for the *Second German Bundestag* in September 1953 shifted the weight of the parties massively in favor of the CDU/CSU. For the first and last time, a party of expellees made its appearance in the *Bundestag*: the *Gesamtdeutscher Block/Bund der Heimatvertriebenen und Entrechteten* (GB/BHE). Smaller parties with representation were the FDP, DP, and Zentrum. The Bavarian Party and the KPD had failed to crack the 5% threshold, which the Federal Election Law passed by the first *Bundestag* had introduced in the meantime.[229] The *second cabinet of Adenauer* was a coalition government made up of the CDU/CSU, FDP, DP, and GB/BHE.

The "Over-Government" of the Occupying Powers

However, the sovereignty of the Federal Republic of Germany had not yet been established with the founding of the Federal Republic and the creation of its highest constitutional organs. The occupying powers, which had been exercising a comprehensive authority over Germany since its defeat in 1945 (restricted at most by international law), were only willing to restrict the control they asserted in their

[228] Bundesministerium für Arbeit und Soziales and Bundesarchiv (eds.), 2005: Geschichte der Sozialpolitik in Deutschland seit 1945, vol. 3, Chap. 1.

[229] According to Art. 137, Para. 2 of the Basic Law, it was a matter for the Parliamentary Council to enact an election law for the election of the first Bundestag: "Gesetz für die Wahl zum Ersten Bundestag vom 15. Juni 1949" BGBl.: 21, in the version of 5 August 1949, BGBl. I, p. 25. The first Federal Election Law by the Bundestag was passed on 15 January 1952 (BGBl. I, p. 21). Ritter and Niehuss (1991: 100).

respective occupation zones.[230] This restriction was laid out by the Occupation Statute that took effect on 21 September 1949.[231] A further restriction followed soon in the Petersburg Agreement between the Federal Republic and the occupying powers on 22 November 1949 (Huber 1951, pp. 611–614), which opened Germany the way to European and Atlantic cooperation (Schwarz 1981, pp. 61–69). Only the Germany Agreement and the accompanying agreements in the version of the Paris Protocol on the Termination of the Occupation Regime in the Federal Republic of Germany of 23 October 1954, put an end to the general control of the occupying powers of Germany effective 5 May 1955.[232] To be sure, even after that a number of provisos remained in place.

When it came to the development of the young social state, the persistence of occupation rule beyond the establishment of the Federal Republic was important only in certain specific areas. The occupying powers intervened with respect to the economic conditions and economic structures (Abelshauser 1983, pp. 65–67, 76–84). They carried out the dismantling of facilities (Harmssen 1951), an activity that ceased only in 1951. The occupying powers insisted on the continuation of policies that were – without this being the particular intention of the occupying powers – part of the program of the social market economy: "decartelization" and trust-busting (see section "The Responsibility of the State for the Economy"). They retained in a special way the control over the law on the restitution of Nazi injustice,[233] aid for displaced persons (see below Chaps. 10 and 11), the decision about the reception of refugees, and so on.

5.3.2 Intellectual Approaches to Social Policy[234]

The Situation

Social issues dominated the politics of the Federal Republic from the outset – in fact, they *had* to dominate it. The hardships of the time were still urgent. Less than 14 months elapsed between the currency reform and the *Bundestag* elections in August 1949. While the benefits of the free market economy and a currency backed by goods had become evident, there were also disappointments. The question of whether a just economic system should focus more on guiding production and distribution in such a way that the needs of the greatest possible number were met as

[230] See the letter by the occupying authorities, dated 11 May 1949, authorizing the Basic Law. Text in Huber (1951, p. 576).

[231] Published along with the authorization of the Basic Law on 12 May 1949; ibid., pp. 576–579.

[232] Further details in Hofmann (1987, pp. 281–283).

[233] Bundesministerium für Arbeit und Soziales and Bundesarchiv (eds.), 2005: Geschichte der Sozialpolitik in Deutschland seit 1945, vol. 3, Chap. 3, no. 12.

[234] Bundesministerium für Arbeit und Soziales and Bundesarchiv (eds.), 2005: Geschichte der Sozialpolitik in Deutschland seit 1945, vol. 3, Chap. 2.

evenly as possible, or whether the experiment of the social market economy should be continued, that is, to let the market generate prosperity and have redistribution create the social justice that the market does not bring about on its own, troubled many. Behind it, however, stood the question of what a new normality of the social system could look like, one that was no longer caught up in the distortions that Nazi rule, war, and the postwar period had left behind.

But the *two legislative sessions* during which the Federal Republic laid the foundation of its social system differed precisely in this perspective about a future normality. The *first legislative session* was entirely consumed by the immediate challenges. The polity had to be rebuilt. The economy had to be revived further, in whatever way the state was able to do so. Not least, a host of social problems called for solutions. The old problem solutions had to be repaired to make them accord with the needs of the times. And many new solutions had to be found for many new social problems. The first legislative session found itself consigned to the path of pragmatism. It was only in the *second legislative session* that society and politics gained some breathing space to ponder fundamental issues. This was a period that saw a unique coexistence of large-scale and profound deliberations and small-scale but still seminal politics.

The Political Accents

The SPD and the CDU had framed the *election campaign of 1949* as a choice between socialism and a social market economy (Toman-Banke 1994, p. 48f.). As the SPD proclaimed: "Our goal is socialism! We call upon our like-minded comrades in city and country to follow us on this path!" Through socialization, state planning, and guidance, the economy was to be oriented a priori to the social. The other side turned the concept of the social free market into its campaign program. In the Economic Council of the Unified Economic Area, the CDU had carried the new free-market course together with the FDP. It saw itself as the party of a new departure for the economy. *Chancellor Adenauer's* declaration on 20 September 1949 (Behn 1971, pp. 11–34) built upon this course. At the same time, though, it affirmed the social task: "The striving to relieve the hardship, for social justice, will be the highest lodestar for all our work." In terms of specifics, though, social problems were addressed very little: war victims, expellees, housing. For the most part they appeared within larger contexts, especially economic policy, *Mittelstand* policy, and agricultural policy. The multitude of hardships and the pragmatism of a new beginning shaped this governmental declaration.

The *election of 1953* continued the confrontation. The SPD concretized its appeal – "Vote left, where the heart beats! Vote Social Democrats! – not least in terms of economic policy: Professor Erhard – CDU is ruining the economy! Whoever votes for the SPD – votes for development!" The CDU countered: "All roads of Marxism lead to Moscow! Therefore: CDU" (Toman-Banke 1994, p. 49f.).

In the governmental declaration of 20 October 1953 (Behn 1971, pp. 35–60), *Konrad Adenauer* addressed a broad spectrum of social problems – and not infrequently in a more differentiated and intensive manner than he had in 1949. Beyond that, however, he also arrived at a central statement:

> So far it has been primarily those active in the process of work who have drawn the visible benefits from the success of the social market economy. It will have to be the special concern of the federal government to integrate the unemployed, and to propose to the *Bundestag* measures through which the economic situation of pensioners, invalids, orphans, and surviving dependants can be further improved. This goal must be achieved along two paths: first, through a further increase in the national product, second, through a comprehensive social reform. Increasing the national product is not only a task of economic policy and fiscal policy, but at the same time also a very important task of social policy. Every further increase in the national product also allows a correspondingly greater consideration for the recipients of social assistance... A reallocation within the social budget is not only justifiable, but necessary in order to be able to help many strata more than has been possible to date. That goal is served by the preliminary work for the implementation of a social reform already initiated by the first federal government. The new government will promote this preliminary work vigorously and submit a comprehensive social program.

Sociopolitical Concepts

The *fundamental discussion* of social policy and its restructuring by the young Federal Republic (Hockerts 1980, pp. 216–242) was focused on *social benefits systems. Two reasons* were crucial for this orientation. *First*: the existing institutions providing social benefits were – at least in their totality – a confusing jumble. They had evolved separately over decades. Now, however, their combined output was needed to get a grip on the profusion of misery and hardship. If nothing else required reform, their lack of transparency did. Second: the expenditures on social benefits were out of all proportion to the available means. Much-needed improvements would widen this gap even more. Could a systematic reorganization help to set priorities in a better way? A first discussion of these two approaches was initiated by the *German Association for Public and Private Welfare* (*Deutscher Verein für öffentliche und private Fürsorge*). In September 1949, at the very time, that is, when the constitutional organs of the young Republic were establishing themselves, the Association held a welfare conference in Bielefeld on the topic: "Welfare in service to the economic and social safeguarding of the population" (Polligkeit 1950). The focus, however, was not only on the accents and priorities sketched above, but also on the future of social benefits that did justice to the values of a liberal social state.

In 1951, a "Social Study Commission" called upon the *SPD parliamentary group* in the *Bundestag* to carry out a comprehensive inventory of the existing social institutions and benefits and examine the possibilities of a systematic reorganization. The governing coalition countered by proposing an Expert Advisory Committee at the Federal Ministry of Labour. Neither initiative materialized (Hockerts 1980, pp. 216–220). In 1952, the "*Committee on Social Policy with the Party Executive of the SPD*" (the chief author was *Ludwig Preller*) prepared a brief working paper – entitled "Foundations of the overall social plan of the SPD" – that contained impulses for a fundamental reorganization: employment policy with the goal of full employment; a system of health protection; coordinated cash benefit systems; and the local cooperation of the carriers of social benefits for the purpose of a standardized system of benefits, especially joint information and counseling offices. A certain pension was to be guaranteed for the elderly or those permanently unable to work (Hockerts 1980, pp. 220–222).

Subsequently, efforts toward reform crystallized also within the *federal government*. In 1953, the year of parliamentary elections, a "*General Office for Social Security Reform*" was set up within the *Federal Ministry of Labour*. *Kurt Jantz*, henceforth a leading figure in the social policy of the government, was appointed as its director (Hockerts 1980, p. 236f.). His priority was the rational development of what already existed. The best possible expression of these guiding ideas was in the report on "The current state of social security and the possibility of a reform of existing law on social security while retaining the distinction between insurance, provision, and welfare," which the Federal Ministry of Labour commissioned *Walter Bogs* to prepare still in 1953 (Bogs 1955). The Ministry of Labour's rival over responsibility for social policy was the *Federal Ministry of Finances*. The financial cost of the social was in those years still seen as an overarching structural element. Later, when social policy had become institutionally linked to a German tradition characterized by the preeminent role of social insurance, that perspective was lost for some time. Social insurance paid for itself. Tax-financed social benefits moved within the parameters made possible by economic growth. In the early states of the Federal Republic, however, the interconnectedness of finance and economic policy in regard to the social was still perceived and assessed. Therein lay a considerable incentive for new orientations. The Ministry of Finance's engagement in social policy gave expression to this. The key figure was *Konrad Elsholz*, head of the "Chief Department for the Social Budget" (Hockerts 1980, pp. 237–242). His work, too, reflected an expert environment of which *Hans Achinger* was the chief representative. Achinger resisted the tendency toward a schematic monetarization of social benefits. He was profoundly committed to the autonomy of a form of public assistance oriented toward the human being, the individual, and his community, and characterized by the self-responsibility of the helpers and those being helped. It was his hope that a liberal polity and a positive development of the economy would be able to open up new possibilities of self-realization for the values of welfare (Achinger 1953, 1954). The result of this could also strike against the interest of finance policy to resist a proliferation of social benefits.

On the whole then, there had emerged during the first legislative session a remarkable web of socio-political stances that was thin but broad. The *second legislative session*, however, opened with a thunderclap that promised to help the forces pushing for a fundamental new beginning to carry the day: the announcement of a "*social reform*" (see Behn 1971, pp. 35–60). What exactly was to be understood by it remained controversial.[235] In any case, the project soon focused on a reform of social benefits (Hockerts 1980, pp. 242–246). However, opinions diverged

[235] See later attempts at interpreting the word in Schulz (1989) and Schäfer (1997, p. 897f.).

considerably also with respect to social benefits[236] – both within the government and even more so in relationship to the social groups, and finally also within academia (von Bethusy-Huc 1956, pp. 64–136; 1976, pp. 58–139; Frerich and Frey 1996, vol. 3, pp. 28–31). Particularly representative was the "*Rothenfels Memorandum*" (Achinger 1955), which was written – at the behest of *Chancellor Konrad Adenauer* – by *Hans Achinger, Joseph Höffner, Hans Muthesius*, and *Ludwig Neundörfer*. None of these four men came from the field of social insurance or similarly accounting-based social services. Their background lay in the social science or, in the case of Joseph Höffner, in theology. Their expertise lay in fields such as welfare, child and youth services, and family – the exception again being Höffner, an authority of Catholic social doctrine. These authors largely freed themselves from the fetters of tradition. They approached the problems in a dispassionate, fundamental, and far-reaching way. Perhaps the most important pervasive principle they put into effect was subsidiarity – by which was meant the primacy of self-responsibility, on the one hand, and the precedence of intermediary structures (private, societal, and governmental in nature) on the other hand. The *Minister of Labour*, meanwhile, initiated the "*Cologne Memorandum*," which was the work of the professors *Walter Rohrbeck, Erich Roehrbein*, and *Carl Meyrich* (Rohrbeck et al. 1955). The expertise that shaped this report came from another realm of the social: that of insurance and social security – accounting-based social benefits. The authors clung to the institutional tradition of German social policy. This counter-report exemplifies the opposition arrayed against a dispassionate, far-reaching, original reform. Increasingly, the consensus about the need for a comprehensive reform focused on improving the benefits, harmonizing the content of regulation, and creating a systematic codification. At the very end of the legislative session, in 1957, there appeared, at the behest of the *Executive of the SPD*, a "*social plan for Germany*," the lead authors of which were *Walter Auerbach* and *Ludwig Preller* (Auerbach et al. 1957). Here, too, the development had long since assimilated to the traditional structures and readied itself to reforming, revitalizing, and at times also supplementing its benefits branches.

5.4 The Structure of the Social Order[237]

5.4.1 The Responsibility of the State for the Economy[238]

The development of economic policy and economic law took place along the lines of the social market economy (Weddigen 1950). The guidance of the economy

[236] Hockerts (1980, pp. 242–318); a comprehensive documentation in Richter (1955–1970).

[237] Bartholomäi et al. (1977); Zacher (1989c, pp. 36–54); Frerich and Frey (vol. 3, 1996, pp. 16–158).

[238] Abelshauser (1987); Glastetter et al. (1991); Weimer (1998, pp. 71–130).

continued to be gradually dismantled (Huber, esp. 1954, p. 213f.). On the basis of occupation law and largely under the responsibility of the occupying powers, property structures were led toward the requirements of a competitive economy through the breakup of combines and monopolies (Huber 1953, pp. 417–478; 1954, pp. 710–785). Competitive behavior remained under the control of the decartelization norms of the occupying powers (Huber 1953, pp. 231–417; 1954, pp. 767–770). The effectiveness of public market boards declined (Huber 1954, pp. 263–281). At the end of the second legislative session, the free-market tool kit was completed with the addition of two essential laws. Fairly obvious was the move to convert the *Bank deutscher Länder* finally into the *Bundesbank* called for in Art. 88 of the Basic Law (BGBl. [1957] I, p. 745). By contrast, passage of the Law against Restrictions on Competition on 27 July 1957 (BGBl. I, p. 1081) came at the end of years of contentious wrangling. The arguments that were advanced in the debate concerned economic policy, legal policy, as well as constitutional law (Huber 1954, pp. 387–416, 767–770; Hüttenberger 1976).

As consistent and straightforward the development was on the essential points, it did not take place without fluctuations when it came to the details. Time and again, doubts emerged about the correctness of the strict free-market course of Ludwig Erhard, who was the Federal Minister of the Economy from 1949 on.[239] Unemployment climbed to over 8% in 1949 and then above 12% at the beginning of 1950. For the remainder of 1950, as well, it hovered around 10%. That provoked not only criticism from German circles, but also intervention by the occupying powers. They pushed for the dismantling of the restrictive monetary policy and the use of state spending programs to support demand. An economic stimulus program seemed unavoidable. But before the decision about it had been made, the Korean War broke out in June 1950. The war drove up the international demand for German investment goods. Germany's economic development experienced a considerable boost. Interventions no longer seemed necessary. However, a second crisis followed close at heel: after the Korea boom came shortages. Guiding measures seemed unavoidable. The occupying powers pushed for steps to secure the supply of necessities, and not least also to guide the production of scarce military goods. German politics and the German economy sought to avoid a turnaround on economic policy. Solutions were found by way of the self-organization and the self-policing of the economy. Another difficulty emerged with respect to investments in the area of heavy industry. Here the legislator felt compelled to intervene with a special law. The Law on Investment Aid from Industry of 7 January 1952 (BGBl. I, p. 7) stipulated that industry raise a one-time contribution of one billion DM to cover the urgent need for investments in coal mining, the iron industry, and the energy sector. Use of the investment funds and the conditions under which they would be granted to the recipients were decided by a board of 19 members, whose decisions concerning the selection of beneficiaries and the amount of funds awarded required the approval of

[239] On what follows see Abelshauser (1993, pp. 76–84).

the Minister of the Economy. The law set off political and constitutional opposition. Was this the expression of "social market economy"?

Economic growth consolidated from 1951 on, however. Unemployment declined continuously beginning that year, while wages rose just as steadily. The concept of the free market economy had been victorious once again. The establishment of the *Bundesbank* and the formulation of its mandate strengthened it as much as the Law against Restrictions on Competition. And the sustained economic upswing contributed no less to the acceptance of the social market economy. Of course, the systematic understanding of what it meant and its integration into the evolved regulations and structures remained controversial.[240] Under the leadership of *Hans Carl Nipperdey* (Nipperdey 1954) it was widely accepted that there was a necessary correlation between the Basic law and the social market economy. That contention was not without challenge (e.g. Krüger 1951, esp. p. 362f.; Hamann 1953, p. 31f.). The Federal Constitutional Court rejected the notion that the social market economy was constitutionally necessary: "The Basic Law guarantees neither the neutrality of the governmental and legislative power on economic policy, nor a 'social market economy' to be guided only by means that conform to the free market" (BVerfGE 4, 7 [17]). This was no impediment, however, to the pursuit of the course of the social market economy in the practice of economic policy.

5.4.2 Work and Income: Dependent Labor[241]

The arrangement of work life was already a focal point of the rebuilding of the country in the first years after the collapse of the Reich. It now continued. However, providing an account of what happened confronts specific difficulties, which will remain typical also for the periods that followed. When it came to the development of work life, *state legislation* had an importance that was remote and largely indirect; and while it was direct in some areas, even then it was fragmentary and at times only sporadic. Instead, the *legal reality of work* life is reflected above all in two processes.[242]

One process takes place in the *multitude of concretizations* by *collective bargaining regulations*, by entrepreneurial and *business structures* and practices, and, finally, by the *shaping of individual contracts* and their actual implementation. This path of development can be effectively traced only with the methods of empirical research. The *other process* takes place in *judicial decisions* – especially by the *labor courts*. The labor courts have to apply not only the labor law enacted

[240] On the discussion at the time see Ballerstedt (1956, pp. 97–102, 135–143, 172–175, 200–207); Zacher (1981, pp. 835–841).

[241] Bundesministerium für Arbeit und Soziales and Bundesarchiv (eds.), 2005: Geschichte der Sozialpolitik in Deutschland seit 1945, vol. 3, Chap. 3, nos. 1 and 2.

[242] Bundesministerium für Arbeit und Soziales and Bundesarchiv (eds.), (2007b), vol. 11 and Bundesministerium für Gesundheit ... (2005), vol. 7. Chap. 3, no. 1.

explicitly by the legislature (e.g. the Federal Vacation Law). Rather, they must trace out the latitude that state law accords the parties to collective bargaining, the parties cooperating on the enterprise level, and the parties to individual labor contracts. In the process, the labor courts have always seen it as their special charge to overcome the distance between the statutory law they are handed and the specific conflicts of values and interests in the labor relationship through the creative legal development of principles. But the reality of work life depends no less on the everyday practice of the courts than it does on these judge-made legal principles of labor law – a practice that can also move along its own "legal paths" in multifarious ways: with settlement proposals that judges introduce into a pending case; with the decisions of lower and mid-level courts, which can be incontestable even when their conformity to the law is problematic; with the decisions of lower and mid-level bodies that are not challenged because the losing party does not have the energy or interest to pursue the case further, and so on and so forth. All in all: the entire legal reality of work life can be grasped only via empirical studies, and those are largely lacking.

Free Collective Bargaining and the Right of Labor Struggle

The structure of free collective bargaining – the organizations of workers (unions) and of employers and a framework for shaping working conditions (collective bargaining agreement law) – is something the young Federal Republic also found in existence. In October 1949, the erection of unified trade unions had come to an end with the establishment of the German Federation of Trade Unions (*Deutscher Gewerkschaftsbund*, DGB) (Beier 1975). In addition to the individual unions of the Federation, there also existed, as a significant general workers' organization, the German Employees Union (*Deutsche Angestelltengewerkschaft*, DAG). And while some other organizations – especially the Christian unions – could be found, their quantitative weight remained low (Schuster 1974).

Unions and employers' associations were conceived of as the pillars of a comprehensive if vague concept of "*social self-administration*" (Zacher 1981, pp. 287–314). Its *core area* was the right to *free collective bargaining* (Zacher 1981, pp. 289–300). The labor struggle (the strike as well as the lockout) was understood as an implication of the right to free collective bargaining (BAGE 1, 291). In the process, the strike was definitively incorporated: into the collective exercise of the interests of the workers by the unions, and thus also into the responsibility of the unions; and into free collective bargaining – into the cooperative structure of working conditions through agreements between unions and employers (BAGE 1, 291; 2, 75; 6, 321). Conversely, the lockout was also recognized as legitimate (BAGE 1, 291). It was regarded as an important instrument for the employer that would allow him to wage an effective labor struggle. It was an expression of parity in the labor struggle. With that, the Federal Labour Court gave early and decisive consideration to the responsibility of the law for the structure of the societal realization of the social through the organized exercise of the interests of workers and employers.

Legislation, meanwhile, has realized the idea of "*social self-administration*" – once again following the path of tradition – beyond the framework of free collective bargaining, indeed, beyond the boundaries of labor law. Participation rights of unions and employers' association developed rapidly within the *framework of law-making, administration, and judicial decisions* (Drews 1958). Among the outstanding examples is the Law on Self-Administration and the amendment to the regulations in the area of social security in 1951.[243] The Law comprehensively reestablished self-administration in social security. It made possible – on the basis of elections by the insured and the employers – a fundamentally equal participation of both social partners in all organs of social security. Another important example was the laws that introduced labor courts and social courts in 1953. Through the participation of the associations in filling the panel of judges, and through the right of the associations to represent their members in court, both laws accorded the unions and the employers' associations significant influence on the judicial realization of the social.

What did the *constitution* have to say about this? Art. 9, Para. 1 of the Basic Law granted all Germans "the right to form corporations and other associations." Art. 9, Para. 3, Sent. 1, GG, meanwhile, granted "the right to form associations to safeguard and improve working and economic conditions... to every individual and to every occupation or profession."[244] Did this mean that a specific freedom of association existed for work and economic life as such? Had that been the case, the Basic Law would have lacked a specific guarantee of the traditional position of the workers' and employers' organizations. On the other hand: if Art. 9, Para. 3, GG intended to guarantee a special freedom of organization to the economic sector – beyond the general freedom of association in Art. 9, Para. 1, GG – that would have created a serious obstacle to the establishment of a competitive system in conformity with the concept of the social market economy.[245] Already in 1954, the Federal Constitutional Court decided to identify Art. 9, Para. 3, GG with the traditional position of unions and employers' associations (BVerfGE 4, 96). In the process, the final integration of the right of free association into the organizational mandate of free collective bargaining was further deepened:

> Thus, if the freedom of association guaranteed in Art. 9, Para. 3 of the Basic Law is not to be stripped of its historically evolved meaning, the fundamental law of Art. 9, Para. 3 of the

[243] Bundesministerium für Arbeit und Soziales and Bundesarchiv (eds.), 2005: Geschichte der Sozialpolitik in Deutschland seit 1945, vol. 3. Chap. 3, no. 4.

[244] Art. 9, Para. 3, Sent. 3, GG, which states that the right to engage in labor struggle could not be restricted by emergency measures was inserted only by the 17th Law to Amend the Basic Law of 24 June 1968 (BGBl. I, p. 709).

[245] On the dispute over the meaning of the provisions in the Basic Law see Zacher (1981, pp. 287–291, 1049–1055).

> Basic Law must also contain a constitutionally protected core area such that a collective bargaining system in the sense of modern labor law must be provided by the state in the first place, and that the parties to these collective agreements are necessarily freely formed associations (BVerfGE 4, 106).

Furthermore:

> If one assumes.... that one of the purposes of the system of collective bargaining agreements is supposed to be a *sensible order of work life*, especially the setting of wages, and the participation of unions and management, the limitations to the capacity to conclude free collective agreements that arise from this regulatory purpose must also take effect within the framework of the freedom of association (BVerfGE 4, 107).

What remained questionable is whether the shaping of working conditions through free collective bargaining was adequate to produce a socially appropriate state of affairs. Was state intervention required? The Federal Republic had already found in place a supplement to free collective bargaining: *the declaration of the general validity of collective bargaining agreements* according to section "1945–1949: Adversity and New Beginning" (p. 120) of the Collective Bargaining Agreement Law. Another supplement was created by the *Homeworking* Act of 1951. It provided for the *fixing* of remuneration and other conditions of homeworking, provided there were no associations or they encompassed only a minority of those involved. Another framework regulation was provided by the 1952 law about the government's stipulation of *minimum working conditions*. This law allowed for the fixing of the "lower threshold of remuneration and other working conditions in an economic sector or a type of employment" (Sect. 4 Para. 4). But even here, the state had to preserve the principle of the "regulation of remuneration and other working conditions.... in free agreement between the parties to collective bargaining through collective contracts" (Sect. 1 Para. 1). As a result, this regulation remained meaningless. While the legislator had at least enacted an explicit regulation with respect to the declaration of the general extension of collective agreements, to homeworking conditions, and to minimum working conditions, the question of *state mediation* remained open. Before 1933, the mediation system had taken on considerable importance (Huber 1954, pp. 452–467). After 1945 it was revived through occupation and state law (Huber 1954, p. 454; Zacher 1981, p. 309f.). The parties to collective bargaining agreements also showed temporary interest in it (Frerich and Frey 1996, vol. 3, p. 96). However, the existing regulations of state mediation were not practiced, nor were new regulations created. On the whole, then, what remained in place was the concept that would determine the normative responsibility for the development of wages and similar working conditions over the subsequent decades: the *bipolar autonomy of unions and employers' associations* – by way of exception also: of unions and an individual enterprise.

Works Constitution and Enterprise Codetermination

If this concept of free collective bargaining was the result of the legislative approach in the Collective Agreement Law of 1949, the law-creating interpretation of Art. 9, Para. 3 of the Basic Law by the courts, and an energetic practice by the parties to collective bargaining, the dimension of collective labor law concerning businesses and enterprises depended primarily on the legitimation and shaping by the legislator. The federal legislature developed further the existing directives of the works constitution law and codetermination law. The federal legislature passed new regulations for these areas with the *Works Constitution Act* of 1952 and the specific elaboration of the works constitution law for the public sector through the *Staff Council Act* of 1955. The intent was not only to arrange the relationship between employers and workers in a way that ensured the societal realization of the social within enterprises. Rather, the works constitution law – unlike the staff council law, which had to be concerned with balancing the self-realization of democracy and the concerns of its servants – was also intended to alter the relationship between capital and labor. The factor "labor" was to be accorded a minimum degree of influence over the factor capital. The most important expression of this tendency was the sending of workers' representatives onto the supervisory boards of corporations.[246]

The struggle over *codetermination* was aimed in the same direction in more general terms. Its further development (Frerich and Frey vol. 3, 1996, pp. 99–103) became a topical issue when the Allied High Commission began, in 1950, to newly regulate the ownership situation of the decartelized but not expropriated iron and steel industry. By way of an implementation directive, the federal government was to decide whether the parity in representation on the supervisory boards established in this sector in 1947 was to continue or not. The conflict was resolved in the Iron and Steel Codetermination Act (*Montan-Mitbestimmungsgesetz*) of May 1951, which preserved the vested rights of workers and expanded parity-based codetermination to the coal mining industry. Tendencies toward concentration in heavy industry later prompted the expansion of iron and steel codetermination also to holding companies (most recently BVerfGE 99, 367).

Other Statutes in Labor Law

In a number of areas, the legislature could not and would not rely on the elaboration of working conditions by collective bargaining, by businesses themselves, or by individuals. As a result, it intervened in a regulatory capacity.[247] The year 1951 saw passage of the Law Regulating the Payment of Wages on Holidays and the

[246] On the history of this institution, which extends back to the year 1922, and on the regulations in the Works Council Act of 1952 see Huber (1954, pp. 555–575).

[247] Frerich and Frey (vol. 3, 1996, pp. 107–112); Bundesministerium für Arbeit und Soziales and Bundesarchiv (eds.), 2005: Geschichte der Sozialpolitik in Deutschland seit 1945, vol. 3, Chap. 3, no. 2.

Protection Against Dismissal Act. In 1952, the Occupation Health and Safety Act was further expanded by the Law for the Protection of Working Mothers. The subsequent development of labor law was marked in 1953 by the Law on the Employment of the Severely Disabled, the further expansion of technical occupational safety by the Law to Amend Titles I-IV, VII, and X of the Commercial Code, and the Labour Court Act. In 1956 there followed the Law on Closing Time. The year 1957, when the second legislative session of the *Bundestag* came to an end, brought further innovations also for labor law: the Law on Job Security in Case of Conscription, the Law on Improving the Economic Security for Workers in Case of Illness (the first law on the continued payment of wages), and the Law about Inventions by Workers.

The legislator was specifying the areas it did not entrust to those involved and their associations. Specifically as a federal legislator, he identified the areas where he regarded the fragmentation through state law as inappropriate. Finally, the legislator specified the areas in which he preferred the direct political decision of parliament over the creation of norms through judicial decision. This specific responsibility of the legislator was evident in clarifying particularly contentious social issues (e.g. the continued payment of wages in case of illness), deciding on new problems whose solution required a high degree also of legal-technical competence (inventions by workers), and providing protection to especially endangered groups (beginning with protection for home workers, mothers, and the severely disabled), and, finally, regulating working conditions in a standardized way for the entire country (e.g. continued payment of wages on holidays). When it came to technical occupational safety, the requirements of regulation and implementation militated against any other approach. The Protection Against Dismissal Act proved to be one core piece of the development of labor law. The practice of the labor courts and the parties to collective agreements used it to develop a comprehensive protection of stable working conditions – as articulated, on the one hand, in restrictions on conditional and time-limited employment relationships,[248] and, on the other hand, in the expansion by way of collective agreements of employment relationships that cannot be terminated. That the institutions of legal protection had to lie in the responsibility of the state legislature (labor court law) was self-evident.

The Law of the Public Sector

Within the German tradition, *dependent work has two manifestations. First, work on behalf of private employers*. It is regulated by labor law – that is, in principle it is a matter of private law, though it is also shaped to a special degree by collective agreements, obligatory private law, as well by public law. *Second, work in service to the state and to public-law "employers" below the state level* (Krause 1982, pp. 40–67). It can be regulated through civil service law – that is to say, through

[248] On the early development see BAGE 10, 65. For a more recent state of affairs see, for example, Zöllner and Loritz (1998, pp. 267–272).

specific public-law statutes. The civil servant is historically the original type. However, over time employment relationships in service to the state were also regulated by labor law with increasing frequency. Civil servants were joined by public sector workers and employees. In part they were subject to the same duties as civil servants – through penal law, the regulations about secrecy, and so on. In part, however, especially through a supplementary provision that complemented pension insurance, workers, and especially white-collar employees, in the public sector enjoyed specific benefits intended to balance out the social differences between them and civil servants. This had to do not least with the fact that these differences could be justified less and less by a clear differentiation of tasks.

As a result, the two-fold division of the legal and social gestalt of dependent work became more complex. On the *one* side, dependent work in service to private employers that was regulated by *labor law* continued. On the *other* side, however, *work in service to the state and other public sector carriers* became differentiated: it could be regulated by both *civil service law* and *labor law*, though in the latter case it was often characterized by special elaborations. The comprehensive phrase used to encompass both kinds became increasingly "*public service*" (*öffentlicher Dienst*). Service relationships based on labor law assumed increasing importance during the First World War, the Weimar period, the Nazi era, and again in the postwar years – with many differences specific to the times. At the same time, the functional justification of legal and social differences between civil servants and those employed in the public sector on the basis of labor law continued to evaporate.

The *reorganization of the public service after 1945* took an ambivalent stance toward this development (Benz 1981; Wengst 1988). The polity that had been brought to its knees was dependent on a good deal of public service. Was the civil service not the most effective way to respond to this situation? However, the necessity of a solution under labor law was as obvious as the problem of the differentiation of the public service. In addition, the question arose as to how much the traditional civil servants had been shaped by the models of a monarchic or authoritarian state, which were incompatible with the new democratic *Rechtsstaat*. This historical critique of the professional civil service was effectively seconded by the interests of the unions. The professional civil service was regulated by state law *(staatliches Gesetz)*. Free collective bargaining – and thus the parity-based right of participation by the unions – did not apply to the configuration of the civil service relationship. Civil servants had always been prohibited from striking. And so there were two conflicting currents, one pushing for the project of a fundamental reorganization, the other pushing for the preservation of continuity.

In this situation, the state of Hesse drew the consequences of a fundamental reform, as part of which "the legal conditions of all workers and employees of public administrations" were to be set up "within the framework of the uniform labor law called for in Art. 29 in accordance with the needs of the administration."[249] The other states retained the principle of the professional civil service, without ruling out a mix of elaborations in the public sector that were based on private law and on public law (Püttner 1987, pp. 1124–1128). The Basic Law took exactly the same approach by essentially using the umbrella term "public service,"[250] while acknowledging that individuals "who stand in a relationship of service and loyalty defined by public law" that "shall be regulated and developed with due regard to the traditional principles of the professional civil service" (Art. 33, Para. 4 and 5, GG) hold a place of special importance within the public service. The 1950 Law on the Provisional Regulation of the Legal Conditions of Persons in Service to the Federation thus set the course in the direction of a reestablishment of the side-by-side existence of a professional civil service and employment relationships based on labor law. Thereafter, a series of statutes rebuilt the civil service law: the Federal Civil Service Act (1953), the Federal Pay Act (1957), and the legal framework for the standardization of civil service law also of the Länder in the form of the Civil Service Framework Law (1957) (Püttner 1987, pp. 1128–1138). The decision to build up the *Bundeswehr* (armed forces) made it necessary to regulate the status of the *soldier* as a specific type under the service law in a way that was in keeping with the democratic *Rechtsstaat*. The Seventh Law to Amend the Basic Law of 19 March 1956 (BGBl. I, p. 111) inserted into the Basic Law the stipulations about the "constitution of the military." That same day saw passage of the Law on the Legal Status of Soldiers, soon followed by the Compulsory Military Service Law (1956). The year 1957 saw regulations of the social environment of military service: the Law for Job Protection in Case of Conscription, the Military Pay Law, the Law Securing the Livelihood of the Dependants of those Called Up for Military Service (Livelihood Guarantee Act), and – as, in principle, the most important piece of the system – the Law to Provide for Former Soldiers of the *Bundeswehr* and their Surviving Dependants (Soldiers' Provision Law). What all these regulations shared with the civil service law is that the soldier's relationship is also a "relationship of service and loyalty defined by public law." However, considerable differences in substance gave rise to a much higher need for regulation: the difference between voluntary and obligatory service, the various types of service limited in duration, as well as the greater risk inherent in soldiering.

While the public sector service law thus underwent a clear elaboration already during this phase, there was no general and fundamental new regulation for those *employed under labor law*. After 1945, the wage and service regulations from the National Socialist period remained initially in place for white-collar employees and workers.[251] New collective wage agreements appeared only in 1961 (Püttner 1987, p. 1138). The development took a different course with respect to the *social security* for workers in the public sector. For them, a system of supplementary insurance had

[249] Art. 135, LVerf.He. On the realization of this article see Engelhardt (1980).

[250] Art. 33, Para. 2–5, Art. 73, No. 1, Art. 131, Art. 132, Para. 2, GG, old version.

[251] Section 6 of the Law for the Temporary Regulation of the Legal Conditions of Employees of May 1950.

been emerging since the 1920s.[252] During the course of the 1950s, the system was adjusted to the development (Hautmann 1984, pp. 5–20) – for the federation and the *Länder* through collective agreement law, for other public-law entities in part through other means (Schneider 1983, p. 214).

5.4.3 Other Gainful Activities

While the polity thus showed a strong concern for dependent workers during the founding phase of the Federal Republic, the interest of politics and the legal system in independent gainful activity remained vague. The most important goal of politics[253] continued to be unleashing the entrepreneurial energies (Abelshauser 1993, pp. 63–76). The means were fundamentally lacking for a subsidy policy that guided income (Huber 1954, pp. 258–261). The Marshall Plan provided important aid, but it would not be available indefinitely (Abelshauser 1993, pp. 54–63). Policies aimed at steering the economy had to run into concerns related to economic policy and constitutional law (Huber 1954, pp. 167–354). Tax law was and continued to be the most effective and simultaneously the most inconspicuous tool kit (Huber 1954, pp. 161–165; Abelshauser 1993, pp. 71–76). In principle, moreover, thoughts about intervention affected only businesses that were part of industrial production. There was a lot of political talk about the *Mittelstand*, but no concepts emerged.[254] The small-scale self-employed were not a principled topic at the time. The situation was different, of course, with respect to the social protection of the free professions and the small-scale self employed (Guderjahn 1971, pp. 161–195).

A fundamental exception was *agriculture*. The Agriculture Act was passed in 1955. The first section of that law spelled out the following program:

> So as to secure for agriculture the participation in the ongoing development of the German economy, and for the population the best possible provision with foodstuffs, agriculture must be enabled – especially with trade, tax, credit and price policies – to compensate the existing natural and economic disadvantages vis-à-vis other sectors of the economy and boost its productivity. At the same time, in this way the social situation of those engaged in agriculture is to be aligned with that of comparable vocational groups.

The federal government was put under obligation to report annually about its relevant measures.[255] With this, the special status of agriculture had been substantively and institutionally enshrined in a unique way.

[252] Schneider (1983, pp. 207–242). On other kinds of social protections of workers in the public sector see Krause (1982).

[253] For the beginning already before the currency reform and before the establishment of the Federal Republic see Abelshauser (1993, pp. 32–45).

[254] For a contemporary view of *Mittelstand* policy see Albrecht and Schüren (1957); for a retrospective view see Scheyban (1996).

[255] § 4 of the Law. Beginning in 1956, the federal government issued an annual "Green Report" about the state of agriculture and presented its measures in a "Green Plan": 1956 (BTDrs. II/2100),

5.4.4 Wealth as a Source of Social Differentiation

The basic social formula assumes that work provides a person with the essential capacity for social self-realization. Wealth can contribute in many ways to the individual, inter-human, and societal self-realization of a person. But people do not depend on wealth in the same way they do on work. Still, wealth has broad social relevance. A person who can live of his or her wealth is not compelled to work. The importance that work and income have for the life of the working person and his community of maintenance is relativized by wealth. After all, wealth can mean that someone has wealth to employ others. The reality of the basic formula thus depends in a new way on wealth: this person becomes a "capitalist." This juxtaposition can easily turn into a stereotype. The person who deploys wealth to employ others becomes the "enemy" of those who live from dependent work. He is placed under social obligation. By contrast, the person who works dependently and does not use the wealth he may have to employ others is not subjected to a comparable obligation. All that explains why wealth has no fixed place in the basic formula.

Wealth, however, is a priori a yardstick of social inequality: economically conditioned and economically relevant inequality. The inequality of wealth is a social irritant. But it holds especially with regard to the inequality of wealth that the social does not seek "equality" as such, but only "more equality," and in a particular way. The differences in wealth have many reasons that legitimize them: from economic success as the use of freedom, to the respect of the liberal legal system for the will of a testator, from individual merit to luck. And respect for these reasons is part of the basic consensus of society – as is the tolerance for the inequalities that follow.

The Challenges at the Time

For the early years of the Federal Republic, *highly disparate historical currents* held special significance. Historically handed down were critical attitudes about the *private ownership of capital*. This corresponded to the guiding ideas of *socialization*, which was supposed to bind the control over capital more strongly to the concerns of the general public and especially the workers. These tendencies were given a special emphasis by the accusation that "capital" had facilitated the rule of the Nazis and had profited handsomely from it. However, the economic dynamism that had emerged since the currency reform, which had quickly relieved the most dire misery and soon held out the prospect of newly achievable prosperity, quickly consigned such plans of structural change to the arsenal of theory. Those plans were not to impede the path of economic prosperity. Although the antagonism between

---

to 1967 (BTDrs. V/1400). In 1968 (BTDrs. V/2540), 1969 (BTDrs. V/381), and 1970 (BTDrs. VI/372), the federal government submitted only a "Green Report," but not a "Green Plan." The reporting system was reformed in 1971. Since then, the government presents annually a "Agrarian Report" and a "Volume of Materials": first time 1971 (BTDrs. VI/1800 and "zu VI/1800").

capital and labor remained alive, the path of socialization – endangered by opposition and economically risky – soon ceased to be seen as the right solution for it. What seemed achievable from the goal of socialization had already been undertaken through *codetermination in the workplace*. Continuing along that path avoided much of the resistance opposing socialization. And it had on its side a clear group interest, that of the workers, and a strong bearer of those interests, the unions.

Analogous to the social critique of the private ownership of capital, the concentration of *ownership of land* was also subject to social criticism. In that regard, as well, the thrust of historical charges against large-scale landholding was brought to bear after 1945. Plans for a *land reform* were supposed to respond to this. But once again doubts quickly arose about how land reform related to the path of economic dynamism. Taking land to settle expelled farmers[256] was a specific issue, one that did not justify a land reform in the sense of negating the concentrated private ownership of land.[257]

However, *the war and the postwar period* had also brought entirely *new problems of wealth policy*. War damage, the damage from expulsions, occupation damages, damages from the dismantling of industrial plants, and, finally, currency reform had affected the wealth of individuals in exceedingly diverse ways. People who had suffered damages and those who had not, the seriously disabled and the slightly disabled confronted one another. But the confrontation could be cast in very different terms: between the haves who could be harmed, and have-nots who could not suffer a comparable harm; or between those who owned much and could suffer great damages, and those who owned little who could suffer little harm. Should restitution attempt an approximation to the conditions that had existed before the harm occurred? Should a settlement take place among those who had had comparable wealth before the harm occurred? Or should that which was left over be generally redistributed – to the harmed and the unharmed alike? The *equalization of burdens*, which the Federal Republic now had to undertake (Schillinger 1985), combined the principle of compensation according to previous conditions with the principle of settlement based on what was left. The gradient of compensation followed primarily the damages suffered. The gradient of burdens imposed was based on what a person had been spared. Not all damages were compensated – either in substance or in size. Not all that was left behind was encumbered – either in substance or in size. The equalization of burdens was thus no critique of the inequality in the distribution of wealth, only a critique of the inequality of disadvantages and advantages.

[256] "Gesetz des Wirtschaftsrates des Vereinigten Wirtschaftsgebietes zur Förderung der Eingliederung der Heimatvertriebenen in die Landwirtschaft (Flüchtlingssiedlungsgesetz) vom 10. August 1946," WIGBl., p. 231.

[257] On the tradition of settlement law and its relationship to land reform see Huber (1954, pp. 67–77).

Change of Social Stratification Within the Framework of the Constitution?

While the inequality of wealth is clearly a challenge to the social, from the outset it remained open what exactly this could mean for politics and the law of the Federal Republic. There was and is no question that the social principle of the Basic Law (Art. 20, Para. 1, Art. 28, Para. 1, Sent. 1, GG) does not clarify this question.[258] The Basic Law specifically recognizes property and the right of inheritance (Art. 14, Para. 1, Sent. 1, GG). It is evident that this also applies to the case of inequality of wealth. That recognition is confronted with the following statement: "Property entails obligations. Its use shall also serve the public good" (Art. 14, Para. 2, GG), which can actualize the law by determining the content and limits of property (Art. 14, Para. 1, GG). In two places the constitution explicitly opens the door to the taking of property: for expropriation (Art. 14, Para. 3, GG) and for socialization (Art. 15 GG). However, expropriation as such does not pursue the goal of a better distribution of wealth; it takes property for the common good (Art. 14, Para. 3, Sent. 1, GG). And while socialization does embody a critique of the private ownership of certain goods, it, too, does not redistribute these goods, but transfers them "to public ownership or other forms of public enterprise" (Art. 15, Sent. 1, GG). Above all, however, expropriation and socialization require compensation (Art. 14, Para. 3, Art. 15, Sent. 2, GG). And compensation means: the status ante quem must be reestablished more or less – with all its inequality. All of this draws narrow boundaries around a redistribution through expropriation and socialization (Zacher 1981, pp. 972–976).

Still, the early interpretation of the Basic Law was not completely resistant to a *change in social stratification*. Was it not possible to come up with scenarios that could be justified as the social obligation of property (Art. 14, Para. 1, Sent. 2, Para. 2, GG) and were therefore not subject to the demands that the constitution imposed on expropriation or socialization? The equalization of burdens, land reform, decartelization, and codetermination were discussed as examples (Zacher 1981, pp. 976–987). In the political reality of that time, a redistribution of wealth took place, if anywhere, then within the framework of the equalization of burdens. The model of land reform quickly lost importance. What remained were changes to business property. As efforts to break up larger structures, these changes served far more to regulate competition than to create social equalization. As codetermination and works council laws, they concerned the relationship between capital and labor, but also between management and labor. But these were not moves that took from the "richer" and gave to the "poorer." The comprehensive medium of social redistribution became money, of which the state could make use by imposing levies (Zacher 1981, pp. 987–994) – this, too, could not be done arbitrarily, though certainly with the intent of taking from those who could afford it and to give it to those

[258] On the discussion at the time about the relationship of the social state to the distribution of goods see Zacher (1981, pp. 810–819).

who were in need of benefits and services. The "social state as tax state" (Vogel 1986, pp. 133–138) had been born.

The Social State Retreats from the Practice of Laying Its Hands on Wealth

With that, the mandate of the social state to create "more equality" had been given a very specific imprint. From the outset, the idea of establishing equality through the distribution of existing goods had been only a qualified part of the social. In the experience of the postwar period, equality through distribution was equality in necessity. It was part of *Daseinsvorsorge*. "Equality" in the sense of *Daseinsvorsorge* is "the public good." Interest in this kind of equality waned as the economy developed. It persisted longest in the controls on housing. A taking and giving, not for the sake of providing for the "public good," but for the sake of a substantive social equality, had quickly come up against its limitations – already in the design of the equalization of burdens, and fully so beyond that. Taking and giving was focused on the taking of money and – though not with the same exclusivity – the giving of money. The taking and giving of money has the advantage of according the greatest possible freedom to those affected by either action. Moreover, it renders the taking and the giving invisible. "More equality with the proviso of inequality" has the greatest chance with the redistribution of money.

That the practice of the social state retreated from a redistribution of wealth after the equalization of burdens found expression equally in the *focus on adjustment and the redistribution of money*. The dynamic nature of incomes facilitated redistribution, whereas the static nature of wealth would have made it more difficult. Of course, the concentration on incomes – burdening them with levies as well as replacing and supplementing them through social benefits – resulted in imbalances. Over the course of time, they would become evident as an overloading of income redistribution. False effects of taking and giving also have to do with this. Contradictions emerged, as well: when opposition to the redistribution of wealth extended to the redistribution of income derived from wealth, and, most of all, when those who have little or no wealth did not cease to include the comparison of wealth into "their" better-worse constellations, while for those who have wealth, it became quickly a matter of course that wealth has nothing to do with the better-worse constellations.

The Formation of Wealth

This picture is congruent with a policy on wealth[259] that had turned away not only from any taking other than the taking of money, but also from any specific taking of wealth, and focused on giving money or – through tax breaks – leaving money untouched. Wealth was not to be redistributed but formed. That became clear first in

[259] Bundesministerium für Arbeit und Soziales and Bundesarchiv (eds.), 2005: Geschichte der Sozialpolitik in Deutschland seit 1945, vol. 3, Chap. 3, no. 16.

the property-promoting dimension of housing policy. The Condominium Act of 1951 expanded the legal ways of acquiring residential property. The Housing Construction Premium Act of 1952 carried out also in terms of benefits law the shift in emphasis on the private formation of property. The Housing Construction and Family Home Act of 1956, and the Law to Amend the 1st Housing Construction Act and the 2nd Housing Construction Act of 1957 deepened this development. It was only later that a general promotion of savings would expand this path. By contrast, the idea of supplementing the codetermination of workers within businesses and enterprises by having them share in a business's capital and profits repeatedly fell by the wayside (Frerich and Frey, vol. 3, 1996, pp. 139–141).

5.4.5 The Family[260]

The basic formula of the social refers the family to support by the earners and the active maintenance by the family members who have taken on family tasks. When the Federal Republic was born, the normative model was still one in which the husband worked and the wife took care of the children and the household. The presumption of the law was also in line with this model (Sect. 1353ff., BGB, old version). Although the Basic Law had guaranteed the *equality of men and women* in general terms (Art. 3, Para. 2, GG), Art. 117, Para. 1, GG had granted a postponement:

> Law which is inconsistent with paragraph (2) of Art. 3 of this Basic Law shall remain in force until adapted to that provision, but not beyond 31 March 1953.

The legislature neglected to adhere to this deadline. As a result, with the expiration of 31 March 1953, law that was contrary to the stated equality ceased to be in force. The application of the law had to fill the gap (BVerfGE 3, 225). The legislature fulfilled its obligation of a new regulation only with the Law on the Equality of Men and Women in the Sphere of Civil Law of 18 June 1957. By contrast, the implementation of the postulate of equality in labor law and in the social benefits law remained also after 1953 – in spite of various legislative steps (Scheffler 1960, pp. 315–323) – all too often a matter of those who applied the laws, especially the courts (W. Bogs 1960, pp. 39–42). In a multitude of decisions, the courts tried to do justice to the principle of equality, without doing violence to the real conditions that were based on traditional ideas.

The Basic Law had also placed a new emphasis on the *value of marriage and the family* (Art. 6, GG). However, in this regard the need for changes to the law was not as clear as it was with the equality of men and women (Zacher 1981, pp. 995–1017; W. Bogs 1960, pp. 42–44). The most important step was the Child Allowance Act of 1954. The demand for a family-suitable income (see above notes 135 and 145)

---

260 Bundesministerium für Arbeit und Sozialordnung and Bundesarchiv (eds.), 2001b: Geschichte der Sozialpolitik in Deutschland seit 1945, vol. 2, Chap. 3, no. 10.

that was put forth after 1945 had not been realized. Only in the public service – led by civil service law – were wages and salaries paid that were to any appreciable degree oriented toward family burdens. In the private sector, the per-capita income of workers and employees remained in place (with exceptions). But the idea that the family-suitable wage was a duty of employers was not so quickly forgotten. Since the individual employer could not bear that obligation, it was collectivized. The organizational model was – strangely enough – accident insurance. The risk of accidents in the workplace was covered by employers grouped together into liability insurance associations (*Berufsgenossenschaften*). These liability insurance associations now had added to them family equalization funds to implement the *child allowance law*. The solution was seen as complementing the tax breaks for the family. The dual system of family equalization began (Frerich and Frey, vol. 3, 1996, pp. 115–118). However, the solution to *family equalization* by way of social insurance law revealed serious shortcomings. Neither the circle of those entitled to benefits, nor workers and other individuals insured against accidents, nor the circle of those liable for payments (employers) had been properly delineated. This quickly gave rise to repairs (Frerich and Frey, vol. 3, 1996, p. 116f.).

The law on child allowance was complemented, hesitantly, by the social *assistance for training* (Frerich and Frey, vol. 3, 1996, pp. 118–121). On the one hand, social benefits systems, especially the social compensation law, were complemented with the addition of relevant benefits (to war orphans and so on). On the other hand, the federal government and the *Länder* agreed on a general program of aid to university students, the so-called Honnefer Model, which took effect on 1 July 1957 (Stephany 1968). Other than that, the social flanking of education policy[261] was largely the task of the *Länder*, who were responsible for the educational system. They slowly instituted free education and the supply of books and materials at no cost.

Among the most revolutionary programs in the Basic Law, Art. 6, Para. 5, GG pertained to family life: "*Children born outside of marriage* shall be provided by legislation with the same opportunities for physical and mental development and for their position in society as are enjoyed by those born within marriage." This passage was regarded as binding, but not in such a way that it would have by itself invalidated contrary law (BVerfGE 8, 210). As a result, all that happened initially were interpretational steps toward change (Krüger 1960, pp. 325–367; Zacher 1981, pp. 1013–1017).

The constitutional program of *protection for mothers* (Art. 6, Para. 4, GG) was picked up by the Maternity Protection Act of 1952, as well as in labor law and social benefits law (Frerich and Frey, vol. 3, 1996, p. 113f.).

The change in the idea of marriage and family was no central theme in legal and social policy at the time. In many cases, the war and the postwar period had thrust women into the role of the "head of the family," especially into the role of the

[261] Bundesministerium für Arbeit und Soziales and Bundesarchiv (eds.), 2005: Geschichte der Sozialpolitik in Deutschland seit 1945, vol. 3, Chap. 3, no. 11.

breadwinner who had to support the family. But this did not initially turn into a discussion with political effect. As a result, social law also found itself challenged by the circumstances of the time in an ambivalent way, not only to realize the equality of men and women, but also to strengthen and develop its traditional structure.[262] Only a decade later did the positive acceptance of the new social reality call into question old family structures and their corresponding reflections in labor *and* social benefits law.

5.4.6 The Social Benefits Systems: Social Provision[263]

The question of whether the traditional structures of provision should be taken over and continued by the Federal Republic preoccupied the discussion over social policy at the time intensely and in multifarious ways (Hockerts 1980). However, the development headed in the direction laid down by tradition. Overall this took place through the adjustment of social insurance to the new political, economic, social, and legal realities. The *Länder* and the Unified Economic Area had already done much to revitalize social insurance. What needed to be done now was above all to create legal unity.[264] Another step along that path was the establishment of social jurisdiction,[265] which picked up the tradition by visibly absorbing into itself the existing legal protection institutions of social insurance, care for war victims, and labor administration (W. Bogs 1979; Christmann and Schönholz 1984, pp. 3–46; Bürck 1984). In essence, however, the development took place within the individual legal areas.

Continued Development of Provision for the Risks of Old Age, Disability, and Death with Surviving Dependants[266]

With respect to *social insurance* in the case of old age, disability, and death with surviving dependants, there was initially a series of benefits adjustments and improvements. More and more, however, the development came to focus on the "*major pension reform*" of 1957 (Hockerts 1990). It became the most important emblem for a revival of social insurance in keeping with the times. Without formal

[262] Largely carried by this view: Ehe und Familie im Sozialversicherungs- und Versorgungsrecht (1967).

[263] Peters (1978, pp. 147–209); D. Zöllner (1981, pp. 136–146); Bundesministerium für Arbeit and Soziales and Bundesarchiv (eds.), 2005: Geschichte der Sozialpolitik in Deutschland seit 1945, vol. 3, Chap. 3, nos. 3–7.

[264] "Gesetz über die Selbstverwaltung und über Änderung von Vorschriften auf dem Gebiet der Sozialversicherung von 1951."

[265] "Sozialgerichtsgesetz" of 1953.

[266] Bundesministerium für Arbeit und Soziales and Bundesarchiv (eds.), 2005: Geschichte der Sozialpolitik in Deutschland seit 1945, vol. 3, Chap. 3, no. 5.

and institutional changes, the pension insurance law of workers and white-collar employees was standardized. Moreover, workers' and white-collar employees' pension insurance, on the one hand, and the miners' pension insurance, on the other hand, were also largely harmonized structurally.[267] For all sectors the rule was: the pension should no longer be merely a supplement to other sources of income, but should guarantee the livelihood. The wage-based, dynamic pension became a core piece of the social benefits system. The reform took a strict stance on the criterion of the need for provision. Voluntary insurance was radically curtailed. Pension insurance concentrated on workers and on a number of other groups in need of protection precisely defined by the law. In line with this was the fact that, parallel to pension reform, the specific social protection of the self-employed was also addressed. The *insurance for tradesmen* was initially temporarily repaired,[268] while a reform had to be postponed to the next legislative session.[269] By contrast, the *old-age assistance for farmers*[270] was a completely new departure. The program of agrarian policy formulated by the Agriculture Act of 1955 found its first major implementation in social policy.

Compared to the development of social security, the other areas of insurance for old age, disability, and surviving dependants did not come to the fore much. Following tradition, *civil service pension* developed parallel to the active service law (Ruland 1983, pp. 92–95). *Occupational provision systems*, which initially existed only in Bavaria, were set up also in a few other states (Frerich and Frey, vol. 3, 1996, p. 59). Work-based old-age pension schemes did not attract any major attention from social policy (Frerich and Frey, vol. 3, 1996, p. 63). By contrast, the largest branch of work-based supplementary provision, the supplementary pension in the public service, was adjusted to the new conditions (see above section "The Law of the Public Sector").

Further Development of Sickness Insurance[271]

The year 1955 became an important one for *sickness insurance*. The Law on the Associations of the Statutory Sickness Funds and the *Ersatzkassen* (substitute funds) (1955) provided a new foundation for the structure, legal status, and tasks of the association of sickness funds. More important still was the reorganization and standardization of relations between doctors, dentists, and sickness funds through the Law to Change the Stipulations of the Second Book of the Reich Insurance

[267] "Arbeiterrentenversicherungs-Neuregelungsgesetz;" "Angestelltenversicherungs-Neuregelungs gesetz;" "Knappschaftsrentenversicherung-Neuregelungsgesetz" – all 1957.

[268] "Gesetz zur vorläufigen Änderung des Gesetzes über die Altersversorgung für das Deutsche Handwerk von 1956."

[269] "Handwerkerversicherungsgesetz von 1960."

[270] "Gesetz über eine Altershilfe für Landwirte von 1957."

[271] Bundesministerium für Arbeit und Soziales and Bundesarchiv (eds.), 2005: Geschichte der Sozialpolitik in Deutschland seit 1945, vol. 3, Chap. 3, no. 6.

Code and the Supplement to the Social Jurisdiction Law (Sickness Fund Physician Act) (1955). The Basic Law had not established a special responsibility for the real provision of medical care to the population. The responsibility of the state that was oriented toward medical personnel and encompassed "admission to the medical profession and to ancillary professions or occupations" was mentioned in a corresponding position among concurrent legislative powers (Art. 74, no. 19, GG). Already the complementary law on the exercise of a profession and the legal organization of the medical professions had remained within the jurisdiction of the state legislatures (Landesgesetzgebung) (Art. 30 and 70 GG). The suitable and economically appropriate provision of medical and other health care services was not recognized as a task area of its own. The "Statute on Panel Doctor Law" saw that almost self-evidently as a task of social insurance. Soon after, in 1960, the Federal Constitutional Court decided (BVerfGE 11, 30) that participation in the care provided by panel doctors was an extension of the basic right for the free choice and exercise of the medical profession (Art. 12, Para. 1, GG). The disproportion between the totality of the task of medical care and the specialized nature of the task of social provision for the case of illness was now perfectly in place. Later reforms would increasingly deepen this disproportion between the creative power of a social insurance that was – for all its expansiveness – particularistic, and the general problem of the socially and economically appropriate provision of medical care. Moreover, with this law, social insurance assumed a certain responsibility – initially inconspicuously so – for the income of panel doctors. This, too, would be the beginning of a development that expanded to an ever growing number of groups of service providers, until eventually the contribution that the health care sector made to the national economy became a justification for health care spending (Sachverständigenrat für die Konzertierte Aktion im Gesundheitswesen 1996, 1997/1998).

5.4.7 Other Areas of Social Benefits

Social Compensation[272]

No area of social benefits was tied to the historical situation of the Federal Republic in so elementary a way as the social compensation law. Of equal urgency in terms of domestic and foreign politics, and of the utmost difficulty, was the *restitution* of National Socialist injustice (Herbst and Goschler 1989; Goschler 1992). The Federal Republic initially supplemented the compensation laws of the *Länder* with the Federal Supplementary Compensation Act (1953), and then replaced them with the Federal Compensation Act (1956). The return of confiscated property was initially regulated by occupation law. Only toward the end of the period under

[272] Bundesministerium für Arbeit und Soziales and Bundesarchiv (eds.), 2005: Geschichte der Sozialpolitik in Deutschland seit 1945, vol. 3, Chap. 3, no. 12.

discussion was the Federal Restitution Law passed (1957). A separate restitution agreement was signed with Israel (10 September 1952).[273] In addition, specific regulations were adopted for the restitution of National Socialist injustice for members of the public service (1951) and in the provision for war victims (1958).

The compensation for damages considered to have been caused, not by persecution, but as the *special sacrifice* of the individual within the national community of fate, was fundamentally regulated in a separate process: for personal damages, and for property damages. The compensation for *personal damages* was the only area that could connect to older traditions – namely the Reich Pension Law. The federal legislature acted swiftly to improve the benefits[274] and to replace the old regulations with a new Federal Pension Act that same year (1950).

The *property damage* caused by war, expulsion, and currency reform formed the subject of the laws on the equalization of burdens. The United Economic Area had entered into this area with its Law to Relieve Urgent Social Hardships – the Immediate Assistance Act – of 8 August 1949. This law was temporary. The Federal Republic therefore once again confronted the question about the principles by which equalization should be carried out. The Currency Equalization Law of March 1952 and the Determination Act of April 1952 were eventually followed by the Equalization of Burdens Act of August 1952. These were joined somewhat later by the Old Savings Act (1953). A differentiated system of one-time and ongoing monetary benefits had been created, which took on essential importance for the material status of the expellees. However, the measures to equalize the damages could not be sufficient – especially since the intended compensation was paid out only over the long term. The *integration* of the expellees required additional help. This was the task of the Federal Expellees' Act (1953). Similar problems were faced by individuals who had been *evacuated* from endangered areas during the war; the Federal Evacuees' Act sought to provide assistance to them.

The circumstances of the time also prompted the state, however, to take responsibility for a series of other, more or less similar problems. There were still *prisoners of war*, and their dependants received subsistence allowance.[275] The *returnees* needed help[276] and expected compensation.[277] Finally, it seemed proper to provide aid to political *prisoners* who, coming from the *German Democratic Republic or other problem states*, sought refuge in the Federal Republic.[278] All in all, then, what emerged was a highly diverse system of social compensation law.

[273] "Ratifizierungsgesetz vom 20. März 1953," BGBl. II, p. 35.

[274] "Gesetz zur Verbesserung von Leistungen an Kriegsopfer von 1950."

[275] "Gesetz über die Unterhaltsbeihilfe für Angehörige von Kriegsgefangenen von 1950."

[276] "Heimkehrergesetz von 1950."

[277] "Kriegsgefangenenentschädigungsgesetz von 1954."

[278] "Häftlingshilfegesetz von 1955."

Unemployment Insurance – Employment Policy[279]

Ever since unemployment aid had been introduced in Germany, it was combined with non-insurance benefits (unemployment assistance) and with job placement services in a complex system. In 1945, the relevant institutions and central agencies of the Reich had collapsed. Local and state labour offices had tried to carry on the work. While that initially continued in the Federal Republic, adjustments to benefits were necessary.[280] The restoration of a uniform administrative structure that was in line with the governmental system of the Federal Republic was the next urgent desideratum. In a first step, the Federal Labour Office (*Bundesanstalt für Arbeitsvermittlung und Arbeitslosenversicherung*) was set up in Nuremberg in 1952. The continued development of the law on job placement and unemployment insurance came to a temporary end in 1956 (Frerich and Frey, vol. 3, 1996, p. 85f.). In this area, as well, the Federal Republic thus took a path that had been charted by history.

Public Assistance[281]

All the hardship that could not find help anywhere else looked to public assistance (welfare). The local communities and charitable organizations worked together to do what they could. The legal foundations for their activities still stemmed from the Weimar period: the Reich Law on the Responsibility to Provide Public Welfare Assistance of 1924 and the Reich Principles about the Precondition, Nature, and Level of Public Welfare of 1924/1931. According to these statutes, public assistance was still seen as the objective duty of the state, but not as a subjective right of the person in need. In this regard, the literature[282] and judicial decisions[283] forced a change. A subjective right to assistance essential to survival was recognized. Principles of the social and constitutional state (Art. 20, Para. 1, Art. 28, Para. 1, Sent. 1, GG), as well as the right to the free development of one's personality (Art. 2, Para. 1, GG) and the right to life (Art. 2, Para. 2, GG) were the decisive arguments. The legislature initially did not pick up this issue, but it did adjust the "objective" welfare law to the changed circumstances.[284] The need for a fundamental reorganization of welfare had to wait.[285] However, toward the end of the period under

[279] Bundesministerium für Arbeit und Soziales and Bundesarchiv (eds.), 2005: Geschichte der Sozialpolitik in Deutschland seit 1945, vol. 3, Chap. 3, no. 3.

[280] "Arbeitslosenversicherungs-Änderungsgesetz vom 29. März 1951"; "Arbeitslosenfürsorge-Änderungsgesetz vom 29. März 1951."

[281] Bundesministerium für Arbeit und Soziales and Bundesarchiv (eds.), 2005: Geschichte der Sozialpolitik in Deutschland seit 1945, vol. 3, Chap. 3, no. 9.

[282] For a compilation see Zacher (1981, p. 767, note 6).

[283] Culminating in 1954 by one of the first decisions of the Federal Administrative Court: BVerwG 1, 159 (161f.).

[284] "Gesetz über die Änderung and Ergänzung fürsorgerechtlicher Bestimmungen von 1953."

[285] Fürsorge und Sozialreform (1956); Die Neuordnung des Fürsorgerechts als Teil einer Sozialreform (1958).

examination, the *Physical Disability Act* (1957) signaled the recognition, at any rate, of the need to respond more specifically to certain life situations than the general welfare law did. It was soon followed by the *Tuberculosis Assistance Act* (1959).

5.4.8 The Meeting of Needs: From *Daseinsvorsorge* to Income Policy

Freeing the meeting of needs from the directives of control and rationing had still begun in the United Economic Area. The Federal Republic proceeded along this line. Price controls were loosened and for the most part lifted (Huber 1954, pp. 313–329). The supply of goods shifted quickly to the market. And the individual possibility of meeting essential needs shifted from rationing and price policy to income policy: to wage policy and social benefits policy (Hoffmann 1958). That is not to say that the legislature was completely released from responsibility for the supply of goods. On the contrary: the appropriate organization of the economy and the specific economic conditions of the time necessitated many new regulations and institutions (Huber 1954, pp. 195–329). But the focal point of the political responsibility moved away from *Daseinsvorsorge* to the functioning of the economy. Sociopolitical intentions were directed less and less at the socially appropriate provisioning of consumers and increasingly at their economic conditions. But while the responsibility of the state for the supply of goods thus changed fundamentally, the *local mandate* of *Daseinsvorsorge* remained in place unchanged (Zacher 1981, pp. 228–242). The communal offerings continued to largely equalize the access to goods and services. A corresponding structuring of needs at times provided easier access for the "socially weaker" (Barocka 1960, pp. 825–832; Zacher 1981, p. 832). However, the *fees* for state services were also selectively tiered – for example, for educational and training offerings, if they were not already free.[286]

Particular emphasis was placed on meeting *housing needs*.[287] The housing shortage was still dire. The first Housing Construction Act was passed in 1950. It made the promotion of housing construction the joint task of the federal government, the states, and the local communities. A broad spectrum of measures promoted especially public housing. At the same time, the control over living space was loosened for the first time, in a way that could itself stimulate housing construction: namely for housing that was built after 1949 with free financing. In 1951, the Condominium Act made it easier to create condominiums by way of private law. The Housing Construction Premium Act of 1952 favored the formation of private property in housing construction. Control over residential living space

[286] Zacher (1981, p. 821); Bundesministerium für Arbeit und Soziales and Bundesarchiv (eds.), 2005: Geschichte der Sozialpolitik in Deutschland seit 1945, vol. 3, Chap. 3, no. 11.

[287] Bundesministerium für Arbeit und Soziales and Bundesarchiv (eds.), 2005: Geschichte der Sozialpolitik in Deutschland seit 1945, vol. 3, Chap. 3, no. 15.

was curtailed further in 1953. The Building Land Procurement Act (1953) was intended to improve the supply of land to build on. In the second legislative session there followed the Federal Rent Act (1955), which gave rent law a fundamentally new shape. Additional laws promoted above all the ownership of residential apartments.[288] These were targeted especially at low-income earners, large families, and the severely disabled. The accomplishments in housing construction at the time were enormous (Schulz 1994).

5.4.9 The Development of Taxes

The movement in tax law (Muscheid 1986, pp. 32–66; Frerich and Frey, vol. 3, 1996, pp. 142–151) was focused largely on the income tax. We can identify two dimensions that substantially supplemented the policy of social benefits: *family equalization* and relief for the *disabled* as well as for persons who, as *persecutees, refugees, expellees, late returnees, individuals who had suffered personal or property damage from the war*, and so on, had been practically affected and harmed by the politics of the preceding period.[289] Characteristic was also the entry into *income tax relief for the elderly*.[290] Family equalization involved especially tax deductions for children and the modalities of spouse taxation. With regard to spouse taxation, the period ended with a bang: the Federal Constitutional Court demanded "income splitting."[291]

5.5 *Summary*

5.5.1 The Features of the Development

The two legislative sessions were characterized by exceptional constructive accomplishments. Following the lead of the United Economic Area, the power of society to generate prosperity was further liberated. After a difficult start, *prosperity and freedom* – prosperity-conditioned freedom and prosperity-creating freedom – spread quickly. The *basic formula* of work, income, the meeting of needs, and the community of maintenance *quickly gained new force*. The *reinvigoration of labor law* provided protection for those who fulfilled the basic formula through dependent labor. The old *social benefits systems* that compensate for the shortcomings that

[288] "Wohnungsbau- und Familienheimgesetz" (II. WoBauG) of 1956; "Gesetz zur Änderung des I. WoBauG und des II. WoBauG von 1957."

[289] "Einkommensteueränderungsgesetz vom 29. April 1950" BGBl. I, p. 95; "Steueränderungsgesetz vom 24. Juni 1953," BGBl. I, p. 413; Bundesministerium für Arbeit und Soziales and Bundesarchiv (eds.), 2005: Geschichte der Sozialpolitik in Deutschland seit 1945, vol. 3, pp. 142–151.

[290] "Strukturneuordnungsgesetz von 1954."

[291] BVerfGE 6, 45; "Steueränderungsgesetz vom 26. Juli 1957" BGBl. I, p. 848.

arise during the implementation of the basic formula were quickly "repaired" and soon also fundamentally improved – especially pension insurance. Added to this was a multitude of new benefit systems that were necessary to deal with the consequences of National Socialist rule. The expellees and refugees were integrated. Tax policy, too, addressed social inequalities.

As *new* as the *social compensation law* was in its variety, the *other social benefits systems* were tied to the past. To be sure, a lot of thought, including fundamental thought, was devoted to new beginnings. Effectively, however, politics remained on the *tracks of the preceding development.* As a result, this period would later be referred to as "*restorative*." However, looking at the exceptional accomplishments of the political system and society in the first 8 years of the Federal Republic, looking at the circumstances under which those accomplishments were achieved, one might ask whether the sort of "different and more things" that a fundamental reform would have had to create was really possible. But because the doable had been done, and essentially done well, the historical path had been affirmed in a unique way. Future politics saw itself set on a track from which it would never again depart, no matter how much it might appear to the contrary at times.

The new course that was charted at the time, however, included not only social compensation law and the integration of the expellees and refugees. A fundamental course of another kind was laid down in the *renunciation of a direct socio-political grasp at the potential of the economy*. The *guidance* of the economy in the sense of *Daseinsvorsorge* was *minimized.* The *socializing resort to capital*, which seemed to find such broad approval in the immediate post-war period, *did not happen.* The intent of making the economy more social by way of a nationalization or other communalization of capital was set aside. The social control of capital was understood as a problem in the field of tension between capital and labor or also in the field of tension between employers and workers. *Works constitution and codetermination* were the names for this direction. With that, however, the *inequality in the distribution of wealth* seems to have generally lost its social resonance. To be sure, the equalization of burdens meant a considerable effort to redistribute to those who had suffered property damage from the war and the postwar period, and from those who had been spared. Other than that, however, the unequal distribution of wealth did not trigger any attempts to correct it through confiscation and redistribution. Instead, the beginnings of a wealth policy were focused on help to acquire wealth. To put it differently: it was focused on the distribution of growth. That put in place a trait that would remain characteristic of the social state that is the Federal Republic: the inequality in the distribution of wealth was no longer the object of a central critique; this social state was oriented entirely toward the inequality and equality of incomes – toward the growth of incomes, the approximation of incomes, and especially also the replacement and supplementation of incomes through social benefits. *Redistribution now concerned incomes*. The equalization of burdens bore the stamp of a historically unique event.

All of this boosted the centrality of the basic formula of work, income, the meeting of needs, and the community of maintenance. But for that very reason, the foundation was also put in place that would cause *family policy* to remain a field of uncertainty. The *basic formula is clear and unambiguous*, to the extent that it refers to *one* person (i.e., as long as the issue is a single person working, earning, and meetings his or her needs), or to the extent that it is carried out within a community of maintenance *by all persons in tandem* (i.e., when both spouses of a childless couple work and meet their needs jointly). But the *basic formula seems hopelessly complex if not all members of the community of maintenance are earners*. At that point it becomes difficult to do justice to the different relationships between the smaller number of earners and the larger number of those with needs. And it is equally difficult to do justice to the fact that not all non-earners in this community of maintenance are passive recipients, that non-earners in fact also contribute important services within this community. In other words: it is difficult to do justice to the problems of those who perform family work – especially if they perform *only* family work. During the period under examination here, the main provider of this work was generally the wife and mother. But regardless of how that may have changed: to this day the family is an essential producer of human welfare. And as a rule that *goes hand in hand with inequalities*: either in the overburdening of individuals who engage in both gainful employment and family work; or in the disadvantaging of those who forego gainful employment to do family work. The period we are looking at reflects especially this *difficulty of the social state*. Both on the benefits side (particularly through the introduction of the child allowance) and on the dues side (through income splitting and an improvement in the child tax deduction) important steps were taken to help families more than before. But it was impossible to do so much for families, and to differentiate so precisely that family work was worth it without discriminating against the gainful employment of family members. This impasse characterized not only the situation of families within the social state of the Federal Republic. It also characterizes the status of family work. Because it is not gainful employment, the social state tends to forget about it.

5.5.2 Classlessness Thanks to Complexity

It was a pragmatic time. And it was an open time – open in the sense that there were hardly any rigid frontlines. The field of social differentiations was exceedingly complex. Worse-better comparisons overlapped in multifarious ways. The employer-employee relationship could take on many forms. But at any rate, it confronted so many other differentiations: between the persecuted and the non-persecuted; between expellees and residents; between victims of the war and those who escaped unharmed; between those who had suffered damage to their property from the war and those who had been able to save it; between those who had had nothing before the calamity and those who did have something before and now had less or maybe the same; between those who had cash wealth before the currency reform and those who had material wealth, and so on. Added to this were gradients between people who had to care for families and those who were alone, or also between acquisitive individuals who could start anew, and the old who were dependent on what was left to them.

This was in a very specific way a *"classless" society*. And it remained that – wrapped in the dynamism of the times. For the opportunities to establish oneself under the new conditions were very broadly distributed.

An important indicator of what was special about that period is the question concerning *poverty*. The "poverty question," too, had taken on a new face. The "conventionally" poor had been joined by so many who were living in an analogous disproportion between their needs and the ability to meet them, but whose history and perspective assigned them a different place: expellees, evacuees, those bombed out of their homes, displaced persons, separated families; people who had wanted to live off their savings, which had now been wiped out by the currency reform; people who had expected in their old age to be supported by their children, who were now dead, and so on. Moreover: the economic dynamism soon pushed into difficulties groups who previously had been able, as independent workers, to live from what was "their own." The political concern for agriculture is only one symptom of this process. The variety of affected persons was enormous. This "*classlessness by force of complexity*" was a crucial foundation for the subsequent development of the social in West Germany.

5.5.3 Complexity, Pragmatism, Principles?

This "classlessness by force of complexity" also reduced the meaning of conceivable principles of the social. What could *equality* mean in the face of so many inequalities?

What could *participation* mean? The important thing was that there was once again economic activity and gainful work, and that participation in it spread rapidly. This was the central opportunity of the time. Social tensions therefore arose vis-à-vis unemployment, for it called this participation into question. And with the importance of participation in a gainful life, social protection, which continued the earned income in case the direct participation was interrupted or terminated, also attracted new interest. It is quite obvious that this kind of participation was in the foreground. Then there was another kind of participation: that of those who had been harmed in the potentialities of the commonality. It found its expression in social compensation law. Finally, there was the elementary participation through the guarantee of a subsistence minimum. This principle was never seriously in question. But neither was it in the foreground. Later, the expectations were directed at a participation in society's opportunities for prosperity. That, in particular, is what would be meant in the future when the demand for "more equality" was raised. This participation found its expression later above all in the systems of social promotion. In that regard, however, the "founding period" still lacked the self-evidence of prosperity.

Talk of *justice* was, naturally enough, as diverse as inequality was complex. Justice was therefore not a useful slogan. The development showed that nobody wanted simply *one kind* of justice. Of course, the hardship of the time demanded a *justice of needs*. But the most important key to progress was the *justice of achievement*. But *the justice of acquired standing* – as a principle – was also not challenged, not by and vis-à-vis those who had been harmed; and most definitely not by those whose justice of achievement had helped them – or was supposed to – in acquiring new standing.

The word *solidarity* encountered a peculiar timidity. It was reminiscent of the "*Volksgemeinschaft*" (national community) that had fallen so deeply into guilt and calamity. How could one make this into a principle with a future? But even those knowledgeable of social policy who had no hesitation to speak of solidarity could not strike a lot of sparks with it. What kind of solidarity was meant? A *vertical solidarity* of the richer with the poorer? Beyond the diversity of differences: yes. But who exactly should give, and who would receive? The solidarity of society with the victims of National Socialist rule and war? Again: yes. But was this the equal solidarity with all victims? And who would be obligated to pay up? What was left was the solidarity with all those in need, as realized by public assistance and welfare! It seemed easier to organize the horizontal solidarity for the shared provision of those affected in the same way, the kind that is typical of social insurance. Thus, *horizontal solidarity* remained from the outset a characteristic of the development of the social state.

The principle of *subsidiarity*,[292] finally, met with a certain trust. For some, there was something of freedom about it. For others, it embodied Catholic social doctrine and thus something that had gained authority also through its opposition to National Socialism. But what did the word actually mean? The general primacy of the societal realization of the social quickly found acceptance – or at any rate, it quickly became reality. But who identified subsidiarity with the free market economy? Strangely enough: the federal state, otherwise the prime example of subsidiarity, could not be meant, either, since the *Länder* did not expect much from either the constitutional order or from social policy. That left the communities. But the social responsibility of the communities barely resonated in a fundamental way. That left the charitable organizations, families, and, of course, the individual. Individuals, however, already had their rights of liberty. Families, too, had their guarantees – and yet so much remained unclear. Finally, as the entire development would show, the place of altruism and of non-profit organizations is not really clarified by any principle of subsidiarity.

The integration of the society of the young polity had succeeded to an astonishing degree. It was borne and dominated by the dynamism of the time. A central experience of society was that of freedom and of self-responsibility in freedom. Another crucial experience was help in hard times. The polity and the society did their utmost not to abandon anyone to their misery without any help at all. To be sure: it was only over the course of time that this turned into protection against hardship. Equality and prosperity were not a general reality. But they could be understood as universal opportunities. The value of protection had already gone through a long history of fractures: inflation, the global economic crisis, the

[292] On the pairing of solidarity and subsidiarity that has recurred to this day see Achinger et. al. (1955, pp. 21–30); von Nell-Breuning (1957).

despotism of the National Socialists, war and collapse. Still, the concern of the state to provide protection and security had proved itself also in many ways: through the continuation of old institutions of social protection or their reorganization, as well as through completely new departures. Crucial above all, however, was that the goals of prosperity, freedom, security, equality, and protection against hardship were affirmed as a shared system of values – as a shared hope.

6 1957–1966: Consolidation

6.1 Political and Societal Premises[293]

6.1.1 Starting Points

The national product had risen throughout the entire founding phase of the Federal Republic. On average for the period, growth rates – though they dropped to an economic low toward 1957 – remained at a level they would not achieve again later.[294] The general supply with goods had reached the level of a "prosperous society." The biggest successes of the time, however, were in the reduction of unemployment and in the ratio of income to the cost of living. The unemployment rate had dropped from 11% in 1950 to 3.7% in 1957, and was then below 1% from 1961 to 1966. Wages grew continuously in both nominal and real terms. The price index had still risen between 1950 and 1951. After a period of decline (1953), the rate of inflation fluctuated between 0.3 and 3.0% until 1964. Hourly productivity had risen across the period at around 6.2% annually. The "economic miracle" was under way (Wildt 1994).

6.1.2 The Political Constellations

The *Third German Bundestag* was elected in 1957. The CDU ran its campaign (Toman-Banke 1994, p. 50) under two slogans that expressed the success of the preceding years: "No experiments/CDU" and "Prosperity for all/CDU/Ludwig Erhard." And the CSU added: "Let us keep building/Adenauer/CSU." Particularly significant was the slogan: "Prosperity for all" (Erhard 1957). It reflected the complex "classlessness" of society and its experience that general prosperity is superior to any tightly managed social care. Society had begun to yield to the equality illusion of growth, which is born of the fact that tomorrow many will

[293] Schwarz (1983); Hildebrand (1984); Stern (2000, pp. 1432–1467); Bundesministerium für Arbeit und Soziales and Bundesarchiv (eds.), 2007a: Geschichte der Sozialpolitik in Deutschland seit 1945, vol. 4, Chap. 1.

[294] Bundesministerium für Wirtschaft (1964; 1966). Neumann (1976).

always have what few have today. “Prosperity for all” was the political coinage minted from that belief. *Willy Brandt* would later refine that statement into “More quality of life.” And it would take from the mid-1970s to the mid-1990s for the realization to sink in how difficult it is to manifest the social once it is not simply realized through growth: when the available social product no longer grows reliably and sufficiently; and perhaps even more so when the conflicting goals within the social increase and the social cannot be continued indefinitely in a straight line. The SPD played on the choice between military and social spending (Gruner 1990, pp. 63–72): “Every tank costs 40 apartments, every fighter jet three schools.” It called for “No Compulsory Military Service/Therefore SPD,” and “Reunification in Freedom!/And End to Inaction!/Security for All/SPD.” “Security” was, of course, a broad concept, but it also encompassed “social security”: “Security for the family – SPD/Old Age Without Worries – SPD.” The FDP dispensed with substantive statements. It contested the CDU’s absolute rule.

The elections were won by the CDU and the CSU in a landslide (Ritter and Niehuss 1991, p. 101). *Konrad Adenauer* formed his third government on the basis of a coalition with the tiny partner of the DP. The socio-political dimension of the government’s inaugural declaration on 29 October 1957 (Behn 1971, pp. 61–81) was not very developed. It contained observations about the social structure (the erosion of the *Mittelstand* between “a small stratum of rulers over the economy and a large class of dependants”), about the necessity of not only creating capital, but also of dispersing it widely, about the state of agriculture, and the state of large families. “Social reform will be carried on. First and foremost.... a reorganization of sickness insurance and accident insurance will be on the table... However, it is also time to draw consequences from the changed social structure of our nation... Large segments of the population who hitherto barely reached the subsistence minimum... have risen into higher income strata” and are thus “largely in a position to provide for themselves.”

The *Fourth German Bundestag* was elected in 1961. The CDU placed all its bets on continuity (Toman-Banke 1994, p. 50f.): “Success and Experience/CDU.” Similarly the CSU: “For Adenauer/Erhard and the Team Successful for 12 Years/ Therefore Better Vote CSU Again.” The FDP, too, dispensed with concrete content: “Erich Mende: A free people needs Free Democrats/FDP.” The SPD had adopted the Godesberg Program in 1959, breaking with the old doctrines and embracing the social market economy (Schwarz 1983, pp. 192–204). But now it was not reflecting any content, but merely the spirit of its transformation: “We are one Family/SPD.”

In the elections the balance shifted slightly in favor of the SPD (Ritter and Niehuss 1991, p. 101). Adenauer’s fourth government rested once again on a coalition with the FDP. The inaugural speech on 29 November 1961 (Behn 1971, pp. 83–108) was delivered by the Vice-Chancellor, *Ludwig Erhard*. It sketched the continuity in social policy. At most the intensity of the elaboration on housing policy deserves special attention.

In 1963, *Konrad Adenauer’s* age caught up with him and he resigned in the middle of the legislative session. *Ludwig Erhard* became Chancellor. The coalition with the FDP continued. Erhard’s inaugural address on 18 October 1963

(Behn 1971, pp. 109–148) was pervaded by the need to commit the prosperous society to the common good. Like *Konrad Adenauer* before him, *Ludwig Erhard* also voiced his conviction that in view of the improvement of living conditions, the "social order" had to give "broader leeway to individual responsibility." Ideas about the concrete implementation were not articulated, however. The socio-political program absorbed the traditional elements.

In 1965, Ludwig Erhard faced the challenge of elections for the *Fifth German Bundestag*. The slogan of security now moved fully into the center of the campaigning (Toman-Banke 1994, p. 51). Its meaning was comprehensive and referred to both domestic and foreign policy – implying policy without putting it in the foreground. CDU and CSU spoke of "Our Security;" the SPD said "Better Safe than Sorry;" the FDP, meanwhile, spoke of "New Paths." The coalition held its own in the elections (Ritter and Niehuss 1991, p. 101). Still, the SPD won 39.3% of the votes, its best result to date, and overtook the CDU. The seeds of change had been planted. But Ludwig Erhard still formed his second government. In his inaugural address on 10 November 1965 (Behn 1971, pp. 149–187), he articulated in the opening the "connection between economic stability and political security." Furthermore: "The reference points... of politics... must no longer be the war and the postwar period....The postwar period is over." The politico-moral approaches in Erhard's first inaugural address were now pushed further to become the guiding images of the "achievement society" and the "formed society." The financial constitution of the federal state, which had occupied nearly all inaugural addresses, was now to be changed for the first time in the direction of a "joint enterprise of the federation and the states." The path to the "shared tasks" had been embarked upon. Social policy was to be developed further on a number of individual issues.

6.1.3 Fundamental Thinking About Social Policy[295]

The time of blueprints for a "social policy of the first order" (Kaufmann 1998, pp. 307–322) was now over. The pragmatism of the founding period of the Federal Republic had made central decisions. Interpreting, situating, and evaluating the given seemed to be the task of these years. In 1958, *Hans Achinger*, with his book *Sozialpolitik als Gesellschaftspolitik* (Social Policy as Societal Policy) subjected the societal consequences of socio-political approaches to an elementary analysis (Achinger 1971). *Elisabeth Liefmann*-Keil's *Ökonomische Theorie der Sozialpolitik* (Economic Theory of Social Policy) appeared in 1961 (Liefmann-Keil 1961). In 1962, *Ludwig Preller* presented a broad, innovative spectrum of questions and answers in his *Sozialpolitik. Theoretische Ordnung* (Social Policy: Theoretical Structure) (Preller 1976). *Viola Gräfin von Bethusy-Huc* provided a first

[295] Bundesministerium für Arbeit und Soziales and Bundesarchiv (eds.), 2007a: Geschichte der Sozialpolitik in Deutschland seit 1945, vol. 4, Chap. 2.

comprehensive overview in her book *Sozialleistungssysteme der Bundesrepublik Deutschland* (Social Benefits Systems of the Federal Republic of Germany) (von Bethusy-Huc 1976), along with the first critical analysis of the institutional conditions of their development. This work was particularly significant. For a long time now, the need had been articulated to give the social benefits a common structure. And already a decade earlier, Walter Bogs had written a systematic analysis of the functional interlocking of social benefits (W. Bogs 1955). By now, the totality of social benefits had been developed further in multifarious ways. A synopsis seemed more urgently needed than ever before: in the sense of the right structure of benefits, but also to educate the public awareness. After all, social benefits had by now become the central identity of the social. It was in keeping with the spirit of the times that in 1965, as well, scholars and practitioners formed an association devoted to the overarching cultivation of the entire system of social benefits, first under the name *Sozialgerichtsverband*, later under the name *Sozialrechtsverband* (Wannagat 1975, pp. 17–31; Friedrich-Marczyk 1984, pp. 170–216; Zacher 1991b, pp. 7–27). The integration of social benefits law into a whole, which integrates the differences of history, regulatory practice, financing, associational embeddedness, legal protection, and so on, instead of letting them stand as partitioning walls, was beginning to assert itself.

The intellectual framework of the time now included also the discussion over the relationship between *constitution and social policy*. It was no longer conducted in the spirit of social programs on the "Weimar" model, and no longer over the primacy of constitutional state or social state. Rather, what now began was the detailed work of how the social state and the constitutional state intertwined. The *Federal Constitutional Court* began to make itself felt as a factor in social policy. The years 1959–1961, in particular, saw a series of crucial decisions. The Court approved compulsory insurance for the free professions (BVerfGE 10, 354; 12, 119), and ruled the objective barriers to accreditation for panel doctors unconstitutional (BVerfGE 11, 30; 12, 144). The early child allowance legislation, which had financed the allowance through employers' contributions and organized along the lines of accident insurance, was accepted as "social insurance" in the meaning of Art. 74, no. 12 of the Basic Law.[296] The development was underscored when the *43rd Annual Convention of German Lawyers in 1960* ("*Deutscher Juristentag*") in Munich picked up the issue. For the first time the Deutsche Juristentag set up a "Committee on Social Law;" the theme: "The influence of constitutional legal norms on the social security law" (Verhandlungen des 43. Deutschen Juristentages 1960).

Toward the end of the period under discussion, the federal government issued a new call for thoughts about an overall reform of social benefits. Between 1964 and 1966, *Hans Achinger, Walter Bogs, Helmut Meinhold*, and *Wilfrid Schreiber* authored a report on "Social Security in the Federal Republic of Germany" that

---

[296] BVerfGE 11, 105. On the further development of the Federal Constitutional Court's intervention in social policy during this period see Bley (1974, pp. 321–333); Rüfner (1974-68-93); Wand (1974, pp. 52–67).

has come to be known as the "*Sozial-Enquête*" (Soziale Sicherung in der Bundesrepublik Deutschland 1966). This report was a last shot at a "social policy of the first order." But that period did not know what to do with it.

6.2 The Development of the Social System[297]

6.2.1 The Responsibility of the State for the Economy[298]

Still in 1957, the federal legislature had passed the fundamental law dealing with the competitive system, the Law against Restrictions on Competition, and had given an effective order to the central institutions of the currency system with the *Bundesbank* Act. The system of the economic constitution was now carried further: through the *Law on the Formation of an Expert Council to Examine the Overall Economic Development* of 14 August 1963.[299] The law set up an independent advisory council of experts and described its mandate as follows (Section "The Fundamental Interpretation of What Can Be Concretely Observed in History"):

> In its report, the Advisory Council shall describe the overall state of the economy and its projected development. In the process it shall examine how, within the framework of the free market system, price level stability, high employment, and a foreign economic balance can be simultaneously ensured against a backdrop of steady and appropriate growth. The report shall also include education and the distribution of income and wealth. In particular, the Advisory Council shall identify the causes of current and possible tensions between overall economic demand and overall economic supply, which threaten the goals enumerated in the second sentence. The report shall be based on various assumptions, and their differential effects shall be described and assessed. The Advisory Council shall identify undesirable developments and possibilities of avoiding or eliminating them, though it must not issue any recommendations for specific economic and social policy measures.

This law was highly significant. First, this was the first time that the central *goals of economic policy* were codified: *price level stability, high employment, foreign economic balance*, and *steady and appropriate growth* (Hoffmann 1959). Moreover, it was declared that the goal should be attained "*within the framework of the free market system.*" To be sure, this is expressed only as a directive to the Advisory Council. However, it makes sense only if the federal government, which must justify its policies in response to the report of the Advisory Council, affirms this normative framework. Second, "*education and the distribution of income and*

---

[297] Zacher (1989c, pp. 54–62); Frerich and Frey (vol. 3, 1996, pp. 53–157).

[298] Abelshauser (1993, esp. pp. 98–116); Glastetter et al. (1991); Weimer (1998, pp. 132–184). Sachverständigenrat zur Begutachtung der gesamtwirtschaftlichen Entwicklung, see note 294 above.

[299] On the discussion at the time: Giersch and Borchardt (1962); von Beckerath and Giersch (1963).

wealth" were also named as topics of comparable political interest. Third, the law stipulated *not only the report by the Advisory Council, but also the obligation by the federal government to justify itself publicly*. The government must issue a response to the report to the legislative bodies (Sect. 6, Para. 4). The *public* is included in this process; the Advisory Council makes its report public (Sect. 6, Para. 3).

6.2.2 Work and Income

Labor law was improved further,[300] for example, by the Youth Occupational Safety Law (1960) and the Federal Holiday Act (1963). The most important developments, however, took place in practice. This period was characterized by a level of full employment that occurred only one more time thereafter, 1969–1971, and was then never achieved again. Economic growth and rising productivity made possible generous collective wage agreements – generous not only with respect to wages, but above all also with respect to contractual and working conditions (von Kevelaer and Hinrichs 1985, pp. 52–75). The state of the market strengthened the hand of workers and unions to push through relevant demands. Accordingly, case law also perceived room to expand and fine-tune the protection of workers. Thus, in the 1960s two currents that were very different in substance came together to trigger the development of labor law in which the advantage of the worker would have the presumption of correctness on its side. One current was the typical social disadvantage of dependent workers. The other current was their historically unique power in the market place. The two currents could well have led to different solutions for different groups of people and different problems. As it was, however, a consensus emerged that what the market power of workers could bring about also seemed socially necessary, while workers with a powerful position in the market also participated in the social protection of disadvantaged workers.[301]

Independent gainful work did not receive comparable care and attention from the social state. Nevertheless, *agricultural policy* was now joined by a new political interest in the *Mittelstand*.[302]

---

[300] Beginning in 1964, the development of labor law was periodically documented in G. Müller (1964–1981; relevant for our period are vols. 1 (1964) – 4 (1967)); see also Bundesministerium für Arbeit und Soziales and Bundesarchiv (eds.), 2007a: Geschichte der Sozialpolitik in Deutschland seit 1945, vol. 4, Chap. 3, nos. 1 and 2.

[301] For a critical look back see Rüthers (1995, pp. 326–333; 1996).

[302] "Bericht über Maßnahmen der Bundesregierung zur Förderung der kleinen und mittleren Betriebe der gewerblichen Wirtschaft," BTDrs. III/689; "Bericht über die Lage der Mittelschichten," BTDrs. III/2010; "Erklärung der Bundesregierung über eine zusammenfassende Initiative zur Förderung des gewerblichen Mittelstandes und der freien Berufe," BTDrs. III/2757.

6.2.3 Social Benefits

In the area of social benefits,[303] the issues that the first two legislative sessions did not get to were addressed. The *Law on the Insurance of Tradesmen* (1960) completed the reform of pension insurance for independent tradesmen. *Accident insurance* was reformed in 1963 and updated. In 1964, the new *Federal Child Allowance Act* changed family equalization – which had been set up in 1954 as a branch of social security – into a tax-financed system of assistance and promotion. By contrast, a reform of health insurance got off the ground twice but failed each time (Frerich and Frey, vol. 3, 1996, p. 68f.).

The Reform of Social Assistance and Child and Youth Welfare in Particular

In 1961, the Federal Social Assistance Act replaced the old welfare with modern *social assistance*.[304] That same year saw a reform of *youth welfare law*.[305] Of these two reforms, the transition from the old welfare to modern social assistance was by far the more significant step. What case law had already rendered a matter of course – namely, the legal entitlement to assistance – was now made the basis of law. The recipient of aid was thus also recognized by the law as a subject who could expect and lay claim to aid. No less important, however, was the distinction between the general "subsistence aid" and "aid in special life situations." While the "subsistence aid" continued to represent the minimum general participation through the guarantee of a decent subsistence minimum (now, of course, in a way that reflected the general improvement in conditions), the "aid in special life situations" (in case of sickness, maternity, disability, old age, and so on) was aimed at a participation in the opportunities of society in a way that was particularly appropriate to the situation.

Still, it is right to mention the two reforms in the same breath. It was no coincidence that they represented *the end to the series of major reforms* in social benefits law after the establishment of the Federal Republic. *All other benefit areas* dealt chiefly with calculated cash benefits (pensions etc.) and professional services (medical treatment). Those were and remained the preferred objects of this democratic constitutional and social state. They attracted the more assertive, more broadly reflected interests. With them, politics could present itself to its clientele

[303] Peters (1978, pp. 147–213); D. Zöllner (1981, pp. 147–153). Beginning in 1963, the development of social insurance law and adjoining areas of the law was documented: Maunz and Schraft (1963/1968; relevant for our period are vols. 1/2 (1963) – 6 (1967)); Bundesministerium für Arbeit und Soziales and Bundesarchiv (eds.), 2007a: Geschichte der Sozialpolitik in Deutschland seit 1945, vol. 4, Chap. 3, nos. 4–9.

[304] Bundesministerium für Arbeit und Soziales and Bundesarchiv (eds.), 2007a: Geschichte der Sozialpolitik in Deutschland seit 1945, vol. 4, Chap. 3, no. 9.

[305] Bundesministerium für Arbeit und Soziales and Bundesarchiv (eds.), 2007a: Geschichte der Sozialpolitik in Deutschland seit 1945, vol. 4, Chap. 3, no. 10.

much more effectively. Behind social security stood especially the engagement of the unions (at times also of the employers' associations), behind social compensation stood the lobbying of the associations of war victims, expellees, and so on. By contrast, *social assistance and youth welfare* involved only in part *cash benefits*, largely within the framework of social assistance. And those benefits were supposed to be determined by each individual case, that is, they were not preset by a formula. Unlike with pension benefits, for example, politics cannot – or only with great difficulty – gauge how many affected individuals will react in what way to changes in the regulations governing these benefits. Moreover, the *service benefits* were not characterized by the kind of self-contained professionalism one found, for example, with services provided by doctors, other healing professionals, or rehabilitation facilities. Social services are in a very different way open to the hardship they are supposed to relieve, and to the people they are intended to help. And their offerings are not always seen as an advantage. In any case: social assistance and youth welfare reflect "interests" that cannot be organized, or only marginally so. Poverty, atypical conditions, deviance, and so on, are not amenable to effective collective assertion. It thus comes as no surprise that the reform of social assistance and youth welfare was the last to be undertaken. It may have required precisely the pacified, prosperous period we are talking about here for these reforms to be accomplished, as well.

But there is another reason why the two reforms take on special importance. As I have already said: both social assistance and – especially – youth welfare are realized essentially through *services*.[306] Providing these services, from the time there was "poor relief" and "youth welfare," was split between the local communities and the "free carriers," the "charitable organizations." The latter were and are groups with the most varied motives and competencies: churches, congregations, organizations affiliated with the churches, local associations, philanthropic groups, or also parallel organizations to the political parties, to ideologies, to vocational or social "estates." After 1945, these forces were highly important. At the same time, however, there was room for them to create new structures. The field of charitable welfare was occupied by a (not legally) circumscribed group of organizations: Innere Mission (later Diakonisches Werk), Caritas, Paritätischer Wohlfahrtsverband, Rotes Kreuz, and so on (Die freie Wohlfahrtspflege 1956). When the legislature reformed social assistance and youth welfare, it confronted the question of what place it should assign to these carriers in the implementation of the laws. It decided on a framework of restrictions for both the communal and the "charitable" side, which was boiled down to the subsidiarity of communal carriers vis-à-vis the "charitable" carriers (Lerche 1963; Zacher 1964). The Federal Constitutional Court approved this regulation (BVerfGE 22, 180 [204]):

[306] Bundesministerium für Arbeit und Soziales and Bundesarchiv (eds.), 2007a: Geschichte der Sozialpolitik in Deutschland seit 1945, vol. 4, Chap. 3, no. 14.

> By no means does it follow from the principle of the social state that the legislature may only stipulate official measures in realizing this goal... The legislature is therefore at liberty to stipulate the support from private welfare organizations in attaining the goal.

This *participation of societal forces* in implementing the social assistance and youth welfare law was of far-reaching importance. On the one hand, the freedom to help had thus been extended into the legally regulated sphere of social services. And the variety of providers expanded the freedom of those seeking and receiving services to choose among multiple options. Moreover, religious, political, and social currents were given an opportunity to shape the aid they provided. With that, additional leeway was opened up to the freedoms linked to the corresponding orientation – of religious creed, political action, the free expression of opinion, and so on. And this once again on both sides: on the side of those who organized and provided services, and on the side of those who needed and received services. The sphere of social services was given a significantly *more pluralistic character*. On the other hand, however, what emerged was a *mixed system* that had its own problems. For it was not merely the case that the construction of the law had simply made room for the primacy of the societal realization of the social. Rather, the societal realization of the social was absorbed into the legal program. The crucial element was financing. The broad sphere that was opened up to "charitable" carriers could only be filled if the state and the local communities assigned the money they would have spent on their own and direct implementation to the "charitable" carriers who were taking on the implementation for them. In this way, the financing conditions turned into a body of regulations for the working of the societal forces. And conversely: the societal processes of supply and demand guided the state financing programs. Both aspects were left vague so as not to call into question the societal autonomy of the carriers involved. This overlap led to problems of orientation – precisely also within the carriers. The purposive rationality of their actual motivation – altruism, ideological orientation, and so on – was joined by the "operational" rationality of the use of the organization. Those in charge were tempted to arrange the services in such a way that the organization had to contribute as little as possible – or nothing – to carrying out the mission, and might even be able to use the outside funds to pay for the organization's "general expenses." The longer this went on, the more aberrations it produced occasionally even entailing personal disasters. Only in the 1980s and 1990s did these symptoms lead to clarifying deliberations.[307]

Supraindividual Programs

Supraindividual benefit programs began to develop already from the 1950s as a significant supplement to social benefits regulated by law (Zacher 1981, pp. 106–112).

[307] Bundesministerium für Arbeit und Soziales and Bundesarchiv (eds.) Geschichte der Sozialpolitik in Deutschland seit 1945, vol. 5 (2006a), 6 (2008a), 11 (2007b), and Bundesministerium für Gesundheit und Soziale Sicherung and Bundesarchiv (eds.) (2005), vol. 7, Chap. 3, no. 14 in each.

In addition to public education campaigns and the informal exertion of influence on associations and other key actors, we are talking primarily about subsidy and subvention programs (financing programs). With that, the federal government expanded its political maneuvering room. It had more money than the *Länder* – at least the financially weaker ones. By providing the funds, it could regulate the distribution without regard to its possible legislative authority. The *Länder* had little chance to close themselves to this expansion of the federal government. The price for such a move would have been the charge that they were withholding available funds from the areas in question. The prosperity of the 1960s gave this development a strong boost. In addition to programs demanded and legitimated by law, especially for agriculture, we find programs that were aimed above all at dealing with the direct and indirect consequences of the war (expellees, resettlers from the "Soviet Zone," late resettlers, late returnees, foreign refugees, stateless foreigners, and so forth), to promote social services and youth work, and to promote regional and sectoral economies.[308]

6.2.4 Wealth

When it came to the problem of wealth,[309] the period opted emphatically for measures to aid the formation of wealth: the 1958 Law on Bonuses for Housing Savers; the 1959 Law on Bonuses for Savings; the 1961 First Wealth Formation Act; the 1965 Second Law to Promote the Wealth Formation of Employees. Added to this were actions to issue "people's shares (*Volksaktien*)": in 1959 of Preussag stocks; in 1960 of VW stocks, in 1965 of stock of the Vereinigte Elektrizitäts- und Bergwerks AG (Hirche 1961; Molitor 1980, pp. 282–299).

6.2.5 The Meeting of Needs: Housing

Social assistance to cover basic needs continued to focus on housing.[310] Housing controls were scaled back further. Accordingly, rental law was newly regulated.[311] The rental subsidies, which the Federal Rental Law of 1955 had already provided

[308] Kommission für die Finanzreform (1966, pp. 178–202); Adami (1970).

[309] Bundesministerium für Arbeit und Soziales and Bundesarchiv (eds.), 2007a: Geschichte der Sozialpolitik in Deutschland seit 1945, vol. 4, Chap. 3, no. 16.

[310] Bundesministerium für Arbeit und Soziales and Bundesarchiv (eds.), 2007a: Geschichte der Sozialpolitik in Deutschland seit 1945, vol. 4, Chap. 3, no. 15.

[311] "Gesetz über den Abbau der Wohungszwangswirtschaft und über ein soziales Miet- und Wohnrecht" of 1960.

for, were expanded and turned into the housing allowance.[312] With that, an important process had reached a certain conclusion. A housing law of *Daseinsvorsorge*, manifested in rationed living space, rent control, and rigid renters' protection, had been reshaped into a liberal and social housing law, which built on the market and the self-responsibility of those in search of housing, but was supplemented by assistance for the "socially weaker."

Of importance in this development is also that the housing allowance represented the creation of the first *special assistance and promotion system* (Zacher 1987b). Previously there had existed, alongside the contribution-financed social insurance, only a limited canon of tax-financed social benefits systems: the civil service pension, the social compensation systems, the general support system of welfare, and youth welfare that was focused on services. Beyond that, tax-financed social benefits systems had not been introduced. The child allowance, too, had been initially attempted as social insurance. With the housing allowance, the development crossed the Rubicon to the formation of specific, tax-financed assistance and promotion systems. Child allowance would follow in 1964. And in the subsequent period, special tax-financed assistance and promotion systems would be the real "growth sector" of social services.

6.3 Consensus and Dissent

The productivity of the economy, full employment, and the continuously progressing integration of the expellees produced a certain general satisfaction with the achievements of the 1950s and their underlying principles. Even more so than at the end of the second legislative session, the *integration* of society under the banner of prosperity, freedom, security, equality, and protection against hardship was the experience of reality – even if the dynamism of this development continued to be the crucial medium that made possible the commonality of this experience. But as the self-evident nature of this experience grew, so did questions as to whether the condition that seemed to be emerging "all on its own" could and should be optimized through political assistance. As a result, there emerged – first in the background, but slowly pushing to the fore – a political current that expected from more social intervention a new link between prosperity, security, liberty, and equality, which should be able to abolish within itself the protection against hardship.

[312] "Gesetz über die Gewährung von Miet- und Lastenbeihilfen" of 1960; the renaming into "housing allowance" *(Wohngeld)* was done by the "Wohngeldgesetz" of 1965.

7 1966–1982: Development – High Point – Turnaround

7.1 The Political Premises[313]

7.1.1 The End of the Postwar Period – The Beginning of an Unimagined Future

The period from 1966 to 1982 was characterized by the profound historical caesura of the mid-1970s (Hobsbawm 1994, pp. 257–286, 403–432). One can place this caesura within a narrower framework: as the end of the postwar period; the end of a long economic upswing; the beginning of the economic shortage of monetary goods being joined by the ecological shortage of goods, whose monetary value cannot express their communal value; and as the transition from colonialism to the postcolonial world divided into blocs. One can also place it within a wider context that reaches back to the nineteenth century: as the transition from the industrial age to the era of services; from the age of transportation to the age of communication; from the age of chemistry and physics to the age of biology and medicine, as well as to the age of information technology. All of these are only examples for the many currents that collide in the early and the mid-1970s. At any rate, this period also saw a questioning of the social state as a result of the time it took to realize it. That holds true for the liberal social state, whose effects, perception, and assessment change as it becomes a matter of course, while its capacity to respond creatively to a change in the conditions under which it operates declines. But it applies also to the "namesake" of the social state, the socialist state, whose disfunctionality from the all-embracing political control over the distribution of goods through a closed system of power was becoming increasingly evident. While talk of the "crisis of the social state" emerges in the "free" world, it is becoming clear in the socialist countries that the adherence to the "unity of economic and social policy" was demanding more and more sacrifice of quality of life – that the shortcomings of the systems were not in fact coming to an end with the reconstruction, but were proving to be permanent and actually increasing. In the Federal Republic, this caesura had its own context: in the form of the social, political, and legal development of the young, post-catastrophic state, the quick succession of new experiences, the rapid economic flourishing, and the relationship to the "Western" and "Eastern" worlds.

The social policy of the Federal Republic reflected this caesura in three very distinct periods. The time of the Grand Coalition (1966–1969) completed the social state of the postwar period. It set itself the task of clarifying its rationale and realizing it in institutions (Hildebrand 1984). The liberal-social era of Willy Brandt (1969–1974) was ambivalent. The social state consolidated by the Grand Coalition

[313] Stern (2000, pp. 1445–1535); Bundesministerium für Arbeit und Soziales and Bundesarchiv (eds.) Geschichte der Sozialpolitik in Deutschland seit 1945, vols. 5 (2006a) and 6 (2008a), Chap. 1.

seemed self-evident and ready to be transcended. But the world of the "post-socialist welfare states" was already much "newer" than the actors involved in transcending the social state were able to foresee (Bracher et al. 1986). The liberal-social era of Helmut Schmidt (1974–1982) already lies on the other side of this profound caesura. It was characterized by a two-fold challenge: the transformation of the social state by transcending it, and the transformations of the conditions of its existence and development (Jäger and Link 1987).

From the inside, German social policy appears as follows. The *period of the Grand Coalition* was marked by the need for *institutional reforms*. It achieved what could be achieved only on the *basis of a broad consensus*. In constitutional terms: it achieved the things that presupposed a constitution-altering majority in the *Bundestag* and the *Bundesrat*. This period stood under a negative and a positive sign. The negative sign: during the previous years, many of the problems that were becoming apparent had not been addressed – the Erhard era had left behind a pent-up need for reform. The positive sign: the CDU/CSU and the SPD were together providing a leadership elite that was creative and effective enough to do what was needed by consensus.

But the years before had left behind not only this pent-up need for reform in state politics. The success of the first 17 years of the Federal Republic had also given rise to the question of whether this could not have achieved even greater freedom and equality. The Grand Coalition had only occasional answers. To answer with a simple "Yes" was not the matter of a broad majority. It was the natural privilege of those who had previously been in the minority. It was a matter for the Social Democrats, the minority in parliament, and of the Free Democrats, the minority in the government. Making full use of this "Yes" was the spirit of the *Brandt era*. The 5 years of this era were not enough to realize all the things one could conceive under the banner of this "Yes." All the more so because all the things that were now begun to convert the nation's prosperity into more freedom and more equality brought forth more and more ideas about still more freedom and equality.

Thus, when the leadership of the social-liberal coalition passed from *Willy Brandt* to *Helmut Schmidt*, the thrust behind this demand for more freedom and equality was still highly potent. But it was generating frictions – increasingly so as time went on. The clarity of social goals (presumed or real) that had characterized the start of the Brandt era evaporated. The more the development proceeded, the louder the dissenting voices grew: about alternatives, priorities, the evaluation of effects. And especially about whether the division of labor between the societal realization of the social and the state's realization of the social was still correct. The oil price shock of 1973 that triggered a sharp decline in growth was a warning shot. And the development of inflation and unemployment kept alive the concern about the proper relationship between the economy and social policy, until in the end the doubts had grown strong enough to effect another change. When the time had come, the pent-up need for reform that had characterized the year 1966 was no longer a topic.

7.1.2 The Time of the Grand Coalition

All three periods were times of great movement. During all three periods, that movement was fed by energies that had built up before 1966 and were released by the change in 1966. That change was brought about when the FDP left the coalition with the CDU/CSU and Chancellor Erhard resigned. The CDU/CSU and the SPD entered into a coalition. *Kurt Georg Kiesinger* became Chancellor of the government based on this coalition. In terms of social policy, this government opted for continuity. However, it did undertake substantial reforms in financial and economic policy whose social importance was significant.[314]

During the period of the Grand Coalition, the public in the Federal Republic reshaped itself in new ways. The year 1968 falls into this period: the student revolt began, and along with it a wealth of discontent and opposition was articulated and became active. Much of this had been accumulating independently in separate private and public spheres, and it now came together into a broad process of public unrest. Much of it was constructive, much of it mere negation. And yet, the common denominator seemed to be that of a fundamental modernization. In the process, the possibilities that the prosperity of the young Federal Republic had opened up were accepted as given, indeed, as immune to threat. But the system that had produced this prosperity was to be developed further, overcome, and perhaps also destroyed. The politics of the parties, parliaments, and governments was deeply shaken. Which elements of all that was going on could, should, or had to be incorporated into the work of representative democracy? How should one deal with attitudes and demands that were incompatible with the explicit and implicit principles of the young polity?

7.1.3 The Brandt Era

In the campaign of 1969 (Toman-Banke 1994, p. 51f.) the SPD appropriated the denominator of modernization: “We are creating the modern Germany. SPD/We have the right men.” Likewise the FDP: “F.D.P./We are getting rid of the old relics!” As the only opposition party to the Grand Coalition, it evidently felt closest to the new spirit of departure. Differently so the CDU: “CDU/Securely into the 1970s.” Finally, the CSU believed that it could embed the modernization trend into a “sensible” context: “CSU/Modern thinking/resolute action/better living.”

In the elections to the *Sixth German Bundestag*, the gains were all on the side of the SDP (Ritter and Niehuss 1991, p. 101). The social-liberal coalition was formed, with *Willy Brandt* as Chancellor. Contrary to many expectations, his inaugural address of 28 October 1969 (Behn 1971, pp. 205–235) was devoid of spectacular pronouncements on social policy. The outlook for a further development of the free

[314] Inaugural address by Chancellor Kurt Georg Kiesinger on 13 December 1966 in Behn (1971, pp. 185–204).

market economy remained within the parameters of the social market economy. Social policy was emphatically friendlier to workers and unions, which found expression, for example, in advances in the area of codetermination and personnel representation, which was seen within the context of a general democratization, but above all in the slogan "Humanization of the working world." At the same, time, however, much was articulated that was intended to improve the living conditions of everyone: of the disadvantaged but also of society as a whole. Perhaps the most innovative emphasis was on education policy and on the equality of opportunity connected with it.

The majority of the governing coalition had been 254:242. Beginning with the election of the Chancellor, it shrank continuously (Jäger 1986, pp. 67–76). Time and again, members of the governing parliamentary groups felt they could no longer support the course of the government. As a result, the CDU/CSU tried in April 1972 to elect *Rainer Barzel* Chancellor by way of the constructive vote of no confidence. The attempt failed. But the problem of the deadlock between the government and the opposition was not resolved. In September of 1972, Chancellor Brandt asked for a vote of confidence, and the result was 233:248. *Willy Brandt* suggested to the President that he dissolve the *Bundestag*, and he agreed. Early elections took place in November 1972, the first time in the history of the Federal Republic.

During the campaign for the *Seventh German Bundestag* (Toman-Banke 1994, p. 52), the CDU focused on the dispute over the "*Ostverträge*" (treaties signed between West Germany and several Eastern Bloc states). The CSU headlined *Franz Josef Strauß*: "Knowledge and Energy/Bavaria for Germany/CSU." The FDP had articulated in its "Freiburg Theses" how it envisaged the modernization of the state and society: "FDP/Let reason prevail." The SPD focused on its chancellor: "Germans/We can be proud of our country. Elect Willy Brandt/SPD/ Social Democrats."

The elections showed the SPD at its height. The FDP also made substantial gains (Ritter and Niehuss 1991, p. 101). The mandate of the governing coalition was emphatically affirmed. *Willy Brandt* became Chancellor again. In his inaugural address on 18 January 1973 (Presse- und Informationsamt der Bundesregierung 1973, pp. 45–56), he spelled out the general denominator of the social that would remain characteristic of his time in office: "Quality of life" or "Progress in liberty and justice." "Quality of life is more than living standard. It is the enrichment of our life beyond income and consumption... . It depends increasingly on how much good neighborliness exists among us, and what the common institutions are able to offer... Quality of life... has become a central concept of our political work... It means for us: freedom, also freedom from fear and want, security also through human solidarity." The speech was accordingly replete with plans that transcended the traditional spectrum of the social in the direction of a general lifting of living conditions. The new political importance of the environment was especially obvious. However, the core areas of the social were to be developed and expanded no less.

But Willy Brandt had only 18 months left in office to carry out the program. In the spring of 1974 he was brought down by a scandal involving his innermost circle (Jäger 1986, pp. 117–126). Moreover, the political maneuvering room of the governing coalition had been shrinking since 1972. The Länder in which the CDU/CSU governed alone or was the dominant force had gained the majority in the Bundesrat (Schüttemeyer 1990; Fromme 1990, pp. 381–400). For the first time in the history of the Federal Republic there was a principled, sustained confrontation between a majority of the Bundesrat, on the one side, and the government and "its" Bundestag majority, on the other. It would remain that way until the end of the social-liberal coalition in 1982.

7.1.4 The Schmidt Era

Brandt's successor was *Helmut Schmidt*. In his first inaugural address on 17 May 1974 (Presse- und Informationsamt der Bundesregierung 1974, pp. 9–27), the new Chancellor laid out a broad spectrum of themes and plans. The stronger concentration on concrete elements and on the framework of the social – now, of course, irreversibly expanded – is unmistakable. In 1972, the Club of Rome had sounded the *Götterdämmerung* of economic growth (Meadows 1972). And in the fall of 1973, the "oil crisis" had triggered the most severe economic downturn of the postwar period.[315] The speech by the matter-of-fact Chancellor breathed the spirit of the sobering times.

In 1976, *Helmut Schmidt* faced elections to the *Eighth German Bundestag* (Toman-Banke 1994, p. 52f.). The SPD promoted the continuation of its consolidating policy of reform: "Model Germany." But it also pushed the person of the Chancellor: "The better man must remain Chancellor: Helmut Schmidt. That's why: SPD." The FDP also placed the emphasis on consolidation: "Vote Performance/FDP." The CDU exaggerated its opposition to the reform policy of the social-liberal coalition: "For love of Germany: Freedom instead of Socialism/CDU/Secure/social and free." Similarly the CSU: "CSU/1976/Germany Faces the Decision/Freedom or Socialism."

Like the *Landtag* elections earlier (Ritter and Niehuss 1991, pp. 157–179), these elections showed that approval of the policy of the social-liberal government had passed its peak (Ritter and Niehuss 1991, p. 101). Still, the continuation of the SPD/FDP coalition was beyond question. *Helmut Schmidt's* inaugural speech on 16 December 1976 (Presse- und Informationsamt der Bundesregierung 1976, pp. 1285–1308) began – unusually enough, though characteristic for the anxieties of the time – with a statement about the "pension issue." The governing coalition, Schmidt declared, had decided on measures to consolidate the financing of pension insurance. Those measures had run into intense opposition. The remainder of the address was at pains to combine realism and sobriety with an expansive view of the problems and a

[315] Sondergutachten des Sachverständigenrates zur Begutachtung der gesamtwirtschaftlichen Entwicklung vom 17. Dezember 1973 "Zu den gesamtwirtschaftlichen Auswirkungen der Erdölkrise" (BTDrs. 7/1456).

positive outlook. The Chancellor called upon his fellow Germans to realize "that growth is not infinite, and that reforms do no not necessarily mean that the state can continuously provide new, additional benefits."

The year 1980 brought elections for the *Ninth German Bundestag* (Toman-Banke 1994, p. 53). Franz Josef Strauß was the chancellor candidate for the CDU/CSU. An unprecedented polarization of public opinion was in the offing. The SPD went with Helmut Schmidt. The FDP set a government of Schmidt/Genscher against Strauß. The CDU proclaimed: "Franz Josef Strauß/Chancellor for Peace and Freedom." The CSU chimed in: "Vote Strauß/Stop Socialism." The SPD held its position, the FDP gained votes (Ritter and Niehuss 1991, p. 102). *Helmut Schmidt* became Chancellor once again. In terms of domestic policy, his inaugural speech on 24 November 1980 (Presse- und Informationsamt der Bundesregierung 1980, pp. 1049–1064) was above all a program of consolidation. "More jobs," "Unions and codetermination," "Opportunities through structural change," "Education for boys and girls," "Social protection," "Living in city and country," "Integration of foreigners," "Marriage and family," and "Opportunities of women" were the social headings for rather disparate sections.

The social-liberal coalition broke apart in September 1982; the FDP left the SPD-led government (Jäger 1986, pp. 188–263). In October 1982, the *Bundestag* elected Helmut Kohl Chancellor.

7.1.5 A Time of Contradictions

This period was characterized by the extreme diversity and contradictory nature of the forces that became effective, of the ideas that were articulated, and of the expectations that were directed at politics. A flood of open and covert dissent washed over society and public opinion. A considerable portion of it was directed outward. This was the time of the new *Ostpolitik*, and also the time of the Federal Republic's entry into the United Nations. Those developments cannot be discussed here. But it is obvious that there were interactions between foreign and domestic politics. Cooperation with the "socialist" countries opened the government to the suspicion that it would not shy from "Socialism" also at home. And in fact, there were forces which wanted that and said as much. But they played the smaller role where suspicion became a weapon in political competition. On the other hand, a successful domestic policy was necessary to hold one's ground in the competition with the "socialist" countries. It was probably necessary least of all to keep one's own citizens from embracing Socialism, but certainly to preserve and strengthen the power of freedom, democracy, and the *Rechtsstaat* to radiate into the "socialist" countries – through all the walls of isolation and propaganda. Finally, there was also the side-by-side existence of a socialist German Democratic Republic and the liberal social state of the Federal Republic of Germany.[316]

But leaving all that aside, there was plenty of confusion in domestic politics. All of a sudden, the game had expanded beyond the platform of the young Federal Republic and its constitutional system. Disobedience and violence persisted: from the movement of 1968 to the terror of the RAF. They forced the state onto a defensive posture that could easily be experienced as dubious. The "old Federal Republic" had early on outlawed the anti-constitutional parties on the Right and the Left.[317] Thereafter, anti-constitutional endeavors had been only a marginal theme. Now, however, an ever growing number of – mostly young – people were willing to place themselves outside of the basic liberal, democratic order. They were able to put the state into an embarrassing situation – for example, when it refused to accept them into public service. Yet the chief strain of the time was the abundance of diverging guiding principles and interests also within the sphere that social consensus and the constitutional order set aside for the competition of ideas and their realization (Zacher 1972b, pp. 241–266). "Emancipation" and "participation" were among the great magic words of the time. But the most important was "democracy." "Democratization" could be readily used to justify every kind of leveling imposed by some on others and every interference by some in the affairs of others. After all, "quality of life" was the central value at that time. Whatever seemed to increase well-being was legitimated by this value. Seemingly endless was the variety of ideas that were put forth! It was a time when everyone was lecturing everyone. And it was a time of multifarious conflicts. Sentiments of euphoric harmony inspired broad segments of society – because many interests seemed to be finding a voice at the same time, as though they were all in agreement, while their collision became clear only later on.

7.2 The Development of the Constitution

7.2.1 The Development of the Constitutional Text

By the time the Grand Coalition came to power, the Basic Law had already undergone 14 constitutional amendments, and the pent-up demand for reform could be achieved only with further amendments (Hofmann 1987, esp., pp. 292–298). The period of the Grand Coalition, alone, recorded 12 constitution-amending laws. When the criticism of the Basic Law continued to widen, the *Bundestag*, through resolutions

---

[316] For a semi-official comparison of the social policy of the two German states see Bundesminister für Innerdeutsche Beziehungen, 1971, 1974, 1987: Bericht der Bundesregierung und Materialien zur Lage der Nation. Bonn: (1971), pp. 125–185; (1974) pp. 441–500; (1987) pp. 555–595.

[317] "Verbot der Sozialistischen Reichspartei durch Urteil des Bundesverfassungsgerichts vom 23. Oktober 1952" BVerfGE 2,1; "Verbot der Kommunistischen Partei Deutschlands durch Urteil des Bundesverfassungsgerichts vom 17. August 1956" BVerfGE 5, 85.

on 8 October 1970, and 22 February 1973, set up a Commission of Inquiry to look into questions of constitutional reform. With that the high point had passed. The Commission issued only very restrained recommendations for a change of the constitution.[318] In essence, the Commission affirmed that the constitutional system of the Basic Law was effective and appropriate. The relevant constitutional organs expressed their agreement by silence.

The explicit changes to the constitution that occurred during this period concern two central topics (leaving aside technical issues, especially procedural ones). The first was replacing the Allied reserve powers with a German *emergency law*.[319] That amendment relates to the social as follows: the guarantee to strike also under the emergency law (Art. 9, Para. 3, Sent. 3, GG, new version); with that the mention of the right to strike and its incorporation into free collective bargaining in the Basic Law; and the introduction of compulsory military service to prepare for a state of defense (Art. 12a, GG, new version).

The other issue led to a whole sequence of changes: strengthening the *state's mandate to ensure an adequate development of economic conditions*. That mandate was conceived increasingly as a responsibility encompassing the entire state, the federation and the states. That is why the separation of jurisdictions between the federal government and the states was increasingly relativized. Accordingly, an ever growing number of joint policies were institutionalized. There was a prehistory to this development. A number of constitution-changing laws had previously already changed the financial constitution of the Basic Law and in the process had communalized sources of financing.[320] What followed now was a move to demand that the budgets of the federal government *and* the *Länder* "take due account of the requirements of the overall economic equilibrium" (Art. 109, Para. 2, GG, new version). This obligation was deepened and broadened (Art. 109, Para. 3, Art. 115, Para. 1, Sent. 2, GG, new version). This was followed by the institutionalization of the "joint tasks."[321] What characterized the latter was that the federal government participated "in the discharge of responsibilities of the Länder, provided that such responsibilities are important to society as a whole and that federal participation is necessary for the improvement of living conditions" (Art. 91a, Para. 1, GG). Expanding and building new scientific colleges, improving regional economic structures, improving the structure of agriculture, and providing coastal protection are listed as such joint tasks. The same amendment created a similar regulation for "education planning" and the "promotion of scientific projects and research institutions of higher education" that were of "supraregional importance" (Art. 91b, GG). In direct connection with this, the federal government

[318] See the Interim Report in 1973, BTDrs. VI/3829, and the Final Report of 1976, BTDrs. 7/5924.

[319] "17. Gesetz zur Ergänzung des Grundgesetzes vom 24. Juni 1968," BGBl. I, p. 709.

[320] "Gesetz vom 20. April 1953," BGBl. I, p. 130; "Gesetz vom 25. Dezember 1954," BGBl. I, p. 517; "Finanzverfassungsgesetz vom 13. Dezember 1955," BGBl. I, p. 817; "Gesetz vom 24. Dezember 1956," BGBl. I, p. 1077.

[321] "21. Gesetz zur Änderung des GG (Finanzreformgesetz) vom 12. Mai 1969," BGBl. I, p. 359.

was authorized to "grant the Länder financial assistance for particularly important investments by the Länder and municipalities (associations of municipalities)" that served "to avert a disturbance of the overall economic equilibrium" or to "equalize differing economic capacities within the federal territory," or to "promote economic growth" (Art. 104a, Para. 4, Sent. 1, GG). Alongside the "*overall economic equilibrium*," "*economic growth*" had that also found reception into the constitution. The responsibility of the state for the economy had been recognized by the Basic Law. Finally, that same law intensified the systems of shared taxes and financial equalization (Art. 105–108, GG, new version).

Finally, the federal government's legislative powers were extended to educational and training grants (Art. 74, no. 13, GG, new version), economic guarantees for hospitals and the regulation of hospital charges (Art. 19a GG), and salaries in public service also in the *Länder* (Art. 75, Para. 2, GG, new version).[322] In other ways, too, the jurisdiction of the federal government to make regulations in the area of public service – with special emphasis on the role of the *Bundesrat* – was expanded further (Art. 74a GG).[323] At the end of this development, the formula of the *social federal state* had a substantially different meaning than before. The state as a whole had been strengthened, the politics of the federal government and the states was now more intertwined than before.

7.2.2 Constitutional Understanding – Constitutional Reality

The Goal of the Social State

However, the understanding and practice of the constitution also changed beyond explicit amendments to the Basic Law. The *goal of the social state* took on new valence. The widespread doubts in the early years of the Basic Law as to what a "social state" might mean had long since been removed by the self-evident understanding that the Federal Republic was to be a "social state" in the sense of what was shared by the modern social movement: a state of help against misery and poverty; a state that guaranteed a decent subsistence minimum to everyone (BVerfGE 40, 121 [133]); a state that wants more equality[324] and protects the weaker members (BVerfGE 26, 16 [37]); a state that protects against the "vicissitudes of life" (BVerfGE 21, 352 [375]) and compensates for damages that are the responsibility of the community (BVerfGE 1, 97 [105]). This was understandable given what was in place historically,[325] and it provided a basis for

[322] "22. Gesetz zur Änderung des GG (Finanzreformgesetz) vom 12. Mai 1969," BGBl. I, p. 363.

[323] "28. Gesetz zur Änderung des GG (Art. 74a GG) vom 18. März 1971," BGBl. I, p. 206.

[324] On the duty of the social state "to ensure an equalization of social antagonisms and thus a just social order" see BVerfGE 22, 180 (204).

[325] For an analysis of the existing social order as "the basis for knowing in interpretation" see Kittner (1984: Art. 20, Para. 1–3 IV, margin nos. 25, 30–32; 2nd ed. 1989: Art. 20, Para. 1–3 IV,

continuing the development of what was historically given.[326] That these goals can only be reached if the state sees itself as responsible also for the economy was self-evident from the outset. What was problematic is *how* the state was to live up to this responsibility (Zacher 1981, pp. 835–841). The principles of the social free market were only slowly taking shape. In the 1960s, when economic growth had not only become a matter of course, but was also understood to be essential to the success of the social state, the duty of the state to make "provisions for growth" was discovered (Ipsen 1966, p. 222; Stern 1984, p. 902, note 156). From the perspective of the principle of the social state this meant: the state has the charge to increase prosperity and broaden the participation in it (Zacher 1987a, pp. 1078–1082). Of course, the subsequent development of the economy has shown that the issue is more generally a "broader responsibility of the state for the well-being of the economy" (Stern 1977, p. 703; 1984, p. 902).

This normative core principle of the social state left behind the anxious question of the late 1940s whether this new state had any kind of responsibility for society's wellbeing. It does have a responsibility. The only question now could be about the content and direction of this responsibility. By contrast, the question about the social obligation of the individual now received only an ambivalent answer. Social obligation of the "socially stronger," the "richer": yes – but not of the general public, no social obligation of each individual. The social state entitles the individual. That it must also potentially place everyone under obligation in order to potentially entitle everyone remains an unpopular truth. If the social goal of the state was to carry on the history of social policy as it had been developing since the end of the eighteenth century, it was to be a history of improvements, a history of the liberation of the greatest possible number and the social obligation of the smallest possible number. The 1960s and 1970s seemed to many like the fulfillment and end point of this history. Social rights: yes – social obligations: no.

But the social goal of the state became multi-valent also in a positive sense. The guiding concepts of the time – democratization, emancipation, participation, quality of life – also expanded the responsibility of the state, far beyond anything that was traditionally part of the social. And much of that could still be understood as a broadening of equality. Much could be understood in the sense that the improvement in the general living conditions diminished the relevance of economic inequality. Much could be understood as a new, more comfortable Daseinsvorsorge in conformity with the nation's prosperity and civilizational development. But where in this scenario would the social end? Where would the limitations be? (von Ferber 1967). Moreover, this was a time when a more general understanding of the welfare state was also spreading internationally: as "the institutional outcome of

margin no. 25, 30–32). On the differentiation between the concrete development of the social and the principle of the social state and critique about the customary practice of equating the two see Hartwich (1970).

[326] On the above-mentioned contents from the period see the comprehensive accounts in Stern (1977, pp. 678–732; 2nd ed. 1984, pp. 891–914); Obermayer (1979, pp. 8–16).

a society's assumption of legal and therefore formal and explicit responsibility for the basic well-being of all of its members" (Girvetz 1968, p. 512). Was the "quality of life" state not precisely this welfare state? And should it not also be the new social state? Could one – indeed, was it permissible – to withhold from this new departure the legitimation through the social goal of the state in the constitution? (Zacher 1977a, pp. 207–270).

The Social Rechtsstaat

The *Rechtsstaat* was shaping the social more and more.[327] Especially the basic rights were exerting an influence on the fashioning of social law.[328] But the most comprehensive effect of the *Rechtsstaat* on the development of the social was that the social was realized in conformity with the law (Auerbach 1974). The elements that constituted the *Rechtsstaat* institutionally and formally – the need for legal regulation; the principle of legal security, protection of legitimate expectations, and the prohibition against excessive action; subjective entitlement; comprehensive judicial legal protection of the individual and the independence of the courts; finally, the comprehensive control of the legislature through the touchstone of the constitution – intensively determined the reality of the social. The social is directed to law as an essential medium (Wege 1977; Henke 1980; Voigt 1980; Kübler 1984). The *Rechtsstaat* prescribes procedures of conflict resolution. The *Rechtsstaat* regulates the stages and forms of decision. It guarantees controls and ensures publicity and obligatoriness. All this enriches the social state with the values of the *Rechtsstaat*. The price is that the social must endure the nature and structure of the law. The *social is juridified*. As a result, it becomes one-sided. What of the basis rights is protected, and what is not? What does the legislature pick up, and what does it not? (Zacher 1974–1979, pp. 51–64). Where is the legal protection of subjective rights effective, and where is it not?[329] For example, which person who is dependent on care is able to assert his rights in a care relationship? (Verhandlungen des 52. Deutschen Juristentages 1978a) How can the normative control of the Federal Constitutional Court intervene? (Gerstenmaier 1975). What do judges take up, and what do they not?[330] A major reason for why the sequences of one-sided social law, at the beginning of which stands *juridification*, continue with *economization, professionalization, and bureaucratization*, lies in these conditions of the *Rechtsstaat*. If one can reduce the wealth of social interventions to the common denominator of legal, economic, service-providing, pedagogical, and environment-shaping interventions,

[327] Schriftenreihe des Deutschen Sozialrechtsverbandes 1975, pp. 32–49 ("Die verfassungsrechtliche Relevanz des Sozialrechts").

[328] Grundrechte im Leistungsstaat (1972); Schriftenreihe des Deutschen Sozialrechtsverbandes (1972; "Freiheit und Bindung im Recht der sozialen Sicherheit").

[329] On the further intellectual framework at the time see Neumann (1984).

[330] Schriftenreihe des Deutschen Sozialrechtsverbandes (1972; "Rechtsfortbildung durch die sozialgerechtliche Rechtsprechung").

the intensity of legal guidance and control declines precisely as we move down this very sequence of categories (Krause 1981, pp. 239–255). The problematic nature of social services is closely connected with this. Because social policy developed ever more dynamically from the late 1960s on, all of these objective necessities of the social *Rechtsstaat* became increasingly effective.

However, the spirit of the time pushed for allocating to the institutions of the *Rechtsstaat* an active role in the unfolding of the social. The most important process went in the direction of interpreting the basic rights also as rights of participation (Wiegand 1974, pp. 657–663). In 1972, the Federal Constitutional Court for the first time spoke of a right of freedom – the right to freely choose one's place of training (Art. 12, Para. 1, Sent. 1, GG) as a right of participation (BVerfGE 33, 303 [330 f.]). The consequence was the fundamentally free access of all *Gymnasium* graduates to university. This was followed by the question about the property-law protection for entitlements to services under social law:[331]

> What would argue for it is that the guarantee of property, in its freedom-guaranteeing function, aims at ensuring for the individual the economic precondition for a self-responsible conduct of life,. . . that in the modern industrial service society the great majority of citizens secure their economic livelihood less through private material wealth, but through the employment contract and through the communally-born *Daseinsvorsorge* that flows from it, and that precisely this *Daseinsvorsorge* was historically always closely linked to the notion of property (BVerfGE 40, 65 [83]).

The Federal Constitutional Court approached this consequence step by step.[332]

The question of whether the social *Rechtsstaat* required supplementation through the catalog of *social rights* was vigorously debated (Böckenförde et al. 1981; Brunner 1971; Hernekamp 1979; Lücke 1982, pp. 15–60). Could the constitution of a social state settle for the classic rights of freedom, equality, procedure, and status? Did it not have to accord social rights the same guarantees? The question, however, did not find a positive answer. It could not find a positive answer: for the sake of the social, for the sake of democracy, for the sake of the *Rechtsstaat* itself. Could the *Rechtsstaat* serve as the interpreter and executor of social programs? Was it permissible for the institutions of the *Rechtsstaat* to dispose over the goods that would be necessary for it to do so? Was it permissible for them to determine the distribution of these goods to people? Or should social rights be entrusted to their own institutions of interpretation and implementation? How should they be legitimized? And if they were, would this relativize the *Rechtsstaat*? A semantic way out was to combine the basic rights and the social goals of the state, and occasionally also statutory principles, into a norm or a normative fabric and declare them rights, at least verbally: thus, a right to education (Clevinghaus 1973), work (Wank 1980; Braun 1982; Pietzker 1984), housing, and health (Seewald 1981; Jung 1982).

[331] Schriftenreihe des Deutschen Sozialrechtsverbandes (1982; "Verfassungsrechtlicher Eigentumsschutz sozialer Rechtspositionen").

[332] BverfGE 42, 263 (293); 50, 290 (339); 68, 193 (222). But it was only in 1985 that it defined the property-law protection of social entitlements: BVerfGE 69, 272 (299–304).

Social Democracy – The Definition of the Social by Democracy

More lasting still is the effect of the dependence of the social on the institutions of democracy. This, too, would have to assert itself with particular clarity now that the social state could and did break away from the priorities of the founding years. The conditions of the postwar period had created something like a "classless" society. The long phase of economic growth had created wide scope for a general expectation of ever more equality at an ever higher level. Democratic politics of the late 1960s and the 1970s could thus expect the assertion that the mandate of the social had not yet been fulfilled to have broad appeal. Democracy and social conditions together brought about that the mandate of the social was not restricted to what was "below." On the contrary: inequality was now detected and articulated in an open-ended multitude of worse-better comparisons. Every worse-better comparison by itself justified social intervention. By contrast, the question of where the concrete worse-better comparison should be situated within a comprehensive system of social states was increasingly of only relative importance. Especially the "middle voters" were interested in disconnecting the worse-better comparison from a consistent top-bottom schema. And the political forces offered them plenty of help to do just that.

Parallel with this tendency toward the generalization of the social, *poverty* was also rediscovered – *had* to be rediscovered. While in the early phase of the Federal Republic hardship had still been a very widespread, very multifaceted phenomenon pervading the most varied conditions of life, though very different from conventional poverty, and while full employment and economic growth in the 1960s, along with the reform of the social assistance law, may have in fact marginalized it, poverty now became visible in a new way.[333] The generalization of the social invariably entailed the danger that the specific nature of a hardship receded into the background. To put it more pointedly: the rule of the "middle voter" displaced the "swing voter," even if the latter's social interest was the more urgent one – especially since his electoral behavior displayed neither the same rationality as that of the typical "middle voter," nor an equally effective organization. And both of these features are associated with poverty.

That this period also saw the emergence of the "*new social question*" (Widmaier 1978; Groser and Veiders 1979; Geißler 1980) is part of the same context. The "new social questions" were a consequence of the generalization of the social – more precisely: the multiplication of the worse-better comparisons. They are a response to the differential political perception of the worse-better comparisons that have multiplied. "Old social questions" often prove better able to assert themselves democratically than "new social questions," even if the social urgency of the latter might be greater. But that is not all. Even among the newly perceived worse-better comparisons, not all have the same political chances. Here the old formula of the

[333] Klanfer (1969); Neundörfer (1969, pp. 201–214); Kortmann (1976, pp. 144–149); Kögler (1976); von Brentano (1978); Hauser et al. (1981).

"social question" is a good method for calling attention to problems that are being neglected. The interwoven processes of democracy and the social find an apt expression in the proliferation of "social questions."

Social Democracy – Workers' State – Union State

One of the temptations of the time was to understand *democracy* not only as a structural principle, but also as an *objective-normative principle* that could be directed toward institutional participation, as well as toward material participation.[334] Thus, the principle of democracy was invoked to underscore social demands. Above all, however, a change in the structures of integration and subordination was called for, not only in the realm of the state, but also in the societal and even private sphere. Participation was supposed to create equality and self-determination, to "democratize." It was in that sense that the expansion of rights of codetermination and participation on the part of workers was seen as socially *and* democratically legitimated. To be sure, the discovery of democracy as a normative material program had many goals and contents, but the interests of the workers were the most important example.

Workers had carried the label of "the disadvantaged" from the nineteenth and early twentieth centuries into the situation of growing participation in prosperity. The revival of the term "working class," pushed by both the movement of 1968 and some of the unions and their intellectual backers, was in accord with this. That term was reminiscent of the "old social question." The expansion of the designation "working class" to all "wage-dependent workers" affirmed the formalization of "disadvantage" – the linkage of the social claim primarily to a status, and only secondarily to a real condition. The growing democratic weight of the workers made it easier to do this. The circumstances of the time gave rise to a special proximity between the *constitution of society in the state* and the self-constitution of the workers within the unions (Zacher 1977b). This had a *demographic* reason in the rising ratio of workers within society. It had a *democratic* reason in the democratic weight of the workers organized into unions. This refers not only to the weight of their votes, but also to the dependency of everything that went on in society and the state on the workers. People at that time, having attained a high level of urban civilization and facing the increasing spread of technology, were keenly aware of how vulnerable all public and private life was to the denial of services. Finally, this proximity of democratic state constitution and union self-constitution of the workers had a reason that was grounded in the *social state*: in the social concerns of workers, a reason that many themselves also understood as "democratic." The meaning of the "workers' question" as the "social question" and the

[334] Das demokratische Prinzip im Grundgesetz. VVDStRL no. 29 (Berlin, 1971), esp. the essay by Martin Kriele; see also above Chaps. 1, 2 and 3.

social mandate of this "social democracy" seemed as much aligned as the claim of workers to participation and state democracy. The unions played a special role in the "social democracy" of those years (Löwisch 1975, pp. 53–58; Popp 1975; Gießen 1976; Gerhardt 1977). To be sure, the parity between unions and employers' associations within the framework of "social self-administration" that was invoked in the early years continued to be a medium of participation in social and political decision-making power. Increasingly, however, it was being called into question as an inappropriate restriction on the special position of the unions. All in all: the "social democracy" at the time was largely understood as a "workers' state" and a "union state" and was used as such.

Association State – Corporatism

The example of the unions also points to the change that has generally taken place in the relationship between the state and the self-organization of society. From the outset, the construction of the Federal Republic was accompanied by the societal and political effectiveness of associations. Their interaction became differentiated and intensified. The political climate of the Brandt-Schmidt era gave this development new impulses and new directions. Society expressed itself with more variety and vigor than ever before: in initiatives, protests, revolutionary actions. Politics was more ambitious than ever before. The demand on the part of politics for a pacifying legitimation grew. And the power of representative democracy to grant pacifying legitimation became disproportionate. And so the "association state" intensified into *corporatism*. In a growing number of contexts, the interests and readiness of state decision-making bodies coincided with the interests and readiness of societal forces – representative organizations, directly affected actors (businesses etc.), but also public law institutions in which (as with the carriers and associations of social insurance) societal forces were bundled together – to negotiate, and possibly jointly legitimate, political and especially legislative solutions. Slowly, the political system of the country was being changed in this way.

Reporting – Planning – Expertise

During this period, *change* became a *value in itself*: the perception of change, the promotion of change, the guidance of change.[335] At the same time, politics began to reveal *itself to the public* on an unprecedented scale: through reports (Derlien 1975, pp. 42–47), forecasts, projections, and programs on the most varied topics and with the most varied degree of obligatoriness (Jochimsen 1971, pp. 1236–1244).

[335] On the establishment of a "Commission for economic and social change" see Jahreswirtschaftsbericht 1971 der Bundesregierung (BTDrs. VI/1760), sections 90, 100; Ergebnisse: Wirtschaftlicher und sozialer Wandel in der Bundesrepublik Deutschland (1976).

This new practice concerned not least social policy.[336] What had begun in the second legislative session with the report on agriculture and the two-step report by the Social Advisory Committee and the federal government on the state of pension insurance,[337] and had continued in the fifth legislative session with the Youth Reports and the Accident Prevention Reports, now expanded into a broad spectrum of *specialized reports*, but was simultaneously developed into a *general social reporting*. Beginning in 1968, the federal government drew up a *social budget* (Berié 1970). From 1970 on, the social budget appeared in conjunction with *periodic social reports*, in which the federal government outlined social projects and their implementation (Bartholomäi 1974, pp. 57–78).

With that, politics and the law were also drawing closer again to the word "*plan*."[338] Ever since economic guidance had yielded to the free market economy, the word had been taboo. Increasingly, its rejection had been directed also against a socialist planned economy as was practiced in Central and Eastern Europe. Now, however, it proved necessary again to develop new instruments, spell out political intentions, guide processes, and, above all, guarantee coordination among subjects. Reports, forecasts, and projections were supposed to respond to this in a non-binding way. The most important examples served to promote coordination with the federation: the medium-term financial planning of the federal government and the states, or the framework plans on how to carry out the joint tasks.[339] There were no examples from the narrower sphere of social policy.

Finally, politics intensified its engagement with *expertise*. This was especially significant, as long as it was an institutionalized, periodic dialog between politics and expertise, the kind that was first established in 1957 in the form of the pension insurance report by the Social Advisory Council and the federal government, then found a thematically much more expansive application in 1963 through the establishment of the Council of Economic Advisors, and then especially in 1967 in the Stability and Growth Act (Schneider 1968). Ad-hoc requests for reports from expert committees are comparable only to a limited extent: for example, the Codetermination Commission,[340] the Transfer Inquiry Commission, which was tasked with determining the influence of state transfer payments on the disposable income of private households (Transfer-Enquete-Kommission 1979; 1981), the Expert Commission for the Social Protection of Women (Bundesminister für Arbeit und Sozialordnung 1979), or the Expert Commission on Old-Age Pension Schemes (Sachverständigenkommission 1983a, b, c). Still, these committees were also able

[336] On the reports see Frerich and Frey (vol. 3, 1996, p. 731f.).

[337] The report by the Social Advisory Council was given the title "Social report," which concealed its special topic, pension insurance.

[338] See the series "Planung" ed. by J. H. Kaiser, vol. 1 (1965), vol. 2 (1966), vol. 3 (1968), vol. 4 (1970), vol. 5 (1971). Schneider (1967); Arndt and Swatek (1971).

[339] On this and the relevant instruments of economic policy see Zacher (1973, pp. 33–51).

[340] Sachverständigenkommission zur Auswertung der bisherigen Erfahrungen bei der Mitbestimmung in Unternehmen, 1970: Bericht, BTDrs. VI/334.

to contribute significantly to debates over social policy with a more reasoned foundation.

However, what was neither intended nor achieved with *any of these instruments was a comprehensive account, explanation, and assessment of social policy* (beyond the steps of legislation and the calculations of the costs of social benefits and their financing). Other limitations were connected to this practice. Reports of actions took precedence over analyses of effects. And the gradient between legal, economic, service-providing, competency-conveying, and environment-shaping intervention found a new expression. If an overarching report covered at best the manifestations of legal and economic intervention, the service-providing, competency-conveying, and environment-shaping interventions receded well into the background.

7.2.3 "Crisis of the Social State" or Crisis of the Democratic Constitutional and Social State?

The era was characterized by the will of constitutional democracy to realize the social. The "postwar period" was over. The time of the Grand Coalition and especially the time of Chancellors Brandt and Schmidt felt responsible for exploring and implementing what was still possible. That also entailed a change in the relationship between the state and society. Where the postwar misery could be managed in any case only by everyone doing what he or she was capable of doing, regardless of their position, the founding period of the Federal Republic was a great interweaving of political and societal accomplishments. Where Ludwig Erhard had in the end emphasized the role of society to the point where the latter was sick and tired of hearing about it, the essential things were now expected to come from politics. And politics promised to deliver the essential things.

This expectation rested on the experience of reconstruction and growth. The previous period – since 1948/1949 – knew only improvements in social protection and expansions of social benefits, embedded in a general rise in prosperity. The "business model" for the new departure was to not only continue this development, but to maximize it fully. Because of a lack of any directly comparable experience, the inherent limits to growth in this system were not perceived. Because the economic prosperity of the postwar decade was considered a success of economic policy, there was belief that it could be made to continue. Both perceptions turned out to be wrong, and the result was a debate about the "*crisis of the social state*."[341] The real issue was – then and now – to recognize and take seriously the developmental laws of the social, and to accept the burden of the decisions that become necessary because and when these developmental laws come to pass (Külp and Haas 1977).

[341] A compilation of the "crisis literature" in Zacher (1987a, p. 1079f.); Zacher (1989c, p. 86f.). For additional background see Spieker (1986).

The constitutional statement about the social does not relieve anyone of this burden. It stands apart from the matter itself; it points the way but is open, always uncertain in concrete terms. The social, however, is nothing static and nothing finite – neither as a normative program, nor as a reality. The social is a process, an unending process, because the external circumstances, especially also conditions within society and the state, are constantly changing. And they change precisely also as a result of the social. Every social intervention alters the conditions for the behavior of people and how they behave – and it does so in ways different from what the intervention predicted. Even without any alteration, over time the behavior-guiding effects of nearly every social intervention change. The consensuses that (may have) carried an intervention do not necessarily support the reality that emerges from it or may simply be attributed to it. The same holds true for the external circumstances under which the social develops and exerts its effects. They, too, escape the claim to complete guidance by politics and the law. They, too, are "validity conditions" of old consensuses, and every change can call them into question. Every change can thus necessitate new decisions. In the end, even the best social state will always be so unfinished that the hope for a development for the better must remain open for human beings. It was precisely developments – or more precisely: surprises, disappointment, disturbances – of this kind that triggered the general talk of the "crisis of the social state" in the 1970s. These developments were part of the essence of the social, but they are not its "crisis." To be sure, this essence is a challenge to democracy and possibly also to the *Rechtsstaat*, which bear the institutional responsibility for the social. These systems must continually redefine the social, a definition that no norm preempts for them (Budschin 1976; Bethusy-Huc 1976, pp. 222–305). If *democracy and the Rechtsstaat* cannot cope with this essence of the social, that is *their crisis* and always also the *crisis of the society* that has constituted itself into a democracy and a constitutional state. Only the observer who understands that "social state" means this interconnection of the social, the *Rechtsstaat*, and democracy has a right to speak of the "crisis of the social state."

7.3 The Development of the Social System[342]

7.3.1 Responsibility for the Economy[343]

During the time of the Grand Coalition, the responsibility of the state for the economy was given powerful expression. At the same time, the tool kit for global guidance was expanded. The potentialities of the federal government and the

[342] Zacher (1989c, pp. 62–95); Frerich and Frey (vol. 3, 1996, pp. 16–157, 159–423); Sozialberichte der Bundesregierung, BTDrs. (1970) VI/643; (1971) VI/2155; (1972) VI/3432; (1973) 7/1167; (1974) 7/2853; (1976) 7/4953; (1978) 8/1805; (1980) 8/4327.

[343] Abelshauser (1993, pp. 106–170); Glastetter, Högemann and Marquardt (1991, pp. 185–316). Bundesministerium für Wirtschaft (1964/1966/1982); Jahreswirtschaftsberichte der Bundesregierung (1968–1982).

Länder were bundled. The state as a whole was committed to the essentials of a joint economic policy. The central steps were the Law for the Promotion of Stability and Economic Growth (1967)[344] and the Law on the Principles of the Budget Law of the Federal Government and the States (Budget Principles Law – 1969).[345] The key economic ideas of overall economic equilibrium, of the regulation of the market economy, the stability of prices, high employment, foreign trade balance, and steady and appropriate economic growth, which the Law on the Council of Economic Advisors of 1963 had introduced into legal language for the first time, were now increasingly recognized by the law.[346] The reports by the Council of Economic Advisors, and the Annual Economic Report by the federal government in response to the Council's Annual Report became the starting points of "orientational data," by means of which the federal government – in a purely consultative mechanism called "concerted action"- sought to bring influence to bear also on local communities, the unions, and the business associations (Sect. 3, StWG). Beyond that, financial and budgetary planning, tax law, and public loans were presented and regulated as the most important tools for guiding the economy (R. Schmidt 1971, pp. 180–226). The regime of a stability policy of global guidance attained little importance (Schneider et al. 1975). When, beginning with the oil crisis of 1973, budget politics became increasingly difficult, this found expression in a series of budget supplementary acts that changed the laws on both benefits and taxes and levies (list in Zacher 1989c, p. 88, note 314). By contrast, the specific interventionist tool kit of the Stability and Growth Act was barely used. The concerted action "exploded" at the end of 1977. When employers challenged the constitutionality of the Codetermination Act of 1976, the unions withdrew from the concerted action (Watrin 1982, p. 785). That had no effect on the fundamental importance of the Growth and Stability Act to the clarification of the goals of economic policy and the global orientation of economic guidance. In addition, the reports by the Council of Economic Advisors and the government's Annual Report on the State of the Economy emerged as the core pieces of a differentiated system of information about the development of economic policy and its assessment. Together with the joint forecasts by the large German economic research institutes, the reports from the Deutsche Bundesbank, and the publications of the Federal

[344] "Gesetz zur Förderung der Stabilität und des Wachstums der Wirtschaft" (StWG), passed on 8 June 1967 BGBl., p. 582.

[345] "Gesetz über die Grundsätze des Haushaltsrechts des Bundes und der Länder" (HGrG), passed on 18 August, 1969, BGBl. I, p. 1273.

[346] In addition to Sect. 1 StWG and Sect. 2 of the Law on the Council of Economic Advisors, also the following: on the overall economic equilibrium – Art. 104a, Para. 4, Sent. 1; Art. 109, Para. 4; Art. 115, Para. 1, Sent. 2 of the Basic Law, new version; on the free market system of the Law Against Restrictions on Competition; on the stability of monetary value, which is linked to price stability – Sect. 3 Bundesbank Act.; on high employment – Sect. 1 of the Work Promotion Law of 1969; on economic growth – Art. 104a, Para. 4, Sent. 1 of the Basic Law, new version.

Office of Statistics, as well as the reports from the Advisory Council of the Federal Ministry of Economics, they constituted an efficient concept of reporting on and justifying the development of the economy and economic policy. The core piece of monetary policy was and continued to be the *Bundesbank*.[347]

However, the spirit of the Brandt era, and in the Schmidt era also the difficulties of that time, confronted the economy with new challenges. Both the faith in the self-regulation of the free market economy and the confidence in the tool kit of global guidance seemed shaken. The question of whether politics should assume more economic responsibility appeared to arise anew (Weizsäcker 1979). The "quarrel over the constitution of the economy" that had been carried on in the first years of the Federal Republic was given new fuel (Tettinger 1977, pp. 1617–1621). The idea of planning became concentrated especially in the direction of investment control (*Investitionslenkung*) (Krüper 1975, pp. 21–43). And the demands for institutionalized union influence on the economy were – parallel to the advance of codetermination in the workplace and businesses – also voiced in the sense of an exaggerated codetermination (Vilmar 1975, pp. 3–33; Schultz 1977, pp. 13–21). However, none of these considerations progressed beyond the discussion stage. The quandaries at the time drove home not only the problems, but also a new awareness of the value of the social market economy. To be sure, it was necessary to confront its conceptualization with the current projects and ideas (Issing 1981; Zacher 1981). Its message had to be articulated anew and in keeping with the times.[348] In 1979, when the Federal Constitutional Court had to decide on the constitutionality of the Codetermination Act of 1976, it did reiterate that the legislature could "pursue any economic policy it deemed appropriate," but the court also emphasized that it could not curtail individual freedoms (BVerfGE 50, 290 [338]).

7.3.2 Work and Income

Dependent Work[349]

No other development of the social expressed the climacteric, in retrospect zenith-like character of this era quite like that of dependent labor. Into the Schmidt era, dependent labor was marked by the self-evidence of general growth and the possibility of full employment. Still, the first two decades of the Federal Republic had left social problems of the workers unaddressed. The notion that workers are

[347] On the state of the economy policy tool kit in 1970 see Zacher (1973).

[348] On the "*Reinigungskrise der Globalsteuerung*" (crisis of cleansing global guidance) see Bundesministerium für Wirtschaft (1975/76, pp. 152–155; 1987, pp. 895–962).

[349] G. Müller (1967–1981; vols. 4–18), Dieterich and G. Müller (1982); Bundesministerium für Arbeit und Soziales and Bundesarchiv (eds.): Geschichte der Sozialpolitik in Deutschland seit 1945, vols. 5 (2006a) and 6 (2008a), Chap. 3 in each.

the primary creditors of the social state had not exhausted itself through the social progress of the time. This juxtaposition of a general rise in prosperity (also and especially a rise in the prosperity of workers) and the outstanding "debts" to the workers created a certain resistance on the part of labor policy visions to the criterion of inequality. Demands by the workers removed themselves from being embedded within a larger cosmos of differences in prosperity. Steps for the benefit of workers seemed social by definition. Tradition and the electoral calculation of social democracy demanded as much. To be sure, the great majority of workers did not embrace the fact that the "new Left" in the "period of 1968" spoke again of the "working class." Nevertheless, such talks reinforced society's awareness of the worker's historical claim to the social.

As a result, the status of the worker – and public service is emphatically included here[350] – became the most protected status in society. The "*workers' society*" saw itself as a society of those in dependent gainful employment (Offe 1984a, pp. 13–43), and for reasons of industrial rationality as well as reasons of socio-political technique, dependent labor was typified into the "*normal employment relationship*" (Behrens et al. 1987, pp. 24–34). The working hours for a day, a week, a year were defined – in the sense of a "full-time job" in such a way that the labor potential that the gainfully employed person could and should employ for dependent work thanks to a social convention was fully utilized, but generally not overtaxed. Another characteristic for the normal employment relationship was that it was oriented toward stability. That stability meant, on the one hand, the principled negation of conditions, time limitations, and dismissal. On the other hand it meant a continuity of status that was already prefigured in the civil servant law since the nineteenth century. The temporal pulse of the daily, weekly, or monthly exchange of labor and pay was extended very widely. As a result, a long-term security of living conditions developed within the labor relationship. The principle of seniority – this, too, a key element of civil service law – made it seem more and more self-evident that working conditions should improve over the course of a working life. All this was achieved – against the backdrop of broad full employment and an employment policy that optimized the demand for work – through a continuously expanded, internalizing protection in the labor relationship. Added to this was the emphatic development of the social inclusion of the workers, as well. The social environment in the workplace was joined increasingly by *participation* in life in the workplace (works constitution), in management (through codetermination), in the development of working conditions above the particular workplace and business, and in public life in general (through union organization).

[350] See, for example, Gutachten der Deutschen Revisions- und Treuhand A. G. Zur Frage des Besoldungsrückstandes. BTDrs. VI/3504; Vergleich des beamtenrechtlichen Versorgungssystems mit den Versorgungssystemen für Arbeitnehmer im öffentlichen Dienst und in der privaten Wirtschaft. Gutachten der Treuhand-Aktiengesellschaft, Wirtschaftsprüfungsgesellschaft. BTDrs. 7/5569.

What became increasingly important, however, was that the *social benefits* supplemented the labor market and labor relations. The system of provision, of social insurance, and of provision under civil service law extended the ability to earn an income and meet basic needs into situations when social risks have materialized (illness, disability, old age, etc., as a guarantee of maintenance even beyond death). Under certain circumstances, compensation systems could have similar effects. The systems of assistance and promotion, both the specialized ones like child and housing allowance and the general one of welfare, relativized the importance that attached to earnings from dependent work for meeting needs and providing maintenance. They increased the freedom to choose between various forms of gainful employment, or between work and non-work. The active and passive employment policy bundled in the system of work promotion complemented this development effectively. What was later called the "decommodification of labor" – the complete uncoupling of labor from its character as a commodity (Esping-Andersen 1990) – was never practiced as emphatically as during this phase.[351]

In this way, dependent work evolved increasingly into a totality of social fulfillment and social protection. It had considerable advantages over both independent work and unpaid work – domestic work as well as uncompensated work outside the family in private or public contexts. This situation was widely recognized. The ratio of the self-employed as part of the working population declined steadily. The ratio of dependent workers as part of the gainfully employment population rose steadily.

The Further Development of Labor Law

In 1969, the First Labour Law Consolidation Act improved the protection against dismissal. That same year, the continued payment of wages in case of sickness was newly regulated and standardized for workers and employees. In 1972, the Temporary Employment Act addressed a new kind of employment relationship. In 1974, the law for the severely disabled was developed further. That year also saw a reorganization of the law governing home-based work and the Law to Improve Work-based Pension Provision.[352] The maternity leave was introduced in 1979, supplementing the period of protection under the maternity law. In the area of *individual labor law*, however, the crucial developments did not take place by way of legislation, but by way of the practice of collective bargaining agreements and the decisions of the labor courts. In no other area did the protection of the worker come into its own as it did in the decisions by the labor courts, as well as in the scholarly discussion of labor law: on the one hand vis-à-vis the employer's concrete situation of prosperity, on the other hand vis-à-vis the functional contexts in which

[351] On the preceding see Zacher (1997).

[352] Bericht der Bundesregierung über die Erfahrung mit der Durchführung der betrieblichen Altersversorgung, BTDrs. 8/2377.

labor was performed and on the basis of which it was paid (W. Zöllner 1990, pp. 1–8; Hanau 1998, pp. 69–79).

New movement also came into the *law governing industrial actions*. The dissolution of parity-based "social self-governance" in favor of the unions found expression in an intense disagreement about the admissibility of the lockout (Bieback et al. 1979). The strike, so the argument went, was to remain legitimate as the weapon of the "socially" legitimated workers and their unions. The lockout, on the other hand, as the weapon of the employers, who were not pursuing an immediate "social" interest, was to remain prohibited. The Federal Labour Court responded with graduated restrictions on lockouts (Konzen and Scholz 1980, pp. 1593–1600).

In the face of these developments of labor law following their own inherent dynamic, the attempt by the Brandt government to *codify labor law* – parallel to the plan for a Social Security Code – stood no chance.[353]

By contrast, the law on *codetermination* showed significant legislative developments. In 1972, the new Labour Management Relations Act expanded the rights of workers and their representatives in companies and enterprises. In 1976, finally, following years of political disputes, the spectacular Law on the Codetermination of Workers (Codetermination Act) was passed, which essentially structured the codetermination of workers on the supervisory boards on the basis of parity. Highly controversial in terms of constitutional law (Badura et al. 1977; Kübler et al. 1978), the Federal Constitutional Court confirmed the constitutionality of the law in 1979 (BVerfGE 50, 290).

Another development of fundamental importance occurred in the area of *occupational safety*. One of the goals of the period was to lead working life and labor law to the expectations and possibilities of a prosperous society. "*Humanization of the working world*" was the central slogan for this goal (Rohde 1974, pp. 101–120). While all areas of labor law contributed to its realization, the focal point lay in occupational safety law. In the area of technical occupational safety, the Law on Technical Labour Equipment was passed as early as 1968. In 1973, the Law on Company Medical Officers, Safety Engineers, and other Experts brought substantial progress. This was supplemented by passage of a wealth of special regulations. Training was newly regulated as early as 1969 by the Vocational Training Act. In 1976 there followed the Law for the Protection of Young People in Employment.

Lastly: Doubts

Even though the social status of workers – of workers as a type of individual existence, as well as of workers as a social entity – and the political and legal

[353] "Kommission zur Erstellung eines Arbeitsgesetzbuches," in AuR 10 (1970), 371; Ramm (1972, pp. 13–19); Bundesminister für Arbeit und Sozialordnung (1977); specifically on the codification of the law governing industrial actions see the podium discussion at the 51st Congress of German Lawyers (Verhandlungen des 51. Deutschen Juristentages 1976).

recognition of their union representation seemed to be continuously improving, there was a growing number of signs that a high point may have been reached. There were economic symptoms: the weakness and fragility of growth, inflation, and unemployment. And above all there were symptoms in the social benefits law, which descended into ever stronger spasm of cutbacks. Although the status of workers as expressed in the individual and collective conditions of work held its own, it could no longer conceal the fact that the utopia of a "workers' state", in which the universality of a normal employment relationship provided an ever growing number of people with a maximum of prosperity, security, and freedom, was proving unrealistic to the same degree that it was being realized (Habermas 1985, pp. 141–163). The working society found itself in a crisis, as did the workers' society (Matthes 1983; Offe 1984b). In the end, this also heralded consequences for labor law and labor relations.[354]

7.3.3 Other Gainful Employment – Other Work

Independent Gainful Employment

The basic formula of work, income, meeting of needs, and maintenance took on a specific meaning during this period. The understanding and practice of this formula now focused, in a matter-fact-way that was previously unknown, on dependent gainful employment. Of course, independent gainful work remained a possibility for fulfilling the basic formula. However, the *fulfillment of the basic norm through dependent gainful employment assumed* – in a way that is immeasurable – *normative status*. That applied to the responsibility of the individual to earn an income through work. The freedom of work referred to both independent and dependent work. But where it became an indirect duty, a "burden," it was understood as the duty of dependent work. This concentration of the basic formula on dependent work applied even more so to the responsibility of the polity and society to make possible the fulfillment of the basic formula and to ensure that it was socially tolerable. The responsibility of politics for *full employment* concerned dependent gainful employment – not just any kind of gainful employment, not just any kind of work. And the responsibility of the policy toward dangers and shortcomings in the implementation of the basic formula remained selective.[355] A significant comparison that persisted was how extensively workers – through protection against dismissal, social

[354] See, for example, the debate at the 52nd Congress of German Lawyers on the topic "Sind im Interesse einer gerechten Verteilung der Arbeitsplätze Begründung und Beendigung der Arbeitsverhältnisse neu zu regeln?" (Verhandlungen des 52. Deutschen Juristentages 1978b); debates on the topic "Möglichkeiten der Sanierung von Unternehmen durch Maßnahmen im Unternehmens-, Arbeits-, Social- und Insolvenzrecht," (Verhandlungen des 54. Deutschen Juristentages 1982).

[355] Bericht betreffend die Lage der freien Berufe, BTDrs. 8/3139; Der Beruf im Sozialrecht, SDSRV, vol. 5 (Wiesbaden, 1969).

security, and (formal and informal) employment policy – were protected in those years if they lost their job, while the self-employed bore the entire risk of "failure." Within the circle of the self-employed, the farmers[356] – with extensive support from income policy and social security – were a notable exception, though that special status was, of course, not evident in the prosperity of every single farmer.

In all of this, the history of the social state played a significant role. That is true, on the one hand, for the concentration of the "social question" in the nineteenth century on the "workers' question". Even though the fate of many self-employed persons (small tradesmen, smaller farmers, and so on) was similarly characterized by hardship and need as that of wage workers already in the nineteenth century, indeed as the fate of the poorer among the wage workers, it was only workers who carried the historical-political banner of the "social question" through history. The other historical association that took shape in the value-judgments of the time found nourishment in the fact that the self-employed person is often also an employer, a "capitalist." He is something like the "class enemy." Abstracting from this situation, politics and the practice of labor law declared every worker in need of protection and *every* employer as obligated to provide protection, even if the actual differentials in prosperity, the actual dependencies were quite different. That seems to be one reason why independent gainful work became less and less attractive to those entering the working world – unless the decision to forego the guarantees of dependent work was clearly compensated by secure income opportunities (real or perhaps only presumed).

The readiness to draw a distinction grew where independently working individuals entered into a dependency on a third party that was similar to an employment relationship. Home workers and cottage industry were examples that the Federal Republic had already encountered. Now, the protection of labor law was expanded for "*worker-like individuals*" by way of general clause.[357]

Non-gainful Work

No less significant was the intensification of the basic formula for non-gainful employment: for domestic work as well as private, societal, or communal unpaid work outside of the family. The expansion of social protection and the social development of dependent gainful employment deepened the gap to unpaid work. Of the elements making up the meaning of work, only the real effectiveness remained common to all forms of work. Private, societal, or communal unpaid

[356] On the "Green Reports" see above note 255; see also the "Agrarian Reports" from 1971 (BTDrs. VI/1800) to 1983 (BTDrs. 9/2402).

[357] See the introduction of §12a of the Collective Bargaining Agreement Act through the Home Working Amendment Act of 20 October 1974, BGBl. I, p. 2879. Analagous to this, the employment relationship under social security law – the key concept that placed workers under the protection of social security – was reinterpreted. See the decisions by the Federal Social Court concerning chief physicians (BSGE 32, 38), on the independent workers at radio stations (BSGE 36, 262).

work outside of the family for the most part still conveyed a direct, non-private social inclusion. But it lacked the element of compensation and of social protection that flowed from it, just as it lacked the broadening of social inclusion that was accorded workers through works constitutions, codetermination, and the participation of the union in society and the polity. Domestic work remained entirely limited to its real effectiveness. Its social inclusion remained purely private in nature. By contrast, earnings and social protection depended entirely on the person who bore the responsibility for earning and maintenance within the family. That, however, heightened the tension between the linearity of the basic formula as long as the number of earners in a community of maintenance equaled the number of consumers, and the nonlinearity of the basic formula as soon as the number of earners in a community of maintenance was smaller than the number of consumers.

Two basic problems with which every industrial society, especially every society with a free-market economy, is familiar are thus exacerbated. The *first* basic problem concerns *families*. This problem of families is chiefly a problem for *women*. It lies in the relationship of tension between the production of welfare by domestic work and the social status of those who perform it. The *second* problem concerns the supra-familial, societal *interaction* and all *communal work* that does not assume the form of dependent gainful employment (or corresponding public offices). This applies not only but especially to so-called "honorary" social services. At any rate, we are dealing also with an important dimension of the societal realization of the social. Because the social gap between dependent gainful employment and unpaid work widens, the attractiveness and reasonableness of relevant activities that benefit others declines.

7.3.4 Problems of Wealth

Wealth policy[358] was largely pursued as the promotion of *wealth formation*. In the process, new emphases were continually set: promoting low and middle income earners and large families (Tax Amendment Act of 1969); the wealth formation of workers (Third Law for the Promotion of Wealth Formation of Workers, 1970), especially also in public service (Law on Benefits with Effects on Wealth for Federal Civil Servants, Professional Soldiers, and Voluntary Soldiers, 1970; First Law on the Standardization and Reorganization of Compensation Law in the Federation and the States, 1971); expansion of investment opportunities with bonus rewards for savings (Law to Amend the Savings Act, 1972). Thereafter, the state's wealth policy petered out. Attempts at placing company shares in the hands of workers, at a wealth formation policy by way of collective bargaining agreements, and so on had essentially no results. The parties involved focused on

[358] Frerich and Frey (vol. 3, 1996, pp. 136–149); Bundesministerium für Arbeit und Soziales and Bundesarchiv (eds.): Geschichte der Sozialpolitik in Deutschland seit 1945, vols. 5 (2006a) and 6 (2008a), Chap. 3, no. 16 in each.

income policy – though in a broad sense: beyond earned income on earnings replacement income and earnings-supplementing income from social benefits.

Private wealth formation reached an unprecedented generality during that period, but at the same time also a new dimension of *inequality* (Miegel 1983). The de-sensitization of the social toward inequality in wealth entered into a new phase. The inequality in wealth became a crucial field on which to play out the proviso of inequality. After 1945, the inequality in the distribution of wealth had still been an issue of social concern and criticism. With the economic upswing, the critique of the unequal distribution of capital and land was swallowed up in the dynamism of the new uses to which capital and land were put. The focus shifted increasingly toward the equality of opportunities for creating new private wealth. However, a peculiar social-state schizophrenia emerged as new wealth was in fact acquired and inherited. The inequality of incomes remained – within broad parameters of tolerance – the object of social criticism. By contrast, the inequality of wealth was increasingly declared to be a "private matter." Income from wealth was privileged vis-à-vis earned income and the income from dependent work.[359]

At the same time, a new side of the issue of "wealth" became apparent: liabilities. The "crisis of the social state" was reflected in private economic entities. They, too, displayed the symptoms of contradictory goals, disappointed growth expectations, and unforeseen changes. The phenomenon of private *debt*[360] increased in the final phase of the period under examination. It became a specific cause of social inequalities and thus a specific occasion of social intervention.[361]

7.3.5 The Family[362]

Equality of Men and Women

The *equality of men and women* was faced with new challenges. During the building phase of the Federal Republic, a wealth of traditional inequality had been swept aside. What now emerged was the need to adjust family and social

[359] On the criticism by the Federal Constitutional Court of the "sparing" treatment of earnings from capital see BVerfGE 84, 273; for a border-line case of "workless income" see Bundesministerium der Finanzen (1976).

[360] See also "Bericht der Bundesregierung über die Erfahrungen mit dem Zweiten Gesetz zur Änderung des Abzahlungsgesetzes", BTDrs. 7/1398.

[361] It is remarkable that the first edition of the Fachlexikon der sozialen Arbeit (1980), published by the Deutscher Verein für öffentliche und private Fürsorge, still lacked an entry on *Verschuldung* (debt). In the second edition (1983) we find the word *Schuldenregulierung*, though without further material. The third (1993) and fourth (1997) editions have the entry *Schuldnerberatung* with further material; see Bundesministerium für Arbeit und Soziales and Bundesarchiv (eds.), 2008a: Geschichte der Sozialpolitik in Deutschland seit 1945, vol. 6, Chap. 3, no. 9.

[362] "Erster Familienbericht," BTDrs. V/2532; "Zweiter Familienbericht," BTDrs. 8/3121; Bundesministerium für Arbeit und Soziales and Bundesarchiv (eds.) Geschichte der Sozialpolitik in Deutschland seit 1945, vols. 5 (2006a) and 6 (2008a), Chap. 3, no. 10 in each.

law even better to the reality of marriage (Ehe und Familie im Sozialversicherungs- und Versorgungsrecht 1967). In 1968, the 47th Congress of German Lawyers dealt with the topic "Is it advisable to change the legal regulations concerning the social protection of non-working wives during and after marriage, especially in the case of divorce?" (Verhandlungen des 47. Deutschen Juristentages 1968). What became evident is that the issue was no longer only the equal treatment of men and women, but increasingly also the equal treatment of women themselves – the working wife, the housewife only, the mother, the housewife burdened with providing nursing care, and so on, the wife who took on only one of these roles, the wife who took on two of these roles, the wife who took on several of these roles. However, the discussion led initially only to a regulation of old age, disability, and survivor insurance in case of divorce. In 1976, *pension adjustment* was introduced through the First Law on the Reform of Marriage and Family Law. Efforts at a reform of divorce law had shown that a reform of alimony was possible only if the settlement among spouses could also include entitlements from social provision, especially pension insurance, civil service pension, and possibly a work place-based pension. Pension adjustment was the answer. However, this did not resolve the broader problem of a social protection of spouses that was fair and equal. In two decisions, the Federal Constitutional Court demanded such a solution (1975: BVerfGE 34, 169; 1978: BVerfGE 48, 346 [365]).

But a discussion that ranged far beyond this issue revealed less and less understanding for the conventional system of social protection, which was oriented toward the traditional distribution of roles between men and women regarding gainful work, domestic work, and maintenance. Already the unequal status of women in the working world was becoming a growing problem.[363] In 1977, the federal government appointed a commission, which submitted its report in 1979 (Bundesminister für Arbeit und Sozialordnung 1979). However, the socio-political turmoil at the time prevented a quick decision. The Federal Constitutional Court intervened once again – this time from an entirely new perspective. In 1980, the Court reviewed the differences in the taxation of the civil service pension and the pensions from the statutory pension insurance as well as the supplementary pension insurance from the public sector. It ruled that the principle of equality was being violated, and that the legislature was obligated to revise the system (BVerfGE 54, 11). The question of a revamping pension schemes that met the requirement of equality now overlapped with the question of a new regulation that did justice to the equality between men and women. Another Expert Commission that was appointed in 1981 was to broaden the basis for a decision that would meet the demands for equality in both areas (see note 364 above). A decision was only made in one of the subsequent periods under examination.

[363] Debates at the 50th Congress of German Lawyers on the topic "Welche rechtliche Maßnahmen sind vordringly, um die tatsächliche Gleichstellung der Frau mit den Männern im Arbeitsleben zu gewährleisten?" In: Verhandlungen des 50. Deutschen Juristentages (1974).

Additional Developments

While child allowance and tax breaks for parents had coexisted in the so-called dual system since the 1950s, the 1974 Law on the Reform of the Income Tax, of Family Equalization, and Savings Incentives (Income Tax Reform Law) concentrated *family equalization* on child allowance. The tax breaks were essentially eliminated. Before that, the equality aspect was developed by way of two parameters: the child allowance addressed the inappropriate inequality resulting from the different burdens from children; the income tax regulation addressed the inappropriate inequality resulting from equal taxation in spite of different burdens from children. The second criterion was now dropped.[364]

The expansion of the *social protection for young people* (kindergartners, primary and secondary school students, university students, and so on)[365] was one of the characteristic features of that time. A highly contentious debate erupted over the reorganization of *youth welfare services*, however. While the federal government and the governing majority in the *Bundestag* wished to emphasize a public education mandate, the opposition and the majority in the *Bundesrat* advocated for the rights of parents. The *Bundestag* and the *Bundesrat* blocked each other.[366]

7.3.6 Social Benefits Systems[367]

If this period turned the social state into a "workers' state," it made it equally into a "*social benefits state*." The penchant to measure the social by quantitative expenses and quantitative allowances can find no more effective expression than in the expansion of the system of social benefits. But that means that they also become the first site for the "crisis of the social state" (Auswirkungen von Inflation, Konjunktur und Unterbeschäftigung auf das System der sozialen Sicherheit 1978).

Social Provision

For social insurance (Peters 1978, pp. 147–233; D. Zöllner 1981, pp. 153–178) this period was a time for a robust advancement. Just as during these years participation in the world of work and the economy developed, the policy of social insurance was also guided by this goal. This was not a time of questioning, not a time of fundamental

---

[364] The Federal Constitutional Court did not consider this regulation unconstitutional: BVerfGE 43, 108; in subsequent, decisions, however, it modified that position: BVerfGE 82, 60 (89f.), 198; 87, 153 (170).

[365] *Jugend und soziale Sicherheit*, SDSRV, vol. 11 (Bonn-Bad Godesberg, 1974).

[366] For an account of the events see Zacher (1999a: Teil D VIII, before p. 1).

[367] Maunz and Schraft (vol. 6: 1967; vol. 7: 1968; vols. 8: 1969 – 12: 1973); Wannagat (vol. 1: 1979 – vol. 5: 1983); Bundesministerium für Arbeit und Soziales and Bundesarchiv (eds.) Geschichte der Sozialpolitik in Deutschland seit 1945, vols. 5 (2006a) and 6 (2008a), Chap. 3, nos. 4–9 in each.

new beginnings. Rather, it was a time of expansion – of the protected circle of persons, of the protected risks, of benefits, and above all of the existing institutions, and later repeatedly of reduction, adjustment to unexpected developments, simply a "flinching" in the face of what was called the "crisis of the social state."

a) In particular: pension insurance[368]
   In the area of *pension insurance*, the Finance Amendment Act of 1967 established obligatory insurance for all *white-collar employees* – regardless of their occupational status or level of income. In 1969, the Third Pension Insurance Amendment Act reformed the financing of pension insurance. Where the 1957 pension reform had tried a so-called *Abschnittsdeckungsverfahren* (a special type of pay-as-you-go system), financing was now clearly switched to the *Umlageverfahren* (a completely pay-as-you-go-financed system). The year 1972 saw the most significant reform of pension insurance since 1957. The Law on the Further Reform of the Statutory Pension Insurance and on the Fifteenth Adjustment of Pension as well as on the Adjustment of Cash Benefits from the Statutory Accident Insurance (Pension Reform Act) introduced the *flexible pensionable age*, initially set at 63 (for the severely disabled at 62). It *opened* pension insurance to many individuals previously excluded from it, especially to the *self-employed* and to non-working *housewives*. Because of its particular modalities, this opening of pension insurance would prove particularly problematic. The possibility of joining was tied to the option of a retroactive insurance back to 1956. Because of these retroactive payments, older insured individuals could collect their pensions right away. Pension insurance had become one of the most profitable investment vehicles (Hermann 1990, pp. 119–122). On the other hand, this wave of new joiners and retroactive insurance in connection with the *Umlageverfahren* led to a financing illusion. The funds that flowed in quickly were spent just as quickly, while the acquired entitlements extended into a distant future. With the introduction of a *minimum pension*, the reform wanted to create an equalization of cases in which, because of a regional or sector-specific wage disparity or past wage discrimination against pay for women, the actually insured compensation did not provide an adequate basis for a long-term benefit.
b) Sickness insurance[369]
   In 1970, the Law on the Further Development of the Law on Statutory Sickness Insurance (*Second Sickness Insurance Amendment Act*) expanded protection for *white-collar employees*, who were subject to obligatory insurance only up to a certain income limit. Tests for the early diagnosis of diseases were adopted into the benefits catalog of sickness insurance. In 1972, the Law on the Further

[368] Bundesministerium für Arbeit und Soziales and Bundesarchiv (eds.): Geschichte der Sozialpolitik in Deutschland seit 1945, vols. 5 (2006a) and 6 (2008a), Chap. 3, no. 5 in each.
[369] Bundesministerium für Arbeit und Soziales and Bundesarchiv (eds.): Geschichte der Sozialpolitik in Deutschland seit 1945, vols. 5 (2006a) and 6 (2008a), Chap. 3, no. 6 in each.

Development of the Law of Statutory Sickness Insurance (*Law on the Sickness Insurance of Farmers*) closed the last large gap in the social protection for farmers. In 1973, the Law on the *Improvement of Benefits* in the Statutory Sickness Insurance (Benefits Improvement Act) provided a temporally unlimited legal entitlement to hospital nursing care and introduced sick pay if a worker was given a leave of absence to care for a sick child.

c) Other developments
The *Artist Social Insurance Act* (1981) included self-employed artists and writers in the protection of sickness insurance and pension insurance.[370] The social protection of *civil servants* was also reformed. Social protection against the risks of an occupational accident, old age, disability, and death was newly regulated in 1974 through a Civil Servant Provisioning Law that was standard throughout the country. The 1970s were also a time in which the social protection for *ministers* and *members of parliament* was regulated in a manner similar to what was in place for civil servants, though in detail usually more favorable (Zacher 1984b, pp. 91–99). At *Land* level the expansion of the *professional pension funds* for the *free professions*, which had been going on – with considerable variations among the *Länder* and professions – since the 1950s, reached a kind of conclusion (Frerich and Frey, vol. 3, 1996, p. 58f., 242). A significant supplementation took place only in the 1980s with the pension fund for lawyers (Reusch 1984, pp. 98–102).

d) Universalization versus differentiation
On the whole, a peculiar hybrid development occurred in the area of provisioning. On the one side, the circle of persons included in the protection systems expanded continuously. Their totality approached a "universalistic" concept: of a social protection that was aimed at the totality of all inhabitants or the totality of all gainfully employed persons. On the other side, social protection retained the selective principle by which it had developed from the very beginning: the differentiation by occupational group and life situation. However, the more broadly and more densely the net of social provision was spun, the more problematic the differentiations between the subsystems became. The decision of the Federal Constitutional Court of 1980, which had challenged the unequal net effect of the various old-age pension systems as unconstitutional, made this problem starkly apparent.

Social Compensation Law[371]

Social compensation law witnessed a new departure during this era. Historically the development of social compensation law had been backward-looking: at the

[370] See the preceding "Bericht der Bundesregierung über die wirtschaftliche und soziale Lage der künstlerischen Berufe" (Künstlerbericht), BTDrs. 7/3071.

[371] Bundesministerium für Arbeit und Soziales and Bundesarchiv (eds.) Geschichte der Sozialpolitik in Deutschland seit 1945, vols. 5 (2006a) and 6 (2008a), Chap. 1, no. 12 in each.

damages caused by National Socialist rule, the war, and the postwar period. Over the course of time, however, it became evident that *peacetime society* was also creating *problems that required analogous responses*. The issue here was not so much compensation for injustice. The young constitutional state was doing its utmost to prevent injustice on the part of the state. But where it did happen, there was the tried-and-true offense of a breach of official duties, the legal consequence of which was and is full restitution (Art. 34 GG, sect. 839 BGB). The issue was also not the compensation for property sacrifices. The Basic Law had clearly stated that expropriation imposed in the interest of the common good had to be compensated (Art. 14, Para. 3, GG). What remained problematic were sacrifices of life and limb for which the polity was responsible or for which it was willing to shoulder responsibility. There was no secure tradition for recognizing and compensating them.[372] A number of cases in which compensation seemed called for (harm during the exercise of an honorary position, when rendering emergency aid, while giving blood, in connection with life-saving measures and other first aid, and so on) had been resolved by the legislature within the framework of accident insurance: so-called "*unreal accident insurance*" (Krasney 1998, pp. 407–439). In due course, however, another solution inserted itself: the compensation for damages on the *model of assistance for war victims*. Comparable bodies of regulation like the Military Pensions Act[373] picked up this obvious model.[374] But was this model also suitable outside of a service law context? In 1953, the Federal High Court of Justice had awarded compensation in case of harm caused by publicly ordered immunizations (BGHZ 9, 83). To stipulate the nature and scope of the compensation in concrete terms, the legislature of Hesse[375] pointed to the regulation of the Federal Maintenance Act. In 1971, the federal legislature picked up this suggestion.[376] The question about a general system of social compensation law for the peacetime society emerged anew.[377] In 1975, the General Part of the Social Code brought the final decision: "Whoever suffers harm to his health, for the consequences of which the state community takes responsibility in compensation for a special sacrifice or for other reasons, is entitled" to benefits in accordance with the Federal Maintenance Act.[378]

---

[372] On this and what follows see Zacher (1972a).

[373] Also the Federal Border Guard Law and the Alternative Civilian Service Law.

[374] See also the Prisoner Assistance Act.

[375] "Hessisches Impfschadengesetz vom 6. Oktober 1958," GVBl., p. 147.

[376] "Zweites Änderungsgesetz zum Bundesseuchengesetz."

[377] Debates at the 49th Congress of German Lawyers on the topic "Empfiehlt es sich, die soziale Sicherung für den Fall von Personenschäden, für welche die Allgemeinheit eine gesteigerte Verantwortung trägt, neu zu regeln?", in: Verhandlungen des 49. Deutschen Juristentages (1972).

[378] Section 5, 24 SGB I (quote Sect. 5, Para 1). This must be supplemented by Art. II Sect. 1 no. 11 of the Social Code – General Part – of 11 December 1975, BGBl. I, p. 3015, according to which the Federal Maintenance Act will be considered "as special part of the Social Code... until its incorporation into the Social Code." In 1976, then, the Law on Compensation for Victims of

Assistance and Promotion Systems

Systems of assistance and promotion, in particular, experienced a significant *expansion* during this period. Previously there had only existed the general system of welfare/social assistance and the specialized systems of youth welfare, child allowance, and housing allowance. The year 1970 saw the addition of *education assistance* (Federal Education Assistance Act), 1971 the addition of *postgraduate assistance* (Law for the Promotion of Junior Scientists and Scholars at the Universities).[379] A *maintenance advance* for young children was introduced in 1979.[380] Finally, in 1980 *legal aid* was created, replacing the old poor law.[381] The number of tax-financed benefits that were universal in nature had thus substantially increased. The goal of not only guaranteeing individuals a subsistence minimum (which was characteristic of the old welfare even more so than for the new social assistance), of not only securing their participation in the world of work and the economy (through social insurance and other institutions of provision), but directly opening up to them an appropriate participation in society's opportunities of prosperity, had been emphatically underscored.

Work Promotion

In 1969, the old Law on Employment Exchanges and Unemployment Insurance was replaced by the Employment Promotion Act.[382] This also amounted in substance to a thorough *reform of the entire system of employment promotion*. The main goals were assuring full employment, securing optimal job opportunities by promoting professional qualifications, and protecting against downward social movement as a result of unemployment or short-time work. Promotion of winter construction was introduced as a new benefit. The Federal Office of Labour Exchanges and Unemployment Insurance was renamed to Federal Labour Office. With its tripartite structure (the central office in Nuremberg, the state labour offices, and the labour exchanges), whose organs (made up in three equal parts) encompass – in addition to the unions and the employers' associations – also the federal government, the *Länder*, and the municipalities, it overlays the federal scheme of separate jurisdictions and spheres of activity of the federal government and the *Länder*. The Employment Promotion Act clearly put forth this employment

Violent Crimes once again picked up the regulations of the Maintenance Act, in 1994 the Penal Rehabilition Law did the same.

[379] Bundesministerium für Arbeit und Soziales and Bundesarchiv (eds.), 2008a: Geschichte der Sozialpolitik in Deutschland seit 1945, vol. 6, Chap. 3, no. 11.

[380] Bundesministerium für Arbeit und Soziales and Bundesarchiv (eds.), 2008a: Geschichte der Sozialpolitik in Deutschland seit 1945, vol. 6, Chap. 3, no. 10.

[381] "Gesetz über die Prozeßkostenhilfe;" "Beratungshilfegesetz."

[382] Bundesministerium für Arbeit und Soziales and Bundesarchiv (eds.): Geschichte der Sozialpolitik in Deutschland seit 1945, vols. 5 (2006a) and 6 (2008a), Chap. 3, no. 3 in each.

bureaucracy as the carrier of a comprehensive mandate of an active (ensuring employment) and passive (social protection against unemployment) employment policy.

In 1974, *bankruptcy compensation payment* was created. It guaranteed that if a business went into bankruptcy, workers would be paid the full net wages and salaries for the last 3 months of employment.

Supraindividual Benefits and Finance Programs

Supraindividual programs took on new importance. The changes to the financing system enacted during the time of the Grand Coalition and the introduction of joint tasks reorganized the spheres and responsibilities of the federal government and the states. The Growth and Stability Pact for the first time called for reporting: in general terms in that the annual economic report had to outline the "economic and finance policy planned for the current year;"[383] in specific terms in that a Subsidies Report every 2 years is to provide an overview of the financial assistance that is given from federal funds "for certain purposes to agencies outside of the federal administration."[384] These stipulations improved the political control of the financial programs. Even more so, they contributed to legitimizing the supraindividual benefits and financing programs. Since the 1950s, those programs had already been playing an increasing role also as instruments of social policy. Supraindividual benefits and financing programs countered regional inequality with the utmost vigor and varied tools (Eberstein 1971ff.): as part of the federal government's financial equalization (Art. 107, Para. 2, GG), through investment assistance to equalize differing economic capacities (Art. 104a, Para 4, Sent. 1, GG), and through the joint task of "improvement of regional economic structures" (Art. 91a, Para. 1, no. 2, GG). A special role in this process fell to aid programs for the border regions[385] and Berlin,[386] as well as for coastal regions (Art. 91a, Para. 1, no. 3, GG). Another focal point for supraindividual programs was the promotion of the economy: to secure the overall economic equilibrium and economic growth (Art. 104a, Para. 4, Sent. 1, GG). Prominent here, in addition to investment programs (Sect. 10ff., StWG), were financial aids to maintain enterprises or economic sectors, to carry out structural adjustments, to promote advances in productivity, the growth of businesses and economic sectors, and the development of new methods and directions of production (Sect. 12, Para. 2 StWG). These mostly sectoral subsidies[387] quickly became

[383] Section 2 Para. 1, no. 3 StWG. On the annual economic reports see above note 343.

[384] Section 12 StWG. On the Subsidies Reports at that time see: 1966–68 BTDrs. V/2423; 1967–70 BTDrs. VI/391; 1969–72 BTDrs. VI/2994; 1971–74 BTDrs. 7/1144; 1973–76 BTDrs. 7/4203; 1975–78 BTDrs. 8/1195; 1977–80 BTDrs. 8/3097; 1979–82 BTDrs. 9/986.

[385] First regulated through the "Zonenrandförderungsgesetz vom 5. August 1971," BGBl. I, p. 1237.

[386] First regulated through the "Berlinhilfegesetz vom 7. März 1950," BGBl., p. 41.

[387] "Antwort der Bundesregierung auf die Große Anfrage zur sektoralen Strukturpolitik" BTDrs. 8/1607.

very broad in scope. The programs in favor of agriculture, which became massive in scope early on,[388] were joined by subsidies for mining, the steel industry, ship building, and fishery.[389] Added to these was a large number of programs that were intended to moderate or compensate for social inequalities, not by way of regional or economic-sectoral equalization, but directly: group-based programs for expellees, resettlers, ethnic German emigrants, need-based programs, for example to improve the supply of housing, programs of wealth formation, programs to improve social services, and so on. In part they merely quantified statutory directives. In part, however, they complemented and replaced one another.[390]

7.3.7 Social Benefits Systems: Overarching Aspects[391]

Quantitative Social Policy – Qualitative Social Policy – Social Policy Through Law and Money

Alongside the development of working conditions and the influence of workers on the economy and the polity, the improvement and multiplication of social benefits was one of the hallmarks of the period. The expenditures devoted to social benefits have become *the* criterion of what the social state is. That applies internally: the federal government's social reporting identifies primarily the "costs" and not the effects; and during elections, the input (what the system costs) and the output (what is paid out) of the social benefits systems becomes a prominent argument. It also applies externally: welfare states now compared each other (and do so until this day) by the share of their domestic product devoted to social expenditures (e.g. Alber 1989; 1999). It is a time of *quantitative* social policy. However, that could not suffice for a policy of "quality of life." Quantitative social policy required a counterpart: a qualitative social policy was recognized as a necessary "added value". This was accommodated by the development of "*social indicators*". As yardsticks of human welfare (Zapf 1972, pp. 267–279; Zacher 1974, pp. 15–51; R. Werner 1975) they were to add to the quantitative tool kit of statistics and budget calculations a set of tools with a qualitative orientation.

Nevertheless, the *juridification* and *monetarization* of social benefits proceeded. The law remained the central medium for the regulation of social benefits. By comparison, the attractiveness of service-providing, pedagogical, and environment-shaping intervention lagged behind.[392] It remained poorly developed. Its political

---

[388] On the Agrarian Reports see notes 255 and 356.

[389] See the Subsidies Reports (note 384) and the reports in note 302.

[390] On the state of affairs before the new regulations see note 308 above.

[391] Bundesministerium für Arbeit und Soziales and Bundesarchiv (eds.): Geschichte der Sozialpolitik in Deutschland seit 1945, vols. 5 (2006a) and 6 (2008a), Chap. 3, no. 4 in each.

[392] Bundesministerium für Arbeit und Soziales and Bundesarchiv (eds.): Geschichte der Sozialpolitik in Deutschland seit 1945, vols. 5 (2006a) and 6 (2008a), Chap. 3, no. 15 in each.

perception was less socio-political and more "politically oriented" in nature. Left-Right models, progressive-conservative polarizations, and the like shaped the discussion at the time. Still, the liberal, emancipatory trait of the period did introduce a new element also in the area of social benefits, especially in social services. Those affected developed new methods of *collective self-help* (self-help groups), which gave expression to their status as subjects and provided an ever more diverse and effective supplement to the system of social services (Moeller 1980, p. 655f., 2nd ed. 1986, p. 732f.; Kraft 1986, p. 26f.).

An Exposition of the System as a Whole

The benefits systems had been growing since the beginning of the Federal Republic. In terms of their history, however, the various systems led separate lives. Their institutions had a significantly different management, very specific bureaucracies, an extremely varied associational embeddedness, and a unique "clientele" each. Even the scholarly study ran along separate tracks – in the social sciences as well as jurisprudence. The science of social insurance was pursued by different individuals than the science of public welfare or youth services. And there was no science of social compensation law or of the new subsidies and promotion programs. But the denser the web of social services had become, the more the totality of social services concerned potentially everyone. Society was being ever more intensively pervaded by the totality of social benefits. Accordingly, its success depended increasingly on the total effect of social benefits. The shortcomings in their coordination were becoming an irritant. Science and scholarship began to address this problem.[393]

The Codification of Social Benefits Law

The key contribution that politics and jurisprudence could make to an overall account of social benefits law was a codification of social benefits law. Hence, the desideratum of a codification had accompanied the development of the social benefits systems from 1949 on (Hockerts 1980, esp. pp. 195–299). The Brandt era set out to tackle the problem.[394] A commission created the concept for the *Social Code*. Book One, "*General part*," appeared in 1975. The first Chapter of Book Four, "*Joint provisions for social insurance*" was enacted in 1976.[395] Book Ten followed in 1980/1982: "*Administrative procedures, protection of social data, cooperation of*

[393] Gitter (1969); Möglichkeiten und Grenzen der Vereinfachung und Vereinheitlichung des Sozialversicherungsrechts (1970); Über- und Unterversorgung in der Alterssicherung (1979); Empfiehlt es sich, die Voraussetzungen für Sozialleistungen an leistungsgeminderte Personen zur Herstellung der Nahtlosigkeit neu zu regeln? (1980).

[394] On the background and development see 25 Jahre Sozialgesetzbuch – Anspruch und Wirklichkeit (1995).

[395] Later turned into Book Four.

benefit providers and their relationships to third parties." Then came a long break. The codification was continued only *6 years later*: with Book Five, "*Sickness insurance*" (1988), Book Six, "*Pension insurance*" (1989), Book Eight, "*Child and youth services law*" (1990), Book Eleven, "*Long-term nursing care*" (1994), Book Seven, "*Accident insurance*" (1996), and Book Three, "*Employment promotion*" (1997). The fate of the originally included topics of training assistance, the law concerning the severely disabled, social compensation, child allowance, child-raising allowance, housing allowance, social assistance, and the repeatedly called for book on disability law is currently uncertain.

The codification *enshrined* the *traditional institutions* of social benefits law. The attempt to use the codification for a completely new beginning in shaping social benefits law would have caused the undertaking to fail. The critical political and social forces – especially the carriers that administered the various benefits systems, and their associations – were not willing to call the traditional structures of social benefits law into question. The central guideline of the codification was thus: "Codification with limited substantive reform." But even within these parameters, the *codification was not comprehensive*. It *excluded the following: private-law solutions* (e.g. work-based pensions), *internalizing solutions* (both internalizing solutions in which social problems are directly settled between private individuals, as in labor law (excluding the law on the severely disabled), private housing law, consumer protection law, regulations of nursing homes and homes for the elderly, etc., as well as internalizing solutions of a public-law nature that combined situations of administrative and service law with regulations of social protection, as in civil service law, judge-made law, and soldier's law, as well as in pension law for ministers and parliamentarians), *regulations* that were regarded as *historically unique* (such as the Law on the Equalization of Burdens or the Law on Compensation for National Socialist Injustice), *social law regulated by the Länder* (especially the law of professional pension systems for the free professions), but also the *law of judicial procedures* (as regulated in the Administrative Court Procedures Code and in the Social Courts Act).

The codification began with "*social rights*" (Sects. 1–10 of Book One). With these "social rights" the legislature was quite obviously trying to respond to the desire at the time of adding a catalog of "social rights" to the fundamental rights of the Basic Law. In reality, of course, the social rights merely carried on the traditional institutions of the social benefits law. That is not the case for Sect. 1 of Book One, which attempted an *independent concretization of the principle of the social state* with respect to social benefits law:

> (1) The law of the Social Code shall, for the purpose of realizing social justice and social security, design social benefits inclusive of social and educational assistance. It shall contribute to:
> - securing a dignified existence.
> - creating equal prerequisites for the free development of one's personality, especially also for young people,
> - protecting and promoting the family,
> - making it possible to earn a living through freely chosen work,
> - averting or compensating for special burdens of life, also through assistance for self-help.

(2) The law of the Social Code shall also contribute to making sure that the social services and institutions necessary to fulfill the tasks listed in Sect. 1 are available in a timely and sufficient manner.

The "social rights" in Sects. 3–10 of Book One, on the other hand, must be described as a *triumph of the institutionalism of German social policy*. All the "social rights" laid down there say is that there is a right to the rights accorded in the traditional institutions of social benefits law incorporated into the Social Code. The best example is the "right to social security" (Sect. 4):

(1) Within the framework of this Code, everyone has a right of access to social security.

(2) Anyone who is insured in social security has a right, within the framework of the statutory sickness, accident, and pension insurance, including old age assistance for farmers, to

1. the necessary measures to protect, preserve, improve, and restore health and the ability to produce

and

2. economic security in case of sickness, maternity, reduction of earnings capacity and old age.

The surviving dependants of the insured person also have a right to economic security.[396]

To avoid any misunderstanding that these "rights" were only references to established rights, they were preceded by the statement that "entitlements can be asserted or derived from them only to the extent that their prerequisites and content are determined in detail through the stipulations in the special parts of this Code" (Sect. 2, Para. 1, Sent. 2, SGB I).

If the "social rights" could hardly live up to their claims, the *Social Code* as a whole did take on *great importance for allowing the included areas of social benefits to coalesce into a functional unity*. While it consolidated the traditional institutions, it did substantially improve the overall effectiveness of the social benefits systems. And it did not stand in the way of reforms that essentially followed the lines of demarcation of the traditional institutions.

Regulations for the Disabled[397]

Even independent of the Social Code, functional commonalities were brought to bear across institutional boundaries during this time. More precisely: while the overall system remained "historically" grounded thanks to its institutional bonds –

[396] The long-term care insurance was later inserted in Sect. 2.

[397] Schulin (1980); Die soziale Sicherung der Behinderten (1981); Bundesministerium für Arbeit und Soziales and Bundesarchiv (eds.): Geschichte der Sozialpolitik in Deutschland seit 1945, vols. 5 (2006a) and 6 (2008a), Chap. 3, no. 8 in each.

sickness, pension, and unemployment insurance in a “history of provision”; accident insurance and social compensation in a “history of responsibility”; assistance and promotion systems in one situation – definitive, common elements now pushed to the fore. The most important example is the *Law on the Adjustment of Rehabilitation Benefits* (1974), which introduced a comprehensive coordination of the measures and benefits for the integration of physically, mentally, and emotionally handicapped individuals through essentially all areas of benefits – with the exception of welfare. In spite of the program spelled out in Sects. 10 and 29 of Book One of the Social Code, which seemed to point in this direction, a further integration of disability law did not take place. But one should at least mention the *Law on Nursing Homes and Homes for the Elderly* (1974), which sought to guarantee minimum standards in an important area of social services. Politics declined to effect a comprehensive regulation of situations involving care-giving.[398]

7.3.8 Needs

Beginning with the currency reform, and in the wake of rationing and price controls on the one hand, and the invigoration of the economy on the other, the meeting of needs had been entrusted increasingly to the development of individual income. Over the course of time, however, there arose a new necessity for the social state to address the meeting of needs. The primary instrument now was externalized social benefits systems. An important step had already been taken with the Federal Social Welfare Law in 1961. Its “assistance in special life situations” (Para. 3 [Sects. 27–75] BSHG) guaranteed – under the premise of the subsidiarity essential to social assistance – the meeting of a number of needs for indigent persons: especially needs of medical care, special needs of the disabled and elderly, and the need for nursing care. However, *internalizing interventions* also proved indispensable.

With respect to *consumer protection*,[399] new private-law solutions were found beyond the Law on Nursing Homes and Homes for the Elderly: the Law Governing Standard Business Conditions of 1976.

A particular concern at the time was the promotion of *child-rearing, education, training, and continuing education*.[400] The measures developed into a rich ensemble. On the one side, it was primarily a matter of the *Länder* to provide free access (free education, free learning materials, complete coverage or reduction of public transportation costs to get to school, exemption from university fees). On the other side, the subject-oriented promotion systems of *training grants* and *post-graduate*

[398] Debates at the 52nd Congress of German Lawyers on the theme “Empfiehlt es sich, soziale Pflege- und Betreuungsverhältnisse gesetzlich zu regeln?” in: Verhandlungen des 52. Deutschen Juristentages (1978a).

[399] “Berichte der Bundesregierung zur Verbraucherpolitik” BTDrs. VI/2724, 7/418.

[400] Bundesministerium für Arbeit und Soziales and Bundesarchiv (eds.): Geschichte der Sozialpolitik in Deutschland seit 1945, vols. 5 (2006a) and 6 (2008a), Chap. 3, no. 11 in each.

subsidies were now added. A substantial contribution also came from the *Employment Promotion Act*, which promoted qualifications for working and professional life through subject-oriented and institutional benefits.

In the area of *medical care*,[401] the subject-oriented methods of sickness insurance and social welfare were no longer sufficient to guarantee the adequacy of the offerings. It was therefore an important innovation that securing the economic condition of *hospitals*, including the regulation of hospital rates, was taken over by a comprehensive state responsibility (Hospital Financing Act of 1972, Federal Hospital Charges Regulation of 1973).

The most diverse set of tools continued to belong to the need for *housing*.[402] Lively political and legislative activity prevailed in all areas of the housing sector. Of continuing importance was the role that internalizing solutions played once again: the Law to Improve Tenancy Law and Limit Rent Increases and the Law on Protection Against Termination of Rental Agreements for Living Space (1971). In 1974, the Law on Protection Against Termination was incorporated into the Civil Code as a permanent law.

7.3.9 Taxes and Dues, a Comprehensive View of Transfer Payments

Tax policy was employed only sporadically with a specific socio-political intent (Muscheid 1986, pp. 67–199; Frerich and Frey, vol. 3, 1996, pp. 142–151, 401–409). The most important examples are the measures to promote housing construction and wealth formation, as well as the broad removal of the income tax from the dual system of family equalization (1974). But there were many changes in individual areas (e.g. to provide relief for the disabled, to promote work-based pension insurance, and so on). The importance of tax law – and beyond that of the entire fiscal code (Hansmeyer 1983) – for the social state (Schmähl 1982, pp. 251–296) was much more evident in financing requirements.[403] The growth of the social budget hit a sensational and all-time high in 1957 at 23.1%, but it quickly returned to normal. From 1960 to 1969 it fluctuated between 74% and 11%; from 1970 to 1975 it hovered between 13% and 15%; beginning in 1976 it dropped below 10%, and thereafter it varied between 8.2% (1980) and 3.4% (1982). The "crisis of the social state" had begun. While social benefits law was involved chiefly through cuts to benefits, the part played by tax law was complex. The repeal or reduction of social tax breaks was joined by a variety of other changes.

---

[401] "Gesundheitsbericht", BTDrs. VI/1667; Soziale Sicherung und medizinische Dienste (1971); Arzt und Gesellschaft (1977); Bundesministerium für Arbeit und Soziales and Bundesarchiv (eds.): Geschichte der Sozialpolitik in Deutschland seit 1945, vols. 5 (2006a) and 6 (2008a), Chap. 3, no. 6 in each.

[402] Bundesministerium für Arbeit und Soziales and Bundesarchiv (eds.): Geschichte der Sozialpolitik in Deutschland seit 1945, vols. 5 (2006a) and 6 (2008a), Chap. 3, no. 15 in each.

[403] Albers and Dreissig (vols. 1–5, 1974–1977); Hansmeyer (1983).

Together with the growing *need to* grasp the *social benefits systems as a single entity*, to allow them to exert their effects and critically evaluate them as such an entity (Pfaff 1983), the *taxation of income and social benefits* was now increasingly included in the examination. One attempt at a comprehensive analysis was the appointment of an Expert Commission to Determine the Influence of State Transfer Payments on the Disposable Income of Private Households (Transfer Inquiry Commission).[404] The effects of this investigation were slight. The more comprehensively the existing social benefits systems *and* tax breaks were presented and compared, the more the results lost their clarity. By contrast, the individual vested rights could be readily perceived. Once again, and even more interesting, is the *resistance here that is linked to a highly differentiated institutionalization.*

One important example is the *taxation of pensions and annuities.*[405] Every reform alters the conditions governing the level, distribution, and taxation of pension expenditures. Every reform alters the net level of benefits and thus the real effect of the system of provision. Every reform alters the relationship between the individual expenses for provision and the individual benefits from the system. Every reform of *one* system must be set against the existing and future taxation of pension expenses *for all other* systems of old-age protection and of the benefits *from all other* systems of old-age protection. But not only that. The problems enter into the details in other ways, as well. Let us take the example of pension insurance. Assuming pensions are taxed like other income, to what degree would pensions have to be raised so that they would achieve their socio-political purpose also in the future? Would the pension insurance be responsible for this increase, while taxes flowed to the federal government and the states? Should a withholding tax be levied, as with the payroll tax? Would it be justified to have pension insurance bear the cost of the withholding process? In the face of all of these problems, a reform of the taxation of pension systems has not happened to date. With that, not only has the taxable portion of benefits from pension insurance been retained, but retirees still have the opportunity not to pay any tax at all. Pension insurance schemes are under no obligation to deduct a withholding tax. But they do not even inform the pension recipients that they themselves are responsible for the tax on their pension as part of their income tax statement. Thus, pensioners have not only been left with a "cheap" way of taxation, but also with the presumption of innocence if they do not pay even this tax.

7.4 Summary

For the history of the social state in the Federal Republic of Germany, the period under discussion (Grube and Richter 1977; Standfest 1979) is something like the middle section of a classic drama: rise, climax and reversal. That is not to say it is

[404] See Transfer-Enquete-Kommission (1979; 1981), and Heilmann (1976).

[405] Sachverständigenkommission Alterssicherungssysteme (1983a, vol. 1, pp. 140–177 (161–176)); Littmann (1983, note 364), in ibid., vol. 2; Bundesministerium der Finanzen (1986); Birk (1987).

the middle section of a tragedy. The constitutional structures that carry the social state have proven capable of dealing with the reversal – of giving the social state a future also after the climax. Needless to say, though, many continue to wonder and ask why the high point did not become a permanent plateau. Or if that is not possible: why politics did not return to the high point quickly. We need not look into these questions in connection with this analysis of social policy in Germany. Instead, I will ask here how this period fulfilled the normative mandate of the social. Let me give this general answer: it exhausted the multiplicity of what the social can be in a special way. At the high point it became clear that the coincidence of fulfillment had its limitations. In the turnaround phase the competition among the various dimensions of the social gave rise to conflicts, or at least tensions, criticism, and open questions.

The elementary social mandate of *equality* certainly guided this period in a special way. But this aspiration of equality was not directed so much at a differentiation toward a social "bottom". The ideal of the time was to neutralize the danger of the "bottom" through the dynamism of the "normality of the middle". But the demarcation against a social "top" was also not a major concern of the period. Many more were doing much better all the time, why should not even more do better? That view reconciled equality with *freedom* to a special degree. But the fact that this differentiation toward the top was not only left to personal achievement, but was also secured through legal regulation and social benefits, became a problem. This became most evident in labor law, whose protection was completely uncoupled from differences in prosperity among those it covered and the differences in prosperity between the protected and their employers. And the radical distinction between the inequality of income, which the social state took note of, and the inequality of wealth, to which it paid only marginal attention, was part of this context. Still other aspects were evident in the provisioning systems. Because ever broader and better-earning circles were incorporated into social insurance, it was becoming more and more obvious that its cost-benefit ratio – to say the least – was not reliably more favorable toward the "bottom" and less favorable toward the "top."

But *equality* also became problematic in the sense that it spread *freedom*. To be sure, the purpose of social intervention oriented toward equality is to generalize freedom – to provide ever more people access to the same spheres of freedom. Yet the consensus about this weakens when the issue revolves around the use of that freedom – especially also where the issue is who will bear the risk of freedom. The more and the more quickly freedom spread, the more the discomfort grew about how it was being used "at the expense of" and "to the disadvantage" of others. Doubts arose: What was just, what was merely unconsidered? What was use and what was abuse?

Social *participation* was also mediated to an optimum degree at this time. The oldest form of participation mediated by social policy, the guarantee of the subsistence minimum, was already assured – chiefly in the form of social welfare. During a time of full employment, the participation in industrial society that was linked to the resolution of the "workers' question" experienced a historically unique realization – not only in the employment relationship, but also in the social benefits systems that pervaded and surrounded the working life and in the forms of participation in the workplace, the enterprise, and public life. What that period added in particular was participation in society's opportunities for prosperity, as they were opened up especially by the special assistance and promotion systems, but also by other arrangements for meeting needs. Why, then, the turnaround? On the one hand, no doubt, because these systems and arrangements were not set up to respond to sharp declines in economic growth. On the other hand, because these arrangements overextend themselves if they impair the guiding effect of individual responsibility. Participation must be borne primarily by personal contributions and performance. That is an essential part of the meaning of the basic formula. Only as long as this remains a matter of course can the social arrangements that surround personal responsibility bring about what they are intended to: lessening the dangers that threaten the person who has embarked upon this path. In other words: participation must be primarily a matter of distribution and only secondarily a matter of redistribution. The fact that this was no longer a certainty was one source of the irritation that led to the turnaround.

The social principle of *solidarity* was a principle at this time only in a very broad, macrocosmic sense. The society constituted in the polity was as such in a state of solidarity with its weaker members. But *vertical solidarity* – the solidarity of the stronger with the weaker, the richer with the poorer – had ceased for the general public to be the individual achievement of each person. The principle of an equality "open toward the top" included that "solidarity toward the bottom" by society at large should not create a personal burden. The contribution that every person had to make to this solidarity was neutralized: broad paths of redistribution separated those who gave from those who received. And nothing guaranteed an appropriate relationship between the capacity to give and the share of what was given. Of course, real and direct solidarity existed also during this period. But that was a matter either of those who – as social workers, care-givers, and so on – provided this solidarity as employees of the relevant institutions, or of altruistic individuals who fell between the cracks of the workers' society – those, precisely, who did not engage in altruistic work for a living and therefore not only earned nothing from it, but also failed to acquire any social security by doing so. But even those who practiced direct solidarity professionally found themselves increasingly in a difficult situation (and still do so today). I am referring chiefly to all care providers. Those who provide care do not assert their interests in the same way as those who engage in some other form of work. Society and the state rely on this inner commitment of the caregiver to his or her work. Aside from vertical solidarity, there is *horizontal solidarity*: the solidarity of the "normal person" threatened by the typical risks of life with the other "normal people" affected by these typical risks. This solidarity among the "normal" is the typical solidarity of social insurance. The inequality it addressed was a very specific one: the inequality between the normally healthy with the sick, between the active and the elderly, between those with a job and those who have been unemployed for not too long.

The principle of *security* fit this period in a special way. Not even the "crisis" called into question the security expected from the social systems. At most overall economic developments pointed to the limits of security, and here especially inflation. Of course, insecurity was directly experienced where individuals were affected by unemployment. Thus, security, too, started to get caught up within the grinder of the turnabout.

Subsidiarity was given a special emphasis during this time. Subsidiarity could be experienced as an entitlement. In the interplay of protection against outside control and the differentiated systems of social security and social protection, individuals could experience spheres of freedom that might be understood as subsidiarity of the general vis-à-vis the freedom of the individual: the individual could trust that a general body would act on his behalf if his freedom was inadequate to solve his problems, even if the use of his freedom had caused these problems in the first place. But the subsidiarity that makes the general public intervene *only* when the individual has reached his limits was relativized. The equality-creating diffusion of freedom limited freedom. That is *not* the case in the same way for *families*. The autonomy and the self-preferentiality of the family remained largely untouched. Of course, the inner life of the family was altered from the outside in a peculiar way. While courts and the legislature expanded the self-determination rights of children vis-à-vis their parents, the parental obligation to maintain their children was extended well into the age of majority (Zacher 1989b, p. 293 f., pp. 296–302). In the enthusiasm for emancipation characteristic of that time, the representatives of a society with fewer and fewer children burdened the parents who still had children with ever new obligations. A very different sphere in which there was and is much talk of "subsidiarity" is the area of "public welfare" – of *services* especially in connection with social assistance and child and youth services. At issue are the already mentioned reservations that favor societal forces undertaking tasks that would otherwise have to be done by municipal or state agencies or providers. "Subsidiarity" is here a name for "plurality." This plurality of social services was preserved, and it acquired some new emphases.

Finally, there is this question: Did this period succeed in *integrating society*? This is a particularly difficult question. This was a time of great political antagonisms: the movement of 1968, clashes over emergency laws, terrorism, and a time also of a powerful extra-parliamentary peace movement. That, however, was the problem of a more general *political integration* of society. *Social integration* had the task of overcoming the doubts as to whether this polity was distributing its prosperity correctly. The Grand Coalition sought to provide clarification. But only the Brandt era answered the need for new, attractive models. Yet its politics increased both the approval of some and the opposition – or at least the reluctance – of others. The *set of goals of prosperity, freedom, security, equality, and protection against hardship* remained unchallenged normatively and in real terms. But there was growing dissent about the meaning of the various goals and their ranking by priority. At its high point, this dissent could take on the form of confrontation. In the phase of the turnabout, the constellation of approval, rejection, and doubt became more diverse. The differences of opinion focused on how society was to move forward: on how the various tracks on which the goals were moving forward should relate to one another. Yet the consensus about the set of goals remained intact.

8 1982–1990: The Administration of the Crisis, New Solutions for the Future, and the Agglomeration of Frictions

8.1 The Political Premises[406]

Helmut Kohl, elected Chancellor through a constructive vote of no confidence without new *Bundestag* elections, formed his first cabinet in 1982. His government was based on a coalition between the CDU/CSU and the FDP. In his *inaugural address* on 13 October 1982 (Presse- und Informationsamt der Bundesregierung 1981, pp. 561–582), the Chancellor announced an emergency program whose first points were: "Creating new jobs" and "securing the social net." The steps that were announced to create new jobs concerned economic policy. At the end, though, the Chancellor transitioned to social policy:

> All in all, with this emergency program we are setting the course for renewal:
> – away from more state, toward more free market,
> – away from collective burdens, toward personal performance,
> – away from fossilized structures, toward more flexibility, individual initiative, and greater competitiveness.

Kohl then went on to speak specifically about "securing the social net":

> This policy of renewal is the only promising path to consolidate also the financial foundations of our social net. To that end, we must ask our fellow citizens to make sacrifices. For that we need their willingness for solidarity. This solidarity demands a pause in social policy. What needs to be asked of pensioners, welfare recipients, civil servants, and others, must apply to all.

This was followed by the announcement of a reduction in benefits levels and a suspension of the expected improvements in the area of pension insurance, care for war victims, unemployment insurance, sickness insurance, and so on. The talk was of "flexibility in work life," but also of the "participation of broad segments in the necessary wealth formation in the economy."

Kohl's address devoted a separate section to subsidiarity:

> [T]he economic problems are grave, and they demand all our strength. But many people are still suffering from poverty today; they suffer from loneliness, a lack of a feeling of safety, a lack of humanity. They lack goods they cannot buy in the free market and most definitely cannot receive from the state... The free market economy is a necessary but not sufficient condition for a free, happy, prosperous, just, and well-ordered society... The final fate of the free market economy will be decided beyond supply and demand....

[406] Stern (2000, pp. 1535–1579); Bundesministerium für Gesundheit und Soziale Sicherung and Bundesarchiv (eds.), 2005: Geschichte der Sozialpolitik in Deutschland seit 1945, vol. 7, Chap. 1.

> Family, neighborhood, charitable organizations, initiative and self-help groups, and social services can create more civic feeling and civic responsibility than large and anonymous institution will ever be able to.
>
> Our social policy will help wherever it is possible to awaken, build up, and maintain voluntary social initiatives by citizens.

Further comments concerned youth and family, and not least also the difficulties that women faced in combining family and work.

In December 1982, Chancellor Kohl asked for a vote of confidence. Since nearly all delegates of the governing coalition abstained, he lost the vote. At the suggestion of the Chancellor, the President dissolved the *Bundestag* on 7 January 1983, and scheduled new elections for 6 March 1983. The CDU conducted the campaign with the following slogans (Toman-Banke 1994, p. 53f.): "Unemployment, debt, bankruptcies/Never again SPD!/Jobs, peace, future/Together we can/CDU/Secure/ Social and free." And the CSU added: "Hope for Germany/CSU/Both votes," and "A ray of hope/6 March/CSU." The FDP had to wrestle with another about-face, this time from partnership with the SPD to partnership with the CDU/CSU: "Freedom requires courage/Therefore FDP/The Liberals." The SPD was laconic: "SPD/In Germany's interest." It personalized the contest: "Germany once again needs a chancellor who can do it. Hans-Jochen Vogel." The SPD and the FDP emerged from the elections for the *Tenth German Bundestag* weaker, while the CDU/CSU became stronger (Ritter and Niehuss 1991, p. 102). *Helmut Kohl* formed his *second cabinet*, which was based once again on a coalition of the CDU/CSU and the FDP. In his *inaugural address* on 4 May 1983 (Presse- und Informationsamt der Bundesregierung (1983, pp. 611–637), the Chancellor articulated seven key ideas:

> I. Personal freedom and meaningful work, prosperity for all and social safety can be achieved with the spirit and productivity of the social free market economy.
>
> II. We want a society with a human face. Mutual humanity is the civic spirit in action... That is why we encourage our citizens to ask not only, 'Who is helping me?', but also, 'Whom am I helping?'....
>
> III. We want a modern society. We can manage the social and technological transformation of our time only as a productive industrial society....
>
> IV. We are returning the state to the core of its tasks, so that it may truly fulfill them in a reliable manner. Entitlements cannot grow more than the productivity and productive motivation of the citizens. He who has rights also has obligations.

Essentially, Chancellor Kohl was announcing the continuation of his policy – which comes as no surprise only 6 months after forming his first government.

The *Eleventh German Bundestag* was elected on 25 January 1987. During the campaign (Toman-Banke 1994, p. 54; Gruner 1990, pp. 80–95) the CDU asked for the renewal of its mandate: "Keep it up, Germany/CDU/The Future." The CSU emphasized its dual role in Bavaria and on the federal level: "Thanks/Your trust is our mandate for Bavaria and Germany/CSU." The FDP struck a performance-oriented tone: "The future through achievement." The SPD articulated more concrete problems: "So our children might live: Get tough on environmental polluters/ SPD," or "SPD/Majority for fair taxes." But it also had more general slogans: "So justice might govern, not social coldness."

The elections left the CDU/CSU and SPD weaker, the FDP and The Greens stronger (Ritter and Niehuss 1991, p. 102). However, the CDU/CSU and the FDP were able to continue their coalition. *Helmut Kohl* formed his *third cabinet*. In contrast to its predecessors, the inaugural address on 18 March 1987 (Presse- und Infomationsamt der Bundesregierung, 1987, pp. 773–795) broke with crisis management. With new clarity it addressed ecological tasks. Social policy was dominated by continuity. Under the heading "A productive economy makes possible social stability and practical solidarity with the weaker members in our society," the address stated, among other things:

> We want to preserve the high performance standard of medical care in our country. For all these reasons we need a general overhaul of the social sickness insurance with the goal of greater efficiency with justifiable contribution rates. A comprehensive structural reform in the health care system will be initiated without delay. . . .
>
> A special task for society as a whole is social protection for those in need of nursing care, which, given the manifold problems and the great financial dimensions, can be solved only gradually. . . .
>
> Our pension insurance, as it has existed since the reform under Konrad Adenauer, remains the core of our social protection. The citizens of the Federal Republic of Germany can trust that in old age they will receive an adequate pension in return for the contributions they have paid throughout their working lives. The pension is and remains safe.
>
> The child-raising periods in pension law will be gradually extended also to older mothers. . . .
>
> The demographic development makes a structural reform of pensions unavoidable. As we see it, pensions and available worker incomes shall develop with equal weight. The insurance periods that are exempt from contributions or have reduced contributions will be newly regulated. . . The federal government will submit a draft for a structural reform of pension insurance by the beginning of 1988.

A special emphasis was placed on agriculture: "Heimat should be tangible, and especially the rural areas must have a future."

8.2 *The Climate of Social Policy*[407]

8.2.1 The Time of the Big Change

The events of 1982/1983 now placed the political seal on a change that had already been under way since the middle of the 1970s. If the years before had been a time of an impetuous departure, the years since have been more like a time of compromise between ideal and reality. Hence it also had to be a time of uncertainty and dissent. It was a time of a growing, and frequently also productive political perception of social changes (Opielka and Ostner 1987). Where the Brandt era had believed that

[407] Bundesministerium für Gesundheit und Soziale Sicherung and Bundesarchiv (eds.), 2005: Geschichte der Sozialpolitik in Deutschland seit 1945, vol. 7, Chap. 2.

social change could and should be a goal – or at least a subject – of politics, this social change had now long since become *independent*. In part the social state had triggered this *social change*; and that change now reverberated back upon the social state as one of the causes of its "crisis." In part, the developments had taken place also independently of the special conditions and effects of the social state (Lutz 1987). But they contributed no less to its "crisis." The full magnitude of the changes would only become clear in the 1990s, *after* German reunification had brought a broad and deep front of new challenges to social policy, and *after* the collapse of Communism gave globalization – which had been looming economically and technologically for quite some time – free rein around the world. The time under examination here could anticipate neither German unification and its economic and social consequences, nor the dimension that globalization assumed after the Iron Curtain had come down nearly everywhere in the world. But the changes in society had become impossible to overlook. And they had repercussions for the social state.

When the political turnaround came, the disquieting symptoms had already persisted for some time. Although economic growth, which had crashed to nearly zero in the middle of the 1970s, had recovered robustly during the second half of the decade, between 1980 and 1982 it once again hovered around zero and then continued at an unstable and modest level. Only in 1989/1990 did it rise again markedly (Bundesministerium für Wirtschaft 1982, 1988, 1989, 1990). This was accompanied by a rate of inflation unknown since the period around 1950. The rise in prices had already begun in the early 1970s, had peaked in 1974 at 7%, declined, but then hovered once again between 5.2% and 6.3% from 1980 to 1982. The unemployment rate had increased only moderately in the 1970s, from 0.7% (1970) to 4.7% (1975). It became the terror of the 1980s: 9% and more from 1983 to 1986. Only toward the end of the decade was there some kind of recovery down to 7.2% in 1990. All reasons enough to be worried.

Although this was not the dominant pattern of perception and discussion at the time, in retrospect one can say that *the basic formula of work, income, the meeting of needs, and maintenance lost its guiding force*. In due course, demands for a general minimum income (Miegel and Wahl 1985; Opielka and Vobruba 1986; Klanberg and Prinz 1988) funded from tax revenues would demonstrate that the growing challenge to the basic formula would be the most comprehensive element of the problem.

8.2.2 Challenges of the Time

Changes in Work

Dependent gainful employment had run into difficulties. Over the course of the 1960s and 1970s, the *normal employment relationship* had continued to take on implications of participation in prosperity, equality, freedom, and security. With that, it became increasingly attractive for an ever growing part of the adult population. At the same time, *the demand* for work performance organized in this way declined. In a world that was becoming increasingly technological and scientific, capital, knowledge, and management were becoming relatively more important to earnings and profits than the factor "labor." In addition, the effects from international competition were accumulating – though by no means on the scale that would become apparent from 1989/1990 on. Thus, the reasons for the decline in the demand for *dependent* work were becoming more and more complex. Economic reasons were joined by structural reasons. Moreover, the growth in the supply of dependent labor continued. The paradigm of full employment was being increasingly called into question. The demand for dependent labor was focused on workers considered optimal – in terms of their qualifications and productiveness, their age, place of residence, and so on.

At any rate: if the first piece of the basic formula had been interpreted since the 1960s such that everyone had the possibility – and thus also the responsibility – to earn an income from *dependent* work, this was no longer self-evident. The contradiction between the general development of the economy and the negative development of unemployment could have suggested that in addition to dependent work, *other forms of gainful employment* – especially self-employed work – should be brought to bear once again. However, this correlation was only drawn occasionally and very gradually. The alternative between gainful employment and *unpaid work* – domestic work, charitable work, societal and community work – was more clearly articulated. With respect to domestic work, the legislature set out again to counteract its disadvantages in social law.[408] That was not the case for charitable, societal, and community-based unpaid work.

The changes were clearer, at any rate, in dependent work (Veränderungen in der Arbeitswelt und soziale Sicherung 1986). Essential elements of the normal employment relationship from which social policy had previously proceeded – in particular, a lifetime of work stretching from the completion of education and training until retirement – were losing their validity (Mückenberger 1985, pp. 415–434, 457–475). Moreover, the manifestations of an open or hidden *shift of work or unemployment* into the social benefits systems were increasing: into passive employment policy (short-term work subsidy), into active employment policy (assistance for qualifications, assistance for employment),[409] into social protection (disability or "early retirement"),[410] into social welfare.[411] Likewise, there were increasing attempts to deviate from the typology of labor and social insurance law (ostensible self-employment), but above all – and for a long time already – a

[408] Bundesministerium für Gesundheit und Soziale Sicherung and Bundesarchiv (eds.), 2005: Geschichte der Sozialpolitik in Deutschland seit 1945, vol. 7, Chap. 3, nos. 5 and 10.

[409] Bundesministerium für Gesundheit und Soziale Sicherung and Bundesarchiv (eds.), 2005: Geschichte der Sozialpolitik in Deutschland seit 1945, vol. 7, Chap. 3, no. 3.

[410] Bundesministerium für Gesundheit und Soziale Sicherung and Bundesarchiv (eds.), 2005: Geschichte der Sozialpolitik in Deutschland seit 1945, vol. 7, Chap. 3, no. 5.

[411] Bundesministerium für Gesundheit und Soziale Sicherung and Bundesarchiv (eds.), 2005: Geschichte der Sozialpolitik in Deutschland seit 1945, vol. 7, Chap. 3, no. 9.

breaking away also from economic law and especially tax law (moonlighting, shadow economy) (Cyprian 1984; Schwarze 1990; Werner 1990).

Demography

Another development concerned population structures. While *rising life expectancy* was a familiar trend already in the 1960s, the late 1960s and 1970s added the experience of a general *decline in the birthrate* and thus the prospect of a continuously growing imbalance in the generations.[412] Family structures, in particular, were changing. The focus on the two-generation household had become the norm and was being overtaken more and more by the trend toward a single-generation household. *Marriages* had become less stable, and non-marital life partnerships were increasingly competing with marriage. *Marriage and family* were drifting apart in multiple ways. In this way, "the ground was cut from under" social protection which – like pension insurance, old-age, and survivor insurance – was built on the typology of long-term life situations.[413] On the other hand, there was growing unease that provision for old age did not sufficiently take into account the family burden of those who have and raise children, even though it is they who provide the future contributors for the old-age security. This was felt to be all the more disconcerting the weaker the willingness was to have children, and the more burdensome it seemed to forego an income and a separate social security in favor of raising children (Schmidt 1988).

Equality of Men and Women

Closely connected to this is the problem of the *equal treatment of men and women* (Weg 1988, pp. 677–687; Buhr et al. 1988, pp. 655–658; Hohmann-Dennhardt 1988, pp. 673–677). In labor law, opinions on what was to be done diverged sharply (Frerich and Frey, vol. 3, 1996, pp. 206–211). In social benefits law, a good deal had already been done to bring about equality. But in contrast to labor law, where the issue was "simply" the equal treatment of men and women, social benefits law revealed more and more that the equal treatment of men and women was the smaller problem, in terms of regulatory technique, compared to the equal treatment of women amongst themselves: of working women, full-time housewives, child-raising mothers, women who provided nursing care at home, women who assumed only one of these roles, women who combined two or more of these roles. Of course these conflicts were not simply women's problems. Men, too, could be affected by

[412] Bundesminister für Jugend, Familie und Gesundheit (1978, 1979); Bundesministerium für Wirtschaft (1973–1986; "Der Wissenschaftlicher Beirat. . ."); "Bericht über die Bevölkerungsentwicklung in der Bundesrepublik Deutschland. 1. Teil: Analyse der bisherigen Bevölkerungsentwicklung in Modellrechnungen für künftige Bevölkerungsentwicklung," BTDrs. 8/4437, "2. Teil: Auswirkungen auf die verschiedenen Bereiche von Staat und Gesellschaft," BTDrs. 10/863.

[413] Der Wandel familiärer Lebensmuster und das Sozialrecht (1985); Zacher (1989a, pp. 955–983).

them. But as a rule, the social biographies of women were more diverse and complicated in this way. This had an effect especially on the long-term systems of social security – chief among them, pension insurance (Frauen und Alterssicherung 1988).

Health Care – Meeting the Need for Nursing Care

The problem areas of the *health care system* and *nursing care*, in particular, were pushing for solutions. The continuous developmental problems of sickness insurance (Frerich and Frey, vol. 3, 1996, pp. 262–279) had exogenous and endogenous causes.[414] Exogenous causes were primarily the ageing of the population, changes in diagnoses, and the development of the field of medicine. Endogenous causes were imbalances in the system of statutory sickness insurance, which resulted in constant, undesirable developments regarding the costs and the distribution of expenses and opportunities for profit.

In the previous period already, rehabilitation had presented itself as an area that called for regulation and implementation that cut across the various systems. Something similar had become apparent for the specific problems of the disabled,[415] though no comprehensive and internally coherent regulations were in fact passed. Increasingly, though, it was becoming clear that at least potential need for nursing care required a separate solution (Soziale Sicherung bei Pflegebedürftigkeit 1987). That debate would eventually lead to a substantial further development of the system of social protection.

Individualization

Another challenge to the social state lay in *individualization* (Zapf 1987; Hoffmann-Nowotny 1988). This development was part of the emphasis on social protection and safety, and its intent of spreading freedom. But individualization was much more generally a product of freedom and prosperity. Individualization meant the freedom to shape one's own life. Individualization took seriously the freedom that this constitutional democracy was promising. It took seriously the prosperity that the free market economy had generated. And it took seriously that the social not only spread participation in this prosperity, but also the freedom that this prosperity offers. The more self-evident freedom, prosperity, and the social had become, the more self-evident it was to draw from this the consequences in the sense of

---

[414] Gäfgen (1986); Sachverständigenrat für die Konzertierte Aktion im Gesundheitswesen (1987; 1988; 1989; 1990); Die Strukturreform der Krankenversicherung (1988).

[415] See the "Berichte der Bundesregierung über die Lage der Behinderten und die Entwicklung der Rehabilitation: Erster Bericht", BTDrs. 10/1233; "Zweiter Bericht", BTDrs. 11/4455; for the subsequent period see also "Dritter Bericht", BTDrs. 12/7148; "Vierter Bericht", BTDrs. 13/9514; "Antwort der Bundesregierung: Ende des 'Jahrzehnts der Menschen mit Behinderungen'" BTDrs. 12/3555.

individualization. As that happened, however, two difficulties became evident. One difficulty was that the success of the political and social system had much to do with a high degree of normality – one could also say: of conformity. The typecasting of working life as reflected in the normal employment relationship was such a normality. The same rationality was also apparent in the systems of social protection, which presupposed this "thoroughly normalized" work life. This was clearest with pension insurance. But time again, when part-time work was to be taken on, it became obvious just how much the other safety systems also ran into difficulties when the precondition of normality was not given (Landenberger 1987, pp. 15–29; Bäcker 1988, pp. 595–629). And individualization manifests itself no less in the change of familial patterns of life or in the approach to health and other life risks.

Individualization confronted multifarious problems of how to shape the law in response. How should the law react? Should it facilitate individualization and promote it? Should it rebuff it and fight it? The other difficulty I will look at here is closely tied to these questions. It arises from the fact that individualization generates costs. Someone must bear those costs: either the person who "individualizes" himself or herself, or the entity that bears social responsibility for him or her – the family, the employer, the community of insured, the general community of solidarity that are the taxpayers. Therein lies a dilemma. What is the "liberal social state" worth if it does not assume the risks that come with the freedom of individualization? But where are the limitations within which it is reasonable to impose on others the consequences of one's own exercise of freedom? Debates about whether certain sports or other risky behaviors should be excluded from the protection of health insurance, or whether certain behaviors in the workplace should forfeit or reduce the protection of unemployment insurance are examples of this problem. And where the issue is the consequences of individualization for marriage and family life, it becomes clear just how much the mere thinking about individualization has to do with values.

8.2.3 The Challenge to the Social State

All this befell a social state under siege on many fronts (Zacher 1984a, pp. 1–12). The social state had profoundly transformed society. It was become increasingly clear that many of the processes it had made possible or had initiated had become self-perpetuating. And one could no longer ignore that every new intervention would have not only the intended effects, but also others that were unforeseen. Moreover, the effects of the social changed as the social developed. It had been one thing to protect exploited workers. It was another to develop the world of dependent work ever more in the direction of equality, freedom, security, and participation. It had been one thing to open access to medical care to the disadvantaged. It was another to guarantee the entire society – without a meaningful individual contribution to the concrete expense – a maximum of health care services. It had been one thing to protect the old against hardship and dependency. It was another to turn old age for the greatest possible number of citizens into a phase of new freedom and new participation. All this together justifies speaking about the self-exhaustion of the social state.

But the social state was also under siege because these realizations were only very gradually and very unevenly absorbed by society and politics. There were some who saw that the balance between distribution and redistribution had long since been upset, while others wanted to push ahead on the path of redistribution. In between and all around were many to whom too much of one thing and too little of another made sense only within very concrete contexts of their own interests or experience. There were some who believed that the role of the state and the extent of its intervention had long since grown too large and who felt that the private and the societal were being suppressed. There were others for whom there could not be enough state or enough intervention. But most of them felt that way only for very concrete cases in which they were being affected one way or the other. Finally, one of the big and complex disagreements of the time concerned tying social benefits to particular purposes.[416] The regulation of social benefits also takes place against the backdrop of a particular picture of reality, which explains why they make sense – or in most cases: why they are necessary. However, the legislator is not able, or willing, to incorporate all the essential traits of this picture into the wording of the law. In general, all those involved in a law would be unable to agree on all the caveats and clarifications that are in the air. As a result, all social laws create latitude for how to understand and use them. This gives rise to all kinds of disagreements about which use is legally or morally right or wrong. These differences of opinion are subject to a structural pattern that preoccupies the apparatus of the social state as much as it does its society. While the latitude is understood – indeed, praised – by one side as an expression of freedom, the other side denies it or reduces it by way of interpretation and brands its use as misuse. The truth lies between these two extremes when it comes to the creation of laws, the interpretation of the laws, and the social rules on how they should be used. But that only increases the explosive social potential that lies in this disagreement, instead of diminishing it. In any case, this problem has made a substantial contribution to the difficulties that arose for the social state from this dissenting back-and-forth within society.

Finally, the social state was also contested insofar as it has become increasingly evident, over the course of time and in view of changing conditions under which it works, how the autonomous mechanisms inherent in the federal state, the constitutional state, and especially democracy shape the social. The result of all of this was that the unease, both with the social state and with a "turnaround" politics that was convinced that the traditional development of the social state had to be "pruned back" did not cease and talk of the "crisis" of the social state continued.

[416] For a contemporary perspective see Eichenhofer (1982, pp. 137–141); from a later perspective Lessenich (1998, pp. 91–108).

8.2.4 The Social Goal of the State in the Constitution

During these years, the principle of the social state as laid down in the Basic Law (Art. 20, Para. 1, Art. 28, Para. 1, Sent. 1, GG) was understood once again in the traditional sense: as the guarantee of a subsistence minimum, the guarantee of social safety, as "more equality" for the weaker members of society (von Hippel 1982), and as the responsibility of the state for an economic system that did justice to these goals (Stern 1984, pp. 877–938; Zacher 1987a). The expansion of the social toward a more general notion of the well-being of society lost in importance. The comprehensive project "quality of life" had fallen into the turmoil that had afflicted the Schmidt era. At the same time, it was recognized that the state must not be reduced to the mandate of the social, just as it could not be meaningful to seek to describe its task as the guarantee and promotion of "quality of life." A debate over the tasks of the state had already begun in the 1970s (Bull 1977), and it continued in the 1980s.[417] Safety (in a diverse sense from external to internal safety), freedom, culture, communication, welfare, and other mandates and goals were discussed. Finally, the protection of the environment assumed special importance. A number of state constitutions[418] and eventually also the Basic Law (Art. 20a, GG, new version)[419] incorporated the protection of the "natural foundations of life" into their text. That development contributed substantially to freeing the constitutional principle of the social state from being invoked for all dimensions of individual and societal well-being. The social goal of the state is *the constitutionally normative positivization of the basic social norm of this society*.

However, especially in regard to its specific meaning, the social principle of the constitution was increasingly faced with a new challenge. During the period when the social order had been erected and expanded, that principle had served to legitimize its growth. But beginning in the mid-1970s, there were more and more movements of retreat. What did the social state principle have to say about this? There was talk about a "prohibition against going backwards" (Schlenker 1986). However, the constraints of the circumstances did not allow placing existing regulatory conditions above the responsibility for a continued development of the social system that did justice to the current situation. Of course, the Federal Constitutional Court decided in 1980/81 (BVerfGE 53, 257; 58, 81) to recognize property protections for "acquired" social rights. But even that could amount only to a relative protection.[420]

[417] Bundesminister des Innern/Bundesminister der Justiz (1983); Staatszwecke im Verfassungsstaat – nach 40 Jahren Grundgesetz (1990).

[418] A list in Pestalozza (1995, p. XLIV).

[419] Inserted through the "Gesetz zur Änderung des Grundgesetzes vom 27. Oktober 1994," BGBl. I, p. 3146.

[420] On the relationship between the social state principle and the basic right of property in protecting against a dismantling of the social see Kittner (1989: Art. 20 Para. 1–3 IV, margin

8.3 *The Development of the Social System*[421]

8.3.1 Responsibility for the Economy

The economic system at that time was based on the principles of the social free market.[422] The consensus behind this continued to stabilize (Fischer 1989).

8.3.2 Work and Income

While the retraction of social regulations in the preceding period had been limited to social benefits law, now there were also changes in the area of labor law.[423] Not only the high unemployment rate, but also the many changes in work life gave cause to rethink the regulations in labor law. There was consensus on this, and also on the issue that instruments of employment promotion should be further activated.[424] There was disagreement about whether work, while maintaining its strict formalization, should be newly distributed by shortening the weekly and yearly working hours and the lifetime work period, or whether it should be made more flexible by promoting part-time work, limiting the protection against dismissal, allowing temporary contracts, and opening it up to more to temporary work. The latter was the position of the governing majority. The former was the position of the unions and the parliamentary opposition. The legislator could tackle only some of the problems. Much was left to the practice of *collective bargaining agreements and the actual management of businesses*. That process gave rise to changes that were not insubstantial. The standard weekly hours for workers, which had dropped between 1969 and 1978 from 40.7 to 40.1, and stood at 40 h between 1980 and 1984, were cut to 39.4 h in 1985 and 38.1 in 1990.[425] The legislature made an attempt to *shorten the working lifetime*. In 1984 it introduced early retirement. In 1989, it replaced the early retirement regulation with the so-called *Altersteilzeit*

---

nos. 29, 79). For a further discussion of this question see H. Bogs (1998, pp. 65–83); Neumann (1998, pp. 401–411).

[421] Zacher (1989a, pp. 95–118); Frerich and Frey (vol. 3, 1996, pp. 259–423); "Sozialberichte der Bundesregierung 1983" (BTDrs. 10/842), 1986 (BTDrs. 10/5810), 1990 (BTDrs. 11/7527).

[422] Glastetter, Högemann and Marquardt (1991, pp. 317–364); Weimer (1998, pp. 317–364); Bundesministerium für Wirtschaft (1982; 1988; 1989; 1990); "Jahreswirtschaftsberichte der Bundesregierung" 1982 (BTDrs. 9/1322) to 1990 (BTDrs. 11/6278).

[423] See by way of supplementation Das Arbeitsrecht der Gegenwart (1983–1989); Bundesministerium für Gesundheit und Soziale Sicherung and Bundesarchiv (eds.), 2005: Geschichte der Sozialpolitik in Deutschland seit 1945, vol. 7, Chap. 3, nos. 1 and 2.

[424] Bundesministerium für Gesundheit und Soziale Sicherung and Bundesarchiv (eds.), 2005: Geschichte der Sozialpolitik in Deutschland seit 1945, vol. 7, Chap. 3, no. 3.

[425] The numbers for white-collar workers differ only minimally from those for blue-collar workers: 1969: 41.8; 1977: 40.1; 1978–1984: 40.0; 1985: 39.6; 1990: 38.2.

(early retirement by way of reduced working hours). Particularly controversial were the two Employment Promotion Acts that sought to make labor law and employment promotion more flexible. The law of 1985 allowed temporary work contracts, expanded the possibility of using temporary workers, provided exceptions to the protection against dismissal, and restricted the obligation to put severance plans in place. The Employment Promotion Act of 1990 extended these and a number of other regulations and added other measures of employment policy. The measures to *combat moonlighting and illegal employment* that had already been taken during the preceding period[426] were intensified.[427]

Self-employment drew hardly any political interest.[428]

The inaugural address in 1983 had given cause to expect that politics would give more attention to *unpaid work*. And in fact, improvements were made for domestic work. By contrast, nothing was done for *unpaid work outside of the family*.

8.3.3 Wealth

Wealth formation[429] received new impulses at the time, which were directed above all at participation in productive assets. Of course, that requires the participation of the parties to collective bargaining agreements and of businesses. The result was considerable differences in the effect of these measures. And with the persistence of unemployment, the instability of familial conditions, the risks of individualization, and the "cuts in the social net," the negative wealth problem of *debts* also grew (Reifner and Laatz 1989, pp. 213–235).

8.3.4 The Family

When it came to marriage and the family,[430] the legislature was enjoined, first of all, to respond to the demand by the Federal Constitutional Court (1975: BVerfGE

[426] "Gesetz zur Bekämpfung der illegalen Beschäftigung" (1981); "Arbeitsförderungskonsolidierungsgesetz" (1981).

[427] "Gesetz zur Einführung eines Sozialversicherungsausweises und zur Änderung anderer Sozialgesetze von 1989;" other measures listed in Frerich and Frey (vol. 3, 1996, p. 196f.).

[428] "Antwort der Bundesregierung auf die Große Anfrage der CDU/CSU und der FDP betreffend Lage und Perspektiven des selbständigen Mittelstandes in der Bundesrepublik Deutschland", BTDrs. 10/6090; "Bericht der Bundesregierung über die sozialrechtliche Stellung der mithelfenden Ehegatten, von selbständig Erwerbstätigen sowie über die Möglichkeiten ihrer Einbeziehung in das bestehende System der sozialen Sicherung," BTDrs. 11/5182; on the state of agriculture see "Agrarberichte" 1982 (BTDrs. 9/1340) to 1991 (BTDrs. 12/120).

[429] Bundesministerium für Gesundheit und Soziale Sicherung and Bundesarchiv (eds.), 2005: Geschichte der Sozialpolitik in Deutschland seit 1945, vol. 7, Chap. 3, no. 16.

[430] Bundesministerium für Gesundheit und Soziale Sicherung and Bundesarchiv (eds.), 2005: Geschichte der Sozialpolitik in Deutschland seit 1945, vol. 7, Chap. 3, nos. 5 and 10.

34, 169; 1978: BVerfGE 48, 346 [365]) to regulate *the maintenance of surviving family members* within the framework of pension insurance in a way that accorded with the constitutional provision of the equality of men and women. The Law on the New Regulation of Pensions for Surviving Family Members and on the Recognition of Child-raising Periods in the Statutory Pension Insurance of 1985 abandoned all earlier plans to establish a separate system for women – or in neutral terminology: for spouses running the household. Instead, the legislature decided on the so-called "*Anrechnungsmodell.*" The inequality in the pension for surviving family members, which lay in the fact that men always left their wives a pension, while women could leave one for their husbands only if they had provided most of the maintenance for them during their lifetime, was removed. The same principle now applied in all branches of social security in case of death and surviving family members: every spouse leaves an entitlement for the other spouse. But then the issue was to prevent excessive protection. With respect to social security, this was done by requiring that the surviving spouse had to count some of his or her gainful income (including the public-law supplementary replacement income, for example, for pension insurance).

While the revision of social law on the basis of equality had thus made a substantial step forward, much remained to be done for families, that is, for those with children. That was all the more so in that marriages and families have become increasingly fragile over time, and the context of marriage and family has become disconnected from traditional patterns (Der Wandel familiärer Lebensmuster und das Sozialrecht 1985).While the legislature that passed the pension law for surviving family members and the law on child-raising periods could not manage to set up a separate social protection for spouses who ran households and raised children, it did try in other ways to help those who had children and devoted themselves exclusively to raising them – at least when the children were infants. Initially it stipulated that 1 year of child-raising for each child would be counted under pension law as a contribution period or a quasi-contribution period. That same year, the Law on the Granting of Child-Raising Allowance and Parental Leave added the protection under labor law and the specific social benefit of the child-raising allowance for 10 months, from 1988 for 12 months, and from 1989 for 15 months after the birth of a child. The Pension Reform Law 1992 (1989) brought further improvements with respect to the inclusion of child-raising periods under pension law. In this way, the freedom of parents – in actual practice, the freedom of mothers – to combine family and work was expanded. At least a modest step was thus taken toward recognizing domestic work for the added value it offered, namely, that of providing social protection – something that was by now self-evident for dependent employment.

Another problem, however, became increasingly pressing: the imbalance inherent in the basic formula *between the* (presumably small) *number of earners* and the (presumably larger) *number of consumers* in a family. The problem cannot be solved by social benefits law alone. This is conclusively also a problem of *tax law* (F. Klein 1987, pp. 773–801). With the Tax Reduction Act of 1986/1988 (1985), the federal legislature reestablished the dual system of family equalization and provided a number of tax breaks for families. The Tax Reduction Expansion Act of 1988 and the Tax Reform Act of 1990 continued this policy. Eventually, however, the Federal Constitutional Court established a new, lasting emphasis in May 1990:[431]

> When taxing income, an amount equal to the subsistence minimum of the family must remain tax exempt; only the income over and above that can be subject to taxation.
>
> The starting point for a constitutional judgment is the principle that the state must leave the subject liable to taxation his income free of taxation to the extent that it is needed to create the minimum conditions for a humane existence. This constitutional precept follows from Art. 1, Para. 1, GG, in conjunction with the principle of the social state from Art. 20, Para. 1, GG. Just as the state is obligated under these constitutional norms to guarantee the indigent citizen these minimum requirements, if necessary through welfare payments (see BVerfGE 40, 121 [133]), he may not deprive the citizen of his own earned income up to this amount. If follows further from the indicated constitutional norms, but also from Art. 6, Para. 1, GG, that when it comes to taxing a family, the subsistence minimum of all family members must remain tax exempt (BVerfGE 82, p. 85).

Another development relevant to family policy reached its conclusion: the replacement of the Youth Welfare Act of 1961 by a *new Child and Youth Services Act* in 1989. With respect to the difficult issues of how parental rights could be reconciled with the need for public childcare and educational offerings outside of the school, the law formulated largely balanced solutions. What remained controversial was the question of whether there should be a right to place toddlers in daycare facilities. The municipal providers resisted this "financially unfeasible" right. Still, the legislature provided this entitlement.[432] However, the difficulty of implementing the law soon prompted the legislature to introduce grace periods.[433]

All told, the period brought a number of advances in family policy: the further implementation of equality for men and women in social law; an improved adjustment of income tax law to the situation of families; building blocks in social and labor law to give parents greater freedom to combine family and work; finally, a compromise regarding the supplementing child-raising within the family with offerings outside of school. Still, some quandaries remain – quandaries less of the legislature and more within society. Parents who wish to combine job and family by putting their children in daycare find only very limited support. But parents who are willing to interrupt their working lives to devote themselves to child-raising also

[431] BVerfGE 82, 60; concurring BVerfGE 82, 198; see also BVerfGE 99, 246, 268, 273.

[432] Section 24, Para. 1, SGB VIII in the original version: "From age three until entry into school, a child is entitled to attend a kindergarten. For children under the age of three and for school-age children, places in full-day centers and, should the well-being of the child require it, places in childcare shall be made available."

[433] Section 24 a SGB VIII, version of the "Zweiten Gesetzes zur Änderung des Achten Buches Sozialgesetzbuch vom 15. Dezember 1995," BGBl. I, p. 1775; see "Antwort der Bundesregierung auf die Kleine Anfrage 'Platzsituation und Personalbedarf im Zusammenhang mit der Umsetzung des Rechtsanspruchs auf einen Kindergartenplatz ab 1. Januar 1996'," (BTDrs. 12/3822); "Beschlussempfehlung und Bericht des Ausschusses für Frauen und Jugend: Für einen gerechten Lastenausgleich zwischen Bund und Ländern zur Sicherung des Anspruchs unserer Kinder auf einen Kindergartenplatz ab 1996," (BTDrs. 12/6792); "Antwort der Bundesregierung: Sicherung des Rechtsanspruchs auf einen Kindergartenplatz ab Januar 1996," (BTDrs. 13/722).

find only limited compensation, at least with respect to pension insurance. One might speak of half-heartedness. But one could also speak of pluralism. Could the polity cover the burdens of both options? If not: would it really be better to make one of the two options the rule by way of state fiat?

8.3.5 Social Benefits Systems[434]

Initially, the issue in the Kohl era – as in the Schmidt era preceding it – was to adjust the benefits systems to what was possible for the polity. Thus, further cuts were necessary (Zacher 1989c, p. 89 f.). But there was more than crisis management, as substantial reforms of the existing systems were carried out. The experience of "crisis" was increasingly being blotted out by the experience of constructive solutions.

Provision Systems

The development of social provision demonstrates a certain contradiction. On the one hand, there were increasing signs that the development especially of working life, of families, and the age structure of the population would cause problems for the social insurance systems. On the other hand, the social insurance systems, in particular, experienced a robust development.

The *Health Care Reform Act*[435] of 1988 brought a creative, comprehensive, and thorough-going reform of sickness insurance. It tried to combine the best possible medical care with tolerable costs. The law expressed this in a multitude of principles that were supposed to guide the actions of those involved: effectiveness, efficiency, economical pricing, frugality, necessity, humaneness, adequacy, expediency, appropriateness, uniformity, state of medical knowledge, medical progress, rules of the medical profession, quality of care, security of provision, and so on. However, this normative guidance can be hardly more than rhetoric. Crucial for reality are the mechanisms of negotiation, decision-making, and oversight which are used by the sickness funds, their associations, physicians, other providers, state agencies, and so on to make concrete the conditions under which the system becomes effective. With the new regulation of sickness insurance, the legislature created a corporatist system without parallel.

Pension insurance[436] also underwent a fundamental reform. That reform was deliberated in the eleventh legislative session and passed (1989) to take effect at the

[434] Jahrbuch des Sozialrechts der Gegenwart (1982–1990).

[435] Die Strukturreform der Krankenversicherung (1988); Bundesministerium für Gesundheit und Soziale Sicherung and Bundesarchiv (eds.), 2005: Geschichte der Sozialpolitik in Deutschland seit 1945, vol. 7, Chap. 3, no. 6.

[436] Bundesministerium für Gesundheit und Soziale Sicherung and Bundesarchiv (eds.), 2005: Geschichte der Sozialpolitik in Deutschland seit 1945, vol. 7, Chap. 3, no. 5.

beginning of 1992. The challenges were pressing: the change in the working world and the decline in the normal employment relationships that could be drawn on for funding, the quantitative and qualitative change of old age, the transformation of the entire population structure, the massive imbalances in the generational succession, the change in family structures, but also the need to upgrade domestic work, the equality of men and women, as well as equality among women. The Pension Reform Act of 1992 addressed especially these latter problems. The change in the working world hardly reverberated yet. The law built on the tradition of German pension insurance, especially on the principles of the reform of 1957, assessed the experiences of the intervening years, and modernized pension insurance. That also included the elimination, as much as possible, of the differences between the various pension schemes for workers and employees (worker pension insurance, white-collar pension insurance, miners' pension insurance).

While the *diversity of old age pension schemes* had proved a problem at the end of the previous period, the only thing the Pension Reform of 1992 could contribute to its solution was the standardization of social security for workers. Civil servant pension insurance, supplementary pension insurance in public service, old age pension for farmers, and occupational pension schemes all followed their own development. However, politicians often felt compelled to initiate changes analogous to those introduced by pension reform.

The discussion over social protection in case of a need for long-term care (Soziale Sicherung bei Pflegebedürftigkeit 1987) continued. With the introduction of "benefits in case of a permanent need for intensive nursing care," the Health Care Reform Act of 1988 offered a first solution beyond the "nursing care assistance" regulated in the Federal Social Welfare Act.

Assistance and Promotion Systems

The tax-financed assistance and promotion programs bore the brunt of the recession. Both the late Schmidt era and the early Kohl era pruned back especially this area. In the process, the development of the *child allowance*[437] was not straightforward. Constantly new ideas of social justice for families – involving either a concentration of family equalization on the child allowance, or the "dual" incorporation of tax law – gave rise to a steady stream of new solutions. By contrast, *training grants* were cut back.[438] Post-graduate grants were abolished again in 1984. The *Länder* often stepped into the gap this created. They created programs for the social promotion of primary and secondary students, as well as support for post-

[437] Bundesministerium für Gesundheit und Soziale Sicherung and Bundesarchiv (eds.), 2005: Geschichte der Sozialpolitik in Deutschland seit 1945, vol. 7, Chap. 3, no. 6.

[438] Bundesministerium für Gesundheit und Soziale Sicherung and Bundesarchiv (eds.), 2005: Geschichte der Sozialpolitik in Deutschland seit 1945, vol. 7, Chap. 3, no. 11.

graduate students.[439] For once, the historical pattern of the "social federal state," that socio-political tasks pass from the *Länder* to the federal government, was reversed. In view of the close connection of these assistance and promotion programs with the educational systems and with the primary responsibility of the *Länder* for that system, and above all because this has also made the separate social-state responsibility of the *Länder* a little more visible again, there is something positive about this development. Of particular import was the development of *social welfare*.[440] It suffered a series of cutbacks, especially during the first years of this period. On the other side, its tasks had been growing since the middle of the 1970s.

Employment Promotion

To the extent that unemployment was the greatest concern of the period, the promotion of employment and social protection in case of joblessness also faced a special challenge.[441] In the process, the temptation to covertly expand the labor market through job creation measures increased. The legislature followed the line that it should not, if at all possible, alter the economically determined reality of the labor market through the instruments of employment promotion any more than was inevitably part of any active employment policy. More difficult was the answer to another question: which contribution should the budget of the Federal Labour Office make to limiting and balancing the federal budget? The government ratio had to be limited so as to preserve and promote the economy's self-healing powers. But unemployment posed an increasing threat to society, the polity, and to countless individual lives. Out of this conflict there emerged a constant flow of new modifications of employment promotion and benefits in case of unemployment – both benefit cuts and benefit expansions.

Overarching Aspects[442]

The supraindividual performance and financing programs were continued without any essential changes – apart from reforms to wealth formation.[443]

---

[439] A compilation of the *Länder* regulations concerning the promotion of primary and secondary school students can be found in Ramsauer and Stallbaum (1988, pp. 160–165).

[440] Bundesministerium für Gesundheit und Soziale Sicherung and Bundesarchiv (eds.), 2005: Geschichte der Sozialpolitik in Deutschland seit 1945, vol. 7, Chap. 3, no. 9.

[441] Bundesministerium für Gesundheit und Soziale Sicherung and Bundesarchiv (eds.), 2005: Geschichte der Sozialpolitik in Deutschland seit 1945, vol. 7, Chap. 3, no. 3.

[442] Bundesministerium für Gesundheit und Soziale Sicherung and Bundesarchiv (eds.), 2005: Geschichte der Sozialpolitik in Deutschland seit 1945, vol. 7, Chap. 3, no. 4.

[443] "Subventionsberichte" der Bundesregierung: 1981–1984 (BTDrs. 10/352), 1983–1986 (10/3821), 1985–1988 (11/1138), 1987–1990 (11/5116).

The "crisis of the social state" awakened the willingness to rethink the "right" structure of social benefits.[444] In the course of the development, the "social achievements," as controversial as they might have been when they were first introduced, had soon come to seem very self-evident, indeed necessary, becoming something of a natural law. The mental attachment and guarantees of vested rights, and especially the powers of self-preservation of the institutions that had been established, did their part to endow what had been created and what existed with a higher claim to validity than anything that might exist in their place. The patchwork of corrections that had been undertaken with growing frequency since the middle of the 1970s revealed the arbitrary nature of many creations – or in positive terms: their disposability. But along with this experience of disposability there also arose the awareness of a responsibility to think comprehensively and fundamentally about the problems and a solution. This hinted at the vision of an autonomous, comprehensive, internally consistent rationality of the social. And it provided impressive impulses for systematically working through sub-areas. The Health Care Reform Act, and the Pension Reform Act, later also the law of long-term nursing care were examples of this, notwithstanding all the inadequacies that were attached to them.

Moreover, the trend toward making the totality of the social benefits systems visible also continued. The core of the health care reform of 1988 was inserted into the Social Code as Book Five. After the "general parts" that had been created between 1975 and 1982, this was the first "special part" of this codification, whose framework would now be quickly filled in – though it is still not complete (25 Jahre Sozialgesetzbuch 1995). Other developments allowed social insurance, at any rate, to become visible as an overarching entity, in spite of its extreme organizational fragmentation (Sozialversicherung 1988). The associations into which kindred insurance carriers organized themselves (Hein 1990) assumed additional importance. And fiscal equalizations and other financial associations created behind the various social insurance carriers extensive underlying communities of solidarity (Gössl 1992).

8.3.6 Taxes – Dues – An Overarching View

The interconnection between tax burdens and tax breaks, social insurance contributions, and social benefits (Bundesministerium der Finanzen 1986) was certainly part of the themes of the period – from the report by the Expert Commission on Pension Schemes to the decision of the Federal Constitutional Court on the taxation of family incomes.[445] However, new solutions for an overarching analysis

---

[444] Verhandlungen des 55. Deutschen Juristentages (1984); Übergreifende Soziale Risiken – Übergreifender sozialer Schutz (1990); Gesetzesgestaltung und Gesetzesanwendung im Leistungsrecht (1989); Verhandlungen des 59. Deutschen Juristentages (1992b, vol. 1).

[445] Sozialfinanzverfassung (1992); see also Schreyer (1983, pp. 95–113).

or even a fair reorganization of the interaction between various levies and benefits did not come into view.

8.4 Summary

8.4.1 Poverty – Wealth

This period combined an efficient "*crisis management*" with essential and largely *successful reforms*. But it had one central *deficit*: poverty was becoming increasingly visible.[446] That development has causes that reach back a long way. Even a prosperous society with full employment will always be accompanied by poverty – by situations and life stories that cannot be integrated or cushioned, and also by irregular conceptions of participation. The risks of individualization will find victims no matter the circumstances. The irritations of working life, the cutbacks in social benefits, and the general disappointment of growth expectations that set in around the middle of the 1970s added entirely new causal processes. And this development deepened in the course of the 1980s. The networks that kept society together toward the bottom, such as the family, were loosening. More and more often, the calculations on which individuals had grounded their life plans, whether in terms of family, profession, the economy, and social law, were voided. And the more the sphere of a slide into sub-normality expanded, the greater became the temptation to give in to this drift into sub-normality. As problematic as this picture may be: the coexistence of the normal employment relationship and full employment had disciplined society. To the extent that first full employment and then the normal employment relationship weakened, society also lost the guiding effect of this discipline. It must be noted again and again that families with children could come to the edge of poverty much more quickly than any individual or even couples without children. The social state did not adjust adequately to the fact that there now existed a kind of poverty for which the instrument of social welfare, created in 1961 under the banner of growth and full employment, was not sufficiently intensive, differentiated, and sensitive – not in terms of legal regulations, and not in terms of its practical implementation. What was and is even more important and even more difficult to grasp: the social state changes nothing about a process that had become juridified and oriented toward money, and which saw itself far too little as a personal service to the disadvantaged and the threatened. The social state was – to use the key word of the Swedish welfare state – the Volksheim

[446] "Antwort der Bundesregierung auf eine Große Anfrage der GRÜNEN zu 'Armut und Sozialhilfe in der Bundesrepublik Deutschland': BTDrs. 10/6055; "Antwort der Bundesregierung auf eine Große Anfrage der SPD zu 'Armut in der Bundesrepublik Deutschland' und eine Große Anfrage der GRÜNEN zu 'Arbeit und Armut in der Bundesrepublik Deutschland'," BTDrs. 10/6634; Leibfried and Tennstedt (1985); von Bethusy-Huc and Beckmann (1989, pp. 121–124); see also Informationszentrum Sozialwissenschaften (1988).

("people's home") of the "middle voter." The latter determined the priorities, and those priorities were oriented toward a "normality that was open toward the top."

The social state was also not able to tackle the *problem of wealth* – all the less so the more this wealth had become general. Society had quickly and for some time now become accustomed to adding up the possibilities of a liberal social state: to *privatize prosperity* and *socialize social risks*. There is a yawning contradiction between this utilization of a general solidarity for one's personal risks, and the effort to rebuff the general solidarity from laying hands on private prosperity. But it is the "political judgment" of the "middle voter" to leave this contradiction in place or do something about it: he decides in favor of the contradiction. This clearly has its costs. Those costs fall primarily on families with children – especially across the generations. Wealth tends to accumulate most readily among those who have no children: they can earn more, save more, bequeath more. The typical "individualization" of singles and childless couples took on a specific social problematic from this perspective. But with the demographic changes in society, these groups accounted for a growing number of voters, while the children of those who bore society's burden of children remained voiceless. The tendency to socially neutralize wealth received a new impetus in that the concern that social policy could damage the productivity of the economy – to put it differently: redistribution could choke off distribution and thus itself – became more widespread.

8.4.2 The Emphases of the Social

The pathos of *social equality* was not the dominant political sentiment of those years. The social state had to learn that there were limits to "equality through growth," and as a democratic social state it also learned that differentiations that express the proviso of inequality (Molitor 1984, pp. 27–29), especially the opening "toward the top," are accepted. The interaction of a private, societal, and state production of the social and the non social (thesis) with an effective political correction (antithesis) leading toward equal/unequal conditions (synthesis) was and remains the consensus of this society and polity. That era paid more attention to the vitality of the thesis than to what it accomplished for equality. For the sake of the validity of this thesis, it was also willing to rein in the antithesis. It accepted that in the end this shifted the equality/inequality relationships of the synthesis toward inequality. Its priority was the level of the synthesis.

Of the three main manifestations of *social justice*, the justice of achievement and the justice of acquired standing come to the fore in a special way during this period. The justice of needs was the (relative) loser. Of the three expressions of *social participation*, participation in economic life and the life of gainful employment was given comparatively the greatest emphasis – not least also within the systems of social provision. Participation in society's general opportunities for prosperity lost in importance in specific areas. However, it was not negated. What the previous period had put in place along these lines was essentially preserved. The general participation in the minimum life opportunities of society was not questioned, though provisions intended to secure them lost some of their effectiveness. Perhaps too much of a good conscience was at work: the minimum participation should be guaranteed for everyone, but it was overlooked that access to this participation could also be subject to change. *Security* continued to be a fundamental principle of the social. Perhaps one could say: security was the most effective constant within the value system of the social. *Subsidiarity* was given more weight again as a principle. One might question whether the boundaries were correctly drawn – whether it was quite concretely recognized or misjudged what can be left to the individual, families, other small groups, societal forces, and so on without a loss of effectiveness.[447] *Solidarity* developed in a lopsided fashion. *Horizontal solidarity* expressed itself effectively in the development of the social insurance systems. By contrast, *vertical solidarity* disappeared even more so than previously into the realm of abstraction.

The integration of society lost intensity. The *unity of prosperity, freedom, security, equality, and the defense against hardship* lost its coherence. Proximity and distance of the various segments of society to the individual values of the cluster of values increased noticeably – both in the sense of the experience of individual values, and in the sense of the valuation given to them. Yet this game remained open. The decline in integration did not intensify into disintegration.

9 The Profound Change – 1989/1990 and After

9.1 The Fundamental Transformations around 1989/1990

9.1.1 General Observations

The world changed profoundly around 1990.[448] Many developments that have been on everyone's lips since then as "globalization" had been looming for quite some time. Now, however, they took on an entirely new scope. Communism collapsed. The totalitarian and dictatorial character of the Soviet Union began to dissolve. The forces that had been agitating for changes toward greater freedom in the Soviet Union's Central and Eastern European satellite states, some of them for a long time, gained new power and spheres in which to act. The hegemonial structures of global Soviet imperialism lost their power-political base. The rigid division of the world into the "free West" and its zones of influence, the "Communist sphere of power" and its zones of influence, and the "block free" states came to an end. The state

[447] This gave rise to a Left-Right quarrel ("socialist" and "social democratic" versus "liberal" and "conservative") that was specific to the period; see Heinze (1985); Sicking (1989); Wegner (1989); Sachße (1994, pp. 717–738).

[448] For a socio-political diagnosis see Kaufmann (1997a; 3rd ed. 1998); on the developments in constitutional politics see Stern (2000, pp. 1560–1579, 1723–2174).

under the rule of law and democracy were able to spread far beyond their "western" countries of origin. What spread even faster was the capitalist economic system – at times only individual elements of it. It did not necessarily depend on the state under the rule of law and democracy preceding it. It had found ways and means of adjusting also to dictatorships and making deals with them. Now that the systems of power were changing in many countries, it was able – by taking advantage of the unrest as much as of consolidation – to rapidly expand further. For Europe there was the added factor that the European Communities were continuing to integrate with the utmost dynamism. Essential steps were taken in quick succession: The Single European Act in 1986/1987, the Maastricht Treaty in 1992/1993, which included both the foundation of the European Currency Union as well as the establishment of the "European Union;" the deepening of this development through the Amsterdam Treaty of 1997/1999.

All of these developments had profound significance for the Federal Republic of Germany. The outstanding event, however, was that the political process by which Communist rule over Central and Eastern Europe was loosened and eventually dissolved cleared the way for the unification of West and East Germany. A revolutionary movement that had been growing in East Germany for some time brought about the opening of the border on 9 November 1989. Subsequently, a new political structure inserted itself alongside the still operating organs of the East German system: the "Central Roundtable." It was the mandatary of the revolution. It held the representatives of the old system politically – not legally – accountable. The *Volkskammer* was newly elected on 18 March: East Germany had a democratically legitimated representation. It revised the constitution and was able to negotiate the relationship to the Federal Republic of Germany (Fiedler 1995, pp. 3–34; Luchterhand 1995, pp. 35–54; Würtenberger 1995, pp. 101–130).

9.1.2 German Unification[449]

The Monetary, Economic, and Social Union

A first comprehensive step was the Treaty establishing "Monetary, Economic, and Social Union" of 18 May 1990, which took effect on 1 July 1990 (BGBl. II, p. 537; Grosser 1998). Although it was soon overtaken by the Unification Treaty, it was extremely important to subsequent developments. It brought the economic and social systems of the German Democratic Republic very close to the economic and social systems of the Federal Republic of Germany. Even before that the GDR had undertaken a series of reforms that amounted to a liberalization of the economic and working life (Frerich and Frey, vol. 3, 1996, pp. 466–491). However, it was only the Monetary, Economic, and Social Union that set the definitive course: in the

[449] Bundesministerium für Arbeit und Soziales and Bundesarchiv (eds.), 2007b: Geschichte der Sozialpolitik in Deutschland seit 1945, vol. 11, Chap. 1 and 2.

direction of a unification of the two German states, and the agreement that the economic and social system of initially both German states, later the united Germany, would follow – without significant restrictions – the principles that had evolved in the Federal Republic. In the process, the Treaty on the Monetary, Economic, and Social Union also took on fundamental importance for the understanding of the economic and social systems in West Germany. To be sure, the two parties to the Treaty agreed that it was not only laws and organizational structures that should be adopted, but beyond that also the essential elements of what constituted the substance of the economic and social system in the Federal Republic, even if it had so far not assumed an explicit, legal-normative form. But could that become the content of a treaty without being articulated as its text? The parties to the Treaty denied that it could. And they tried to give verbal expression to the previously unwritten substance of the economic and social system – and perhaps also: to elevate norms that determined the practice without having attained the quality of law into legal norms.

Critical importance was accorded in this process to the "common will" of the parties to the Treaty "to introduce also in the GDR the social market economy as the foundation for the further economic and social development, with social equalization and social protection and responsibility toward the environment" (Preamble). Along those lines, Art. 1, Para. 3 of the Treaty stated:

> The basis of the economic union is the social market economy as the joint economic system of both parties to the Treaty. It is determined especially by private property, performance-based competition, free price formation, and in principle complete freedom of movement for labor, capital, goods, and services.

And the joint protocol about guiding principles that is attached to the Treaty provided this explanation:

1. Economic performance shall be achieved chiefly in the private sector and through competition.
2. Freedom of contract is guaranteed. The freedom of economic activity must be interfered with as little as possible.
3. Business decisions are free from the dictates of a plan,. . ..
4. Private businesses and the free professions must not be treated worse than state-owned and cooperative enterprises.
5. Price formation is free, unless there are compelling, overall economic reasons for the state to set prices.
6. The freedom of acquisition, the disposition over and use of land and other means of production is guaranteed for economic activity.
7. Enterprises that are wholly or partly owned by the state shall be run according to the principles of profitability. They shall be competitively structured as soon as possible and transferred into private property to the extent possible. In the process, opportunities shall be created especially for smaller and mid-size companies.
8. With respect to the postal and telecommunications system, the regulatory and organizational principles of the Postal Services Restructuring Act of the Federal Republic of Germany shall be gradually implemented.

In three specific contexts, the text of the Treaty made statements that supplemented the social market economy. Art. 11, Para. 1 created a peculiar link between the concept of the social market economy and the fundamental canon of values in West Germany's economic system:

> The German Democratic Republic guarantees that the economic and fiscal policy measures will be consistent with the social market economy. The measures will be taken such that they contribute, within the framework of the free market system, simultaneously to price stability, a high level of employment, foreign economic equilibrium, against a backdrop of steady and appropriate growth.

Immediately following, Art. 11 Para. 2 formulated a separate goal of free market structural policy, which it then related straightaway to the social market economy:

> The German Democratic Republic will create the framework conditions for the development of market forces and private initiative, so as to promote structural change, the creation of modern jobs, a broad basis for small and mid-size businesses as well as the free professions, and protection of the environment. Enterprise law will be designed such that it is based on the principles of the social market economy as described in Art. 1, with free decision-making by businesses about products, volume, production processes, investments, employment relationships, prices, and the appropriation of earnings.

Less insightful was the statement on the social dimension of the social market economy (Art. 1 Para. 4):

> The social union… is determined especially by work regulations consistent with the social market economy, and a comprehensive system of social protection based on the principles of a justice of achievement and of social equalization.

With that, the principle of the social market economy for the first time achieved the rank of a legal norm (Rupp 1997, pp. 129–148).

As for the rest, the Treaty revolved around *two dimensions: one dimension* – it could naturally be kept short – clarified the premises of the social market economy in democracy and the rule of law in line with the Basic Law (Art. 2 of the Treaty; Sect. A I of the Joint Protocol on Guiding Principles); the *other dimension* identified the details by which the legal systems and policies of the German Democratic Republic and the Federal Republic of Germany were to realize the Monetary, Economic, and Social Union (Art. 3, 4, 8–34 of the Treaty; Joint Protocol on Guiding Principles, especially Sects. A II and III and B; Appendices I-IX). In principle, the *currency union* took place at a ratio of 2 (East German Mark) to 1 (Deutschmark). Out of social considerations, savings up to a certain basic amount, tiered according to age, were converted 1:1. Likewise, wages, salaries, scholarships, pensions, rents, and leases were converted at 1:1 (Art. 10 Para. 5 of the Treaty; Art. 5–11 of Appendix I to the Treaty). The regulations pertaining to the establishment of a *social union* aimed at approximating the work regulations and social benefits systems of the German Democratic Republic to the legal and institutional conditions in the Federal Republic (Art. 17–25; no. A III of the Joint Protocol on Guiding Principles; Appendix II Sect. IV, Appendix III, Sect. III), and at a greater mutual openness of the systems in East and West for migratory movements (no. B IV 1 and 2 of the Joint Protocol on Guiding Principles; Appendix V no. VI). Focal points were labor law and social insurance law.

In addition, the GDR committed itself to set up a system of social assistance (Art. 24 of the Treaty).

Parallel to the treaty negotiations and to the procedures for parliamentary ratification, the *GDR* developed a fairly lively *legislative activity* in an effort to fundamentally reshape the economic and social order, change it in the direction of a state under the rule of law, democracy, and a free market economy, and in the process lead it toward the system that had developed in the Federal Republic. At the same time, however, there were repeated attempts to take into account the values of the East Germans and the resistance to rapid change of concrete circumstances. This legislative activity continued also after the Treaty establishing a Monetary, Economic, and Social Union had taken effect – now, of course, within its framework (Frerich and Frey, vol. 3, 1996, pp. 485–548).

The Unification Treaty

Immediately following the signing of the Treaty establishing a Monetary, Economic, and Social Union, that is, even before it had taken effect, work began on a more far-reaching union of the two Germanies (Schäuble 1991; rev. ed. 1993). The negotiations confronted a *fundamental choice*. Art. 23 of the *Basic Law* had stipulated that "other parts of Germany" that did not belong to the states of the Federal Republic could join, whereupon the Basic Law was to take effect there. However, the Basic Law had also opened up the possibility that *the German people would unify* and *adopt a "freely chosen" constitution* (Art. 146, GG). What it meant was "the entire German people," who, according to the last sentence of the Preamble to the Basic Law, remained called upon to "complete the unity and freedom of Germany in free self-determination" These choices corresponded to different ideological and political considerations, and they entailed different technical problems. The path of *Art. 23 of the Basic Law* meant the continuation of the constitutional order of the Federal Republic and thus also the continuation, in principle, of the legal system of the western state in the united Germany. Continuity of the legal system of the Federal Republic was thus the rule, elements adopted from the joining part could be only the exception. The path according to *Art. 146 of the Basic Law*, by contrast, meant the fundamental equality for "the entire German people." Whether this should and could also mean a fundamental equality of the guiding notions and values that were essential in the two German states, which had once existed side by side, had to depend on the circumstances – and on how they were brought to bear by "the entire German people" in its "free decision" and were recognized by it. But the alternatives also had technical implications. Accession was technically the simpler solution. The continuity of the system of the Federal Republic made it easier to acknowledge the need for and appropriateness of exceptions and to design relevant solutions. The unification of the "entire German people" could potentially be just as easy if this "entire German people" decided in favor of a corresponding rule-exception modality. But it could become infinitely complicated if the "entire German people" opted for the attempt to achieve the unity of Germany by way of a fundamental re-creation through the establishment of a pan-German law and constitution (Tomuschat 1990, pp. 70–100). The *parties to the negotiations* from West and East Germany *decided in favor of accession* – for the solution in accordance with Art. 23 (Badura 1995, pp. 171–198). Already the Preamble of the Treaty had pointed down this path. The Unification Treaty followed it. Once the negotiations had progressed sufficiently far, the *Volkskammer* of the German Democratic Republic adopted the declaration of accession on 23 August 1990. The Treaty was signed on 31 August 1990. Following ratification by the parliaments of the Federal Republic and the German Democratic Republic, the Unification Treaty took effect on 3 October 1990 (BGBl. II., p. 885).

The *Treaty*, which the *Bundestag* and the *Bundesrat* had adopted with constitution-amending majorities,[450] put the Basic Law into effect also in the states that had emerged out of the former GDR (Art. 3). The Basic Law was amended only where it had a direct bearing on the unification process (Art. 4.) However, the "government of the two contracting parties" recommended "to the legislative bodies of the united Germany that within 2 years they should deal with the questions regarding amendments or additions to the Basic Law" (Art. 5). The legal system of the Federal Republic was in principle extended to the acceding territory (Art. 8); accordingly, the law of the GDR was essentially abrogated – though with a wealth of exceptions (Art. 9, Appendices I and II to the Unification Treaty). Likewise, the economic law, labor law, social benefits law, and tax law of the Federal Republic were introduced in the "new *Länder*." The exceptions, especially the modalities of the transition, were numerous and varied.[451] But the principle remained: sooner or later, the legal system was to be uniform.

Once the decision had been made in favor of accession, the Unification Treaty had the task of extending the *Basic Law and the legal system* of the Federal Republic to the acceding territory and of defining and fleshing out the modalities of the transition and the exceptions. The drafters of the Treaty did not face the task of saying anything about which *constitutional and legal reality* was meant by this. Neither the Treaty nor the Treaty Act could do more than extend the normative conditions of this constitutional and legal reality of the Federal Republic to the whole of Germany. It had been different with the Treaty establishing a Monetary, Economic, and Social Union. The issue there was an approximation to the constitutional and legal reality as lived in the Federal Republic, without simply transferring the normative system of the Federal Republic to the GDR. There the issue that the contracting parties were concerned with had to be addressed. Hence the statements in that Treaty about the social market economy. Hence, conversely, the absence of relevant statements in the Unification Treaty. Still, the positive assertion of the social market economy in the first treaty did not vanish with the Unification Treaty. The *Unification Treaty affirmed that the*

[450] See Declaratory Formula of the Unification Treaty Act of 23 Sept. 1990, BGBl. II, p. 885.

[451] For details see Bundesministerium für Gesundheit und Soziale Sicherung and Bundesarchiv (eds.): Geschichte der Sozialpolitik in Deutschland seit 1945, (2005), vol. 7 and Bundesministerium für Arbeit und Soziales and Bundesarchiv (eds.): Geschichte der Sozialpolitik in Deutschland seit 1945, (2007b) vol. 11, Chaps. 1 and 2.

obligations from the Treaty establishing Monetary, Economic, and Social Union remained valid (Art. 40). With that, the entire commitment to the social market economy was also retained.

The principled unity of the constitutional and legal system of all of Germany does not mean that this constitutional and legal system *has the same effects in the old and the new territory of the Federal Republic* (Görlitz and Voigt 1992). There are four essential layers of reasons for this. The *first layer* is to be found in positive law: these are the transition regulations – the exceptions which state what is to be different in the "new Länder" compared to the "old Federal Republic." The *second layer* lies in the *contrast between continuity and discontinuity*. The law that continues to be valid in the old Federal Republic carries on individual, collective, or all-encompassing "stories" that have evolved with the law itself. In the accession territory, that same law carries on individual, collective, or all-encompassing "stories" that began under a different law. And how well the new law fits the old "stories" depends on the modalities of the transition – if any transition is even capable of navigating the interruption. The *third layer* lies in the *living conditions in the "new Länder,"* which are in so many ways so essentially different from the old Federal Republic (Glatzer and Noll 1992). It is true that the law must always be ready to deal with different living conditions. In many respects it will be true that for the differences encountered by the identical legal norm, parallel examples can be found in "East" and "West" – examples for both the "fit" of the legal norm and for the "non-fit," for its beneficial and unpleasant effect, for its functionality and the limits of its functionality. Still, it must be assumed that many legal prescriptions will typically bring forth different effects in the "*new Länder*" from those in the old Federal Republic. The *fourth layer, finally, lies in the subjective perception of the norms*. Citizens who lived in the GDR grew up in a legal system that could not be taken at its word – but which therefore also had the "freedom" to make promises whose fulfillment was left open. By contrast, politics in the GDR had possibilities of altering realities without doing so through the law. In the Federal Republic, the law had to – and has to – be taken at its word. The possibilities of politics to alter realities without a legal basis for doing so are tightly constrained. A "right to housing" or a "right to work" has a different meaning, depending on the experience in this system or that system. Germany's unity, as prepared by the Treaty establishing Monetary, Economic, and Social Union and completed by the Unification Treaty, is a phenomenon with inherent tensions: caught between the pole of unity and the pole of a different history and its aftereffects in the present (Kocka 1995).

The drama of this situation is obvious. The division of Germany had lasted more than four decades. The differences in political and social conditions encompassed nearly all spheres of life.[452] And I am not talking only about the differences during

[452] Frerich and Frey (vol. 2, 1996); M. Schmidt (2013, German Social Policy, vol. 4); see also all the following volumes Bundesministerium für Gesundheit und Soziale Sicherung and Bundesarchiv (eds.): Geschichte der Sozialpolitik in Deutschland seit 1945, vol. 8 (2004), and

the time of division. The drama of the situation is grounded not least in the fact that the economy of the former GDR was not compatible with the economic conditions that became apparent in 1990 and continued to develop. That had to do especially with the developments in the partner states of the Soviet-dominated joint economic sphere. The factor "capital" of the former GDR economy had been devalued "over night," as it were. Capital that was now to be put to work in the *new Länder* had to be newly acquired and newly invested. That took and takes not only time. Since this was and is being done under the premise of the utmost boost in productivity and global competition, it was soon evident that any reconstruction of the factor "capital" would reduce the offers for the use of the factor "labor." All in all: a deep divide of economic and social differences exists between "East" and "West" (Kaase 1996, pp. 385–396; Harich 1996, pp. 447–464; R. Geißler 1996, pp. 611–625; Gros 1996, pp. 740–756; Hauser 1999, pp. 3–9). The Basic Law that constitutes this unified Germany has charged the social federal state with seeing to the uniformity of living conditions within the Federal Republic. It confronts a fundamentally new challenge (Depenheuer 1997, pp. 149–227). And the social confronts a new inequality.

9.1.3 European Integration

During the same period, the supranational framework of the Federal Republic of Germany has continued to evolve dynamically. That development began in 1951/1952 with the establishment of the *European Coal and Steel Community.*[453] On the "basis of a common market" (Art. 2 and 4), it was to work for, among other things, "the improvement of the living and working conditions of the labor force" (Art. 3 (e)). The year 1957 brought the Treaty establishing the European Economic Community, accompanied by the Treaty establishing the European Atomic Energy Community.[454] Its goal more generally was that of "constantly improving the living and working conditions of their peoples" (Preamble). This was joined by the mandate of "reducing the differences existing between the various regions and... mitigating the backwardness of the less favored" (ibid.). However, the vehicle for achieving "a harmonious development of economic activities, a continuous and balanced expansion, an increased stability, an accelerated raising of the standard of living and closer relations between the Member States" was to be once again a "Common Market" flanked by "progressively approximating the economic policies

Bundesministerium für Arbeit und Soziales and Bundesarchiv (eds.): Geschichte der Sozialpolitik in Deutschland seit 1945, vol. 9 (2006b), 10 (2008b), 11 (2007b), and Bundesministerium für Gesundheit und Soziale... (2004), vol. 8.

[453] Bundesministerium für Arbeit und Soziales and Bundesarchiv (eds.), 2005: Geschichte der Sozialpolitik in Deutschland seit 1945, vol. 3, Chap. 3, no. 17.

[454] Bundesministerium für Arbeit und Soziales and Bundesarchiv (eds.): Geschichte der Sozialpolitik in Deutschland seit 1945, vols. 3 (2005), 4 (2007a), 5 (2006a), 6 (2008a), Chap. 1, no. 17 in each.

of the Member States" (Art. 2).[455] *Social policy* proper was to remain, in principle, in *national hands*. However, the European Economic Community was to establish a European Social Fund "to improve opportunities of employment of workers in the Common Market and thus contribute to raising the standard of living" (Art. 3, 123–128). Equal pay for men and women for equal work was guaranteed (Art. 119). Other than that, the Treaty relied on processes of information and exchange to bring about an equalization of the social systems (Art. 117, 118, 120, 122). An important special feature was the mandate that the Council "shall, in the field of social security, adopt the measures necessary to effect the free movement of workers" (Art. 51). That mandate was soon fulfilled.[456] For a long time, the so-called "Migrant Worker Act" formed the most important piece of a European system of social law (Schulte and Zacher 1991). Other than that, the European Economic Community was slow to develop further.

It was only with the *Single European Act of 1986/1987* that the European Community, which had grown robustly in the meantime (the founding members – Belgium, Germany, France, Italy, Luxembourg, and The Netherlands – had been joined by Denmark, Greece, Spain, Ireland, Portugal, and Great Britain), took a significant step forward.[457] The concept of the Common Market was given a new quality. The widespread desire to combine more European social policy with more European market found only limited approval: in a new legal basis for harmonizing regulations (Art. 100a), though it excluded "fiscal provisions, those relating to the free movement of persons, and those relating to the rights and interests of employed persons" (ibid., Para. 2); and in a mandate to improve the working environment "as regards the health and safety of workers" (Art. 118a). In addition, the Commission was given the task "to develop the dialogue between management and labour at the European level" (Art. 118b). This Act was supplemented in 1989 by the "Community Charter of the Fundamental Social Rights of Workers," though it was only able to document the consensus of the member states (with the exception of Great Britain) without creating any new law. Of great significance to the equalization of regional differences within Europe were the regulations about a "policy to strengthen economic and social cohesion", especially through the European Structural Funds (Social Funds, Regional Funds, European Agricultural Guidance and

[455] The basic decision in favor of the free market is the core of the entire system. The "improvement of the living and working conditions of labour" and the "equalisation of such conditions" was to be achieved also through the "functioning of the Common Market" (Art. 117).

[456] "VO Nr. 3 des Rates über die soziale Sicherheit der Wanderarbeitnehmer vom 25. September 1958," ABl. 1958, p. 581, amended ABl. 1961, p. 831; later replaced by "VO 1408/71/EWG des Rates zur Anwendung der Systeme der sozialen Sicherheit auf Arbeitnehmer und deren Familien, die innerhalb der Gemeinschaft zu- und abwandern, vom 14. Juli 1971" ABl. 1971, L 149/2, amended ABl. 1973, L 128/22.

[457] Europäisches Sozialrecht (1992); Bundesministerium für Arbeit und Soziales and Bundesarchiv (eds.): Geschichte der Sozialpolitik in Deutschland seit 1945, vols. 5 (2006a) and 6 (2008a), Chap. 3, no. 17 in each.

Guarantee Funds), the European Investment Bank, and the Cohesion Funds (Art. 4b, 123–125, 130a–e, 198d, 198f).

The 1990s

While the Single European Act was still being put in place, the member states set to work on the *Maastricht Treaty* of 1992/1993.[458] The supranational *European Community* – the new name of the European Economic Community – was now wrapped in a community of international law: the *European Union*. A number of institutional innovations served the greater effectiveness of European policy. However, the material mandate of the European Community was also developed further on a number of points. That applies especially to the expansion of the Economic Community into a Currency Union. The mandates of the Community were now described as follows (Art. 2):

> The Community shall have as its task, by establishing a common market and an economic and monetary union and by implementing the common policies or activities referred to in Art. 3 and 3a, to promote throughout the Community a harmonious and balanced development of economic activities, sustainable and non-inflationary growth respecting the environment, a high degree of convergence of economic performance, a high level of employment and of social protection, the raising of the standard of living and quality of life, and economic and social cohesion and solidarity among Member States.

The more detailed shape of the Economic and Currency Union (Art. 3a and b, Art. 102a-109 m) emphasized the "principle of an open market economy with free competition" (Art. 3a Para. 1, Art. 102a). In addition, the importance of the following principles was highlighted: "stable prices, sound public finances and monetary conditions and a sustainable balance of payments" (Art. 3a Para. 3). The European currency system, in particular, is obligated to pursue these goals (Art. 105 Para. 1). As for social policy proper, the Maastricht Treaty introduced nothing essential. Great Britain opposed an expansion of socio-political competencies. The other member states then created a new legal basis with the "Protocol on Social Policy" and the "Agreement among Member States of the European Community with the Exception of the United Kingdom and Northern Ireland on Social Policy." Art. 1 of the Agreement declared "the promotion of employment, the improvement in living and working conditions, appropriate social protection, social dialogue, the development of the labor potential with regard to a sustained, high level of employment, and the fight against exclusion" to be the common goals of the Community and the member states. To that end, Art. 2 established a number of competencies. Among them, special importance attaches

[458] Bundesministerium für Arbeit und Soziales and Bundesarchiv (eds.), 2007b: Geschichte der Sozialpolitik in Deutschland seit 1945, vol. 11, Chap. 3, no. 17.

to the law-making power in the area of social security and the social protection of the worker (Art. 2 Para. 3).[459]

The next threshold in the development was crossed with the *Amsterdam Treaty* of 16/17 June 1997.[460] With this treaty, new possibilities of action in social policy were created for the European Union and – most importantly – the European Community.[461] The tasks and competencies previously regulated in a special agreement (without the United Kingdom) were incorporated into the Treaty (Art. 136–145 EGV).

On the Importance of the European Community for German Social Policy[462]

Within the sphere of European competencies established in this way, the effects of European law and European politics on German social policy and the corresponding areas of German law also intensified. That holds to a lesser extent for the socio-political *action programs*. By contrast, the *guidelines* that the European legislator enacted especially for the area of labor law[463] and occupational safety law[464] became quite important. In the area of social benefits law, on the other hand, it was chiefly the *European Court of Justice* that spelled out and expanded the meaning of European treaty and ordinance law through its decisions (Schulte and Zacher, vol. 1, 1979, pp. 353–390; vol. 2, 1980, pp. 359–395; vol 3, 1981, pp. 419–454; Schulte 1982–1998, vols. 4–20). In the process a remarkable new development occurred, chiefly in the 1990s. European social law remains largely coordination law – that is, law that brings together various national legal systems into consistent solutions, if those systems (as in the case of the migration of workers within Europe) concern the same topic. The decisions of the European Court of Justice emphatically developed these regulations so as to guarantee and promote the *freedom of movement for workers within Europe. By now, the freedom of movement*

[459] On social policy as the task of the European Community according to the Maastricht Treaty see Willms (1997a), Art. 51; Schulte (1997), Art. 117–118; Willms 1997b, Art. 118a; Currall (1997), Art. 119–122; Docksey et al. (1997), after Art. 122; Schulz (1999), Art. 123–125: 903–1455.

[460] "Zustimmungsgesetz vom 8. April 1997," BGBl. 1998, II, p. 386; went into effect on 1 May 1999.

[461] For the Union: Art. 1, no. 5 (=Art. 2 EGV in the version of the AV), for the Community: Art. 2, no. 22 (=Art. 136–143 EGV in the version of the AV); Zentrum für Europäisches Wirtschaftsrecht der Rheinischen Friedrich-Wilhelms-Universität Bonn (1999); Haverkade and Huster (1999); for a survey of the socio-political tasks and competencies of the European Community/Union see Oppermann (2000, pp. 693–718).

[462] Leibfried and Pierson (1998); Bundesministerium für Arbeit und Soziales and Bundesarchiv (eds.): vols. 6 (2008a), 11 (2007b) and Bundesministerium für Gesundheit...: (2005), vol. 7, Chap. 3, no. 17 in each.

[463] Bundesministerium für Arbeit und Soziales and Bundesarchiv (eds.): vols. 6 (2008a), 11 (2007b), and Bundesministerium für Gesundheit...: (2005), vol. 7, Chap. 3, no. 1 in each.

[464] Bundesministerium für Arbeit und Soziales and Bundesarchiv (eds.): vols. 6 (2008a), 11 (2007b), and Bundesministerium für Gesundheit...: (2005), vol. 7, Chap. 3, no. 2 in each.

of workers has become a multi-layered, differentiated *freedom of movement for the citizens* of the European Union, with equally multi-layered, differentiated consequences for social security. In addition, the *free movement of services and goods* assumed an indirect importance also for the free movement of individuals and their entitlement to social benefits: for example, the freedom of an outside provider of health services to offer his services in Germany; or the freedom of a European citizen who has a right to nursing care benefits in Germany to seek out and receive those benefits in Italy. By incorporating the free movement of citizens and social benefits increasingly into social benefits law, the structures and operations of the national social benefits systems were changed in ways not previously imagined (Schulte and Barwig 1999). Finally, of special significance is the emphatic manner in which European guidelines and the European Court of Justice are bringing the equal treatment of men and women into the German legal system (Currall 1997).

The most important development, however, is not to be found in the substantive intrusions into German social policy. Rather, it is found in the Europeanization of its framework conditions. If the social is defined by the task of equalizing or moderating economically conditioned and economically relevant inequalities, it is of the utmost importance if the political and legal control over economic conditions passes onto the European level to the degree it has happened. To be sure, the principle of the free market constrains the powers of politics. But still: the market itself is a European and no longer a national one.

9.1.4 Globalization[465]

Finally, the national conditions of the social have changed fundamentally through the process of globalization. Globalization makes it possible, *first*, for capital to seek out the most profitable place to invest all over the world. *Second*, it allows *global trade* to bring to bear the most favorable *manufacturing conditions* by means of the quality and price of products in a global competition. *Third*, it makes it easier in many cases also *for people* to *migrate*: for those in search of work to find a job; for those suffering to find a chance to survive. With that a global competition over the chance to work has emerged. It is carried out to a lesser degree through the migration of labor, and to a much greater degree such that labor, where it can be found, is exposed to the conditions of a – potentially – global competition: a competition for capital, the deployment of which makes dependent gainful employment possible in the first place; and a competition of products produced by labor and capital.[466] In the process,

[465] Kaufmann (1997a, esp. pp. 114–130); Bundesministerium für Arbeit und Soziales and Bundesarchiv (eds.), 2007b: Geschichte der Sozialpolitik in Deutschland seit 1945, vol. 11, Chaps. 1 and 2.

[466] United Nations (1997); International Labour Office (1995, 1996); Campbell (1994).

the quality and price of work almost never determine on their own the interest of capital in investment and the competitiveness of the products. Rather, quality and the costs of labor enter into a complex overall calculation of investment and production conditions. This globalization is of the utmost importance to the politics of the social state and the further development of the consensuses and conventions of the society of a social state.[467] Until now, state policies, as well as the policies of the societal forces, have been characterized by the crucial relevance of the national (in Western Europe also: the European-supranational) framework. Through globalization, the control of national states over economic and social conditions has been diminished in a way that is historically unparalleled.

The Development of the Factor Labor

The factor labor is under pressure (Archer and Malinvaud 1998a, b; Archer 1999). All decisions about an adjustment of the factor labor, and especially its costs, must be made under the burden of uncertainty whether they are justified, necessary, and sensible relative to other investment and production conditions, and relative to various groups of workers (qualified vs. less qualified, younger vs. older, natives vs. immigrants, and so on). And every interest group confronts the question which alternative distribution of opportunities and sacrifices its own power and influence can achieve. The old conventions about the normal employment relationships, about the work performance and burden it entailed, about the (internalizing) social protection linked to it, about the (externalizing) social safeguards connected with it, and finally about the overall edifice of social benefits that pervades and surrounds the problem areas of work, income, the meeting of needs, and maintenance, are being fundamentally called into question (OECD 1997). All groups within society, along with the media, associations, parties, experts, parliamentarians, and the actors in the governments at the federal and state level are struggling to find a new orientation.

The national society finds itself in economic and political competition with potentially all other societies in the world (Zacher 1999b, pp. 1–47). That means first of all: it is in *competition not only with old-industrialized, liberal welfare states*, which have also been shaped by the guiding ideas of the free market economy and social protection, and especially also by the key ideas of full employment and the normal employment relationship. It is also competing economically and politically with states whose social development has been fundamentally different – provided those states have reached a degree of economic, technological, and communicative development that allows them to participate in the international competition over the conditions of production. That means, on the one hand, that

[467] Afheldt (1995); Schmähl and Rische (1995); Boyer and Drache (1996); Ortmann (1997, pp. 585–596); Mayer (1997, pp. 29–38); Midgley (1997); Hanesch (1999, pp. 3–10); Franzmeyer (1999, pp. 25–31); Rieger and Leibfried (1995).

German society has interrelationships with the *post-socialist societies*.[468] The economy in those countries is in multifarious ways subject to processes involving the dismantling of centrally planned economic structures and the decentralized new formation of the productive factors capital, land, and labor. That is an unsettling event of trial and error, failure and success. It is above all a process that is characterized by free potentialities: perhaps free capital, but above all free labor. This process also knows many paths into poverty. In all of these societies, the situation of a labor force with few opportunities is conveyed not only via the price of products, but directly also through the migration of job seekers – whether temporary or permanent. On the other hand, the national society, as it struggles with new solutions, is also competing with the *developing countries*, whose work world never experienced the kind of formalization that was realized in the old-industrialized welfare states of the West in a liberal form, in the socialist states in the form of a planned economy. Work life in the developing countries is caught between, on the one hand, the modernity of the urban, formal sector, in which work life is organized analogously to the industrialized countries, and, on the other hand, the archaic conditions of the premodern village community, the pre-modern family unit, the pre-modern household, where everyone contributes to maintenance in accordance with his role, and where the needs of everyone are met in accordance with the shared norm, the shared possibilities, and the distribution of roles (von Benda-Beckmann 1988). Between these extremes lies the informal urban sector, with its full diversity of small traders and service-providers, hourly wage earners and day laborers, and otherwise the mostly underemployed, and the informal rural sector, with the most diverse forms of pre-industrial agriculture (International Labour Office 1984/1989). All of these layers can be surrounded and pervaded by poverty – a poverty that can no longer be grasped by all of these categories of work (World Bank 1990). And the working conditions in those countries also enter into the global competition (World Bank 1995): via the value and price of products and via the migration of the factor labor. The old-industrialized, liberal welfare states all face similar challenges, but their responses differ.[469] Widespread is the strategy of banking on the return of the old full employment and the normal employment relationship, for example, with the help of measures toward improved professional qualifications, intensive efforts at an active employment policy, and other economic and socio-political steps. Other strategies are aimed at new conventions for society as a whole: a new, "smaller" and thus "easier," "more readily" distributable employment relationship, which distributes work time and work income in such a way that all those capable of working can participate adequately in gainful work – in other words, that a new full employment is created. Still other strategies bank on society, in free agreement, dividing up the work unequally, meaning that a corresponding willingness to pursue part-time work, community work, and possibly

[468] World Bank (1996); Wollmann et al. (1995); Brunner (1996).

[469] Aust and Bieling (1996, pp. 141–166); von Maydell (1997, pp. 1–39); H. Werner (1998, pp. 3–14); Hanesch (1998, pp. 15–26); Mau (1998, pp. 27–37); Schmid and Niketta (1998).

also family work solves the problem. Other societies and policies pursue the direction of a further spread within the labor market, which pays maximal compensation to the most capable, whose production secures the superiority in the competition, while the wages of the least productive can be exposed to downward competition with the cost of labor in less productive countries. Or is it possible to erect a new world of work and gainful employment which – in order to make sure that the most productive sector of employment performs with maximum efficiency – does have room for the traditional employment relationship, but places it within an ensemble of multifarious forms of independent gainful work, dependent gainful work, and (familial or charitable) unpaid work?[470]

But whatever politics undertakes, and whatever the direction in which society develops: can the "golden age" of full employment and the normal employment relationship return? It was linked with the special circumstances of the 1960s and early 1970s: with economic growth; with a still ongoing process of industrialization; and with the fact that the "decommodifying" and individualizing effect of social protection and of the social benefits systems was only in its infancy. At the pinnacle of this development, the social state combined with dependent work a level of prosperity, equality, freedom, and security that had no historical parallel as the social condition of a large majority of the population. The relationship between the economic, cultural, and other societal premises of this good fortune and the configurations of its realization was so tight that it was threatened by any change in its conditions.

The Development of the Factor Capital

As much as globalization puts the factor labor under pressure, it opens up new opportunities to the factor capital. Those opportunities lie essentially in the fact that capital can operate globally. Not only that it can do so, but that it does. This is simply one of the most important changes in our time. For the welfare states of the 1960s and 1970s, it went without saying that all factors of production saw themselves as national and behaved nationally: the factor land in any case; also the factor labor, which was improving and developing its social position precisely by way of the national political system, and the migration of which was severely circumscribed; but also the factor capital, and above all management, too, which integrated these factors. There are obvious reasons why the national effective space was relevant also for management. And there are likewise rational reasons why the factor capital behaved largely nationally – for example, limiting risks through the transparency of the national operating conditions and the ability to influence them, the advantage of national communications and personal networks, the heightened opportunity to combine economic earnings with societal and political recognition,

---

[470] On family work see Lohkamp-Himmighofen (1994, pp. 3–13); Gilbert (1994, pp. 175–196); on charitable and communal work see Anheier and Seibel (1990); Riedel and Strümpel (1996, pp. 11–35); see esp. also Rifkin (1995, pp. 249–274).

and so on. On the whole, of course, the fact that capital limited itself to the national setting escapes any other explanation than that of the persistent dominance of national thinking and behavior. Be that as it may, the national effect of capital was the rule. Of course there were exceptions. Multinational companies soon formed the most spectacular category of these exceptions. But they did so *because* they were the exception. Now, however, capital has shaken off the national ties.

This has transformed the operating conditions of the social state more so than almost anything else. The state lives from the fruits of its economy. These are the fruits of labor, capital, land, and the knowledge used in the process, and finally of management, which brings these factors together. The nation state in general and the *social state*, in particular, were *accustomed to distributing the burdens of the polity* – and not least also its social expenditures – *among all of these factors. Now, capital is withdrawing from this, in three ways. First: whether it stays within a country* or comes into a country depends on the opportunities it is offered and the burdens it is expected to bear. As a result, the factor capital has acquired influence on national finances and especially also on the social budget and the distribution of the social burdens. Second: capital can move to other countries. To be sure, not only with specific opportunities, but also with specific risks – but it can go. And by going, it *essentially evades its contribution to the national burdens.* And since capital, wherever it goes, can decide once again what share of the national burdens to accept, it is able to reduce its share of the national burdens globally. The factor land and the secondary elements of knowledge and management cannot make up for this loss. Thus, the *factor labor* becomes around the world the pack animal of *national costs* – especially also of national social expenses. Third: the global movement of capital driven by the goal of the maximum return *casts the global economy into an unrest* that is extreme and has an enormous impact. It also alters the conditions under which the national social state operates. National states are tightly constrained in their ability to control, guide, or compensate for these changes. And the international community as such has not developed a set of instruments to organize these effects from globalization in an overarching way. As of now, it is not clear what can be reasonably done without abolishing the benefits of a free global economy (World Bank 1997).

Labor and Capital

At this point we must remind ourselves of the paradigm from which the organizing concepts of the "social partnership" and "social self-governance" once evolved. These organizing concepts built on the fact that labor and capital were mutually interdependent in shared spheres of becoming active and preserving their interests, that within this sphere they could and should resolve joint problems cooperatively and autonomously and in so doing also take some of the burden off the social state. The union-based organization of labor is an essential implication of these concepts. The development that labor and capital have undergone in recent times can leave neither the union organization of labor nor the cooperation model of labor and capital untouched – whether the old forms will have new effects, or whether new forms must be found (International Labour Office 1997).

9.1.5 The Challenged Social State

All of these changes befell a social state that was already under siege from various troubles. More precisely: that applies to the "old Federal Republic." But the FRG mattered most if the economic and social conditions in the former GDR were to be improved and eventually developed toward "western standards." It very quickly shaped the developments in the East in essential ways – thanks to the adoption and transfer of its political, legal, economic, and social system to the "other Germany." And in many respects the problems were in fact related. At any rate: none of the symptoms of a "crisis of the social state" in the "old Federal Republic" had been resolved over the course of time. Most had deepened and intensified. That is true of the *developments handed to the social state* (Deutscher Bundestag 1994/1998): the ageing of the population, the changes in the structure of the family, the growth in medical costs (Sachverständigenrat für die Konzertierte Aktion im Gesundheitswesen 1991, 1992, 1994, 1995, 1996, 1997/1998), the raising of other civilizational standards and its costs, the changes in the world of work and gainful employment, and so on.

Added to this is that the *economic conditions for the operation of the social state* have worsened. After the economy had recovered toward the end of the 1980s, *economic growth* in the territory of the old Federal Republic declined sharply in the second half of 1991, contracted in 1993, and remained at a very low level for the rest of the decade. In the first few years, during which collapse and rebuilding overlapped, the East German economy was unable to compensate and soon fell in line with the low level of growth in the West.[471] The *unemployment rate* had remained stubborn well into the phase of economic recovery. From 1983 to 1988 it had remained at over 8%. Only in 1989 did it drop to 7.9%, in 1990 to 7.2%, in 1991 to 6.3%. In 1992 it already reacted to the reversal of economic growth and rose to 6.6%, and to 8.2% in 1993. The new federal states contributed to this trend with a rate of 10.3% (1991), which rose to 14.8% as early as 1992. And the unemployment rate remained the most dramatic number in the years that followed. In the West it grew from 8.2% in 1993 to 11.0% in 1997, in the East from 15.8% in 1993 to 19.5% in 1997 – for the Federal Republic as a whole, then, from 9.8% in 1993 to 12.7% in 1997. For the social state, this development, in particular, was important on multiple levels: because of the challenge that unemployment always poses to the social state; because of the social benefits that must be paid to the unemployed and their families; because of the strategic and financial problems of an active employment policy on an ever larger scale; and increasingly also because

[471] Bundesministerium für Wirtschaft (1989; 1998; "Jahresgutachten…").

of the loss of contributions and tax revenue, which affects all social benefits systems, but specifically the contribution-based systems of social insurance.[472]

The *manifestations of ageing inherent in the social state* also continued to exert their effects. They, too, had become stronger and more important rather than weaker: the institutional rigidity, the change in behavior from what was intended by social policy to calculations of private advantage, the individualizing dissolution of the regular patterns of life, and so on. The guiding – indeed: disciplining – function that emanates from full employment had grown progressively weaker. Parallel to that, the effects of employment promotion and of social protection in case of unemployment changed. Moreover, for the most varied reasons, social benefits systems that are not immediately intended to compensate the shortfall in income in case of unemployment were nevertheless used that way – either because, as in the case of early retirement or disability, they were accorded growing importance (also socio-politically) as an alternative to work and unemployment; or because the general frustration boosted the readiness to resort to social benefits systems beyond their original purpose. At the same time, however, in the course of these changes there were growing disagreements about how social protection should be set up. How should individuals, how should society be guided by the social benefits systems?[473] Should the basic formula of work, income, the meeting of needs, and maintenance be intensified or loosened? Are there forms of behavior that should be ostracized and prevented as an abuse of social protection and social benefits? With *growing urgency* the question was discussed what could and should be done *to relieve "the economy" of the costs of the social state*. This was the period of the discussion over the "*Standort Deutschland*" ("Germany as a place to do business").[474] The social implications of this discussion were and continue to be complex. One of the front lines ran between the factors labor and capital. Capital, now in its new situation of competition, demanded sacrifices from labor: in wage policy, through more flexible employment conditions, and so on. But capital also demanded exemption from the social expenses. At the expense of whom? At the expense of the factor labor? But labor was supposed to become less expensive. And so the factor labor itself was to be relieved from the social costs. Where, then, would the costs go? And were costs the only issue? What does a socially pacified factor labor, what does a socially pacified society mean for the factor capital? The individual demands were for the most part self-evident, but all considerations taken together were hopelessly contradictory.

---

[472] Döring and Hauser (1995); Pitschas (1998, pp. 755–775); Lampert (1997); Wandel der Arbeit und soziale Sicherung (1998); Hauser (2000).

[473] E.g. Individualverantwortung und Sozialversicherungsschutz (1997).

[474] Hilbert (1994); Borchert et al. (1997a, b); Eckart and Paraskewopoulos (1997); Bundesministerium für Wirtschaft (1995).

9.2 The Development in the Unified Germany

9.2.1 The General Political Development[475]

On 2 December 1990, the *twelfth Bundestag* – the first of the unified Germany – was elected. The CDU/CSU campaigned with the slogan "Yes to Germany/Yes to the Future/Together we can do it/CDU/Freedom/Prosperity/Security." The CSU focused on its specialty: "Bavaria strong for Germany/CSU/December 2nd/Vote Bavarian." The FDP put Hans-Dietrich Genscher front and center: "Vote Genscher. Vote FDP/FDP/The Liberals/A liberal Germany." The slogans of the SPD were: "Oskar Lafontaine/The New Way/SPD/Ecological, social, economically strong" (Toman-Banke 1994, p. 54).

In the elections (Ritter and Niehuss 1995, p. 38), the CDU/CSU and the FDP together achieved once again a governing majority. The PDS was now represented in parliament for the first time. *Helmut Kohl* formed his *fourth cabinet*. His *inaugural address* on 30 January 1991 (Presse- und Informationsamt der Bundesregierung 1991, pp. 61–76) placed domestic policy under three significant headings: "We want to achieve a good future for the people in all of Germany: prosperity and justice in the social market economy;" "We want to promote the diversity of our country and preserve creation: culture and environment in a livable *Heimat*;" "We want to strengthen the human bonds and protect the law: safety and security in the family and society." His elaborations combined the social problems of German unification broadly with the social problems of the old Federal Republic. They were thoroughly borne by the optimism of 1990: by the positive economic trend and the overly optimistic assessment of economic conditions (derived from both the self-representation of Socialism and the self-imposed censorship of "co-existence"), especially the industrial potential of the former GDR. Kohl did not know that both of these premises would soon collapse. In terms of social policy, the speech addressed a broad spectrum of issues. But the profound change of conditions in the new states, in the Federal Republic as a whole, in Europe (in Western Europe as much as in Central and Eastern Europe), as well as throughout the world was barely perceived. And so nothing was said about the challenges that would arise from this. A legislative session got under way during which politics and society had to come to terms with changes on a scale that no other previous session had encountered. The magnitude of the challenge was soon out of proportion to the possibilities of government policy to respond. From 1982 on, the governing majority in the *Bundestag* had been able to count on a corresponding majority in the *Bundesrat*. That majority was lost in 1991. Assuming all states governed by the CDU/CSU/FDP voted in agreement, a "governing majority" in the *Bundesrat* generally came about only if states with a "mixed" government, in which the

---

[475] Bundesministerium für Arbeit und Soziales and Bundesarchiv (eds.), 2007b: Geschichte der Sozialpolitik in Deutschland seit 1945, vol. 11, Chap. 1.

SPD governed together with the parties of the coalition government on the federal level, went along. Beginning in 1996, then, the opposition parties in the Bundestag had a majority in the Bundesrat (König 1999, p. 32f.).

Elections for the *Thirteenth German Bundestag* were scheduled for 16 October 1994. The CDU/CSU picked up on the fact that the economic climate had changed between 1993 and 1994 (from negative growth of 1.6% to positive growth of 2.3%): "For continued improvement/CDU/Securely into the future." The CSU proclaimed: "Freedom instead of *Volksfront*/CSU/Vote for Bavaria." The FDP knew what was at stake: "This time everything is in the balance. F.D.P./The Liberals." The SPD intoned: "Look forward to the change, Germany/SPD" (Toman-Banke 1994, p. 54 f.).

The majority of the CDU/CSU and FDP in the Bundestag shrank, but was still large enough to elect the chancellor (Ritter and Niehuss 1995, p. 38). *Helmut Kohl* formed his *fifth cabinet*. It would be his last. His *inaugural address* on 23 November 1994 began with the headline (Presse- und Informationsamt der Bundesregierung 1994, pp. 985–992): "Courage for a change in thinking – strength for renewal." Still, the text was more a continuation of traditional themes than an engagement with the fundamental changes of the time. The Chancellor believed that activating society was critical: "Less state – more self-responsibility;" "Betting on a renewal – winning the future" – a headline that had in mind above all the invigoration of the economy, not least of small and mid-size businesses; and, finally, "Strengthen families – secure social justice."

9.2.2 The Change as Reflection in Constitutional Politics

The manifold developments, convulsions, and innovations of the period found expression to a considerable degree in the constitutional texts of the Republic and the *Länder*. There were three sources for this. The first source was the *constitutional development in the old Federal Republic* – on the federal as well as the *Länder* level. On the *federal level* there had been 13 changes to the Basic Law between 1949 and 1965, that is, in a period of 15 years. By contrast, there were 19 constitutional amendments in the 10 years from 1967 to 1976. Thereafter there was a hiatus in constitutional changes (with the exception of an amendment to Art. 21 GG concerning the financing of parties) until the Unification Treaty. The *Länder* had had their great constitution-creating period already before the enactment of the Basic Law. To be sure, a number of states (Schleswig-Holstein, North-Rhine Westphalia, Lower Saxony, Berlin, and – after the merger of the states of Baden, Wuerttemberg-Baden, and Wuerttemberg-Hohenzollern – Baden-Wuerttemberg)[476] enacted constitutions only after the Basic Law had gone into effect. In contrast to the state constitutions in the pre-Basic Law period, these constitutions contained either no or only selective substantive statements in terms of social

[476] A compilation in Pestalozza (1995, pp. XXI-XXX).

programs – though on the whole there were plenty of them.[477] Later, environmental protection, in particular, was inserted into the state constitutions.[478]

The second source that fed the demand for constitutional changes was the call for an appropriately *joint constitution for the unified Germany*. Once it had been decided that German unification should not be accomplished directly through the creation of a new, united German state and through passage of a joint, new constitution (Art. 146, GG), but through the accession of the GDR to the FRG (Art. 23, GG), the question arose all the more urgently what needed to be changed in the Basic Law to make it ready – beyond the immediate amendments related to the accession (Art. 4 of the Unification Treaty) – to serve as the future constitution of the united German state. Art. 5 of the Unification Treaty therefore stipulated:

> The Governments of the Contracting Parties recommend to the legislative bodies of the united Germany that within 2 years they should deal with the questions regarding amendments or additions to the Basic Law as raised in connection with German unification, in particular
> - with regard to the relationship between the Federation and the Länder. . ..
> - with regard to the possibility of restructuring the Berlin-Brandenburg area. . ..
> - with considerations on introducing state objectives into the Basic law, and
> - with the question of applying Art. 146 of the Basic Law and of holding a referendum in this context.

A third source that fed the constitutional changes in the 1990s was the *establishment of the Länder on the territory of the former GDR*. The *Länder* that had been set up within the Soviet-occupied zone had still had a place in the first constitution of

[477] Thus on the social goal of the state (Preamble LVerf.Be 1950; Preamble, Art. 23 Para. 1 LVerf. BW; Preamble, Art. 3 Para. 1 LVerf.HH); on the right to work (Art. 12 Para. 1 Sent. 1 LVerf.Be 1950; Art. 24 Para. 1 Sent. 3 LVerf.NRW); on the protection of labor power (Art. 12 Para. 2 LVerf. Be 1950; Preamble LVerf.HH; Art. 24 Para. 1 Sent. 2 LVerf.NRW); on the right to vacation (Art. 24 Para. 3 LVerf.NRW); on the protection of Sundays and holidays (Art. 22 Para. 1 LVerf.Be 1950; Art. 3 Para. 1 S. 1 LVerf.BW; Art. 25 Para. 1 LVerf.NRW); on codetermination (Art. 26 LVerf.NRW); on the right of industrial action (Art. 18 Para. 3 LVerf.Be 1950); on cooperatives (Preamble LVerf.HH; Art. 28 Sent. 2 LVerf.NRW); on family work (Art. 5 Para. 2 LVerf.NRW); on the guarantee of charitable, esp. church-based, welfare (Art. 6, 87 LVerf.BW); on the appropriateness of income (Art. 24 Para. 2 LVerf.NRW); on the property of farmers (Art. 29 Para. 2 LVerf.NRW); on the right to housing (Art. 19 Para. 1 LVerf.Be 1950); on the right to an education (Art. 11 Para. 1, 14, 85 LVerf.BW; Art. 8 Para. 1 Sent. 1, 9 LVerf.NRW); on adult education (Art. 22 LVerf.BW; Art. 17 LVerf.NRW; Art. 9 Para. 2 LVerf.SH); on the protection of marriage and the family (Art. 5 Para. 1 LVerf.NRW); on child and youth protection (Art. 13 LVerf. BW; Art. 6 Para. 2 LVerf.NRW); on maternity protection (Art. 5 Para. 1 Sent. 3 LVerf.NRW); on parental rights (Art. 15 Para. 3 LVerf.BW; Art. 8 Para. 1 Sent. 2 LVerf.NRW); on the educational mandate of the churches and charitable associations (Art. 6 Para. 3 LVerf.NRW); on the guarantee of the subsistence minimum (Art. 14 LVerf.Be 1950); on the equality of men and women (Art. 6 Para. 2 LVerf.Be 1950); on the social obligations of the economy (Art. 16 LVerf.Be; Art. 24 Para. 1 Sent. 1 LVerf.NRW); on the formation of common property (Art. 27 Para. 1 LVerf.NRW); against the abuse of economic power (Art. 16 LVerf.Be 1950, Art. 27 Para. 2 LVerf.NRW); and on full employment (Art. 12 Para. 1 Sent. 2 LVerf.Be 1950).

[478] Art. 3 Para. 2, 141 LVerf.Bay; Art. 31 Para. 1 LVerf.Be 1950; Art. 11 a LVerf.Br; Art. 26 a LVerf.He; Art. 29 a Para. 1 LVerf.NRW; Art. 59 a LVerf.Sl; Art. 7 LVerf.SH.

the GDR, but had been abolished in 1952 (Kilian 1995, pp. 55–100). They had to be recreated and, not least, given new constitutions. This offered the inhabitants in the new *Länder* an opportunity to give expression to their values – derived from their experiences in the GDR – also on the level of constitutional texts, provided they were in accordance with the Basic Law (Häberle 1993; von Mangoldt 1993; Starck 1994).

Changes to the Basic Law

The development that the Basic Law had undergone since 1990 was only in part conditioned by German unification. A number of amendments were attributable to the privatization and break-up of the transportation and telecommunications sectors.[479] Other changes concerned the adjustment of the federal system to the exigencies of European unification,[480] the reform of the asylum law,[481] rights of intervention in the interest of domestic security,[482] and a technical reform of electoral law.[483] The legislature also had to deal repeatedly with questions about the federal financial system.[484] Finally, the *Bundestag* and the *Bundesrat* also had to live up to the promise of Art. 5 of the Unification Treaty to establish German unity also in constitutional terms.[485] The basis for this was created by a Joint Constitutional Committee of the *Bundestag* and the *Bundesrat*.[486] It had a broad program, which concerned the relationship between the federation and the *Länder*, the basic rights, the goals of the state, direct democracy, the law of parliament, electoral law, and a number of other issues. The final recommendation of the Commission on 28 October 1993, focused on a closely circumscribed catalog. And the constitutional changes that were eventually made fell short even of these recommendations. Of importance to the social were the following: the duty of the state to "promote the actual implementation of equal rights for women and men" and to "take steps to

[479] "37. Gesetz zur Änderung des Grundgesetzes vom 14. Juli 1992," BGBl. I, p. 1254; "40. Gesetz zur Änderung des Grundgesetzes vom 20. Dezember 1993," BGBl. I, p. 2089; "41. Gesetz zur Änderung des Grundgesetzes vom 30. August 1994," BGBl. I, p. 2345.

[480] "38. Gesetz zur Änderung des Grundgesetzes vom 21. Dezember 1992," BGBl. I, p. 2086.

[481] "39. Gesetz zur Änderung des Grundgesetzes vom 28. Juni 1993," BGBl. I, p. 1002.

[482] "45. Gesetz zur Änderung des Grundgesetzes vom 26. März 1998," BGBl. I, p. 610.

[483] "46, Gesetz zur Änderung des Grundgesetzes vom 16. Juli 1998," BGBl. I, p. 1822.

[484] "43. Gesetz zur Änderung des Grundgesetzes vom 3. November 1995," BGBl. I, p. 1492; "44. Gesetz zur Änderung des Grundgesetzes vom 20. Oktober 1997," BGBl. I, p. 2470. Kesper (1997). Bundesministerium der Finanzen 1992; 1995).

[485] "42. Gesetz zur Änderung des Grundgesetzes vom 27. Oktober 1994," BGBl. I, p. 3146. H. Klein (1995, pp. 557–602); Bart (1996); Berlit (1996, pp. 17–89).

[486] "Bericht der Gemeinsamen Verfassungskommission gem. Beschluß des Deutschen Bundestages" BTDrs. 12/1590, 12/1670, and "Beschluß des Bundesrates," BRDrs. 741/91. Published by the Deutscher Bundestag, Referat Öffentlichkeitsarbeit (Bonn 1993); see also Deutscher Bundestag, 1996: Materialien zur Verfassungsdiskussion und zur Grundgesetzänderung in der Folge der deutschen Einigung. Bonn.

eliminate disadvantages that now exist" (Art. 3, Para. 2, Sent. 2, GG); an expansion of the prohibition against discrimination (Art. 3, Para. 3, GG) by adding disability; the new demarcation of the concurrent legislative powers of the federation, which now stipulated that the federal government had the right to legislate "to the extent that the establishment of equivalent living conditions throughout the federal territory of the maintenance of legal or economic unity renders federal legislation necessary in the national interest" (Art. 72, Par. 2, GG);[487] a reorganization of the integration of the social insurance carriers into the spheres of competency of the federation and the states (Art. 87, Para. 2, GG). In addition, the social goal of the state has now been joined by the mandate to "protect the natural foundations of life and animals" (Art. 20a, GG). No less notable is the multitude of proposals that the Joint Constitutional Commission and the constitution-amending legislature rejected: special rights for children; constitutional pronouncements on the compatibility of family and work, and a special constitutional recognition of the family's contributions to education and care-giving; an expansion of the protective sphere of Art. 6, Para. 1, GG, to long-term life partnerships other than marriage; the determination of state goals regarding employment, housing, social security, and education; finally, constitutional statements about a sense of shared humanity and a spirit of community.

New Developments in the Constitutional Law of the Länder

In the constitutions of the new federal states, the social goal of the state is generally affirmed,[488] at times linked to the affirmation of the European Social Charter.[489] Highlighted are the right to work[490] and the state's task of full employment and the promotion of employment,[491] the protection of the workforce,[492] the prohibition against child labor,[493] the protection of Sunday and holidays,[494] codetermination in the workplace,[495] codetermination above the enterprise level, free collective

[487] Previously, Art. 72, Para. 2, GG, had contained a differentiated catalog of prerequisites each of which had its own legitimizing effect. Taken together, though, they opened the door to federal legislation much wider than the clause now in effect. But the most important change in detail is that the words "equal living conditions" was replaced with "equivalent living conditions."

[488] Preamble, Art. 2 Para. 1 LVerf.Bb; Preamble, Art. 2 LVerf.MV; Art. 1 Sent. 2 LVerf.Sn; Preamble, Art. 2 Para. 1 LVerf.SnA; Preamble, Art. 44 Para. 1 Sent. 2 LVerf.Th. – see also Art. 1 Para. 2 LVerf.Nd.

[489] Art. 2 Para. 3 LVerf.Bb. – The constitutional affirmation of a united, social Europe is now also found in Art. 3a LVerf.Bay.

[490] Art. 7 Para. 1 LVerf.Sn.

[491] Art. 48 Para. 1 LVerf.Bb; Art 39 LVerf.SnA; Art. 36 Sent. 1 LVerf.Th.

[492] Art. 48 Para. 3 Sent. 1 LVerf.Bb.

[493] Art. 27 Para. 8 LVerf.Bb; Art. 28 Para. 2 LVerf.Sn.

[494] Art. 14 Para. 1 LVerf.Bb.

[495] Art. 50 LVerf.Bb; Art. 26 LVerf.Sn; Art. 37 Para. 3 LVerf.Th.

bargaining and the right to industrial action,[496] protection against dismissal for trainees, mothers, and so on.[497] Remarkable is the attention that the new constitutions devote to family work.[498] Emphasis is also placed on charitable activities and the freedom of relevant institutions.[499] Property is guaranteed, though its obligations to the common good are highlighted.[500] Occasionally we also hear about a broad dispersion of property and of the promotion of the wealth among workers and employees.[501] Differentiated programs are devoted to realizing the right to housing.[502] Vigorous language is used to talk about access to education[503] and participation in cultural life.[504] With respect to the health care system, emphasis is given to preventive health care for children.[505] Marriage and the family are recognized and promoted in an emphatic and differentiated manner.[506] "Special care is given to mothers, single parents, large families, and families with disabled members."[507] Child and youth protection[508] is given special contours through the stress on the complementary and supportive tasks of the federal government.[509] Social benefits are supposed to "make possible a dignified and autonomous shaping

[496] Art. 51 LVerf.Bb; Art. 25 LVerf.Sn; Art. 37 LVerf.Th.

[497] Art. 48 Para. 4 LVerf.Bb.

[498] Art. 26 Para. 4 LVerf.Bb; Art. 22 Para. 2 LVerf.Sn; Art. 24 Para. 2 Sent. 1 LVerf.SnA; Art. 17 Para. 2 LVerf.Th.; see also Art. 12 Para. 5 und 7 LVerfBe 1995.

[499] Art. 19 LVerf.MV; Art. 109 Para. 3, 110 LVerf.Sn; Art. 32 Para. 3, 33 LVerf.SnA; Art. 41 LVerf.Th.

[500] Art. 41 Para. 1 u. 2 LVerf.Bb; Art. 31 LVerf.Sn; Art. 18 Para. 1 u. 2 LVerf.SnA; Art. 34 Para. 1 u. 2 LVerf.Th.

[501] Art. 41 Para. 3 LVerf.Bb.

[502] Art. 47 Para. 1 LVerf.Bb. Right to housing: Art. 7 Para. 1 LVerf.Sn; state task housing : Art. 17 Para. 3 LVerf.MV; Art. 40 Para. 1 LVerf.SnA; Art. 15, 16 LVerf.Th.

[503] Art. 29, 33 LVerf.Bb; Art. 8, 16 Para. 4 LVerf.MV; Art. 7 Para. 1, 108 LVerf.Sn; Art. 25 Para. 1, 30 Para. 2 Sent. 2 LVerf.SnA; Art. 20, 29 LVerf.Th; s. auch Art. 20 Para. 1 LVerfBe 1995; from the "old states" see the new constitutions of the states Lower Saxony and Schleswig-Holstein: Art. 4 Para. 1 LVerf.Nd and Art. 9 Para. 3 LVerf.SH.

[504] Art. 34 Para. 3 LVerf.Bb; Art. 11 Para. 2 LVerf.Sn; Art. 36 Para. 3 LVerf.SnA; Art. 30 Para. 2 Sent. 3 LVerf.Th.

[505] Art. 9 Para. 3 LVerf.Sn; Art. 19 Para. 4 LVerf.Th.

[506] Art. 26 Para. 1 LVerf.Bb; Art. 22 Para. 1 LVerf.Sn; Art. 24 Para. 1 LVerf.SnA; Art. 17 Para. 1 LVerf.Th; s. auch Art. 12 Para. 1 LVerf.Be 1995. In Brandenburg also "other long-term life partnerships" (Art. 26 Para. 2); see also Art. 12 Para. 2 LVerf.Be 1995.

[507] Art. 26 Para. 1 Sent. 2 LVerf.Bb. On maternity protection see also Art. 22 Para. 5 LVerf.Sn; Art. 17 Para. 3 LVerf.Th; see alsoArt. 12 Para. 6 LVerf.Be 1995.

[508] Art. 27 Para. 3 Sent. 1 and Para. 5 LVerf.Bb; Art. 14 Para. 1 and Para. 3 LVerf.MV; Art. 9 LVerf.Sn; Art. 24 Para. 3, 4 LVerf.SnA; Art. 19 Para. 1 LVerf.Th.

[509] Art. 27 Para. 5 Sent. 2 LVerf.Bb; Art. 14 Para. 2 LVerf.MV; Art. 22 Para. 3 and 4 LVerf.Sn; Art. 11 Para. 1 and Para. 2, 24 Para. 2 Sent. 2 LVerf.SnA; Art. 18 Para. 2 and 3, 19 Para. 3 LVerf.Th.

of one's life."[510] The provision of the subsistence minimum is guaranteed.[511] Likewise, social security is guaranteed.[512] One state guarantees social compensation to the victims of National Socialism and Communism.[513] Some constitutions extend the prohibition against discrimination beyond Art. 3, Para. 3 of the Basic Law.[514] The equality of men and women is emphatically affirmed and developed in the direction of positive promotion.[515] The old and the disabled are guaranteed equality and equal living conditions.[516] The economic system is to be a socially just free market.[517] The possibilities of socialization are kept open.[518]

9.3 The Development of the Social System[519]

The *constitutional development* did not change the fundamental currents of the past decades. The decision of the Unification Treaty to place the united Germany on the track of the old Federal Republic was not called into question. But the difficulties of equalizing the unequal were enormous.[520] The new challenges to the social state were met in very different ways. A discussion with a multitude of competing voices erupted: for and against the status quo, for and against less social protection and fewer social benefits, for and against the costs of the social state, for and against the values it realized.[521] But the willingness of society to truly accept reforms that

[510] Thus for social security Art. 45 Para. 1 Sent. 2 LVerf.Bb; similarly for "social assistance and welfare" Art. 17 Para. 2 Sent. 2 LVerf.MV; see also Art. 22 Para. 1 Sent. 2 LVerfBe 1995.

[511] Art. 45 Para. 2 LVerf.Bb.

[512] Art. 45 Para. 1 LVerf.Bb; Art. 7 Para. 1 LVerf.Sn; see also Art. 22 Para. 1 Sent. 1 LVerf.Be 1995.

[513] Art. 116 LVerf.Sn.

[514] Art. 12 Para. 2 LVerf.Bb; Art. 2 Para. 3 LVerf.Th; see also Art. 10 Para. 2 LVerfBe 1995.

[515] Art. 12 Para. 3 LVerf.Bb; Art. 13 LVerf.MV; Art. 8, 18 Para. 2 LVerf.Sn; Art. 7 Para. 2, 34 LVerf.SnA; Art. 2 Para. 2 LVerf.Th; see also Art. 10 Para. 3 LVerf.Be 1995; in the "old *Länder*" see now Art. 118 Para. 2 LVerf.Bay, new version; Art. 3 Para. 2 Sent. 3 LVerf.Nd; Art. 6 LVerf.SH.

[516] Art. 17 Para. 2 Sent. 1 LVerf.MV; Art. 7 Para. 2 LVerf.Sn; Art. 38 LVerf.SnA. Only for the disabled: Art. 12 Para. 4 LVerf.Bb; Art. 2 Para. 4 LVerf.Th; see also Art. 11 LVerf.Be 1995; see also the program of "institutions for counseling and care in old age" (Art. 22 Para. 2 LVerf.Be 1995); see the relevant Art. 118 a LVerf.Bay, new version.

[517] Art. 42 Para. 2 Sent. 1 LVerf.Bb; Art. 38 LVerf.Th also emphasizes the ecological character of the free market.

[518] Art. 41 Para. 5 LVerf.Bb; Art. 32 Para. 2 LVerf.Sn; Art. 18 Para. 4 LVerf.SnA.

[519] Frerich and Frey (vol. 3, 1996, pp. 463–647); Ritter (1996, pp. 393–408); Sozialberichte der Bundesregierung 1993 (BTDrs 12/7130), 1997 (BTDrs. 13/10142); Bundesministerium für Arbeit und Sozialordnung (ed.) (1994); Bundesministerium für Arbeit und Soziales and Bundesarchiv (eds.), 2007b: Geschichte der Sozialpolitik in Deutschland seit 1945, vol. 11, Chap. 2.

[520] Kleinhenz (1991); Kleinhenz (1992a); Hauser (1996a); Kommission zur Erforschung des sozialen und politischen Wandels in den neuen Bundesländern (KSPW) (1996).

[521] A selection can be found in Lampert 1997; (1998, pp. 429–463).

interfered with vested rights remained small. Especially the "middle voter" wanted his cake and eat it too. And so for politics – already kept busy by the process of German unification, European integration, and the changes in the international community – the most sensible approach was to stay the course. Social policy, too, continued along the track of the old Federal Republic. The social state challenged on many fronts did not respond with innovation: not with revolution, barely with evolution. The inertia of the institutions supported this development. *The questions of principle remained unanswered.*

9.3.1 The Responsibility for the Economy[522]

The process of unification *affirmed* the *social market economy* in a special way. Through its efficiency and performance, it formed a central motive behind the desire of the citizens of the GDR to join the Federal Republic. Through the Treaty establishing Monetary, Economic, and Social Union and the Unification Treaty, the social market economy was normatively codified. But the overall development, too, *invigorated the economic forces*. If the period around 1970 tended to accord a high rank to the politically feasible redistribution alongside – if not ahead of – distribution produced by a competitive society, and if the period around 1980 entertained concerns about the precedence of redistribution, around 1990 the understanding and significance of distribution continued to expand. There was quite generally a new climate of openness in economic policy. Politics and society worked hand in hand to spread new values: to see globalization not as a threat but an opportunity, to understand that innovation is a necessity, to rekindle the courage to be independent, and to break the monopoly of the life model of dependent gainful employment. The federation *and* the states realized that the adjustment of the German economy to the global changes in technology, communications, and commerce demanded new framework conditions for them.[523]

Two problems, however, remained as the specific challenges of the time. One of these can slowly fade into history. It is the *transformation* of the centralized state economy of the GDR into a decentralized, "private-capitalistic" economy (Turek 1996, pp. 662–671). We are talking about the process of privatization, which has

[522] Weimer (1998, pp. 365–467); Jahresgutachten des Sachverständigenrates (1989, 1998); "Jahreswirtschaftsberichte der Bundesregierung" 1990 (BTDrs. 11/6278) – 1999 (BTDrs. 13/10107).

[523] "Bericht über die Deregulierungsmaßnahmen der Bundesregierung," BTDrs. 12/7468; "Bericht der Bundesregierung zur Zukunftssicherung des Standortes Deutschland," BTDrs. 12/5620; "Bericht der Bundesregierung über den Stand der Umsetzung der Maßnahmen zur Zukunftssicherung des Standortes Deutschland und des Aktionsprogramms für mehr Wachstum und Beschäftigung," BRDrs. 171/94; "Fortschrittsbericht zum Bericht der Bundesregierung zur Zukunftssicherung des Standortes Deutschland," BTDrs. 12/8090; see also Bundesministerium für Wirtschaft (1996).

been completed (Oppenländer 1997). And we are talking about the overbalance of public financing in the economy of the new states.[524]

The other challenge: the two-stage process of the *emigration of economic policy from the purview of the national competency* of the Federal Republic. The first stage: the emigration to the European Community. This is primarily an emigration of competencies and regulatory schemes. But it is also a process of the emigration of economic activities. Very different the second stage: the process of the emigration of economic activities to global processes. This process is unbalanced. Ordering competencies follow the global integration of economic activities only inadequately. This applies to the regulatory sphere that every free market economy needs; and it holds for the social supplementation that a social market economy needs. In this regard the social market economy of the Federal Republic has become increasingly vulnerable over time. But the global market economy also falls short on this criteria – it is in no way on the road to a social market economy.[525]

9.3.2 Work[526]

The system of gainful labor is under challenge by the development like never before. What can be done to adjust the degree to which dependent gainful employment has become the typical norm and the extent of social protection that characterizes it to the evolving conditions without compromising their essence? These are question above all for labor law (Hanau 1997, 1999, pp. 179–194; Löwisch 1999, pp. 69–80), but also for the law on social security, indeed for all assistance and promotion systems that have always had a hand in shaping the reality of the basic formula (Mückenberger 1990, pp. 158–179; Zacher 1999b). Reality is outpacing the characterizations of labor relationships. The prime example of that is the "pseudo self-employed" (Wank 1997). Instead of inquiring into the meaning of the new developments and developing it in a positive way, labor law and social insurance law are trying to "capture" the "pseudo self-employed" with the old categories of labor and social law.[527] In fact, the development of labor law –

---

[524] Boss and Rosenschon (1996). Also: "Materialien zur Deutschen Einheit und zum Aufbau in den neuen Bundesländern, "BTDrs. 13/2280; "Jahresbericht der Bundesregierung zum Stand der Deutschen Einheit 1997," BTDrs. 13/8450; "Jahresbericht der Bundesregierung zum Stand der Deutschen Einheit 1998," BTDrs. 13/10823.

[525] It is notable that the "Sachverständigenrat zur Begutachtung der gesamtwirtschaftlichen Entwicklung" in this decade of globalization has addressed the need for efforts to bring about a new global economic system only twice: Bundesministerium für Wirtschaft (1994/95, p. 241; 1995/96, pp. 239–245).

[526] Das Arbeitsrecht der Gegenwart (1990–1998); Kommission für Zukunftsfragen der Freistaaten Bayern und Sachsen (1996, 1997); Bundesministerium für Arbeit und Soziales and Bundesarchiv (eds.), 2007b: Geschichte der Sozialpolitik in Deutschland seit 1945, vol. 11, Chap. 3, nos. 1 and 2.

[527] "Gesetz zu Korrekturen der Sozialversicherung und zur Sicherung der Arbeitnehmerrechte vom 19. Dezember 1998" BGBl. I, p. 3843, esp. Art. 3.

especially that of judge-made law – is having a very hard time escaping its character as an end in itself.[528] But the issue is not only to adequately reform the employment relationship and the social benefits systems that envelop it. For society as a whole the issue is also to relativize the difference between work that is done in the typified relationships of dependent employment, and work that is performed as independent gainful employment, and possibly also as cooperatively organized gainful work. And the issue is also – if in a different way – to relativize the difference between (dependent and independent) gainful work and the work that is performed as unpaid work within the family and outside the family, or as community-oriented work. Do the values whose legal expression labor law has solidified in such an extreme way – protection from and in a state of dependency, protection against typical dangers and shortcomings, security against inappropriate changes – not have meaning outside of labor law? It cannot be that all legal relationships that call for consideration of these values must be declared work or employment relationships.[529]

But the labor system is being called into question not only with regard to individual employment relationships: it is also being challenged with respect to its structures involving the unions[530] and industrial relations (social partnership) (Kleinhenz 1992b, pp. 14–24; Zohlnhöfer 1996).[531] Changes at all levels of union organization in the practice of free collective bargaining and of codetermination provide clues to a development whose outcomes cannot be foreseen at this time.

Labor law and the practice of labor law pose tasks especially for German unity (von Maydell and Wank 1996). Art. 30 of the Unification Treaty assigns the "all-German legislator" the task

1. to recodify in a uniform manner and as soon as possible the law on employment contracts and the provisions on working hours under public law, including the admissibility of work on Sundays and public holidays, and the specific industrial safety regulations for women;
2. to reorganize public law on industrial safety and bring it into line with present-day requirements in accordance with the law of the European Communities and the concurrent part of the industrial safety law of the German Democratic Republic.

The idea of a codification of labor law had already been floated in the Weimar Constitution (Art. 157, Sent. 2). It was picked up again in the Brandt era. Now it is in trouble again with regard to the law on employment contracts.[532] Not so the

---

[528] On the transition of the "leadership" role from labor courts to the Federal Constitutional Court and the European Court of Justice see Hanau (1998).

[529] See above notes 357 and 527. See also the "Agrarberichte" 1971 (BTDrs. VI/1800) to 1983 (BTDrs. 9/2402).

[530] Modernisierung (1992); Neue Industriepolitik im gesellschaftlichen Konsens? (1995).

[531] On "social self-administration" see issue no. 10 (1993) of the "Deutsche Rentenversicherung" with contributions by, among others, Lutz Freitag and Franz Ruland.

[532] Verhandlungen des 59. Deutschen Juristentages (1992/1993a); Bundesministerium für Arbeit und Soziales and Bundesarchiv (eds.), 2007b: Geschichte der Sozialpolitik in Deutschland seit 1945, vol. 11, Chap. 3, no. 1.

codification of occupational health and safety law.[533] Of course, the mass of problems was left to practice to deal with (e.g. Sander 1997; Deich and Kohte 1997).

The concern of the social state for the *self-employed* is more diffuse than ever.[534] The political responsibility for the income of *farmers* has long since passed to Europe.[535] Other than that, the social state has assumed a – highly problematic – income responsibility above all for the income of doctors and other professional groups active in the health care system. To the supraindividual programs for regional, sectoral, and structural promotion,[536] whose income effects can be as considerable as they are diffuse, there has been added a new focal point: aid to the new federal states (see above note 524).

9.3.3 The Community of Maintenance[537]

The social situation of marriage and the family continues to be replete with "unequal inequalities": between marriage and non-marital partnerships, singles with and without children, couples with and without children, couples with many children and those with few, singles who focus on child-raising, couples in which both partners work, and so on.[538] And as society ages, the constellations involving the role of the elderly within families and the care of the middle generation for the elderly are increasingly felt.[539] Here, too, we find a multitude of inequalities. Has enough already been done to honor the *production of welfare* that is achieved by families? In fact, politics has done a great deal to moderate the disadvantages that one parent suffers if he or she focuses on domestic work. Politics must also be highly commended for not fixating on a single model – whether it is the model of the gainful employment of both parents and outside care for the children, whether it is the model of a strict allocation of gainful employment and domestic work to one parent each. But does that really amount to what is required to properly situate the family economically? Once again it took the Federal Constitutional Court to bring a

[533] Bundesministerium für Arbeit und Soziales and Bundesarchiv (eds.), 2007b: Geschichte der Sozialpolitik in Deutschland seit 1945, vol. 11, Chap. 3, nos. 1 and 2.

[534] "Fortschreibung des Berichts über die Lage der freien Berufe," BTDrs. 12/22.

[535] See "Agrarberichte" 1990 (BTDrs. 11/6387) to 1995 (BTDrs. 13/400), and the "Berichte der Bundesregierung über die Integration in den Europäischen Gemeinschaften" cited below in notes 630 and 689.

[536] See on this the Jahreswirtschaftsberichte (note 522) and Subventionsberichte 1987–1990 (BTDrs. 11/5116), 1989–1992 (12/1525), 1991–1994 (12/5580), 1993–1996 (13/2230).

[537] "Familien und Familienpolitik im geeinten Deutschland – Zukunft des Humanvermögens" BTDrs. 12/7560; Bundesministerium für Arbeit und Soziales and Bundesarchiv (eds.), 2007b: Geschichte der Sozialpolitik in Deutschland seit 1945, vol. 11, Chap. 3, no. 10.

[538] One example: BVerfGE 87, 234: comparison of unemployment benefits in the case of the unemployment of one or both partners among "dual earners," "single earners," those permanently separated or not separated, and finally, with singles.

[539] "Altenbericht (erster) der Bundesregierung," BTDrs. 12/5897.

development for which politics did not have the strength to a conclusion: the Court guaranteed the family the right to a subsistence minimum with respect to the income tax.[540]

The *Unification Treaty* paid special attention to the divergent developments in the "old Federal Republic" and in the GDR (Art. 31):

> (1) It shall be the task of the all-German legislator to develop further the legislation on equal rights for men and women.
> (2) In view of the different legal and institutional starting positions with regard to the employment of mothers and fathers, it shall be the task of the all-German legislator to shape the legal situation in such a way as to allow a reconciliation of family and occupational life.

This mandate poses difficulties (Verhandlungen des 60. Deutschen Juristentages (1994) not least because the different preferences in East and West Germany are deeply connected with the divergent guiding models and with differences in the systems of labor and social law. One of the most serious issues concerns the provision of social services where the compatibility of family and work can be ensured only by way of services.[541] So far there has been no specific answer from the "all-German legislator."[542]

9.3.4 Wealth[543]

The social approach to the problem of wealth has developed in an extremely divergent way. The broad *exclusion of wealth from the social worse-better comparison* (Huster 1997) was affirmed. In 1995, the Federal Constitutional Court decided (BVerfGE 93, 121) that wealth can be taxed only where it can be presumed to yield earnings (and may not be taxed away in any other way). A taxation that went beyond the effective presumed earning capacity of wealth is not permissible. What was still regarded as self-evident during the first years in which the Basic Law was in effect – the possibility of a social reallocation also of wealth – had thus been

[540] BVerfGE 82, 60, 198; 87, 153; 99, 246, 268, 273. – "Bericht über die Höhe des Existenzminimums von Kindern und Familien" BTDrs. 12/6329; also BTDrs. 13/381; on the state of tax law see also Lehner (1998, pp. 511–524).

[541] See above note 432, and by way of supplement "Antwort der Bundesregierung auf die Große Anfrage betreffend Situation der Kindergärten, Krippen und Horte in den neuen Bundesländern" BTDrs. 12/661.

[542] "Familien und Familienpolitik im geeinten Deutschland – Zukunft des Humanvermögens. Fünfter Familienbericht" BTDrs. 12/7560; the "Gesetz zur Durchsetzung der Gleichberechtigung von Frauen und Männern" ("Zweites Gleichberechtigungsgesetz vom 24. Juni 1994" BGBl. I, p. 1406) has a tightly circumscribed range of effect.

[543] Bundesministerium für Arbeit und Soziales and Bundesarchiv (eds.), 2007b: Geschichte der Sozialpolitik in Deutschland seit 1945, vol. 11, Chap. 3, no. 16.

called into question.[544] The Federal Constitutional Court, of course, sees the problem in a broader context:

> Whether and to what extent the wealth tax could be used, within a different framework of tax law, as an instrument of redistribution, does not need to be decided here, since it does not, in the current overall tax law, have a redistribution effect of any significance... A possible change in the law of redistributive burdens and benefits is not the subject of the current certification procedure.

The privileging of wealth is heightened under the current economic conditions in that wealth, in the form of capital, escapes the framework of the nation state and thus also largely evades its national obligations (Bundesministerium der Finanzen 1999). The reform of the inheritance and gift tax (BGBl. [1991] I, p. 468), at any rate, brought at most an adjustment of the tax law to the reality of inheritance and gifting activities, but it was not an expression of an alternative approach.

Wealth caused another vexation in connection with German unification. The *citizens of the GDR* had only *modest opportunities to form wealth*. Therein lay one of the most profound differences between the society of the old Federal Republic and the society in the new states (Hauser et al. 1996, pp. 156–181). An equalization of burdens between the "haves" in the old Federal Republic and the "have-nots" in the new states did not take place. Rather, the regulation of property questions in East Germany, tax breaks, and instruments of promotion have had the result that the distribution of assets not only between East and West, but also within the East, has developed in a way that is felt by many to be unfair (Glatzer and Kleinhenz 1997; Lampert 1998, p. 110f.).

9.3.5 Social Benefits Systems[545]

The energy of social benefits policy was largely absorbed by the problems of German reunification and by the adjustment to the economic and social developments. Still, there were also some fundamental reforms.

Social Provision

The focal point of the development was in every regard the *systems of social insurance*. The law governing the statutory *sickness insurance*[546] had to be reformed repeatedly. One should single out the Health Care Structure Act (1992),

---

[544] BVerfGE 93, 135; for a critique of the decision see the dissenting opinion by the judge Böckenförde, ibid., 149–164.

[545] Jahrbuch des Sozialrechts der Gegenwart (1991–1998); Bundesministerium für Arbeit und Soziales and Bundesarchiv (eds.), 2007b: Geschichte der Sozialpolitik in Deutschland seit 1945, vol. 11, Chap. 3, nos. 3–9. On the progress of codification see: 25 Jahre Sozialgesetzbuch (1995).

[546] Bundesministerium für Arbeit und Soziales and Bundesarchiv (eds.), 2007b: Geschichte der Sozialpolitik in Deutschland seit 1945, vol. 11, Chap. 3, no. 6.

which further deepened the corporatist character of health insurance. Still, there was no long-term, satisfactory balancing of the development of costs, the expectations of the insured, and the income expectations of the service providers. The statutory *accident insurance* was reformed in 1996 and incorporated into the Social Code (SGB VII).[547] In 1997, finally a reform of *pension insurance* was agreed upon, which was supposed to tackle the problem of the ageing of society within the system.[548] However, a multi-layered discussion doubted that it was possible to solve the pension problem without bringing new elements into the equation and strengthening overarching, general structures.[549]

The most significant development in the area of social provision came with the introduction of *social long-term care insurance* and its incorporation into the Social Code (SGB XI).[550] There are many notable aspect to this (Schulin 1998, pp. 1029–1046) insurance. First, that the path of social insurance was chosen, even though there were alternatives under discussion – on the one hand, a tax-financed assistance system, and, on the other hand, private insurance. Second, of note is the widening of the circle of the insured to include individuals whose social protection in case of illness is otherwise guaranteed by civil service or official law (Sect. 23, Para. 3 and 4, Sect. 24, SGB XI), private insurance (Sect. 23 SGB XI), or social compensation law (Sect. 22 SGB XI). No other social insurance law has approximated the principle of universal coverage as much as this one. The incorporation of private insurance into the circle of possible carriers makes use of new possibilities for a partnership between social insurance and private insurance (Sect. 1, Para. 2, Sects. 10, 21–23, 61, 110 f. SGB XI). The most spectacular development, however, must be seen in the broad scope for the recruitment of nursing-care services – individual care providers, services, and in-patient establishments. This recruitment begins with individual help, especially from the family, includes volunteers and non-profit organizations as well as institutions of administrative *Daseinsvorsorge*, and also brings free market coverage of the need for nursing care into the system (Sects. 36–45, 69–92 SGB XI). Finally, it is recognized that the need for nursing care within society as a whole cannot be "taken care of" by a branch of social protection, but that it remains instead a shared responsibility of all parties involved – those in need for care, their families, society, and all levels of the polity (Sects. 6–13, 69 SGB XI). It is significant, especially

[547] Bundesministerium für Arbeit und Soziales and Bundesarchiv (eds.), 2007b: Geschichte der Sozialpolitik in Deutschland seit 1945, vol. 11, Chap. 3, no. 7.

[548] Gesetz zur Reform der gesetzlichen Rentenversicherung – Rentenreformgesetz 1999 – von 1997; Bundesministerium für Arbeit und Soziales and Bundesarchiv (eds.), 2007b: Geschichte der Sozialpolitik in Deutschland seit 1945, vol. 11, Chap. 3, no. 5.

[549] See, for example, Bundesministerium für Wirtschaft (1998; "Grundlegende Reform der gesetzlichen Rentenversicherung…"); Schmähl (2000, pp. 50–71).

[550] "Gesetz zur sozialen Absicherung des Risikos der Pflegebedürftigkeit – Pflegeversicherungsgesetz – von 1994;" Bundesministerium für Arbeit und Soziales and Bundesarchiv (eds.), 2007b: Geschichte der Sozialpolitik in Deutschland seit 1945, vol. 11, Chap. 3, no. 6.

because of the modernity of this law, how little attention it received in the public discussion. Society and politics were not interested in learning the lessons to which this law was already giving expression.

Social security assumed special significance within the framework of *German unification*. The Unification Treaty stipulated the transfer of the West German social security system to the new states.[551] The largest structural change this entailed concerned health insurance, since medical care in the GDR was organized into a state health service (Mrotzek 1997, pp. 17–216). In social insurance, the western communities of solidarity had to share in the burden of rebuilding the East.[552] That was especially true of pension insurance. The federation assumed only part of the pensions for East German retirees; the remainder had to be borne by the community of solidarity that is pension insurance. In this way those paying into pension insurance financed pensions whose "contribution history" had occurred under the GDR, while pension insurance sees itself as the solidarity of the "active" with the "old," who had carried the system with their contributions during their "active" years. As a result, the financing of the "Eastern pensions" ran into the limits of acceptance. In fact, those covered by social insurance in the "West" contributed more to the costs of German unity than "simple tax payers."[553] On the other hand: all of the – very numerous – pension schemes that had existed in the GDR were transferred into the pension insurance. However, the process of integration through which this was achieved led to such a low configuration of benefits that the latter invariably had to be perceived as unfair. And the Federal Constitutional Court did set limits to this mode of transition (BVerfGE 100, 1, 59, 104, 138).

Other Social Benefits Systems – Social Services

The tax-financed *assistance and promotion programs*[554] and the systems of *social compensation*[555] did not undergo a pronounced legislative development. Too many changes in both working life and social benefits[556] and services[557] had to be

[551] See Appendix I to the Unification Treaty, Chap. VI, subject area D, Chap. VIII, subject areas E, F, G, H, I; Appendix II to the Unification Treaty, subject areas E, F, G, H, I.

[552] For accident insurance see BSGE 79, 23; for sickness insurance see Engelhard (1994, p. 1412).

[553] On the numbers see "Materialien zur Deutschen Einheit" BTDrs. 13/2280: 114–116. Still, the Federal Social Court (BSGE 81: 276) ruled that this regulation was not unconstitutional.

[554] Bundesministerium für Arbeit und Soziales and Bundesarchiv (eds.), 2007b: Geschichte der Sozialpolitik in Deutschland seit 1945, vol. 11, Chap. 3, nos. 3, 9–11, 14, 15.

[555] Bundesministerium für Arbeit und Soziales and Bundesarchiv (eds.), 2007b: Geschichte der Sozialpolitik in Deutschland seit 1945, vol. 11, Chap. 3, no. 12.

[556] Bundesministerium für Arbeit und Soziales and Bundesarchiv (eds.), 2007b: Geschichte der Sozialpolitik in Deutschland seit 1945, vol. 11, Chap. 3, no. 9.

[557] Bundesministerium für Arbeit und Soziales and Bundesarchiv (eds.), 2007b: Geschichte der Sozialpolitik in Deutschland seit 1945, vol. 11, Chap. 3, no. 14.

grappled with. The transition to the new Länder[558] led to considerable rearrangements with regard to social assistance (Wienand et al. 1997).

The social benefits system that was most directly challenged by unemployment was *employment promotion*.[559] It was subject to constant political directives – and especially also to a relationship of tension between the growing need and the shrinking revenue from contributions and public funds. Eventually, employment promotion was fundamentally reformed. In 1997, the promotion of employment was incorporated into the Social Code.[560] The substantive reform connected with it brought in many ways a new understanding of the responsibility on the part of both citizens and the polity for earning the basis of a livelihood.

The problem of social *services*[561] became more acute. The persistent unemployment, in conjunction with the inadequacies of the social benefits systems, had released more and more individuals from the integrative system that was linked to the normal employment relationship and full employment. Poverty in a variety of manifestations became visible ever more clearly.[562] To counter this trend, the system of social law focused on the monetary benefit systems of unemployment insurance, unemployment assistance, and welfare. Within the sphere of freedoms that these monetary and juridified systems leave, people are fundamentally left to their own devices. They are not personally helped – not in a way appropriate to their vexing and perilous situation. Moreover, institutions and society do not receive any reliable feedback about how they are faring. That may have something to do with the general unwillingness to accept and provide personal support. Instead, the parties involved prefer to agree that the administration of juridified monetary systems is the assistance that is most suitable to the emancipation of those in need. But what if those individuals cannot live up to this claim of emancipation? Is the steering of freedom through juridified monetary systems enough to promote emancipation? Moreover: the system of social services is set up for pluralism. This is a great benefit and should not be squandered. But it does have a flipside: the plurality of services leads to competition among the services. Where is the service behind which stands – when this is needed – the mandate and authority of the polity?[563]

---

[558] See Appendix I to the Unification Treaty, Chap. VIII, subject areas E and K, Chap. X, subject area H, Chap. XIV, Chap. XVI, subject area B.

[559] On the transition see Appendices I and II of the Unification Treaty, in each Chap. VIII, subject area E.

[560] "Gesetz zur Reform der Arbeitsförderung (Arbeitsförderungsreformgesetz) von 1997"; see Bundesministerium für Arbeit und Soziales and Bundesarchiv (eds.), 2007b: Geschichte der Sozialpolitik in Deutschland seit 1945, vol. 11, Chap. 3, no. 3; on German unity see Kinitz (1997).

[561] Bundesministerium für Arbeit und Soziales and Bundesarchiv (eds.), 2007b: Geschichte der Sozialpolitik in Deutschland seit 1945, vol. 11, Chap. 3, no. 14.

[562] "Armut in der Bundesrepublik Deutschland" BTDrs. 13/1527; "Bericht der Bundesregierung über Maßnahmen zur Bekämpfung der Obdachlosigkeit," BTDrs. 13/5226; Neumann (1999, pp. 27–32).

[563] On the threat to the municipal services see Ortmann (1997).

On the other side there is an intensification of the tendencies toward a new rationality in services.[564] The dangers inherent in the undifferentiated jumble of altruistic motivation and organization-preserving thinking in terms of economic viability, of non-profit principle and the free-market quest for profit, of administrative calculations of covering costs and alternative strategies of private economic activity, but above all in the undifferentiated mix of social-state mandate and basic-right freedoms were perceived ever more clearly – not only in the practice of the charitable and municipal providers, but as the long-term care law revealed, also by the legislator. Still, many inconsistencies and contradictions still wait to be resolved.

Social Security or Basic Pension?

Social insurance once again proved its vitality during those years. It became an essential medium for the social realization of German unification. And it made possible a good solution to the problem of the need for long-term care. Still, it ran into difficulties (Riedmüller 1994; Leisering 1995). Those difficulties arose centrally from the origins of social insurance as workers' insurance. Normal employment relationship, full employment, and "workers' society" were the ideal basis for its effectiveness. The change in working life, especially unemployment, led to strains on the financing and benefits side. And the selectivity that came with the focus on workers and employees led to growing tensions with a general social notion of social protection that was pushing for universality. That tension was felt all the more as the particularity of the various systems were increasingly absorbed into overarching contexts: within the various branches through a growing net of burden equalizations; in relationship to the polity in that social insurance relieved it of some of its burdens ("non-insurance benefits") (Krause 1980, pp. 115–163; Ruland 1995, pp. 28–38; Vogler-Ludwig 1997, pp. 161–176; Kostorz 1998) and in that the polity involved the tax payer in the financing (especially through the federal subsidy to the pension insurance).

Social insurance is concerned in almost in all cases – with the exception of unemployment insurance –with a generational transfer. When it comes to pension insurance, that is its most important task. As a result, the changes in the age structure of the population affect the operating conditions of social security. The new position of capital additionally limits the possibilities of involving it in the financing of social insurance. A host of other problems could also be enumerated. At the same time, it is becoming clear that the institutional form of social insurance draws very narrow boundaries around an appropriate reform. The calculability of social insurance and especially also the group allocation that is part of its selectivity makes the interests that are at stake in any change especially apparent. And that feeds the strength of the opposition. Added to this are the associational interests that are tied to the organizational structures, and the competency (for self-preservation)

[564] Die soziale Arbeit in den 90er Jahren (1991); Öhlschläger and Brüll (1996); Rauschenbach et al. (1996); Speck (1999); see also Pitschas (1996b, pp. 7–40).

of the management of the carriers and their affiliated associations. Pension insurance is affected in a special way by the contradiction between the temporal horizon of its task and the temporal pulse of democracy.

Given all of this, a variety of reasons have led to suggestions about a tax-financed basic pension (Hauser 1996b). It could redefine the relationship between work and social security. It would abolish the tension between the forward-looking dimension of social protection that makes provisions for the future, and the dominance of the present over both the economic and political conditions of what is possible and desired. By making provision beyond the basic pension fundamentally a private responsibility and probably leaving it also to societal organization (Miegel and Wahl 1985), it would strengthen individual responsibility, activate societal forces, take some pressure off politics, and limit the citizens' tendency to give in to socio-political temptations. The strata of society would result directly from the multiplicity of people's circumstances and ways of dealing with one another, and would not be artificially constructed by the structures of a selective social security. The move from a society of workers to a society of citizens would be accomplished (Biedenkopf 1997). But what would be the price for this? This is not the place to discuss that question. Only one thing seems obvious: the basic formula that has carried the social system since its inception would be abolished.

9.3.6 Taxes, Dues, Households – An Overall View

The overall view of the financial effects of the *social processes of giving and taking* fell into even greater disorder than before (Sozialrecht und Steuerrecht 1998). The social benefits systems underwent a restless development – on the one hand because of the fluctuations in the inflow of funds from contributions and tax revenues (Die Finanzierung des Sozialleistungsrechts in der Zukunft 1999), and on the other because of continual interventions by the legislator in the benefits law. Because of the standoff between the governing majority in the *Bundestag* and the opposition's majority in the *Bundesrat*, tax reform (Bundesministerium für Wirtschaft 1998, pp. 1873–1895) had to wait until the spring of 2000. Needless to say, the constitutional necessity of harmonizing tax law and social benefits law was all the more urgent.[565]

Alongside benefits and tax law, the *supraindividual programs* retained their importance.[566] However, *German unification* added a new problem. The gap between the economic power of the old Federal Republic and that of the new federal states could be balanced out only through enormous financial transfers from West to East. This was done via the budgets of the federal government and

[565] See above sections 7.3.9 and 8.3.6. See also Lehner (1993), and Probleme einer Integration... (1996).

[566] On the Jahreswirtschaftsberichte see note 522; on the Subventionsberichte see note 536. See also Huckemann (1997).

the states and the financial equalization between them (Bauer 1997). It was done through the financing of the joint tasks of the federation and the states and through the "German unity" fund. It was done through promotion programs on the federal level. It was done through the social insurance budgets. It was also done through the inflow of private wealth, which led to tax reductions in the West or to revenues for the *Treuhandanstalt* in the East (Freese 1995). With that, any control over the social effects of the financial system has been lost.

9.4 Summary

9.4.1 The Power of the Institutions

This period is characterized by the historical-institutional shaping of the social. Especially the fundamental nature and the urgent multiplicity of challenges seem to refer politics and society most emphatically to the existing institutions of the social. In the general turmoil, they convey the expectation of permanence, reliability, and predictability. As concerns about being disadvantaged by the developments grow among the population, the institutions attract onto themselves the hope of being able to protect vested rights, make change for the worse measurable and thus easier to fight. In the best case, the fact that the institutions are taken for granted provides a useful topography for new demands and desires: advantages and disadvantages, expenses and relief can be persuasively – and if necessary, reassuringly – mapped out on them.

But a more positive interpretation has its own justification. With so much change to be managed, can one justify experiments in this situation? It is not better to use the tried-and-true mechanism, whose ways of operating are largely known and which are deeply rooted in society, politics, and the law? To be sure: all of these mechanisms have revealed their problems and limitations. But all the alternatives are afflicted with infinitely more uncertainty. The historically evolved solutions are carried by the multiplicity of identifications on the part of the interested parties and those affected. That has distorted and alienated them. Above all, though, it has anchored them. New solutions would no doubt have their partisans, as well. But they are likely to have more opponents than the existing ones. And most of those interested and affected might only stand back and watch, take a wait-and-see attitude, remain aloof, and not identify – potentialities of instability.

And so it is in many ways understandable and reasonable that politics and society have so clearly opted for what exists, and still do. Still, the question remains whether the existing institutions were not also put at risk by the expectation and demand that they negotiate the transition from the societal, economic, political, and legal conditions under which they developed over decades to largely new societal, political, and legal premises. In other words: the question remains whether the traditional institutions can and will perform their services under the new conditions in the way they have done in the past.

9.4.2 The Social in the United Germany, in Supranational Europe, in the "Global" World

But wherever the institutions of the social are called into question and are supposed to be redesigned, it must be concretely asked why the old must be replaced and what the new is supposed to achieve. The question must be raised about the normative foundation of the social. And in the light of the multifarious and weighty developments that coincided during these years, this normative foundation, in particular, is showing new features. It should be obvious that *social equality, social justice, social participation, solidarity, subsidiarity*, and *security* mean *something new and exciting* after German reunification, in the face of Europeanization, and, finally, in a globalizing world – if its not obvious, then they are not being taken seriously enough.

Ever since *German unification, equality* has confronted a new challenge: the inequality between East and West Germany. And ever since, *participation* also means the participation of those who live in the new states in those things that are better "in the West." The talk about *social justice* is deeply unsettled. What is conventionally meant by justice of achievement, justice of acquired status, and justice of needs does not capture what the people in "the East" expect from justice. And yet it must be possible to get closer to the truth about these things. Does the justice of achievement mean what was achieved "over there," even if it cannot be measured in the way it is done "here"? What can the justice of acquired status mean if the system negated precisely individual acquisitions? But justice of needs alone is not adequate to explain what needs to be done about the inequality between "East" and "West." And neither is the justice of opportunity in the face of a history in which the opportunities of some were so unequal to the opportunities of others. *Solidarity* is now surely the solidarity of the "West" with the "East." But solidarity by its nature flows in all directions. What can solidarity of the "East" with the "West" mean? And what does "subsidiarity" mean in this context? What can be better done by the citizens of the new *Länder*, their societal forces, their municipal and state entities? Compared to whom? Surely not only compared to the "West." Surely also compared to each other and the world. *Security* is probably the one concept that least refers to something new.

And what do all of these principles mean vis-à-vis *Europe* and the *world*? More 3precisely: what do they mean in the relationship between Germany and Europe, between Germany and the world? What are they supposed to mean within Europe and the world? What must change in their understanding within Germany because there is a Europe and a world, and because Germany is now tied into Europe and the world in a completely new way? The social clearly faces profound changes also in this regard. How valid is the claim of equality, participation, justice, or solidarity if it cannot hold up to the dimension of Europe and the dimension of "one world," "one humanity"? But what kind of system is feasible in view of the differences in Europe, and especially in view of the differences in the world?

9.4.3 The Principles of the Social in Germany in the 1990s

But what kind of understanding has carried the socio-political development in the Federal Republic? *Equality* was surely the central value of the social also in those years. But it has become more complex. The tolerance of inequalities has grown. The proviso of inequality was more blatant. The things that were accepted as self-evident lost some of their space, as did the consensuses. Yet the negation of inappropriate inequality is an essential basic norm of this society.

The emphases of *social justice* have accordingly shifted further. The justice of achievement and the justice of acquired status have grown more important. The justice of needs has receded, although its claim is not being challenged in any essential way.

What does *social participation* mean today? The development of the 1980s and 1990s concentrated entirely on participation in the economic and acquisitive society: on the primary participation therein through gainful employment, on the secondary participation through the systems of social protection (social security, civil service pension, and so on). The systems of compensatory participation in society's opportunities for prosperity (the special assistance and promotion programs such as child allowance, training grants, housing allowance, etc.) are fragile and have remained at the mercy of the political adjustment to the economic and societal circumstances. The guarantee of a minimum participation in the sense of social welfare has not adequately kept pace with reality – partly for political and economic reasons, partly probably because of a lack of attention. The result has been the emergence of an imbalance. The participation in the acquisitive and economic society expanded in opportunities without losing protections. The other types of access to participation lost effectiveness. But would that not also have been the time to reform the institutions that update participation in the acquisitive and economic life as social protection in such a way that they, too, would answer to the laws of the acquisitive and economic life? The discussion over the capital cover of pension insurance shows in this regard a considerable willingness to be inconsistent. The middle voters and the politicians who count on them continue to pursue maximum privilege: through the advantages of the primary distribution *and* the advantages of the redistribution directed by them. And would this not have been the time, on the other hand, to reform the systems of minimal participation, especially social welfare, such that they accompany people not only with legally regulated monetary benefits, and but also with personal services on a sufficiently intensive level? That they not only posit emancipation, but help to achieve it?

Corresponding questions arise regarding the principle of *solidarity*. More than ever, the principle of *horizontal solidarity*, as expressed in the social insurance, was expanded. By contrast, the principle of *vertical solidarity*, help for the people at the bottom rung of society, lost force.

The principle of *security* developed the same way. On the one side, security continues to be the principle within the strongest consensus in this society. But the increase in poverty, especially also the rise in homelessness, shows not only that there are too few services helping people along. It also shows, above all, that the principle of "security" was narrowed down: to the participation in the acquisitive and economic society, and to its updating in the form of social protection. The person who can no longer gain access to this participation or cannot hold on to it may soon be on the way down – he or she is no longer safe. "Security" was understood less and less as a task of the system overall, a task that must follow the societal developments, and especially the realities of social threats.

This focus of the development of participation in acquisitive and economic life also led to misunderstandings of *subsidiarity*. It goes without saying that the primacy of acquisitive and economic life invigorates subsidiarity. But the development was heading for a harsh "either-or." It is not only the person whose skills and abilities meet the requirements of the acquisitive and economic life who should fall under the principle of subsidiarity; there must be room in that principle also for the person who needs help to help himself – more precisely: who simply cannot help himself without outside assistance.

The *integration* of society has retained its old foundation: the commonality of the values *prosperity, freedom, security, equality, defense against hardship* – common ground in the recognition of these values and common ground in their experience. Especially within the European and global context, this commonality is an essential feature of German identity. At the same time, the process whereby the various segments of society strike an increasingly specific relationship of closeness to or distance from the individual values has continued (Sachße and Engelhardt 1990). In the process, the patterns overlap, so there are no unbridgeable rifts. Of course, one of these patterns is especially important: the people in the "old Federal Republic" and in the "new states" are prompted, by their own particular experiences, interests, and values, to impart a typical structure to the constellation of prosperity, freedom, security, equality, and the defense against hardship.

9.4.4 The New Meaning of the Social Federal State

The meaning of the "social federal state" developed from the inception of the Federal Republic into the 1980s in the direction that the federation is the decisive shaper – especially the crucial legislator – of the social. Accordingly, the most important socio-political function of the *Länder* is to participate in the federal government's formative activity (especially through the *Bundesrat*), or (as in the commissions between the federal government and the *Länder* to carry out the joint tasks) to cooperate with the federal government. Moreover, the *Länder* are essentially in charge of carrying out federal laws and can thus determine the style and climate of their implementation. But that, too, is only of limited significance when the implementation of a law is reserved for the self-governing bodies (social insurance carriers, municipalities, and so on).

This distribution of roles changed substantially in the course of the 1980s and then especially in the 1990s. To be sure, nothing essential changed with respect to the design of the law on social protection and social benefits and its implementation. However, under pressure from technical and economic changes at the time, the framework conditions of economic activity and work, indeed of life as such, took on an entirely new significance. Where capital is invested, where qualified workers are available, where new and useful knowledge is available, where the best possible management is at work, where manufacturing can be competitive – all this depends to a high degree on the cultural, civilizational, political, and administrative givens: not only on the immediate technical and economic conditions, on energy, transportation, communications, and so on, but also on educational opportunities, internal security, public health and medical care, administrative and legal procedures, the openness and incorruptibility of the officials, the efficiency of public planning, and son, as well as on the lifestyle of the people and the attractiveness of an area. The individuality of the states can have a bearing on all of this: because of the existing characteristics of history, the landscape, etc.; because of societal forces that are developing in the respective state; or, finally, because of the political and administrative integration of the polity that is the state. The 1980s, and even more so the 1990s, have shown that the powers that remain in the hands of the states offer crucial opportunities combining the uniqueness of their space, the resources of their society, and the structures and operating modes of politics, the bureaucracy, and the legal system into different, characteristic "conditions as a place for business." As a result, the states have gained a new significance not only for economic, but precisely also for social conditions. They are no longer merely regional branches of the unitary social state of the Federal Republic. More so than before, they are once again individual polities – and also individual social states.

The Federal Republic of Germany – A Difficult, Fractured, and Open Nation State

10 Social State and National State: The Relation and Its Dramatic Changes

10.1 The Working Hypothesis of the National Social State

The *welfare state came into being as a nation state*. As much as the development of the welfare state was promoted and sustained by the international current of social ideas, the realization of the welfare state was a matter of nation states. The social became part of the national identity. From the outset, the economic, societal, political, and not least also intellectual conditions that brought forth the social questions and both made possible and shaped the answers, worked to impart a pronounced national character to the welfare states. The paths that were chosen in the process have left a lasting imprint on the subsequent development. That is *especially true for the German social state*. The German tradition of political thought provided essential foundations for the development of the social state (Maier 1980). Because the member states of the German Confederation had to deal with the contradiction between their social legislation and the small scale of their effective sphere, they contributed substantially to the beginnings of international social law (Perrin 1983). The social insurance laws of the Bismarck period provided powerful impulses to the social policy of the entire civilized world (Alber 1979, pp. 123–210; Köhler and Zacher 1981, 1983). In the twentieth century (Hockerts 1998, pp. 267–279), the creation of constitutions after 1945 initiated the series of states that were constitutionally referred to as "social states." In the model of the "social market economy," the Federal Republic has demonstrated the possibility that the market economy and social policy can be reconciled in a fruitful symbiosis. The social is in a very special way part of Germany's national identity (Ritter 1998a). But the *social state of the Federal Republic of Germany was never simply a nation state*. What we are considering here as the German polity – the German bloc of the three western occupation zones under occupation law, the "western state" of the Federal Republic, and the reunited Germany – differed and differs in multiple ways from the simple model of a nation state.

If the welfare state is thought of as "national," it is not the national homogeneity of society that is in the foreground. Rather, ethnic homogeneity or heterogeneity, social stratifications, clashes, or commonalities, regional differentiations and so on are among the conditions under which the social has developed and under which the social state has realized itself. They can also burden a "national" state. When I speak here of a "*nation state*," I mean something much simpler and more robust: that *the state territory, the nation that constitutes the state, and the state power define a coherent social, legal, and political world*. The basic notion of a national social state is that of a polity whose citizens usually also live in the land and whose inhabitants are usually also its citizens – a polity whose members usually realize the basic formula of the social within the land, and whose state power is capable of keeping under control, through its legal system and administrative institutions, the dangers and shortcomings that arise in the implementation of the basic formula. Finally, this picture includes that the state is sovereign, that is, it decides autonomously on the shape of politics and the law of the welfare state. Especially for the social state, which is also a *Rechtsstaat* and a democracy, the congruence between the effective sphere of democracy, the *Rechtsstaat*, and the social state is essential.

If the nation, as in the case in Germany, is historically divided – into smaller, historically conditioned entities that merge into a larger polity – this nation state has a more complicated design. That is true for democracy. It is true for the *Rechtsstaat*. But it is also true of social integration. Internationally and historically, we can find various models of how the emphases are distributed and which preconditions and consequences flow from that. Germany history sought the solution in the dominance of the larger unit. The social state could develop only in the way permitted by the directives of the federal state, the powers of the federation and the states, and the cooperation between the federal government and the states. But the federal state also repeatedly strengthened the social state. In the edifice of central state and member states, state and society could and can enter into a closer relationship than would be possible in a unitary state. That can counteract social problems and help solve them. Especially the most recent period, which has demanded a willingness and commitment to deep change from the state and society, offers new examples of this. All in all: a national social state that is a unitary state may be different from a national social state that is a federal state, but the differences need not be fundamental in nature. Germany, at any rate, became a federal state by becoming a social state, and a social state by becoming a federal state.

10.2 The Inter-state Openness of the National Social State

This "model" of a national social state that I have sketched is theory. *The state is not closed*. Its responsibility is not limited to the citizens who live in its territory. Its responsibility is not limited to the events that transpire on its territory. Its *responsibility extends also to "the foreigners"*: to the people who do not hold its citizenship or any citizenship and yet reside in its territory – either temporarily (to travel, for recreation, in search of an education, to work, in search of business, to meet contracts etc.) or permanently (for family reasons, to work, to live here from personal assets or other income, to find refuge, etc.). And it can *also have a responsibility for "foreign lands"*: for circumstances that occurred or occur in another country and yet have implications for the nation state – because they affect individuals who are its citizens, or because they entail damages for which it or its citizens are liable. The more the systems of social protection and social benefits developed, the more the contexts of the national social state's dealings with "foreigners" and with "the outside world" have become differentiated. The only question with regard to "the foreigner" before the development of the modern social sate was whether he was allowed to be and remain in the land, to pursue work or seek in some other way to participate in the life opportunities of the native society. But once poor relief began, the question was already whether it extended to "the foreigners" simply because of their presence. After the establishment of social insurance, it went without saying that it also included "the foreigner" who was participating like a citizen in the working and economic life of the country. But since there now existed these new ways of participation, the question rose anew whether there should not be some kind of distinction: *a distinction in the right to be here; or a distinction in the right to participate here*. But the dealings with the "outside world" also became more complicated. Was it permissible for the protection of social insurance to end at the state's borders? In case of illness? In case of disability or old age? For the native? For the foreigner? What about the person who fell ill abroad? What right should the foreign worker have to "consume" his pension back in his own homeland, to which he returned after working in Germany? Or: if accident insurance covers the harm caused during work, should that protection lapse if work takes a person out of the country?

Increasingly, the development of the social state called for functional and credible demarcations and extensions (Schuler 1988, pp. 203–215). Just as within the emerging social states the freedoms were shaped no longer only by limitations and obligations, but also by social protection and social benefits, which guided and changed the reality of freedoms, freedom of movement between states now demanded regulations to bring interstate migration in line with the nationality of the systems of social protection and social law (Schuler 1988, pp. 198–304). The *principles that stood behind the development of the social demanded clarification what they could and should mean beyond the* – personal and/or territorial – *boundaries of the national.* The principle of the general national participation (which marked poor relief and marks social welfare) suggests other kinds of demarcations than the principle of participation in working and economic life (as extended into social provision through social insurance and civil service pension) or the principle of participation in society's opportunities for prosperity (as expressed in the special assistance and promotion programs of child allowance, housing allowance, and the like). The general, vertical solidarity of all productive members with the poorest suggests very different demarcations than the specific solidarity of those bound together through a shared provision. What does "social protection" mean beyond the borders? (Schuler 1988, pp. 97–117). What does the crossing of – personal or territorial – national borders demand of justice? (Schuler 1988, pp. 198–215).

This opening and demarcation of the national social state toward "foreigners" and "the outside world" was, naturally, *initially a matter for each state.* It soon became apparent, however, that objective justice and efficiency demanded *international regulations*: first *bilateral*, but then *multilateral* and especially *general international conventions.* Of course, this development was not spurred only by the social. Part of this process was also to overcome opposition that had arisen to the social. National differences in social policy led to differences in economic competition. And so it was not only the concern to help the values of the respective national system of social law to achieve an appropriate and wide extension that found expression in the development of international social law. It was no less so the concern about distortions in competition that could result in differences among socio-political standards. Be that as it may: the Treaty of Versailles, with a list of basic demands in favor of workers, created a first catalog of social rights binding under international law,[567] but at the same time also the International Labour Organization (ILO).[568] The ILO quickly developed the technique of conventions and recommendations to improve, harmonize, and standardize the national legal systems for both labor law and social insurance law.[569] In addition, the development of international social law proceeded through bilateral instruments, whereby the focus was, of course, on social insurance (Wickenhagen 1957, pp. 39–43; 2nd ed. 1982; 3rd ed. 1997). The dual interactive process had established itself, at the center of which stood the national development of social policy. The latter was, on the one hand, increasingly subject to the influence of internationally designed regulatory models. On the other hand, it had become necessary to supplement the national legal systems with inter-state regulations.

---

[567] Art. 427 of the Treaty of Versailles, 28 June 1919, RGBl., p. 687.

[568] Art. 387–427.

[569] Internationales Arbeitsamt (1931). On more recent developments see International Labour Organization (1996).

10.3 The Irregularity of the "National" Social State of the Federal Republic of Germany

When the development we are examining here began after 1945, the nation state thus already stood within a self-evident tradition of international openness and integration. Reconnecting to that tradition would have been nothing special for the social state that was erected after 1945 in the "western zones." However, its problems went far beyond the usual scope. They arose from the fact that the new polity concerned not only "its" territory, but bore responsibility also for people and situations that involved other territories. They arose from the fact that this polity initially did not have a "national people," but did bear responsibility – for a variety of reasons – for many people. And they also arose from the fact that his new polity from the outset was not to have the kind of sovereignty that characterized the nation state; instead, it was to be initially subject to foreign rule, in order to later integrate itself more and more into a deeply layered edifice of supranational and international communities. All this has continually changed in the six decades since then.

11 What Distinguished and Distinguishes the Federal Republic of Germany (and What Preceded It) from a National Social State

11.1 Occupation Period – Länder *– Unified Economic Area*[570]

After the collapse of the Third Reich, what was a *German state*? And if there was none: Had a different state taken its place? The most pragmatic, obvious starting point for reflecting on these questions is the *territory of the four occupation zones, including Berlin* – the territory that was also subject to the authority of the Allied Control Council. It is the territory of Germany of 1937 minus northern East Prussia annexed by the Soviet Union, minus the region east of the Oder-Neiße line that was placed under Polish administration, and minus the Saar region, which the French occupying power quickly and decisively separated from its occupation zone. Beginning in the spring of 1948, "Control Council Germany" no longer had a four-power Control Council, and Berlin from the summer of 1948 no longer had a four-power headquarters. Instead, the occupation zones assumed an independent existence under their respective military governments and beyond the originally intended scope. The zonal governments permitted the beginnings of new German statehood: everywhere in the form of states; in the American zone also in the *Länderrat* (Council of States), in the British zone in the Central Zone Offices and

---

[570] See above Chapter 4.; Bundesministerium für Arbeit und Sozialordnung and Bundesarchiv (eds.), 2001b: Geschichte der Sozialpolitik in Deutschland seit 1945, vol. 2, Chap. 1, esp. 2.1., Chap. 2, esp. 2.1., Chap. 3, no. 17.

the Zonal Advisory Council, and, finally, jointly for the American and British zones in the administration of the Unified Economic Area. The occupying powers remained everywhere the final authority. What existed in the three "western zones" in this way was the precursor to the Federal Republic of Germany.

The zones and their states had something like a *"natural" substrate*. This was the territory as defined by the occupying powers. This was the people who had always lived there, most of whom were German citizens. But the latter had no citizenship status with reference to these polities that was regulated anywhere and could have been ascertainable.[571] Moreover, there was no thought given to demarcating these entities from one another like states. And there were also *many other people who "belonged"* – or who wanted "to belong". These were individuals who were *Germans* or had reason to be treated as Germans: German citizens whose roots were in a different state, a different zone, or in a different part of "Germany in the borders of 1937," but who had now ended up in one of the zones as a result of the war or the postwar circumstances; Germans who had previously lived somewhere in the world, but who had now returned (Krohn 1997), been brought to, or been expelled into this "Control Council Germany;" individuals whom National Socialist policy had claimed as "ethnic Germans" (*Volkstumsdeutsche*), and who – coming from wherever – were now living in "Control Council Germany;" individuals who had been expelled from another country which had declared them to be Germans.[572] But this "Control Council Germany" was home not only to these "natives." There were also many *"foreigners."*[573] These were all those whom the Nazi tyranny had brought into the country: in concentration camps, in prisons, in forced labor camps. Finally, there were the "foreigners" who had fled Stalin's Soviet Union and perhaps already the coming Communist rule in Central and Eastern Europe. For all of them, the "territory" in which they now were had a fundamental responsibility. When it came to the "foreign" victims of Nazi rule, this responsibility was a primary concern of the occupying powers.[574] They should not have to depend on the good will and possibilities of the Germans. But the phenomena were multifarious, and the responsibility for these "foreigners" also devolved increasingly upon the German authorities.

History, however, advanced still further claims. Did this "Control Council Germany," its zones or its states have a responsibility for Germans living in *territories that had been part of "Germany in the borders of 1937,"* but which

---

[571] The constitutions of Baden (Art. 53 LVerf.Baden), Bavaria (Art. 8 LVerf.Bay), and of Rhineland-Palatinate (Art. 75, Para. 2 LVerf.RP) did stipulate citizenship in the states, but it required legal regulation that did not come about anywhere.

[572] Bethlehem (1982); Schulze, von der Brelie-Levien and Grebing (1987); Bundesministerium für Arbeit und Sozialordnung and Bundesarchiv (eds.), 2001b: Geschichte der Sozialpolitik in Deutschland seit 1945, vol. 2, Chap. 3, no. 12.

[573] U. Müller (1990); Königseder and Wetzel (1994); Jacobmeyer (1985); Bundesministerium für Arbeit und Sozialordnung and Bundesarchiv (eds.), 2001b: Geschichte der Sozialpolitik in Deutschland seit 1945, vol. 2, Chap. 3, nos. 12 and 13.

[574] von Schmoller et al. (1957): "B. Besonderer Teil, 1. Teil: Beschränkungen der völkerrechtlichen Handlungsfähigkeit, 3. Kapitel: § 32. Die Rechtsstellung der 'DP' in Deutschland."

were not now *part of "Control Council Germany"* in East Prussia, in the territories east of the Oder-Neiße line, or in the Saarland? What were the repercussions for people in the *territories that Germany had annexed after 1937*: in Austria, in the Sudeten region, in the Memel region, in Danzig, in the Protectorate of Bohemia and Moravia? What responsibility existed for the people who had lived there during the period of German rule, especially if they had entered into a special relationship to the social institutions of the Reich (e.g. through social insurance)?[575] All the more so if they had suffered some harm from the Reich or in some other way in Germany's name? What should apply to the people in the *territories that the Reich had attacked, conquered, and occupied* – especially if it de facto annexed these territories, like Alsace-Lorraine, or subjected them – like Poland (Szurgacz 1998) – to a colonial regime as the "General Government"?

And finally, what about all the people whom the National Socialist state had persecuted, expelled, despoliated, and stripped of their citizenships, and who were now living wherever they had found refuge? For them, too, the question needed to be raised who was responsible, who was in charge of giving that responsibility a legal form, and what it should mean.[576]

The time was too turbulent and too short to clarify many of these questions. The occupying powers pushed for compensation and restitution toward the victims of racial, political, and religious persecution. German agencies also strove to provide assistance to the refugees and expellees who were now living in the land. Most questions remained unresolved. The conditions were as confusing as the jurisdictions were unclear and the means inadequate.

11.2 The Founding Phase of the Federal Republic of Germany (1949–1957)

11.2.1 Structures[577]

With the founding of the two German states in 1949 there arose *two polities, each of which was organized like a self-contained nation state*. However, in the case of the "western" state, the Federal Republic of Germany, that was conceivable only by *accepting contradictions*. The *Basic Law* posited that even after the establishment of the Federal Republic there existed a *larger Germany*, on whose behalf the German Reich had acted until the collapse of its system of government (Preamble, Art. 23, GG, old version). The move to constitute the West German state was not

[575] Some information on this is in Majer (1993).

[576] Bundesministerium für Arbeit und Sozialordnung and Bundesarchiv (eds.), 2001b: Geschichte der Sozialpolitik in Deutschland seit 1945, vol. 2, no. 12.

[577] See above section 5.2; Bundesministerium für Arbeit und Soziales and Bundesarchiv (eds.), 2005: Geschichte der Sozialpolitik in Deutschland seit 1945, vol. 3, Chap. 3, no. 17.

intended to create a system of government only for its territory and people. Rather, the intent was to do whatever was possible to create the beginning of a system of government also for the larger Germany. Legally that was expressed in the theory of the *partial identity of the Federal Republic of Germany with the German Reich*. This theory rejected both the assumption that the Federal Republic was the legal successor to the German Reich (for according to the prevailing doctrine, the German Reich had not fallen), and the assumption that the Federal Republic was identical with the German Reich (that would have negated not only the reality of the German Democratic Republic, but also the continuing rights of the occupying powers to jointly govern over "Germany as a whole") (Bernhardt 1987, pp. 321–349; Stern 2000, pp. 1091–1169). This, then, was the specific *ambiguity that had been imposed upon the Federal Republic of Germany*, and which also showed its effects in the realm of the social. On the one hand, nothing else was conceivable but that the *Federal Republic thought of itself as a nation state*: the state power through which "the German People in the Länder of Baden, Bavaria, Bremen, Hamburg, Hesse, Lower Saxony, North Rhine-Westphalia, Rhineland-Palatinate, Schleswig-Holstein, Wuerttemberg-Baden, and Wuerttemberg-Hohenzollern" established for themselves a "temporary state order" (Preamble, Art. 23, GG, old version).[578] On the other hand, it still remained to be determined what consequences arose from the fact that this *Federal Republic of Germany acted for the German Reich and was obligated to bring about the unification of "Germany as a whole*," without actually being the German Reich or "Germany as a whole." *Internally* the issue was to take into account the reality of the German Democratic Republic and to live up to the claims of the larger Germany (Ress 1987, pp. 449–545). *Beyond Germany* the issue was to find the proper boundary between the virtual existence of the larger Germany – its historical responsibility, the powers of the victorious powers arising from it, and the right and obligation of the Federal Republic to act on behalf of this larger Germany and work toward its reunification – and the separate existence of the Federal Republic that came into being in 1949 and the relations arising from it.

In addition, the new Federal Republic also had to respect the *structures of occupation law* that concerned "Control Council Germany" and its occupation zones. To be sure, the institution of the Control Council was dormant and was not revived. The three western occupying powers had reserved for themselves the final say over the Federal Republic, which they exercised in accordance with the occupation statute. Only in 1955 – when the Germany Treaty (*Deutschlandvertrag*) and its accompanying agreements went into effect[579] – were the rights of the occupying powers put into provisos agreed upon in the form of a treaty (Stern 2000, pp. 1376–1432). But there were further difficulties that attached to

[578] Unlike the Preamble, Art. 23, GG, also spoke of the territory of the *State of Berlin*.

[579] "Vertrag vom 26. Mai 1952 über die Beziehungen zwischen der Bundesrepublik Deutschland und den Drei Mächten" and "Vertrag vom 26. Mai 1952 zur Regelung aus Krieg und Besatzung entstandener Fragen in der Fassung des Protokolls über die Beendigung des Besatzungsregimes in der Bundesrepublik Deutschland vom 23. Oktober 1954," "Zustimmungsgesetz vom 24. März 1955," BGBl. II, p. 213. On the accompanying agreements see I. Münch (1968, vol. 1, pp. 234–273).

this quasi-nation state that was the Federal Republic. West Berlin was a state within the Federal Republic only with certain limitations (Scholz 1987, pp. 351–383). Border questions remained open (Stern 2000, pp. 1116–1128), especially with regard to the territories east of the Oder-Neiße line. By virtue of the duty to work toward reunification, the Federal Republic had potential obligations also toward those territories and the Germans who lived in them. The Saarland (Thieme 1960, pp. 423–462), too, remained part of Germany. At the latest when the Saarland was able to accede to the Federal Republic in accordance with Art. 23, Sent. 2, GG, old version (BGBl. [1956] I, p. 1011) – the accession took effect on 1 January 1957 – it was clear that the Saarland had been part of the "whole Germany" from the beginning (BVerfGE 4, 157, esp. 170–176).

But what gave the *Federal Republic* the capacity to act was its *development as a quasi-nation state*. Its foundation of values and its political and legal system determined the development *within* the Federal Republic *and* they determined its relations *with its international environment* – as complicated as that could be in view of the parallel existence to the German Democratic Republic, with a view toward Germany as a single entity, and at times also with regard to the Saarland or the territories east of the Oder-Neiße line. This Federal Republic was shaped from the outset by the "constitutional decision of the Basic Law in favor of international cooperation" (K. Vogel 1964). This option of the Basic Law for international cooperation finds its broadest expression in Art. 24, GG. It speaks of the transfer of sovereign powers to intergovernmental institutions, of a system of mutual collective security involving limitations upon its rights of sovereignty, and of a general, comprehensive, and obligatory system of international arbitration. But the willingness to engage in international cooperation manifested itself also in other ways (Art. 25, 26, 32, 59, 73, no. 1, GG). This *international cooperation*[580] had to begin, naturally enough, with *bilateral relations*. But part of what was new at that time was that *international organizations* were beginning to play an exceptional role. The first step toward *collective European cooperation* that the Federal Republic could take in 1949 was to join the *European Organization for Economic Cooperation* (OEEC), the future Organization for Economic Cooperation and Development (OECD) – which was originally trans-Atlantic, but eventually included also Japan, Australia, and New Zealand.[581] It had been founded in 1948 and served to coordinate the implementation of the Marshall Plan and the political stabilization of Western Europe. The Marshall Plan and the OEEC were crucially important in allowing the idea of a development based on the market economy, but also the real possibilities of free market, to be successful (see above

[580] Bundesministerium für Arbeit und Soziales and Bundesarchiv (eds.), 2005: Geschichte der Sozialpolitik in Deutschland seit 1945, vol. 3, Chap. 3, no. 17; on the treaties and organization see Zacher (1976); Däubler et al. (1994); see also Bundesgesetzblatt Teil II, Fundstellennachweis B. Völkerrechtliche Vereinbarungen. Verträge zur Vorbereitung und Herstellung der Einheit Deutschlands. Abgeschlossen zum 31. Dezember 1998.

[581] Founded in 1960; Germany joined in 1961. Bührer (1997).

Benz 1983b, p. 434). In 1950, Germany joined the *Council of Europe*. After the Western European Union,[582] the Council of Europe had been the second large creation by which the states of "free Europe" demonstrated their willingness to collaborate constructively in the wake of the catastrophes of the two World Wars. The Council of Europe developed quickly into an important community of values and law. By joining it, the Federal Republic, on the one hand, partook of its legitimacy, and, on the other hand, acquired the opportunity to make significant contributions to the development of pan-European values and law. At the same time, the Federal Republic also gained access to the global international community of states. In 1950 it joined the Food and Agriculture Organization of the United Nations (FAO), in 1951 the World Health Organization (WHO), the General Agreement on Tariffs and Trade (GATT), the United Nations Children Fund (UNICEF), and the International Labour Organization (ILO). In 1952, finally, it was admitted to the World Bank and the International Monetary Fund. That was both a recognition of the strength of the German economy and a move to reinforce German economic policy (Albrecht 1954). But the social state of West Germany took the most important step toward formal participation in a socio-political organization of global reach by joining the International Labour Organization. The German Reich had withdrawn from that organization in 1933. While the war was still going on, the General Conference of the International Labour Conference met to formulate the basis for the work after the war. The "Declaration Concerning the Aims and Purposes of the International Labour Organization" (the so-called Philadelphia Declaration) of 10 May 1944 (Zacher 1976, pp. 84–86) formed an essential foundation for the socio-political forces in the postwar period. As early as 1946, the International Labour Organization was annexed to the United Nations as the first specialized agency. Through its membership in the ILO, the Federal Republic of Germany also gained its first central access to the system and social policy of the United Nations (Köhler 1988).

In Europe, meanwhile, the development intensified in a completely new way. The road toward a supranational Europe began in 1952 with the establishment of the *European Coal and Steel Community*. Through this road, the conditions of the social for the states that entered into the supranational community gradually underwent significant changes. National law, national politics, national administration, but also the citizens of the member states had to subordinate themselves to the directives of the law of the supranational community. At the same time a new framework emerged for all these areas – for national law, national politics, national administration, and above all the economies of the member states and the economic activities within the members states, and in the final analysis also for a broad area of the societal: the framework of a common European law, of common European policies, and with these two also a new quality of common transnational economic activities and coexistence. The European Coal and Steel Community quickly

[582] Treaty of Brussels (Treaty of Economic, Social and Cultural Collaboration and Collective Self-Defense), 17 March 1948.

became important for the mining economy. However, the treaty on this first European community contained hardly any social charges.[583] But in 1957 there followed the founding of the *European Economic Community* and the *European Atomic Energy Community*. While the latter had marginal significance for the development of the legal, political, economic, and societal environment of the national social state, and even less for national social policy and for the legal organization of the social on the national level, the European Economic Community became extraordinarily important in both areas over the long term.

When the founding phase of the Federal Republic came to an end in 1957 with the conclusion of the second legislative session of the German *Bundestag*, the country was already firmly integrated into the European and global community of states. The Federal Republic was largely its own master. With the Germany Treaty it had acquired "sovereignty in name" – legally limited in favor of "its" three occupation powers, and with respect to Germany as a whole in favor of the four victorious powers. The remaining restrictions were without any meaning on a day-to-day basis. The Saarland has been part of the Federal Republic since 1957. The two German states existed and operated side-by-side (and against each other). Berlin was divided. But the "western sectors" essentially had the status of a federal state of the Federal Republic. Thus the structures had also stabilized within Germany. At the same time, the Federal Republic had entered into a complex interaction with a great diversity of other spheres and polities: with the "other parts of Germany" (Art. 23, Sent. 2, GG); with many states in the world, with which it addressed shared social problems through formal treaties and other forms of bilateral and multilateral cooperation; with the Europe of the Council of Europe and with the Europe of the European Economic Community; with the trans-Atlantic community of the "free western world;" with the community of the industrialized states oriented toward free market economies.

11.2.2 People[584]

"Domestic Society": The Effective Sphere of the Social State

This already says something essential about the relationship that this social state has and can have to the people in the land and outside the land, and for what kinds of relationships it can be invoked. The responsibility of the social state "does not extend universally to all persons and life situations in the world; its reference is internal. It is limited… to the *domestic society*, understood as the totality of the material and social life conditions (an edifice of interaction processes determined

[583] Art. 3b: the organs of the community were to "promote the improvement of the living and working conditions of the labor force."

[584] Bundesministerium für Arbeit und Soziales and Bundesarchiv (eds.), 2005: Geschichte der Sozialpolitik in Deutschland seit 1945, vol. 3, Chap. 3, nos. 13 and 17.

by a system of norms) at home. The domestic society is the primary point of reference for the state's concerns and its mandate to realize social justice and social security; it represents the most general socio-political demarcation of responsibility against foreign systems of social law. This societal belonging is essentially and primarily defined territorially, namely through the resident rules of domestic domicile and usual residency, but also of domestic employment. In its economic and social dimension, the domestic society is primarily a territorial society. Second, the principle of the social state encompasses the social situations for which the domestic generality is causally or finally responsible or which it has assumed. Thus, alongside the personal principle of demarcation of *societal membership* stands the *objective/material principle of allocatability* with respect to special risks and social conditions" (Schuler 1988, p. 210f.). But "neither the societal membership of persons nor the allocatability of risks and social conditions to a generality constituted into a state are uniformly defined, nor do they represent in this generality a usable yardstick for the socio-legal demarcation in the specific case." Rather, "the domestic socio-political jurisdiction and responsibility varies, depending on the special occasions, goals, and purposes of the various social benefits systems and the nature of the social benefit in question" (Schuler 1988, p. 211).

Thus, the demarcation of the *personal sphere of jurisdiction of a national social state* is already complex under the "most normal" of circumstances. In the process, citizenship rarely appears directly. In fact, it is a rather formal criterion, one that cannot say anything definitive about "membership in society." Nevertheless, citizenship is the basis for a right to membership in the federation – a right to reside in the territory of the state (Art. 11, Art. 16, Para. 2, GG), a right, that is, to establish and maintain an essential precondition for membership in the domestic society. On the other hand, citizenship can also be important where the social state is called upon for living conditions that occur abroad. The personal connection of citizenship can serve as the criterion for the person in question having a sufficient relationship to the "domestic society" to have access to its solidarity.[585]

On the other hand, the social state may differentiate vis-à-vis the foreigner not only by denying or withdrawing the right to enter the "domestic society," but also by qualifying the solidarity towards foreigners living within the land.[586] By contrast, where access to a provisioning system depends on participation in domestic working and economic life, what matters is the local connection.[587] And objective criteria are in the foreground also where the responsibility is causal: (Schuler 1988, pp. 210–212): in social compensation law, the question whether the German polity is responsible (Sect. 1 ff. BVG); in accident insurance, the question whether liability, which is collectivized through accident insurance, is subject to German

---

[585] See in the current law for social assistance to Germans abroad Sect. 119 BSHG, or for pension payments abroad Sects. 114, 272, 318 SGB VI.

[586] In the current law see Sect. 119 BSHG, Sect. 1, Para. 3 BKGG, Sect. 1, Para. 1a BErzGG.

[587] In current law see Sects. 3, 7, 9–11 SGB IV.

law (Schlegel 1996, p. 287; Raschke 1996, pp. 1403–1411). However, the German social state can limit its responsibility for the compensation of damages to "domestic society."[588]

The Complexity of "Domestic Society" in the Federal Republic of Germany[589]

Now, the *particular* problem of the young Federal Republic did *not* lie in this kind of demarcation of "domestic society." It lay in the restless *complexity of the domestic society*. The "domestic" that was its state territory had been created only in 1945 in the form of three occupation zones, and had been brought together only in 1947 in the United Economic Area for the American and British zones, which was later, on the eve of the establishment of the Federal Republic, extended also to the French zone. The "state of Berlin" in turn was only one part of Berlin. And above all: the people living in this "domestic" had only in part a "natural," evolved connection to it. The others had come to this "domestic society" for the most varied reasons of being German: as German citizens, as ethnic Germans, as individuals tied in some way to the fate of the German nation. Or they were victims of the National Socialist tyranny, escapees, expellees, those without a homeland.

The Basic Law erected this new "*domestic society*" on the *definition of who was "a German"* (Art. 116, GG). This notion of "a German" was grounded primarily in German citizenship (Art. 116, Para. 1, GG).[590] But that criterion could not be sufficient. The Basic Law saw (and sees) as a German also the person "who has been admitted to the territory of the German Reich within its borders of 31 December 1937 as a refugee or expellee of German ethnic origin or as the spouse or descendant of such a person" (Art. 116, Para. 1). The Basic Law thus saw itself compelled to make two openings. First: to go beyond the criterion of German citizenship in establishing the "domestic society." Second: to accept, alongside the "domestic society" defined by its connection to the state territory of the Federal Republic (Art. 11, Art. 16, Para. 2, Sent. 1, GG, old version), another "domestic society" defined by the territory of the German Reich as constituted on 31 December 1937. What that meant for the relationship to the GDR is obvious. And the federal legislator soon found himself compelled to control access to the Federal Republic through a Law on the Emergency Admission of Germans into the Federal Territory (22 August 1950; BGBl. I, p. 367). A clarification of who was a German without being a citizen came in 1953 with the Law regarding the Affairs of Expellees and Refugees (19 May 1953, BGBl. I, p. 202; E. Klein 1995, pp. 623–662).

But solutions had to be found also for those individuals who were now living on the territory of the Federal Republic of Germany without being Germans and

---

[588] On social compensation law see Sects. 7 and 8, BVG, on accident insurance law Sect. 3, nos. 2, 3, 4, SGB IV.

[589] Bundesministerium für Arbeit und Sozialordnung and Bundesarchiv (eds.), 2005: Geschichte der Sozialpolitik in Deutschland seit 1945, vol. 3, Chap. 3, nos. 12, 13, 17.

[590] On the principled use of the notion of German citizenship by the Basic Law see also Art. 16, Para. 1, Art. 73, no. 2.

without being able to or wanting to become Germans. A first step was the 1951 Law on the Legal Status of Homeless Foreigners on Federal Territory (BGBl. I, p. 269). The connection to the historical development is immediately apparent through the description of the individuals in question (§1):

> A homeless (*heimatloser*) foreigner is a foreign citizen or a stateless person who... can prove that he is under the care of the international organization that has been charged by the United Nations with looking after displaced persons or refugees,... is not a German... and resides in the territory covered by the Basic Law or in Berlin (West).

These homeless foreigners were granted the right of residence and free movement within the federal territory (§ 12). They were given "equal standing to German citizens in social security, unemployment insurance, and unemployment aid" (§ 18), and the same with regard to the benefits of "public welfare" (§ 19). The admission of the *politically persecuted* was guaranteed in the Basic Law in the form of right to asylum (Art. 16, Para. 2, Sent. 2, GG, old version).[591] Internationally, this was in line with the 1951 Geneva Convention on Refugees, which the Federal Republic ratified in 1953.[592]

Still in the 1950s, the spectrum of the "domestic society" had been expanded with the addition of *foreign workers*.[593] The legal prelude was an ordinance from the Federal Ministry for Labour on 22 February 1952.[594] Inclusion in the "domestic society" was entirely dominated by employment. A residence permit went along with recruitment and entry into employment. And the end of employment essentially also ended the right of residence. During the period of employment and residence, social participation was guaranteed, on the one hand, through the wage and supplementary work-based benefits, and, on the other hand, by the institutions of social protection for workers. The long-term protection against the risks of old age, disability, and death with surviving dependants had to take into account that the worker, when he is entitled to these benefits, had returned to his native country or that his family entitled to survivor benefits had remained in the native country or had gone back. The legal regulation was therefore a task for the conflict of laws – one-sided nationally, bi- or multi-lateral in international law, or supranational. The calculus could simply not be that smooth. And so over the course of time a second tier of manifestations arose, which devolved, on the one hand, into the normalcy of foreign fellow citizens, and, on the other hand, into a multitude of conflicts and tensions. These manifestations emerged especially out of the incongruity between the duration of employment and duration of residence, between participation by the worker himself and the participation of his family, between participation in the

[591] Now Art. 16a as amended by the "Gesetz zur Änderung des Grundgesetzes vom 28. Juni 1933" BGBl. I, p. 1002.

[592] "Zustimmungsgesetz vom 1. September 1953" BGBl. II, p. 559.

[593] Bundesministerium für Arbeit und Soziales and Bundesarchiv (eds.), 2005: Geschichte der Sozialpolitik in Deutschland seit 1945, vol. 3, Chap. 3, nos. 12 and 13.

[594] BAnz no. 43/1952, 1. Remarkably enough, this ordinance was reminiscent of the Decree on Foreign Workers of 23 January 1933.

working and acquisitive economy through labor law and social insurance and the further-reaching participation – be it through the minimum participation through social welfare, be it through the general participation in prosperity through special assistance and promotion programs (child allowance and so on).

While the "domestic society" of the quasi-nation state of the Federal Republic was thus enriched from the outside, this *social state* also *radiated outward in many ways*. Already the traditional nation state usually has a clientele abroad: citizens who are entitled to its help also abroad; citizens to whom it must provide benefits from social provision or social compensation also abroad; as well as non-citizens to whom it owes – by virtue of its own legal system or of regulations agreed under international law – benefits from social provision or social compensation also abroad.[595] For the "West German" social state, a *special emphasis lay on this dimension* of its operations. This resulted at the outset from the fact that many of its former citizens had *fled abroad to escape the persecution* of the National Socialists, and who – for the most varied reasons – had no desire to return to Germany, or were no longer able to do so. The Basic Law promised that former German citizens "who, between 30 January 1933 and 8 May 1945, were deprived of their citizenship on political, racial or religious grounds, and their descendants, are re-granted German citizenship on application" (Art. 116, Para. 2, GG). But independent of that, restitution and compensation payments also had to be made to individuals living abroad. Restitutions agreements were also entered into with a number of states: first with Israel (1952), later (1959–1964) with various "western" European states.[596] Over the course of time, the foreign orientation of the social benefit activity on the part of the Federal Republic increased through the large number of those who were *temporarily incorporated into the working life in the Federal Republic*, and who, upon leaving, took with them entitlements to benefits, especially from pension and accident insurance. Initially, the individuals with such entitlements were recruited from the large number of those who, after the war, had lived in the "tri-zone region" and later in the Federal Republic, and who then returned to their homelands or – in most cases – emigrated to third countries. Later, the stream of those entitled to benefits abroad was fed above all from the large number of guest workers.

Of the utmost complexity was the problem concerning the *Germans in and from the German Democratic Republic* (Das Sozialrecht im geteilten Deutschland 1968). For this concerned not only those who came from the GDR to the FRG *to stay there (resettlers)* (Heidemeyer 1994; Schumann et al. 1996). Rather, there were also those who came to the Federal Republic for *only a short time, as visitors*, but who depended on financial assistance and, in cases of special circumstances (e.g. illness), on the protection of the social benefits systems. Finally, there were also Germans who traveled *from the Federal Republic to the German Democratic*

[595] Schuler (1988, pp. 291–300, 475–509, 651–665, 740–750, 756–764).

[596] Bundesgesetzblatt II Fundstellennachweis B 1998, p. 662.

Republic. Once again, some did so to stay there, others only for a short time. The unparalleled difficulties of a "double domestic society" – the narrower "domestic society" of the Federal Republic of Germany and the wider "domestic society" of all of Germany and all Germans – were brought to bear here to a special degree. Neither the non-recognition of the GDR nor the recognition of all Germans as citizens of the Federal Republic could lead to seeing the inhabitants of the GDR as simply entitled to benefits according to German social benefits law. In this regard, legal practice generally resorted to *specific legal concepts* (K. Vogel 1968, pp. 45–64). Fundamental was the legal concept of the "*interlocal social law.*" While "international social law" determines the relationship between the national systems of social law of separate, independent states, "interlocal social law" regulates the relationship between two legal subsystems within a single state (especially between the systems of social law of two member states in the federation). Qualifying the relationship between the systems of social law of the Federal Republic of Germany and the German Democratic Republic as "interlocal" exceeded the conventional use of the term. Still, it could be used first of all to do justice to the position of the Basic Law that the German Democratic Republic was not a foreign land. And it accorded perfectly with the position of the law of the Federal Republic that the citizens of the GDR were also in principle "Germans." Finally, this qualification of the relationship as "interlocal" created the necessary substantive leeway for an appropriate shaping of the law. Even without a recognition of the GDR, its system of social law could be considered as a self-contained, functioning system that should not be intervened in – through insurance obligations, through the export of benefits, or in any other way. The assignment of individuals to the various legal systems of social insurance was carried out on the basis of the "*residency principle*" developed by case law.[597] On the other hand, for citizens who came to the Federal Republic from the GDR there was the opportunity to situate them within West German social law in such a way that their East German "social biography" benefited them as much as possible (*integration principle*). Because of the temporal dimension of the benefit basis and the benefit output, this was particularly important for pension and accident insurance law.[598] In addition to integration into the benefits systems of social protection, resettlers also benefited from compensation payments, the benefits from the law on the equalization of burdens, and the integration assistance from the Federal Expellees Act.[599] Other assistance also came from non-statutory programs (Frerich and Frey, vol. 3, 1996, p. 36f., pp. 311–324).

[597] As has been done by the Federal Social Court (*Bundessozialgericht*) in its established jurisdiction since BSGE 3, 286 (292).

[598] In the process, the "Fremdrenten- und Auslandsrentengesetz vom 7. August 1953" (BGBl. I, p. 848) still proceeded from the principle of compensation, which referred essentially to the law and economic conditions of the country of origin. On the "integration principle" (*Eingliederungsprinzip*) see Schuler (1988, p. 299f., pp. 553–569, 652).

[599] Bundesministerium für Arbeit und Soziales and Bundesarchiv (eds.), 2005: Geschichte der Sozialpolitik in Deutschland seit 1945, vol. 3, Chap. 3, no. 12.

The Development of a Transnational European "Domestic Society"[600]

But *Europe*, too, set out to join the national "domestic societies" of the European states willing to work together into a transnational European "domestic society" (Schregle 1954; Hampel 1955). For this coalescing of Europe, the *freedom of movement* of citizens within the respective combined states represented an essential medium. However, the national welfare states have integrated their "domestic societies" through the norms and institutions of social protection and social benefits in such a way that departure from a "domestic society" usually entails a loss of rights and entitlements, while entry into another "domestic society" often opens up only a reduced participation in its social protection and social benefits. These migratory losses in social participation are particularly evident where – as is the case especially in social provision against long-term risks (old age, disability, death with surviving dependants) – the foundation and level of rights and entitlements are time-dependent. Time spent in *one* country does not have the same value, or none at all, in *another* country. Any given national law, if it regulates passage from one national system of social law to another on its own and thus unilaterally, has little interest in mitigating or even eliminating these "social costs" of migration between states. Bilateral regulations by way of treaty between the states involved reflect a greater interest in giving consideration to the concerns of the other side. But two states rarely have the intention of uniting their territories into a sphere of maximum transnationality. And if they do, then the issue is not that of bringing together a community of *multiple* states. The new institutions of European union, the Council of Europe and the European Communities, thus faced a new task with their goal of promoting freedom of movement by opening the social benefits systems to migration.

The *Council of Europe* addressed this task in 1953 by presenting three conventions intended to facilitate the migration between the signatory states in terms of social law: the European Interim Agreement on Social Security Schemes Relating to Old Age, Invalidity and Survivors; the European Interim Agreement on Social Security other than Schemes for Old Age, Invalidity and Survivors; and the European Convention on Social and Medical Assistance. Not until 1955 did it address the issue of freedom of movement directly: through the European Convention on Establishment. Of course, in keeping with the character of the Council of Europe as an international body of international law, these conventions were restrained. Most of all, they could obligate only *those* member states who signed them.

The development in supranational Europe proceeded in two stages. The *European Coal and Steel Community* set up in 1952 articulated the issue of the freedom of movement of workers only in a fragmented and very restrained way

[600] See above section "European Integration"; Bundesministerium für Arbeit und Soziales and Bundesarchiv (eds.), 2005: Geschichte der Sozialpolitik in Deutschland seit 1945, vol. 3, Chap. 3, no. 17.

(Art. 69 EGKSV). And the treaty had nothing to say about complementing freedom of movement with social provisions. At the same time, migration within the sphere of the treaty increased to such a degree that the necessity of a joint regime of social protection became evident. A multi-lateral agreement to supplement the treaty was prepared to coordinate the national systems of social security accordingly.[601] The development was overtaken by the establishment of the *European Economic Community*. Founded in 1957, it guaranteed the freedom of movement of workers (Art. 48–51 EWGV). Art. 51 declared:

> The Council... shall, in the field of social security, adopt the measures necessary to effect the free movement of workers, in particular, by introducing a system which permits an assurance to be given to migrant workers and their beneficiaries:
> (a) that, for the purposes of qualifying for and retaining the right to benefits and of the calculation of these benefits, all periods taken into consideration by the respective municipal law of the countries concerned, shall be added together; and
> (b) that these benefits will be paid to persons resident in the territories of the Member States.

The "migrant worker ordinance"[602] that was based on this provision was a first, though highly effective, step toward creating within supranational Europe a "domestic society of the second degree."

11.2.3 Institutions and Norms

But these constellations also meant that from the outset, the Federal Republic was integrated into structures and organizations that limited it. That was true for *Germany as a whole* as well as the reserved rights of the victorious powers to

---

[601] In the development of the law of the European communities, the concept of "*coordination*" was articulated to refer to normatizations that concerned factual situations involving several national legal systems. Typical are thus cases of migratory workers whose social biography takes them through several member states. We are talking about equivalents to the usual expressions "*Kollisionsrecht*", "*Konfliktsrecht*" (conflict of laws), and "international law" in the specific sense of international private law, international administrative law, and so on. The conceptual counterpart to "coordination" in European law is "*harmonization*." It refers to norms that are given to national social law, also – and precisely – to the extent that it is purely "domestic social law" (with no foreign references). Since these directives are contained within international law, that is, they have a coordinating effect on multiple national legal systems, they "harmonize" national legal systems. "Harmonization" can also be limited to basic principles. It can selectively pick out specific items. But it can also attempt to undertake a denser web of normatizations – all the way to a complete, comprehensive regulation that would have to be adopted in place of the prevailing national law. The expression "harmonization" includes all of these variations. See Schuler (1988, pp. 61–64).

[602] "VO Nr. 3 des Rates über die soziale Sicherheit der Wanderarbeitnehmer vom 25. September 1958," ABl., p. 561, amended ABl. 1961, p. 831. Later replaced by the "VO 1408/71/EWG des Rates zur Anwendung der Systeme der sozialen Sicherheit auf Arbeitnehmer und deren Familien, die innerhalb der Gemeinschaft zu- und abwandern, vom 14. Juni 1971" ABl. L 147/2, amended ABl. 1973, L 128/22.

exert control over this entire Germany. It was true of the *smaller Germany of the three western occupation zones*: of the condominium that the three occupying powers had initially reserved for themselves also vis-à-vis the Federal Republic, and of the treaties which, beginning in 1955, defined the reciprocal rights and obligations of the occupying powers and the Federal Republic. And it applied to the *international organizations*, membership in which was so important for the young Federal Republic: especially the *Council of Europe* and the *International Labour Organization*. Within the framework of these organizations, the Federal Republic was able to have a hand in shaping the rebuilding of postwar Europe and the global international community. But it also had to integrate itself. To be sure, what the majorities in these international organizations decided could constrain the Federal Republic only within very narrow boundaries. The conventions developed by the Council of Europe and the agreements and conventions drafted by the International Labour Organization were always only an offer to the member states. But both the influence that the Federal Republic could exert on these organizations, and the legitimacy conveyed by belonging to them depended crucially on the degree to which the Federal Republic itself embraced what they developed as international law. It had to be important to the social state of the Federal Republic to find within the norms of the International Labour Organization a framework for itself that was both acceptable and useful. At the same time, though, it had to be equally important to the young German social state to participate in the social development of the world through the consultations, decisions, and norms of the International Labour Organization, as well as through the technical services of the latter.

By contrast, what the Council of Europe could mean for the young German state was thematically broad. The mandate of the Council was not limited to the social. It reaffirmed its

"devotion to the spiritual and moral values which are the common heritage of their peoples and the true source of individual freedom, political liberty and the rule of law, principles which form the basis of all genuine democracy" (Preamble to the Statutes).

Its mandate concerned a community of laws and values. The most significant manifestation of that mandate was the European Convention for the Protection of Human Rights and Fundamental Freedoms of 4 November 1950, which the Federal Republic ratified in 1952 (BGBl. II, pp. 685, 953). This convention demonstrates in the most elementary way the importance of the general legal culture to the development of the social state. It forms an essential foundation for the fact that the welfare states in the Europe of the Council became "liberal welfare states." And yet, the Council of Europe also faced the challenges of the social directly. The coordinating conventions of 1953 to accompany the right of establishment were a first step.

In 1955, once the occupation regime essentially came to an end with the Germany Treaty, the Federal Republic was able to join the *North Atlantic Treaty Organization* (est. 1949). With that, it became even more integrated into the web of trans-Atlantic relations. Analogously, the Federal Republic joined the *Western*

European Union.[603] The latter had not only a military, but also a cultural and economic-social mandate (Art. I and II of the Brussels Treaty). It realized that mandate especially through a first European agreement on guest workers (17 April 1950), which the Federal Republic joined in 1960.

The building of the *supranational Europe* was of a new quality. The *European Coal and Steel Community*, the *European Atomic Energy Community*, and – above all – the *European Economic Community* changed Europe in a unique way – and from the outset also and especially the "social Europe." The immediate theme of the European treaties was – using the categories of the German social state – the responsibility for the economy. The member states of the EEC, "directing their efforts to the essential purpose of constantly improving the living and working conditions of their peoples" (Preamble, EWGV, old version), declared that it was the "aim of the Community, by establishing a Common Market and progressively approximating the economic policies of Member States, to promote throughout the Community a harmonious development of economic activities, a continuous and balanced expansion, an increased stability, an accelerated raising of the standard of living" (Art. 2, EWGV, old version). The improvement in living and working conditions would be achieved in part from "the functioning of the Common Market which will favour the harmonisation of social systems" (Art. 117, EWGV, old version). Other than that, the treaty was restrained when it came to a direct influence of the European Community on national social policies. The instruments were limited to studies, opinions, and consultations (Art. 118, EWGV, old version) and to periodic reports (Art. 122, EWGV, old version). The treaty went beyond these parameters only on two issues: regarding the immediate "application of the principle of equal remuneration for equal work as between men and women workers" (Art. 119, EWGV, old version), and regarding the creation of the European Social Fund "to improve opportunities of employment of workers in the Common Market and thus contribute to raising the standard of living" (Art. 3i, 123–128, EWGV, old version). Nevertheless, the creation of the supranational Europe has substantially altered the conditions of the social in the member state and in their environment.

11.3 The Federal Republic of Germany from After the Founding Phase to German Reunification (1957–1990)

11.3.1 Structures[604]

The situation of "*all of Germany*" changed fundamentally during this period (Kleßmann 1988/1997). In 1961, the building of the wall in Berlin deepened the division of Germany in a shocking way and infused a new dynamic into the

[603] Established by the Treaty of Economic, Social, and Cultural Collaboration and Collective Self-Defense (Brussels Treaty) of 17 March 1948.

[604] Bundesministerium für Arbeit und Soziales and Bundesarchiv (eds.): Geschichte der Sozialpolitik in Deutschland seit 1945, vols. 4 (2007a), 5 (2006a), 6 (2008a), and Bundesministerium für Gesundheit and Bundesarchiv (2005), vol. 7, Chap. 1 and 3, no. 17 in each.

polemical relationship between the two German states. In 1969, the Brandt government set out to guide this relationship onto a constructive path, without calling into question the indispensable premises: the imperative of reunification, and the impermissibility for the two German states to refer to each other as foreign countries. However, a resolution to the situation of "all of Germany" could not be limited to the Federal Republic and the German Democratic Republic. With the fate of the Saarland now resolved through its accession to the Federal Republic, it also had to take a position on the legal status of those other territories of the German Reich in the borders of 1 January 1937, which belonged neither to the FRG nor the GDR: the legal status of northern East Prussia annexed by the Soviet Union in 1945, and the legal status of the territories east of the Oder-Neiße line that had been placed under Polish administration by the Potsdam Agreement. Through the Treaty of Moscow and the Treaty of Warsaw, which were signed in 1970 and took effect in 1972, the Federal Republic recognized the status quo, subject to the rights of the four victorious powers and a peace treaty. A Berlin Agreement among the four occupying powers in 1971 complemented the ensemble of agreements and treaties. In 1972/73 there followed the Basic Treaty between the two German states. It cleared the way for the admission of the FRG and the GDR into the United Nations (1973). The Treaty between the Federal Republic and Czechoslovakia in 1973/74 concluded the sequence of *Ostpolitik* treaties (Bernhardt 1987; Scholz 1987). Since then, the territories east of the Oder-Neiße line have been definitively removed from the pan-German responsibility of the Federal Republic – though of course without ceasing to be relevant as the homeland of ethnic Germans (E. Klein 1995). The relationship between the two German states was regulated in such a way that they recognized each other as states, although the Federal Republic maintained that the German Reich continued to exist, which meant that the GDR could not be a foreign country in its eyes. Moreover, inhabitants of the GDR, who are German citizens according to the law of German citizenship, remained citizens of the Federal Republic (Art. 116, Para. 1, GG) even when they were recognized and claimed by the GDR as its citizens.[605]

The *supranational Europe* expanded during this phase: beyond the original member states of Belgium, Germany, France, Italy, Luxembourg, and the Netherlands, to include also Denmark, Ireland, and Great Britain (1973), Greece (1981), and Spain and Portugal (1986). In 1967, the Merger Treaty, which largely combined the three European Communities institutionally into a single entity, affirmed the overarching character of European integration. But only the Single European Act (1986/87) set in motion the development of treaty law that would continue in the Treaties of Maastricht (1992/93) and Amsterdam (1997/99). The Single European Act imparted a significant new vigor to the Common Market and thus also new importance to the national social state (see above section "European

[605] These provisos were underscored and developed with special emphasis by the Federal Constitutional Court: BVerfGE 36, 1. On the issue as a whole see Ress (1987); Dolzer, vol. 1 (1987, pp. 547–590).

Integration"). Of course, the explicit and direct socio-political changes to the EEC Treaty remained minimal: the authority to set guidelines to encourage improvements in the working environment (Art. 118a, EEA); the power to "adopt the measures for the approximation of the provisions laid down by law, regulations or administrative action in Member States which have as their object the establishment and functioning of the internal market," also in regard to social policy (though it did not apply "to fiscal provisions, to those relating to the free movement of persons nor to those relating to the rights and interests of employed persons") (Art. 100a); finally, the mandate to the Commission "to develop the dialogue between management and labour at the European *level" (Art. 118b). Efforts at greater socio-political competency were opposed by Great* Britain. This deadlocked situation gave rise to the Charter on the Fundamental Social Rights of Workers in 1989 (Däubler et al. 1994, pp. 926–934). However, it was only able to demonstrate the political consensus of all member states with the exception of Great Britain.

11.3.2 People and Spaces[606]

The "Double Domestic Society" of the Constitutional State of the Federal Republic of Germany

The *narrower "domestic society" of the Federal Republic of Germany* became more and more a natural state of affairs during these decades. Of course, the political consciousness of the people who understood and felt themselves to be citizens of this state was exceedingly peculiar. The "*double domestic society" of Germany* prevented an uninhibited self-awareness as a political people – especially since the constant reminders of recent history made it difficult to have an emotional orientation to "the people." Similarly, the *variety of conceivable conceptions of the territory of a German state* – the German Reich, the German Reich within the borders of 1 January, 1937, the two German states, or the Federal Republic alone – was an obstacle to a natural bond to one's own "land." History had discredited the power of the state, which was in need of legitimacy. That legitimacy came from the constitution, the Basic Law (Isensee 1987, pp. 591–661). And much of the international recognition of this polity was also derived from this constitution, which had stood the test of time. It was this constitution that united the "domestic society" into a national people (*Staatsvolk*). The sphere in which the constitution was in force defined the territory of the state. And it was the constitution that established the authority of state power. The word "*Verfassungspatriotismus*" (constitutional patriotism) aptly captures this peculiarity. The common denominator of this society

[606] Bundesministerium für Arbeit und Soziales and Bundesarchiv (eds.): Geschichte der Sozialpolitik in Deutschland seit 1945, vols. 4 (2007a), 5 (2006a), 6 (2008a), and Bundesministerium für Gesundheit and Bundesarchiv (2005) vol. 7, Chap. 1 and 3, nos. 12, 13, 17 in each.

and its state was the constitution – not the definition of the people, not the definition of territory. This constitution was a constitution *for* the Germans and *for* Germany (Preamble, Art. 11, 16, 23, 116, 146, GG). This entailed a specific openness of this country to all those who could and did claim that they were Germans in one way or another. But the constitution had also stipulated another kind of openness: the openness of refuge – for Germans, too, but not only for them (Badura 1998, pp. 1–14). The political asylum is also an element of this constitutional state.

The Germans

The Germans who had always lived in the land that was now the state territory of the Federal Republic of Germany could continue to regard themselves as the core of the "*domestic society*" – they and their children. But the Germans who had come into the "Trizone" around the time the war ended in the years that followed had long since become their equals. And all the Germans who immigrated later were unquestioned members of this "domestic society." The notion of the "partial identity" of the Federal Republic with the German Reich developed a very practical relevance in this regard: the Federal Republic, even though it was not the German Reich and not its legal successor, was the land of all Germans, the land in which they could feel at home. The basic right to freedom of movement – from the outset not only as a right to move freely *within* the territory of the federation, but also as the right to move *to* the Federal Republic[607] – was the right of all Germans (Art. 116, GG), and not only of German citizens in the narrower and formal sense. All other basic rights, provided they were not human rights or, like the right to asylum (Art. 16, Para. 2, Sent 2, GG, old version; Art. 16a, GG, new version), a right for foreigners, were rights for Germans. To the degree to which the basic rights contribute to constituting the "domestic society," all Germans who de facto integrated themselves into it were "born" members of the "domestic society" of the Federal Republic of Germany.[608]

The period of the mass expulsion of Germans, especially from countries in Central and Eastern Europe, was by now over. The reasons and circumstances of immigration became more varied. Expulsions did continue to exist, but their manifestations were more subtle. In many places, the Germans became isolated and felt stripped of the ability to cultivate and pass on their ethnic identity. Finally, for many it seemed like the chance of a lifetime to move from the Communist-dominated states in Central and Eastern Europe to the liberal, economically flourishing Federal Republic. The more access to the Federal Republic was opened up in this way, the more important it became to define the preconditions under which it could be asserted, to regulate the process that clarified these preconditions, and to offer assistance that promoted integration. The essential foundations for the

[607] BVerfGE 2, 266 (271); 43, 203 (211).

[608] Only the indefeasibility of German citizenship was articulated in the narrower, formal sense as the right of German citizens: Art. 16, Para. 1, GG.

demarcation of the group of persons to which all of this applied had already been laid down by the Federal *Expellee and Refugee* Law of 1953 (E. Klein 1995, pp. 624, 629–637). The social assistance toward equality and integration took place from different perspectives: through the social compensation law (the equalization of burdens law) (Frerich and Frey, vol. 3, 1996, p. 35f.), through inclusion in social provision (especially via the foreign pension law, which regulated the valuation of a person's "social biography" in the pension and accident insurance law of the Federal Republic),[609] and finally by integration assistance (granted on the basis of various law, in part also stipulated in mere benefits programs) (Frerich and Frey, vol. 3, 1996, pp. 316–327).

The *relationship* of the "West German" social state *to the German Democratic Republic,* to the *Germans who lived there,* and to *those who came from there to the Federal Republic* continued to be more complicated. It is difficult to ascertain the social practice in a comprehensive way. Fundamental pronouncements were avoided as much as polemical benefits practices. That was true especially for the time of the new direction of the *Ostpolitik* and after.[610] The doctrine of the partial identity of the Federal Republic with the German Reich was kept warm "at the lowest possible flame."[611] For the Germans *in* the GDR, the Federal Republic clung to the principle of integration (*Eingliederungsprinzip*), according to which their socio-legal status was determined by the law of the GDR.[612] Germans who resettled from the GDR, however, were fundamentally put in the position in which they would have been, had the "social biography" they lived through in the GDR taken place in the Federal Republic. This intention found its most enduring realization in the pension and accident insurance law.[613] Added to this were compensation payments, benefits from the equalization of burdens law, and integration assistance from the Federal Expellees and Refugees Law. Additional assistance came in part from non-statutory programs (Fredrich and Frey, vol. 3, 1996, p. 36f., pp. 316–327),

[609] First regulated through the "Fremdrenten- und Auslandsrentengesetz vom 7. August 1953," BGBl. I, p. 848; newly regulated through the "Fremdrenten- und Auslandsrenten-Neuregelungsgesetz vom 25. Februar 1960" BGBl. I, p. 93. Since then known as the "Fremdrentengesetz" (Foreign Pensions Law).

[610] On the conditions that framed the forty-year history of inter-German relations see Haendecke-Hoppe and Lieser-Triebnigg (1990).

[611] Quaritsch (1995, p. 351). Explicit bi-lateral socio-political regulations existed only for the health care system: "Abkommen vom 25. April 1974 zwischen der Regierung der Bundesrepublik Deutschland und der Regierung der Deutschen Demokratischen Republik auf dem Gebiet des Gesundheitswesens. Zustimmungsgesetz vom 20. November 1975" BGBl. II, p. 1729.

[612] BVerfGE 28, 104; 71, 66; 95, 143. In legal language, attention was paid to avoid the pair of terms "*Ausland*" (foreign countries] and "*Inland*" (in-country]. For example, Sect. 30, Para. 1 of the General Part of the Social Code (SGB I) gave this definition: "The regulations of this Code apply to all persons who have their domicile or usual residence in the area in which it is valid." See also Dolzer (1987, p. 584).

[613] First through the "Fremdrenten- und Auslandsrentengesetz", later through the "Fremdrentengesetz."

though largely from the Refugee Assistance Act of 15 July 1965 (BGBl. I, p. 612). Finally, persons who had been imprisoned were entitled to benefits from the Prisoner Assistance Act of August 1955.[614] For its part, the German Democratic Republic also applied the integration principle to individuals who had resettled there (Cäsar 1968, pp. 157–166).

The Non-Germans in the Federal Republic

What changed even more so than the immigration of Germans into the Federal Republic during this period was the immigration and *share of non-Germans*. The *non-Germans who were in Germany at the end of the war because of the Nazi tyranny* had mostly left the country again. Immigration to Germany was shaped, on the one hand, by the political conditions in the large number of states – scattered across the world – that had totalitarian or authoritarian governments or were in a state of chaos and anarchy. Germany thus took on new importance as a *refuge*. On the other hand, there was growing immigration in response to the demand from a Germany with increasingly full employment for *foreign workers* – and a corresponding demand by foreigners for work. When employment declined in the Federal Republic in the 1970s, there was an overhang of demand for work compared to the demand for workers. Moreover, not all foreign workers were willing and able to respond by suspending or terminating their employment by returning to their home countries, especially if the foreign workers had brought their families to Germany or had established families in Germany. Then there was the desire on the part of individual family members to stay – especially to be educated here and find work of their own. Whatever the reason: the primary immigration of foreign workers resulted in *secondary phenomena of immigration*. All of these situations raised questions of support and integration.[615] Finally, there was a *third dimension of immigration: individuals who were seeking primarily to participate in the conditions of life in Germany*, which, for political, economic, societal or civilizing, cultural, ethnic, or religious reasons were better than the conditions in their homelands. The spectrum of circumstances under which they set out to emigrate to Germany was very broad and differentiated. It ranged from cases of expulsion, persecution, discrimination, and similar hardships, to cases where immigrants were seeking to participate in the working life or merely in the prosperity (and especially the social benefits) of the Federal Republic.

The legal system of the Federal Republic had to come to terms with these phenomena (Schuler 1988, pp. 775–786). From the outset, a distinction had to be made between *two levels*. One level concerned *access to the Federal Republic* and

[614] "Gesetz über Hilfsmaßnahmen für Personen, die aus politischen Gründen in Gebieten außerhalb der Bundesrepublik Deutschland in Gewahrsam genommen wurden (Häftlingshilfegesetz) vom 6. August 1955", BGBl. I, p. 498.

[615] "Aktionsprogramm der Bundesregierung zur Ausländerbeschäftigung vom 6. Juli 1973", in: Presse- und Informationsamt der Bundesregierung (1973, p. 693).

residency in it.[616] The other level concerned *participation in the social life of the Federal Republic*. That level was again divided into *two sub-levels*: *active participation in the living possibilities* in the Federal Republic through dependent or independent gainful employment, through education and training, through unpaid work, and so on; and *participation in the social benefits systems* of the Federal Republic (Die sozialrechtliche Stellung der Ausländer in der Bundesrepublik Deutschland 1983). Both sub-levels encompassed a complex diversity of issues: the limit and control of participation, the distribution of participation, the conveyance of appropriate participation at least for the individuals who were in the country (Soziale Arbeit 1988, pp. 29–47). New issues were constantly arising at the sub-level of social benefits: inclusion in the minimum living conditions of society (through the general assistance system of social welfare), inclusion in society's opportunities for prosperity (through the specific assistance and promotion programs of child allowance, housing allowance, and so on), and the self-evident inclusion by workers in the participation conveyed through working and economic life (via social insurance); participation *during* the residence in the Federal Republic and *continued participation* in the provision systems – especially the long-term systems in case of old age, disability, and survivors – also *after* a return to the native country. Considerable differentiations were made with respect to every one of these issues. In the process, the right to asylum, thanks to its anchoring in the Basic Law (Art. 16, Para. 2, Sent. 2, GG, old version) formed a special area, the relevance of which would be felt also quantitatively only at the end of the 1960s. In 1965, the Federal Republic gave itself, in the "*Ausländergesetz*," for the first time a comprehensive and differentiated system of residency law for foreigners. In 1976, the country joined the Agreement about the Legal Status of Stateless Individuals (BGBl. II, p. 473). Over the course of time, the fundamentally equal treatment of asylum seekers with those who had been granted asylum had become a problem. Restrictions were put in place in 1981. Possibilities of working were limited for asylum seekers.[617] To the same extent this closed off access to social insurance. That same year, social welfare for asylum seekers was also cut for the first time.[618] The differentiation and restrictions on the status of foreigners with respect to residence, employment, and social law, which had begun with the "*Ausländergesetz*," continued.

Another special area was *freedom of movement by virtue of European Community law*: starting from the freedom of movement of workers (Art. 48–51, EWGV) and its supplementation in terms of social law through the "Migrant Worker Ordinance," specific regimes of European freedom of movement and corresponding

[616] The "Ausländergesetz vom 28. April 1965" (BGBl. I, p. 353) was a first coherent regulation. On the historical development of foreigner law (*Fremdenrecht*) see Renner (1998, pp. 1–37).

[617] "Sechstes Gesetz zur Änderung des Arbeitsförderungsgesetzes vom 3. August 1981", BGBl. I, p. 802.

[618] Section 120, Para. 2, BSHG, in the version of the "Zweites Haushaltsstrukturgesetz vom 22. Dezember 1981", BGBl. I, p. 1523.

social law emerged for the self-employed,[619] service providers and service recipients,[620] and for students.[621] At the same time, it proved necessary over time to enact corresponding laws for example for the continued stay of individuals with a right of residence after the expiration of their primary residency permit.[622] In 1969, the German legislator codified the consequences for German law that arose from the European development.[623] And the social protection of those who took advantage of freedom of movement had to be developed further accordingly (Barwig et al. 1997; Hänlein 1998, pp. 91–105).

The External Extension of the German Social State

The extension of the German social state to individuals living abroad increased in multiple ways. With *Germans* living abroad temporarily or permanently in growing numbers, protection through German social benefits law became more and more relevant (Schuler 1988, pp. 291–300, 475–509, 651–665, 740–750, 756–764). *Foreign workers* returned to their native countries temporarily or permanently and were entitled to social benefits under these circumstances. *Compensation* for Nazi injustice, especially to individuals living abroad, was challenged by the constant emergence of new constellations of cases.[624] As already noted, restitution agreements were concluded with a number of West European countries. Various benefits were granted on the basis of principle of equity, beyond what the Federal Republic recognized as a legal basis. With respect to the claims of forced laborers that had been employed in the German Reich, the Federal Republic invoked the London Debt-Settlement Agreement of 27 February 1953,[625] according to which the review of claims against the German Reich by individual states and their citizens stemming from the Second World War would be put off until their final regulation in a peace treaty. However, that did not resolve the problem (Ferencz 1986).

This time also saw a growing universal concern on the part of the Federal Republic for the *Third World*. From the beginning, there had been efforts in the

---

[619] Art. 52–57, EWGV. On the development of social protection for this group of individuals see Willms (1997a) on Art. 51, margin numbers 9 and 50.

[620] Art. 66 EWGV. On the development of social protection Willms (1997a), margin number 12.

[621] On the freedom of movement for students see Haag (1997) on Art. 8a, margin number 2.

[622] On the right to remain for former "migrant workers" and the self-employed, family members, survivors, and so on, see Troberg (1997) on Art. 56, margin nos. 13 and 14. On additional rights of residence see Haag (1997) on Art. 8a, margin no. 2; Troberg (1997) on Art. 56, margin no 16.

[623] "Gesetz über Einreise und Aufenthalt von Staatsangehörigen der Mitgliedstaaten der Europäischen Wirtschaftsgemeinschaft (Aufenthaltsgesetz/EWG) vom 22. Juli 1969", BGBl. I, p. 927. By now repeatedly amended.

[624] Bundesministerium für Arbeit und Soziales and Bundesarchiv (eds.): Geschichte der Sozialpolitik in Deutschland seit 1945, vols. 4 (2007a), 5 (2006a), 6 (2008a), Bundesministerium für Gesundheit and Bundesarchiv (2005), vol. 7, Chap. 3, no. 12 in each.

[625] BGBl. II, p. 333. Schwarz (1987).

direction of *development aid*.[626] In the 1960s, however, this dimension became manifest in a new way: for example, with the Federal Republic joining the International Development Association (IDA) (BGBl. 1960, II, p. 2137), through the establishment of a separate Ministry for Economic Cooperation (Ritter and Niehuss 1991: 107), and through the beginning of continuous reporting on development aid.[627] This was joined increasingly by humanitarian aid in natural and political catastrophes.[628] In 1973, finally, the Federal Republic moved comprehensively onto the level of universal international law by joining the United Nations.

11.3.3 Institutions and Norms[629]

Institutions

This period was characterized not least by a substantial expansion of the web of international institutions and norms into which the social policy and the socially relevant law of the Federal Republic was increasingly integrated. In *supranational Europe*,[630] this development with respect to the establishment of freedom of movement, its social protection of occupational safety, and – to a limited degree – the equality of men and women, was manifested in formal European laws (through guidelines, occasionally also through ordinances). The reforms of the European Social Fund[631] required formal changes to the law, even though political and financial decisions were of greater importance. Other than that, there was series of political attempts to advance a common socio-political development for Europe.[632] The chief themes were poverty, employment, works constitution, equality of men and women, the disabled, and time and again first steps toward an overarching socio-political conception for the European Community. The most important carrier of the development of European law during this time of relative stagnation, however, was the European Court: through its decisions – repeatedly received with displeasure in Germany – on the social protection of freedom of

[626] Carl-Duisberg-Gesellschaft (1960); Deutsche Stiftung für Entwicklungsländer (1962).

[627] Development Aid Reports, from the first report (BTDrs. 7/1236) to the ninth report (BTDrs. 12/4096).

[628] "Berichte der Bundesregierung über die deutsche humanitäre Hilfe im Ausland", BTDrs. 8/2155, 9/2364, 10/6564, 11/7508, 12/7737.

[629] See section "European Integration"; Bundesministerium für Arbeit und Soziales and Bundesarchiv (eds.): Geschichte der Sozialpolitik in Deutschland seit 1945, vols. 4 (2007a), 5 (2006a), 6 (2008a), and Bundesministerium für Gesundheit (2005), vol. 7, Chap. 3, no. 17 in each.

[630] "Berichte der Bundesregierung über die Integration in den Europäischen Gemeinschaften", from report 1967 (BTDrs. V/2127) to report 1990 II (BTDrs. 12/217); Frerich and Frey, vol. 3, (1996, pp. 426–459).

[631] Schulz (1999), preliminary remarks to Art. 123–125, margin numbers 5–11.

[632] Especially the "Sozialpolitische Aktionsprogramm (des Rates) vom 12. Februar 1974," ABl. 1974, no. C 13: 1.

movement in Europe (Schulte and Zacher 1991), and through its decisions on the equality of men and women (see above section "On the Importance of the European Community for German Social Policy"). The *Council of Europe* (Frerich and Frey, vol. 3, 1996, p. 459f.) supplemented the Convention on Human Rights with a codification of social rights: the European Social Charter of 1961, which the Federal Republic ratified in 1964 (BGBl. II, p. 1261). This was followed in 1964 by the European Code of Social Security, which the Federal Republic ratified in 1970 (BGBl. II, p. 909).

Once the Federal Republic joined the *United Nations*, the global human rights regime of the United Nations could also be taken over for the Federal Republic as binding. The Universal Declaration of Human Rights on 10 December 1948, had had great authority in Germany from the time it was issued. Moreover, it had been possible for the Federal Republic, even before joining the UN, to formally adopt the International Convention on the Elimination of All Forms of Racial Discrimination (BGBl. 1969, II, p. 961). Now, the FRG was able to ratify also the International Covenant on Civil and Political Rights of 19 December 1966 (BGBl. 1973, II, p. 1533), and the International Covenant on Economic, Social, and Cultural Rights of the same day (BGBl. 1973, II, p. 1569). With that, the Federal Republic was now fully part of this global system of human rights – though of course, it now also subjected itself to its oversight. When it came to the development of labor and social law, the agreements, recommendations, and conferences of the International Labour Organization continued to be of the utmost importance (Frerich and Frey, vol. 3, 1996, p. 461f.). But responsibility for the economy now also meant participating in shaping a new global economic system.[633]

The International Normative Framework of the German Social State

The Federal Republic of Germany was now integrated into a *fundamental international* – global and European – *system* that confirmed the foundations of its own policies and law. That system is carried by the guiding ideas of *social justice*,[634] *social welfare*,[635] and the *social rights of human beings*.[636] However, this guiding image is dominated by the idea of constant social growth: of further social progress

[633] "Gutachten vom 20. November 1976. Fragen einer neuen Weltwirtschaftsordnung, in: Bundesministerium für Wirtschaft (1987, "Der wissenschaftliche Beirat...", pp. 777–838); Bundesministerium für wirtschaftliche Zusammenarbeit (1978).

[634] Preamble, Statutes of the ILO, Para. 1; Second Declaration of Philadelphia; Preamble EEA, Para. 3.

[635] Preamble to the EuSCh.

[636] AEMR; IPWSKR; EMRK, Preamble to the EuSCh.; Preamble to the EEA; Preamble, Para. 9, Art. 2, Art. 3, Art. 136–145, EGV in the version of AV.

and a further improvement in living conditions.[637] The European Social Charter[638] goes so far as to add to the obligation "to establish or maintain a system of social security," not only that of maintaining this system "at a satisfactory level," but also the duty "to endeavor to raise progressively the system of social security to a higher level." This *focus on social growth* is understandable in view of the period during which the earliest of these norms were laid down. It is also understandable in view of the different standards of the countries addressed by these norms. Still, it also expresses a lopsided optimism that should have been replaced since the 1970s and 1980s with a more realistic experience: the optimism that the social could only get better and better all the time. The fixation on this growth goal is a central reason for the difficulties the Federal Republic and many other countries are having adjusting to the need to realize the values of the social also under fundamentally altered conditions – worse conditions compared to what one was accustomed to.

The *basic formula* is essentially confirmed in these documents. Full employment is a central value.[639] The individual has a right to work, but also the obligation to earn his living through work.[640] Concern over appropriate working conditions finds multiple expressions.[641] In the process, the attention is focused on dependent labor – in part implicitly, in part explicitly. By comparison, independent gainful work is neglected. The law of the European Community knows the issue as a problem of the freedom to provide services (independently) and the free movement of goods, that is, not so much in a social context.[642] The European Social Charter also guarantees *every* gainful employment certain protection in case it is pursued in another country (Part II Art. 18 EuSCh). Unpaid work is barely mentioned (Art. 5 b, Art. 11 Para. 2 c UN Convention on Women). Work is supposed to earn a wage that allows for a

[637] Preamble and Art. 55a, UN Charter; Preamble EuSCh; Art. 2, 3i, 117, EWGV; Preamble and Art. 2, EGV in the version of AV.

[638] Art. 12, nos. 1–3, EuSCh.

[639] Art. 55a UN Charter; Art. 6, Para. 2, IPWSKR; III a, Declaration of Philadelphia; ILO Convention 122: Employment Policy; Part II, Art. no. 1, EuSCh.; Art. 2, EGV in the version of MV; Art 2, Art. 126, EGV in the version of AV.

[640] Art. 23, no. 1 AEMR; Art. 7, IPWSKR; Part I, no. 2, Part II, Art. 2 and 3, EuSCh.

[641] Art. 23, no. 1, AEMR; Art. 7, 11, 12, IPWSKR; Preamble ILO Constitution; III d, Declaration of Philadelphia, in addition a majority of the Conventions and Recommendations of the International Labour Organization; Part I, nos. 2, 3, 7, 8, EuSCh; Art. 118, 120, EWGV; Art. 2, no. 22, AV. A special role was played by the shaping of working conditions by the unions and employers' associations (their freedom to engage in industrial action, especially the right to strike, and free collective bargaining): Art. 23, no. 4, AEMR; Art. 22, IPBPR; Art. 8, IPWSKR; Preamble ILO Constitution; I d, Declaration of Philadelphia; on this see ILO Convention 87: Freedom of Association and Protection of the Right to Organize; ILO Convention 98: Right to Organize and Collective Bargaining; Art. 11, EMRK; Part I, nos. 5 and 6, Part II, Art. 4, 5 and 6, EuSCh; Art. 118, EWGV.

[642] Art. 48ff., 52ff., 59ff., 78, 118 a, Para. 2, EWGV.

suitable living standard, also for the community of maintenance.[643] Special attention is paid to the equality of pay for men and women.[644]

The *community of maintenance* is fundamentally addressed separately as a personal, societal, but also community-supporting good. Social problems are also considered.[645] In keeping with the different scope of the potential sphere of validity of individual documents and in accordance with the different purposes to which they are connected, the problems of *meeting needs* are addressed in multifarious ways: housing,[646] clothing,[647] food,[648] education (including vocational training and advanced training),[649] cultural participation,[650] medical care and the promotion of good health,[651]and, finally social services (here, too, neglected).[652] More recently, consumer protection[653] and environmental protection[654] have also been emphasized.

In terms of *social benefits*, the minimum subsistence[655] and a corresponding right to *welfare*[656] are guaranteed. However, the program of *social protection*[657] is

---

[643] Art. 23, no. 3, AEMR; Art. 7 a, I, IPWSKR; Preamble ILO Constitution; III d, Declaration of Philadelphia; Part I, no. 4, Part II, Art. 4, no. 1, EuSCh.

[644] Art. 7 a, ii, IPWSKR; Art. 11, Para. 1 d, UN Convention on Women; Preamble ILO Constitution, ILO Convention 100: Equal Remuneration; Part II, Art. 4, no. 3, EuSCh; Art. 119, EWGV; Art. 119, EGV in the version of MV; Art. 141 EGV in the version of AV.

[645] Art. 16, nos. 3, 25, 26, AEMR; Art. 10, 13, Para. 3, IPWSKR; Art. 11, Para. 2, UN Convention on Women; III h, Declaration of Philadelphia; Art. 8, 12, EMRK; Part I, nos. 7, 16, 17, Part II, Art. 16, 17, EuSCh.

[646] Art. 25, no. 1, AEMR; III i, Declaration of Philadelphia.

[647] Art. 25, no. 1, AEMR.

[648] Art. 25, no. 1, AEMR; III i, Declaration of Philadelphia.

[649] Art. 26, no. 1, AEMR; Art. 6, Para. 2, 13, 14, IPWSKR; Art. 10, 11, Para. 1 c, UN Convention on Women; Preamble ILO Constitution; III c and j, IV, Declaration of Philadelphia; Art. 2, Supplementary Protocol no. 1 to EMRK; Part I, nos. 9 and 10, Part II, Art. 1, nos. 3 and 4, Art. 9 and 10, EuSCh; Art. 118, 125, Para. 1, 128, EWGV; Art. 3 p, Art. 123, Art. 126f., EGV in the version of MV; Art. 125, Art. 140, EGV in the version of AV.

[650] Art. 27, no. 1, AEMR; Art. 15, Para. 1 a, b, IPWSKR; III i, Declaration of Philadelphia; Art. 3 p, 128, EGV in the version of MV.

[651] Art. 25, no. 1, AEMR, Art. 12, IPWSKR; III f, IV, Declaration of Philadelphia, ILO Convention 130 on Medical Care and Sickness Benefits; Part I, no. 11, Part II, Art. 11, EuSCh; Art. 3 o, 129, EGV in the version of MV; Art. 95, Para. 3, 152, EGV in the version of AV.

[652] Part I, no. 14, Part II, Art. 14, EuSCh.

[653] Art. 129 a, EGV in the version of MV, Art. 95, Para. 3, 153, EGV in the version of AV.

[654] Art. 130 r, EWGV; Art. 6, 95, Para. 3, 174, EGV in the version of AV.

[655] Art. 25, no. 1, subclause 1 AEMR.

[656] Art. 25 no. 1, subclause 1 AEMR; Part I, no. 13, Part II, Art. 13, EuSCh.

[657] Art. 22, 28, AEMR; Art. 9, IPWSKR; Preamble ILO Constitution; ILO Convention 102: Social Security Minimum Standards, and numerous other recommendations of the ILO; Part I, no. 12, Part II, Art. 12, EuSCh; Art. 51, 118, Para. 1, EWGV; Art. 2, nos. 12, 22, AV (now Art. 42; 136–143, EWGV in the version of AV).

dominant, especially of social insurance.[658] In a diversity almost too vast to grasp, *equality* is a theme in all of these documents:[659] also in the sense of dismantling differences in prosperity,[660] equality for the disadvantages (especially the disabled),[661] and especially in the sense of the equality of men and women,[662] the prohibition against discrimination,[663] the protection of minorities,[664] and the equality of foreigners (especially of migrant workers).[665]

The *responsibility of the state for the economy* is addressed by these documents in very different ways. The *international* documents of international law focus – apart from the common goal of a high level of employment – on the aspect of economic progress (Art. 55 a, UN Charter) and on making economic activities stable and steady. European treaties, by contrast, are essentially set up to realize themselves through a Common Market. They presuppose private property.[666] Other than that, the policies of the *European Communities* – such as the economic policy of the Federal Republic of Germany – is committed to price and currency stability, equilibrium in external trade, growth, and full employment.[667] In connection with the establishment of a European currency system, the orderly financial affairs of the member states have become particularly important.[668]

As a result of the fundamental *concordance of the German social system with the norms of international law*, the *international legal system* acts much more to affirm

[658] Art. 25 no. 1, subclause 2 AEMR, Art. 9, IPWSKR; Preamble ILO, Constitution and numerous Conventions and Recommendations by the ILO on sickness insurance, accident insurance, and pension insurance.

[659] Art. 1, nos. 3, 55 c, UN Charter, Art. 1, 6, 7, AEMR.

[660] II a, Declaration of Philadelphia; Art. 3, Para. 2, EGV in the version of AV.

[661] ILO Convention 159: Vocational Rehabilitation and Employment of Disabled Persons; Part I, no. 15, Part II, Art. 15, EuSCh.

[662] Preamble UN Charter; Preamble AEMR; Art. 3, IPBPR; Art. 3, IPWSKR; UN Convention on Women; Art. 119, EWGV; Art. 2, EGV in the version of AV.

[663] Art. 2, AEMR; UN Convention on Racial Discrimination; Art. 2, Para. 1, IPBPR; Art. 2, Para. 2, IPWSKR; Art. 14, EMRK; Preamble EuSCh; Art. 12, 13, EGV in the version of AV.

[664] Art. 27, IPBPR.

[665] ILO Convention 118: Equality of Treatment in Social Security; Art. 7, 48–51, EWGV, Art. 39–42, EGV in the version of AV.

[666] Exception: common property of fissionable materials (Art. 2f., 86ff., EAGV).

[667] Thus already the Directive 74/121/EWG of the Council on Stability, Growth, and Full Employment in the Community, 18 February 1974.- On the current goal of price and currency stability: Art. 2, 3 a, Para. 3, 109 Para. 1, 109 e, Para. 2, 109 f, Para. 2, 109 j, Para. 1, EGV in the version of MV; on equilibrium in external: Art. 3 a, Para. 3, 109 h, 109 I, EGV in the version of MV; on the goal of growth: Art. 2, EGV in the version of MV; on full employment: Art. 2, 118, Para. 1, EGV in the version of MV; Art. 127, EGV in the version of AV.

[668] For the Federal Republic see Art. 109, Art. 115, GG. For Europe see Art. 3 a, 104 c, 109 e, Para. 1 and 4, 109 j, Para. 1, EGV in the version of MV; Art. 4, Para. 3, 104, EGV in the version of AV.

national law than to direct and constrain it.[669] International law usually picks up consensuses that have emerged within the community of states. International law that is diametrically opposed to a standard of national law has the chance to assert itself only in exceptional cases: for example, if a group of influential states supports the progressive content and is able to push it through in the face of reluctant members of the international community. As a result, *conflicts between the norms of international law and the legal system of the Federal Republic of Germany*[670] have therefore remained marginal. For the most part, conflicts between German law and international law were prompted by structural peculiarities of German law, but not by principled opposition against international values. One of the problem areas in this regard concerns *public service*, whose specific German organization is not very well understood internationally and accepted only to a limited extent. For example, the hiring practice that sought to keep "radicals" from public employment was sanctioned as a violation of the ILO Convention no. 111 Against Discrimination in Employment and Occupation. The law that prohibits civil servants from striking has been seen as a violation of the ILO Convention no. 87 on the Freedom of Association and Protection of the Right to Organize as well as of the guarantee of the right to strike in Art. 6, no. 4, EuSCh, the use of strike-breaking civil servants as a violation of the ILO Convention no. 87, and the refusal of collective bargaining with teachers as a violation of the ILO Convention no. 98 about the Right to Organize and Collective Bargaining. Another problem area that led to difficulties is the specific German understanding of the *right of industrial action and free collective bargaining* as a self-contained ordering system that is dominated by the goal that the autonomy of collective bargaining shared by the unions and the employers (employers' associations) should be able to shape working conditions. The impermissibility of a protest strike against a legislative act was criticized as a violation of both ILO Convention no. 87 and of Art. 6, no. 4, EuSCh, and the impermissibility of "wild" strikes not organized by the unions and under their responsibility as a violation of Art. 6, no. 4, EuSCh. On occasion there were other disagreements with the bodies charged with implementing international law: for example, over the *admission of union representatives into enterprises* (violation of Convention No. 87), and over the *work of prisoners* (violation of ILO Convention No. 29 on Forced Labour). The bodies charged with implementing the European Social Charter have criticized especially *regulations at the expense of migrant workers*: procedures pertaining to the law on foreigners (violation of Art. 18, no. 2, EuSCh), restrictions on family reunions (Art. 19, no. 6, EuSCh), disadvantages in the workplace protection law (Art. 19, no. 4, EuSCh), and exclusions of non-EU citizens from state child-raising allowance (*Landeserziehungsgeld*) in the state law of Baden-Wuerttemberg and Bavaria (Art. 16, EuSCh).

[669] See Lörcher (1991, pp. 97–104; 1994, pp. 284–293); Adamy (1995, pp. 165–175). "Antwort der Bundesregierung auf die Kleine Anfrage der Abgeordneten Georg Andres u. a. und der Fraktion der SPD" – BTDrs. 12/2959: "Die sozialpolitische und rechtliche Bedeutung der Normen der Internationalen Arbeitsorganisation sowie ihrer sonstigen Aktivitäten auf internationaler und innerstaatlicher Ebene" (BTDrs. 12/3495).

[670] On what follows see Däubler, Kittner and Lörcher (1994, p. 201f., p. 609f.).

Considerably different is the relationship between German law and the *law of the European Communities. European Law* – especially the so-called *secondary law* of ordinances and directives, thanks to substantive boosts to European legal development from the Single European Act, the Maastricht Treaty, the Amsterdam Treaty, and increasingly also thanks to the *primary law* of treaties – is much denser and more detailed than international systems limited to the essential elements. Time and again, the supranational European law transcends the premise of a priori general consensuses and embarks upon unforeseeable interpretations and practices. A significant role is played above all by the fact that the supranational European legal system possesses in the European Court a most unique institution. The European Court is the meeting place for the legal thinking and legal experiences of all member states: they form the intellectual arena in which the challenge of the specific case gives rise to the response of the mostly completely novel community law. By now, this has intensively shaped many areas of national law.[671]

11.4 The United Germany[672]

11.4.1 Structures

The unification of Germany as agreed upon and carried out in 1990 put an end to the ambivalent relationship of the Federal Republic of Germany, first, to its own state territory and its own nation, and, second, to the wider territory of a "Germany as a whole" and to the indefinite nation of "all Germans." Likewise, German unification ended the other ambivalence, namely that this open responsibility on the part of the Federal Republic to a "larger Germany" and for "all Germans" was complicated by the existence – and since the Basic Treaty – the recognition of the "other German state." Through the Unification Treaty, through the Treaty on the Final Settlement with Respect to Germany ("2 + 4 Treaty") on 12 September 1990 (BGBl. II, p. 1317), and through the accompanying treaties with the Soviet Union,[673]

[671] Bundesministerium für Arbeit und Soziales and Bundesarchiv (eds.): Geschichte der Sozialpolitik in Deutschland seit 1945, vols. 4 (2007a), 5 (2006a), 6 (2008a), and Bundesministerium für Gesundheit... (2005), vol. 7, Chap. 3, nos. 1–10, 13, 17 in each.

[672] See above Chapter 9; Bundesministerium für Arbeit und Soziales and Bundesarchiv (eds.), 2007b: Geschichte der Sozialpolitik in Deutschland seit 1945, vol. 11, Chap. 3, no. 17.

[673] "Vertrag zwischen der Bundesrepublik Deutschland und der Union der Sozialistischen Sowjetrepubliken über die Bedingungen des befristeten Aufenthalts und die Modalitäten des planmäßigen Abzugs der sowjetischen Truppen aus dem Gebiet der Bundesrepublik Deutschland (Truppenabzugsvertrag) vom 12. Oktober 1990" BGBl. II 1991, p. 258;

"Abkommen zwischen der Regierung der Bundesrepublik Deutschland und der Regierung der Union der Sozialistischen Sowjetrepubliken über einige überleitende Maßnahmen (Überleitungsabkommen) vom 9. Oktober 1990", BGBl. II, p. 1655ff.

Poland,[674] and the Western powers (Schweitzer 1995, p. 222f.), it was made clear that the *united state territory of the Federal Republic of Germany and the German Democratic Republic* constitutes that "*Germany as a whole*" that can lay claim to the continuity of the German Reich (Frowein 1995, pp. 477–487). The *Germans in the old Federal Republic of Germany and the former German Democratic Republic are the political nation of this "Germany as a whole*." Section 2 of the Preamble to the Basic Law in the version of Art. 4 of the Unification Treaty expresses this:

> The Germans in the *Länder* of Baden-Wuerttemberg, Bavaria, Berlin, Brandenburg, Bremen, Hamburg, Hesse, Lower Saxony, Mecklenburg-Western Pomerania, North Rhine-Westphalia, Rhineland-Palatinate, Saarland, Saxony, Saxony-Anhalt, Schleswig-Holstein, and Thuringia have achieved the unity and freedom of Germany in free self-determination. This Basic Law is thus valid for the entire German people.

With that, Germany once again acquired the character of a nation state.[675]

At the same time, the *loss of sovereign statehood* toward the outside proceeded. That holds true institutionally for the supranational *Europe*.[676] It holds true, in an only marginally institutionalized but no less potent way, for the process of *globalization*.[677]

11.4.2 People[678]

Germans and Non-Germans in the Federal Republic

Needless to say, the state territory as well as the national people in this united Federal Republic of Germany continue to bear the imprint of history. The *dividing line between the old Federal Republic and the old German Democratic Republic* will remain visible for the unforeseeable future: in the infrastructure, in the architecture, in the economic conditions, and in much more. And the people are carrying the divided history with them: not only by virtue of their education and experience, not only in their human and social connections, but also in the form of their social

[674] "Vertrag zwischen der Bundesrepublik Deutschland und der Republik Polen über die Bestätigung der zwischen ihnen bestehenden Grenzen vom 14. November 1990", BGBl. II 1991, p. 1328; "Nachbarschaftsvertrag vom 17. November 1991," BGBl. II 1991, pp. 1314, 1328.

[675] See above section "German Unification"; Bundesministerium für Arbeit und Soziales and Bundesarchiv (eds.), 2007b: Geschichte der Sozialpolitik in Deutschland seit 1945, vol. 11, Chap. 1 and 2.

[676] See above section "European Integration"; Bundesministerium für Arbeit und Soziales and Bundesarchiv (eds.), 2007b: Geschichte der Sozialpolitik in Deutschland seit 1945, vol. 11, Chap. 1 and 2, Chap. 3, no. 17.

[677] See above section "Globalization"; Bundesministerium für Arbeit und Soziales and Bundesarchiv (eds.), 2007b: Geschichte der Sozialpolitik in Deutschland seit 1945, vol. 11, Chap. 1 and 2.

[678] Bundesministerium für Arbeit und Soziales and Bundesarchiv (eds.), 2007b: Geschichte der Sozialpolitik in Deutschland seit 1945, vol. 11, Chap. 1 and 2, Chap. 3, nos. 12, 13, 17.

biography – in the form of their professional and economic opportunities, their wealth, and their social entitlements. There is no other area in which the law carries greater responsibility for how these differences will be carried forward than long-term social provision (in case of old age, disability, and survivors).[679] But the abundance of worse-better comparisons between the spheres of life and the individual social contingencies is a comprehensive problem that will challenge politics and law in Germany for some time to come.[680]

But the historical burden of the German people remains alive also in another respect. As a result of the ethnic and territorial imperialism of Nazi Germany, the Basic Law recognized as German any person "who has been admitted to the territory of the German Reich within the boundaries of 31 December 1937 *as a refugee or expellee of German ethnic origin*" (Art. 116, Para. 1, GG). For many different reasons, this opening was given a broad interpretation by statutes and case law (E. Klein 1995, pp. 630–637). In connection with the exhaustion and eventual collapse of Communist rule, the people who were living in Central and Eastern European countries and had the necessary connections now had new reasons and opportunities to emigrate to Germany and seek admission. At the same time, it was becoming clear that the actual circumstances were drifting further and further away from what the Parliamentary Council had in mind when it drafted Art. 116, Para. 1, GG. The legislator therefore defined the notion of the ethnic German and the related term of the "*Spätaussiedler*" ("late ethnic German repatriate") in a new and more restrictive way,[681] without calling into question the essential substance of Art. 116, Para. 1, GG (Ruhrmann 1994). But restrictions were also imposed on the social benefits for *Spätaussiedler*.[682] Moreover, the integration of this group of people proved increasingly a specific problem that could not be solved only with cash benefits, but required above all services. To that extent, the cooperation of various carriers – the *Länder*, the municipalities, charitable carriers – is necessary (Haberland 1994, pp. 447–448; 1995, pp. 38–40, 86–90, 116–120).

The image of the *non-Germans in the Federal Republic of Germany* continued to intensify the characteristics that had already taken shape during the previous decades (Münz, Seifert and Ulrich 1997). On the one hand, the normality intensified, but so did the differentiation of migration within the *supranational Europe*: of workers, the self-employed, service providers and service users,

[679] See above section "Social Benefits Systems"; Bundesministerium für Arbeit und Soziales and Bundesarchiv (eds.), 2007b: Geschichte der Sozialpolitik in Deutschland seit 1945, vol. 11, Chap. 3, no. 5.

[680] See above Chapter 9.; Bundesministerium für Arbeit und Soziales and Bundesarchiv (eds.), 2007b: Geschichte der Sozialpolitik in Deutschland seit 1945, vol. 11, Chap 1.

[681] "Art. I des Gesetzes zur Bereinigung von Kriegsfolgengesetzen vom 21. Dezember 1992" BGBl. I, p. 2094; Sect. 6 of the "Gesetz über die Angelegenheiten der Vertriebenen und Flüchtlinge i. d. F. der Bekanntmachung vom 2. Juni 1993" BGBl. I, p. 829.

[682] For an account of current law see Bundesministerium für Arbeit und Sozialordnung (1998, pp. 719–726).

students, pensioners etc. And then there appears the freedom of movement of the "citizens of the union" which the Treaty of Maastricht had promised (Art. 8, 8 a, EGV in the version of the MV). Analogous migrations can be observed from other "old-industrialized" countries in a similar political and societal state – of course, without the privileged status of an EU European (Jorens and Schulte 1998). On the other hand, people continue to seek refuge in the Federal Republic as victims of persecution, as refugees, as the homeless and stateless, and so on. There continues to remain a broad array of cases which cannot be readily assigned to these typical conditions. With globalization it is not only capital that is on the move. People, too, are migrating around the world – whether in search for jobs, whether simply as human beings who want to live better or merely survive. The Federal Republic has a great power of attraction for this stream of humanity. Added to this is a regional, neighborly problem. The collapse of Communism has given people in the Central and Eastern European countries new reason and new possibilities to migrate. The Federal Republic found itself challenged in many different ways to grant or deny freedom of movement, admission, and participation. Thanks to the right of asylum enshrined in constitutional law, its interpretation and application became the central field of the debate. The legislature responded with the "asylum compromise". The 39th Law to Amend the Basic Law (28 June 1993, BGBl. I, p. 1002) replaced the simple basic right to asylum (Art. 16, Para. 2, Sent. 2, GG, old version) with an intensely differentiating regulation (Art. 16a, GG, new version). The corresponding implementation regulation can be found in the Asylum Procedure Law of 1993 (27 July 1993, BGBl. I, p. 1361). The socio-legal side of the problem was newly regulated through an Asylum Seeker Benefits Law (21 December 1993, BGBl. I, p. 2374). Moreover, the new category of "civil war refugees"[683] was added to that of "contingency refugees".[684] On the whole this gives rise to an increasingly "seasoned" differentiating clarification of the status – under foreigner and social law – of foreigners and the stateless who live or wish to live in the Federal Republic of Germany.[685]

The Reaching Out of the German Social State

The extension of the German social state to individuals – Germans or non-Germans – living abroad also received a new emphasis. For those who had a social benefits relationship to the previous *GDR,* the temporary *continued application of the*

[683] Section 32 a of the "Ausländergesetz," new version.

[684] "Gesetz über Maßnahmen für im Rahmen humanitärer Hilfsaktionen aufgenommene Flüchtlinge vom 22. Juli 1980" BGBl. I, p. 1059.

[685] On the older state of the law see Schraml (1992); see also above section "The Comprehensive Explanations of the Social". Supplemented by Bommes and Halfmann (1998); Bommes (1999).

relevant treaties was ordered.[686] A long-term solution was or is to be discussed and agreed upon with the respective contracting parties (Art. 12 of the Unification Treaty).

However, German unification created a new situation also for *compensation for National Socialist injustice*. The division of the world into the "free West" and the Communist-dominated countries had created difficulties for the assertion of claims, as had the division of the Greater German Empire into the "successor states" of the FRG, the GDR, and Austria. The London Debt Agreement had postponed war compensation from the Federal Republic to western treaty states – also at the expense of their citizens – until a peace treaty. Meanwhile, the Moscow Protocol of 22 August 1953, on the Waiver of German Reparations Payments and on Other Measures to Ease the Financial and Economic Obligations of the GDR that are Connected with the Consequences of the War,[687] had a similar significance for the relationship of the GDR to the Soviet Union and Poland. Now, after German unification and the final end to the state of war through the "2 + 4 Agreement", a new atmosphere emerged. Those affected saw new prospects for asserting claims to restitution (Barwig et al. 1998). On the one hand, they sought compensation directly from where they had been harmed – thus, forced laborers from the firms that had employed them.[688] But states, too, especially Central and Eastern European states, are picking up the compensation claims of their citizens, as some kind of trustees and thus skirting the clauses renouncing reparations in past treaties.

11.4.3 Institutions and Spheres

Supranational Europe[689] intensified not only institutionally. It also donned the new legal and political mantle of the *European Union*. And it expanded in 1995 with the accession of Austria, Finland, and Sweden. The web of framework conditions that the *European Community* wove for the development of the social in the member states and in their European totality became steadily denser and more lasting. However, the immediate European social policy did not give up its traditional selectivity. Still, the development of the "social Europe" also moved forward. As before, it was chiefly the European Court that pushed integration ahead. While since the founding of the European Economic Community, the law on coordinating the national social benefits systems that accompanied the freedom of movement of

[686] "VO über die vorübergehende weitere Anwendung verschiedener völkerrechtlicher Verträge der Deutschen Demokratischen Republik im Bereich der sozialen Sicherheit vom 3. April 1991" BGBl. II, p. 614.

[687] *Europaarchiv* 8 (1953), pp. 5974–5981.

[688] On the legal situation BVerfGE 94, 315.

[689] "Berichte der Bundesregierung über die Integration der Bundesrepublik Deutschland in die Europäischen Gemeinschaften" 1991 I (BTDrs. 12/1201); 1991 II (BTDrs. 12/2218) and so on (semi-annually).

workers had been the medium to allow the national systems of social law to coalesce into the minimum of a common European order of social law, the freedoms of services and the movement of goods now emerged ever more clearly as additional drivers to compel a certain functional unity of national social benefits systems – even at the price of calling into question what nations took for granted (Schulte and Barwig 1999).

The Europe of the *Council of Europe* took on a fundamentally new importance through the collapse of Communism in Central and Eastern Europe. More countries joined in the 1990s: Albania, Bulgaria, Estonia, Georgia, Latvia, Lithuania, Macedonia, Moldavia, Poland, Rumania, Russia, Slovakia, Slovenia, Czechia, Ukraine, and Hungary. It is obvious that this lowered the degree of the legal-normative commonalities, and even more so the real commonalities among the member states. It is equally obvious that the influence of single member states like Germany would decline. Nevertheless, these developments did recognize elementary commonalities across Europe. The shared value system of the Human Rights Convention surely plays the biggest role in this.[690]

However, the *world community* altered its appearance and reality more profoundly than everything else. Where it had been dominated since the Second World War by the *international* relations and organizations of states, the *transnational* effect of societal factors now moved to the front at an unparalleled pace. In accordance with this, the mechanisms and institutions of international law and the international community of states increasingly revealed functional deficits. They were not prepared for this new regulatory task of channeling transnational actions and transnational developments. Likewise, national politics and legal systems were confronted with an erosion of their power. In the historical hour when Germany became once again a nation state, that statehood was relativized not only by a multifarious integration into supranational and international structures. It also faced a fundamentally new reality that escaped the level of the national.

Where We Stand Today

12 The Normative Core of the Social

During the five decades that form the topic of this study, the reality of the social has developed in ways that would defy even the most imaginative predictions. That

[690] On the state of ratification of the Human Rights Convention see *Bundesgesetzblatt* II 1999, Fundstellennachweis B, 303–306. By contrast, see the state of ratification of the European Social Charter (ibid., 433), the European Code of Social Security (ibid., 447f.), the European Agreement on Social Security (ibid., 332), and the European Convention on Social Assistance (ibid., 332). The human rights-integration of the Europe of the Council of Europe was always more intensive that the socio-political integration. In the 1990s, however, these areas drifted apart dramatically.

applies to the change in the challenges it has faced, and to the change in the conditions on the basis of which these challenges had to and could be responded to. It applies to the extent and ways in which the social was realized, as well as to the problems that grew out of that realization. And it applies, finally, to the levels and perspectives by which the national totality of social policy and social law became differentiated, and to the dimensions on which the social policy and social law of the Federal Republic of Germany opened up to the outside world and integrated themselves into larger contexts. Nevertheless, the *normative core* that formed the understanding of the social from the beginning has been preserved: namely, that it is *social to create more equality in the economically conditioned and economically relevant circumstances of life*, and to prevent them from developing in the opposite direction toward greater inequality. Another element has remained consistent: that the primary concern is to *limit the range of differences toward the "bottom," so that every person is guaranteed an existence worthy of a human being.*

But the counterpart to these core values has also survived: the *proviso of inequality*. Not only that it was never simple "equality" that was meant. Not only that what was meant by "more equality" was concentrated on the economically conditioned and economically relevant inequalities, that is, on changing those inequalities among people which – one may posit – society and the state, law and politics can control and in fact change. No, especially with respect to the economically conditioned and economically relevant inequalities, this society has reserved for itself the proviso that things should not become and be *too* equal. The freedom to set oneself apart from others in better ways, especially in terms of more prosperity, should be retained – whether we are talking about the change between the advantages of primary economic distribution and the advantages of secondary redistribution, or about the different opportunities to derive advantages from the various principles of secondary redistribution. The entire course of the development can be explained by this basic template: by the juxtaposition of the principle of "more equality" and the proviso of inequality. Neither aspect can be thought of alone. The consensus was not and is not simply toward inequality. Inequality is affirmed because the principle of "more equality" is anterior to it. But the principle of "more equality" is only affirmed because the proviso of inequality leaves room for freedom, luck, fate, achievement, and also political assertiveness.

Normatively the path that social policy has taken over these five decades has been mapped out only very approximately. The formula that "social" means "more equality," but at the very least a dignified existence for everyone, is inherently highly indeterminate. And the proviso of inequality deepens that indeterminacy. The substance of problems is as infinite as the shape of conceivable solutions. The causes, too, behind which contexts, values, and realities will coalesce into politically relevant problems that call for solutions are infinite in their variety. What then, determined the path that was taken? The real social conditions, the ideas with which they were perceived and assessed, the elements handed down by history, the institutional structures of the federal state, of the *Rechtsstaat*, and of democracy, the constellations of party politics, the orientation and the power of social organizations, the institutional representatives of the status quo and changes to it, and time and again individual actors – experts, special interest representatives, bureaucrats, and above all politicians: these are the forces that determined the path. These conditions of social evolution did not keep the development tethered to the social "bottom," to the issue of guaranteeing a subsistence minimum. They made worse-better comparisons in the most varied spheres of prosperity the object of social responsibility and socio-political calculation. Not least they accepted that the social concern over a worse-better comparison, which had originally drawn political attention as a phenomenon of the lower spheres of prosperity (in the form of obvious hardship and need), migrated upward as the social claims of those concerned shifted increasingly into the higher sphere of prosperity. The most important example of this is the long path from the workers' policy of the nineteenth century to the employees' policy in the second half of the twentieth century.

The common denominator for this expansion of the social across ever more problem areas was the *power of the "middle voter*." He is in the maximum position to use the relativity of the worse-better comparisons to realize his own concerns. The middle voters have available an extensive configuration of coalitions. And they also have available a broad array of substantive options, especially the merger of participation in the primary distribution with participation in the secondary redistribution. The "middle voter" has the most varied and effective interest in combining the social demand for "more equality" with the proviso of inequality into a principle of maximum advantage.

It was therefore unavoidable that in the 1960s and late 1970s, the specifically social was integrated into farther-reaching projects of social well-being. The "prosperity for all" of *Konrad Adenauer* and of *Ludwig Erhard* and *Willy Brandt's vision of "more quality of life"* encapsulated this development. The evolution of German social policy seemed to be 'leading to what was internationally defined at that time as the "*welfare state arrangement*": an indefinite responsibility of the state for a general well-being. In any case, the 1960s and 1970s witnessed a process by which the social not only expanded, but was opened up toward the "top." This led to disagreements about the meaning of the social that have remained a source of friction to this day, and which are commonly referred to as the "crisis of the social state." Still, the *"welfare state arrangement" did not simply replace the social principle*. That is most clearly demonstrated by the discussion over the goals of the state. The *social goal of the state* always retained a specific place. From the beginning, other goals – like that of being a state of culture – stood alongside, and more goals – like the protection of the natural foundations of life – kept being added on. In spite of all the distortions that reappeared time and again, and in spite of all expectations that had to be newly articulated, all social debate is still centered on the negation of economically conditioned and economically relevant inequality that exceeds a certain – though never generally definable – level of what is tolerable.

13 Persistence and Challenge: The Basic Formula of Work, Income, the Meeting of Needs, and Maintenance

13.1 Work and Income

Social responsibility was always seen against the assumption of a normality of societal life. It is expressed in the *basic formula*, according to which *every adult* (who is not yet elderly and tied up by family work) *has the possibility and bears the responsibility to earn an income through work and thereby meet his own needs and those of his community of maintenance.* This normality was the pattern that formed the backdrop to thinking about social responsibility. Although the basic formula was not made explicit anywhere, it was the precondition against which the social responsibility had to be understood from the beginning of this period and against which social responsibility could be understood over the course of time. This social responsibility refers first of all to the fact that the rule determines the reality: that it is possible to live in the sequence of work, income, maintenance and the meeting of needs, and that the economically conditioned or relevant inequalities that arise when some can live the normality of the rule and others cannot are avoided. It further refers to the question of how help can be offered if the rule does not take: if there is not enough work and income from work. It refers to the dependencies that emerge in the realization of the rule and need to be controlled. And, finally, it refers to the question of which dangers must be counteracted as the rule is realized, and which shortcomings can arise during its realization and must be compensated for lest there emerge inequalities that must be judged inappropriate because of their causes or effects. Thus there had evolved what the social policy of the postwar years encountered. At first glance, the basic formula seems to have held up to the developments over time. But a closer look reveals that while the basic formula has not been replaced by any other rule, its validity is being called into question.

The *disturbance* emanates above all from the *element of work.* I am referring to gainful work – independent, cooperative, or dependent gainful employment. The formula presupposes that there are sufficient opportunities for gainful work. And it expects that the "social citizen" will make use of them. That holds for *gainful work as such.* However, *dependent gainful work* assumes a *special place.* The responsibility of society and state is focused on it: on the realization of the rule through the supply of dependent gainful employment and on the protection of dependent workers against this dependency and against the threats and shortcomings that dependent work can entail. But the responsibility of the "social citizen" to work is also concentrated on dependent work. *Dependent gainful employment* became the rule, against which independent and cooperative gainful work was presented as the exception. The *normal employment relationship and full employment* seemed the *fulfillment of this rule. All of this is now under siege.* Society and the state seem permanently unable to provide full employment – at least within the normal employment relationship. The contrast between work and unemployment, between those who have a job and those who do not has itself become of the great inequalities of the times. That has also impaired the mechanisms of social protection that are connected to the normal employment relationship and which, in case of deficits in jobs, the ability to work, or income, make up for income, the capacity to meet needs, or the maintenance that can be provided from income. To what degree independent work could close the gap remains an open question. That cooperative gainful work remains the exception goes without saying. On the other side, the "decommodified" *embedding of dependent work in an ever denser web of social benefits systems has long since curtailed the responsibility of the individual to engage in earning through work.* The long and sustained shortage of dependent work has further weakened the effectiveness of the responsibility to work.

The *social state* is confronted by *weighty decisions* in this regard. Can it hope for developments that will *lead back* to the *normal employment relationship and full employment* of the kind experienced in the 1960s and 1970s? Can it, by *varying the working conditions* – in the sense of different work time structures, less stability, a specific link of work and social benefits in employment policies – organize work in such a way that the level of employment approaches a "full employment in terms of a head count," even if it is not a "full employment in terms of time"? Is it not imperative to abolish the contradiction by which it is assumed *in favor* of the worker or employee that he or she needs protection, and *to the disadvantage of* the self-employed that he or she does not? Is it not the case that the normal employment relationship comes with a relative maximum of participation, equality, freedom, and security, while the self-employed, no matter how small his income, how imperiled his enterprise might be, essentially does not enjoy a comparable protection? Is it not the case that labor law protects the employee against the employer even when the latter is the one who is actually "dependent?" Is the self-employed, however vulnerable his position might be, not being placed on the side of the "class enemy" – the capitalist? How else can one explain the self-evident way in which the expansion of social protection to the self-employed took place fundamentally, in terms of rationale and substance, in such a way that those among them "resembling employees" were given the status of "employees"? Experience has shown that there has been an excess of typecasting on both sides of the equation of gainful work. Thus we would be well advised to take a close look what exactly the social state – developing the values that social policy has taken on with regard to gainful work – really needs to provide for on both sides of the equation, what can be left to the participants, society, and above all the market economy – indeed, what should be reserved for the market economy. In this way one could arrive at a more open system of all gainful work that differentiates in a more objectively appropriate way. That could also reduce the excessive strain on the social system. This social system has provided too many incentives to become an employee and then disappointed with underemployment. And it has contributed to making the option of self-employment unattractive, and has also linked it too much to the chance at "big money." In the end, though, the absence of the self-employed worker was keenly felt because he relieves the labor market: he does not claim a dependent job for himself and may even offer jobs to others.

Must the solution be sought also in a new status for *unpaid work* – work in the family, the private sector, or for the benefit of society and the community? Should this work also generate earnings? How should those earnings be measured, and who should pay for them? Should unpaid work lead to social protection – over and above what is today already extended to family work? On what scale and at whose expense? Under what conditions does this strengthen the basic formula? Under what conditions does it weaken it?

Or *is it necessary to abandon the basic formula?* That is the thrust of proposals for a *tax-financed universal minimum income*. If that happened, gainful employment would probably remain as an opportunity, but would no longer be a "duty." How would that change society? How would that change the systems of social protection? What effect would it have on public finances?

The question about the *"future of work" is a central question* for the future of the social as such. Moreover: any significant change in work also alters the organization of workers and their interests – which means, above all: the unions. Work and its organization are mutually dependent. Flexibility within the organization could thus facilitate a reform of work. Rigidities within the organization could impede a reform of work. Given the position of the unions within the institutional framework of the social, that relationship between work and its organization contains important potential for development or stagnation. But there is more: the change in work could eventually weaken union organization, on which free collective bargaining, the social partnership, and "social self-administration" are built, and in the end even cut the ground from under them. In the same way, capital that disconnects itself from "its" society, from "its" policy, could call these patterns of organization into question. How might this development be avoided? How could the gaps that gave rise to it be closed again?

13.2 The Meeting of Needs

The basic formula proceeds from the assumption that work and income form the basis for the meeting of needs. This normality was extremely constrained during the first phase of the period we have examined. The meeting especially of the general needs of life (food, clothing, housing, etc.) was entrusted to the state's *Daseinsvorsorge*, as expressed in rationing and price controls. At that time, income (possibly replaced with or supplemented by other sources of financial ability to meet needs, especially through previously acquired commodities of trade or cash assets in amounts that were useful for the black market) was a necessary but not a sufficient condition for meeting needs. Beginning with the currency reform, the market economy quickly regained its importance. Once again, the *meeting of needs* became *primarily a question of income*. The *normality of the basic formula* had been essentially restored. However, the necessity of special arrangements arose in a number of areas to ensure an adequate meeting of needs. One such area was the *need for housing*. The dismantling of the controlled housing economy required a transition. Even after the market economy had been in principle revived, there was a need for internalizing regulatory mechanisms (tenant protection, price controls), for individual promotion (subsidies, tax breaks), for supply incentives through promotion programs, and, finally, for externalizing assistance (housing allowance). Over the course of time, this complementarity kept changing shape. In principle, though, the laws of the market economy and the determinative nature of income prevailed.

Meeting the needs linked to *child-raising and education* diverged. The institutional expenditures for schools, after-school programs, universities, and so on were essentially assumed by the state – though municipalities, in particular, were tenaciously reluctant to do so when it came to kindergartens and day-care centers, and there was a range of differentiated solutions concerning the programs for adult education (especially vocational training and continuing education). The general living expenses of those being raised and educated/trained remained essentially a matter for the parents or the trainees themselves. However, a multitude of measures of social relief and promotion took these needs into account: through child allowance, education grants, post-graduate funding; through subsidies to social benefits, for example, in pension insurance; through tax breaks; through survivor pensions in social security and social compensation; through benefits of employment promotion, vocational promotion, and rehabilitation.

The guarantee of *medical provision* was entrusted chiefly to the *statutory sickness insurance*. At the same time, this *particular* system of social protection is supposed to provide *overall* guidance, a mandate that became ever broader and more intensive. With that, the statutory sickness insurance evolved to assume ever greater responsibility not only for the conditions of the benefits, but also for the existential conditions of the benefit providers, while the benefit providers were increasingly placed under a collective obligation to contribute to the functioning of the system. The problem of combining a specific task of social protection with a global guiding function becomes clear when one considers how many different subsystems supplement the statutory sickness insurance with respect to its protective task: civil service law – system of aid (*Beihilfe*); medical care (*Heilfürsorge*) under law pertaining to soldiers and alternative service; accident and pension insurance; welfare/social assistance; private insurance. The circle of persons included in the statutory sickness insurance, and the concrete meeting of medical needs by statutory sickness insurance, expanded for a long time, but was then reduced again beginning in the second half of the 1970s. The relationship between the overall guiding function of statutory sickness insurance and its specific protective task was made even more difficult by this development. On the whole, all of this achieved a relative maximum of medical care for essentially the entire population. However, the result of the imbalances in the two very differently structured levels of medical care – guiding the supply and guaranteeing social protection – was that the conflicts increased and the intervals of political intervention became shorter. Whether this can be seen as a reasonable price for the high level of medical care with a limited – or better: not entirely uncontrolled – growth in costs, or whether there are better solutions, is a question we must continue to ask.

The need for *nursing care services* was initially entrusted to families and to charitable associations and the municipalities. The costs – unless specific systems (social compensation, accident insurance, and so on) were responsible – were left either to the capacity of those affected or to welfare/public assistance. However, over the course of time the demand for nursing care services increased steadily. The 1990s therefore saw a solution in terms of social insurance: statutory long-term care insurance. It represents a considerable innovation. First, the size of the group for which this kind of insurance became mandatory has no parallel in the history of social provision. Second, this insurance adjusted in a positive way to the very different ways in which care is provided today. That care includes services provided by the family, the private sector, charitable organizations, the market economy, as well as communal providers. Third, the law makes clear that in spite of these technical solutions in terms of provision, long-term care remains an indefinite task and effort for all of society and the entire polity.

The number of sensitive areas in which specific provisions had to be made to achieve an adequate meeting of needs was therefore considerable. Beyond that, the need for a broad *consumer protection* proved increasingly urgent. In principle, however, the basic formula has not been called into question. The crucial importance of income for demand and the crucial importance of the market economy for supply are regarded as an optimal system. And the difficulties of regulating the meeting of needs any other way are obvious – if unavoidable.

13.3 The Community of Maintenance

Values and realities have changed substantially when it comes to the community of maintenance. There is much that the social order has already adopted: the equality of men and women in marriage and the family, the instability of marriage and the family, or the drifting apart of marriage and the family. Other developments tend to have more indirect, diffuse consequences: the decline in the number of children, the near-disappearance of three-generation households, all other shrinkage of the household. The consequences for old age security or for social services are obvious. Concretizing them, however, is another matter altogether. *The* great problem continues to be the *imbalance between the number of earners and the number of those dependent on maintenance* – and even more fundamental than that: the likelihood arising from the nature of the basic formula of an imbalance between the number of earners and the number of those dependent on support. To put it the other way around: the problem is that those involved optimize the quantitative effects of the basic formula if they keep the number of earners and the number of consumers within the same community of maintenance the same.

The way in which the basic formula combines work, income, and community of maintenance seeks to bring together two elementary values of this society and its polity: on the one side, the freedom and responsibility of individuals to provide for themselves and their families through work; on the other side, the privacy and autonomy of the family. Wherever individuals provide for themselves, it must also be their freedom and thus responsibility to provide for those closest to them. Wherever a family exists, it is fully private and autonomous only when its members provide for it. The development – and this is of crucial importance – has held on to both basic values. But it must not be overlooked that the linkage of work, income, and family creates a multi-layered potential for inequality – and accordingly a multi-layered challenge to the social responsibility of the polity. The linear relationship between those who earn and those who are supported in the single-person household, the household of a "dual income" couple without children, and so on, also confronts the non-linear relationship between those who earn and those who are supported where the community of maintenance includes children who are too young to work, and even more so where one parent devotes herself or himself to caring for the family and therefore does not pursue gainful employment. But a non-linear relationship exists also where one partner in a childless couple "remains at home." The variety of conceivable constellations is large and need not be fleshed out here.

The social system responded to the problem initially by insuring families – without contributions – in sickness insurance, survivors' insurance, pension and accident insurance, pension schemes for civil servants, judges, soldiers, and officials, in social compensation law, and by offering tax breaks. Over the course of time, the spectrum of equalization measures was substantially expanded: parental leave and child-raising allowance, child allowance, maintenance advance, housing allowance pegged to family size, exemption from school fees until university, education grants, credited time in pension insurance and civil service pension schemes, spousal splitting, and consideration for children in income tax law. The polity has made an effort to respond in a differentiated manner to the non-linearity in the relationship between earners and the community of maintenance. It discovered how difficult it is to make credible distinctions in a thicket of equalities and inequalities. Over time, however, it was not only the structures of equalization that multiplied, but also the claims to an equalization of disadvantages. Wherever the social state mitigates inequalities, other inequalities become newly visible. In no other area has this fate of the social state realized itself as much as in that of the community of maintenance. Especially since it is also here that very different freedoms demand respect: for example, the freedom of parents to combine family and work, as well as the freedom of one parent to focus on family work. And new claims of freedom are constantly arising: non-marital life partnerships demanding their place next to marriage; non-married parents demanding a place next to married parents, and so on.

The difficulties of offering solutions that are in keeping with equality grow where an area of the social is mired in problems for reasons of its own. That applies, for example, to social services. The shortage of publicly financed (or at least adequately supported) day-care centers for children is being increasingly seen as a deficit in equality. More complex – though no less pressing – are the problems of old age security. It is in trouble not only because of the changes in the age structure, or only because of the decline in dependent gainful employment. One of its great difficulties is the inherent contradiction between the universality of the principle of old age security and the far-reaching differentiation in the way it is realized: through tax-funded schemes (pension schemes for civil servants, judges, soldiers, and officials; supplementary pension insurance in the public sector), through contribution-financed schemes (professional provision, private insurance), through company and/or contribution-financed schemes (work-based pensions), and above all through a primarily contribution-financed and secondarily tax-financed social insurance, which services non-contribution-based entitlements to old age pensions on a large scale. What can be expected of a justice of the "generational contract" if in the one case the middle generation pays contributions, while the older generation is taken care of by the tax-financed system? And conversely: what can be expected of a justice of the "generational contract" if the middle generation – civil servants, for example – pays no contributions, while the older generation is cared for with the contributions from others? What can be expected of a justice of the "generational contract" between those who, because they are not (or no longer married), "cash in" *only* "their" pension, while among others, who are married, the old age pension of the one spouse can be followed by the survivor's pension of the other spouse – and this in a comparison between tax-financed, contribution-financed, and social security schemes? Finally, what can be expected of a justice of the "generational contract" if some only pay taxes and contributions, while others are also raising children? – and lastly: if the children of some later pay only taxes, and the children of others pay taxes and contributions?

Do these difficulties show that the *basic formula* is being *called into question* also on this point? The multiplicity of solutions through which "more equality" was created for the communities of maintenance shows that effective equalizations *are* possible. That even better solutions must be searched out says nothing definitive against the fundamental approach of the basic formula. And what would a different formula look like that would do justice to the family as a productive community, in the sense of both a self-responsibility for work and income and the private "production of welfare"?

13.4 In the Shadow of the Basic Formula: Wealth

The basic formula traces a line along the typical course of a life. With that it also traces a line along which the necessity of intervening against inappropriate worse-better comparisons typically becomes apparent. The basic formula orients itself toward the experience of the general. That applies to the experience of social reality – that is, the experience of work, income, the meeting of needs, and maintenance – and to the experience of politics and the law – that is, the experience of social protection and social benefits. It is from this highlighting of what is typical that the basic formula derives its system-sustaining power. But the life of the individual does not unfold only against the backdrop of this normality; it can deviate considerably from the "normal line." Politics and the law essentially have two possibilities of responding to that situation: ignoring the gap between the formula and reality, or adjusting social intervention to it. Of course, politics and the law can also – pragmatically – do something in between. That is the case with wealth. The basic formula neglects the aspect of wealth. Relevant wealth is not a rule from which the social proceeds. To put it in extreme terms: wealth *can* be; work and income *must* be. Thus, the basic formula of politics and the law does not invariably direct the gaze at the inequality of wealth as a social problem.

However, the inequality of wealth varies the reality of the basic formula in real life. Wealth can generate or replace income. To the extent that income is the meaning of work, wealth can thus render work superfluous. Wealth can be used to meet needs and provide maintenance. Wealth also offers a different kind of access to the economy. To the extent that the meaning of work is to participate in economic life, wealth is an alternative also in this regard. As a result, the inequality of wealth was still a substantial social topic in the 1940s and 1950s. The *redistribution of wealth* was part of the original stock of social ideas, and the equalization of burdens is its most important example. To the extent, however, that the dynamic of work and income moved to the fore, social concern limited itself to the *opportunity to create wealth*. The question whether the inequality between rich and poor can be a social irritant not only in terms of income, but also in terms of wealth, was raised less and less frequently – all the way to the Federal Constitutional Court, which accorded the wealth tax only a marginal place. *Social redistribution* thus seems to mean: *taking from income and giving in place of or in addition to income*. But not even this formula holds. For the most part, "social redistribution" means: taking from work income and giving to income; for in both the law governing the contributions within statutory sickness insurance and in income tax law, income from wealth is privileged over income from work. Nowhere else was the proviso of inequality brought to bear more than in the growing distance between the inequality of wealth and the social question.

In the *late 1980s*, and especially in the *1990s*, this disproportionality of social policy toward wealth reached *new and dramatic meaning* – in two very unequal contexts, to be sure. The *first* context concerned wealth *in the form of capital*. It is an essential element of *globalization* that capital frees itself from the national context in which it has been embedded, and in which it has contributed in crucial ways to the "golden age" of the welfare state, and thus largely removes itself from national social solidarity. The *second context* in which the exclusion of wealth from the social question assumed greater importance was and is *German unification*. By 1990, West German society had had four decades during which its members could create wealth. The citizens of East Germany had lived through more than four decades during which they were largely prohibited from creating wealth. This difference brought to mind the equalization of burdens from the 1950s, but this approach was not picked up. In fact, politics even accentuated the difference. Anyone who had acquired expropriated property in the German Democratic Republic had to expect a claim to restitution. Finally, generous tax breaks were offered to promote investment in the new *Länder*. In practice, this became, among other things, a great opportunity for citizens of the old *Länder* to create wealth in the East.

Wealth has a counterpart: *debt*. In the prosperous society, the problem of debt takes on new social importance. The danger of indebtedness grew in the most varied social circumstances. Debt became a "poverty trap." As a result, debt counseling became a specific dimension of social services. In the 1990s, the restructuring of bankruptcy law dealing with individuals who had run up excessive debt – debtors and the families dependent on them, as well as their creditors – created a new perspective in the form of personal bankruptcy. In the final analysis, though, the social state comes up against a limit of possible intervention here. Excessive debt is a multi-sided process that involves the responsibility of multiple actors. It cannot be a matter for the social state to impose the risks that arise from it on the general public. What remains is this: to guide the process through normative and service-providing intervention in a timely fashion and eventually accompany it in a mediating role.

13.5 In the Shadow of the Basic Formula: Levies, Subsidies, and Supra-Individual Transfer Programs, and – Most of All – the Net Balance of All Transfers

The more a legal system replete with and supplemented by the social developed, the clearer it became that the law shapes life through several approaches. It imparts a *primary order* to the *autonomy* of human beings. This is chiefly the task of private law. But it also imparts to it a *secondary order*, which *extends* the *life possibilities* of the individual beyond the sphere that he could fill through his own effort; in doing so, however, it not only expands his *autonomy*, but also imposes *an obligation on it*. This is the domain of social law. Another pairing concerns the *resources* through which a person realizes his or her autonomy. These resources arise from what a person *has*, what he *acquires*, and what he *is given* (from his wealth, his income, and the social benefits that replace or supplement income), and from what *is taken from him* so the community can fulfill its tasks (not least also that of social redistribution). Thus a *positive income and wealth law* faces a *negative income and wealth law*. And finally, though, all these individual circumstances and the systems that establish and secure them are encased by the *conditions* which the society and the state *generally establish* – by virtue of legal regulation or without it. While these conditions are in many different ways essential for the realization of an individual life, their effect is not aimed at the *individual*, but at *individuals*.

The basic formula is in keeping with these distinctions. Or to put it differently: the public – societal, political, professional, academic – discussion of the social is oriented toward the line of the basic formula. The "spotlights" of the basic formula fall on the *arrangements of individual life* and its fulfillment. They leave in the "*shadow*" *general conditions* of the individual life circumstances. The "spotlights" of the basic formula illuminate the *"have-side" of resources*; the *"taking-side"* is left in the *"shadow."* This is in accordance with an essential difference between social services and levies. The *sole* purpose of *services* is to shape individual life conditions in a socially appropriate way. The primary task of *levies* is to generate funds. That they should do this in a socially fair way is one condition for their legitimacy. That they also serve as an instrument of a socially appropriate realization of life might be an added function.

Thus, the development of *taxes* is determined by their social meaning only in a secondary – often also sporadic, uncertain – way, while the development of social benefits is determined primarily by their social purpose. Moreover, far less accountability is demanded and given (should one add: for now?) when it comes to the social effect of taxes than when it comes to the social effect of services. That applies even to the *income tax*, even though it is of the greatest social import – in its principles as well as in its exemptions. It also applied to the *wealth tax*. And it applies to the *indirect taxes*, whose social effects are so difficult to discern. The social shaping, perception, and assessment of the *other levies* (dues, fees, and special levies, as for example the equalization payments within a sector of the economy) are accordingly uncertain. On the surface, *social insurance contributions* might seem easy to grasp because of their proportionality. In reality, though, their social effects through the regulations governing their assessment (work income versus other income; contribution assessment ceiling), their allocation (employee/employer share versus sole responsibility of the insured or the employer), their consideration when it comes to taxes and their effect on benefits laws (sole insurance of the payee versus co-insurance of the family; value of services and material benefits; limits to material and cash benefits) are hardly less transparent than the social effects of taxes.

On the side of *benefits*, the possibility of their social assessment decreases with the *distance to the individual conditions*. That already applies to *subsidies*, whose benefit is always uncertain: in terms of their size (how much of them is truly "deserved"?), but also in terms of their subject (who benefits from them: the recipient, the general public, the state?). This applies to the provision and delivery of *social services*. Their individual effects, too, cannot be perceived in the way in which the individual effects of social cash benefits can be "counted." And it applies to all *assistance and promotion programs for disadvantaged areas* (regions, sectors) of societal and especially economic and political life (for the purpose of modernization, to build infrastructure, to compensate for disadvantages, and so on). As intensely as they are political fought for and eventually defended: as yardsticks of social states of being they do not count in the same way as monetary social benefits that are given to the individual to replace or supplement his income. Over the course of time, however, it is precisely these supra-individual benefits programs that have an increasing share of the redistribution processes. And there is no mistaking that they have contributed essentially to equalizing differences in prosperity. One might think of the great *sectoral* redistribution processes (especially in favor of agriculture and mining). One might think of the great *regional* redistribution processes: whether they are embedded in the territorial financial equalization (on the federal or municipal level), or whether they concern specific, circumscribed areas (coastal regions, border regions, other structurally weak regions). These regional redistribution processes assumed an extreme level in the wake of *German unification*. Finally, one might think of the financial equalization schemes of the various branches of *social insurance*, which serve the goal of sectoral and regional equalization.

The political dynamic of the social is focused on individual social protection and individual social benefits. That goes along with substantial differentials with respect to the institutional conditions of the social. It makes a considerable difference to the federal state, the *Rechtsstaat*, and democracy whether social protection and social benefits or taxes and other levies are regulated, whether individual benefits are systematized or supraindividual benefit programs are devised and set up, indeed, even whether individual monetary benefits are promised or services set up whose provision still has something general and undetermined about it, while the concrete effect remains uncertain. These differences have no uniform tendency. The normative background and the institutional relevance change from one area to the next. One might think, for example, of the different constitutional directives and the different decision-making processes in which labor law is shaped, social insurance law regulated, the income tax newly assessed, the federal financial equalization carried out, or promotion programs decided upon if the overall economic equilibrium is threatened. The mere fact how little these problems are seen and appreciated shows that the "shadow" that the basic formula casts over all of this is no coincidence.

It is in accord with all of this that there is no *reliable institutional empiricism about the net balances of transfers*, and no relevant *public accounting for them*. Not only that this is too difficult to achieve. There is a lack of interest – on the part of those concerned and politics. Those affected by them measure their satisfaction and discontent primarily according to the individual effects. They evidently shy away from the potential for disappointment that lurks in an overall accounting, which could reveal their share in an overarching balance sheet of advantages and disadvantages. Politics cannot dispense with addressing groups, and with articulating what the groups receive from politics. Their reaction is an important element in the democratic competition over power. The more diffuse a group's reaction, the less consideration is given to it. But politics also shies away from relativizing the political "benefit" that flows to the individual by making a total account of everything. Similarly: this democratic, constitutional, and social state presents its social effects only superficially, mathematically, selectively, and in an extremely imbalanced way; it attempts no deeply penetrating, overall accounting and information; conversely, the society that is constituted in this state demands only a formal, limited account and accountability.

14 Innovation, Persistence, and Expansion: The Institutions of the Social

The basic formula traces a line of essential situations that trigger the social responsibility of society and state, but it does not spell out the methods by which the state assumes this responsibility and the criteria that guide it in the process. The system of the methods and these criteria was historically conditioned and has remained so.

14.1 The Responsibility of the State for the Economy: The Social Market Economy

14.1.1 Genesis and Standing the Test of Time

The basic formula presupposes an economy in which it can realize itself as a meaningful normality. The responsibility for the economy is therefore the most comprehensive responsibility for a socially appropriate realization of the basic formula. It is a responsibility of society *and* of the state. Still, it is a special responsibility of the state, because it determines the organization of economic activity and thus controls the conditions under which society can fulfill its economic responsibility. With respect to this specific responsibility of the state, a fundamental decision was made early on. The beginnings after 1945 certainly reflected a way of thinking that sought to orient the effectiveness of the economy directly toward social goals through specific structures and social guidance. This was in keeping with a long history of socialist and conservative-statist ideas. It was in keeping with the discussions of the Weimar period. In its technical tools of economic guidance it was also in keeping with the war economy that the National Socialist state had left behind. And above all it was in keeping with the hardship of the postwar period, which could be addressed initially only through a comprehensive economic *Daseinsvorsorge* (providing the necessities of life). But the year 1948 brought the fundamental change: toward the market economy and competition – toward the self-sustaining economic integration of the economy. The forces that carried this change staked the future on the prosperity effects of an economy optimized according to its inherent laws. They were aware of the need for social supplementation. But they also knew that a certain minimum measure of this social supplementation was traditionally given, and that the integration of the economy could thus count on this supplementation. The social market economy had been born and it prevailed. A *new paradigm of the state's responsibility for the economy* had been created.

Since then, the concern for the competitive economy and the stability of the currency has formed the center of economic policy. Guaranteeing economic efficiency is primary. In principle it must not be reduced through social guidance. Social conditions either emerge directly out of the optimized economy, or they must be created by means of what the economy generates through institutions of the polity, especially through redistribution. This boundary is not cast into fixed rules. To a not inconsiderable extent it is entrusted to political discipline – in the final analysis, to the voter. In the 1960s the legislator affirmed the system: by formulating relevant basic values – the market economy system, overall economic equilibrium, growth, price stability, high employment, and equilibrium in the external sector; by setting up institutions to provide advice and accountability, and, less successfully, by creating the general tool kit of global guidance envisaged by the Stability and Growth Act. First and foremost, however, it was the *volonté générale* that secured the social market economy.

In the *process of German unification*, the social market economy experienced its most pronounced affirmation. In the Treaty on Monetary, Economic, and Social Union, it was for the first time enshrined in a legal text. The Unification Treaty adopted this as an essential foundation for the common future of the united Germany.

14.1.2 Challenges

Especially the state's responsibility for the economy was challenged in an unparalleled way by the development in the 1980s and even more so in the 1990s: by the profound technological and structural changes in economic activity, as well as by Europeanization and globalization. These challenges call for answers from domestic and foreign policy.

Domestically, the chief challenge is to create the preconditions that will allow Germany as a place for business to keep pace in the competition over technological innovation and to remain – or: become – attractive in the competition over capital. Both of these dimensions are an accomplishment of society and the state as a whole, which cannot be reduced to aspects of economic, social, or technology policies. In the final analysis, all areas of public life are relevant: the creativity, openness, and stability of society, infrastructure in the broadest sense, public safety, the standard of civilization, and cultural life. This invests the *Länder* with a new importance. Many of the conditions that determine the potentialities, their development and efficiency, but also Germany's international attractiveness, are under the control of the *Länder*, not the federal government. And many of the potentialities – from the "type of people" to nature – are regional. After decades of unitary desolation, the *social federal state* is seeing signs of new life. Within the closer circle of problems involving the state's responsibility for the economy, central importance continues to attach to the dilemma that the share that *capital and labor* bear of the communal burden, and especially of the burden of social redistribution, is to be reduced, without it being apparent who is to assume these burdens in their stead.

Externally the issue is to contribute, within the framework of the international community, to the creation of a *new economic order* for Europe and the world, one that combines economic efficiency with respect for shared values (e.g. ecological and bio-ethical ones) and sensible social redistribution. The global economic society needs a global economic order. What the social market economy of the Federal Republic needs in Europe and in the world is a framework that substitutes as best as possible for what the national social market economy loses in terms of its operating conditions through Europeanization and globalization. In the process, the preconditions under which an answer can be searched for and found are very different for Europe and the world. For *Europe*, the developments within the framework of the European Union are proceeding – all imperfections and risks notwithstanding – along a path that is strewn with many problems, but is fundamentally comprehensible and – one hopes – manageable. The difficulties of the *world* have not been mastered.

14.2 The Structures of Social Intervention

14.2.1 Goals and Institutions

If the responsibility of society and the state for the economy has the mandate to make the normality of the basic formula possible as a reality and secure it, the institutions of social intervention have the task of counteracting the inequalities that arise in the process of realizing the basic formula: reducing dependencies, controlling dangers, and compensating for deficits. As for how this task could be fulfilled, the development from 1945 found a model that was deeply committed to the goal of equality *and* to the proviso of inequality. That arose from the tradition of German social policy and the institutions that were effective at the time and were holding the society and the polity "above water" in the years of the catastrophe. Across the decades, society and politics have varied and enriched this model, but they have never called it fundamentally into question.

The program in which the claim to equality and the proviso of inequality pervade each other intensely was from the outset characterized by internal contradictions. However, those inner contradictions were and are never seen fundamentally as flaws, but as an opportunity, indeed, a necessity so as to realize different aspects of equality, justice, participation, and solidarity side-by-side and together. Within this system one can distinguish three blocks:

First: the *guarantee of a subsistence minimum for everyone*, as it had developed in public welfare. This institution had the most general relationship to the basic formula. It must always step in where the basic formula does not take hold and the subsistence minimum of people is therefore imperiled. The inequality it opposes is a very simple one: the inequality between people whose subsistence minimum would be in danger without this institution, and all those people to whom their own productive capacity or a more specific system of social intervention provide at the least the subsistence minimum, and usually a higher standard of living. The equality at issue in this institution runs along a minimum threshold. It is the equality of *at least* the subsistence minimum. In no other system is the basic social value of human dignity as nakedly apparent as here. Nevertheless: that human dignity be preserved is therefore precisely its essential task. The social justice at issue is the justice of need. The participation at stake is a participation whose measure is the subsistence minimum. The solidarity that realizes itself in it encompasses the entire society – it is vertical in nature. But the claim to redistribution stops precisely where the subsistence minimum is guaranteed.

Second: the guarantee of social protection, as it has developed in social provision, especially social insurance and social compensation. These institutions proceed from the normality of the basic formula. They pick up where disturbances occur: because the capacity to work drops out of the picture, because it does not earn an income, because income is in an obvious imbalance to needs and/or the community of maintenance, because the earner who has provided maintenance disappears, and so on. Social protection is supposed to mitigate or moderate the difference between the way things would be without this disturbance, and the way things would unfold after this disturbance in the absence of assistance. Here, then, is where the two basic types of social protection differ: provision (especially social insurance) and social compensation. Provision is directed at disturbances that typically have a certain probability of occurring, which means that collective action can be taken to protect against them. Social compensation targets disturbances that are not accepted as the typical part of the course of a life; rather, their consequences must be compensated because the disturbance was illegitimate, was imposed by the community as a special sacrifice, or for which the community is in some other way responsible.

Social insurance, socio-politically the most important phenomenon of social provision, is demarcated by two inequalities: toward the "bottom" through the inequality in the capacity to make provision – that is, vis-à-vis those who are unable to make provisions for themselves collectively; toward the "top" through the inequality in the need for provision – that is, vis-à-vis those whose wealth makes it seem unnecessary to organize provision for them within the responsibility of the polity. And the equality to which it sees itself obligated is a very peculiar one: an intertemporal or – more generally – an intersituational one. It is the maximum possible equivalence between the life situation before a disturbance and the life situation during or after a disturbance. "Social safety" (*soziale Sicherheit*) is one name for this equivalence. The station in life that has been achieved and manifests itself in income is an essential protected good of this equivalence. Social insurance intertwines the justice of achievement, the justice of acquired status, and the justice of needs. It extends the participation in the acquisitive and economic society that expressed itself in the course of the basic formula right up to the disturbance into the time after the disturbance has occurred. It realizes the solidarity of a narrower community: the community of those who, positing a similar capacity to make provision and a similar need for it, take collective measures to provide against similar risks. This solidarity is primarily horizontal in nature. To what extent – in fact: even in which direction – this solidarity is also vertical in nature is very uncertain. *Other institutions of social provision* (externalizing: private insurance; internalizing: pension schemes for civil servants, judges, soldiers, and officials) vary this basic model.

Social compensation also compares the hypothetical development that would have occurred without the disturbance with the real development resulting from the disturbance. The inequality it targets is the inequality between those who suffered no injustice and upon whom no sacrifice was imposed, and those who did suffer an injustice or upon whom a sacrifice was imposed. But there is also an intertemporal or intersituational element here: the conditions of life before the harm become the criteria for compensation. Here, too, elements of the justice of achievement, the justice of acquired status, and the justice of needs become intermingled. The participation that is realized is the very participation that was interrupted by the harm. The solidarity that is realized is that of the general political community – a solidarity that becomes concrete according to the measure of the particular responsibility, which affects the polity, or which the polity has taken on.

Third: the creation of "more equality" through the abolition or control of dependency relationships or through the conveyance of participation in prosperity. The basic formula is realized time and again in dependency relationships: in the employment relationship, in the relationship of meeting needs, and not least in the community of maintenance. "More equality" usually means: internalizing guarantee of freedom, security, and participation. The inequalities that the law targets in the process are concrete. The justice at issue can be the justice of achievement, the justice of acquired status, and the justice of needs. Participation is directed toward an appropriate share of the general legal goods of freedom, security, and participation. Likewise, the solidarity that is realized is primarily the solidarity of the general legal community, even though secondary communities of solidarity can emerge in narrower contexts (in the workplace, in the union, within the framework of free collective bargaining, and so on).

However, participation is also directed at a share of societal prosperity – or more modestly: an appropriate share of the life opportunities of society. Neither the general guarantee of a subsistence minimum nor the unfolding of the basic formula through institutions of social protection can provide a comprehensive assurance of an *appropriate participation in prosperity*. That is why supplementary institutions of social redistribution are needed: the *special assistance and promotion systems*. They are supposed to guarantee especially equal opportunity of access to the basic formula: for example, through training assistance and job promotion. They are supposed to ensure an adequate meeting of needs where that is not possible by way of the basic formula: for example, through the housing allowance. They are supposed to moderate or abolish the imbalance between the earnings capacity of the bread winner and the needs of the community of maintenance: for example, through child raising allowance and the child allowance. The inequality targeted by the assistance and promotion programs is the inequality of participation in prosperity. The justice that they realize is the justice of needs, as well as the justice of opportunity as – in equal measure – a precept of the justice of needs and a preliminary stage to the justice of achievement. The participation that is being made possible is the participation in society's general life opportunities. And the solidarity that concretizes itself in the assistance and promotion systems is the general solidarity of the community constituted in the polity.

14.2.2 Social Provision

Social provision through *social insurance shapes the overall system in a preeminent way*. This is connected with the important position held by the protection of workers and employees – for social insurance is *at its core the protection of workers and employees*. But it is also connected with *financing through contributions*. It gives social insurance a robust functional autonomy, and – in particular – removes it from the structure of the federal state's financial constitution. *Self-administration* gives it an effective basis of institutional persistence and assertiveness. All of this has to do with the idea of special communities of the insured. It perpetuates the *selective approach* of German social policy – an important mechanism for uniting the claim of equality with the proviso of inequality. The internalizing variant of provision in the form of the pension schemes for civil servants, judges, soldiers, and officials affirms this approach, as does the externalizing variant of occupation-based pension schemes.

Social insurance was modernized, expanded to include ever broader circles of individuals, and expanded in terms of the substantive area in which is was effective – most recently in the development of the new social insurance in cases of long-term care. Nevertheless, the principle of *social insurance* has run into difficulties. A central reason for this can be found in the *crisis of dependent work*. As a protection for workers, social insurance is suffering from the decline of dependent gainful employment and from the change in the way it manifested itself. Another challenge to social insurance lies in the development of the *age structure* among the population. To be sure, this is primarily a problem of old-age protection. In reality, however, the change in the age structure has substantially altered also the functional conditions of all social insurance systems. In the case of sickness insurance, we must add the rise in *medical possibilities* and also the rise in medical *costs*. Especially sickness and pension insurance are suffering from an *evolutionary dilemma* beyond these problems. On the one hand, these two branches of social insurance have become increasingly generalized. In each case that happened in a specific way. In *pension insurance*, this expansion happened above all through a process of including ever broader groups of individuals and a simultaneous extension to ever more "insurance courses" beyond those of gainful employment and contribution payment that were originally typical of pension insurance – most recently through the incorporation of the pension entitlements earned in the German Democratic Republic. Another dimension of "generalization" arose from the ever more intensive inclusion of pension insurance in society's broader model of protection in old age. That model extends beyond pension insurance to the pension schemes for civil servants, judges, soldiers, and officials, to the supplementary pension in the public sector, to workplace-based pension schemes, to professional pension schemes, to private insurance, indeed, even to the private formation of wealth, and which includes a comparison not only of benefits, but also of the prior histories and the relationship of the costs of provision and benefits to taxation – a claim to equalization that nobody who would be negatively affected by it would be willing to honor.

For *sickness insurance*, the process of generalization initially also took place through an expansion of the groups of individuals included; since the 1980s, however, that trend has been in reverse. The benefits provided by statutory sickness insurance were also expanded repeatedly. However, the most important track of the "generalization" of the statutory sickness insurance lies in the fact that since the 1970s and 1980s it has been given ever greater and more developed overall responsibility for medical care: responsibility to provide an adequate supply, to provide a supply that can be paid for, and to ensure adequate payment to the providers. And this happened even though the statutory sickness insurance's mandate of social protection covers only about half of the expenditures for medical care.

In spite of these developments, however, pension insurance and sickness insurance have retained their selective approach.

The tension between the conditions that formed the basis of the development of social insurance, the functions and structures toward which it evolved, and the societal, technological, and economic conditions under which it operates is therefore steadily increasing. But the inherent institutional laws of democracy and the *Rechtsstaat* supported the given and the particular. The result is a growing danger of dysfunctionality. Just how important these conditions of democracy and the *Rechtsstaat* are can be seen in the case of pension insurance, for example. Its concept – like the concept of old-age security as such – must be justified in the face of the likely developments in the decades ahead. But elections are "now" – all 4 years for the *Bundestag* and in between for the parliaments of the *Länder* (*Landtage*). And the law protects the entitlements of those who are alive *now*. In other words: who could complain about the excessive burden of the coming generations who are supposed to pay, in the twenty-first century, the contributions that will be needed to maintain the level of pensions promised in the twentieth century? Or about the shortcomings in the protection of those who will be the "elderly" in 30 years, and whose pensions can no longer be paid out in full because the contributions required to do so would be impossibly onerous? On the other hand: the financing from contributions forces us to think in specific ways about whether future benefits can be paid for. The fact that the pension schemes for civil servants, judges, soldiers, and officials is financed from taxes seems to make this kind of thinking unnecessary.

As a result, the picture that social provision offers is highly contradictory. The achievements of its institutions and the social happiness of this society are enormous. But taking responsibility for its proper development seems particularly difficult for the democratic constitutional and social state. The selective approach successfully resists any all-encompassing examination. The future obligation of provision is always subject to the superior power of contemporary interests. Unaccustomed questions about social provision arise also from Europeanization and globalization: for example, the question about the Europeanization of benefits from sickness and long-term care insurance; or the question whether it might not be necessary, if capital evades its national incorporation into the pay-as-you-go financing, for processes of capital cover to ferret out the capital where it is currently working. Social insurance, the "flagship" of German social policy, is mired in deeper problems than is generally recognized.

14.2.3 Social Compensation

Among the peculiarities of the time is the development of social compensation. The starting point was there: in the tradition of the claim of special sacrifices derived from the General Prussian Code (*Preußisches Allgemeines Landrecht*) and in the care for victims of the war, and via a more remote analogy also in accident insurance and the history of liability law. The flood of harm that National Socialist policy unleashed on so many in so many different contexts made it necessary to understand and distinguish the diversity of cases, and to standardize them for appropriate solutions. The most important distinction was between restitution of the injustice inflicted by racial, religious, and political persecution, and the compensation for special sacrifices made by individuals as members of the German people or that were in some other way the specific responsibility of the German state. The most important extension was that in addition to "personal harm" (bodily harm, impaired health, death), harm to wealth (from obstructions to gainful employment, through the loss of assets due to destruction, confiscation, or some other causes) was also recognized. Later it became clear that this amounted to a recognition of criteria that had to be considered – beyond the liquidation of a catastrophe – also in the relationship between a civil peace-time society and its democratic constitutional state. The most innovative example is probably compensation for the victims of crime.

Currently the historical dimension seems to be breaking open again. The reunification of Germany, the collapse of Communist rule in Central and Eastern Europe, and the new everyday reality of a global world have opened up new possibilities for many individuals living abroad to file claims for harm done to them by Nazi Germany or for which Nazi Germany was responsible. It is possible that the restitution of National Socialist injustice will thus enter into a new phase.

14.2.4 "More Equality"

"More Equality" Through Directives of Social Protection and Participation

The classic field in which "more equality" was realized primarily through the *internalizing development of existing law* is *labor law*. Throughout its long history, the law has sought to grant workers, first, a minimum measure, and then an ever rising level of freedom, equality, security, and participation in the employment relationship. In the Federal Republic, this development proceeded rapidly and concentrated a maximum of these values in the normal employment relationship. That led to inequalities: in relationship to non-normal employment relationships, to numerous types of self-employed gainful work, and to unpaid work, but also in the relationship between "job-holders" (in the public sector and otherwise) and the jobless. Finally, it led to a considerable societal, political, and especially legal-political inflexibility. That development seems to have passed its peak. However, it is too soon to tell what reality will emerge from this and which legal and political solutions will be found. One difficulty in this process will be the fact that labor law has long since lost the sole power of shaping conditions in the working world. It can take meaningful action only in agreement with social benefits law, and especially with social insurance law. After all, the issue cannot be only the creation of new legal regulations. The crucial point is for society – in agreement with politics and the law – to find new patterns of life and new consensuses.

However, the development of internalizing protection does not remain limited to the field of work and income. In the area of the *meeting of needs*, as well, it was necessary to introduce "more equality" into existing legal relationships: for example, beyond renter protection in consumer protection, especially in the law on general business conditions, and through the protection of people living in nursing and retirement homes. Further developments also occurred in the law dealing with the *community of maintenance* – especially as it relates to children. The Care Law comprehensively ensured for "more equality" for those who were no longer able to take care of their own affairs.

"More Equality" Through Social Benefits

Creating social equality through externalizing, tax-financed *assistance and promotion systems* is a *stylistic feature of the period under review*. As potential precursors one might consider at most the higher-level social assistance (so-called group welfare in favor of minors, the severely disabled, war victims, and so on) according to the 1924 Reich Ordinance on the Obligation to Provide Welfare and the family subsidies paid during the Third Reich. By contrast, a considerable network was created in the Federal Republic beginning in the 1960s: child allowance, child-raising allowance, maintenance advance, training grants (for a while also post-graduate grants), housing allowance, and so on. We must also include the "assistance in special life situation" according to the Federal Social Assistance Act (*Bundessozialhilfegesetz*). Child and Youth Services also fulfill corresponding tasks. Finally, the old "poor law" was replaced by counseling assistance and legal aid to make it possible to assert legal entitlements.

During the times of economic and social growth, these benefit systems imparted a special sheen to the social state. However, they also proved to be particularly endangered: endangered by the change in socio-political priorities and by the economic development and the resulting financial constraints. The assistance and promotion systems have repeatedly experienced times of benefit reduction – explicitly or through the failure to adjust benefit rates to the development of needs and their costs – and occasionally also times of renewed invigoration. Unlike social insurance, they have no special source of financing. They have not moved into proximity to acquired property. They do not have the moral background of claims to compensation. They do not have the equally diverse and deeply rooted institutional representation that characterizes social insurance. Already the representation of social assistance and of child and youth services through charitable associations and by the municipalities is diffuse and not very effective compared to social insurance. And all of the other benefits have no comparable backing. After all, the benefits of the special assistance and promotion systems are for the most part "estimated" variables, and this also reduces their ability to resist encroachments.

In Particular: Employment Promotion

A particular role attaches to the system of employment promotion: a complex system that promotes individual access to work through counseling and assistance in obtaining skills and finding a job, supports the supply of jobs through relevant subsidies, brings together supply and demand through information and placement services, counteracts the losses of jobs through compensation for reduced hours and other measures, and, finally, makes up the loss of income in case of joblessness through the social insurance payments of unemployment benefits. Employment promotion is the specific instrument by which the state lives up to its responsibility of making sure that income can be earned through work. At the same time, it is the specific instrument for providing the individual an opportunity to meet his obligation to earn income through work. But it is also the central, systematic place where – especially by virtue of the conditions under which the benefits of employment promotion replace the income from work – certain spaces of freedom from work are created.

Of course, in this regard employment promotion is supplemented in a deeply tiered way by nearly all social benefits systems. And all of the various pieces are interconnected in a fundamental and inextricable interdependence: the *development of work influences the reality of the social benefits systems; and the practice and effect of social benefits systems influence the development of work.* It is obvious that the change in work and the change in the political intent toward work also change the ideas about the optimal promotion of employment. The Employment Promotion Act of 1969 was a law borne of prosperity, of full employment, of freedom to work, and of the procurement of opportunities. The late 1970s and especially the 1980s changed a good deal in this equation. Book Three of the Social Code, which replaced that 1969 law in 1997, posited the reality of underemployment and the scarcity of funds. It emphasized the responsibility of every person to engage in gainful work, and it understood employment promotion above all as assistance to the individual in living up to that responsibility. It will presumably be necessary to accompany and support the further development of work life through a further opening up also of employment promotion.

"More Equality": The Diversity of Instruments, the Infinitude of Inequalities

Beyond these particular focal points, "more equality" has been and is used to justify diverse instruments: to shape public expenditures (taxes, dues, fees, etc.); to promote societal offerings (especially through subsidies); to improve regional living conditions (through the development of infrastructure, the expansion of services, through other promotion programs and, finally, financial allocations); to compensate for sectoral disadvantages (through subsidies and other promotion programs); to guarantee universal access to essential goods and services (e.g. through price controls, forced consolidation, but also through institutions of *Daseinsvorsorge*); to place private individuals under obligations in favor of the disadvantaged (e.g. the severely disabled); to shape administrative and legal processes, and so on.

Finally, the process by which inequalities have proliferated is characterized by the greatest diversity, indeed, infinitude. The social question was based on inequalities pertaining to groups – beginning with the elementary inequality of the poor vis-à-vis all those who are not "poor;" and then also the inequality of workers vis-à-vis others who are gainfully employed, but also vis-à-vis the poor. They were followed by other groups that are likewise constituted by their disadvantages within working life: small farmers, leaseholders, and settlers. Further inequalities emerged with respect to the coverage of needs: renters, leaseholders, and so on. The family and a person's position in life also offered a rich source of inequalities: families with many children, mothers, children, young people, and the elderly. And there is no need to spell out once again the great variety of inequalities that arose from the responsibility of third parties or the community for harm or damages. But new perspectives were constantly emerging: the typical threats to those being educated (kindergartners, school-age children, trainees in the working world, and students), the disabled and those in need of nursing care, or individuals who had particular difficulties integrating. Other categories arose from foreignness within this state and society: refugees, emigrants and resettlers, prisoners from Communist countries, asylum-seekers, guest workers, and so on. And old problems assumed new forms: poverty, homelessness, street children, and so forth. Alongside these individual fates stand the large-scale inequalities of sectors (agriculture, mining, etc.) and of regions (mountain regions, coastal regions, border regions, regions particularly affected by structural changes), and now also the difference between "Germany West" and "Germany East." At any rate, this much is true: *new inequalities are emerging, and the old inequalities are being reassessed.*

All these examples of *inequality are national in nature*. By virtue of territorial, personal, or functional connections, they fall within the responsibility of the German state. Until now, the *inequalities in the world* and toward the world were taken note of as something substantially different, and the response to them was fundamentally different. *Development aid* is the central example. *European unification* has already shown that the expansion beyond the framework of the nation state also adds *new inequalities*. They demand a corresponding participation in joint responses. At times they relativize, indeed, alter the existing national inequalities. But how could a *global economic and social system* be constructed without placing the inequalities in the world and vis-à-vis the world into a coherent relationship to the existing national differences? What would a global cosmos of inequalities look like? What would be the consequence for the traditional inequalities defined within the national framework?

14.2.5 The Guarantee of the Subsistence Minimum

The guarantee of the subsistence minimum is the oldest layer of the German social state. After 1945, as well, it belonged – in the form of welfare – to the basic stock of the social. In 1961 it was adjusted – as social assistance – to the values and living conditions of the time. It was the effective "net below the net." That it also contributed in the process to the "decommodified" freedom of a choice between social benefits and work was not a problem at a time when the discipline of the basic formula was still general and was affirmed by the condition of full employment. However, in time there was a growing discontent, in that this "decommodification" became for one part of the population social benefits in the good sense, while for others the use of freedom from work remained a form of abuse of the system. The rise in unemployment and financing problems also brought growing doubts about the correctness of the way social assistance was set up. Social assistance became a victim of the policy of belt-tightening – not only on the part of the legislature, but also on the part of the municipalities, to whom the actual implementation and its financing are entrusted. Not that social assistance was touched in principle. However, the ways in which it became possible for individuals – contrary to all assurances of the law – to fall between the "net below the net" multiplied and widened: the roads to poverty became more varied.

One essential reason behind this development is also that social assistance – at least the reality of social assistance – is characterized by the primacy of legal and monetary mechanisms. This is not sufficient to spare and save individuals from poverty or lead them out of it. That requires – to invoke Franz-Xaver Kaufmann's catalog of interventions once more – alongside legal and economic intervention also service-providing, pedagogical (social competency-conveying), and ecological (environment-shaping) intervention. But all of those dimensions are too feebly developed. There are many reasons for this. In the democratic competition for power, services do not reliably score points. The *Rechtsstaat* can do little to regulate them. Those affected by social policies see in money and laws the greatest possible respect for their freedom, but in services a potential threat to it. And those who are supposed to provide services also feel more secure in the realm of monetary, legally regulated assistance. After all, service providers have their own problems. They compete with one another over the recipients of their help. But service-providing, competency-conveying, and environment-shaping intervention cannot always be only pleasant, let alone a form of positive advertisement – especially not at first glance.

14.2.6 The Problem of Services

Very generally, social services proved a peculiarly insecure, non-standardized, contested, and imperiled area of the social. This does not apply in the same way to the professional services that are not specifically social in nature, for example, medical care. I am referring to the specifically social services of counseling, care, education and attendant care, housing, and nursing care. These services have always made a substantial contribution to the realization of the social. At the same time, however, they were characterized by unevenness in quality, style, the application and use of resources, and, finally, the guiding ideas behind them:

depending on the tasks and circumstances, all these aspects differed from one state to the next, from organization to organization, from municipality to municipality, and from institution to institution. This diversity and the competition between institutions and providers have positive effects: plurality of offerings and a choice for the clientele, as well as incentives and leeway for giving concrete shape to services and developing them further. But the diversity also entails disadvantages: the spheres that make possible individual development and progress can also be spheres of stagnation. The diversity of offerings also means divergences in quality and in the conditions under which services are provided. If all of this is added to the individuality and intimacy of service activities, the result is also a lack of transparency.

The distance that the *Rechtsstaat* and democracy keep to services opens the way to providers and their staff to develop freely. However, the dispensing with guidance and oversight that goes along with this can also lead to a loss of legitimacy and suitability on the part of services. Social services cannot be normatized in the same way that social monetary benefits can. But even for services there is – at least in theory – an optimal, normative clarification of their mission, implementation, and available resources. Since that optimum is difficult to define, it is an inherent part of the basic potential of dissatisfaction with services among all those involved. Yet whatever that optimum might be: exceeding it can be just as disadvantageous as not reaching it. The situation in Germany is characterized by a deficit in clarification and a deficit of responsibility, for which the distribution of the roles among the federal government and the states is a major reason. The federal government has the legislative authority for individual services laws (especially for social assistance and child and youth services). It regulates services related to these laws. In the process, it must respect the authority of the states and municipalities to implement them, and the autonomy of the "charitable" providers. If they regulate anything, the states for their part stand between the directives of the federal government and respect for the autonomy of the municipalities and the "charitable carriers."

The federal government, the *Rechtsstaat*, and democracy meet in the differential of political interest that declines as one moves from the center to the periphery and from the formal to the informal. The concentration of the socio-political discussion on federal laws marks the starting point of this differential. By contrast, the social activities by local communities on the ground are neglected. This is the lower end of the differential. This situation is reinforced by the fact that the de facto local activities are divided up between local governments and "charitable carriers." Services, however, are always concrete, they always happen "on site." Once gain we see how the development is conditioned by the institutions.

Lastly, the deficit in services is the expression of a *shortcoming in society as a whole*. This society wants to have services available and to use them. But it does not want to provide them itself in the same way, nor pay for them. Using services is self-evident to everyone. The willingness to provide services is far less pronounced in this society. And society and politics also have an ambivalent relationship to those who provide services. On the one hand, they respect them; on the other hand, they rely on their idealism and possibly also their personal commitment to provide help. As a result, society and politics always run the risk of paying service-providers poorly. Hence democracy, too, is always uncertain whether to take up the cause of these service-providers. And society as a whole has a relatively high degree of tolerance toward the risk that services will lag behind demand or will be provided in a less-than-optimal way.

15 Constants

15.1 The Complementary Totality of Society and State

15.1.1 The Deeply Tiered Co-existence and Interaction of Society and State

The period under discussion here, but also the contemporary situation, is characterized by the *dual interaction* that was described in the introduction through the image of the dialectical locus of the social. *First*, the interaction of *a priori activities* (in the picture of dialectics: the thesis) with *deliberately corrective activity* (the antithesis), which combines into a new *overall effect* (the synthesis) that is not identical with either the a priori or the corrective activity; *second, the interaction of the private and the public, of society and the state*. This two-fold interaction has its counterpart in a *two-fold need for differentiation*. The corollary to this two-fold need for differentiation is *two-fold danger of confusion*. The *first differentiation* must be the one *between the corrective intervention and the totality of social activities*. The corresponding danger of confusion lies in the fact that the *corrective intervention is equated with the social*. This confusion neglects the social achievement of the a priori activities. It likewise neglects that the overall effect emerges continually from the fact that the a priori activities are changed and supplemented by the corrective intervention. The *second differentiation* must be the one *between the share of the state* also of a priori activities, but especially of the corrective intervention, *and the share of private and societal elements* in a priori and corrective activities and thus of the overall effect. The corresponding *danger of confusion* is that the share of the state in the overall social activities is equated – pars pro toto – with the social. Both dangers of confusion overlap and intensify in the *danger that the share of the state in corrective intervention is simply identified with the social as such*. This danger exists especially for the *social state*, which is *not infrequently perceived and understood in a way that is substantially* – if not exclusively – guided by *its task of corrective intervention*. In reality, though, the social state is responsible not only for its specific share of corrective intervention. It is also responsible for its share of a priori activity, for the scope of private and societal forces to participate in a priori activities (secured and limited especially by the law), for the share that the latter are permitted to assume in corrective intervention, and thus for an optimal overall development.

With that, important lines of the overall development become visible. First: the coexistence and complementarity of society and state as forces for the realization of the social. The coexistence and interaction of state and society may have been seen differently in the first years of the postwar period than after currency reform and the founding of the Federal Republic – in other words: after the freeing of the economy in the United Economic Area and after the comprehensive constitution of a free society by the Basic Law. The economically prostrate society of the first few postwar years may have perceived the role of the state as more strongly interventionist. But the essential role of the private was as unquestioned as the necessary interaction of society and state. The establishment and workings of associations and "charitable" carriers are the best example of this. After the establishment of the social market economy, the development was shaped by the crucial importance of all structures and modes of operation within society. There may still have been a certain ebb and flow: in favor of the state (as in the Brandt era) or in favor of society (as in the early and mid-1960s and possibly once again in the 1980s and 1990s). But these were nuances, nothing more. The liberal social state had been accepted. And that is what it continued to be: a social state that presupposes, includes, and complements itself with freedom.

15.1.2 And Yet: The Utilization and Overestimation of the State – The Openness and Uncertainty of the Role of Society

The *second line*: *the political, financial, and legal effectiveness of the state* – its share of the a priori activities, but especially its share of corrective intervention – is *emphasized and overestimated* in a lopsided way. As a result, the overall effects of the dialectical structure of the social are attributed in a lopsided manner to the state and its corrective intervention. Too much is expected – and at times, too much is feared – from its intervention.

By comparison, the social accomplishment of private and societal forces remains hazy. There is a good reason for this: the private and societal forces must not and should not be at the disposal of the state – at least not in a way that interferes with or even abolishes their private and societal character, their quality of being free and independent. But the price for this is a lack of clarity what should be attributed to societal forces and what to the state when it comes to the success or failure of the system as a whole. That applies especially to the fact that the private and societal forces are at work not only in the dimension of the thesis, the a priori activities, but also and particularly in the dimension of the antithesis, the corrective intervention. What can and should be accomplished by immediate help and advocacy, by self-help and outside help, by altruism and self-interest, by professional and non-professional engagement, by gainful work and unpaid work – all this remains open. The allocation of the "*production of welfare*" to the various factors and mediums has been and remains a sphere of uncertainty.

15.1.3 Social Market Economy and Social State

A *third line: the polarity between the market economy and the state* assumes a *special status* within this juxtaposition. The focus here is on the tension between the market economy's share of a priori activities and the state's share of corrective intervention. The economy appears as *the* challenge of the socially interventionist state. The state's social intervention in turn appears as a potential threat to the market economy. However, it is the market economy that contributes to the overall system the prosperity that the social intervention of the state cannot generate, while the social intervention of the state contributes the social pacification and integration that the economy cannot accomplish on its own. This polarity attained its determinative importance in tandem with the social market economy – and has retained it with that economy. The tension between the market economy and the state's social intervention rose exponentially during the Brandt era. The Schmidt era began to dial back these pretensions on the part of the state. The Kohl era went further in opening up new fields of activity for the economy. The trend toward privatization has expanded the share of the private market economy borne by the private sector and has tended to reduce the share of the state's economic activity – whether in the form of economic enterprises, whether in the form of performing institutional tasks. At the same time, the share that the private economy can take on in the realization of the social has become apparent once again. The statutory long-term care insurance, going beyond the existing model of statutory sickness insurance, assigned a crucial (constructively differentiated) role to the societal provision of care by private persons (especially families), by non-profit providers, and by private sector enterprises. And the reduction in the protection of statutory sickness insurance and the growing uncertainty about the future of the statutory pension insurance created new interest in the market economy's production of social protection.

The current of development that ran from the establishment of the market economy in the 1940s and 1950s, to the experiment of its maximum social utilization in the 1970s, to another expansion of its spheres of freedom in the 1980s, *affirmed the value that society and politics assign to the market economy as the productive pillar of the entire system.* The market economy became a guiding principle. If it appeared that the state's corrective intervention might endanger the ability of the economy to generate prosperity, public opinion became alarmed and politics adjusted the relationship between the economy and the state to this sentiment.

15.1.4 The Profile of the Market Economy – The Diversity of Societal Welfare Production

A fourth line is connected with this: within the societal contribution to the social, there is a clear differential between the market economy and the diversity of non-market forces. The relative self-contained nature of the market economy's structure of interests and modes of operation sets it apart from the multifarious complexity of all other manifestations of society's share of social activities: the existence side-by-side of individual freedom (the concern of the individual for himself), private coexistence (especially through the realization of marriage and family), and the development of societal forces (the formation of groups, associations, and organizations) in the a priori activities; of individual help, of private cooperation and mutual support, a great variety of societal forces of collective self-help (from the self-help group and the cooperative to the special-interest organization), of altruistic outside help (by small groups or the benefits from large charitable organizations, the use of the wealth of foundations), and the economically rational (non-profit entrepreneurial) offerings of benefits by the corrective intervention. The public perception and assessment of this diversity of structures, functions, and motives is one thing, the public perception and assessment of the market economy is another. Linked to this difference are ignorance and uncertainty – and a trend toward neglect – about the "production of welfare" that does not come from the state or the market economy. That runs counter to its real importance. But there are reasons for this. At any rate, it is the expression of the self-evidence of freedom out of which welfare is "produced."

15.2 The Social at the Mercy of the Facticity of Its History and the Institutional Conditions of Its Development

15.2.1 The Appearance of Normative Guidance and the Power of Conditions

The development that has been traced here is carried by the *assumption that the social is normatively determined*. However, that assumption holds only in a very broad and vague sense: *abstract certainty with concrete uncertainty*. That applies to the *legal normatization* of the social: to the social goal of the state and to all the programs of constitutional or international law it seeks to explain. It applies to all *pre- and meta-legal norms* that mean the social, and to all the normative concepts that are used to exemplify the social: social equality, social justice, social participation, social inclusion, social protection, social integration. They all encompass a rich variety of meanings and are to the highest degree capable of and in need of concrete articulation. Each of these norms has specific parameters: beyond those parameters the framework of meaning has been abandoned and it becomes clear that invoking them amounts to their misuse. But those parameters are very broad, and within them much is possible and little is imperative.

Whoever is in the driver's seat can legitimize any solution he decides upon as social as long as he remains within these parameters. Since every one of the principles that are employed to exemplify the social encompasses a wide range of meanings, nearly every condition and nearly every change can be denounced as falling short: as "unsocial," "socially unjust," "lacking in solidarity," "exclusionary" and so on. The development of the social is *thus determined by the institutional structures* in which crucial aspects can be defined, and *by the forces that are at work in these structures*. These are not only the institutional structures of the polity as constituted, but the entire edifice of all private, societal, and governmental structures in which norms are formulated and brought to bear, conditions are shaped and realized, and – finally – institutions are created. The diversity of contexts and processes in which the social is thus thought about, articulated, and made real – for example, the considerable influence exerted by academia, the churches and other bearers of ideas, by journalism and the media, along with the amorphous diffusion of sentiments and so on – eludes any definitive description. In the final analysis they all lead to the state, in which the power to determine what is "social" is concentrated (but not exclusively so). But this state, too, speaks with many voices – on various issues, in various places, and at various times. In spite of the central role of the state, the diversity of the social thus remains considerable and its development open. Time and again what matters are the institutional structures, who influences them, and who has the say within them. As a result, the particular concrete expression of the social always has a prehistory of causes that is difficult to illuminate: societal conditions, the potential for analyzing, assessing, and articulating them, carriers of interests and ideas, and so on; and the circumstances under which these energies and stimuli interact with the organizational, functional, and normative conditions of the polity. For it is only by virtue of this interaction that they lead to the decisions of heightened significance that are peculiar to the state. To understand the development of the social in the Federal Republic of Germany, it is therefore of the utmost importance what impact the real conditions, ideas about their assessment, and the forces that sought to guide their evolution could and did have within the concrete constitutional edifice of the federal state, the *Rechtsstaat*, and democracy.

On the whole, then, the normative impulse of the social – essential but weak in its ability to provide guidance – confronts the determinative importance of real conditions and forces, and the structures within which social problems are turned into problem solutions. However, the critical discussion of the development sees it the other way around. It accords the norm fairly high importance. In the process, the openness of the norm is to a large extent instrumentalized – at least when the critical discussion is driven by a political intent. The difficulty of deriving the social from the norm is used to declare what is wanted and demanded as self-evidently social, and what is opposed as self-evidently asocial. Those who agree with this assessment – because it accords with their own interests, values, or prejudices – will be happy to adopt the "obviousness" of the social. And those who do not agree – because it goes against their interests, values, or prejudices – often find it difficult to make any headway against this "obviousness." By contrast, the role that the concrete constellations in society and politics – as well as the conditions of their effectiveness – play within the constitutional structure of the federal state, the Rechtsstaat, and democracy, is neglected, even blinded out. Who, when putting forth a social demand, would, instead of asserting that it is "socially obvious," justify it by arguing that the societal, political, and legal conditions are favorable for asserting a particular interest, a particular value, or a particular prejudice? And who, if he does not have the power or at least the opportunity to push through his "social obviousness," would say why it fits into the calculus of his interests or values to advocate his "social obviousness" nonetheless?

The concrete manifestations are many and varied. The discussion invokes the social norm to justify, fight for, or defend demands or vested rights as socially imperative, or to denounce an existing condition as "asocial." The indeterminacy of the social norm becomes the argumentative reservoir of both change *and* inertia. Vested rights are defended as "social achievements." Existing conditions are accused of being "socially backward" and "social progress" is called for. A connection is made between historical constellations of power or powerlessness, between used or lost opportunities and what is defended as a "social achievement" or judged in need of correction as a "sin of the past." However, justifying current politics by asserting that the existing circumstances in conjunction with the institutional conditions open up or close the way for this content or that would seem cynical. But in actuality, the institutional conditions and the powers at work within them dominate the path of the social.

15.2.2 The Neglect of the Autonomous Rationality of the Social

Wherein lies the *shortcoming*? It lies in the fact that there is not enough long-term, structural, unbiased, comprehensive, and honest thinking about the relationship between the normative power, diversity, and openness of the social and the real and institutional conditions under which society and the polity become cognizant of social problems and articulate social solutions. It lies in the fact that the politics of the social *appears* to justify itself on the normative basis of the social, while in reality it can be explained chiefly from the constellations of political integration and assertiveness. Next to that, the *normative mandate of the social atrophies*. The responsibility for a rational development of the basic norm in its totality is covered up by the assertion of "social obviousness" by actual politics on behalf of what exists and what is desired. The given societal and political forces and the institutional conditions of their effectiveness decide not only *how many* problems are seen and *how many* problem solutions are devised. They also decide *which* problems are seen and *which* problem solutions are adopted. Unless the stock of norms of the social is to be simply put at the mercy of the real, existing circumstances and institutional conditions by which problems are identified and solutions arrived at, it is precisely this process by which the social is made concrete that requires study, explanation, and evaluation. It must be asked what the normative framework of the social – an increase in economically conditioned and economically relevant equality under the proviso of inequality, the protection of human dignity, social justice, participation and inclusion, solidarity and social protection, subsidiarity and freedom, and social integration – can mean for specific life situations, which social problems the normative framework of the social establishes, and what problem solutions it leads to. This would have to be juxtaposed to the factual contexts that are addressed as problems under the given societal and institutional conditions, and which solutions are eventually adopted. Only in this way would it be possible to identify – on the basis of historical experience – the structural bias arising from the societal and political forces and from the institutional conditions of their efficacy. Only this can generate the societal, political, and especially legal energy to correct imbalances. Only in this way can the social develop from within, can a separate and comprehensive rationality of the social arise, can the reality of the social be held up against its idea. Only in this way can the social point the way to the future from within itself.

One characteristic of the entire period under discussion here is precisely the willingness to understand and define the social on the basis of what was done and put in place "in the name of the social," and what of this concrete reality became (and continuously becomes) visible and tangible as a potential for criticism and further development. The role of the social norm is ambiguous. It is held aloft to defend the existing as social or criticize it as "asocial." The concepts derived from the norm are used in the same way: equality and the violation of equality, participation and exclusion, justice and injustice, solidarity and lack of solidarity, security and the lack of security, subsidiarity and "total provision," integration and disintegration. But society does not face up to the comprehensive rational responsibility that is connected to all these ideas and concepts – at best it does so with timidity and too little patience. It is indispensable for the social to be entrusted to the institutions of the federal state, the Rechtsstaat, and democracy. There is no comparable way in which social policy could legitimize itself. But the fact that the social is at the mercy of the institutional conditions of the federal state, the Rechtsstaat, and democracy – that is the problem.

The stubborn refusal of society and politics to look at this problem critically has the potential for becoming one of the central ways in which this "democratic and social *Rechtsstaat*" could put itself at risk. An *expert institution* that could confront democracy and the *Rechtsstaat* with a comprehensive diagnosis of the social conditions and with a comprehensive system of possible therapies, thereby increasing the responsibility within the *Rechtsstaat* and democracy, in fact, making it possible in the first place, would be a compromise for uniting the "inherent logic" of the social with the – undiminished – legitimacy of the federal state, the *Rechtsstaat*, and democracy. But neither politics nor the social forces with the power to assert themselves want to give up the chance to realize their own interests, their own values, or their own prejudices, also – and especially – when it is difficult to justify them against an objective, independent unfolding of the meaning of the social.

16 The Crisis of the Social State?

Since the 1970s, there has been talk about a "crisis of the social state." The subsequent development of societal conditions, but especially of the international community, has repeatedly invigorated this discussion. It has become more general and many more voices have joined in. It has increasingly become a widely held opinion that the social state cannot survive without significant changes. There is more and more talk of the "renovation" of the social state. But the "crisis" is also being perceived in a more relaxed way. Are we really dealing with a "crisis"? With the phase in the course of an illness that decides whether a patient will live or die? Yes and no. On the one hand, we are dealing with problems that were only slowly understood (or had to be understood) as being a permanent part of the social state. On the other hand, we are in fact facing problems which, if they are not resolved, could lead to the disintegration of the social state.

16.1 The Message of More Equality Cannot Be in Question

At times certain voices seem to suggest that the *social state* is being *fundamentally* called into question. That *cannot* be. *Constitutionally it cannot be*. The only way that would be possible is if the goal of the social state were stricken from the constitutions of the federal state and the states. And it cannot be in terms of *international and European law*, unless the Federal Republic of Germany withdraws from all organizations and conventions committed to social concerns. But *even aside from positive law*, it is simply *unthinkable* that Germany would walk away from the social.

The social is an *expression of equality among people*. It took a long time before that equality began to find acceptance throughout the civilized world in the eighteenth and nineteenth century. It is one of the *irreversible discoveries in human history*. With some delay, it was also recognized that equality among people would invariably have consequences for the real conditions under which people live. At the same time, however, it had to be recognized that the realities in which people live cannot be shaped and altered at will. A reasonable understanding realized that it cannot be a matter of society let alone the state to make people themselves more equal than they are. Personal inequalities must not be coerced into equality. The more essential a particular freedom is to the development of the human personality, the less disposable are the inequalities that arise from the utilization of the freedoms that are available. As a result, the responsibility of society and the polity for the equality of living conditions focuses on what can be shaped and altered while preserving the individuality of the person – his or her dignity and freedom. To put it differently: it focuses on the inequalities that do not lie directly and exclusively within the individuality of a human being. But a reasonable understanding also realized that equality as such is not feasible. First, because human beings are unequal, and every increase in equality therefore can also spawn new inequalities. Second, because conditions cannot be altered at will. The societal and political responsibility for equality was therefore narrowed down to distinguishing between appropriate and inappropriate inequalities and to counteract the inappropriate ones. It was narrowed down to a responsibility for "more equality." But since this is what is possible for society and the state to do on behalf of the reality of equality among people, the *responsibility of society and the state toward economically conditioned and economically relevant inequalities among people can no longer be retracted* also in this sense.

16.2 The Social Is and Remains a Process

Yet these reflections do not define a problem, develop a yardstick for assessing it, or advance the construction of a solution. As urgent as the message of the social is, it is also broad, multifarious, and open. *By contrast, all concretization is selective.* All corrective social intervention, in particular, is dependent on emphasizing some contents while neglecting others. At most the overall structure of a priori activity, corrective intervention, and the overall effect resulting from it may approximate the optimal development. But imperfections, imbalances, and shortcoming will always remain – and they bring forth ever new demands for change.

These effective interconnections between the open infinitude of social goals and the selective way in which they are made concrete differ depending on whether the *economy and the social are in a phase of growth or in a phase of stagnation or even decline*. In the growth phase, the social is unfolded through more benefits, more social protection, and on rare occasions also through lower taxes and dues. In the stagnation phase, the differences between the social goals and the concrete manifestations become more urgent. In the retraction phase, the control of the social state over the development of the conditions loosens. Even if necessary explicit adjustments are not made, implicit adjustment effects nevertheless take place. Explicit adjustments are either justified by aiming for what is the comparatively "most social" state under the given conditions; or they distinguish in terms of clientele by sparing those groups that are "more relevant" in the democratic competition over power the sacrifices that are demanded from "less relevant" voters. If periods of growth distribute and allocate increases, periods of retraction allocate reprieves from cutbacks.

Solutions to social problems are created under specific political, legal, economic, and societal conditions. If things go badly, they fail to do justice even to these conditions and are therefore in need of correction. If things go well, they do justice to these conditions. However, the conditions are always changing. And *not infrequently it is the problem solutions themselves that sooner or later alter a problem or the conditions for its solution*. Regulatory mechanisms of the social have *one* effect when they are created, and *different* effects once society has accommodated itself to them. Benefits that are intended to help when individuals are affected by the vagaries of fate, can – whether or not that was the intent of the legislator – create spheres in which individuals can create their own lives. But well beyond that, social benefits, in particular, alter societal conditions. One need only recall the kind of development of medical care that statutory sickness insurance has made possible. All that has repercussions for the overall situation of society and the polity, and thus also for the possibilities of devising social interventions and their effects.

All of this *is perceived by individuals, their groups, and by societal and political forces as a struggle over the allocation of resources*. The conditions as they are, the conditions as they could be, and the conditions that can or seem to arise from imminent changes are reckoned in terms of disadvantages and advantages. These calculations, too, can change. New values and new experiences, and above all new living situations of individuals and groups, can produce new assessments of the advantages and disadvantages. Journalists, expert commentators, and political actors can add their weight to one side of the scale or the other, and new constellations can make possible new strategies for realizing specific goals.

The difference between any ideal of the social and any realization of the social – an inevitable product of the very nature of the thing – is intensified by the fact that the *institutional conditions* under which the social is made concrete *correspond to specific tendencies toward selectivity*. Under the given societal conditions, the institutions of the federal state, the *Rechtsstaat*, and democracy have an inherent tendency to favor the middle and neglect the periphery, to favor the horizontal and neglect the vertical, to favor the central and neglect the particular, and, finally, to favor the formal and neglect the thing itself – and to do so in a multitude of different contexts. That, in turn, multiplies the occasions *for perceiving and criticizing the difference between what can be conceived as the social and what is realized as the social*.

The *institutions* that are responsible for concretizing the social are for their part *set up* to recognize and pick up on perspectives of change and to *utilize the possibilities of change*. They legitimize themselves through their ability to formulate the social in new and "better" ways, and to lead social reality closer to this new and "better" social. This is least true of the *federal state*. It is evident, though, that the social policy of the individual states, even though it is fundamentally confined to the spheres of implementing and supplementing federal laws, can contribute substantially to sounding out and making use of the possibilities of variety. The *Rechtsstaat* works independently chiefly through the courts. Their particular function is to supplement the motives of politics with the values and principles of the law, and the effect of powerful societal and political currents with respect for individual interests and views that can be asserted in civil court. However, the most potent effect emanates from the m;echanisms of *democracy*. The competition of the political parties for power constantly provides new occasions for articulating the differences between what is and what could be and to woo the voters with them. In the final analysis, though, that is true not only for the "machinery" of state institutions. Societal forces work in a similar fashion: advocacy groups, the media, experts, and so on. They and politics constantly stimulate public opinion into new critiques of what is and new ideas about possible changes.

The social state must live with all of this. And the society that wants the social must live with all of this. In the final analysis, the *procedural, developmental openness* of the social is an *anthropological necessity*. No social state can be so perfect that there are no individuals within it who do not regard themselves as disadvantaged, who do not regard the social state as unjust (and may have reason for doing so). And there will be even more who will see the social state as it exists as a "next best thing". For all of them, the procedural, developmental openness of the social state provides a necessary hope for more equality, more justice, something better, something more social.

16.3 What Is Meant by the "Crisis of the Social state"?

In the early years of the social state of the postwar period, a few individuals might have spoken of the "crisis of the social state." But "crisis" was not a common denominator in the talk of the social state – not for three decades, until the middle of the 1970s. And that was the case even though the social state was continuously evolving. But these were developments of growth – a more or less linear expansion. It was the period of that illusion of equality that arises when more people tomorrow have what only a few have today. Politics "served" the various groups in a kind of "circular process" again and again, gradually – not equally, some more, some less, but in the end most of them. Democracy established itself also socially as the form of government of the smallest persistently neglected minority.

This established development did not come to an end until the *middle of the 1970s*. Movements of contraction were superimposed upon movements of expansion. Conflicts arose: strategic conflicts, valuation conflicts, interest conflicts, allocation conflicts. The victorious March of the social state ground to a halt. It proved to be open to challenge. And a more profound criticism was now also heard. The institutions of the democratic constitutional and social state, for whom it had been so easy to justify and utilize the growth of the social state, confronted a new, difficult task: to legitimize themselves no longer through growth, but through their management of stagnation and recession, no longer through the allocation of gains, but through the persuasive allocation of disadvantages and sacrifice. This change was all the more dramatic in that it began when the socio-political climate was still driven by the years that had witnessed the greatest social growth. In reality this was *not a crisis of the social state*. It was the *transition to the complete normality of the social state*. Until then, the "social state" had been identified with a "permanently growing social state." But one should have known all along that neither the conditions of the social state nor the manifestations of the social state would and could continue to grow indefinitely. What emerged was at most the *challenge of a painful learning process*. Both public awareness and the institutions of society and the polity had to learn that the social state cannot be only a fair-weather phenomenon, but must prove itself as an all-weather phenomenon. Still, talk of the "crisis of the social state" has persisted. The general experience never returned to the "fair-weather social state." Institutions barely had the chance any more to legitimize themselves through an unambiguous growth of the social. This difference between the early experience of the "fair-weather social state" and the reality of the "everyday social state," and later the continuing difficulty of realizing and experiencing the social state under changing conditions, was permanently characterized as a symptom of crisis. That is how unpopular normality is.

But the current situation goes beyond this normality. Two reasons are crucial for this. The *first reason*: the present condition of the social state is characterized primarily by the fact that the *circumstances* under which the problem solutions currently in place were designed *are undergoing substantial change – to an unusual extent, with unusual impact, and with unusual density*. This is happening through *outside developments*: such as the technological changes in work, the economy, and the public, and the transformation of the relationship between the factors land, capital, labor, knowledge, and management. The change in the circumstances is also driven by *developments that the social state itself had a hand in triggering*: such as individualization, the change in reproductive behavior, family structures, and the age pattern; a rise in the level of civilization, especially also in medical care; and numerous other changes in the working and acquisitive life. Lastly, the conditions of the social state change through *developments that are inherent in the social state*: the maximal utilization of the scope granted to individual interests and strategies; the growth and inertia of particular institutions, and so on. With that, the functioning of essential institutions of the social state is called into question – at least over the medium to long term. Essential social problems seem to call for new solutions.

The development of the social state has taken place since 1945 – and most certainly since 1948/49 – in a continuous evolution. New things were developed out of what existed. Substantially new things were added to what existed in a homogenous way. That approach no longer seems adequate for mastering the challenges of the present. What is needed is a level of creativity, competence, and leadership that was never so starkly necessary in the political sphere of the social in the six decades we have looked at. If that challenge is not met, the social state will soon fall short. The realization of the social could fall behind the level that has become self-evident ever since the postwar misery was overcome.

The *second reason* why the existing problems depart from the normal processes of the social state lies in the challenges of the *denationalization* of the social: in *Europeanization and globalization.* This denationalization manifests itself in two dimensions: in the *expansion of the real problem contexts* and in the *shift of the jurisdiction for problem solutions.* However, what is happening in both dimensions is not a complete shift from the narrower national realm into the broader European or global realm. Rather, what is taking place in both dimensions is a *comprehensive complication.* The real problem contexts will have their national, European, and global reference points. But they will also interact over and above all three of these levels. And the jurisdiction for problem solutions will also not simply pass to a new, higher level. It will retain its importance (altered, of course) on the old levels, while at the same time having to develop on the new ones. The carriers of the problem solutions will also have to interact: not only because of the complementarity of their substantive jurisdictions, but also because of the role of national governments on the supranational and international level. In the final analysis, though, the national level will retain a maximum of importance and also responsibility in both directions – that is, vis-à-vis the problem contexts *and* the jurisdictions for problem solutions. The only difference is that it is becoming vastly more difficult to do justice to that responsibility.

Even more so than the actual socio-political challenges, these Europeanizing and globalizing *changes are without precedent.* And that means that creativity, competence, the power of persuasion, and assertiveness are needed like never before. What is needed is a global order and a global politics that interpret and realize the negation of inappropriate inequality as a global principle. The longer the contradiction between the globalization of activities and the absence of a congruent order persists, the more national social policy will suffer from it without being granted relief from the transnational and international sides. By comparison, the European framework is more intensively developed. But Europe, too, needs a further clarification and decision about the proper relationship between the supranational community and national and supranational responsibility. Just as the national social state in the nineteenth century did not arise from the understanding of the general public, but out of the leadership of individual personalities and groups, the social global community will not grow out of the direct understanding on the part of national governments and international organizations. It will need the leadership of individual personalities, individual national governments or – probably most of all – groups of national governments. And Europe, too, will need fundamentally new ideas to prevent the discrepancy in national social policies from having a negative impact on the supranational community and to allow the latter to become the framework for a social statehood that is open to the future.

In view of this dual challenge to the social mandate from the development of societies and their polities and from the denationalization of structures and activities, the talk of the "crisis of the social state" is now fully justified. It is to be hoped that the crisis will meet forces that are up to the task.

References*

Abelshauser W (1983–1993) Wirtschaftsgeschichte der Bundesrepublik Deutschland (1945–1980), 1st edn 1983, 7th edn 1993. Frankfurt am Main

Abelshauser W (1987) Die langen fünfziger Jahre. Wirtschaft und Gesellschaft der Bundesrepublik Deutschland 1949–1966. Düsseldorf

Achinger H (1953) Soziale Sicherheit – Eine historisch-soziologische Untersuchung neuer Hilfsmethoden. Stuttgart

Achinger H (1954) Zur Neuordnung der sozialen Hilfe. Konzept für einen Deutschen Sozialplan. Stuttgart

Achinger H (1971) Sozialpolitik als Gesellschaftspolitik, 2nd edn. Hamburg

Achinger H et al (1955) Neuordnung der sozialen Leistungen. Denkschrift, auf Anregung des Herrn Bundeskanzlers erstattet. Köln

Adami N (1970) Die Haushaltspolitik des Bundes von 1955–1965. Bonn

*Note on changes in the name of the Federal Ministry of Labour in the Federal Republic of Germany: The *Bundesministerium für Arbeit und Sozialordnung* (Federal Ministry of Labour and Social Order) was split into the *Bundesministerium für Gesundheit und Soziale Sicherung* (Federal Ministry of Health and Social Security) and a section of the *Bundesministerium für Wirtschaft und Arbeit* (Federal Ministry of the Economy and Labour) in October 2002, to be merged again in November 2005 under the name *Bundesministerium für Arbeit und Soziales* (Federal Ministry of Labour and Social Affairs).

Adamy W (1995) Bedeutung internationaler Arbeitsnormen für die deutsche Arbeits- und Sozialpolitik. Soziale Sicherheit 44:165–175

Afheldt H (1995) Ausstieg aus dem Sozialstaat? Gefährdungen der Gesellschaft durch weltweite Umbrüche. Aus Politik und Zeitgeschichte B 25/26:3–12

Alber J (1979) Die Entwicklung sozialer Sicherungssysteme im Licht empirischer Analysen. In: Zacher HF (ed) Bedingungen für die Entstehung und Entwicklung der Sozialversicherung. Berlin, pp 123–210

Alber J (1989) Der Sozialstaat in der Bundesrepublik Deutschland 1950–1983. Frankfurt am Main

Alber J (1999) Der deutsche Sozialstaat im Licht international vergleichender Daten. In: Flora P, Noll H-H (eds) Sozialberichterstattung und Sozialstaatsbeobachtung. Frankfurt am Main New York, pp 41–72

Albers W, Dreissig W (eds) (1974/1977) Öffentliche Finanzwirtschaft und Verteilung. Vol 1 (1974). Vol 2 (1974). Vol 3 (1977). Vol 4 (1977). Vol 5 (1977). Berlin.

Albrecht G (ed) (1954) Deutschland und die Weltwirtschaft. Verhandlungen auf der Tagung des Vereins für Socialpolitik in Bad Nauheim. Berlin

Albrecht K, Schüren P (1957) Der Mittelstand zwischen Bedrängnis und Bewährung in der sozialen Marktwirtschaft. Düsseldorf

Altenbericht (erster) der Bundesregierung (1993) Bundestagsdrucksache 12/5897

Ambrosius G (1977) Die Durchsetzung der sozialen Marktwirtschaft in Westdeutschland 1945–1949. Stuttgart

Anheier HK, Seibel W (1990) The third sector: comparative studies of non-profit organizations. New York Berlin

Apelt W (1964) Geschichte der Verfassung der Weimarer Republik, 2nd edn. Berlin.

Archer M (ed) (1999) Towards reducing unemployment. Proceedings fifth plenary session of the Pontifical Academy of Social Sciences 3–6 Mar 1999. Vatican City

Archer M, Malinvaud E (eds) (1998a) The future of labour and labour in the future. Proceedings second plenary session of the Pontifical Academy of Social Sciences 20–23 Mar 1996. Vatican City

Archer M, Malinvaud E (eds) (1998b) The right to work: towards Full employment. Proceedings third plenary session of the Pontifical Academy of Social Sciences 23–26 Apr 1997. Vatican City

Arndt A (1946) Das Problem der Wirtschaftsdemokratie. Süddeutsche Juristenzeitung 1:137–141

Arndt H, Swatek D (eds) (1971) Grundfragen der Infrastrukturplanung für wachsende Wirtschaften. Verhandlungen des Vereins für Socialpolitik in Innsbruck 1970. Berlin

Arzt und Gesellschaft (1977) Schriftenreihe des Deutschen Sozialrechtsverbandes (until vol 22 (1982) Deutscher Sozialgerichtsverband), vol 15

Auerbach W (1974) Klärung um den sozialen Rechtsstaat. In: Christmann A, Hesselbach W, Jahn M, Mommsen EW (eds) Sozialpolitik. Ziele und Wege. Köln, pp 271–278

Auerbach W et al (1957) Sozialplan für Deutschland, Gutachten erstattet auf Anregung des Vorstandes der SPD von Berlin. Hannover.

Aust A, Bieling H-J (1996) Arbeitsmarkt- und Beschäftigungspolitik in Westeuropa – Zwischen strategischer Konvergenz und institutioneller Vielfalt. Zeitschrift für Sozialreform 42:141–166

Auswirkungen von Inflation, Konjunktur und Unterbeschäftigung auf das System der sozialen Sicherheit (1978) In: Schriftenreihe des Deutschen Sozialrechtsverbandes (until vol 22 (1982) Deutscher Sozialgerichtsverband), vol. 16

Bachof O (1954) Begriff und Wesen des sozialen Rechtsstaats. In: Veröffentlichungen der Vereinigung der Deutschen Staatsrechtslehrer. Issue no. 12. Berlin, pp 37–84

Bäcker G (1988) Normalarbeitsverhältnisse und soziale Sicherung, Sozialversicherung und/oder Grundsicherung? Sozialpolitische Handlungsnotwendigkeiten und –alternativen bei Dauerarbeitslosigkeit und Ausbreitung ungeschützter Arbeitsverhältnisse. Zeitschrift für Sozialreform 34:595–629

Badura P (1987) Die Parlamentarische Demokratie. In: Isensee J, Kirchof P (eds) Handbuch des Staatsrechts, vol 1. Heidelberg, pp 953–986

Badura P (1995) Die innerdeutschen Verträge, insbesondere der Einigungsvertrag. In: Isensee J, Kirchof P (eds) Handbuch des Staatsrechts, vol 8. Heidelberg, pp 171–198
Badura P (1998) Deutschland – Heimat und Zufluchtsort. In: Ruland F, von Maydell BB, Papier H-J (eds) Verfassung, Theorie und Praxis des Sozialstaats. Festschrift für Hans F. Zacher zum 70, Geburtstag. Heidelberg, pp 1–14
Badura P, Rittner F, Rüthers B (1977) Mitbestimmungsgesetz 1976 und Grundgesetz – Gemeinschaftsgutachten. München
Ballerstedt K (1956) Wirtschaftsverfassungsrecht. Die öffentliche Verwaltung 8:97–102, 135–143, 172–175, 200–207
Ballerstedt K (1958) Wirtschaftsverfassungsrecht. In: Bettermann KA, Nipperdey Hans C, Scheuner U (eds) Die Grundrechte. Vol 3/1. Berlin, pp 1–90
Barocka E (1960) Die Berücksichtigung sozialer Gesichtspunkte bei der Erhebung von Gebühren und Beiträgen für kommunale Abwasseranlagen, ihre Möglichkeiten, Problematik und Grenzen. Deutsches Verwaltungsblatt 75:825–832
Bart H-L (1996) Die Grundgesetzreform nach der deutschen Einheit. Akteure, politischer Prozeß und Ergebnisse. Opladen
Bartholomäi R (1974) Sozialplanung. In: Christmann A, Hesselbach W, Jahn M, Mommsen EW (eds) Sozialpolitik. Ziele und Wege. Köln, pp 57–78
Bartholomäi R et al (eds) (1977) Sozialpolitik nach 1945. Geschichte und Analysen. Bonn-Bad Godesberg
Barwig K et al (eds) (1997) Sozialer Schutz von Ausländern in Deutschland. Baden-Baden
Barwig K, Saathoff G, Weyde N (eds) (1998) Entschädigung für NS-Zwangsarbeit. Rechtliche, historische und politische Aspekte. Baden-Baden
Bauer H (1997) Die finanzverfassungsrechtliche Integration der neuen Länder. In: Isensee J, Kirchhof P (eds) Handbuch des Staatsrechts, vol 9. Heidelberg, pp 259–304
Behn HU (1971) Die Regierungserklärungen der Bundesrepublik Deutschland. München Wien
Behrens J, Leibfried S, Mückenberger U (1987) Sozialpolitische Regulierung und Normalisierung des Arbeitsbürgers. In: Opielka M, Ostner I (eds) Umbau des Sozialstaats. Essen, pp 24–34
Beier G (1975) Volksstaat und Sozialstaat. Der Gründungskongreß des DGB in München 1949 und Hans Böcklers Beitrag zur Stellung der Gewerkschaften in Gesellschaft und Staat. In: Vetter HO (ed) Vom Sozialistengesetz zur Mitbestimmung. Köln, pp 359–397
Beier G (1981) Gewerkschaften I: Geschichte. In: Albers W (ed) Handwörterbuch der Wirtschaftswissenschaften, vol 3. Stuttgart, pp 641–659
Benda E (1994) Der soziale Rechtsstaat. In: Benda E, Maihofer W, Vogel H-J (eds) Handbuch des Verfassungsrechts der Bundesrepublik Deutschland, 2nd edn. Berlin New York, pp 719–797
Benda E, Maihofer W, Vogel H-J (eds) (1994) Handbuch des Verfassungsrechts der Bundesrepublik Deutschland, 2nd edn. Berlin New York
Benz W (1981) Deutsche Opposition gegen alliierte Versuche zur Reform des öffentlichen Dienstes 1945–1952. Vierteljahreshefte für Zeitgeschichte 29:216–245
Benz W (1983a) Vorform des "Weststaats": Die Bizone 1946–1949. In: Eschenburg T (ed) Jahre der Besatzung: 1945–1949. Geschichte der Bundesrepublik Deutschland, vol 1. Stuttgart, pp 375–458
Benz W (1983b) Das Ende der Besatzung. In: Eschenburg T (ed) Jahre der Besatzung 1945 – 1949. Geschichte der Bundesrepublik Deutschland, vol 1. Stuttgart Wiesbaden, pp 515–536
Berié H (1970) Das Sozialbudget. Grundlagen, Methoden und Verfahren. Bonn-Bad Godesberg
Berlit U (1996) Die Reform des Grundgesetzes nach der staatlichen Einigung Deutschlands. Jahrbuch des öffentlichen Rechts der Gegenwart (new edition) 44:17–89
Bernhardt R (1987) Die deutsche Teilung und der Status Gesamtdeutschland. In: Isensee J, Kirchhof P (eds) Handbuch des Staatsrechts, vol 1. Heidelberg, pp 321–349
Bethlehem S (1982) Heimatvertreibung. DDR- (Deutsche Demokratische Republik) Flucht. Gastarbeiterzuwanderung. Stuttgart
Beutler B (1973) Das Staatsbild in den Länderverfassungen nach 1945. Berlin
Bieback K-J et al (eds) (1979) Streikfreiheit und Aussperrungsverbot. Neuwied

Biedenkopf K (1997) Von der Arbeits- zur Bürgergesellschaft. In: Hradil S (ed) Differenz und Integration. Die Zukunft moderner Gesellschaften. Verhandlungen des 28. Kongresses der Deutschen Gesellschaft für Soziologie in Dresden 1996. Frankfurt New York, pp 54–71

Birk D (1987) Altersvorsorge und Alterseinkünfte im Einkommensteuerrecht. Verfassungsrechtliche Vorgaben, gesetzliche Regelungen, Neuordnungsmodelle. Köln

Blättel I, Fromen W (1984) Die ehrenamtlichen Richter in den sozialgerichtlichen Instanzen. In: Deutscher S (ed) Entwicklung des Sozialrechts - Aufgabe der Rechtsprechung. Festgabe zum 100-jährigen Bestehen der sozialgerichtlichen Rechtsprechung. Köln, pp 107–138

Bley H (1974) Die Relevanz verfassungsgerichtlicher Grundentscheidungen im materiellen Sozialrecht. Dargestellt aufgrund der Rechtsprechung des Bundesverfassungsgerichts. Die Sozialgerichtsbarkeit 21:321–333

Blum R (1980) Marktwirtschaft, soziale. In: Albers W et al (eds) Handwörterbuch der Wirtschaftswissenschaften, vol 5. Stuttgart, pp 153–166

Blum R (1988) Soziale Marktwirtschaft. In: Görres-Gesellschaft (ed) Staatslexikon, 7th edn, vol 4. Freiburg Basel Wien, pp 1240–1250

Blumenberg-Lampe C (1973) Das wirtschaftspolitische Programm des “Freiburger Kreises”. Entwurf einer freiheitlich-sozialen Nachkriegswirtschaft. Nationalökonomen gegen den Nationalsozialismus. Berlin

Böckenförde E-W (ed) (1976) Staat und Gesellschaft. Darmstadt

Böckenförde E-W (1987) Demokratie als Verfassungsprinzip. In: Isensee J, Kirchhof P (eds) Handbuch des Staatsrechts, vol 1. Heidelberg, pp 887–952

Böckenförde E-W, Jekewitz J, Ramm T (eds) (1981) Soziale Grundrechte. Fünfter rechtspolitischer Kongreß der SPD (Sozialdemokratische Partei Deutschlands) vom 29. Februar bis 2. März 1980 in Saarbrücken. Heidelberg

Bogs H (1998) Artikel 14 GG (Eigentum) als Vertrauensschutz-Basisnorm für Rentenversicherte? Ein Plädoyer für andere Wege verfassungsgerichtlicher Kontrolle von Sozialstaatsumbau. In: Ruland F, von Maydell BB, Papier H-J (eds) Verfassung, Theorie und Praxis des Sozialstaats. Festschrift für Hans F. Zacher zum 70. Geburtstag. Heidelberg, 65–83

Bogs W (1955) Grundfragen des Rechts der sozialen Sicherheit und seiner Reform. Berlin

Bogs W (1960) Die Einwirkung verfassungsrechtlicher Normen auf das Recht der sozialen Sicherheit. In: Verhandlungen des 43. Deutschen Juristentages, vol 2, part G. Tübingen, pp 5–65

Bogs W (1979) Sozialrechtspflege vor Einführung der Sozialgerichtsbarkeit, insbesondere Verfassung und Verfahren des Reichsversicherungsamts. In: Deutscher Sozialgerichtsverband (ed) Sozialrechtsprechung. Verantwortung für den sozialen Rechtsstaat. Festschrift zum 25-jährigen Bestehen des Bundessozialgerichts, vol 1. Köln, pp 3–24

Böhm F (1946) Die Bedeutung der Wirtschaftsordnung für die politische Verfassung. Süddeutsche Juristenzeitung 1:141–149

Bommes M (1999) Migration und nationaler Wohlfahrtsstaat. Ein differenzierungstheoretischer Entwurf. Opladen

Bommes M, Halfmann J (eds) (1998) Migration in nationalen Wohlfahrtsstaaten. Theoretische und vergleichende Untersuchungen. Osnabrück

Borchert J, Lessenich S, Lösche P (eds) (1997) Standortrisiko Wohlfahrtsstaat. Jahrbuch für Europa- und Amerika-Studien 1. Opladen

Boss A, Rosenschon A (1996) Öffentliche Transferleistungen zur Finanzierung der deutschen Einheit: Eine Bestandsaufnahme. Kieler Diskussionsbeiträge Nr. 269. Institut für Weltwirtschaft. Kiel

Boyer R, Drache D (eds) (1996) States against markets. The limits of globalisation. London New York

Boyer C, Henke K-D, Skyba P (eds) (2008) Deutsche Demokratische Republik 1971–1989. Bewegung in der Sozialpolitik, Erstarrung und Niedergang (Geschichte der Sozialpolitik in Deutschland seit 1945, vol. 10, edited by Bundesministerium für Arbeit und Soziales, Bundesarchiv). Baden-Baden

Bracher KD, Jäger W, Link W (1986) Die Ära Brandt: 1969–1974. Geschichte der Bundesrepublik Deutschland, vol 5/I. Stuttgart

Braun W (1982) Die Zukunft der Arbeitsgesellschaft und das Recht auf Arbeit. Wuppertal

Braun M, Mohler PH (eds) (1998) Soziale Ungleichheit in Deutschland. Blickpunkt Gesellschaft 4. Opladen

Briefs G (1965) Gewerkschaften I (Theorie). In: von Beckerath E et al (eds) Handwörterbuch der Sozialwissenschaften, vol 4. Stuttgart Tübingen Göttingen, pp 545–561

Brohm W (1987) Sachverständige Beratung des Staates. In: Isensee J, Kirchhof P (eds) Handbuch des Staatsrechts, vol 2. Heidelberg, pp 207–248

Broszat M, Henke K-D, Woller H (eds) (1988) Von Stalingrad zur Währungsreform. Zur Sozialgeschichte des Umbruchs in Deutschland. München

Brück GW (1984) Solidarität und Subsidiarität in ihrer wechselseitigen Bedingtheit. Sozialer Fortschritt 33:197–200

Brunner G (1971) Die Problematik der sozialen Grundrechte. Tübingen

Brunner G (ed) (1996) Politische und ökonomische Transformation in Osteuropa. Berlin

BTDrs. = Bundestagsdrucksachen (parliamentary papers and documents, including drafts of laws). Published by Deutscher Bundestag. (Example 12/7560. The first number calls the electoral period of the parliament, the second one is the sequential number of the document. From the 8th electoral period beginning 14 December 1976 online see Homepage Deutscher Bundestag/Drucksachen und Plenarprotokolle online

Bucher P (ed) (1990) Nachkriegsdeutschland 1945–1949. Darmstadt

Buchheim C (1998) Die Errichtung der Bank deutscher Länder und die Währungsreform in Westdeutschland. In: Deutsche Bundesbank (ed) Fünfzig Jahre Deutsche Mark: Notenbank und Währung in Deutschland seit 1948. München, pp 91–138

Budschin HJ (1976) Die Formung der staatlichen Sozialpolitik in der Bundesrepublik Deutschland. Berlin

Buhr P, Leibfried S, Meyer T, Riedmüller B (1988) Individualisierung und soziale Sicherung der Frau. Zeitschrift für Sozialreform 34:655–658

Bührer W (1997) Westdeutschland in der OEEC. Eingliederung, Krise, Bewährung. München

Bull H-P (1977) Die Staatsaufgaben nach dem Grundgesetz, 2nd edn. Königstein im Taunus

Bull H-P (1988) Der Sozialstaat als Rechtsstaat. Zeitschrift für Sozialreform 34:13–39

Bundesminister des Innern/Bundesminister der Justiz (1983) Bericht der Sachverständigenkommission "Staatszielbestimmung/Gesetzgebungsaufträge". Bonn

Bundesminister für Arbeit und Sozialordnung (ed) (1977) Entwurf eines Arbeitsgesetzbuchs – Allgemeines Arbeitsvertragsrecht. Bonn

Bundesminister für Arbeit und Sozialordnung (ed) (1979) Vorschläge zur sozialen Sicherung der Frauen und der Hinterbliebenen. Gutachten der Sachverständigenkommission. Bonn

Bundesminister für Arbeit und Sozialordnung (ed) (1983a) Sachverständigenkommission Alterssicherungssysteme: Darstellung der Alterssicherungssysteme und der Besteuerung von Alterseinkommen, Gutachten der Sachverständigenkommission, 2 vols. Bonn

Bundesminister für Arbeit und Sozialordnung (ed) (1983b) Sachverständigenkommission Alterssicherungssysteme: Anlagenband B zum Gutachten der Sachverständigenkommission. Bonn

Bundesminister für Innerdeutsche Beziehungen (ed) (1971, 1974, 1987) Bericht der Bundesregierung und Materialien zur Lage der Nation. Bonn, pp 125–185 (1971); 441–500 (1974); 555–595 (1987)

Bundesminister für Jugend, Familie und Gesundheit (ed) (1978) Konsequenzen des Geburtenrückgangs für ausgewählte Politikbereiche. In: Schriftenreihe [of the Ministry]. vol. 58. Stuttgart

Bundesminister für Jugend, Familie und Gesundheit (ed) (1979) Ursachen des Geburtenrückgangs – Aussagen, Theorien und Forschungsansätze zum generativen Verhalten. In: Schriftenreihe [of the Ministry], vol 63. Bonn

Bundesministerium der Finanzen (ed) (1976) Wissenschaftlicher Beirat beim Bundesministerium der Finanzen. Gutachten über Probleme und Lösungsmöglichkeiten einer Bodenwertzuwachsbesteuerung. Bonn
Bundesministerium der Finanzen (ed) (1986) Wissenschaftlicher Beirat beim Bundesministerium der Finanzen: Gutachen zur einkommensteuerlichen Behandlung von Alterseinkünften. Bonn
Bundesministerium der Finanzen (ed) (1992) Wissenschaftlicher Beirat beim Bundesministerium der Finanzen: Gutachen zum Länderfinanzausgleich in der Bundesrepublik Deutschland. Bonn
Bundesministerium der Finanzen (ed) (1995) Wissenschaftlicher Beirat beim Bundesministerium der Finanzen: Gutachen Einnahmeverteilung zwischen Bund und Ländern. Probleme und Lösungsmöglichkeiten. Bonn
Bundesministerium der Finanzen (ed) (1999) Wissenschaftlicher Beirat beim Bundesministerium der Finanzen: Gutachen Reform der internationalen Kapitaleinskommensbesteuerung. Bonn
Bundesministerium für Arbeit und Sozialordnung (ed) (1994) Sozialstaat im Wandel. Bonn
Bundesministerium für Arbeit und Sozialordnung (ed) (1998) Übersicht über das Sozialrecht, 5th edn. Bonn
Bundesministerium für Arbeit und Sozialordnung (ed) (1999) Statistische Übersichten zur Geschichte der Sozialpolitik in Deutschland seit 1945. Vol West. Authored by Berié H. Bonn
Bundesministerium für Arbeit und Soziales, Bundesarchiv (eds) (2001–2008) Geschichte der Sozialpolitik in Deutschland seit 1945, 11 vols. Baden-Baden (single volumes: see below, see also footnote on the page 391)
Bundesministerium für Arbeit und Sozialordnung, Bundesarchiv (eds) (2001a) Geschichte der Sozialpolitik in Deutschland seit 1945, vol 1: Grundlagen der Sozialpolitik. Baden-Baden
Bundesministerium für Arbeit und Sozialordnung, Bundesarchiv (eds) (2001b) Geschichte der Sozialpolitik in Deutschland seit 1945, vol 2: Die Zeit der Besatzungszonen 1945–1949. Sozialpolitik zwischen Kriegsende und der Gründung zweier deutscher Staaten. Edited by Wengst U. Baden-Baden
Bundesministerium für Arbeit und Soziales, Bundesarchiv (eds) (2005) Geschichte der Sozialpolitik in Deutschland seit 1945, vol 3: Bundesrepublik Deutschland 1949–1957. Bewältigung der Kriegsfolgen, Rückkehr zur sozialpolitischen Normalität. Edited by Schulz G. Baden-Baden
Bundesministerium für Arbeit und Soziales, Bundesarchiv (eds) (2006a) Geschichte der Sozialpolitik in Deutschland seit 1945, vol 5: Bundesrepublik Deutschland 1966–1974. Eine Zeit vielfältigen Aufbruchs. Edited by Hockerts HG. Baden-Baden
Bundesministerium für Arbeit und Soziales, Bundesarchiv (eds) (2006b) Geschichte der Sozialpolitik in Deutschland seit 1945, vol 9: Deutsche Demokratische Republik 1961–1971. Politische Stabilisierung und wirtschaftliche Mobilisierung. Edited by Kleßmann Ch. Baden-Baden
Bundesministerium für Arbeit und Soziales, Bundesarchiv (eds) (2007a) Geschichte der Sozialpolitik in Deutschland seit 1945, vol 4: Bundesrepublik Deutschland 1957–1966. Sozialpolitik im Zeichen des erreichten Wohlstandes. Edited by Ruck M, Boldorf M. Baden-Baden
Bundesministerium für Arbeit und Soziales, Bundesarchiv (eds) (2007b) Geschichte der Sozialpolitik in Deutschland seit 1945, vol 11: Bundesrepublik Deutschland 1989–1994. Sozialpolitik im Zeichen der Vereinigung. Edited by Ritter GA. Baden-Baden
Bundesministerium für Arbeit und Soziales, Bundesarchiv (eds) (2008a) Geschichte der Sozialpolitik in Deutschland seit 1945, vol 6: Bundesrepublik Deutschland 1974–1982. Neue Herausforderungen, wachsende Unsicherheit. Edited by Geyer MH. Baden-Baden
Bundesministerium für Arbeit und Soziales, Bundesarchiv (eds) (2008b) Geschichte der Sozialpolitik in Deutschland seit 1945, vol 10: Deutsche Demokratische Republik 1971–1989. Bewegung in der Sozialpolitik, Erstarrung und Niedergang. Edited by Boyer Ch, Henke KD, Skyba P. Baden-Baden
Bundesministerium für Gesundheit und Soziale Sicherung, Bundesarchiv (eds) (2004) Geschichte der Sozialpolitik in Deutschland seit 1945, vol 8: Deutsche Demokratische Republik 1949–1961. Im Zeichen des Aufbaus des Sozialismus. Edited by Hofmann D, Schwartz M, commissioned by Institut für Zeitgeschichte. Baden-Baden

Bundesministerium für Gesundheit und Soziale Sicherung, Bundesarchiv (eds) (2005) Geschichte der Sozialpolitik in Deutschland seit 1945, vol 7: Bundesrepublik Deutschland 1982–1989. Finanzielle Konsolidierung und institutionelle Reform. Edited by Schmidt MG. Baden-Baden

Bundesministerium für Wirtschaft (ed) (1964–1999) Jahresgutachten des Sachverständigenrats zur Begutachtung der gesamtwirtschaftlichen Entwicklung 1964/1965; 1966/1967; 1975/1976; 1982/1983; 1989/1990; 1994/1995; 1995/1996; 1998/1999

Bundesministerium für Wirtschaft (ed) (1973, 1987, 1998) Der Wissenschaftliche Beirat beim Bundesministerium für Wirtschaft: Sammelband der Gutachten 1948 bis 1972 (Göttingen 1973); Sammelband der Gutachten 1973 bis 1986 (Göttingen 1987); Sammelband der Gutachten 1987 bis 1997 (Stuttgart 1998)

Bundesministerium für Wirtschaft (ed) (1998) Der Wissenschaftliche Beirat beim Bundesministerium für Wirtschaft: Grundlegende Reform der Gesetzlichen Rentenversicherung

Bundesministerium für wirtschaftliche Zusammenarbeit (ed) (1978) Der Wissenschaftliche Beirat beim Bundesministerium für wirtschaftliche Zusammenarbeit: Auf dem Weg zu einer neuen Weltwirtschaftsordnung. Schriftenreihe, vol 30. Stuttgart

Bundestagsdrucksachen, see BTDrs.

Bürck H (1984) War die Spruchtätigkeit des Reichsversicherungsamtes, der Versicherungsämter, der Versorgungsgerichte und der Schiedsgerichte nach damaligem und heutigem Rechtsverständnis Rechtsprechung? In: Deutscher Sozialrechtsverband (ed) Entwicklung des Sozialrechts. Aufgabe der Rechtsprechung. Festgabe aus Anlaß des 100-jährigen Bestehens der sozialgerichtlichen Rechtsprechung. Köln, pp 139–170

Campbell D (1994) Foreign investment, labour immobility and the quality of employment. International Labour Review 33:185–204

Carl-Duisberg-Gesellschaft (1960) Entwicklungshilfe – Entwicklungsländer. Ein Verzeichnis von Publikationen in der BRD (Bundesrepublik Deutschland) und Westberlin 1950–1959. Köln

Cäsar P (1968) Die sozialrechtlichen Ansprüche bei Übersiedlung aus der BRD (Bundesrepublik Deutschland) in den anderen Teil Deutschlands. In: Schriftenreihe des Deutschen Sozialrechtsverbandes (until vol 22 (1982) Deutscher Sozialgerichtsverband), vol 4: Das Sozialrecht im geteilten Deutschland. Wiesbaden, pp 157–166

Christmann A, Schönholz S (1984) Die Errichtung des Reichsversicherungsamtes und seine geschichtliche Entwicklung. In: Deutscher Sozialrechtsverband (ed) Entwicklung des Sozialrechts. Aufgabe der Rechtsprechung. Festgabe aus Anlaß des 100-jährigen Bestehens der sozialgerichtlichen Rechtsprechung. Köln, pp 3–46

Clevinghaus B (1973) Recht auf Bildung. Grundlagen und Inhalt. Bremen

Currall J (1997) Zur Sozialpolitik als Aufgabe der Europäischen Gemeinschaft nach dem Vertrag von Maastricht, Art. 119–122. In: von der Groeben H, Thiesing J, Ehlermann C-D (eds) Kommentar zum EU-/EG-Vertrag, 5th edn, vol 1. Baden-Baden

Cyprian R (1984) Schattenwirtschaft, Alternativökonomie. Edited by Institut für Arbeitsmarkt- und Berufsforschung. Nürnberg

Czada R, Schmidt MG (eds) (1993) Verhandlungsdemokratie, Interessenvermittlung, Regierbarkeit. Festschrift für Gerhard Lehmbruch. Opladen

Das Arbeitsrecht der Gegenwart. Jahrbuch für das gesamte Arbeitsrecht und die Arbeitsgerichtsbarkeit. Edited by Müller G, vol 1 (1964) – vol 18 (1981). Edited by Dieterich T, Müller G, vol 19 (1982) – vol 20 (1983). Edited by Dieterich T, Kissel OR, vol 21 (1984) – vol 25 (1988). Edited by Kissel OR, vol 26 (1989) – vol. 31 (1994). Edited by Dieterich T, vol 32 (1995) – vol 36 (1999). Berlin

Das demokratische Prinzip im Grundgesetz (1971) Veröffentlichungen der Vereinigung der Deutschen Staatsrechtslehrer. Issue no. 29, insbesondere das Referat von Martin Kriele. Berlin New York, pp 46–80

Das parlamentarische Regierungssystem und der Bundesrat - Entwicklungsstand und Reformbedarf (1999) Veröffentlichungen der Vereinigung der Deutschen Staatsrechtslehrer. Issue no. 58. Berlin New York

Das Sozialrecht im geteilten Deutschland (1968) In: Schriftenreihe des Deutschen Sozialrechtsverbandes (until vol 22 (1982) Deutscher Sozialgerichtsverband), vol 4. Wiesbaden
Däubler W, Kittner M, Lörcher K (1994) Internationale Arbeits- und Sozialordnung, 2nd edn. Köln
Degenhart C (1983) Anmerkungen zum aktuellen Problemstand. In: Achterberg N, Krawietz W, Wyduckel D (eds) Recht und Staat im sozialen Wandel. Festschrift für Hans Ulrich Scupin. Berlin, pp 537–553
Deich I, Kohte W (eds) (1997) Betriebliche Sozialeinrichtungen. Opladen
Depenheuer O (1997) Das soziale Staatsziel und die Angleichung der Lebensbedingungen in Ost und West. In: Isensee J, Kirchhof P (eds) Handbuch des Staatsrechts, vol 9. Heidelberg, pp 149–258
Der Beruf im Sozialrecht (1969) Schriftenreihe des Deutschen Sozialrechtsverbandes (until vol 22 (1982) Deutscher Sozialgerichtsverband), vol 5. Wiesbaden
Der Gleichheitssatz (1988) Veröffentlichungen der Vereinigung der Deutschen Staatsrechtslehrer. Issue no. 47. Berlin
Der Grundrechtseingriff (1998) Veröffentlichungen der Vereinigung der Deutschen Staatsrechtslehrer. Issue no. 57. Berlin New York
Derlien H-U (1975) Das Berichtswesen der Bundesregierung. Zeitschrift für Parlamentsfragen 6:42–47
Der Wandel familiärer Lebensmuster und das Sozialrecht (1985) Schriftenreihe des Deutschen Sozialrechtsverbandes (until vol 22 (1982) Deutscher Sozialgerichtsverband), vol 27. Wiesbaden
Deufel K (1986) Freie Wohlfahrtspflege. In: Görres-Gesellschaft (ed) Staatslexikon, vol 2, 7th edn. Freiburg im Breisgau Basel Wien, pp 687–694
Deutsche Bundesbank (ed) (1998) Fünfzig Jahre Deutsche Mark: Notenbank und Währung in Deutschland seit 1948. München
Deutsche Rentenversicherung (ed) (1993) Soziale Selbstverwaltung. Issue 10. With contributions by, among others, Lutz Freitag: Soziale Selbstverwaltung – ein Auslaufmodell? Franz Ruland: Funktion und Tradition sozialer Selbstverwaltung am Beispiel der gesetzlichen Rentenversicherung. Frankfurt am Main
Deutsche Stiftung für Entwicklungsländer (ed) (1962) Entwicklungshilfe – Entwicklungsländer. Ein Verzeichnis von Publikationen in der BRD (Bundesrepublik Deutschland) und Westberlin 1960. Berlin
Deutscher Bundestag (ed) (1991) Bericht der gemeinsamen Verfassungskommission. Bundestagsdrucksachen 12/1590, 12/1670
Deutscher Bundestag (ed) (1994/1998) Enquete-Kommission Demographischer Wandel - Herausforderungen einer älter werdenden Gesellschaft an den Einzelnen und die Politik. Erster Zwischenbericht (1994); Zweiter Zwischenbericht (1998). Bonn
Deutscher Bundestag (ed) (1996) Materialien zur Verfassungsdiskussion und zur Grundgesetzänderung in der Folge der deutschen Einigung. Bonn
Deutscher Sozialgerichtsverband (ed) (1979) Sozialrechtsprechung. Verantwortung für den sozialen Rechtsstaat. Festschrift zum 25-jährigen Bestehen des Bundessozialgerichts, vol 1. Köln
Deutscher S, Wannagat G (eds) (1984) Entwicklung des Sozialrechts - Aufgabe der Rechtsprechung. Festgabe zum 100-jährigen Bestehen der sozialgerichtlichen Rechtsprechung. Köln
Deutscher Verein für öffentliche und private Fürsorge (ed) (1997) Forum sozialer Arbeit
Die Finanzierung des Sozialleistungsrechts in der Zukunft (1999) Schriftenreihe des Deutschen Sozialrechtsverbandes (until vol 22 (1982) Deutscher Sozialgerichtsverband), vol 45. Wiesbaden
Die freie Wohlfahrtspflege (1956) Beiträge zu einem Sozialatlas. Köln
Die Neuordnung des Fürsorgerechts als Teil einer Sozialreform: Gesamtbericht über den Deutschen Fürsorgetag 1957 in Essen (1958) Schriften des Deutschen Vereins für öffentliche und private Fürsorge. Köln Berlin

Die soziale Sicherung der Behinderten (1981) Schriftenreihe des Deutschen Sozialrechtsverbandes (until vol 22 (1982) Deutscher Sozialgerichtsverband), vol 21. Wiesbaden

Die sozialrechtliche Stellung der Ausländer in der Bundesrepublik Deutschland (1983) Schriftenreihe des Deutschen Sozialrechtsverbandes (until vol 22 (1982) Deutscher Sozialgerichtsverband), vol 24. Wiesbaden

Die soziale Arbeit in den 90er Jahren (1991) Neue Herausforderungen bei offenen Grenzen. Gesamtbericht über den 72. Deutschen Fürsorgetag 1990 in Hannover. Frankfurt am Main

Die Strukturreform der Krankenversicherung (1988) Schriftenreihe des Deutschen Sozialrechtsverbandes (until vol 22 (1982) Deutscher Sozialgerichtsverband), vol 30. Wiesbaden

Die Umwandlung der Arbeits- und Sozialordnung (1996) With contributions by von Maydell BB et al Edited by Kommission zur Erforschung des sozialen und politischen Wandels in den neuen Bundesländern. Opladen

Die verfassungsrechtliche Relevanz des Sozialrechts (1975) Schriftenreihe des Deutschen Sozialrechtsverbandes (until vol 22 (1982) Deutscher Sozialgerichtsverband), vol 14. Bonn-Bad Godesberg

Dieterich T, Müller G (eds) (1982/1983) Das Arbeitsrecht der Gegenwart. Jahrbuch für das gesamte Arbeitsrecht und die Arbeitsgerichtsbarkeit, vol 19 (1982), vol 20 (1983). Berlin

Docksey C, Séché J-C, Currall J (1997) Zur Sozialpolitik als Aufgabe der Europäischen Gemeinschaft nach dem Vertrag von Maastricht, after Art. 122. In: von der Groeben H, Thiesing J, Ehlermann C-D (eds) Kommentar zum EU-EG-Vertrag, 5th edn, vol 1. Baden-Baden

Dolzer R (1987) Die rechtliche Ordnung des Verhältnisses der Bundesrepublik Deutschland zur Deutschen Demokratischen Republik. In: Isensee J, Kirchhof P (eds) Handbuch des Staatsrechts, vol 1. Heidelberg, pp 547–590

Döring D, Hauser R (eds) (1995) Soziale Sicherheit in Gefahr. Die Zukunft der Sozialpolitik. Frankfurt am Main

Dörrie K (1997) Freie Wohlfahrtspflege. In: Fachlexikon der sozialen Arbeit, 4th edn. Frankfurt am Main, pp 350–353

Drews G (1958) Die Gewerkschaften in der Verwaltungsordnung. Heidelberg

Dürig G (1953) Verfassung und Verwaltung im Wohlfahrtsstaat. Juristenzeitung 8:193–204

Dürig G (1955) Der deutsche Staat im Jahre 1945 und seither. In: Veröffentlichungen der Vereinigung der Deutschen Staatsrechtslehrer. Issue no. 13. Berlin, pp 27–55

Eberstein HH (1971) Handbuch der regionalen Wirtschaftsförderung (Loseblatt). Köln

Eckart K, Paraskewopoulos S (eds) (1997) Der Wirtschaftsstandort Deutschland. Berlin

Ehe und Familie im Sozialversicherungs- und Versorgungsrecht (1967) Schriftenreihe des Deutschen Sozialrechtsverbandes (until vol 22 (1982) Deutscher Sozialgerichtsverband), vol 2. Wiesbaden

Eichenhofer E (1982) Der Mißbrauch sozialer Leistungen. Die Sozialgerichtsbarkeit 29:137–141

Empfiehlt es sich, die Voraussetzungen für Sozialleistungen an leistungsgeminderte Personen zur Herstellung der Nahtlosigkeit neu zu regeln? (1980) Schriftenreihe des Deutschen Sozialrechtsverbandes (until vol 22 Deutscher Sozialgerichtsverband), vol 19. Wiesbaden

Engelhard W (1994) Finanz- und Risikostrukturausgleiche. In: Schulin B (ed) Handbuch der gesetzlichen Krankenversicherung. München, pp 1409–1423

Engelhardt H 1963ff. (1980) Art. 135. In: Zinn GA, Stein E with Barbinski B et al (eds) Verfassung des Landes Hessen. Baden-Baden

Engelhardt WW (1981) Selbstverantwortung, Solidarität, Subsidiarität und andere Sinnstrukturen einer industriellen Gesellschaft. In: Herder-Dorneich P (ed) Dynamische Theorie der Sozialpolitik. Berlin, p. 55–80

Entstehungsgeschichte der Artikel des Grundgesetzes (1951) Edited by von Doemming K-B, Füßlein RW, Matz W. In: Jahrbuch des öffentlichen Rechts der Gegenwart (new edition), vol 1:43 f

Erhard L (1957) Wohlstand für alle. Edited by Langer W. Düsseldorf

Eschenburg T (1983) Jahre der Besatzung 1945–1949. Geschichte der Bundesrepublik Deutschland, vol 1. Stuttgart Wiesbaden

Esping-Andersen G (1990) The three worlds of welfare capitalism. Cambridge
Etzel M (1992) Die Aufhebung von nationalsozialistischen Gesetzen durch den Alliierten Kontrollrat. Tübingen
Eucken W (1948) Die soziale Frage. In: Salin E (ed) Synopsis. Festgabe für Alfred Weber. Basel, Heidelberg, pp 113–131 (See: Hohmann: Grundtexte zur sozialen Marktwirtschaft)
Eucken W (1989) Grundlagen der Nationalökonomie, 9th edn. Berlin (first published 1940)
Europaarchiv (1953) Institut für Europäische Politik und Wirtschaft (ed.). Oberursl 8:5974–5981
Europäisches Sozialrecht (1992) Schriftenreihe des Deutschen Sozialrechtsverbandes (until vol 22 (1982) Deutscher Sozialgerichtsverband), vol 36. Wiesbaden
Evers A, Olk T (eds) (1996) Wohlfahrtspluralismus. Opladen
Fachlexikon der sozialen Arbeit (1980/1983/1993/1997) Published by the Deutscher Verein für öffentliche und private Fürsorge. Four eds. Frankfurt am Main
Fait B (1985) In einer Atmosphäre der Freiheit. Die Rolle der Amerikaner bei der Verfassungsgebung in den Ländern der US-Zone (Amerikanische Besatzungszone) 1946. Vierteljahreshefte für Zeitgeschichte 33:420–455
Fait B (1998) Demokratische Erneuerung unter dem Sternenbanner. Amerikanische Kontrolle und Verfassungsgebung in Bayern 1946. Düsseldorf
Familien und Familienpolitik im geeinten Deutschland – Zukunft des Humanvermögens. Fünfter Familienbericht (1993) of the Familienberichtskommission at the Bundesministerium für Familie und Senioren. Edited by Deutscher Bundestag. Bonn. Bundestagsdrucksache 12/7560
Fechner E (1955) Sozialer Rechtsstaat und Arbeitsrecht. Recht der Arbeit 8:161–168
Ferencz BB (1986) Lohn des Grauens. Die Entschädigung jüdischer Zwangsarbeiter. Frankfurt am Main
Fiedler W (1995) Die deutsche Revolution von 1989. Ursachen, Verlauf, Folgen. In: Isensee J, Kirchhof P (eds) Handbuch des Staatsrechts, vol 8. Heidelberg, pp 3–34
Fischer W (ed) (1989) Währungsreform und soziale Marktwirtschaft. Erfahrungen und Perspektiven nach 40 Jahren. Jahrestagung des Vereins für Socialpolitik in Freiburg im Breisgau 1988. Berlin
Fitting K (1948) Kontrollratsgesetz Nr. 22 und deutsche Betriebsräte-Gesetzgebung. Recht der Arbeit 1:89–92
Forsthoff E (1938) Die Verwaltung als Leistungsträger. Stuttgart Berlin
Forsthoff E (1959) Rechtsfragen der leistenden Verwaltung. Stuttgart
Forsthoff E (ed) (1968) Rechtsstaatlichkeit und Sozialstaatlichkeit. Darmstadt
Franke SF (1993) Steuerpolitik in der Demokratie. Das Beispiel der Bundesrepublik Deutschland. Berlin
Franzmeyer F (1999) Kippt die Globalisierung den Sozialstaat? Aus Politik und Zeitgeschichte B 49:25–31
Frauen und Alterssicherung. Auswirkungen veränderten Erwerbsverhaltens – sozialpolitisches Colloquium Berlin (1988) Die Angestelltenversicherung 35:261–323
Freese C (1995) Die Privatisierungstätigkeit der Treuhandanstalt. Frankfurt am Main
Freiheit und Bindung im Recht der sozialen Sicherheit (1972) Schriftenreihe des Deutschen Sozialrechtsverbandes (until vol 22 (1982) Deutscher Sozialgerichtsverband), vol 9. Wiesbaden
Frerich J, Frey M (1993/1996) Handbuch der Geschichte der Sozialpolitik in Deutschland, 1st edn 1993; 2nd edn 1996, vol 1: Von der vorindustriellen Zeit bis zum Ende des Dritten Reiches, vol 2: Sozialpolitik in der Deutschen Demokratischen Republik, vol 3: Sozialpolitik in der Bundesrepublik Deutschland bis zur Herstellung der Deutschen Einheit. München Wien
Friedrich-Marczyk M (1984) 25 Bände Schriftenreihe des Deutschen Sozialrechtsverbandes 1965 – 1984. In: Schriftenreihe des Deutschen Sozialrechtsverbandes (until vol 22 (1982) Deutscher Sozialgerichtsverband), vol 25. Wiesbaden, pp 170–216
Fromme FK (1990) Die beiden "Kammern" im Widerstreit. In: Wilke D, Schulte B (eds) Der Bundesrat. Darmstadt, pp 381–400

Frowein JA (1995) Die Identität der Bundesrepublik Deutschland als Völkerrechtssubjekt. In: Isensee J, Kirchhof P (eds) Handbuch des Staatsrechts, vol 8. Heidelberg, pp 477–487
Fuchs M (1992) Zivilrecht und Sozialrecht. Recht und Dogmatik materieller Existenzsicherung in der modernen Gesellschaft. München
25 Jahre Sozialgesetzbuch – Anspruch und Wirklichkeit (1995) In: Schriftenreihe des Deutschen Sozialrechtsverbandes (until vol 22 (1982) Deutscher Sozialgerichtsverband), vol 40. Wiesbaden
Fürsorge und Sozialreform (1956) Gesamtbericht des Deutschen Fürsorgetages 1955 in Frankfurt am Main. Köln
Gabriel K, Herlth A, Strohmeier KP (1997) Solidarität unter den Bedingungen entfalteter Modernität. In: Gabriel K, Herlth A, Strohmeier KP (eds) Modernität und Solidarität. Konsequenzen gesellschaftlicher Modernisierung. Für Franz-Xaver Kaufmann. Freiburg im Breisgau Basel Wien pp 13–27
Gäfgen G (ed) (1986) Ökonomie des Gesundheitswesens. Jahrestagung des Vereins für Socialpolitik in Saarbrücken 1985. Berlin
Gaudier M (1993) Pauvretés, inégalités, exclusions: renouveau des approches théoriques et des pratiques sociales. Institut international d'études sociales Genève. Série bibliographique no. 17. Genève
Geck LH (1963) Über das Eindringen des Wortes sozial in die deutsche Sprache. Göttingen
Geißler H (1980) Die neue soziale Frage, 3rd edn. Freiburg im Breisgau
Geißler R (1996) Sozialer Wandel. In: Weidenfeld W, Korte K-R (eds) Handbuch zur deutschen Einheit (Neuausgabe 1996). Frankfurt am Main, pp 611–625
Gerhardt M (1977) Das Koalitionsgesetz. Berlin
Gerstenmaier K-A (1975) Die Sozialstaatsklausel des Grundgesetzes als Prüfungsmaßstab im Normenkontrollverfahren. Justitiabilität und Justitiabilisierung der Sozialstaatsklausel des Grundgesetzes. Berlin
Gesetzesgestaltung und Gesetzesanwendung im Leistungsrecht (1990) In: Veröffentlichungen der Vereinigung der Deutschen Staatsrechtslehrer. Issue no. 48. Berlin New York
Geyer MH (ed) (2008) Bundesrepublik Deutschland 1974–1982. Neue Herausforderungen, wachsende Unsicherheit (Geschichte der Sozialpolitik in Deutschland seit 1945, vol. 6, edited by Bundesministerium für Arbeit und Soziales, Bundesarchiv). Baden-Baden
Giersch H, Borchardt K (eds) (1962) Diagnose und Prognose als wirtschaftswissenschaftliches Methodenproblem. Verhandlungen der Arbeitstagung des Vereins für Socialpolitik in Garmisch-Partenkirchen 1961. Berlin
Gießen K.-H (1976) Die Gewerkschaften im Prozeß der Volks- und Staatswillensbildung. Berlin.
Gilbert N (1994) Sozialpolitik und Familienbeziehungen im Wandel. Internationale Revue für Soziale Sicherheit 47:175–196
Girvetz HK (1968) Welfare state. In: International Encyclopedia of the Social Sciences, vol 16. New York London, pp 512–520
Gitter W (1969) Zweckwidrige Vielfalt und Widersprüche im Recht der Sozialversicherung. In: Schriftenreihe des Deutschen Sozialrechtsverbandes (until vol 22 (1982) Deutscher Sozialgerichtsverband), vol 6. Wiesbaden
Glastetter W, Högemann G, Marquardt R (1991) Die wirtschaftliche Entwicklung in der Bundesrepublik Deutschland 1950 bis 1989. Frankfurt am Main
Glatzer W, Kleinhenz G (eds) (1997) Wohlstand für alle? Opladen
Glatzer W, Noll H-H (eds) (1992) Lebensverhältnisse in Deutschland. Ungleichheit und Angleichung. Frankfurt am Main
Görlitz A, Voigt R (eds) (1992) Rechtsvereinheitlichung. Pfaffenweiler
Goschler C (1992) Wiedergutmachung. Westdeutschland und die Verfolgten des Nationalsozialismus (1945–1954). München
Gössl TMJ (1992) Die Finanzverfassung der Sozialversicherung. München
Grimm D (1987) Solidaritätsprinzip. In: Herzog R et al (eds) Evangelisches Staatslexikon, 3rd edn. Stuttgart, columns 3144–3147
Grimm D (1994) Verbände. In: Benda E, Maihofer W, Vogel H-J (eds) Handbuch des Verfassungsrechts der Bundesrepublik Deutschland, 2nd edn. Berlin New York, pp 657–673

Gros J (1996) Wirtschaft. In: Weidenfeld W, Korte K-R (eds) Handbuch zur deutschen Einheit. Neuausgabe 1996. Frankfurt am Main, pp 740–756

Groser M, Veiders WW (1979) Die neue soziale Frage. Melle

Grosser D (1998) Das Wagnis der Währungs-, Wirtschafts- und Sozialunion. Politische Zwänge im Konflikt mit ökonomischen Regeln. Stuttgart

Grube F, Richter G (eds) (1977) Der SPD-Staat. München

Grundrechte im Leistungsstaat (1972) In: Veröffentlichungen der Vereinigung der Deutschen Staatsrechtslehrer. Issue no. 30. Berlin

Gruner P-H (1990) Die inszenierte Polarisierung. Die Wahlkampfsprache der Parteien in den Bundestagswahlkämpfen 1957 und 1987. Frankfurt am Main

Guderjahn K (1971) Die Frage des sozialen Versicherungsschutzes für selbständige Erwerbstätige. Vom Entstehen der deutschen Sozialversicherung bis zur Gegenwart. Bonn-Bad Godesberg

Haag M (1997) Zur Freizügigkeit der Studenten, Art. 8a. In: von der Groeben H, Thiesing J, Ehlermann C-D (eds) Kommentar zum EU-/EG-Vertrag, 5th edn, vol 1. Baden-Baden

Haberland J (1994/1995) Die Aufnahme und Eingliederung von Spätaussiedlern. In: Nachrichten des Deutschen Vereins für öffentliche und private Fürsorge: (1994), pp 477–448; (1995), pp 38–40, 86–90, 116–120

Häberle P (1993) Die Verfassungsbewegung in den fünf neuen Bundesländern. Jahrbuch des öffentlichen Rechts der Gegenwart 41:69–92

Habermas J (1985) Die Krise des Wohlfahrtsstaates und die Erschöpfung utopischer Energien. In: Habermas J (ed) Die neue Unübersichtlichkeit. Frankfurt am Main, pp 141–163

Haendecke-Hoppe M, Lieser-Triebnigg E (eds) (1990) 40 Jahre innerdeutsche Beziehungen. Berlin

Hamann A (1953) Rechtsstaat und Wirtschaftslenkung. Heidelberg

Hampel G (1955) Die Bedeutung der Sozialpolitik für die Europäische Integration. Kiel

Hanau P (1997) Deregulierung des Arbeitsrechts - Ansatzpunkte und verfassungsrechtliche Grenzen. Berlin, New York

Hanau P (1998) Entwicklungslinien im Arbeitsrecht. Der Betrieb 51:69–79

Hanau P (1999) Das Arbeitsrecht am Ende unserer Generation. In: Hadding W (ed) Festgabe Zivilrechtslehrer 1934/1935. Berlin New York, pp 179–194

Hanesch W (1998) Soziale Sicherung im europäischen Vergleich. Aus Politik und Zeitgeschichte B 34–35:15–26

Hanesch W (1999) Der Sozialstaat in der Globalisierung. Aus Politik und Zeitgeschichte B 49:3–10

Hänlein A (1998) Arbeitsaufnahme von Drittstaatsangehörigen in Deutschland. In: Kaufmann O, Kessler F, von Maydell BB (eds) Arbeits- und Sozialrecht bei grenzüberschreitenden Sachverhalten. Baden-Baden, pp 91–105

Hansmeyer K-H (ed) (1983) Staatsfinanzierung im Wandel. Verhandlungen auf der Jahrestagung des Vereins für Socialpolitik in Köln 1982. Berlin

Harich R (1996) Lebensbedingungen. In: Weidenfeld W, Korte K-R (eds) Handbuch zur deutschen Einheit. New edn. Frankfurt am Main, pp 447–464

Harmssen GW (1951) Am Abend der Demontage. Sechs Jahre Reparationspolitik. Bremen

Hartwich H-H (1970) Sozialstaatspostulat und gesellschaftlicher Status quo. Opladen

Hauser R (ed) (1996a) Sozialpolitik im Vereinten Deutschland, vol 3. Berlin

Hauser R (1996b) Ziele und Möglichkeiten einer sozialen Grundsicherung. Baden-Baden

Hauser R (1999) Die Entwicklung der Einkommensverteilung und der Einkommensarmut in den alten und neuen Bundesländern. Aus Politik und Zeitgeschichte B 18:3–9

Hauser R (ed) (2000) Die Zukunft des Sozialstaats. Jahrestagung des Vereins für Socialpolitik Rostock 1998. Berlin

Hauser R, Cremer-Schäfer H, Nouvertnè U (1981) Armut, Niedrigeinkommen und Unterversorgung in der Bundesrepublik Deutschland. Bestandsaufnahme und sozialpolitische Perspektiven. Frankfurt am Main

Hauser R et al (eds) (1996) Ungleichheit und Sozialpolitik. Opladen

Hautmann G (1984) Die Zusatzversorgung im öffentlichen Dienst und ihre Rechtsverhältnisse. Heidelberg
Haverkade G, Huster S (1999) Europäisches Sozialrecht. Baden-Baden
Heidemeyer H (1994) Flucht und Zuwanderung aus der SBZ (Sowjetische Besatzungszone), DDR (Deutsche Demokratische Republik) 1945/1949 - 1961: Die Flüchtlingspolitik der Bundesrepublik Deutschland bis zum Bau der Berliner Mauer. Beiträge zur Geschichte des Parlamentarismus und der politischen Parteien, vol 100. Düsseldorf
Heiden D (1995) Sozialisierungspolitik in Hessen, 1946–1967: Vom doppelten Scheitern deutscher Traditionssozialisten und amerikanischer Industriereformer. Münster
Heilmann M (1976) Die Umverteilung der Einkommen durch den Staat in der Bundesrepublik Deutschland 1960–1972. Göttingen
Hein M (1990) Die Verbände der Sozialversicherungsträger in der Bundesrepublik Deutschland. München
Heinze RG (ed) (1985) Neue Subsidiarität. Leitidee für eine zukünftige Sozialpolitik. Opladen
Heisig M (1995) Armenpolitik im Nachkriegsdeutschland (1945–1964). Frankfurt am Main
Henke W (1980) Die Sozialisierung des Rechts. Juristenzeitung 35:369–378
Hentschel V (1996) Ludwig Erhard. Ein Politikerleben. München
Herbst L, Goschler C (eds) (1989) Wiedergutmachung in der Bundesrepublik Deutschland. München
Hermann C (1990) Entwicklungslinien der 100-jährigen Geschichte der gesetzlichen Rentenversicherung: Die Zeit von 1957–1991. In: Ruland F (ed) Handbuch der gesetzlichen Rentenversicherung. Festschrift aus Anlaß des 100-jährigen Bestehens der gesetzlichen Rentenversicherung. Commissioned by Vorstand des Verbandes Deutscher Rentenversicherungsträger. Neuwied Frankfurt am Main, pp 105–139, 119–122
Hernekamp K (1979) Soziale Grundrechte. Berlin
Herrmann W (1956) Arbeitgeberverbände. In: von Beckerath E et al (eds) Handwörterbuch der Sozialwissenschaften, vol 1. Stuttgart Tübingen Göttingen, pp 285–291
Herzog R (1987) Subsidiaritätsprinzip. In: Herzog R et al (eds) Evangelisches Staatslexikon, 3rd edn. Stuttgart, columns 3563–3571
Hilbert J (1994) Wirtschaftsstandort und Zukunft des Sozialstaats. Marburg
Hildebrand K (1984) Von Erhard zur Großen Koalition: 1963–1969. Die Geschichte der Bundesrepublik Deutschland, vol 4. Stuttgart Wiesbaden
Hirche K (1961) Das Experiment Volksaktie. Köln
Hirsch F (1977) Social limits to growth. London (Die sozialen Grenzen des Wachstums, 1980). Reinbek bei Hamburg
Hobsbawm E (1994) Age of extremes. The short twentieth century 1914–1991. London
Hockerts HG (1980) Sozialpolitische Entscheidungen im Nachkriegsdeutschland. Alliierte und deutsche Sozialversicherungspolitik 1945–1957. Stuttgart
Hockerts HG (1990) Die Rentenreform 1957. In: Ruland F (ed) Handbuch der gesetzlichen Rentenversicherung. Festschrift aus Anlaß des 100-jährigen Bestehens der gesetzlichen Rentenversicherung. Commissioned by Vorstand des Verbandes Deutscher Rentenversicherungsträger. Neuwied Frankfurt am Main, pp 93–104
Hockerts HG (1996) Die historische Perspektive – Entwicklung und Gestalt des modernen Sozialstaats in Europa. In: Sozialstaat – Idee und Entwicklung; Reformzwänge und Reformziele. With contributions by Hockerts HG et al. Edited by Walter-Raymond-Stiftung, vol 35. Köln, pp 27–48
Hockerts HG (1998) Drei Wege deutscher Sozialstaatlichkeit – Das NS-Regime, die"alte" Bundesrepublik und die DDR (Deutsche Demokratische Republik) in vergleichender Betrachtung. In: Ruland F, von Maydell BB, Papier H-J (eds) Verfassung, Theorie und Praxis des Sozialstaats. Festschrift für Hans F. Zacher zum 70. Geburtstag. Heidelberg, pp 267–279
Hockerts HG (2001) Perodisierung des Gesamtwerks. Abgrenzung der Bände. In: Bundesministerium für Arbeit und Sozialordnung, Bundesarchiv (eds) Geschichte der Sozialpolitik in Deutschland seit 1945, vol 1: Grundlagen der Sozialpolitik. Baden-Baden

Hockerts HG (ed) (2006) Bundesrepublik Deutschland 1966–1974. Eine Zeit vielfältigen Aufbruchs (Geschichte der Sozialpolitik in Deutschland seit 1945, vol. 5, edited by Bundesministerium für Arbeit und Soziales, Bundesarchiv). Baden-Baden

Höffe O, Hollerbach A, Kerber W (1986) Gerechtigkeit. In: Görres-Gesellschaft (ed) Staatslexikon, vol 2, 7th edn. Freiburg im Breisgau Basel Wien, columns 895–906

Hoffmann WG (ed) (1958) Einkommensbildung und Einkommensverteilung. Verhandlungen der Tagung des Vereins für Socialpolitik in Köln 1956. Berlin

Hoffmann WG (ed) (1959) Finanz- und wirtschaftspolitische Bedingungen stetigen Wirtschaftswachstums. Verhandlungen der Tagung des Vereins für Socialpolitik in Baden-Baden 1958. Berlin

Hofmann H (1987) Entwicklung des Grundgesetzes nach 1949. In: Isensee J, Kirchhof P (eds) Handbuch des Staatsrechts, vol 1. Heidelberg, pp 259–319

Hoffmann D, Schwarz M (eds) (2004) commissioned by Institut für Zeitgeschichte, Deutsche Demokratische Republik 1949–1961. Im Zeichen des Aufbaus des Sozialismus (Geschichte der Sozialpolitik in Deutschland seit 1945, vol. 8, edited by Bundesministerium für Gesundheit und Soziale Sicherung, Bundesarchiv). Baden-Baden

Hohmann-Dennhardt C (1988) Soziale Sicherung der Frau im Widerspruch von Familien- und Sozialpolitik. Zeitschrift für Sozialreform 34:673–677

Hoffmann-Nowotny H-J (1988) Gesamtgesellschaftliche Determinanten des Individualisierungsprozesses. Zeitschrift für Sozialreform 34:659–670

Hohmann K et al (eds) (1988) Grundtexte zur sozialen Marktwirtschaft, vol 2. Stuttgart, New York, pp 1–101 (See: Eucken: Die soziale Frage)

Hondrich KO, Koch-Arzberger C (1992) Solidarität in der modernen Gesellschaft. Frankfurt am Main

Hradil S, Schiener J (1999) Soziale Ungleichheit in Deutschland, 7th edn. Opladen

Huber ER (ed) (1949–1951) Quellen zum Staatsrecht der Neuzeit, 2 vols. Tübingen, vol 1: Deutsches Verfassungsrecht im Zeitalter des Konstitutionalismus, 1806–1918 (1949); vol 2: Deutsche Verfassungsdokumente der Gegenwart, 1919–1951 (1951)

Huber ER (1953/1954) Wirtschaftsverwaltungsrecht, vol 1 (1953); vol 2 (1954). Tübingen

Huber ER (1956) Der Streit um das Wirtschaftsverfassungsrecht. Die Öffentliche Verwaltung 8:97–102, 135–143, 172–175, 200–207

Huckemann S (1997) Finanzhilfen im kooperativen Föderalismus. Wiesbaden

Hudemann R (1988) Sozialpolitik im deutschen Südwesten zwischen Tradition und Neuordnung 1945–1953. Mainz

Huster EU (1997) Reichtum in Deutschland, 2nd edn. Frankfurt am Main

Hüttenberger P (1976) Wirtschaftsordnung und Interessenpolitik in der Kartellgesetzgebung der Bundesrepublik 1949–1957. Vierteljahreshefte für Zeitgeschichte 24:287–307

Individualverantwortung und Sozialversicherungsschutz (1997) In: Schriftenreihe des Deutschen Sozialrechtsverbandes (until vol 22 (1982) Deutscher Sozialgerichtsverband), vol 42. Wiesbaden

Informationszentrum Sozialwissenschaften (ed) (1988) Armut in einem reichen Land. Literatur- und Forschungsdokumentation 1984 – 1987. Bonn

International Labour Office (1984/1989) World labour report 1 (1984); 4 (1989). Genf

International Labour Office (1995) Wold employment 1995. Genf

International Labour Office (1996) Wold employment 1996/1997. Genf

International Labour Office (1997) World labour report 1997/1998. Genf

International Labour Organization (1996) International labour coventions and recommendations 1919–1995, vols 1–3. Genf

Internationales Arbeitsamt (ed) (1931) 10 Jahre Internationale Arbeitsorganisation 1919–1929. Genf

Ipsen HP (1966) Diskussionsbeitrag zu "Gesetzgeber und Verwaltung". In: Veröffentlichungen der Vereinigung der Deutschen Staatsrechtslehrer. Issue no. 24. Berlin, pp 221–224

Isensee J (1968) Subsidiaritätsprinzip und Verfassungsrecht. Berlin

Isensee J (1983) Das Grundrecht auf Sicherheit. Zu den Schutzpflichten des freiheitlichen Verfassungsstaates. Berlin

Isensee J (1987) Staat und Verfassung. In: Isensee J, Kichhof P (eds) Handbuch des Staatsrechts, vol 1. Heidelberg, pp 591–661
Isensee J (ed) (1998) Solidarität und Knappheit. Zum Problem der Priorität. Berlin
Issing O (ed) (1981) Zukunftsprobleme der sozialen Marktwirtschaft. Verhandlungen auf der Jahrestagung des Vereins für Socialpolitik, Gesellschaft für Wirtschafts- und Sozialwissenschaften in Nürnberg 1980. Berlin
Jacobmeyer W (1985) Vom Zwangsarbeiter zum heimatlosen Ausländer. Die Displaced Persons in Westdeutschland 1945–1951. Göttingen
Jäger W (1986) Die Innenpolitik der sozialliberalen Koalition 1969–1974. In: Bracher KD, Jäger W, Link W (eds) Die Ära Brandt 1969–1974. Geschichte der Bundesrepublik Deutschland, vol 5/I. Stuttgart, Mannheim, pp 5–162
Jäger W, Link W (1987) Republik im Wandel: 1974–1982. Die Ära Schmidt. Geschichte der Bundesrepublik Deutschland, vol 5/II. Stuttgart, Mannheim
Jahrbuch des Sozialrechts der Gegenwart (1979–1998) vol 1 (1979); vol 2 (1980); vol 3 (1981); vol 4 (1982); vol 12 (1990); vol 13 (1991); vol 20 (1998). Berlin
Jahresberichte der Bundesregierung zum Stand der deutschen Einheit (1997/1998) Bericht 1997 (Bundestagsdrucksache 13/8450); Bericht 1998 (Bundestagsdrucksache 13/10823). Bonn
Jahreswirtschaftsberichte der Bundesregierung (1968/1990) Bundestagsdrucksachen: (1968) V/2511; (1971) VI/1760; (1982) 9/1322; (1990) 11/6278 – (1999) 13/10107. Bonn
Jehle O (1950/1954) Fürsorgerecht. Handkommentar, 1st edn, 1950; 2nd edn, 1954. München
Jochimsen R (1971) Planung im staatlichen Bereich. In: Presse- und Informationsamt der Bundesregierung (ed) Bulletin. Bonn, pp 1236–1244
Jorens Y, Schulte B (eds) (1998) European Social Security Law and Third Country Nationals. Bruxelles
Jostock P (1946) Grundzüge der Soziallehre und der Sozialreform. Freiburg im Breisgau
Jung E (1982) Recht auf Gesundheit. München
Jugend und soziale Sicherheit (1974) Schriftenreihe des Deutschen Sozialrechtsverbandes (until vol 22 (1982) Deutscher Sozialgerichtsverband), vol 11. Bonn-Bad Godesberg
Kaase M (1996) Innere Einheit. In: Weidenfeld W, Korte K-R (eds) Handbuch zur deutschen Einheit. New edition. Frankfurt am Main, pp 385–396
Kahlenberg FP, Hoffmann D (2001) Sozialpolitik als Aufgabe zentraler Verwaltungen in Deutschland – Ein verwaltungsgeschichtlicher Überblick 1945–1990. In: Bundesministerium für Arbeit und Sozialordnung, Bundesarchiv (eds) Geschichte der Sozialpolitik in Deutschland seit 1945, vol 1: Grundlagen der Sozialpolitik. Baden-Baden
Kaiser JH (ed) (1965/1971) Planung, vol 1 (1965); vol 2 (1966); vol 3 (1968); vol 4 (1970); vol 5 (1971). Baden-Baden
Kaiser JH (1987) Verbände. In: Isensee J, Kirchhof P (eds) Handbuch des Staatsrechts, vol 2. Heidelberg, pp 149–170
Kaufmann F-X (1973) Sicherheit als soziologisches und sozialpolitisches Problem, 2nd edn. Stuttgart
Kaufmann F-X (1982) Elemente einer soziologischen Theorie sozialpolitischer Intervention. In: Kaufmann, Franz-Xaver, Staatliche Sozialpolitik und Familie. München, Wien, pp 49–86
Kaufmann F-X (1997a) Schwindet die integrative Funktion des Sozialstaates? Berliner Journal für Soziologie 7:5–19
Kaufmann F-X (1997b) Herausforderungen des Sozialstaates. Frankfurt am Main
Kaufmann F-X (1998) Der Sozialstaat als Prozeß - für eine Sozialpolitik zweiter Ordnung. In: Ruland F, von Maydell BB, Papier H-J (eds) Verfassung, Theorie und Praxis des Sozialstaats. Festschrift für Hans F. Zacher zum 70. Geburtstag. Heidelberg 1998, pp 307–322
Kaufmann F-X (1999) Sozialstaatlichkeit unter den Bedingungen moderner Wirtschaft. In: Korff W et al (eds) Handbuch der Wirtschaftsethik, vol 1. Gütersloh, pp 800–830
Kaufmann F-X (2013) Thinking About Social Policy. In: Leisering L (ed) German Social Policy, vol 1. Berlin Heidelberg

Kaufmann F-X, Külp B (1988) Soziale Sicherheit. In: Görres-Gesellschaft (ed) Staatslexikon, vol 4, 7th edn. Freiburg Basel Wien, columns, 1274–1281
Kempen OE (ed) (1976) Sozialstaatsprinzip und Wirtschaftsordnung. Frankfurt am Main
Kerber W, Westermann C, Spörlein B (1981) Gerechtigkeit. In: Böckle F (ed) Christlicher Glaube in moderner Gesellschaft, 2nd edn, vol 17. Freiburg im Breisgau Basel Wien, pp 5–75
Kesper I (1997) Bundesstaatliche Finanzordnung. Grundlagen, Bestand, Reform. Göttingen
Kilian M (1995) Wiedererstehen und Aufbau der Länder im Gebiet der vormaligen DDR (Deutsche Demokratische Republik). In: Isensee J, Kirchhof P (eds) Handbuch des Staatsrechts, vol 8. Heidelberg, pp 55–100
Kinitz H (1997) Aufbau der Arbeitsverwaltung in den neuen Bundesländern und die Entwicklung des Arbeitsförderungsrechts seit 1989. Opladen
Kirchhof F (1990) Finanzierung der Sozialversicherung. In: Isensee J, Kirchhof P (eds) Handbuch des Staatsrechts, vol 4. Heidelberg, pp 395–423
Kirchhof P (1990) Staatliche Einnahmen. In: Isensee J, Kirchhof P (eds) Handbuch des Staatsrechts, vol 4. Heidelberg, pp 87–233
Kittner M (1984/1989) Art. 20 Abs. 1–3. In: Azzola A et al (eds) Kommentar zum Grundgesetz für die Bundesrepublik Deutschland, 1st edn 1984; 2nd edn 1989. Neuwied Darmstadt
Klanberg F, Prinz A (eds) (1988) Perspektiven sozialer Mindestsicherung. Berlin
Klanfer J (1969) Die soziale Ausschließung. Armut in reichen Ländern. Frankfurt am Main Wien, Zürich
Klein E (1995) Der Status des deutschen Volkszugehörigen und die Minderheiten im Ausland. In: Isensee J, Kirchhof P (eds) Handbuch des Staatsrechts, vol 8. Heidelberg, pp 623–662
Klein F (1987) Ehe und Familie als verfassungsrechtliches Problem. In: Fürst W, Herzog R, Umbach DC (eds) Festschrift für Wolfgang Zeidler. Berlin New York, pp 773–801
Klein HH (1995) Kontinuität des Grundgesetzes und seine Änderung im Zuge der Wiedervereinigung. In: Isensee J, Kirchhof P (eds) Handbuch des Staatsrechts, vol 8. Heidelberg, pp 557–602
Kleinhenz G (1981) Gewerkschaften II: Aufgaben und Organisation. In: Albers W et al (eds) Handwörterbuch der Wirtschaftswissenschaften, vol 3. Stuttgart, pp 659–670
Kleinhenz G (ed) (1991) Sozialpolitik im Vereinten Deutschland, vol 1. Berlin
Kleinhenz G (ed) (1992a) Sozialpolitik im Vereinten Deutschland, vol 2. Berlin
Kleinhenz G (1992b) Tarifpartnerschaft im Vereinten Deutschland. Aus Politik und Zeitgeschichte B 12:14–24
Kleßmann C (1988/1997) Zwei Staaten, eine Nation. Deutsche Geschichte 1955–1970, 1st edn 1988. Göttingen; 2nd edn 1997. Bonn
Kleßmann C (ed) (2006) Deutsche Demokratische Republik 1961–1971. Politische Stabilisierung und wirtschaftliche Mobilisierung. (Geschichte der Sozialpolitik in Deutschland seit 1945, vol. 9, edited by Bundesministerium für Arbeit und Soziales, Bundesarchiv). Baden-Baden
Kleuker M (1993) Gesetzgebungsaufträge des Bundesverfassungsgerichts. Berlin
Köbl U (1979) Allgemeine Rechtstheorie. Aspekte der Gesetzesbindung. In: Deutscher Sozialgerichtsverband (ed) Sozialrechtsprechung. Verantwortung für den sozialen Rechtsstaat. Festschrift zum 25-jährigen Bestehen des Bundessozialgerichts, vol 1. Köln, pp 1005–1094
Kocka J (1995) Vereinigungskrise. Zur Geschichte der Gegenwart. Göttingen
Kögler A (1976) Die Entwicklung von "Randgruppen" in der Bundesrepublik Deutschland – Literaturstudie zur Entwicklung randständiger Bevölkerungsgruppen – Kommission für Wirtschaftlichen und Sozialen Wandel, vol 87. Göttingen
Köhler PA (1988) Sozialpolitische und sozialrechtliche Aktivitäten in den Vereinten Nationen. Baden-Baden
Köhler PA, Zacher HF (eds) (1981) Ein Jahrhundert Sozialversicherung in der Bundesrepublik Deutschland, Frankreich, Großbritannien, Österreich und der Schweiz. Berlin
Köhler PA, Zacher HF (eds) (1983) Beiträge zur Geschichte und aktuellen Situation der Sozialversicherung. Berlin
Kommission Alternative Steuer-Transfer-Systeme (1996) Gutachten Probleme einer Integration von Einkommensbesteuerung und steuerfinanzierten Sozialleistungen. Bonn

Kommission für die Finanzreform (1966) Gutachten über die Finanzreform in der Bundesrepublik Deutschland. Stuttgart

Kommission für Zukunftsfragen der Freistaaten Bayern und Sachsen (1996/1997) Erwerbstätigkeit und Arbeitslosigkeit in Deutschland. Entwicklung, Ursachen und Maßnahmen. Part I (1996), Parts II and III and Leitsätze, Zusammenfassung und Schlußfolgerungen (1997). Bonn

Kommission zur Erforschung des sozialen und politischen Wandels in den neuen Bundesländern (ed) (1996) Die Umwandlung der Arbeits- und Sozialordnung. With contributions by von Maydell BB et al. Opladen

Kommission zur Erstellug eines Arbeitsgesetzbuches (1970). Arbeit und Recht 10:371

König T (1999) Regieren im deutschen Föderalismus. Aus Politik und Zeitgeschichte B 13:24–36

Königseder A, Wetzel J (1994) Lebensmut im Wartesaal: Die jüdischen DPs (displaced persons) im Nachkriegsdeutschland. Frankfurt am Main

Konzen H, Scholz R (1980) Die begrenzte Aussperrung. Zur neueren Aussperrungsjudikatur des Bundesarbeitsgerichts. Der Betrieb 33:1593–1600

Korff W et al (eds) (1999) Handbuch der Wirtschaftsethik, vol 1. Gütersloh

Kort-Krieger U (1994) Wechselwähler. Verdrossene Parteien - routinierte Demokraten. Pfaffenweiler

Kortmann K (1976) Zur Armutsdiskussion in der Bundesrepublik Deutschland. Nachrichtendienst des Vereins für öffentliche und private Fürsorge 56:144–149

Kostorz P (1998) Versicherungsfremde Leistungen in der gesetzlichen Krankenversicherung. Frankfurt am Main

Kraft D (1986) Alternative soziale Dienstleistungsprojekte. In: Fachlexikon der sozialen Arbeit, 2nd edn. Frankfurt am Main, p 26f

Krasney O-E (1998) Die sogenannte unechte gesetzliche Unfallversicherung. Ein Beispiel für Theorie und Praxis des Sozialstaates. In: Ruland F, von Maydell BB, Papier H.-J. (eds) Verfassung, Theorie und Praxis des Sozialstaats. Festschrift für Hans F. Zacher zum 70. Geburtstag. Heidelberg, pp 407–439

Krause P (1980) Fremdlasten der Sozialversicherung. Vierteljahresschrift für Sozialrecht 8:115–153

Krause P (1981) Rechtsprobleme einer Konkretisierung von Dienst- und Sachleistungen. In: Gitter W, Thieme W, Zacher HF (eds) Im Dienst des Sozialrechts. Festschrift für Georg Wannagat. Köln, pp 239–255

Krause P (1982) Landesbericht Bundesrepublik Deutschland. In: Zacher HF, Bullinger M, Igl G (eds) Soziale Sicherung im öffentlichen Dienst in der Bundesrepublik Deutschland, den Niederlanden, Schweden, Belgien und den Europäischen Gemeinschaften. Berlin, pp 17–116

Krohn C-D (ed) (1997) Rückkehr und Aufbau nach 1945. Deutsche Remigranten im öffentlichen Leben Nachkriegsdeutschlands. Marburg

Krüger H (1951) Staatsverfassung und Wirtschaftsverfassung. Deutsches Verwaltungsblatt 65:361–368

Krüger H (1958) Sozialisierung. In: Bettermann KA, Nipperdey HC, Scheuner U (eds) Die Grundrechte, vol 3/1. Berlin, pp 267–324

Krüger H (1960) Uneheliche Kinder. In: Bettermann KA, Nipperdey HC, Scheuner U (eds) Die Grundrechte, vol 4/1. Berlin, pp 325–367

Krüper M (1975) Wirtschaftsplanung und Investitionslenkung. Aus Politik und Zeitgeschichte B 31:21–43

Kübler F (ed) (1984) Verrechtlichung von Wirtschaft, Arbeit und sozialer Solidarität. Baden-Baden

Kübler F, Schmidt W, Simitis S (1978) Mitbestimmung als gesetzgebungspolitische Aufgabe. Baden-Baden

Külp B (1989) Sozialpartner. In: Staatslexikon, vol 5, 7th edn. Freiburg im Breisgau Basel Wien, columns 30–33

Külp B, Haas H-D (eds) (1977) Soziale Probleme der modernen Industriegesellschaft. Verhandlungen des Vereins für Socialpolitik in Augsburg 1976. Berlin
Lampert H (1992) Freiheit als Ziel der Gesellschafts- und der Wirtschaftspolitik in der Bundesrepublik Deutschland. In: Lampert H (ed) Freiheit als zentraler Grundwert demokratischer Gesellschaften. St. Ottilien, pp 19–48
Lampert H (1997) Krise und Reform des Sozialstaats. Frankfurt am Main
Lampert H (1998) Lehrbuch der Sozialpolitik, 5th edn. Berlin
Landenberger M (1987) Flexible Arbeitszeitformen im Spannungsfeld von ökonomischer Liberalisierung und sozialem Schutzbedarf. Aus Politik und Zeitgeschichte B 21:15–29
Larenz K, Canaris C-W (1995) Methodenlehre der Rechtswissenschaft, 3rd edn. Berlin
Lehner M (1993) Einkommenssteuerrecht und Sozialhilferecht. Tübingen
Lehner M (1998) Der Familienlastenausgleich nach dem Jahressteuergesetz 1996. In: Ruland F, von Maydell BB, Papier H-J (eds) Verfassung, Theorie und Praxis des Sozialstaats. Festschrift für Hans F. Zacher zum 70. Geburtstag. Heidelberg, pp 511–524
Leibfried S, Pierson P (eds) (1998) Standort Europa. Europäische Sozialpolitik. Frankfurt am Main
Leibfried S, Tennstedt F (eds) (1985) Politik der Armut und die Spaltung des Sozialstaates. Frankfurt am Main
Leisering L (1995) Grenzen des Sozialversicherungsstaates? Zeitschrift für Sozialrefom 41:860–880
Leisering L (2004) Desillusionierungen des modernen Fortschrittsglaubens. "Soziale Exklusion" als gesellschaftliche Selbstbeschreibung und soziologisches Konzept. In: Schwinn T (ed) Differenzierung und soziale Ungleichheit. Die Soziologen und ihre Verknüpfung. Frankfurt am Main, pp 238–268
Leisering L (ed) (2013) German Social Policy, vols 1–5. Berlin Heidelberg
Lerche P (1963) Verfassungsfragen um Sozialhilfe und Jugendwohlfahrt. Berlin
Lerche P (1964) Föderalismus als nationales und internationales Ordnungsprinzip. In: Veröffentlichungen der Vereinigung der Deutschen Staatsrechtslehrer. Issue no. 21. Berlin, pp 66–104
Lessenich S (1998) "Relations matter". De-Kommodifizierung als Verteilungsproblem. In: Lessenich S, Ostner I (eds) Welten des Wohlfahrtskapitalismus. Der Sozialstaat in vergleichender Perspektive. Frankfurt am Main, pp 91–108
Liefmann-Keil E (1961) Ökonomische Theorie der Sozialpolitik. Berlin Göttingen Heidelberg
Lindlar L (1997) Das mißverstandene Wirtschaftswunder. Tübingen
Littmann K (1983) Besteuerung von Alterseinkommen. Sachverständigenkommission Alterssicherungssysteme: Vergleich der Alterssicherungssysteme und Empfehlungen der Kommission. Gutachten der Sachverständigenkommission 2:425–518
Lohkamp-Himmighofen M (1994) Vereinbarkeit von Familie und Beruf: Die Situation in den 12 Ländern der EG (Europäische Gemeinschaft). Aus Politik und Zeitgeschichte B 7–8:3–13
Lörcher K (1991) Die Normen der Internationalen Arbeitsorganisation und des Europarats - ihre Bedeutung für das Arbeitsrecht der Bundesrepublik. Arbeit und Recht 49:97–104
Lörcher K (1994) Die Normen der Internationalen Arbeitsorganisation und das Arbeitsrecht der Bundesrepublik. Recht der Arbeit 47:284–293
Löwisch M (1975) Der Einfluß der Gewerkschaften auf Wirtschaft, Gesellschaft und Staat. Recht der Arbeit 28:53–58
Löwisch M (1999) Arbeitsrecht und wirtschaftlicher Wandel. Recht der Arbeit 52:69–80
Luchterhand O (1995) Der Aufbau des parlamentarischen Regierungssystems der DDR (Deutsche Demokratische Republik). In: Isensee J, Kirchhof P (eds) Handbuch des Staatsrechts, vol 8. Heidelberg, pp 35–54
Lücke J (1982) Soziale Grundrechte als Staatszielbestimmungen und Gesetzgebungsaufträge. Archiv des öffentlichen Rechts 107:15–60
Luhmann N (1981) Politische Theorie im Wohlfahrtsstaat. München Wien
Luhmann N (1995) Inklusion und Exklusion. In: Luhmann N. (ed) Soziologische Aufklärung 6. Die Soziologie und der Mensch. Opladen, pp 237–264

Lutz B (1987) Technik und sozialer Wandel. Verhandlungen des 23. Deutschen Soziologentages in Hamburg 1986. Commissioned by Deutsche Gesellschaft für Soziologie. Frankfurt am Main New York

Maier H (1980) Die ältere deutsche Staats- und Verwaltungslehre, 2nd edn. München

Maihofer W (1994) Prinzipien freiheitlicher Demokratie. In: Benda E, Maihofer W, Vogel H-J (eds) Handbuch des Verfassungsrechts der Bundesrepublik Deutschland, 2nd edn. Berlin New York, pp 427–536

Majer D (1993) Fremdvölkische im Dritten Reich. Boppard am Rhein

Matthes J (ed) (1983) Krise der Arbeitsgesellschaft. Verhandlungen des 21. Deutschen Soziologentages 1982. Frankfurt am Main

Mau S (1997) Ungleichheits- und Gerechtigkeitsorientierungen in modernen Wohlfahrtsstaaten. Ein Vergleich der Länder Schweden, Großbritannien und Bundesrepublik Deutschland. Arbeitspapier. Wissenschaftszentrum Berlin für Sozialforschung, Abteilung Sozialstruktur und Sozialberichterstattung. Berlin, pp 97–401

Mau S (1998) Zwischen Moralität und Eigeninteresse. Einstellungen zum Wohlfahrtsstaat in internationaler Perspektive. Aus Politik und Zeitgeschichte B 34–35:27–37

Maunz T, Schraft H (eds) (1963/1968) Die Sozialversicherung der Gegenwart. Jahrbuch für die gesamte Sozialversicherung und Sozialgerichtsbarkeit, vol 1/2 (1963), vol 6 (1967), vol 7 (1968). Berlin

Maunz T, Schraft H et al (eds) (1969/1973) Die Sozialordnung der Gegenwart. Jahrbuch und Nachschlagewerk für Wissenschaft und Praxis der gesamten Sozialversicherung, Sozialgerichtsbarkeit, Bundesarbeitsverwaltung, Versorgung, Sozialhilfe, vol 8 (1969), vol 12 (1973). Berlin

Mayer OG (1997) Globalisierung und wohlfahrtsstaatliche Aufgaben. Aus Politik und Zeitgeschichte B 33–34:29–38

Mayntz R (1997) Soziale Dynamik und politische Steuerung. Frankfurt am Main

Mayntz R, Scharpf FW (eds) (1995) Gesellschaftliche Selbstregulierung und politische Steuerung. Frankfurt am Main

Meadows DL (ed) (1972) The limits to growth. New York

Meusel E-J (1999) Außeruniversitäre Forschung im Wissenschaftsrecht, 2nd edn. Köln

Midgley J (1997) Social welfare in global context. Thousand Oaks

Miegel M (1983) Die verkannte Revolution. (1) Einkommen und Vermögen der privaten Haushalte. Bonn-Bad Godesberg

Miegel M, Wahl S (1985) Solidarische Grundsicherung - Private Vorsorge. Der Weg aus der Rentenkrise. Stuttgart

Mielke S, Rütters P (eds) (1987) Organisatorischer Aufbau der Gewerkschaften (1945–1949). Köln

Mintzel A, von Nell-Breuning O (1986) Gewerkschaften. In: Görres-Gesellschaft (ed) Staatslexikon, vol 2, 7th edn. Freiburg Basel Wien, columns 1035–1050

Modernisierung - Gewerkschaften zwischen Marginalisierung und Zukunftsfähigkeit (1992) Gemeinsame Veranstaltung der Hans-Böckler-Stiftung und des DGB-Bildungswerkes. Hattinger Forum. Düsseldorf 1992

Moeller ML (1980/1986) Selbsthilfegruppen. In: Fachlexikon der sozialen Arbeit, 1st edn, 1980, p 655f; 2nd edn 1986, p 732f. Frankfurt am Main

Möglichkeiten und Grenzen der Vereinfachung und Vereinheitlichung des Sozialversicherungsrechts (1970) Schriftenreihe des Deutschen Sozialrechtsverbandes (until vol 22 (1982) Deutscher Sozialgerichtsverband), vol 7. Wiesbaden

Molitor B (1980) Vermögen II: Vermögenspolitik. In: Albers W et al (eds) Handwörterbuch der Wirtschaftswissenschaften, vol 8. Stuttgart, pp 282–299

Molitor B (1984) Der Sozialstaat auf dem Prüfstand. Baden-Baden

Mommsen W (ed.) (1982) Deutsche Parteiprogramme, 3rd edn. München

Mooser J (1984) Arbeiterleben in Deutschland 1900–1970. Klassenlagen, Kultur und Politik. Frankfurt am Main

Mrotzek H (1997) Organisation und Aufbau der Krankenversicherung in der DDR (Deutsche Demokratische Republik) im Prozeß der Schaffung der deutschen Einheit. In: Mrotzek H, Püschel H (eds) Krankenversicherung und Alterssicherung. Opladen

Mückenberger U (1985) Die Krise des Normalarbeitsverhältnisses. Zeitschrift für Sozialreform 31:415–434, 457–475

Mückenberger U (1990) Normalarbeitsverhältnis: Lohnarbeit als normativer Horizont sozialer Sicherheit. In: Sachße C, Engelhardt HT (eds) Sicherheit und Freiheit. Zur Ethik des Wohlfahrtsstaates. Frankfurt am Main, pp 158–179

Müller G (ed) (1964–1981) Das Arbeitsrecht der Gegenwart. Jahrbuch für das gesamte Arbeitsrecht und die Arbeitsgerichtsbarkeit, vol 1 (1964)–vol 18 (1981). Berlin

Müller K (1979) Das Recht der ehrenamtlichen Richter. In: Deutscher Sozialgerichtsverband (ed) Sozialrechtsprechung. Verantwortung für den sozialen Rechtsstaat. Festschrift zum 25-jährigen Bestehen des Bundessozialgerichts, vol 1. Köln, pp 879–910

Müller U (1990) Fremde in der Nachkriegszeit. Displaced Persons - zwangsverschleppte Personen in Stuttgart und Württemberg-Baden 1945–1951. Stuttgart

Müller-Armack A (1956) Soziale Marktwirtschaft. In: von Beckerath E et al (eds) Handwörterbuch der Sozialwissenschaften, vol 9. Stuttgart Tübingen Göttingen, pp 390–392

Müller-Armack A (1974) Genealogie der sozialen Marktwirtschaft. Frühschriften und weiterführende Konzepte. Bern Stuttgart

Müller-Volbehr J (1984) Der soziale Rechtsstaat im System des Grundgesetzes. Juristenzeitung 39:6–14

Münch U (1997) Sozialpolitik und Föderalismus. Zur Dynamik der Aufgabenverteilung im sozialen Bundesstaat. Opladen

Murswiek D (1989) Grundrechte als Teilhaberechte sozialer Grundrechte. In: Isensee J, Kirchhof P (eds) Handbuch des Staatsrechts, vol 5. Heidelberg, pp 243–289

Münz R, Seifert W, Ulrich R (1997) Zuwanderung nach Deutschland. Strukturen, Wirkungen, Perspektiven. Frankfurt am Main

Muscheid J (1986) Die Steuerpolitik in der Bundesrepublik Deutschland 1949 – 1982. Berlin

Mußgnug R (1987) Zustandekommen des Grundgesetzes und Entstehen der Bundesrepublik Deutschland. In: Isensee J, Kirchhof P (eds) Handbuch des Staatsrechts, vol 1. Heidelberg, pp 219–258

Muszynski B (1975) Wirtschaftliche Mitbestimmung zwischen Konflikt- und Harmoniekonzeptionen, theoretische Voraussetzungen, geschichtliche Grundlagen und Hauptprobleme der Mitbestimmungsdiskussion in der Bundesrepublik Deutschland. Meisenheim

Narr W-D, Offe C (eds) (1975) Wohlfahrtsstaat und Massenloyalität. Köln

Neue Industriepolitik im gesellschaftlichen Konsens? Zur Rolle der Gewerkschaften im Umstrukturierungsprozeß von Branchen und Regionen (1995) Dokumentation eines Symposiums der Industriegewerkschaft Metall Bayern, des IMU-Instituts, des Instituts für Sozialwissenschaftliche Forschung und der Hans-Böckler-Stiftung am 19. und 20. Mai 1994 in München. München Düsseldorf

Neumann F (1976) Daten zu Wirtschaft – Gesellschaft – Politik – Kultur der Bundesrepublik Deutschland 1950–1975. Baden-Baden

Neumann M (ed) (1984) Ansprüche, Eigentums- und Verfügungsrechte. Arbeitstagung des Vereins für Socialpolitik in Basel 1983. Berlin

Neumann MJM (1998) Geldwertstabilität: Bedrohung und Bewährung. In: Deutsche B (ed) Fünfzig Jahre Deutsche Mark: Notenbank und Währung in Deutschland seit 1948. München, pp 309–346

Neumann U (1999) Verdeckte Armut in der Bundesrepublik Deutschland. Begriff und empirische Ergebnisse für die Jahre 1983 bis 1995. Aus Politik und Zeitgeschichte B 18:27–32

Neundörfer L (1969) Notstände, die von der Sozialgesetzgebung nicht gedeckt werden. In: Blind A (ed) Sozialpolitik und persönliche Existenz. Festschrift für Hans Achinger. Berlin, pp 201–214

Neuner J (1999) Privatrecht und Sozialstaat. München

Niclauß K (1974) Der parlamentarische Rat und das Sozialstaatspostulat. Politische Vierteljahrsschrift 15:32–52

Nipperdey HC (1949) Das Tarifvertragsgesetz des Vereinigten Wirtschaftsgebietes. Recht der Arbeit 2:81–89

Nipperdey HC (1954) Die soziale Marktwirtschaft in der Verfassung der Bundesrepublik. Heidelberg

Nullmeier F, Rüb FW (1993) Die Transformation der Sozialpolitik. Vom Sozialstaat zum Sicherungsstaat. Frankfurt am Main New York

Obermayer K (1979) Der Sozialstaat als Herausforderung zur Menschlichkeit. Recht der Arbeit 32:8–16

OECD (1997) Social cohesion and the globalising economy: what does the future hold? Paris

Offe C (1984a) Arbeit als soziologische Schlüsselkategorie. In: Offe C. (ed) Arbeitsgesellschaft. Strukturprobleme und Zukunftsperspektiven. Frankfurt am Main, pp 13–43

Offe C (1984b) Arbeitsgesellschaft. Strukturprobleme und Zukunftsperspektiven. Frankfurt am Main

Öhlschläger R, Brüll H-M (eds) (1996) Unternehmen Barmherzigkeit. Identität und Wandel sozialer Dienstleistung. Baden-Baden

Opielka M, Ostner I (eds) (1987) Umbau des Sozialstaats. Essen

Opielka M, Vobruba G (eds) (1986) Das garantierte Grundeinkommen. Entwicklung und Perspektiven einer Forderung. Frankfurt am Main

Oppenländer K (ed) (1997) Wiedervereinigung nach sechs Jahren. Berlin München

Oppermann T (2000) Europarecht, 2nd edn. München

Orthbandt E (1980) Der Deutsche Verein in der Geschichte der deutschen Fürsorge 1880–1980. Frankfurt am Main

Ortmann F (1997) Der Sozialstaat in der Globalisierungsfalle. Zeitschrift für Sozialreform 43:585–596

Papier H-J (1996) Der Einfluß des Verfassungsrechts auf das Sozialrecht. In: von Maydell BB, Ruland F (eds) Sozialrechtshandbuch, 2nd edn. Neuwied Kriftel Berlin, pp 73–124

Pawlita C (1992) Wiedergutmachung als Rechtsfrage? Die politische und juristische Auseinandersetzung um Entschädigung für die Opfer nationalsozialistischer Verfolgung (1945–1990). Frankfurt am Main

Perrin G (1983) Die Ursprünge des internationalen Rechts der sozialen Sicherheit. München

Pestalozza C (1995) Einführung. In: Verfassungen der deutschen Bundesländer, 6th edn. München, pp XI–LXXVII

Peters H (1978) Die Geschichte der sozialen Versicherung, 3rd edn. Sankt Augustin

Pfaff M (ed) (1983) Effizienz und Effektivität staatlicher Transferpolitik in der Wirtschaftskrise. Vorträge bei der internationalen wissenschaftlichen Tagung der Deutschen Forschungsgemeinschaft vom 14. - 16. Juli 1980 in Augsburg Berlin

Pfetsch FR (1990) Ursprünge der zweiten Republik. Prozesse der Verfassungsgebung in den Westzonen und in der Bundesrepublik. Opladen

Piepenbrock R (1964) Der Gedanke eines Wirtschaftsrechts in der neuzeitlichen Literatur bis zum Ersten Weltkrieg. Köln

Pietzker J (1984) Recht auf Arbeit. Bonn

Pitschas R (1996a) Kommunale Sozialpolitik. In: von Maydell BB, Ruland F (eds) Sozialrechtshandbuch, 2nd edn. Neuwied Kriftel Berlin, pp 1257–1305

Pitschas R (1996b) Verrechtlichung von Sozialleistungen im wohlfahrtsdistanzierten Sozialstaat. In: Leistungsrealisierung und Leistungsstörung im Sozialrecht. In: Schriftenreihe des Deutschen Sozialrechtsverbandes (until vol 22 (1982) Deutscher Sozialgerichtsverband), vol 41. Wiesbaden, pp 7–40

Pitschas R (1998) Der "neue" soziale Rechtsstaat. Vom Wandel der Arbeits- und Sozialverfassung des Grundgesetzes. In: Ruland F, von Maydell BB, Papier H-J (eds) Verfassung, Theorie und Praxis des Sozialstaats, Festschrift für Hans F. Zacher zum 70. Geburtstag. Heidelberg, pp 755–775

Plumpe W (1987) Vom Plan zum Markt. Wirtschaftsverwaltung und Unternehmensverbände in der britischen Zone. Düsseldorf
Polligkeit W (ed) (1950) Fürsorge im Dienst der wirtschaftlichen und sozialen Sicherung der Bevölkerung. Verhandlungen und Ergebnisse des Deutschen Fürsorgetages 1949 in Bielefeld. München
Popp K (1975) Öffentliche Aufgaben der Gewerkschaften und innerverbandliche Willensbildung. Berlin
Preller L (1946/1947) Sozialpolitik. Kernfrage des Aufbaus, 1st edn 1946; 2nd edn 1947. Stuttgart
Preller L (1976) Sozialpolitik. Theoretische Ordnung, 2nd edn. Tübingen Zürich
Presse- und Informationsamt der Bundesregierung (ed) (1974/1987) Jahresberichte der Bundesregierung 1974; 1981; 1983; 1987. Bonn
Presse- und Informationsamt der Bundesregierung (ed) (1985) Erinnerung, Trauer und Versöhnung. Ansprachen und Erklärungen zum vierzigsten Jahrestag des Kriegsendes. Bonn
Probleme einer Integration von Einkommensbesteuerung und steuerfinanzierten Sozialleistungen (1996) Gutachten der Experten-Kommission "Alternative Steuer-Transfer-Systeme". Bonn
Pünder T (1966) Das bizonale Interregnum. Die Geschichte des Vereinigten Wirtschaftsgebietes 1946–1949. Waiblingen
Püttner G (1987) Der öffentliche Dienst. In: Jeserich KGA (ed) Deutsche Verwaltungsgeschichte, vol 5. Die Bundesrepublik Deutschland. Stuttgart, pp 1124–1142
Quaritsch H (1995) Wiedervereinigung und Selbstbestimmung – Recht, Realität, Legitimation. In: Isensee J, Kirchhof P (eds) Handbuch des Staatsrechts, vol 8. Heidelberg, pp 321–401
Ramm T (1972) Arbeitsgesetzbuch und politische Entscheidungen. Zeitschrift für Rechtspolitik 5:13–19
Ramsauer U, Stallbaum M (1988) Bundesausbildungsförderungsgesetz, 2nd edn. München
Raschke U (1996) Internationalrechtliche Grundlagen der gesetzlichen Unfallversicherung. In: Schulin B (ed) Handbuch des Sozialversicherungsrechts, vol 2. Unfallversicherungsrecht. München, pp 1397–1457
Rauschenbach T, Sachße C, Olk T (eds) (1996) Von der Wertgemeinschaft zum Dienstleistungsunternehmen, 2nd edn. Frankfurt am Main
Rauscher A (1988) Solidarität. In: Görres-Gesellschaft (ed) Staatslexikon, 7th edn, vol 4. Freiburg im Breisgau Basel Wien
Rauscher A, Hollerbach A (1989) Subsidiarität. In: Görres-Gesellschaft (ed) Staatslexikon, vol 7, 7th edn. Freiburg im Breisgau Basel Wien, columns 386–390
Rechtsfortbildung durch die sozialgerichtliche Rechtsprechung (1972) In: Schriftenreihe des Deutschen Sozialrechtsverbandes (until vol 22 (1982) Deutscher Sozialgerichtsverband), vol 10. Wiesbaden
Reifner U, Laatz W (1989) Überschuldungssituation und Schuldnerberatung in der Bundesrepublik Deutschland – Ein Problemaufriß. Zeitschrift für Sozialreform 35:213–235
Renner G (1998) Ausländerrecht in Deutschland. München
Ress G (1987) Grundlagen und Entwicklung der innerdeutschen Beziehungen. In: Isensee J, Kirchhof P (eds) Handbuch des Staatsrechts, vol 1. Heidelberg, pp 449–546
Reusch HH (1984) Alterssicherungssysteme und Versorgungswerke der Rechtsanwaltschaft. Mitteilungen der Bundesrechtsanwaltskammer 15:98–102
Reutter W (1991) Korporatismustheorien. Kritik, Vergleich, Perspektiven. Frankfurt am Main
Richardi R (1992) Rechtsquellen und arbeitsrechtliche Verwaltungen. In: Richardi R, Wlotzke O (eds) Münchener Handbuch zum Arbeitsrecht, vol 1: Individualrecht I. München, pp 55–183
Richter M (1955–1970) Die Sozialreform. Dokumente und Stellungnahmen. Bonn-Bad Godesberg
Ridder H (1975) Die soziale Ordnung des Grundgesetzes. Opladen
Riedel B, Strümpel C (1996) Neue Reformen ehrenamtlicher Tätigkeit: Internationale Entwicklungen. Eurosozial 59:11–35
Riedmüller B (1994) Grenzen des Sozialversicherungsstaates. Opladen
Rieger E (1992) Die Institutionalisierung des Wohlfahrtsstaates. Opladen

Rieger E, Leibfried S (1995) Globalisation and the western welfare state. An annoted Bibliography. Center for Social Policy Research (Zentrum für Sozialpolitik (ZeS), Universität Bremen. ZeS-Arbeitspapier no. 1/1995. Bremen
Rifkin J (1995) The end of work. New York
Ritter GA (1991) Der Sozialstaat. Entstehung und Entwicklung im internationalen Vergleich, 2nd edn. München
Ritter GA (1996) Probleme und Tendenzen des Sozialstaats in den 1990er Jahren. Geschichte und Gesellschaft 22:393–408
Ritter GA (1998a) Soziale Frage und Sozialpolitik in Deutschland seit Beginn des 19. Jahrhunderts. Opladen
Ritter GA (1998b) Über Deutschland. Die Bundesrepublik in der deutschen Geschichte. München
Ritter GA (ed) (2007) Bundesrepublik Deutschland 1989–1994. Sozialpolitik im Zeichen der Vereinigung (Geschichte der Sozialpolitik in Deutschland seit 1945, vol. 11, edited by Bundesministerium für Arbeit und Soziales, Bundesarchiv). Baden-Baden
Ritter GA (2013) The Politics of German Unification. Social, Economic, Financial, Constitutional and International Iusses. In: Leisering L (ed) German Social Policy, vol 4. Berlin Heidelberg
Ritter GA, Niehuss M (1991) Wahlen in Deutschland 1946–1991. München
Ritter GA, Niehuss M (1995) Wahlen in Deutschland 1990–1994. München
Robbers G (1987) Sicherheit als Menschenrecht. Baden-Baden
Rodgers G, Gore C, Figueiredo JB (eds) (1995) Social exclusion: rhetoric, reality, responses. International Institute for Labour Studies. United Nations Development Programme. Geneva
Rohde H, Humanisierung der Arbeitswelt (1974) In: Christmann A, Hesselbach W, Jahn M, Mommsen EW (eds) Sozialpolitik. Ziele und Wege. Köln, pp 101–120
Rohrbeck W, Roehrbein E, Meyrich C (1955) Zum Problem der Realisierbarkeit der Vorschläge der Rothenfelser Denkschrift über "Die Neuordnung der sozialen Leistungen". Kritische Stellungnahme. Berlin
Ruck M, Boldorf M (eds) (2007) Bundesrepublik Deutschland 1957–1966. Sozialpolitik im Zeichen des erreichten Wohlstandes (Geschichte der Sozialpolitik in Deutschland seit 1945, vol. 4, edited by Bundesministerium für Arbeit und Soziales, Bundesarchiv). Baden-Baden
Rudolf W (1990) Kooperation im Bundesstaat. In: Isensee J, Kirchhof P (eds) Handbuch des Staatsrechts, vol 4. Heidelberg, pp 1091–1132
Rudzio W (1978) Die ausgebliebene Sozialisierung an Rhein und Ruhr. Archiv für Sozialgeschichte 18:1–39
Rüfner W (1974) Das Sozialrecht in der Rechtsprechung des Bundesverfassungsgerichts. Vierteljahresschrift für Sozialrecht 2:68–93
Rüfner W (1979–1998) Das Sozialrecht in der Rechtsprechung des Bundesverfassungsgerichts. In: Jahrbuch des Sozialrechts der Gegenwart, vol 1 (1979): 59–72; vol 20 (1998): 33–44
Rüfner W (1988) Daseinsvorsorge und soziale Sicherheit. In: Isensee J, Kirchhof P (eds) Handbuch des Staatsrechts, vol 3. Heidelberg, pp 1037–1085
Ruhrmann U (1994) Reformen zum Recht des Aussiedlerzuzugs. Berlin
Ruland F (1983) Möglichkeiten und Grenzen einer Annäherung der Beamtenversorgung an die gesetzliche Rentenversicherung - zu den verfassungsrechtlichen Vorgaben der Versorgung der Beamten. In: Sachverständigenkommission Alterssicherungssysteme: Anlagenband B zum Gutachten der Sachverständigenkommission. Edited by Bundesminister für Arbeit und Sozialordnung. Bonn, pp 73–104
Ruland F (1993) Funktion und Tradition sozialer Selbstverwaltung am Beispiel der gesetzlichen Rentenversicherung. Deutsche Rentenversicherung 10:684–703
Ruland F (1995) Versicherungsfremde Leistungen in der gesetzlichen Rentenversicherung. Deutsche Rentenversicherung 12:28–38
Rupp HH (1987) Die Unterscheidung von Staat und Gesellschaft. In: Isensee J, Kirchhof P (eds) Handbuch des Staatsrechts, vol 1. Heidelberg, pp 1187–1223
Rupp HH (1997) Die soziale Marktwirtschaft in ihrer Verfassungsbedeutung. In: Isensee J, Kirchhof P (eds) Handbuch des Staatsrechts, vol 9. Heidelberg, pp 129–148

Rüthers B (1995) 35 Jahre Arbeitsrecht in Deutschland. Recht der Arbeit 48:326–333
Sachße C (1994) Subsidiarität - zur Karriere eines sozialpolitischen Ordnungsbegriffs. Zeitschrift für Sozialreform 40:717–738
Sachße C, Engelhardt HT (eds) (1990) Sicherheit und Freiheit. Zur Ethik des Wohlfahrtsstaates. Frankfurt am Main
Sachße C, Tennstedt F (1988/1992/1998) Geschichte der Armenfürsorge in Deutschland, vol 1, 2nd edn. 1998; vol 2, 1st edn. 1988; vol 3, 1st edn. 1992. Stuttgart
Sachverständigenkommission Alterssicherungssysteme (1983a) Darstellung der Alterssicherungssysteme und der Besteuerung von Alterseinkommen, Gutachten der Sachverständigenkommission, 2 vols. Edited by Bundesminister für Arbeit- und Sozialordnung. Bonn
Sachverständigenkommission Alterssicherungssysteme (1983b) Bundesminister für Arbeit und Sozialordnung (ed) Anlagenband A zum Gutachten der Sachverständigenkommission: Unterlagen zum empirischen und rechtlichen Vergleich der Alterssicherungssysteme. Bonn
Sachverständigenkommission Alterssicherungssysteme (1983c) Bundesminister für Arbeit und Sozialordnung (ed) Anlagenband B zum Gutachten der Sachverständigenkommission: Möglichkeiten und Grenzen einer Annäherung der Beamtenversorgung an die gesetzliche Rentenversicherung. Bonn
Sachverständigenkommission zur Auswertung der bisherigen Erfahrungen bei der Mitbestimmung in Unternehmen (1970) Bericht, Bundestagsdrucksache VI/334
Sachverständigenrat für die Konzertierte Aktion im Gesundheitswesen (1987–1998) Jahresgutachten 1987: Vorschläge für die Konzertierte Aktion im Gesundheitswesen; Jahresgutachten 1988; Jahresgutachten 1989: Qualität, Wirtschaftlichkeit und Perspektiven der Gesundheitsversorgung; Jahresgutachten 1990: Herausforderungen und Perspektiven der Gesundheitsversorgung; Jahresgutachten 1991: Gesundheitswesen im Vereinten Deutschland; Jahresgutachten 1992: Ausbau in Deutschland und Aufbruch nach Europa; Sachstandsbericht 1994: Gesundheitsversorgung und Krankenversicherung 2000; Sondergutachten 1995: Gesundheitsversorgung und Krankenversicherung 2000. Sondergutachten 1996: Gesundheitswesen in Deutschland. Kostenfaktor und Zukunftsbranche. vol 1 (1996). Demographie, Morbidität, Wirtschaftlichkeitsreserven und Beschäftigung; Sondergutachten 1997: Gesundheitswesen in Deutschland. Kostenfaktor und Zukunftsbranche vol 2 (1997/1998): Fortschritt und Wachstumsmärkte. Finanzierung und Vergütung. Baden-Baden
Sander P (1997) Interessenvertretung der Arbeitnehmer im Betrieb. Opladen
Sanmann H (1977) Sozialpartner. In: Albers W et al (eds) Handwörterbuch der Wirtschaftswissenschaften, vol 7. Stuttgart, pp 52–59
Schäfer D (1997) Sozialreform. In: Fachlexikon der sozialen Arbeit, 4th edn. Frankfurt am Main, p 897f
Schäuble W (1991) Der Vertrag. Wie ich über die deutsche Einheit verhandelte, 1st edn, rev edn. 1993. Stuttgart
Scheffler E (1960) Ehe und Familie. In: Bettermann KA, Nipperdey HC, Scheuner U (eds) Die Grundrechte, vol 4/1. Berlin, pp 245–323
Schellhorn W (1997) Öffentliche Träger. In: Fachlexikon der sozialen Arbeit, 4th edn. Frankfurt am Main, p 679
Scheyban A (1996) Handwerk und Kleinhandel in der Bundesrepublik Deutschland. Sozialökonomischer Wandel und Mittelstandspolitik. München
Schillinger R (1985) Der Entscheidungsprozeß beim Lastenausgleich (1945–1956). St. Katharinen
Schlegel R (1996) Kreis der versicherten Personen. Erster Titel. Grundlagen. In: Schulin B (ed) Handbuch des Sozialversicherungsrechts, vol 2. Unfallversicherungsrecht. München, pp 283–287
Schlenker R-U (1986) Soziales Rückschrittsverbot und Grundgesetz. Berlin
Schmähl W (1982) Konzeptionen sozialer Sicherung - Versicherungs- und Steuer-Transfer-System. Vierteljahresschrift für Sozialrecht 10:251–296
Schmähl W (2000) Alterssicherung in Deutschland an der Jahrtausendwende - Konzeptionen, Maßnahmen und Wirkungen. Deutsche Rentenversicherung: 50–71

Schmähl W, Rische H (eds) (1995) Internationalisierung von Wirtschaft und Politik – Handlungsspielräume der nationalen Sozialpolitik. Baden-Baden
Schmid F (1981) Sozialrecht und Recht der sozialen Sicherheit. Die Begriffsbildung in Deutschland, Frankreich und der Schweiz. Berlin
Schmid J (1996) Wohlfahrtsstaaten im Vergleich. Soziale Sicherungssysteme in Europa. Organisation, Finanzierung, Leistungen und Probleme. Opladen
Schmid J, Niketta R (eds) (1998) Wohlfahrtsstaat: Krise und Reform. Marburg
Schmidt A (1988) Alterssicherung und Familie. Probleme. Zusammenhänge. Lösungsperspektiven. Die Angestelltenversicherung 35:477–492
Schmidt-Aßmann E (1987) Der Rechtsstaat. In: Isensee J, Kirchhof P (eds) Handbuch des Staatsrechts, vol 1. Heidelberg, pp 987–1043
Schmidt E (1981) Die verhinderte Neuordnung 1945–1952. Zur Auseinandersetzung um die Demokratisierung der Wirtschaft in den westlichen Besatzungszonen und in der Bundesrepublik Deutschland, 8th edn. Frankfurt am Main
Schmidt MG (1998) Sozialpolitik in Deutschland. Historische Entwicklung und internationaler Vergleich, 2nd edn. Opladen
Schmidt MG (ed) (2005) Bundesrepublik Deutschland 1982–1989. Finanzielle Konsolidierung und institutionelle Reform (Geschichte der Sozialpolitik in Deutschland seit 1945, vol. 7, edited by Bundesministerium für Gesundheit und Soziale Sicherung, Bundesarchiv). Baden-Baden
Schmidt MG (2013) Social Policy in the German Democratic Republic. In: Leisering L (ed) German Social Policy, vol 4. Berlin Heidelberg
Schmidt R (1971) Wirtschaftspolitik und Verfassung. Baden-Baden
Schmidt R (1990) Öffentliches Wirtschaftsrecht. Allgemeiner Teil. Berlin pp 1–33
Schneider E (ed) (1967) Rationale Wirtschaftspolitik und Planung in der Wirtschaft von heute. Verhandlungen auf der Tagung des Vereins für Socialpolitik in Hannover 1966. Berlin
Schneider HK (ed) (1968) Grundsatzprobleme wirtschaftspolitischer Beratung. Das Beispiel der Stabilisierungspolitik. Verhandlungen auf der Tagung des Vereins für Socialpolitik in Baden-Baden 1967. Berlin
Schneider H-P (1983) Zusatzversorgung der Arbeitnehmer im öffentlichen Dienst. In: Bundesminister für Arbeit- und Sozialordnung (ed) Sachverständigenkommission Alterssicherungssysteme: Darstellung der Alterssicherungssysteme und der Besteuerung von Alterseinkommen, Gutachten der Sachverständigenkommission, vol 2. Bonn, pp 207–242
Schneider HK, Wittmann W, Würgler H (eds) (1975) Stabilisierungspolitik in der Marktwirtschaft. Verhandlungen der Tagung des Vereins für Socialpolitik in Zürich 1974. Berlin
Scholz R (1987) Der Status Berlins. In: Isensee J, Kirchhof P (eds) Handbuch des Staatsrechts, vol 1. Heidelberg, pp 351–383
Scholz R (1989) Koalitionsfreiheit. In: Isensee J, Kirchhof P (eds) Handbuch des Staatsrechts, vol 6. Heidelberg, pp 1115–1183
Schräder H (1957) Kommunale Sozialpolitik. In: Peters H (ed) Handbuch der kommunalen Wissenschaft und Praxis, vol 2. Berlin, Göttingen, Heidelberg, pp 265–282
Schraml A (1992) Sozialhilferecht der Ausländerinnen und Ausländer. München
Schregle J (1954) Europäische Sozialpolitik. Erfolge und Möglichkeiten. Köln
Schreyer M (1983) Staatliche Sozialausgaben - Die Regelung der Finanzierungskompetenz in der Bundesrepublik Deutschland. Vierteljahreschrift für Sozialrecht 11:95–113
Schriftenreihe des Deutschen Sozialrechtsverbandes (until vol 22 (1982) Deutscher Sozialgerichtsverband). Vol 2 (1967); vol 4 (1968); vol 5 (1969); vol 6 (1969); vol 7 (1970); vol 8 (1971); vol 9 (1972); vol 10 (1972); vol 11 (1973); vol 14 (1975); vol 15 (1977); vol 16 (1978); vol 17 (1978); vol 19 (1979); vol 20 (1980); vol 21 (1981); vol 23 (1982); vol 24 (1983); vol 25 (1984); vol 27 (1985); vol 28 (1986); vol 29 (1987); vol 30 (1988); vol 31 (1988); vol 32 (1989); vol 33 (1990); vol 34 (1991); vol 35 (1992); vol 36 (1992); vol 40 (1995); vol 41 (1996); vol 42 (1997); vol 44 (1998); vol 45 (1999)
Schröder H-J (ed) (1990) Marshallplan und westdeutscher Wiederaufstieg. Stuttgart

Schuler R (1988) Das internationale Sozialrecht der Bundesrepublik Deutschland. Baden-Baden
Schulin B (1980) Soziale Sicherung der Behinderten, 1980. In: Schriftenreihe des Deutschen Sozialrechtsverbandes (until vol 22 (1982) Deutscher Sozialgerichtsverband), vol 20
Schulin B (1981) Soziale Entschädigung als Teilsystem kollektiven Schadensausgleichs. Köln
Schulin B (1988) Solidarität und Subsidiarität. In: von Maydell BB, Kannengiesser W (eds) Handbuch Sozialpolitik. Pfullingen, pp 85–93
Schulin B (1997) Die soziale Entschädigung im System des Sozialrechts. In: Gitter W, Schulin B, Zacher HF (eds) Festschrift für Otto Ernst Krasney zum 65. Geburtstag. München, pp 463–483
Schulin B (1998) Grundstrukturen der sozialen Pflegeversicherung. In: Ruland F, von Maydell BB, Papier H-J (eds) Verfassung, Theorie und Praxis des Sozialstaats. Festschrift für Hans F. Zacher zum 70. Geburtstag. Heidelberg, pp 1029–1046
Schulte B (1982/1998) Das Sozialrecht in der Rechtsprechung des Europäischen Gerichtshofs. Jahrbuch des Sozialrechts der Gegenwart, vol 4 (1982): 439–481; vol 20 (1998): 461–491
Schulte B (1997) Zur Sozialpolitik als Aufgabe der Europäischen Gemeinschaft nach dem Vertrag von Maastricht, Art. 117–118. In: von der Groeben H, Thiesing J, Ehlermann C-D (eds) Kommentar zum EU-/EG-Vertrag, 5th edn, vol 1. Baden-Baden
Schulte B, Barwig K (eds) (1999) Freizügigkeit und soziale Sicherheit. Baden-Baden
Schulte B, Zacher HF (1979–1981) Das Sozialrecht in der Rechtsprechung des Europäischen Gerichtshofs. Jahrbuch des Sozialrechts der Gegenwart, vol 1 (1979): 353–390; vol 2 (1980): 359–395; vol 3 (1981): 419–454
Schulte B, Zacher HF (eds) (1991) Wechselwirkungen zwischen dem Europäischen Sozialrecht und dem Sozialrecht der Bundesrepublik Deutschland. Baden-Baden
Schulz G (1989) Sozialreform. In: Görres-Gesellschaft (ed) Staatslexikon, vol 5, 7th edn. Freiburg im Breisgau Basel Wien, columns 68–71
Schulz G (1994) Wiederaufbau in Deutschland. Die Wohnungsbaupolitik in den Westzonen und in der Bundesrepublik Deutschland 1945–1949. Düsseldorf
Schulz G (ed) (2005) Bundesrepublik Deutschland 1949–1957. Bewältigung der Kriegsfolgen, Rückkehr zur sozialpolitischen Normalität (Geschichte der Sozialpolitik in Deutschland seit 1945, vol. 3, edited by Bundesministerium für Arbeit und Soziales, Bundesarchiv). Baden-Baden
Schulz O (1999) Zur Sozialpolitik als Aufgabe der Europäischen Gemeinschaft nach dem Vertrag von Maastricht, Art. 123–125. In: von der Groeben H, Thiesing J, Ehlermann C-D (eds) Kommentar zum EU-/EG-Vertrag, 5th edn, vol 3. Baden-Baden, pp 903–1455
Schultz R (1977) Arbeitnehmerkammern und Wirtschafts- und Sozialräte als Instrumente gesamtwirtschaftlicher Mitbestimmung. Aus Politik und Zeitgeschichte B 22:13–21
Schulze R, von der Brelie-Levien D, Grebing H (eds) (1987) Flüchtlinge und Vertriebene in der westdeutschen Nachkriegsgeschichte. Hildesheim
Schumann KF et al (1996) Private Wege der Wiedervereinigung. Die deutsche Ost-West-Migration vor der Wende. Weinheim
Schuster D (1974) Die deutschen Gewerkschaften seit 1945, 2nd edn. Stuttgart
Schüttemeyer S (1990) Die Stimmverteilung im Bundesrat 1946–1990. Zeitschrift für Parlamentsfragen 21:473–474
Schwarz H-P (1981) Die Ära Adenauer: Gründerjahre der Republik, 1949–1957. Geschichte der Bundesrepublik Deutschland, vol 2. Stuttgart Wiesbaden
Schwarz H-P (1983) Die Ära Adenauer: Epochenwechsel 1957–1963. Geschichte der Bundesrepublik Deutschland, vol 3. Stuttgart Wiesbaden
Schwarz H-P (ed) (1987) Die Wiederherstellung des deutschen Kredits. Das Londoner Schuldenabkommen. Stuttgart
Schwarze J (1990) Umfang und Ursachen von Mehrfachbeschäftigung und Schattenwirtschaft. Dissertation. Berlin Frankfurt am Main New York
Schweitzer M (1995) Die Verträge Deutschlands mit den Siegermächten. In: Isensee J, Kirchhof P (eds) Handbuch des Staatsrechts, vol 8. Heidelberg, pp 199–24

Seewald O (1981) Zum Verfassungsrecht auf Gesundheit. Köln

Selbstverwaltung in der Sozialversicherung (1991) Schriftenreihe des Deutschen Sozialrechtsverbandes (until vol 22 (1982) Deutscher Sozialgerichtsverband), vol 34. Wiesbaden

Sicking M (1989) Der "CDU"-Staat und sein politisches Regulierungsmodell. Ein Beitrag zur Interpretation und Kritik der sozialpolitischen Konzeption der konservativen "Wende". Dissertation. Aachen

Simons T (1985) Verfahren und verfahrensäquivalente Rechtsformen im Sozialrecht. Baden-Baden

Sobota K (1997) Das Prinzip Rechtsstaat. Tübingen

Social Exclusion Indicators: Problematic Issues. Collective Paper issued from the Seminar on "Social Exclusion Indicators" held in Brussels, May 1995. European Commission Directorate General XII Science, Reserach and Developement. Brussels

Söllner A (1994) Gesetzgebung oder Richterrecht? In: Söllner A (ed) Das Arbeitsrecht in der Verfassungsordnung des Grundgesetzes. Goldbach, pp 325–335

Soziale Arbeit – ein Bindeglied zwischen Ausländern und Deutschen (1988) Eine Hauptausschußsitzung des Deutschen Vereins für öffentliche und private Fürsorge. Nachrichtendienst des Deutschen Vereins für öffentliche und private Fürsorge 68:29–47

Soziale Sicherung bei Pflegebedürftigkeit – Bestandsaufnahme und Reformbestrebungen (1987) In: Schriftenreihe des Deutschen Sozialrechtsverbandes (until vol 22 (1982) Deutscher Sozialgerichtsverband), vol 29. Wiesbaden

Soziale Sicherung in der Bundesrepublik Deutschland. Bericht der Sozialenquete-Kommission, Anlagenband (1966). Stuttgart

Soziale Sicherung und medizinische Dienste (1971) In: Schriftenreihe des Deutschen Sozialrechtsverbandes (until vol 22 (1982) Deutscher Sozialgerichtsverband), vol 8. Wiesbaden

Sozialfinanzverfassung (1992) Schriftenreihe des Deutschen Sozialrechtsverbandes (until vol 22 (1982) Deutscher Sozialgerichtsverband), vol 35. Wiesbaden

Sozialberichte der Bundesregierung (1970–1990) Bundestagsdrucksachen (1970) VI/643; (1971) VI/2155; (1972) VI/3432; (1973) 7/1167; (1974) 7/2853; (1976) 7/4953; (1978) 8/1805; (1980) 8/4327; (1983) 10/842; (1986) 10/5810; (1990) 11/7527; (1993) 12/7130; (1997) 13/10142

Sozialrecht in der Wechselwirkung der Gewalten (1975) Schriftenreihe des Deutschen Sozialrechtsverbandes (until vol 22 (1982) Deutscher Sozialgerichtsverband), vol 14. Wiesbaden

Sozialrecht und Steuerrecht (1989) Schriftenreihe des Deutschen Sozialrechtsverbandes (until vol 22 (1982) Deutscher Sozialgerichtsverband), vol 32. Wiesbaden

Sozialversicherung – Organisatorische Gliederung und funktionale Einheit der Sozialverwaltung (1988) Schriftenreihe des Deutschen Sozialrechtsverbandes (until vol 22 (1982) Deutscher Sozialgerichtsverband), vol 31. Wiesbaden

Speck O (1999) Die Ökonomisierung sozialer Qualität. Zur Qualitätsdiskussion in Behindertenhilfe und Sozialer Arbeit. München Basel

Spiegelhalter F (1985) Arbeitgeberverbände. In: Görres-Gesellschaft (ed) Staatslexikon, vol 1, 7th edn. Freiburg im Breisgau Basel Wien, columns 235–238

Spieker M (1986) Legitimationsprobleme des Sozialstaats. Bern Stuttgart

Staatszwecke im Verfassungsstaat - nach 40 Jahren Grundgesetz (1990) Veröffentlichungen der Vereinigung der Deutschen Staatsrechtslehrer. Issue no. 48. Berlin

Standfest E (1979) Sozialpolitik als Reformpolitik. Aspekte der sozialpolitischen Entwicklung in der Bundesrepublik Deutschland. Köln

Starck C (1978) Gesetzgeber und Richter im Sozialstaat. Deutsches Verwaltungsblatt 93:937–945

Starck C (1994) Die Verfassungen der neuen deutschen Länder. Heidelberg

Steininger R (1979) Reform und Realität. Ruhrfrage und Sozialisierung in der anglo-amerikanischen Deutschlandpolitik. Vierteljahreshefte für Zeitgeschichte 27:167–240

Stephany G (1968) Das Honnefer Modell. Berlin

Stern K (1977/1984/2000) Das Staatsrecht der Bundesrepublik Deutschland, vol 1: Grundbegriffe und Grundlagen des Staatsrechts, Strukturprinzipien der Verfassung, 1st edn 1977; 2nd edn 1984; vol 5: Die geschichtlichen Grundlagen des Deutschen Staatsrechts, 2000. München

Stern K (1992) Idee und Elemente eines Systems der Grundrechte. In: Isensee J, Kirchhof P (eds) Handbuch des Staatsrechts, vol 5. Heidelberg, pp 45–100

Stern K (1998) Die Notenbank im Staatsgefüge. In: Deutschen B (ed) Fünfzig Jahre Deutsche Mark: Notenbank und Währung in Deutschland seit 1948. München, pp 141–198

Stödter R (1933) Öffentlich-rechtliche Entschädigung. Hamburg

Stolleis M (1982) Rechtsordnung und Justizpolitik 1945–1949. In: Horn N, Luig K, Söllner A (eds) Europäisches Rechtsdenken in Geschichte und Gegenwart. Festschrift für Helmut Coing, vol 1. München, pp 383–407

Stolleis M (1987) Besatzungsherrschaft und Wiederaufbau deutscher Staatlichkeit 1945–1949. In: Isensee J, Kirchhof P (eds) Handbuch des Staatsrechts, vol 1. Heidelberg, pp 173–217

Stolleis M (2013) Origins of the German Welfare State - Social Policy in Germany to 1945. In: Leisering L (ed) German Social Policy, vol 2. Berlin Heidelberg

Subventionsberichte der Bundesregierung: Bundestagsdrucksachen (1981–1984) 10/352; (1983–1986) 10/3821; (1985–1988) 11/1138; (1987–1990) 11/5116; (1989–1992) 12/1525; (1991–1994) 12/5580; (1993–1996) 13/2230

Szurgacz H (1998) Das Polenstatut in der Sozialversicherung in den in das III. Reich eingegliederten Ostgebieten (1939–1945). In: Ruland F, von Maydell BB, Papier H.-J. (eds) Verfassung, Theorie und Praxis des Sozialstaats. Festschrift für Hans F. Zacher zum 70. Geburtstag. Heidelberg, pp 883–894

Tennstedt F (1976) Sozialgeschichte der Sozialversicherung. In: Blohmke M et al (eds) Handbuch der Sozialmedizin, vol 3: Sozialmedizin in der Praxis. Stuttgart, pp 385–492

Tettinger PJ (1977) Neuer Streit um die Wirtschaftsverfassung? Betriebsberater 32:1617–1621

Thieme W (1960) Die Entwicklung des Verfassungsrechts im Saarland von 1945–1958. Jahrbuch des öffentlichen Rechts der Gegenwart (new edition) 9:423–462

Toman-Banke M (1994) Die Wahlslogans von 1949–1994. Aus Politik und Zeitgeschichte B 51–52:47–55

Tomuschat C (1990) Wege zur Deutschen Einheit. In: Deutschlands aktuelle Verfassungslage. In: Veröffentlichungen der Vereinigung der Deutschen Staatsrechtslehrer. Issue no. 49. Berlin, New York, pp 70–100

Transfer-Enquete-Kommission (1979) Zur Einkommenslage der Rentner. Zwischenbericht der Sachverständigenkommission zur Ermittlung des Einflusses staatlicher Transfereinkommen auf das verfügbare Einkommen der privaten Haushalte. Published by Bundesregierung. Der Bundesminister für Arbeit und Sozialordnung, Der Bundesminister für Wirtschaft. Bonn

Transfer-Enquete-Kommission (1981) Das Transfersystem in der Bundesrepublik. Bericht der Sachverständigenkommission zur Ermittlung des Einflusses staatlicher Transfereinkommen auf das verfügbare Einkommen der privaten Haushalte. Published by Bundesregierung. Der Bundesminister für Arbeit, Der Bundesminister für Wirtschaft. Bonn

Treue W (1968) Deutsche Parteiprogramme seit 1861, 4th edn. Göttingen

Trittel GJ (1982) Die Bodenreform - ein Beitrag der Besatzungsmächte zur gesellschaftlichen Strukturreform Nachkriegsdeutschlands 1945–1949. Zeitschrift für Agrargeschichte und Agrarsoziologie 30:28–47

Troberg P (1997) Zum Verbleiberecht für ehemalige Wanderarbeitnehmer und entsprechende Selbständige, Familienangehörige, Hinterbliebene usw., Art. 56. In: von der Groeben H, Thiesing J, Ehlermann C-D (eds) Kommentar zum EU-/EG-Vertrag, 5th edn, vol 1. Baden-Baden

Trometer L (1977) Die Kriegsopferversorgung nach 1945. In: Bartholomäi R et al (eds) Sozialpolitik nach 1945. Geschichte und Analysen. Bonn-Bad Godesberg, pp 191–205

Turek J (1996) Treuhandanstalt. In: Weidenfeld W, Korte K-R (eds) Handbuch zur deutschen Einheit. New edn. Frankfurt am Main, pp 662–671

Über- und Unterversorgung in der Alterssicherung (1979) Schriftenreihe des Deutschen Sozialrechtsverbandes (until vol 22 Deutscher Sozialgerichtsverband), vol 17. Wiesbaden

Übergreifende Soziale Risiken – Übergreifender sozialer Schutz (1990) Schriftenreihe des Deutschen Sozialrechtsverbandes (until vol 22 (1982) Deutscher Sozialgerichtsverband), vol 33. Wiesbaden

United Nations, Department for Economic and Social Information and Policy Analysis (1997) World social situation. United Nations

Veränderungen in der Arbeitswelt und soziale Sicherung (1986) In: Schriftenreihe des Deutschen Sozialrechtsverbandes (until vol 22 (1982) Deutscher Sozialgerichtsverband), vol 28. Wiesbaden

Verfassungsausschuss der Bayrischen Verfassungsgebenden Landesversammlung (1946) Stenographische Berichte über die Verhandlungen, 4 vols. München.

Verfassungsrechtlicher Eigentumsschutz sozialer Rechtspositionen (1982) In: Schriftenreihe des Deutschen Sozialrechtsverbandes (until vol 22 (1982) Deutscher Sozialgerichtsverband), vol 23. Wiesbaden

Verhandlungen des 43. Deutschen Juristentages (1960) Die Einwirkung verfassungsrechtlicher Normen auf das Recht der sozialen Sicherheit, vol 2: Sitzungsberichte, part G. Tübingen

Verhandlungen des 47. Deutschen Juristentages (1968) Empfiehlt es sich, die gesetzlichen Vorschriften über die soziale Sicherung der nichtberufstätigen Frauen während und nach der Ehe, insbesondere im Falle der Scheidung, zu ändern? vol 1: Gutachten, part T, vol 2: Sitzungsberichte, part O. München

Verhandlungen des 49. Deutschen Juristentages (1972) Empfiehlt es sich, die soziale Sicherung für den Fall von Personenschäden, für welche die Allgemeinheit eine gesteigerte Verantwortung trägt, neu zu regeln? vol 1: Gutachten, part E, vol 2: Sitzungsberichte, part P. München

Verhandlungen des 50. Deutschen Juristentages (1974) Welche rechtlichen Maßnahmen sind vordringlich, um die tatsächliche Gleichstellung der Frau mit den Männern im Arbeitsleben zu gewährleisten? vol 1: Gutachten, part D, vol 2: Sitzungsberichte, part L. München

Verhandlungen des 51. Deutschen Juristentages (1976) Kodifikation des Arbeitskampfrechts? vol 2: Sitzungsberichte, part F. München

Verhandlungen des 52. Deutschen Juristentages (1978a) Empfiehlt es sich, soziale Pflege- und Betreuungsverhältnisse gesetzlich zu regeln? vol 1: Gutachten, part E, vol 2: Sitzungsberichte, part N. München

Verhandlungen des 52. Deutschen Juristentages (1978b) Sind im Interesse einer gerechten Verteilung der Arbeitsplätze Begründung und Beendigung der Arbeitsverhältnisse neu zu regeln? vol 1: Gutachten, part E, vol 2: Sitzungsberichte, part M. München

Verhandlungen des 54. Deutschen Juristentages (1982) Möglichkeit der Sanierung von Unternehmen durch Maßnahmen im Unternehmens-, Arbeits-, Sozial und Insolvenzrecht. vol 1: Gutachten, part E, vol 2: Sitzungsberichte, part M. München

Verhandlungen des 55. Deutschen Juristentages (1984) Möglichkeiten der Fortentwicklung des Rechts der sozialen Sicherheit zwischen Anpassungszwang und Bestandsschutz, vol 1: Gutachten, part E, vol 2: Sitzungsberichte, part N. München

Verhandlungen des 59. Deutschen Juristentages (1992/1993a) Welche wesentlichen Inhalte sollte ein nach Art. 30 des Einigungsvertrags zu schaffendes Arbeitsvertragsrecht haben? vol 1 (1992): Gutachten, part D, vol 2 (1993): Sitzungsberichte, part P. München

Verhandlungen des 59. Deutschen Juristentages (1992/1993b) Empfiehlt es sich, die Zuweisung von Risiken und Lasten im Sozialrecht neu zu ordnen? vol 1 (1992): Gutachten, part E, F, vol 2 (1993): Sitzungsberichte, part Q. München

Verhandlungen des 60. Deutschen Juristentages (1994) Welche Maßnahmen empfehlen sich, um die Vereinbarung von Berufstätigkeit und Familie zu verbessern? vol 1: Gutachten, part E, F, vol 2: Sitzungsberichte, part O. München

Vilmar F (1975) Wirtschaftsdemokratie. Aus Politik und Zeitgeschichte B 16:3–33

Vogel K (1964) Die Verfassungsentscheidung des Grundgesetzes für eine internationale Zusammenarbeit. Tübingen

Vogel K (1968) Internationales und interlokales Sozialverwaltungsrecht – Systematische Grundlagen. In: Schriftenreihe des Deutschen Sozialrechtsverbandes (until vol 22 (1982) Deutscher Sozialgerichtsverband), vol 4. Das Sozialrecht im geteilten Deutschland. Wiesbaden, pp 45–64
Vogel K (1986) Der Sozialstaat als Steuerstaat. In: Randelzhofer A, Süss W (eds) Konsens und Konflikt. 35 Jahre Grundgesetz. Berlin New York, pp 133–138
Vogel W (1989) Westdeutschland 1945–1950. Der Aufbau von Verfassungs- und Verwaltungseinrichtungen in den Ländern der drei westlichen Besatzungszonen, 2nd edn. Boppard am Rhein
Vogler-Ludwig K (1997) Versicherungsfremde Leistungen in der Sozialversicherung. Deutsche Rentenversicherung: 161–176
Voigt R (ed) (1980) Verrechtlichung. Königstein im Taunus
Voigt R (ed) (1983) Gegentendenzen zur Verrechtlichung. Opladen
Volkmann U (1998) Solidarität - Programm und Prinzip der Verfassung. Tübingen
von Beckerath E, Giersch H (eds) (1963) Probleme der normativen Ökonomik und der wirtschaftspolitischen Beratung, Verhandlungen der Arbeitstagung des Vereins für Socialpolitik in Bad Homburg 1962. Berlin
von Benda-Beckmann F et al (eds) (1988) Between kinship and the state. Social security and law in developing countries. Dordrecht Providence
von Bethusy-Huc VG (1956/1976) Das Sozialleistungssystem in der Bundesrepublik Deutschland. 1st edn. 1956, 2nd edn. 1976. Tübingen
von Bethusy-Huc VG, Beckmann N (1989) “Neue Armut” und “Neue Soziale Frage”. Sozialer Fortschritt 38:121–124
von Brentano D (1978) Zur Problematik der Armutsforschung. Berlin
von Doemming K-B, Füßlein RW, Matz W (eds) (1951) Entstehungsgeschichte der Artikel des Grundgesetzes. In: Jahrbuch des öffentlichen Rechts der Gegenwart (new edition), vol 1: 43f
von Ferber C (1967) Sozialpolitik in der Wohlstandsgesellschaft. Was stimmt nicht mit der deutschen Sozialpolitik? Hamburg
von Hippel E (1979) Grundfragen der sozialen Sicherheit. Tübingen
von Hippel E (1982) Der Schutz des Schwächeren. Tübingen
von Kevelaer K-H, Hinrichs K (1985) Arbeitszeit und Wirtschaftswunder - Rahmenbedingungen für den Übergang zur 40-Stundenwoche in der Bundesrepublik Deutschland. Politische Vierteljahresschrift 26:52–75
von Mangoldt H (1993) Die Verfassungen der neuen Bundesländer. Berlin
von Maydell BB, Wank R (eds) (1996) Transformation der Arbeitsrechtsordnung in den neuen Bundesländern. Opladen
von Maydell BB et al (1997) Die "Krise des Sozialstaats" in internationaler Perspektive - Denkanstöße für die Bundesrepublik Deutschland. Sozialer Fortschritt 46:1-39
von Münch I (ed) (1968) Dokumente des geteilten Deutschland, vol 1. Stuttgart
von Nell-Breuning O (1957) Solidarität und Subsidiarität im Raum von Sozialpolitik und Sozialreform. In: Boettcher E (ed) Sozialpolitik und Sozialreform. Tübingen, pp 215–226
von Nell-Breuning O (1964) Partnerschaft. In: von Beckerath E et al (eds) Handwörterbuch der Sozialwissenschaften, vol 8. Stuttgart, Tübingen Göttingen, pp 216–223
von Nell-Breuning O (1985) Artikel “Bodenreform”. In: Görres-Gesellschaft (ed) Staatslexikon, vol 1, 7th edn. Freiburg im Breisgau Basel Wien, columns 858–861
von Schmoller G, Maier H, Tobler A (1957) Handbuch des Besatzungsrechts. Tübingen
von Weizsäcker R (1985) Ansprache in der Gedenkstunde im Plenarsaal des Deutschen Bundestages am 18. Mai 1985. In: Presse- und Informationsamt der Bundesregierung (ed) Erinnerung, Trauer und Versöhnung. Ansprachen und Erklärungen zum vierzigsten Jahrestag des Kriegsendes. Bonn, pp 63–82
von Wiese L (1953/1954) Über die Armut. Kölner Zeitschrift für Soziologie und Sozialpsychologie 6:42–62

von Winter T (1995) Sozialpolitische Interessen: Konstituierung politischer Repräsentation und Beteiligung an Entscheidungsprozessen. Baden-Baden

Wagenführ R (1965) Gewerkschaften (II) Einzelne Länder. In: von Beckerath E. et al (eds) Handwörterbuch der Sozialwissenschaften, vol 4. Stuttgart Tübingen Göttingen, pp 562–585

Wand R (1974) Das Sozialrecht in der Rechtsprechung des Bundesverfassungsgerichts. Vierteljahresschrift für Sozialrecht 2:52–67

Wandel der Arbeit und soziale Sicherung (1998) In: Schriftenreihe des Deutschen Sozialrechtsverbandes (until vol 22 (1982) Deutscher Sozialgerichtsverband), vol 44. Wiesbaden

Wank R (1980) Das Recht auf Arbeit im Verfassungsrecht und im Arbeitsrecht. Königstein

Wank R (1997) Empirische Befunde zur "Scheinselbständigkeit". Juristischer Teil: Freie Mitarbeiter und selbständige Einzelunternehmer mit persönlicher und wirtschaftlicher Abhängigkeit. Bonn

Wannagat G (1975) 10 Jahre Deutscher Sozialgerichtsverband. In: Schriftenreihe des Deutschen Sozialrechtsverbandes (until vol 22 (1982) Deutscher Sozialgerichtsverband), vol 14. Wiesbaden, pp 17–31

Wannagat G (ed) (1979–1988) Jahrbuch des Sozialrechts der Gegenwart, vol 1 (1979)–vol 10 (1988). Berlin

Wannagat G, Gitter W (eds) (1989–1998) Jahrbuch des Sozialrechts der Gegenwart, vol 11 (1989)–vol 20 (1998). Berlin

Watrin C (1982) Art. Konzertierte Aktionen. In: Albers W et al (eds) Handwörterbuch der Wirtschaftswissenschaften, vol 9. Tübingen, Göttingen

Weddigen W (ed) (1950) Untersuchungen zur sozialen Gestaltung der Wirtschaftsordnungen. Berlin

Weddigen W (1956) Sozialpolitik (IV). Träger und Methoden. In: von Beckerath E. et al (eds) Handwörterbuch der Sozialwissenschaften, vol 9. Stuttgart, Tübingen, Göttingen, pp 554–563

Weg M (1988) Frauenarbeit und ihre Folgen für die soziale Sicherheit. Zeitschrift für Sozialreform 34:677–687

Wege J (1977) Positives Recht und sozialer Wandel im demokratischen und sozialen Rechtsstaat. Berlin

Wegner B (1989) Subsidiarität und"neue" Subsidiarität in der Sozialpolitik und Wohnungspolitik. Regensburg

Weimer W (1998) Deutsche Wirtschaftsgeschichte. Von der Währungsreform bis zum Euro. Hamburg

Weiß J (1993) Die Entwicklung des Mieterschutzes - Konsequenzen politischen und sozialen Wandels. Dissertation. Berlin

Weisser G (1956) Soziale Sicherheit. In: von Beckerath E et al (eds) Handwörterbuch der Sozialwissenschaften, vol 9. Stuttgart Tübingen Göttingen, pp 396–412

Weizsäcker CC (ed) (1979) Staat und Wirtschaft. Verhandlungen der Arbeitstagung des Vereins für Socialpolitik in Hamburg 1978. Berlin

Wengst U (1988) Beamtentum zwischen Reform und Tradition. Beamtengesetzgebung in der Gründungsphase der Bundesrepublik Deutschland 1948–1953. Düsseldorf

Wengst U (ed) (2001) Die Zeit der Besatzungszonen 1945–1949. Sozialpolitik zwischen Kriegsende und der Gründung zweier deutscher Staaten (Geschichte der Sozialpolitik in Deutschland seit 1945, vol. 2, edited by Bundesministerium für Arbeit und Sozialordnung, Bundesarchiv). Baden-Baden

Werner C (1990) Die Beschäftigungswirkungen der Schattenwirtschaft. Pfaffenweiler

Werner H (1998) Beschäftigungspolitisch erfolgreiche Länder. Lehren für die Bundesrepublik Deutschland? Aus Politik und Zeitgeschichte B 34–35:3–14

Werner R (1975) Soziale Indikatoren und politische Planung. Reinbek bei Hamburg

Wickenhagen E (1957/1982/1997) Zwischenstaatliches Sozialversicherungsrecht. Eine Einführung, 1st edn 1957. Bad Godesberg; 2nd edn 1982. Sankt. Augustin; 3rd edn 1997 with Aulmann, Heinz. Sankt Augustin

Widmaier HP (ed) (1978) Zur neuen sozialen Frage. Berlin

Wiegand D (1974) Sozialstaatsklausel und soziale Teilhaberechte. Deutsches Verwaltungsblatt 89:657–663

Wienand M, Neumann V, Brockmann I (1997) Fürsorge. Opladen

Wildt M (1994) Am Beginn der "Konsumgesellschaft". Mangelerfahrung, Lebenshaltung, Wohlstandhoffnung in Westdeutschland in den fünfziger Jahren. Hamburg

Willms B (1997a) Zur Sozialpolitik als Aufgabe der Europäischen Gemeinschaft nach dem Vertrag von Maastricht, Art. 51. In: von der Groeben H, Thiesing J, Ehlermann C-D (eds) Kommentar zum EU-/EG-Vertrag, 5th edn, vol 1. Baden-Baden

Willms B (1997b) Zur Sozialpolitik als Aufgabe der Europäischen Gemeinschaft nach dem Vertrag von Maastricht, Art. 118a. In: von der Groeben H, Thiesing J, Ehlermann C-D (eds) Kommentar zum EU-/EG-Vertrag, 5th edn, vol 1. Baden-Baden

Winter G (1976) Sozialisierung und Mitbestimmung in Hessen 1946–1955. In: Winter G (ed) Sozialisierung von Unternehmen. Frankfurt am Main, pp 119–153

Wirtschaftlicher und sozialer Wandel in der Bundesrepublik Deutschland (1976) Gutachten der Kommission für wirtschaftlichen und sozialen Wandel. Bonn

Wollmann H, Wiesenthal H, Bänker F (eds) (1995) Transformation sozialistischer Gesellschaften. Am Ende des Anfangs. Leviathan special issue no. 15. Opladen

World Bank (1990) World development report 1990: Poverty. New York

World Bank (1995) World development report 1995: Workers in an integrating world. New York

World Bank (1996) World development report 1996: From plan to market. New York

World Bank (1997) World development report 1997: The state in a changed world. New York

Wulfhorst T (1987) Sozialpartner. In: Herzog R et al (eds) Evangelisches Staatslexikon, 3rd edn. Stuttgart, columns 3240–3250

Würtenberger T (1995) Die Verfassung der DDR (Deutsche Demokratische Republik) zwischen Revolution und Beitritt. In: Isensee J, Kirchhof P (eds) Handbuch des Staatsrechts, vol 8. Heidelberg, pp 101–130

Zacher HF (1964) Freiheit und Gleichheit in der Wohlfahrtspflege. Köln

Zacher HF (1965a) Aufgaben einer Theorie der Wirtschaftsverfassung. In: Coing H, Kronstein H, Mestmäcker E-J (eds) Wirtschaftsordnung und Rechtsordnung. Festschrift zum 70. Geburtstag von Franz Böhm. Karlsruhe, pp 63–109

Zacher HF (1965b) Sozialgerichtsbarkeit und Sozialrecht. Zeitschrift für Sozialreform 11:137–154

Zacher HF (1968a) Soziale Gleichheit. Archiv für öffentliches Recht 93:341–383

Zacher HF (1968b) Freiheitliche Demokratie. München Wien, p 30

Zacher HF (1969) Das Sozialstaatsprinzip in der Rechtsprechung des Bundesverfassungsgerichts. Bayerische Verwaltungsblätter (new edition) 15:113–118

Zacher HF (1972a) Die Frage nach der Entwicklung eines sozialen Entschädigungsrechts. Die Öffentliche Verwaltung 25:461–471

Zacher HF (1972b) Faktoren und Bahnen der aktuellen sozialpolitischen Diskussion. Archiv für Wissenschaft und Praxis der sozialen Arbeit 3:241–266

Zacher HF (1973) Bericht über das in der Bundesrepublik Deutschland geltende Wirtschaftsrecht. In: Kommission der Europäischen Gemeinschaften (ed) Reihe Wettbewerb-Rechtsangleichung. Issue no. 20. Brüssel, pp 33–51

Zacher HF (1974) Soziale Indikatoren als politisches und rechtliches Problem. Vierteljahresschrift für Sozialrecht 2:15–51

Zacher HF (1974–1979) Materialien zum Sozialgesetzbuch (Loseblatt). Percha

Zacher HF (1976) Internationales und Europäisches Sozialrecht. Percha

Zacher HF (1977a) Was können wir über das Sozialstaatsprinzip wissen? In: Stödter R, Thieme W (eds) Hamburg, Deutschland, Europa. Festschrift für Hans Peter Ipsen zum 70. Geburtstag. Tübingen, pp 207–270

Zacher HF (1977b) Staat und Gewerkschaften. Zur Doppelverfassung einer Arbeitnehmergesellschaft. Heidelberg Karlsruhe

Zacher HF (1978) Der Sozialstaat als Prozeß. Zeitschrift für die gesamte Staatswissenschaft 134:15–36

Zacher HF (1980) Richterrecht für Verbände? Die richterrechtliche Ausprägung der Tarifautonomie in der Bundesrepublik Deutschland. In: Oberndorfer P, Schambeck H (eds) Verwaltung im Dienst von Wirtschaft und Gesellschaft. Festschrift für Ludwig Fröhler zum 60. Geburtstag. Berlin, pp 509–536
Zacher HF (1981) Sozialrecht und soziale Marktwirtschaft. In: Gitter W, Thieme W, Zacher HF (eds) Im Dienst des Sozialrechts. Festschrift für Georg Wannagat zum 65. Geburtstag. Köln, pp 715–761
Zacher HF (1982) Zur Anatomie des Sozialrechts. Die Sozialgerichtsbarkeit 29:329–337
Zacher HF (1983) Der Sozialstaat als Aufgabe der Rechtswissenschaft. In: Lüke G, Ress G, Will MR (eds) Rechtsvergleichung, Europarecht und Staatenintegration. Gedächtnisschrift für Léontin-Jean Constantinesco. Köln pp 943–978
Zacher HF (1984a) Der gebeutelte Sozialstaat in der wirtschaftlichen Krise. Sozialer Fortschrift 33:1–12
Zacher HF (1984b) Die Versorgung der Beamten, Richter und Soldaten. Heidelberg
Zacher HF (1984c) Verrechtlichung im Bereich des Sozialrechts. In: Kübler F (ed) Verrechtlichung von Wirtschaft, Arbeit und sozialer Solidarität. Baden-Baden, pp 11–72
Zacher HF (1984d) Vom Lebenswert der Bayerischen Verfassung. In: Kraus A (ed) Land und Reich, Stamm und Nation. Festgabe für Max Spindler zum 90. Geburtstag. München, pp 485–530
Zacher HF (1987a) Das soziale Staatsziel. In: Isensee J, Kirchhof P (eds) Handbuch des Staatsrechts, vol 1. Heidelberg, pp 1045–1111
Zacher HF (1987b) Grundtypen des Sozialrechts. In: Fürst W, Herzog R, Umbach DC (eds) Festschrift für Wolfgang Zeidler. Berlin New York, pp 572–595
Zacher HF (1988) Sozialrecht und Gerechtigkeit. In: Kaufmann A, Mestmäcker E-J, Zacher HF (eds) Rechtsstaat und Menschenwürde. Festschrift für Werner Maihofer zum 70. Geburtstag. Frankfurt am Main, pp 669–691
Zacher HF (1989a) Ehe und Familie in der Sozialrechtsordnung. In: Fiedler W, Ress G (eds) Verfassungsrecht und Völkerrecht. Gedächtnisschrift für Wilhelm-Karl Geck. Köln, pp 955–983
Zacher HF (1989b) Elternrecht. In: Isensee J, Kirchhof P (eds) Handbuch des Staatsrechts, vol 6. Heidelberg, pp 265–328
Zacher HF (1989c) 40 Jahre Sozialstaat - Schwerpunkte der rechtlichen Ordnung. In: Blüm N, Zacher HF (eds) 40 Jahre Sozialstaat Bundesrepublik Deutschland. Baden-Baden, pp 19–129
Zacher HF (1990) Verfassung und Sozialrecht - Aspekte der Begegnung. In: Maurer H (ed) Das akzeptierte Grundgesetz. Festschrift für Günter Dürig zum 70. Geburtstag. München, pp 67–90
Zacher HF (1991a) Ziele der Alterssicherung und Formen ihrer Verwirklichung. In: Zacher HF (ed) Alterssicherung im Rechtsvergleich. Baden-Baden, pp 29–113
Zacher HF (1991b) 25 Jahre Deutscher Sozialrechtsverband. In: Schriftenreihe des Deutschen Sozialrechtsverbandes (until vol 22 (1982) Deutscher Sozialgerichtsverband), vol 34. Wiesbaden, pp 7–27
Zacher HF (1996) Was kann der Rechtsstaat leisten? In: Burmeister J (ed) Verfassungsstaatlichkeit. Festschrift für Klaus Stern zum 65. Geburtstag. München, pp 413–432
Zacher HF (1997) Arbeit, Arbeitslosigkeit und Sozialleistungssysteme in globaler Perspektive. In: Gitter W, Schulin B, Zacher HF (eds) Festschrift für Otto Ernst Krasney zum 65. Geburtstag. München, pp 807–845
Zacher HF (1999a) Sozialgesetzbuch (Loseblatt). Starnberg
Zacher HF (1999b) Der Wandel der Arbeit und der sozialen Sicherheit im internationalen Vergleich. Zeitschrift für ausländisches und internationales Sozialrecht 13:1–47
Zacher HF, Kessler F (1990) Die Rollen der öffentlichen Verwaltung und der privaten Träger in der sozialen Sicherheit. Zeitschrift für ausländisches und internationales Arbeits- und Sozialrecht 4:97–157

Zapf W (1972) Lebensqualität und soziale Indikatoren. Archiv für Wissenschaft und Praxis der sozialen Arbeit 3:267–279

Zapf W (1981) Wohlfahrtsstaat und Wohlfahrtsproduktion. In: Albertin L, Link W (eds) Politische Parteien auf dem Weg zur parlamentarischen Demokratie in Deutschland. Düsseldorf, pp 379–400

Zapf W (1987) Individualisierung und Sicherheit. München

Zentrum für Europäisches Wirtschaftsrecht der Rheinischen Friedrich-Wilhelms-Universität (ed) (1999) Koordinierte Beschäftigungsstrategie – sozialpolitische Neuerungen durch den Vertrag von Amsterdam. Bonn

Zentrum für Sozialpolitik (ZeS), Universität Bremen (ed) (1998) Thesen zur Sozialpolitik in Deutschland. ZeS-Arbeitspapier no. 5/98. Bremen

Zohlnhöfer W et al (eds) (1996) Tarifautonomie auf dem Prüfstand. Berlin

Zöllner D (1981) Landesbericht Deutschland. In: Köhler PA, Zacher HF (eds) Ein Jahrhundert Sozialversicherung in der Bundesrepublik Deutschland, Frankreich, Großbritannien, Österreich und der Schweiz. Berlin, pp 45–180

Zöllner W (1990) Der kritische Weg des Arbeitsrechts zwischen Privatkapitalismus und Sozialstaat. Neue Juristische Wochenschrift 43:1–8

Zöllner W, Loritz K-G (1998) Arbeitsrecht, 5th edn. München

Index of Persons

H.F. Zacher, *Social Policy in the Federal Republic of Germany*, German Social Policy 3, DOI 10.1007/978-3-642-22525-3,

Subject Index

H.F. Zacher, *Social Policy in the Federal Republic of Germany*, German Social Policy 3, DOI 10.1007/978-3-642-22525-3,

G

H

I

T

Y

MIX
Papier aus verantwortungsvollen Quellen
Paper from responsible sources
FSC® C105338

If you have any concerns about our products,
you can contact us on
ProductSafety@springernature.com

In case Publisher is established outside the EU,
the EU authorized representative is:
Springer Nature Customer Service Center GmbH
Europaplatz 3, 69115 Heidelberg, Germany

Printed by Libri Plureos GmbH
in Hamburg, Germany